# THE
# NEW BOOK
# OF
# KNOWLEDGE

# THE
# NEW BOOK
# OF
# KNOWLEDGE

Scholastic Library Publishing, Inc.
Danbury, Connecticut

VOLUME 16

# Q-R

ISBN 0-7172-0540-1 (set)

Q, the 17th letter in the English alphabet, was the 19th letter in the ancient Hebrew, Phoenician, and early Greek alphabets. The Hebrews and Phoenicians called it *qoph*. The Greeks called it *koppa*.

The Phoenician letter names were also used by the Phoenicians as words. Many were names of animals or objects. Some language scholars believe that the Phoenician word *qoph* meant "monkey" and that the letter represented a monkey. One version of the letter *qoph* looked like this: Φ

The Greeks based their alphabet on that of the Phoenicians. The Etruscans adapted the Greek alphabet and in turn passed it on to the Romans. The Romans gave the letter the shape it has in English today. The Romans only used Q before a W sound, which in those days was written with the letter V. Later the letter V was sometimes written U. Thus the Roman QV combination became QU, as in *quick*.

In English, Q is used almost exclusively in the QU combination, whether it appears at the beginning of a word, as in *quince;* in the middle of a word, as in *equal;* or as a final consonant, as in *grotesque*. The QU is usually pronounced KW as in *queen*. It also has the sound of K as in *croquet* or *unique*. The letter Q appears in English without a U following it only in a few words borrowed from Middle Eastern languages. An example of one of these words is the name of the country Iraq, in which the Q is pronounced like K.

The letter Q is used in many abbreviations. The upper case Q is used as an abbreviation for the province of Quebec. The lower case q is used to stand for quart, quarter, or question. In the army, QM stands for quartermaster, or supply officer, and HQ means headquarters. A slang expression for doing something secretly or on the quiet is to do it "on the q.t."

Reviewed by MARIO PEI
Author, *The Story of Language*

See also ALPHABET.

## QADDAFI, MUAMMAR AL- (1942–   )

Colonel Muammar al-Qaddafi (also spelled Qadhafi or Gadhafi) has ruled the oil-rich North African nation of Libya as a dictator since 1969.

Qaddafi was born to a poor Bedouin family near the town of Surt in northern Libya in June 1942. After graduating from the Libyan Military Academy and training at the Royal Military Academy at Sandhurst in England, he became a captain in the Libyan Army in 1966. In 1969, Qaddafi, along with other revolutionaries, overthrew Libya's King Idris I. The charismatic Qaddafi soon consolidated his hold on the government.

A strict Muslim and a strong believer in Arab unity, Qaddafi tried but failed to unite Libya with Egypt, Syria, and other Arab states. His support of terrorism in many parts of the world led to economic sanctions by the United States and air strikes on Qaddafi's headquarters in 1986. Then in 1988, terrorists linked to Libya exploded a commercial jetliner over Lockerbie, Scotland, killing 270 civilians. In response, the United Nations imposed an economic embargo against Libya.

In 1998, in an effort to transform Libya's outcast status, Qaddafi allowed two Lockerbie suspects to stand trial in Europe and pledged $2.7 billion to compensate the victims' families. He denounced terrorism and later condemned the September 11, 2001, terrorist attacks on the United States. He also set about dismantling Libya's chemical, biological, and nuclear weapons programs. As a result, all U.N. sanctions were lifted in 2003, and the United States resumed diplomatic relations with Libya in 2004. Qaddafi was also a key figure in the establishment of the African Union in 2002.

Reviewed by DIRK VANDEWALLE
Author, *Qadhafi's Libya, 1969–1994*

---

## QAEDA, AL

Al Qaeda, an Arabic phrase that means "the base," is an international fundamentalist Islamic terrorist network. Among its goals are to drive Americans and other Westerners out of Muslim nations; destroy the nation of Israel; overthrow Muslim governments "corrupted" by Western influences; and unite all Muslims in a single Islamic nation.

Al Qaeda was formed in 1988 by Osama bin Laden, a Saudi-born millionaire. It began as an organization to recruit and train Muslims to fight against the Soviet occupation (1979–89) of Afghanistan. In the mid-1990's, after the Soviets had been driven out, a fundamentalist Islamic group in Afghanistan called the Taliban seized power. The Taliban allowed Al Qaeda to maintain its base of operations and terrorist training camps there.

Al Qaeda terrorists were responsible for the attacks that took place in the United States on September 11, 2001. Within a month's time, the United States and a coalition of allied forces invaded Afghanistan. They attacked and ousted the Taliban, which had harbored the terrorists, and forced bin Laden and other top Al Qaeda leaders (including second-in-command Ayman al-Zawahiri) to go into hiding. In the years that followed, thousands of Al Qaeda members were killed or arrested.

Today Al Qaeda is estimated to have several thousand members in small operational units (called cells) in as many as sixty countries. Along with allied terrorist organizations in Egypt, Yemen, Uzbekistan, Sudan, and elsewhere, Al Qaeda has been responsible for many additional attacks worldwide. Among them were the 1993 World Trade Center bombing in New York City and the 1998 bombings of the U.S. embassies in Nairobi, Kenya, and Dar es Salaam, Tanzania. Al Qaeda is also believed to be responsible for the 2000 attack on the Navy destroyer the USS *Cole* in Yemen and the March 11, 2004, bombings in Madrid, Spain.

ELAINE LANDAU
Author, *Osama bin Laden and the War Against the West*

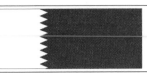

# QATAR

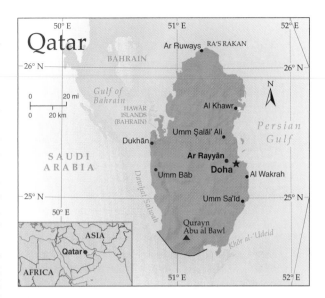

Qatar (pronounced "COTT-er") is a small Arab nation located in Southwest Asia, in a part of the region known as the Middle East. It is situated on the Arabian Peninsula, on the coast of the Persian Gulf. Qatar shares land borders with the nations of Saudi Arabia and the United Arab Emirates. The island nation of Bahrain lies to the northwest.

Qatar is mostly desert. For centuries its people's livelihood depended on herding camels and other livestock, fishing, and diving for pearls in the Persian Gulf. The discovery of large deposits of oil under its barren land in 1939, however, transformed Qatar from a poor nation into a very prosperous one.

▶ **PEOPLE**

Fewer than one in four residents are native Qataris. The great majority of the population is made up of foreign residents who work in the country's oil industry. Most of the foreign workers come from other Middle Eastern countries and from Pakistan and India. Some Europeans and Americans are also employed as oil-industry technicians. The income from oil enables the government of Qatar to provide its people with a number of social welfare benefits. These include free health services and government-supported housing.

**Language and Religion.** Arabic is the official language of the country. English is also used, especially in business. Most of the people are Muslims, and Islam is the official religion of the country.

**Education.** In Qatar, education is free, and schoolchildren also receive free meals, transportation, and clothing. Scholarships are available to qualified students for study abroad or at the University of Qatar in Doha.

▶ **LAND**

The territory of Qatar includes the Qatar Peninsula and a number of small islands in the Persian Gulf. The peninsula is about 100 miles (160 kilometers) long and about 55

Qatar is a small nation on the Arabian Peninsula of Southwest Asia. It is a mostly desert country with an economy based on vast deposits of oil.

miles (90 kilometers) wide. Except for some low hills on the western coast, the landscape is mostly flat and sandy. Qatar's only useful mineral resources are its deposits of oil and natural gas.

**Climate.** Summers are extremely hot, with temperatures averaging 108°F (42°C). Winter temperatures are considerably cooler, averaging 59°F (15°C). There is little rainfall.

▶ **ECONOMY**

Qatar began exporting large quantities of oil in the 1950's. Today crude oil accounts for about 95 percent of the country's export income, and the oil industry employs a majority of the workforce. Qatar's chief manufactured products include refined petroleum, liquefied natural gas, fertilizers, petrochemicals, and steel.

Some wheat, vegetables, and fruits are grown. However, much of the food has to be imported since agriculture is severely limited by the dry climate and lack of fertile soil. The fishing industry processes fish and shellfish harvested in the Persian Gulf.

▶ **MAJOR CITIES**

**Doha**, the capital and largest city, is home to about 75 percent of the population. Situated on Qatar's eastern coast, Doha was at one time a small fishing village. It grew rapidly following the discovery of oil.

Two other towns also developed as a result of the oil industry. **Dukhān** is located at the site where the first oil deposits were discovered. **Umm Sa'īd** is a port on the eastern coast, linked to the Dukhān oil fields by pipeline.

▶ **GOVERNMENT**

Qatar is a traditional monarchy, ruled by an emir (prince). The government is based on a constitution that was approved in 2003. Although the revised constitution kept most of the power in the hands of the ruling family, it provided for the first time for the separation of executive, legislative, and judicial powers. To help with executive duties, the monarch appoints a cabinet called the Council of Ministers. The prime minister serves as head of government. The legislature, the Majlis al-Shura (Consultative Council), is made up of 45 members who are empowered to draft legislation and approve budget proposals. Two-thirds of the council members are elected by the public; the rest are appointed by the emir.

▶ **HISTORY**

Qatar was long governed by the rulers of neighboring Bahrain. In 1872 it came under the domination of the Ottoman Turks, who controlled the peninsula until they were expelled by the British during World War I (1914–18).

In 1916, Britain signed a treaty with the Qataris that brought the territory under British protection and recognized the al-Thani family as hereditary rulers of Qatar. Britain voluntarily ended the treaty agreements in 1971, and Qatar gained full independence. Sheikh Khalifa bin Hamad al-Thani came to power in 1972 and gradually brought Qatar's oil industry under his personal control. In 1995, Sheikh Khalifa was deposed by his son, Crown Prince Hamad, in a bloodless coup d'état.

During the Iraq War in 2003, Qatar became one of the United States' most important allies in the Middle East. U.S. Central Command set up operations there. After the war, the United States shifted its regional air operations to Qatar from Saudi Arabia.

In 2003, Qataris approved a more democratic constitution. That same year, the first woman was appointed to Sheikh Hamad's cabinet, as minister of education.

Reviewed by MAJID KHADDURI
Director, Center for Middle East Studies
Johns Hopkins University

**QUADRILATERALS.** See GEOMETRY.

---

## FACTS and figures

**STATE OF QATAR** is the official name of the country.
**LOCATION:** Arabian Peninsula in Southwest Asia.
**AREA:** 4,416 sq mi (11,437 km²).
**POPULATION:** 800,000 (estimate).
**CAPITAL AND LARGEST CITY:** Doha.
**MAJOR LANGUAGES:** Arabic (official), English.
**MAJOR RELIGIOUS GROUP:** Muslim.
**GOVERNMENT:** Monarchy. **Head of state**—emir. **Head of government**—prime minister (appointed by the emir). **Legislature**—Majlis al-Shura (Consultative Council).
**CHIEF PRODUCTS: Manufactured**—fertilizers, petrochemicals, steel. **Mineral**—petroleum, natural gas.
**MONETARY UNIT:** Qatari riyal (1 riyal = 100 dirhams).

# QUAIL

In the early morning, bird-watchers wait and listen in a woodland area. As they stand quietly, binoculars ready, a small, plump, reddish-brown bird wanders out from the dense foliage and gives a high-pitched whistle, "bob-*white!*" The birdwatchers realize that a Northern bobwhite has just sung its name.

Gambel's quail

The Northern bobwhite is a species of New World quail, which belong to the family Odontophoridae. New World quail are native only to the Americas, although some have been introduced in other parts of the world. Their habitats include moist mountainsides, high-elevation dry brush, desert scrub, chaparral, and agricultural areas.

A separate but related family of birds is the Old World quail. These birds are called partridges and belong to the Phasianidae family, which includes partridges, grouse, turkeys, and pheasants. Old World quail lack the serrations—small, toothlike projections—along their lower bill that New World quail have, and some species have special spurs on their feet. (No species of New World quail have spurs.) This article discusses only New World quail, commonly called quail.

**Characteristics of Quail.** Quail are small- to medium-size birds with short necks, short tails, and short, stout bills. Their short, rounded wings allow for quick takeoffs and flight. Quail feathers range in color from muted browns to gray, with contrasting black-and-white patterns around the face. Most males have a feather or feather cluster that stands up on their heads and is used to attract mates. Vocalizations range from simple repeated whistles to grunts and cackles. The largest species is the long-tailed wood-partridge of Mexico, which is 15 inches (38 centimeters) in length. The smallest is the spot-bellied bobwhite of Central America, which is 7 inches (18 centimeters) in length.

**The Lives of Quail.** Except during nesting, quail live in groups called **coveys**. Sometimes several coveys combine to form a large flock. Their diet includes seeds, roots, flowers, leaves, berries, nuts, and insects. Mating displays by males include strutting, puffing their feathers, and tossing vegetation. Both sexes build the nest, which is usually a scrape in the ground covered with vegetation and concealed in dense brush. Three to fifteen oval eggs, whitish or speckled red or brown in color, are laid one to three times each year. In some species, the parents take turns incubating the eggs. After about 16 to 30 days, the down-covered young hatch and are immediately able to walk and search for food. Both parents tend the young. Quail can live as long as twelve years.

All quail species in the United States are game animals, and their populations are currently strong enough to withstand being hunted by humans for food. However, the populations of some species have declined as large-scale agricultural practices and grazing by cattle have destroyed or significantly changed the birds' habitats.

ALLISON CHILDS WELLS
The Cornell Lab of Ornithology

# QUAKERS

The Society of Friends (or Quakers as they are commonly known) is a Protestant denomination that began in England in the mid-1600's. The Friends were the followers of George Fox, a lay preacher who traveled throughout England spreading his beliefs. Today there are more than 330,000 Quakers in over 40 countries. The largest concentrations are in Africa (156,000), North America (91,000), and Central and South America (60,000).

▶ BELIEFS AND PRACTICES

Although Quakers do not have a formal creed, most share several basic beliefs. Chief among them is the belief that the light of

God is within the heart of every person. This inner light makes it possible for each individual to have a direct relationship with God, without intermediaries such as priests and ministers or the sacraments and rituals found in many other churches. For Quakers, this inner experience of God is best expressed by living a life in harmony with that experience and by doing God's work in the world.

If God is within everyone, then each person should be valued equally, regardless of age, race, gender, or social status. For Fox and his followers, this meant that women as well as men should be allowed to preach. It also meant that everyone was to be treated the same, regardless of their social status. This practice angered many and often landed Fox's followers in prison.

In general, Quakers are pacifists (those who oppose violence as a means of settling disputes), because they believe it is wrong to kill another human being. Quakers are opposed to war and have established the right to be conscientious objectors (those who refuse to bear arms on moral or religious grounds). They help victims of war and work for peace and social justice.

Quakers value simplicity, believing it is easier to experience God's truth without distrac-

George Fox

tions. Worship, for example, takes place in simple meeting-houses or members' homes, rather than ornate churches.

Quakers believe that all human beings form one community and that God can speak to and through any individual. By seeing and affirming the "light within" others, Quakers believe they can build a broader world community.

### ▶ ORIGINS AND HISTORY

George Fox began preaching in England about 1647, when he was in his early 20's. Like thousands of others living in England at that time, he did not like the forms and ceremonies of the Church of England or the strict beliefs of the Puritan preachers. Fox soon developed a following of people who were searching for a new, more spiritual, and more personal kind of religion.

Fox's followers were severely punished for their beliefs. English judges jailed hundreds of them for refusing to attend the established church. They were also jailed for failing to pay church tithes (a tenth of one's income or possessions given to support the church) and for refusing to swear oaths when standing trial. (They believed that oaths were forbidden by the Bible and that if one always told the truth, swearing to do so was unnecessary.)

In spite of cruel and unjust treatment, the early Quakers preached widely in Britain, continental Europe, and elsewhere. Many English settlers in the British West Indies and along the coast of North America became Quakers. By 1700 there were probably 50,000 Friends in Great Britain and almost that many in the New World, with small groups in Ireland, the Netherlands, and Germany.

**A woman addresses a Quaker meeting. For early Quakers, the belief that God is within everyone meant that women should be allowed to preach.**

In Rhode Island, Maryland, and North Carolina they had considerable political power in the 1600's. By 1700 they had organized monthly meetings in all the colonies except South Carolina and Connecticut.

William Penn (1644–1718), a young English convert to Quakerism, received Pennsylvania as a royal grant in 1681. There he began his "holy experiment," governing the colony according to Quaker principles and ideals. Quakers ruled Pennsylvania until 1756, two years after the outbreak of the French and Indian War. Their belief that violence was wrong made it almost impossible for them to carry out the military policies of the colonial government in its war with the French and the Indians.

However, the French and Indian War, as well as the Revolutionary War that followed, allowed the Friends to demonstrate their belief in the value of every person. They attacked slavery, capital punishment, and many other practices they considered evil. They advocated prison reforms and improved care of the insane. They worked for women's rights, education for the poor, and peace with the Indians.

In 1827, due to disagreements over doctrine, a series of Quaker separations began, and the Society of Friends split into several branches. Some branches began to have paid ministers, meetings with regular programs, revival meetings, Sunday schools, and missionary societies. Others continued practicing the faith in its original form.

By the 1900's, the Friends began moving toward greater unity among themselves and with other Christians. In 1917, under the leadership of Rufus M. Jones, all branches joined in forming the American Friends Service Committee. This committee provided opportunities for service by Quakers and others

Pacifism (opposition to war and violence) is a core Quaker belief. Quakers today continue to work for peace and social justice.

whose religious beliefs prevented them from serving in the armed forces.

During and after World War I (1914–18), the committee did relief and reconstruction work in France and other war-torn countries of Europe. They expanded their relief work during and after World War II (1939–45).

They also worked to promote international peace and understanding. In 1947 the American Friends Service Committee and the Friends Service Council of England together received the Nobel Peace Prize.

▸ QUAKERS TODAY

Today there are four main branches of Friends: liberal, conservative (also called Wilburites), pastoral, and evangelical. Both liberal and conservative Friends worship in silence, but members give brief testimonies when they feel moved by the spirit. Pastoral and evangelical Friends have ministers and organized services of worship. Branches also differ in their view of the Bible, with some giving it more authority than others.

Although Quaker membership is slowly growing worldwide, Quakers remain a relatively small group. One reason is that the Quaker ideals—peacemaking, civil rights activism, and a simple lifestyle—do not always fit with mainstream modern culture. In addition, most groups do not actively seek more members.

DONALD B. KRAYBILL
CYNTHIA L. NOLT
Elizabethtown College

See also PENN, WILLIAM.

**QUANTRILL, WILLIAM CLARK.** See OUTLAWS (Profiles).

**QUANTUM THEORY.** See PHYSICS (Quantum Theory).

**QUARANTINE.** See PUBLIC HEALTH.

**QUARKS.** See ATOMS (Other Subatomic Particles).

# QUARRYING

Quarrying is the process by which rock materials are removed from the earth. These materials include sandstone, limestone, marble, granite, and slate. They may be quarried as solid blocks, slabs, or crushed and broken stone. Block or slab rock is most often used for buildings, while crushed rock is used mainly for roadbeds.

## ▶TYPES OF QUARRIES

In some quarries, the rock is in huge, solid masses. Marble and granite usually occur in this form. In some other quarries, the rock forms layers of different thicknesses.

A **pit quarry** is a big hole in the ground. To get to the rock, workers must use ladders or stairs, or they must be lowered and raised by mechanical hoists. The rock itself must be carefully hoisted to the surface.

Another type of quarry, known as a **shelf quarry**, operates above the ground. Rock in shelf quarries is easier to remove because machines can be moved right up to the face of the quarry, and rock can be taken directly away.

In a marble quarry near Carrara, Italy, enormous blocks of rock are carefully cut and hoisted. Marble is prized as a material for buildings and statues.

## ▶OPERATING A QUARRY

Quarries are located where suitable layers of rock have formed. Before the rock can be quarried, the soil, clay, gravel, and other material that cover it must be removed. This process, called **stripping**, can be done with a powerful stream of water that washes away the soil. Earth-moving machines also are used for this purpose.

Because rock is not found in the earth in the shapes and sizes that people need, it must be separated from a large mass. To accomplish this, both vertical cuts and horizontal crosscuts must be made. Cuts are planned so that they can be made at the natural breaks of a rock. Rock in quarries, like all rock, may be found tilted, vertical, or flat. A quarrier usually follows the natural tilts and breaks of the rock when removing it.

The chief methods of separating, or cutting off, a section of rock are drilling, channeling, wire sawing, and blasting. **Drilling** is used to make vertical cuts in the rock. Holes about 1 inch (2 or 3 centimeters) apart are drilled straight down the line of separation. The solid material left between the holes may then be removed by further drilling or split by wedges. In the process known as **channeling**, channels are cut through rocks by a channeling machine. This machine, with its strong chopper blade, cuts a channel about 2 inches (5 centimeters) wide and about 40 inches (1 meter) deep. Another method of separating the rock is by **wire sawing**. First, small holes are blasted in the rock and stakes are driven into the holes. Then a power-driven wire belt is strung between the stakes. As the wire belt moves, it eats its way through the stone, cutting a 1/4-inch (6-millimeter)–wide channel. In **blasting**, explosives are used to separate rock, but this method is used infrequently and only when broken stone is needed.

After the rock is separated, it must be removed from the site. Quarries have huge hoists for lifting the rough blocks to the quarry's rim. The blocks are often cut to be as large and heavy as the hoists can handle. At times, blocks weighing 50 tons or more have been lifted out. From the quarry to the point where they are sawed or split into slabs, the blocks of rock are usually transported by truck or rail for processing.

Reviewed by CHRISTINE E. WILLENBROCK
Building Stone Institute

A natural quartz crystal.

# QUARTZ

Quartz is the most common mineral on earth. It is a part of most rocks. Almost all sand is made up of quartz grains. Quartz has a crystalline structure, but perfect crystals are seldom found. Pure crystalline quartz is six-sided, has sharp pyramids at the ends, and is transparent. Quartz also appears in a form in which the crystals are so tiny they cannot be seen. This form is usually translucent or opaque. Some types of quartz are of great value in industry; other forms are valuable gemstones.

▶ INDUSTRIAL QUARTZ

Quartz is used in many industries. It has special properties that give it particular value. For example, quartz is a very hard substance—harder than a steel file. Most forms of quartz do not split easily. Also, quartz can transmit rays of ultraviolet light, something glass cannot do. Still another property of quartz is its ability to generate a small electric charge when put under pressure.

Because pure quartz transmits the short waves of ultraviolet light better than glass does, clear quartz crystals are melted to make special lenses and prisms and quartz-glass tubes for sunlamps. Less clear quartz crystals are used to make laboratory tubes and crucibles. The quartz crystals may be melted and then fused together to form a glass that is useful for making precise laboratory experiments. Since this glass has a high chemical resistance, it does not affect the chemicals used in experiments. It expands very little when it is hot, and it can be taken from a flame and cooled immediately without shattering. Sand that is rich in quartz is used for making ordinary types of glass.

Quartz sand has many other uses. Because crystals of quartz sand are very strong, large quantities of the sand are used in construction work and foundry molds and as a filter for some liquids. Broken grains of quartz crystals are very hard and sharp. They are used in sandpapers, whetstones, and scouring powders and in sandblasting.

When very clear quartz crystals are cut at a certain angle and placed under pressure, they generate electricity. This characteristic, called **piezoelectricity**, makes quartz useful in radio, television, and radar. Electrical parts using piezoelectric quartz crystals are able to turn vibrations into electrical signals or to do the opposite—turn electrical signals into vibrations. The crystals can be cut so that they vibrate at only one frequency. Thus they can control radio wavelengths. Because only a limited amount of quartz is suitable for this use, scientists have developed ways of growing pure quartz crystals in the laboratory. One of the chief uses of laboratory, or artificial, quartz is in quartz and digital watches. The key part in these watches is a tuning fork, which is made of artificial quartz.

Two building stones are made up almost entirely of quartz. **Sandstone** is a rock made up of quartz sand held together by a natural cement. **Quartzite** is a harder rock than sandstone. It is made up of quartz sand held together by a cement as strong as the quartz itself. **Granite**, the most important building stone, is about 30 percent quartz.

**Flint**, a very hard variety of quartz, was one of the materials used for prehistoric cutting tools. Flint chips easily, forming sharp cutting edges. American Indians made arrowheads of flint. When a piece of flint is struck against steel, sparks are given off. Flint was used with steel to produce sparks in flintlock guns, which were used in the 1600's and 1700's.

▶ GEM QUARTZ

Quartz is the most common gem mineral known. It comes in many varieties. The gems are often very beautiful and relatively inexpensive. Gem quartz comes in crystalline and cryptocrystalline forms.

## CRYSTALLINE GEM QUARTZ

| Gem | Color |
|-----|-------|
| Amethyst | Violet or purple |
| Aventurine | Green, brown, yellow, or black with flakes of mica or hematites |
| Citrine | Yellow-brown |
| Rose quartz | Pale to deep rose-pink |
| Smoky quartz or cairngorm | Varies from smoky yellow to brown and black |

## CRYPTOCRYSTALLINE GEM QUARTZ

| Gem | Color |
|-----|-------|
| Agate | Two or more tones of brownish-red with white bands, or shades of gray and white |
| Carnelian | Deep flesh-red or clear red |
| Chalcedony | Various colors |
| Chrysoprase | Apple green |
| Jasper | Tile-red, dark brownish-red, brown or brownish-yellow |
| Moss Agate | Green intertwined hairlike material appears in this type of quartz |
| Onyx | Usually black and white or brown and white |
| Sard | Orange-brown or reddish-brown |
| Sardonyx | Red and white bands |

Crystalline quartz is the most common type of quartz. However, well-developed clear crystals are rare. Clear quartz crystals, called **rock crystal**, are sometimes found in limestone caves. When they are cut as gemstones, they may sparkle as brightly as diamonds.

The word "crystal" came from ancient Greece. There is a story that mountain climbers saw crystal gleaming in caves near Mount Olympus and called it *krystallos*, meaning "ice."

At one time in the Mediterranean countries rock crystal was used for barter in the same way as salt, gold, and silver. Crystal was mined in the Mediterranean region and the Orient. Now the best clear crystal is found in Brazil. Huge crystals have been found, some weighing well over 300 pounds.

FRANK TUFARO
Executive Secretary
Building Stone Institute

See also GEMS.

---

**QUARTZITE.** See ROCKS (Metamorphic Rock).

# QUASARS

In the 1960's, astronomers noticed a very unusual object in the heavens—a point of light that looked somewhat like a star. A measurement of the distance to this object from Earth, however, showed that it was 2 billion lightyears away. If this had been an ordinary star, it would have been too faint to be seen at such a great distance. This object, therefore, had to be enormously brighter than an ordinary star. When astronomers took into account the star's great distance, they determined that its true brightness was equal to that of hundreds of billions of ordinary stars—as bright as an entire galaxy. This brilliant object and others like it became known as quasi-stellar objects, or **quasars** for short.

Scientists discovered that the quasar's extraordinary brightness was only one of its unusual properties. Even stranger was the fact that its enormous output of energy, which included X-ray and ultraviolet radiation as well as light, seemed to be coming from a region in space that was smaller than our solar system. They wondered how an object that small could produce the energy of hundreds of billions of stars. That many stars could not possibly fit into such a small area.

### A Clue to the Nature of Quasars

Astronomers soon discovered a clue to the strange nature of quasars. When they adjusted their instruments to detect extremely dim objects, they saw the faint image of a galaxy around several of the quasars. This had not been noticed at first because each galaxy was so much fainter than the quasar at its center.

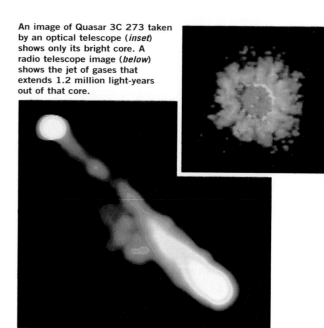

An image of Quasar 3C 273 taken by an optical telescope (*inset*) shows only its bright core. A radio telescope image (*below*) shows the jet of gases that extends 1.2 million light-years out of that core.

When astronomers saw quasars located in the centers of galaxies, they thought of a possible solution to the mystery, one that has become widely accepted. Certain extremely compact objects that generate enormous amounts of energy are called black holes. Quasars might be giant black holes—objects in which the force of gravity is so great, nothing, not even a ray of light, can escape their pull. If quasars are black holes, the source of their brilliance and enormous output of energy becomes clear. The black hole lies in the center of a galaxy, surrounded by stars. These stars spiral inward toward the black hole, drawn by its force of gravity. As each star approaches the black hole, its gaseous body is torn apart by powerful gravitational forces. The atoms of gaseous matter within the disintegrating star accelerate because of these forces, and they begin to collide with one another. These collisions heat the gas, and the hot gas radiates energy into space.

Calculations show that only a giant-sized black hole—perhaps a billion times more massive than an ordinary black hole—could generate the brilliance and enormous energy output of quasars. A giant black hole lurking at the center of a galaxy could explain two remarkable properties of quasars. First, it could account for the enormous amount of energy coming from a quasar. Second, since black holes are exceedingly compact objects, it could account for the fact that the energy comes from a very small region in space.

**Black Holes in Galaxies**

After astronomers conceived the idea that giant black holes might exist in the centers of galaxies, they found it easy to understand why the center of a galaxy was exactly the place where a giant black hole ought to be.

Stars are packed together much more closely in the center of a galaxy than they are anywhere else in one because the gravitational pull of the galaxy tends to draw them toward the center. Stars there are packed together so closely they collide frequently. In the outer part of a galaxy, collisions between stars are very rare, perhaps one every billion years. But near the center of a galaxy, a collision between stars may occur every hour.

When two stars collide, they tend to fuse into one larger star. Additional collisions with this newly enlarged star will produce an even

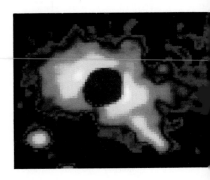

Using instruments that blocked the light coming from Quasar 3C 273 helped astronomers see the image of the elliptical galaxy surrounding it. This helped them determine that quasars often exist at the centers of galaxies.

larger star. Several collisions in a row will create a very large and massive star—the kind that ends its life in an explosion, leaving a black hole behind. As a result of this process, the center of a galaxy may contain many ordinary-sized black holes.

Einstein's theory of relativity explains why a large number of these ordinary-sized black holes in the center of a galaxy are likely to join together to form a single giant-sized black hole. The theory of relativity suggests that a black hole becomes larger as the amount of matter inside it increases. Thus, every time a black hole encounters another object, including another black hole, and swallows it, the black hole grows larger and its gravitational force becomes stronger. This process could eventually result in one giant black hole.

After this giant black hole has formed, the stars of the galaxy continue circling it and are gradually pulled inward by its gravity. If a star comes too close, it is torn apart and swallowed. In the final moments of its existence, the star emits a great burst of energy. These bursts of energy, coming one after the other as stars are consumed, are what cause a quasar's extraordinary energy output.

Quasars are found at the very edge of the visible universe. Because they are so far away, astronomers think that they may reveal what galaxies are like at the early stages of their existence. In looking at quasars, astronomers think they may be observing the early history of the universe.

ROBERT JASTROW
Mount Wilson Institute

See also ASTRONOMY; BLACK HOLES; STARS; UNIVERSE.

**QUAYLE, JAMES DANFORTH.** See VICE PRESIDENCY OF THE UNITED STATES.

# QUEBEC

*The fleurs-de-lis on Quebec's flag (above) and coat of arms (opposite page) recall the province's traditional ties with France. The coat of arms also includes the British lion and a sprig of three maple leaves, a symbol of Canada. The provincial bird is the snowy owl (right), and the provincial flower is the white garden lily (opposite page).*

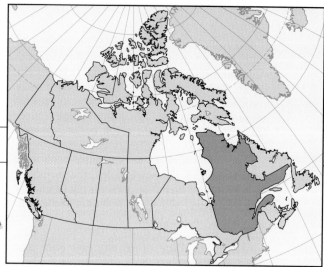

Quebec, Canada's largest province, lies in the eastern part of the country, stretching from the international boundary with the United States to the Arctic.

## ▶ THE LAND

The province of Quebec covers one-sixth of the total area of Canada. The three main land regions that lie within Quebec are the Canadian Shield, the St. Lawrence Lowlands, and the Appalachians.

**The Canadian Shield** covers 80 percent of Quebec. It stretches from the St. Lawrence plain to the Hudson Strait 125 miles (200 kilometers) north of Montreal. This area of ancient rock is cut by important rivers such as the St. Maurice, the Manicouagan, and the Saguenay. Historically, the resources of the Canadian Shield have been its furs, spruce and pine forests, deposits of iron ore, copper, and gold, and its hydroelectric potential.

**The St. Lawrence Lowlands** in southwestern Quebec contain 90 percent of the population. The area has a favorable climate, water routes, and fertile soils. A flat, fertile plain left by glaciers, it is dominated by the St. Lawrence River and the city of Montreal.

**The Appalachian Highlands** are a mountain chain extending from Newfoundland to Alabama in the United States. In Quebec, this region lies south of the St. Lawrence and includes the areas known as the Eastern Townships and the Gaspé Peninsula. Besides timberland and mineral resources, parts of the Eastern Townships are important areas of agriculture and tourism.

### Waterways and Coastline

The St. Lawrence River and Seaway, which links the Great Lakes with the Atlantic Ocean, dominates Quebec geography and transportation history. The province's two major cities, Quebec City and Montreal, are located at strategic points on this river. The Ottawa River is the main tributary of the St. Lawrence. It forms part of the boundary between Quebec and Ontario. Other important tributaries are the St. Maurice and Saguenay in the north and the Richelieu and Chaudière in the south. Several of the province's largest rivers, including La Grande, flow into James Bay and Hudson Bay. Others flow into Ungava Bay. The largest lakes are Mistassini, Minto, Clearwater, and St. John.

Partly surrounded by the waters of Hudson, James, and Ungava bays, Hudson Strait, and the Gulf of St. Lawrence, Quebec has a coastline about 5,000 miles (8,000 kilometers) long.

### Climate

Quebec has an extreme climate, ranging from bitter cold (Arctic) in the northwest to continental—warm summers and cold winters—in the southeast. In northern Quebec at Grande Rivière, the average January temperature is −9°F (−23°C) and the average July temperature is 55°F (13°C). In the south on the St. Lawrence Lowlands, Montreal has an average January temperature of 16°F (−9°C) and an average July temperature of 72°F (22°C). The average frost-free period in the Montreal area is from April 22 to October 23.

The province receives abundant rain and snowfall; average precipitation is 30.5 inches (776 millimeters) of rain and 95 inches (242 centimeters) of snow.

### Natural Resources

Fresh water, hydroelectric potential, forests, and minerals such as iron ore and gold are among Quebec's most valuable natural resources.

Quebec also has a wide variety of wildlife, but many types of mammals, birds, and fish have declined in population over the years, frequently as a result of human activity. For example, Quebec's fishing industry, concentrated in the Gaspé Peninsula and based mainly on cod, haddock, and sole, has declined dramatically from overfishing.

### ▶ THE PEOPLE AND THEIR WORK

Although its area is vast, Quebec's population is concentrated in the south, particularly in the St. Lawrence Lowland. Nearly 50 percent of the population lives in the Montreal region.

Quebec ranks second among the Canadian provinces in population after Ontario. The French were the first Europeans to settle in Quebec, and the majority of today's inhabitants are of French origin. Most of Quebec's residents are French speaking.

Other important population groups in Quebec include those whose origins are elsewhere in Europe, as well as more recent immigrants from Asia, Latin America, and the Caribbean.

Native peoples make up less than 1 percent of the province's population and consist of ten groups: Abnaki, Algonquin, Attikamek, Cree, Huron, Micmac, Mohawk, Montagnais, Naskapi, and Inuit (Eskimos).

### Industries and Products

For many years, farming, forestry, manufacturing, and mining were Quebec's leading economic activities. Today service industries contribute heavily to the provincial economy.

Exports are central to the Quebec economy. More than half of its production of goods and services are exported, much of them to the United States.

**Services.** Service industries employ many people and are the most rapidly growing part of the province's economy. Leading service activities are business, social, and personal services, including education, health care, and services that are related to tourism. Financial services and wholesale and retail trade also are important.

**Manufacturing.** The St. Lawrence Lowland region in Quebec and the adjoining Great Lakes Lowland region in Ontario form the industrial heartland of Canada. Quebec is highly industrialized, and its manufacturing industries contribute about 25 percent of the total Canadian production. Among the province's leading products are textiles and clothing, food and beverages, transportation materials, newsprint and other paper products, and electrical and metal products.

**Agriculture.** At the end of the 1800's, 65 percent of Quebec's income was based on ag-

Percé Rock juts out of the waters off the coast of the Gaspé Peninsula. This picturesque region of Quebec is situated south of the St. Lawrence River.

ricultural production. Today agriculture accounts for less than 2 percent. Nevertheless, Quebec is a leading producer of dairy products, corn, poultry, and hogs. Many truck farms and extensive apple orchards are located near Montreal. Much of Canada's maple sugar and syrup are produced in Quebec.

**Mines and Mining.** Gold and iron ore are Quebec's most important mineral products. Gold is mined in the vicinity of Rouyn-Noranda and Val d'Or. The town of Schefferville is the center of the Quebec-Labrador iron belt, whose iron mines have made Canada one of the world's leading producers of iron ore. Much of the ore is shipped by rail from Schefferville to Sept-Îles for export to the eastern United States. Quebec's other leading mineral products are titanium, limestone, and copper.

**Forest Industries.** Quebec's forests have been of historic importance to the economy for the production of timber, wood pulp, and newsprint and yield almost half of Canada's pulp and paper products. Quebec is a leading newsprint producer. The products of its forests form the province's largest export.

### Transportation and Communication

The St. Lawrence River is the most important feature of Quebec's transportation network. Oceangoing freighters use it to travel 1,000 miles (1,600 kilometers) inland from the Atlantic Ocean to the port of Montreal. From Montreal, the St. Lawrence Seaway allows ships to continue on to ports along the Great Lakes. The Seaway, which was opened in 1959, is vitally important to the transportation of iron ore, grain, and coal. Montreal is a

historic hub of the Canadian rail network, with trunk lines west to Vancouver, east to Saint John and Halifax, and south to the United States. Air transportation from Montreal's Dorval Airport to Toronto and the northeastern United States is extensive. Mirabel Airport, which also is located in Montreal, is a major international airport, particularly for European traffic.

Both French and English newspapers are published in Quebec. *La Presse* and *Le Devoir*, both published in Montreal, are major French-language newspapers. *The Montreal Gazette* is the major English-language daily newspaper. Almost all homes in Quebec have television. Most radio and television broadcasts are in French, but English-language service is available across Quebec.

▶ EDUCATION AND CULTURE

The public school system of Quebec is divided between Roman Catholic and Protestant sectors. There are French- and English-language schools within both systems. Since 1977, the Quebec government has required the children of most immigrants to attend French-language schools.

Quebec has more private schools than any other province. Between high school and the three-year universities, Quebec students are required to attend two-year institutes. These institutes are similar to junior, or community, colleges.

Quebec also has a bilingual university system. The major French-language universities are the Université de Montréal in Montreal, and several campuses of the Université du Québec. The English-speaking population is served by three universities: McGill and Concordia universities, both in Montreal, and Bishop's University in Lennoxville.

The first public library in Canada was built in Quebec City in 1779. Today the province has more than 900 libraries. The National Library of Quebec is located in Montreal.

Quebec has many museums, art galleries, and centers for the performing arts. In Montreal are the McCord Museum of Canadian History, the Canadian Center of Architecture, and the Pointe-à-Callière museum, a center for archaeology and the history of Montreal. The Montreal Museum of Fine Arts has a world-class art collection. Hull offers the Canadian Museum of Civilization, which focuses on art, history, and traditions of Canada's ethnic groups. The performing arts in Montreal include the Montreal Symphony Orchestra, the Grands Ballets Canadiens, and the Montreal Opera company, all at Place des Arts, and the National Theatre School of Canada.

*Opposite page:* The port of Montreal, on the St. Lawrence River, is a leading shipping center. From Montreal, the St. Lawrence Seaway provides access to the Great Lakes.

*Right:* A peaceful scene on Lake Memphremagog, in southern Quebec. The lake is located in an area of the province known as the Eastern Townships.

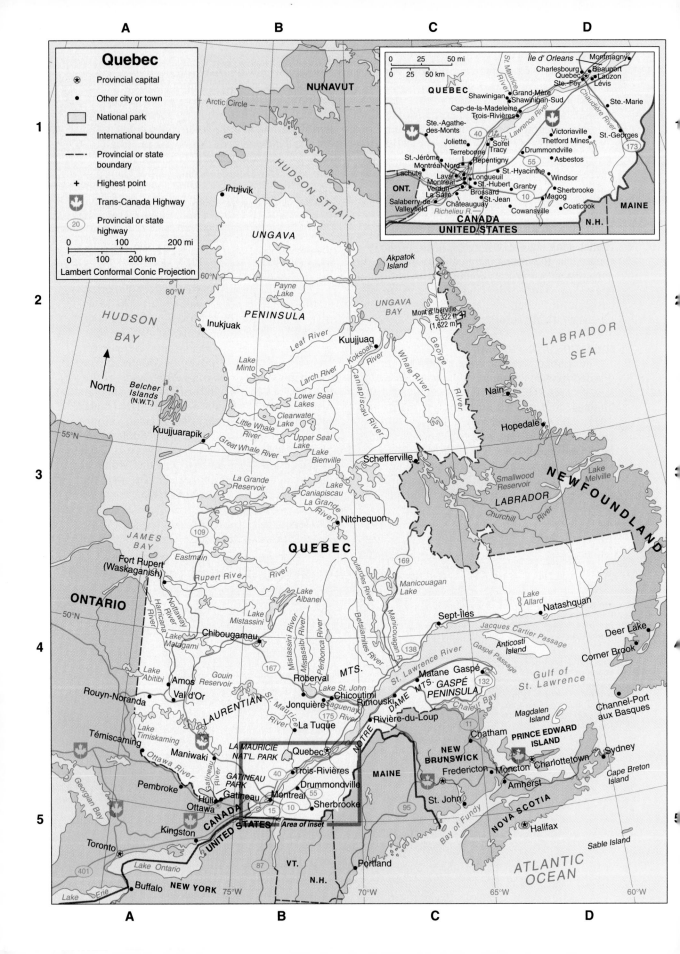

# Quebec

- ✴ Provincial capital
- • Other city or town
- ▢ National park
- ▬ International boundary
- ▭ Provincial or state boundary
- + Highest point
- ⬡ Trans-Canada Highway
- ⬭20 Provincial or state highway

0    100    200 mi
0    100    200 km
Lambert Conformal Conic Projection

**A**  **B**  **C**  **D**

**1**

**2**

**3**

**4**

**5**

NUNAVUT

Arctic Circle

HUDSON STRAIT

Inujivik

UNGAVA

PENINSULA

HUDSON BAY

North

Belcher Islands (N.W.T.)

Inukjuak

Payne Lake

60°N

80°W

Akpatok Island

UNGAVA BAY

Mont d'Iberville 5,322 ft (1,622 m)

LABRADOR SEA

Leaf River

Kuujjuaq

Lake Minto

Larch River

Koksoak River

Caniapiscau River

Whale River

George River

Nain

55°N

Kuujjuarapik

Little Whale River

Clearwater Lake

Upper Seal Lake

Great Whale River

Lake Bienville

Scheffeville

Hopedale

Smallwood Reservoir

NEWFOUNDLAND

La Grande Reservoir

Lake Caniapiscau

La Grande River

Nitchequon

LABRADOR

Lake Melville

Churchill River

JAMES BAY

Eastmain River

109

QUEBEC

169

ONTARIO

Fort Rupert (Waskaganish)

Rupert River

Nottaway River

Harricana River

Lake Matagami

Lake Albanel

Lake Mistassini

Manicouagan Lake

Lake Allard

Natashquan

Deer Lake

50°N

Chibougamau

Gouin Reservoir

167

Mistassini River

Mistassibi River

Péribonca River

Betsiamites River

MTS.

Sept-Îles

138

Jacques Cartier Passage

Anticosti Island

Gaspé Passage

Corner Brook

Amos

Val d'Or

Roberval

Lake St. John

Chicoutimi

Rimouski

Matane Gaspé

GASPÉ PENINSULA

132

Gulf of St. Lawrence

Channel-Port aux Basques

Rouyn-Noranda

LAURENTIAN

St. Maurice River

Jonquière

Saguenay

Rivière-du-Loup

DAME

MTS.

Chaleur Bay

Magdalen Island

PRINCE EDWARD ISLAND

Sydney

Lake Timiskaming

La Tuque

NOTRE

11

Chatham

Témiscaming

Maniwaki

LA MAURICIE NAT'L. PARK

Quebec ✴

Trois-Rivières

MAINE

NEW BRUNSWICK

Charlottetown

Cape Breton Island

Ottawa River

40

Drummondville

Fredericton

Moncton

Gatineau River

GATINEAU PARK

175

Montreal

55

Sherbrooke

Fredericton

Amherst

Pembroke

Hull

Ottawa

Gatineau

15

10

St. John

NOVA SCOTIA

Georgian Bay

CANADA

UNITED STATES

Area of inset

95

Bay of Fundy

Halifax

Kingston

Toronto

401

Lake Ontario

87

VT.

N.H.

Portland

Sable Island

ATLANTIC OCEAN

Lake Erie

Buffalo

NEW YORK

75°W

70°W

65°W

60°W

**Inset (QUEBEC region):**

0    25    50 mi
0    25    50 km

Île d' Orléans

Montmagny

QUEBEC

Charlesbourg

Beauport

Quebec ✴

Ste.-Foy

Lauzon

Lévis

St. Maurice River

Chaudière River

Shawinigan

Grand-Mère

Shawinigan-Sud

Ste.-Marie

Cap-de-la-Madeleine

Trois-Rivières

Victoriaville

Ste.-Agathe-des-Monts

40

Thetford Mines

St.-Georges

Joliette

Sorel

Tracy

Drummondville

Asbestos

173

St.-Jérôme

Terrebonne

Repentigny

55

St.-Hyacinthe

Windsor

Montréal Nord

Lachute

Laval

Verdun

Longueuil

St.-Hubert

Granby

Sherbrooke

ONT.

Montreal

Brossard

St.-Jean

Magog

Coaticook

La Salle

Salaberry-de-Valleyfield

Châteauguay

Cowansville

MAINE

Richelieu R.

CANADA

UNITED STATES

N.H.

## PLACES OF INTEREST

Quebec has a number of places of scenic and historic interest. Most of the historic places reflect the province's French heritage.

**The Citadel,** in Quebec City, situated on Cape Diamond overlooking the city, was built between 1823 and 1832. It was here that Prime Minister Winston Churchill and President Franklin D. Roosevelt met in 1943 and 1944 to discuss World War II. Today it is the summer residence of Canada's governor-general. It contains a military museum.

**Forillon National Park** is a spectacular national park on the ocean featuring rugged coastline and flora of the dunes, salt marshes, and cliffs.

Students relax on the campus of McGill University, in Montreal. The school, established in 1821, is one of Quebec's three English-language universities; all the others conduct classes in French.

**Fort Chambly National Historic Park** is on the Richelieu River, east of Montreal. The fort was originally built by the French in 1665. It was the scene of action during the American Revolution and the War of 1812. Colonel Charles de Salaberry, who defeated the Americans at Châteauguay in 1813, is buried in the Chambly cemetery.

**Notre Dame de Bonsecours,** erected in 1657 and rebuilt in 1771, is the oldest church in Montreal. It overlooks Montreal's harbor.

**Place Royale,** in Quebec City, is one of the oldest districts in North America and the site of the first permanent settlement in New France in 1608. This area between the port and the cliffs was of great commercial importance in the colony's history. The area includes the Notre-Dame-des-Victoires Church, the Old Port National Historic Site, and Quebec's Museum of Civilization.

Other places of interest in Quebec include the ski area of Mont Tremblant, north of Montreal, and the beautiful Gaspé Peninsula, with its small and scenic villages dotting the rugged coastline.

## INDEX TO QUEBEC MAP

## CITIES

Besides the metropolitan regions of Montreal and Quebec City, several other cities in the province of Quebec have populations of more than 50,000. These cities include Gatineau, Sherbrooke, Beauport, Chicoutimi, Hull, and Jonquière.

**Gatineau** is an industrial center in southwestern Quebec.

**Sherbrooke** is the service and cultural center of the Eastern Townships.

**Beauport,** on the St. Lawrence River, is one of the oldest communities in Canada.

Chicoutimi is an important commercial and industrial center.

Hull is an industrial center with a large number of federal government offices.

Jonquière and nearby Chicoutimi form a major center of aluminum production.

Quebec City is the capital of Quebec and the seat of the provincial government. An article on Quebec City follows this article.

Montreal, the largest city in Quebec, is Canada's second largest city and its second major manufacturing center. An article on Montreal can be found in Volume M.

▶GOVERNMENT

Quebec has a one-house legislature called the National Assembly of Quebec. It is made up of 125 members elected for terms of up to five years. There is no fixed period for elections, although they must be held at least once every five years. The two major parties in Quebec are the Liberal Party and the Parti Québécois. While the lieutenant governor is the formal head of state, the decision-making officers are the premier and the ministers of the cabinet. The premier is the leader of the largest party in the National Assembly.

▶FAMOUS PEOPLE

The following are among the many persons who achieved distinction in the history and development of Quebec.

Samuel de Champlain (1570–1635), a French explorer and geographer, is known as the "Father of New France." After founding Quebec in 1608, he built up the fur trade and reinforced French alliances with the Algonquin,

*Above left:* Montreal, Quebec's largest city, is a center of finance, commerce, and industry. Founded in 1642, it is today one of the largest French-speaking cities in the world.

*Left:* The historic buildings and European flavor of Old Quebec City attract artists and tourists alike. Quebec City is the capital of the province of Quebec.

Montagnais, and Huron. A biography of Champlain appears in Volume C.

**Henri Bourassa** (1868-1952), born in Montreal, was the founder and editor in chief (1910–32) of the Montreal nationalist daily newspaper *Le Devoir*. He also served in the House of Commons (1896–99, 1900–07, and 1925–35) and in the Quebec Legislative Assembly (1908–12).

**Sir Guy Carleton** (1724–1808), 1st Baron Dorchester, a British army officer and colonial governor, was born in Strabane, Ireland. He served as both lieutenant governor (1766–68) and governor (1768–78, 1786–96) of Quebec. He also promoted the passage of the Quebec Act (1774) and served as commander in chief of all British forces in North America (1786–96).

**Sir George-Étienne Cartier** (1814–73), Canadian political leader, was born in St.-Antoine. He was a member of the Canadian Legislative Assembly (1848–67) and the Canadian House of Commons (1867–73) and served as attorney general for Lower Canada (1856 and 1864). He became joint prime minister of United Canada (1857–62) with Sir John Macdonald and was noted for his role in the movement toward confederation. Cartier was a minister (1867–73) in the first cabinet of the Dominion of Canada.

**Maurice Le Noblet Duplessis** (1890–1959), Quebec politician, was born in Trois-Rivières. In 1927 he was elected to the Quebec legislature and in 1933 was chosen provincial Conservative Party leader. He founded the National Union Party (1936) and was premier and attorney general of Quebec (1936–39 and 1944–59).

**Sir Wilfrid Laurier** (1841–1919) was Canada's first French-speaking prime minister. A biography of Laurier appears in Volume L.

**Roger Lemelin** (1919–92), author and journalist, was born in Quebec City. His most famous novel, *The Town Below*, is considered by some critics the beginning of a new style in French-Canadian literature.

**Irma LeVasseur** (1878–1964), Quebec's first woman doctor, was born in Quebec City. She began her practice in 1903. She served in Serbia during the typhus epidemic of 1915–17, and set up clinics for children in Quebec City.

**René Lévesque** (1922–87), premier of Quebec and leader of the Parti Québécois (Quebec Party), was born in New Carlisle. He studied law at Laval University in Quebec City. Lévesque was a journalist before entering politics in the 1960's as a member of the Liberal Party. He served in the Quebec legislature and held several cabinet posts. In 1967, Lévesque broke with the Liberal Party after it rejected his views favoring the separation of Quebec from Canada. He formed a separatist political movement, which became the Parti Québécois. In 1976, Lévesque became premier when his party won a majority of the seats in the provincial legislature. He resigned in 1985.

**Louis-Joseph Papineau** (1786–1871) was a lawyer and politician. The key figure in the origins of French-Canadian nationalism, he organized a revolt against the government in 1837.

**Louis Stephen Saint Laurent** (1882–1973), Canadian political leader, was born in Compton. He entered politics at 59 and was minister of justice and attorney general (1941–46) and secretary of state for external affairs (1946–48). He was a member of the Canadian delegation to the San Francisco Conference (1945) to organize the United Nations. He succeeded William Lyon Mackenzie King as prime minister and Liberal Party leader (1948–57). He retired in 1958.

**Pierre Elliott Trudeau** (1919–2000), born in Montreal, became prime minister of Canada in 1968 and served for eleven years. After almost a year out of office, he became prime minister again in 1980. A biography of Trudeau appears in Volume T.

**Georges-Philéas Vanier** (1888–1967), Canadian army officer, diplomat, and governor-general, was born in Montreal. Aide-de-camp to the governor-general of Canada (1921–22 and 1926–28), he later served as representative to the League of Nations. He was minister to France (1939–40), ambassador to France (1944–53), and delegate to the United Nations Conference in Paris (1948). Vanier served as governor-general of Canada from 1959 until his death in 1967.

▶ **HISTORY**

The area that is now Quebec province has been inhabited for some 10,000 years. Native peoples hunted and, in the area south of the St. Lawrence River, grew corn, beans, and squash. Three main language groups existed there: Algonkian, Iroquoian, and Inuit.

## European Settlement

Cod fishing off Newfoundland in the 1400's and 1500's was the main reason for European expansion in the northern part of the continent. Later, a demand in Europe for men's felt hats made of beaver drew French merchants up the St. Lawrence River. In 1608 Samuel de Champlain established Quebec City. After 1642, Montreal became the center of the fur trade.

The colony of New France was directed from the mother country. Within the colony, the governor was responsible for military and diplomatic matters. The Roman Catholic Church was the official church, responsible for education and religious life.

By 1750, France claimed all the land as far west as the mouth of the Mississippi River. But Britain also wanted control of these lands, and war broke out. In 1759 the British defeated the French at a great battle on the Plains of Abraham outside the city of Quebec. A year later, Montreal was captured. Under the Treaty of Paris, signed in 1763, France ceded Canada to the British.

After the American Revolutionary War (1775–83), Americans who remained loyal to Britain as well as those seeking land moved into Canada, creating an expanding English-speaking population. To separate the two groups, the British divided Canada into two provinces in 1791. The province west of the Ottawa River was called Upper Canada (now Ontario); the province east of the Ottawa was called Lower Canada (now Quebec).

## Industrial Development and Confederation

The 1800's saw the transformation of Quebec into an urban, industrial, and capitalist society. More emphasis was placed on individuals, competition, and freedom of property and labor. Although Quebec continued to be predominantly French-speaking, immigration from Great Britain and the United States rapidly resulted in distinct English-speaking areas, particularly in the Eastern Townships, the Ottawa Valley, and Montreal.

This population change was partly the result of Quebec's changing economy. In 1809 the first steamboat service was established on the St. Lawrence River between Montreal and Quebec. In 1817, Canada's first bank, the Bank of Montreal, was established. The opening of the Victoria Bridge across the St. Lawrence River in 1859 and completion of the Canadian Pacific Railway in 1885 allowed goods to be exchanged across Canada.

The period also saw great change in Quebec's political and institutional structures. In 1837 the people of Lower Canada rebelled against British rule. The rebellion was put down. But partly because of it, Upper and Lower Canada were reunited under the Act of Union of 1840.

In 1867 under the British North America Act, Quebec entered the Canadian Confederation as one of the founding provinces. From the outset, Quebec played an important role, often leading demands for greater provincial powers and contributing national leaders such as Wilfrid Laurier, who became the first French-Canadian prime minister in 1896.

---

### IMPORTANT DATES

**1534** Jacques Cartier landed on the Gaspé Peninsula and claimed the new land for France.

**1535** Cartier sailed up the St. Lawrence River to the sites of Quebec City and Montreal.

**1608** Samuel de Champlain established a settlement at the site of Quebec City.

**1642** A permanent settlement was established at the site of Montreal.

**1759** The French were defeated by the British on the Plains of Abraham outside Quebec.

**1763** New France was ceded to Great Britain under the terms of the Treaty of Paris.

**1791** Canada was divided into two separate provinces— Lower Canada (Quebec) and Upper Canada (Ontario)—under the Constitutional Act.

**1840** Upper and Lower Canada were reunited under the Union Act.

**1867** British North America Act brought about the Canadian Confederation of Quebec, Ontario, New Brunswick, and Nova Scotia.

**1885** The Canadian Pacific Railway was completed, linking Quebec with the West.

**1912** Quebec's area was enlarged greatly in the North to include part of the Northwest Territories.

**1918** Women were given the vote in federal elections.

**1940** Women were given the provincial vote in Quebec.

**1968** The Parti Québécois formed as party of independence.

**1977** French became the official language of Quebec.

**1980** In a referendum, Quebec voters rejected independence for their province.

**1990** The Meech Lake Accord collapsed.

**1994** Jacques Parizeau, leader of the Parti Québécois, became premier.

**1995** By a narrow margin, independence was again rejected in a referendum; Parizeau resigned.

**1996** Lucien Bouchard, leader of the Parti Québécois, became premier.

**1998** The Supreme Court ruled that Quebec cannot secede from the rest of Canada without the federal government's consent.

**2001** Bouchard resigned; Bernard Landry, leader of the Parti Québécois, became premier.

**2003** Jean Charest was named premier after the nonseparatist Quebec Liberal Party defeated the Parti Québécois in the provincial elections.

## Recent History

By the early 1900's, manufacturing, mining, and forestry had become the leading sources for jobs, replacing agriculture in importance. Territory east of the Hudson Bay was added to Quebec, nearly doubling its size.

Quebec's conservative political forces remained strong, as the close ties between church and state let the Roman Catholic Church play a major role in education and culture.

Quebec underwent important modernization during the period from the Great Depression of the 1930's to the 1960's. Labor movements expanded, women became increasingly important in the labor force and in public life, and the development of the Canadian welfare state provided new benefits for the young, sick, and aged. Meanwhile, the church loosened its control. French Canadians increasingly emphasized their separate cultural identity in music, theater, and literature. Modernization and the rise of French-Canadian nationalism in the 1960's was known as the Quiet Revolution.

In the 1970's, a radical group of French-Canadian separatists drew attention to the grievances of French Canadians in a series of violent actions. In 1976, René Lévesque, leader of the Parti Québécois, was elected premier of Quebec. A major goal of his government was to separate Quebec from the rest of Canada. But the people of Quebec rejected separation in a 1980 referendum.

Federalists led by Prime Minister Brian Mulroney and the ten provincial premiers signed the Meech Lake Accord in 1987. This recognized Quebec as a distinct society and gave the province additional powers, as well as a veto over constitutional changes. Its failure to be ratified in 1990 led to a strong revival of nationalism, including the Bloc Québécois, a federal party devoted to the province's independence. This movement gained strength in 1994 with the election of Jacques Parizeau, leader of the Parti Québécois, as premier of Quebec. However, independence was rejected in 1995, and Parizeau resigned. In 1998, Canada's Supreme Court ruled that Quebec cannot separate from Canada without the consent of the federal government.

The Parti Québécois continued to hold power under Lucien Bouchard (1996–2001) and Bernard Landry (2001–03). But in 2003, Jean Charest, the leader of the nonseparatist Quebec Liberal Party, became premier.

BRIAN YOUNG
McGill University

# QUEBEC CITY

Quebec City is Canada's oldest city and the capital of the province of Quebec. It is situated on the northern bank of the St. Lawrence River, about 150 miles (240 kilometers) northeast of Montreal. Quebec City combines modern living with the traditions of past centuries. The city is also the cradle of French culture and history in North America—most of the approximately 694,000 people living in Quebec City's greater metropolitan area speak French.

▶ HISTORY

The site of what is now the city of Quebec was visited by the French explorer Jacques Cartier in 1535. But the first permanent settlement was made by Samuel de Champlain in 1608. In 1663 Quebec became the administrative capital of the French province of New France.

One of the most famous battles in North American history was fought on the Plains of Abraham in Quebec. In 1759, on the morning of September 13, the British under General James Wolfe defeated a French army under General Louis de Montcalm. This battle took about 15 minutes, and was part of a global war that resulted in France's loss of its North American empire. It ceded Canada to the British in 1763. For more information, see the article FRENCH AND INDIAN WAR (The Battle of Quebec) in Volume F.

Quebec City was the capital of the British province of Lower Canada (now part of the province of Quebec) from 1791 to 1841 and twice served as the capital of the Province of Canada (1851–55 and 1859–65). After the creation of the Dominion of Canada in 1867, Quebec City was chosen as the capital of the province of Quebec.

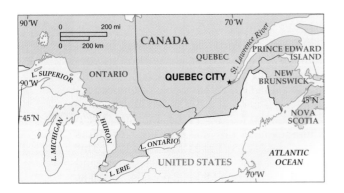

## ►THE CITY TODAY

The metropolitan area of Quebec covers 209 square miles (543 square kilometers). The city itself has an area of approximately 34 square miles (89 square kilometers). It is divided into two sections—the Upper Town and the Lower Town. The Upper Town is situated on Cape Diamond, a cliff that towers above the St. Lawrence River.

High on Cape Diamond, overlooking the St. Lawrence River, is the Citadel. This stone fortress, composed of some 25 buildings, was built by the British between 1823 and 1832.

The heavy walls that still partly surround Upper Town were built during the same period. During World War II (1939–45), the Citadel was the site of famous conferences between Prime Minister Winston Churchill of England and President Franklin D. Roosevelt of the United States. Today it serves as the summer residence of the governor-general of Canada.

Just below the Citadel towers the magnificent Château Frontenac. This beautiful building, which resembles a French castle, was built in 1786. It is now one of the world's most famous hotels. Other outstanding buildings in the Upper Town include the City Hall and the Basilica of Notre Dame. The Hôtel-Dieu du Précieux-Sang, founded in 1639, is one of the oldest hospitals in North America. The legislative buildings are noted for their French Renaissance architecture and the imposing chambers of the National Assembly.

Below Cape Diamond, on a narrow plain along the river, lies the Lower Town, which includes the old financial and commercial section of the city.

*Right:* The Winter Carnival, a popular annual event held in Quebec City, features elaborate ice sculptures as well as parades and fireworks.

*Opposite page:* The stone fortress known as the Citadel can be seen in the foreground of this panoramic view of Quebec City.

In the older sections of both the Lower Town and the Upper Town, narrow, winding cobblestone streets and picturesque stone houses give the look and feeling of a European city. Most of the streets have French names. One of them, Sous le Cap in the Lower Town, is sometimes claimed to be the narrowest street in North America. It is only 8 feet (2.4 meters) wide.

Elsewhere, the city exhibits all the characteristics of a large urban center, with busy expressways and wide streets lined with office towers and shopping centers.

**Economy and Transportation.** Historically, Quebec played a central role in the fur and timber trades that used the St. Lawrence waterway as a gateway to the interior of North America. Later, industries such as shoemaking, tanning, the production of pulp and paper, and shipbuilding flourished. Of these, the last two still have some importance, but manufacturing as a whole has declined since World War II. Service industries, particularly those related to government administration and tourism, play an important role in Quebec City's economy today.

Quebec City is an important transportation center. Major airlines use Jean Lesage International Airport, located in Sainte-Foy, a suburb of Quebec. The city is some 600 miles (970 kilometers) from the Atlantic Ocean, but it is a busy port, handling a great volume of transatlantic trade.

**Education and Culture.** Of the several fine institutions of higher learning in the city, the most noted is Laval University. Founded as a seminary in 1663 by François Laval, the first bishop of Quebec, it is the oldest university in Canada.

Quebec City has many important art galleries, libraries, and theaters. Most theater presentations are in French. Two outstanding musical organizations are the Quebec Symphony Orchestra and the orchestra of the Provincial Conservatory of Music.

There are excellent museums in Quebec City. The Quebec Museum has one of the province's best art collections. The Museum of French America and the Museum of Civilization explore various aspects of Quebec life.

Noted historical sites are Artillery Park and Place Royale. Wendake, a Huron village, is near Quebec City, as is the historic and beautiful Île d'Orleans.

**Sports and Recreation.** Sports are a popular activity in Quebec City. The city is home to the Quebec Rafales of the International Hockey League. Downhill and cross-country skiing at Mont Sainte-Anne and other nearby ski centers are other popular winter activities. Summer sports include golf, bicycling, and hiking.

Quebec City also holds a ten-day Winter Carnival during February. Thousands of people attend this popular event. Festivities include canoe races, ice sculpture competitions, parades, and fireworks. In the summer, the International Quebec Summer Festival takes place. The festival, also a ten-day event, features clowns, jugglers, dance, and music.

Reviewed by BRIAN YOUNG
McGill University

**QUEEN, ELLERY.** See MYSTERY AND DETECTIVE STORIES (Profiles).

## QUEZON, MANUEL (1878–1944)

Manuel Luis Quezon, crusader for Philippine independence, was born on August 19, 1878, in the village of Baler on Luzon Island. His father and mother, both teachers, educated young Manuel. In 1893 he graduated from the Colegio de San Juan and then studied law.

During the Spanish-American War (1898), the United States won control of the Philippines. As a young man, Quezon took part in an uprising against Spanish, and later United States', rule. He was imprisoned for six months for his actions. After his release he resumed his law studies.

Quezon became a lawyer in Baler. In 1906 he was elected governor of Tabayas province, but he resigned to run for the Philippine Assembly. He became the Assembly's floor leader.

From 1909 to 1916, Quezon served in the United States Congress as resident commissioner for the Philippines. He played an important role in the passage of the Jones Act in 1916. The act gave the Filipinos a greater degree of self-rule and a promise of independence. When Quezon returned to the Philippines, he was hailed as a hero. But the United States failed to keep its promise of independence, in spite of Quezon's insistence. For the next 20 years, he served as president of the Philippine Senate. He fought bitterly against interference in Filipino affairs by the American governor-general, Leonard Wood. In 1935 the Philippines gained the status of a commonwealth, which was to serve until independence was granted. Quezon became the first president of the new commonwealth government. He was re-elected president in 1941.

In 1942, during World War II, the Japanese invaded and occupied the Philippines. Quezon escaped to establish a Philippine government-in-exile, first in Australia and then in the United States. On August 14, 1944, Quezon died of tuberculosis. His death came two years before the realization of complete independence for his country. Quezon City in the Philippines is named in his honor.

Reviewed by JULES ARCHER
Author, *The Philippines: Fight for Freedom*

---

## QUICKSAND

You have probably read about quicksand in adventure stories. Perhaps you have seen a movie in which somebody was trapped in quicksand and sank from sight. The whole idea of quicksand seems terrifying, and people were terrified by it for centuries. They believed quicksand had some strange kind of suction that pulled victims under. They believed there was little hope of getting out alive if you ever fell in.

But all this was before scientists studied quicksand and found out what it really is. Despite those movies and adventure tales, the truth is that quicksand cannot hurt you if you know how to handle yourself in it.

Quicksand is not always made of sand. It can be any kind of loose soil. The thing that makes it "quick" is that water is flowing upward through it.

The sand you walk on at a beach is not quick no matter how wet it gets—even when it is underwater. You cannot sink in it. This is because water is just lying on top of it or soaking downward through it. But when water wells up through sand or loose soil, as from an underground spring, it makes the whole sand mass swell. The sand is no longer packed, like beach sand. Each grain rests partly on a cushion of upwelling water. If you step in this, you sink.

But do not believe those old adventure stories. You will not sink out of sight. The depth to which you will sink in any liquid depends on the weight of the liquid. The heavier the liquid, the higher you will float. Since quicksand is heavier than water, you will float higher in it than you do in water.

Quicksand is found most often in valleys, bogs, and river or stream beds. You cannot always recognize it by looking at it, for it may be covered by dead leaves or water or grass. If you ever find you have stepped into quicksand, here's what to do:

(1) Try to run. Some quicksands are just firm enough for this.

(2) If you sink too fast to run, drop anything heavy you are carrying. If you are wearing a pack, unbuckle it and let it fall.

**(3)** Lie flat on your back. The quicksand will buoy you up.

**(4)** Shout for help. If you know help is nearby, just lie still.

**(5)** If no help comes, **slowly** roll yourself to firm ground. This may take you an hour or more, but don't panic. Remember, you can't sink.

**(6)** Whatever you do, make all your movements slow and deliberate. The quicksand must have time to flow around your arms and legs as you move them, and since it's thick, it flows slowly. If you give it time, it will behave just as water does when you're swimming. Otherwise you may pull yourself into an awkward position, and escape will be much more difficult.

MAX GUNTHER
Author, "Quicksand—Nature's
Terrifying Death Trap"

---

**QUILTING.** See NEEDLECRAFT.

## QUOTATIONS

Writers and speakers try to reach others through words, but sometimes the mind fails to come up with the words that will best express an idea. It is then that an apt quotation is likely to fill the need. Ralph Waldo Emerson, American poet and essayist of the 19th century, said, "Our best thoughts come from others."

Many people sprinkle their everyday conversation with quotations. These familiar sayings answer a special need of orators and statesmen, who search for quotations with which they can drive home a point or sum up their speeches. Often the fruit of many years' study is brought together into a single sentence, and nothing adorns a composition or speech better than a fitting quotation. It backs up one's own beliefs. At the same time it shows that those beliefs have been shared by other minds.

"I quote others only in order the better to express myself," wrote Michel de Montaigne, a French essayist who lived during the 16th century. This is another way of saying that, just as a picture sometimes tells more than a thousand words, a single quotation can do the work of many words. Care should be taken, however, not to quote others too often. To do so tends to make a person sound as if he has no thoughts of his own.

Quotations can be long or short, in verse or in prose. They come from countless sources. Writers and people in government have contributed a large number of standard sayings. Lasting quotations have also come from athletes' offhand remarks or sailors' excited battle cries, from advertising slogans and from popular songs.

There are many collections of quotations. Two of the most popular books of quotations are Burton Stevenson's *Home Book of Quotations* and John Bartlett's *Familiar Quotations*. In the indexes of these collections, quotations are grouped according to subject matter. Typical headings are "anger," "beauty," "dog," and so on. If you are vaguely familiar with a quotation and want to look it up, pick out the key word of the quotation. For example, Keats's "A thing of beauty is a joy for ever" would be found among the listings under "beauty."

JACOB M. BRAUDE
Editor, *Speaker's Encyclopedia of Stories,
Quotations and Anecdotes*

A sampling of memorable quotations follows.

### BACON, Francis (1561–1626)

Some books are to be tasted, others to be swallowed, and some few to be chewed and digested. *Essays*

### BIBLE

Am I my brother's keeper?
Genesis 4:9

Go to the ant, thou sluggard;
consider her ways, and be wise.
Proverbs 6:6

Beware of false prophets, which come to you in sheep's clothing, but inwardly they are ravening wolves. Matthew 7:15

A good name is rather to be chosen than great riches. Proverbs 22:1

For the love of money is the root of all evil.
I Timothy 6:10

Let us eat and drink; for to-morrow we die.
I Corinthians 15:32

### BROWNING, Robert (1812–89)

God's in his heaven—
All's right with the world!
*Pippa Passes*, Part I

**BURNS, Robert (1759–96)**

O wad some Pow'r the giftie gie us
To see oursels as others see us!

"To a Louse"

**CAESAR, Gaius Julius (100?–44 B.C.)**

*Iacta alea est* ("The die is cast").
Suetonius, *Divus Julius Caesar* XXXII

**CERVANTES SAAVEDRA, Miguel de (1547–1616)**

A gift-horse should not be looked in the mouth.
*Don Quixote,* Part II, Chapter 62

**COLERIDGE, Samuel Taylor (1772–1834)**

Water, water, every where,
And all the boards did shrink;
Water, water, every where.
Nor any drop to drink.
*The Rime of the Ancient Mariner,* Part II

**EDISON, Thomas Alva (1847–1931)**

Genius is one per cent inspiration and ninety-nine per cent perspiration.
Newspaper Interview, quoted in *Life* (1932)

**EMERSON, Ralph Waldo (1803–82)**

Hitch your wagon to a star.
*Society and Solitude*

**FRANKLIN, Benjamin (1706–90)**

But in this world nothing is certain but death and taxes.
Letter to Jean Baptiste Le Roy
13 November, 1789.
*Writings,* Volume X

**GRAY, Thomas (1716–71)**

Where ignorance is bliss,
'Tis folly to be wise.
"Ode on a Distant Prospect of Eton College"

**HENLEY, William Ernest (1849–1903)**

I am the master of my fate;
I am the captain of my soul.
"Invictus"

**HEYWOOD, John (1497?–1580)**

Two heads are better than one.
*Proverbs*

**JEFFERSON, Thomas (1743–1826)**

That government is best which governs least.
Attributed

**KENNEDY, John F. (1917–63)**

And so, my fellow Americans: Ask not what your country can do for you—ask what you can do for your country.

My fellow citizens of the world: Ask not what America will do for you, but what together we can do for the freedom of man.
Inaugural Address (Jan. 20, 1961)

**LINCOLN, Abraham (1809–65)**

You can fool some of the people all of the time, and all of the people some of the time, but you cannot fool all of the people all the time.
Speech, Bloomington, Ill., May 29, 1856

**LYLY, John (1554?–1606)**

As busy as a bee.
*Euphues and his England*

**PLAUTUS, Titus Maccius (254?–184 B.C.)**

A word to the wise is sufficient.
*Persa*

**POPE, Alexander (1688–1744)**

A little learning is a dang'rous thing.
*An Essay on Criticism*

To err is human, to forgive, divine.
*An Essay on Criticism*

**ROOSEVELT, Franklin D. (1882–1945)**

This great nation will endure as it has endured, will revive and will prosper. So, first of all, let me assert my firm belief that the only thing we have to fear is fear itself—nameless, unreasoning, unjustified terror which paralyzes needed efforts to convert retreat into advance.
First Inaugural Address (Mar. 4, 1933)

**SCOTT, Sir Walter (1771–1832)**

Breathes there the man, with soul so dead,
Who never to himself hath said,
This is my own, my native land!
*The Lay of the Last Minstrel,* Canto VI, Stanza I

**SHAKESPEARE, William (1564–1616)**

The course of true love never did run smooth.
*A Midsummer Night's Dream,* Act I, scene 1

All the world's a stage,
And all the men and women merely players.
*As You Like It,* Act II, scene 7

Brevity is the soul of wit.
*Hamlet,* Act II, scene 2

The better part of valour is discretion.
*King Henry IV,* Part I, Act V, scene 4

This above all: to thine own self be true,
And it must follow, as the night the day,
Thou canst not then be false to any man.
*Hamlet,* Act I, scene 3

**THOMAS A KEMPIS (1380–1471)**

And when man is out of sight, quickly also is he out of mind. *Imitation of Christ*

**TWAIN, Mark (1835–1910)**

The report of my death was an exaggeration.
Cable from Europe to the Associated Press

**WILDE, Oscar (1854–1900)**

I can resist everything except temptation.
*Lady Windemere's Fan,* Act I

R, the 18th letter of the English alphabet, was the 20th letter in the ancient Hebrew and Phoenician alphabets and the 17th letter in the classical Greek alphabet. The Hebrews and Phoenicians called it *rosh*. The Greeks called it *rho*.

Phoenician letter names were also used as words. The word *rosh* meant "head." The form of the letter may have been a simplified picture of a head. The letter *rosh* looked like this: ᑫ

The Greeks based their alphabet on that of the Phoenicians. The early Greeks, like the Hebrews and the Phoenicians, wrote from right to left. Later they wrote from left to right, and many of their letters were reversed. The letter *rho* was one of the letters that changed direction: P

The Etruscans, an ancient people who ruled in Rome in the 6th century B.C., had an alphabet that was based on that of the Greeks. They sometimes added a small stroke to their letter R, so that it would not be confused with their letter P. When the Romans learned the alphabet from the Etruscans, they decided to use only this form of the letter for the R sound. It is the Roman R that is used in English today.

In the United States the R is usually pronounced as in *race*. In some parts of the United States the R is dropped at the end of many words and syllables. This is especially true in the South. In England the tongue is sometimes vibrated when pronouncing the letter, producing a trilled R.

The letter R is used in many abbreviations. In the Navy the letters RA stand for rear admiral. R is an abbreviation for radius in mathematics and for resistance in electricity. The letters R.S.V.P. following an invitation stand for the French words *Répondez s'il vous plaît,* or "Reply, if you please." R may mean registered as in RN for registered nurse. A small r is an abbreviation for the rook in the game of chess.

Reviewed by MARIO PEI
Author, *The Story of Language*

See also ALPHABET.

## SOME WAYS TO REPRESENT R:

The **manuscript** or printed forms of the letter (left) are highly readable. The **cursive** letters (right) are formed from slanted flowing strokes joining one letter to the next.

The **Manual Alphabet** (left) enables a deaf person to communicate by forming letters with the fingers of one hand. **Braille** (right) is a system by which a blind person can use fingertips to "read" raised dots that stand for letters.

The **International Code of Signals** is a special group of flags used to send and receive messages at sea. Each letter is represented by a different flag.

**International Morse Code** is used to send messages by radio signals. Each letter is expressed as a combination of dots (•) and dashes (– –).

The cottontail is one of the most familiar kinds of rabbits. Although rabbits and hares belong to the same family, rabbits are typically smaller than hares and have shorter ears.

## RABBITS AND HARES

Nibbling clover at the edge of a meadow, a cottontail rabbit senses an approaching fox and freezes like a statue—its first line of defense is to escape detection by the approaching enemy. As the fox nears, the cottontail explodes forward and zigzags frantically in flight, its powder puff tail bobbing behind it. As the fox scrambles to catch its prey, the cottontail disappears with a mighty bound into a thicket of tangled brambles where the fox cannot follow.

The cottontail rabbit is one of the most familiar animals in the order Lagomorpha, which includes two distinct families of mammals, the rabbits and hares (Leporidae) and the pikas (Ochotonidae). The hamster-sized pika (also called whistling hare or cony) has small round ears and no visible tail. The 30 species of pikas live primarily in the high mountains and plateaus of Asia, although two species occur in the mountains of western North America. All North American species live in rocky habitats,

Rabbits are born blind, naked, and helpless. By the time they are about 2 weeks old, their eyes are open and their bodies are covered with soft fur.

while those in Asia live among rocks or in open meadows.

The 61 species of rabbits and hares are native to almost all areas except Australia, southern South America, and the islands of the Pacific Ocean. European rabbits and European hares have now been introduced into these areas, where they have flourished.

### ▶ CHARACTERISTICS OF RABBITS AND HARES

Rabbits, hares, and pikas were once considered rodents. They have two pairs of big gnawing teeth, or incisors, in the front of their jaws, as do rodents. But they have a second set of small peg-like upper incisors that sit behind the larger gnawing teeth. Rodents do not have these smaller teeth. Because of this and other differences, the order Lagomorpha was separated from the order Rodentia.

In general, rabbits and hares have big, long ears and stubby tails. They have short front legs and long, powerful hind legs. They are expert runners and leapers. Their diet is almost exclusively plant material, thus they are known as herbivores. Because of this diet, and because plant material is very difficult to digest, rabbits and hares have very large and complex digestive systems. They also engage in a behavior known as **coprophagy**, which means that they eat their own feces. Rabbits and hares expel two types of feces: one is a round dry pellet, the other is a soft sticky black pellet that the animal eats as it is produced. These soft feces generally contain high levels of vitamins and allow food a second chance to be absorbed by the digestive system. If rabbits and hares are prevented from engaging in coprophagy, they often develop malnutrition or die.

Another unusual behavior of rabbits and hares is the lack of care they give their young after birth. Mothers visit their young to nurse them only about once every day. But the milk produced by mother rabbits and hares is extremely rich, so the young are able to survive these long periods between feedings. It is believed that this behavior evolved so that mothers would not bring the attention of potential predators to their helpless young.

**Rabbit or Hare?** Many people think that the words "rabbit" and "hare" refer to the same animal, but there are some distinct characteristics that distinguish one from the other. Hares are generally larger and have longer ears than rabbits. Most hares do not make underground burrows. Instead, they construct nests, called **forms**, on the surface of the ground. Their young are born covered with fur, with their eyes open, and they are ready to hop about almost immediately. Rabbits are normally smaller than hares and have shorter ears. Many species of rabbits construct burrows in which they take cover and make their nests, and their young are normally blind, naked, and helpless at birth. Adding to the confusion over rabbits and hares are the common names of some of these animals. For example, the hispid (bristly) hare is really a rabbit, and the antelope jackrabbit is really a hare.

▶ **RABBITS**

There are 29 species of rabbits, 17 of which belong to the New World group called cottontails. Another species, the European rabbit, is the best known of all rabbits.

The remaining eleven species of rabbits are generally quite distinctive. The Amami rabbit, the only black rabbit, lives exclusively on two small islands in southern Japan. The Zacatuche, or volcano rabbit, occupies only the high altitude volcanoes surrounding Mexico

## RABBITS AS PETS

Rabbits make playful and affectionate pets, and they can be kept indoors just like dogs or cats. Whether you keep your pet rabbit indoors or outdoors, it will need a cage that will serve as its nest. The cage should be large enough for the rabbit to move around in. Outdoor cages must

Palomino rabbit

provide adequate shelter from rain and excessive heat or cold. They must also be strong enough to protect your rabbit from predators, such as coyotes and raccoons. Because rabbits like to chew, you must "rabbit-proof" your house if you keep your pet inside. This means putting all houseplants and electrical and phone cords out of reach. Give your rabbit a collection of safe chewable toys to chew and shred instead. Rabbits can be trained to use a litterbox.

There are many breeds of domestic rabbits to choose from. Small breeds include the Netherland dwarf, which weighs only about 2 pounds (0.9 kilogram) when fully grown. The Flemish giant is the largest breed, with females weighing up to 14 pounds (6 kilograms) or more. Domestics with very long, floppy ears are known as lops, such as the American fuzzy lop. Angora rabbits have long, thick fur. Domestic rabbits come in many colors, such as the overall brownish-orange of palominos and the chocolate and blues often found on harlequins.

For complete information on keeping your pet rabbit happy and healthy, consult a local breeder or pet shop.

City. The hispid hare lives only in the foothills of the Himalayas. The pygmy rabbit lives only in the Great Basin sagebrush region in the western United States. There are two related striped rabbits from southeast Asia, one of which was unknown to science until it was discovered in an animal market in 1995. The riverine rabbit is confined to the Karoo desert of South Africa, and four additional but poorly known rabbit species also live in Africa.

Cottontails occupy a range of habitats from marshes to open grasslands. Most species are relatively solitary, but some form breeding groups with a distinct social order. The Eastern cottontail has the highest rate of reproduction, producing as many as 35 young each year. The lifespan of most cottontails is a bit longer than a year.

While the European rabbit resembles the cottontail, it has very distinctive habits. It is a very social species, and large numbers of animals live in a small area where they dig an extensive burrow system known as a **warren**. Like a breeding group of cottontails, there is a strict social order among the rabbits living within a warren.

All the various breeds of domestic rabbits are descended from the European rabbit. There are now over 100 breeds of domestic rabbits, which are popular as pets and are also raised for their meat and fur.

▶ **HARES**

The 32 species of hares are widely distributed across North America, Europe, Asia, and Africa. They most commonly occupy open grassy areas, but some species live in forests or deserts as well. Hares are fast and normally attempt to escape predators by running instead of seeking cover. Hares produce between one and nine young in each litter. Most hares are solitary, although European and Arctic hares are often very social.

*Top:* Jackrabbits, easily recognizable by their enormous ears, are really a kind of hare. *Bottom:* Snowshoe hares turn white in winter to blend in with the snow.

There are several notable species of hares. The jackrabbits of open desert areas in western North America are easily recognizable by their enormous ears. The snowshoe hare of the far north is named for its broad hind feet, which help it travel across snow. This hare becomes pure white in winter as camouflage, then molts back to a dusky brown during summer.

▶ **RABBITS, HARES, AND THEIR ENVIRONMENT**

Rabbits and hares are often vital parts of the ecosystems they live in. Some species are a source of food for predators, while other species are popular game for hunters. But rabbits and hares are considered pests in some areas. The European rabbit has been introduced to many areas where it has thrived and become very destructive to agriculture. Many techniques have been tried to control rabbit populations in these situations, with variable success.

On the other hand, over 30 percent of all rabbit and hare species are threatened with extinction. These include nearly all the distinctive species, such as the pygmy rabbit, the riverine rabbit, the hispid hare, and the Zacatuche. They are among the most endangered of all mammals worldwide.

ANDREW T. SMITH
School of Life Sciences
Arizona State University

See also RODENTS.

**RABIES.** See DISEASES (DESCRIPTIONS OF SOME DISEASES).

# RACCOONS AND THEIR RELATIVES

Raccoons and related animals all belong to the family group Procyonidae. These mammals range over a wide area of North and South America. They can be found scrambling over the rocky terrain of desert canyons, moving quickly through the treetops of tropical forests, or wading in the shallow waters of lakes, ponds, or swamps.

A mother raccoon teaches its young to find food in shallow water by feeling about with their sensitive front paws.

▶ **CHARACTERISTICS OF RACCOONS AND RELATED ANIMALS**

Members of the Procyonidae family, or procyonids, have sharp teeth and clawed, five-toed feet. Most eat both meat and plant material such as leaves, fruits, berries, and roots. Most have pointed faces with small ears, circles or other markings around the eyes, and long tails ringed by several dark bands.

In general, these animals are good climbers and make their homes in hollow trees. However, they may also nest in caves or among rocks. Most procyonids have a solitary lifestyle; they sleep during the day and come out at night to hunt for food.

▶ **KINDS OF PROCYONIDS**

In addition to raccoons, the Procyonidae family includes ringtails, coatis, kinkajous, and olingos. Some scientists consider the red panda of Nepal and China a member of this family, while other scientists put it in a separate family with the giant panda. For more information, see PANDAS in Volume P.

**Raccoons**

Raccoons are small furry animals that, including the tail, measure up to 40 inches (102 centimeters) long. Brownish gray in color, raccoons have dark fur around their eyes so that they look as if they are wearing masks. Their long bushy tails have several dark bands that alternate with wider, lighter ones.

There are seven species of raccoons. Although they may differ slightly in appearance, all have very similar habits. The most common raccoon is found in southern Canada and throughout the United States and Central America. Another, the crab-eating raccoon, lives in parts of Central and South America. It has shorter fur and longer legs than most other types of raccoons.

Raccoons can be found in woodlands and meadows near ponds, lakes, rivers, and swamps. They spend most of their time on land. However, raccoons are skillful tree climbers, and it is high up in trees that they set up their hideaways, create their nests, and sleep away the worst winter days. In treeless places, raccoons nest in high grasses.

A raccoon's diet is made up of a variety of foods, including fish, lizards, birds, eggs, and insects, as well as fruits and berries. Because they are likely to help themselves to whatever is around—raiding farms to feed on poultry or young corn and searching through garbage containers for food scraps—raccoons are considered pests in some areas.

In the wild, raccoons search in shallow water for prey. Scratching and digging with their sensitive fingers, they feel about in sand and mud for crayfish and other small animals. When raccoons in captivity are given food, they will dip it in water before eating it. This habit has nothing to do with washing or wetting food as was once thought. It is more likely a way for the captive raccoon to satisfy its urge to hunt for water prey.

Raccoons are loners. Males and females meet and stay together only for a short time during mating season. Up to seven young are born at a time. The female and her newborns live together until the young raccoons are able to take care of themselves.

## Ringtails

Ringtails are nimble, graceful animals. They grow to about 32 inches (81 centimeters) in length, with their long bushy tails making up more than half the total length. Soft brownish fur, which is darker on the back than on the belly, covers the body. Like their raccoon cousins, ringtails have distinctive markings—white and black rings alternate along the tail, and a mask of white rings surrounds large dark eyes.

There are two species of ringtails, found chiefly in Mexico and the southwestern United States. However, one species ranges north to southwestern Oregon and Colorado, and the other ranges farther south through Central America. In North America, they are found in rocky country broken by clumps of trees, while in Central America, ringtails prefer living in tropical woodlands.

Even though ringtails are excellent climbers, they spend most of their time on the ground. During the day, they can be found sleeping in hideaways such as a hole in a tree or a cave or other rock shelter. After sunset, they set out to look for food. Ringtails are resourceful explorers, making use of whatever food they find, including small animals, fruits, insects, and plant nectar.

Ringtails are solitary animals. Males and females have their own territories and only come together to mate. Young ringtails, two to four to a litter, are born in the den, where they are raised by the mother. By about 5 months the young are nearly as big as their parents.

*Top:* The ringtail's tail makes up more than half its total body length. *Bottom:* Coatis, or coatimundis, have flexible snouts and long tails that they often carry upright like flagpoles.

## Coatis

The body of a typical coati, or coatimundi, measures up to 26 inches (66 centimeters) long, and the tail may reach 27 inches (69 centimeters). The most distinctive features of the animal are its long, flexible snout, which it pokes into crevices to find food, and its long ringed tail, which it carries straight up like a flagpole. The color of the coati's fur depends on the species (there are three), but most have reddish brown fur.

Coatis can be found from the rocky wooded landscapes of southwestern Arizona to the dense wet forests of Colombia and Venezuela and much of South America. They are good climbers and are as comfortable moving about in the trees as they are on the ground. When threatened, they will often flee into the high treetops.

Unlike other Procyonids, coatis are very active during the day. They spend most of their time foraging for food. Insects, spiders, snails, lizards, fruits, and birds' eggs are all part of their varied diet. As night approaches, coatis climb into the trees to find safe sleeping places or, in treeless areas, snuggle into caves or cracks in rocks.

Coatis are the most social member of the Procyonidae family. Although the males and older coatis move about alone, the females and young coatis travel together. During the mating season, male coatis are allowed into the group. After mating, they are driven out again. The females separate from their companions when they are ready to have their young. Three to six offspring are in each litter. When the newborn coatis are about 5 weeks old, the mother returns with them to the group.

### Kinkajous

There is only one species of kinkajou, a slender animal with red-brown fur, short legs, and sharp-clawed feet. Including its tail, which can be almost as long as its body, it can reach up to 45 inches (114 centimeters) in length. This long tail is prehensile, which means the kinkajou can use it to grasp branches for support as it moves through the treetops.

Tropical forests from southern Mexico to Brazil are home to the kinkajou. During the day, small family groups sleep in tree holes. At night, the animals roam high in the trees searching for food, which can include insects, birds' eggs, and small mammals. The kinkajou also uses its long tongue, almost 5 inches (13 centimeters) in length, to lap up nectar, honey, and soft fruit pulp. Kinkajous usually eat alone, but sometimes several kinkajous pick the same tree to forage in. Then a noisy group forms as each kinkajou jealously protects its food from the others.

After the male and female mate, one or, rarely, two kinkajous are born in the spring or summer. The newborn develops quickly, and soon its tail is fully functional. By 4 months the offspring is nearly independent but continues to sleep with the family group until it finds a mate of its own.

### Olingos

Olingos measure about 38 inches (97 centimeters) long from head to tail. Because of their small build, brown fur, and long tails (as long as the body), olingos are sometimes mistaken for kinkajous. But the olingo's brown-

*Left:* The kinkajou's tail is prehensile—it can wrap around and grasp branches as the animal moves through the trees. *Above:* The olingo resembles the kinkajou, but its long tail is not prehensile.

ish fur is darker on its back than on its belly, and its long, furry tail—which may or may not be marked by several dark rings—is not prehensile like the kinkajou's. Its most distinguishing characteristic is also a built-in defense from predators—it smells bad! When threatened, the olingo discharges a foul-smelling secretion that keeps enemies away.

The dense tropical forests of central and northern South America are home to all five species of olingos. Seldom climbing down to the ground, olingos spend the day sleeping in tree holes. At night they move through the branches searching out food. They will feed on fruits, insects, lizards, and other small animals.

Olingos live alone. They come together to mate, but separate soon afterward. The female gives birth to one offspring, which grows quickly and begins to fend for itself at about 4 months of age.

Reviewed by CYNTHIA BERGER
Science Writer

See also ANIMALS; MAMMALS.

# RACES, HUMAN

Humankind is made up of a number of natural populations, commonly called races. Such races occupy the continents and islands that can support life. These geographical populations developed where groups of people were separated from one another for long periods of time—10,000 years or more. They often experienced very different climates, ate different foods, were subject to different diseases, and therefore developed many differences over time. Yet all humanity has a common origin. People are more alike than they are different. They are all part of the same species, which scientists call *Homo sapiens.*

People around the world may look very different from one another, yet they all belong to the same species— *Homo sapiens.*

### ▶ THE PROPER MEANING OF RACE

When scientists use the word "race," they are referring to the natural populations that make up the species as a whole. Together they form the human species and not the human "race," as it is sometimes incorrectly called. When scientists use the word "race," they mean natural populations, not nations or religions or groups that use the same language. Language, nationality, and religion have only temporary boundaries that can change rapidly in the course of a century or less. In their homelands people have customs and beliefs that are often different from the new ones they may adopt when they move to different lands.

### ▶ HOW DIFFERENCES ARE DETERMINED

For a long time, human populations were described on the basis of the most obvious differences. These were the color of the hair, the form of the hair, and the amount of melanin, or black pigment, in the skin. But many differences can be seen in the skeletons of people as well. Anthropologists, scientists who study people, can tell the difference between an American Indian skeleton and that of a European settler by comparing the shape of the teeth, the form of the skull, and the shape of the bones of the face. Classes of fingerprints also differ from one geographical population to the next. So do the amount of hair on the face, the extent to which men become bald, and the shape and thickness of the bones of the arms and legs.

As might be expected, geographical races that live closer together tend to be more similar. The people of India somewhat resemble the people of Europe. They probably have been separated for only a few thousand years. American Indians resemble the people of Asia in many ways. Some Indians may have come from Asia 10,000 to 20,000 years ago. From the study of blood groups it is clear that the people of Africa and the people of Europe also had common origins before they became separated on different continents.

### Blood Groups

The blood groups, or blood types, that are important in making compatible blood transfusions have been very helpful to anthropologists because blood groups can also be used to distinguish human populations. Using what is called the M-N-S blood group system, scientists have found that most American Indians are of blood group M, but that Australian aborigines (original inhabitants) are usually of blood group N. Probably these two groups have been separated for the longest period of time—30,000 years or more. Europeans, Asians, and Africans have both blood group M and blood group N.

There is another set of blood groups that anthropologists use in the study of races. This is the A-B-O blood group system. American Indians almost never have blood group B, but 30 percent of Asians and 15 to 20 percent of Europeans do have blood group B. So it is thought that American Indians migrated from Asia before blood group B was common there. There are many other blood factors that are helpful to scientists in comparing different geographical populations. Scientists know exactly how blood factors are inherited, which also makes blood groups more useful than skin color or height in comparing races. Furthermore, skin color can be affected by the sun, and growth can be affected by the food eaten in childhood.

### Local Differences

In each geographical population, there are many local differences. The San of South Africa are smaller and have lighter skin than the Masai warriors of East Africa. The Indians who live on the highlands of Central America are clearly different from the Penobscot Indians of Maine in North America. The Scandinavian peoples of Sweden, Norway, and Denmark in northern Europe

are lighter in skin and hair color than the Europeans to the south, who live along the Mediterranean Sea. Such local groups are what anthropologists call local, or microgeographical, races. They show to a lesser degree the differences that come from separation, different environmental conditions, and time.

### ▶ CHANGES IN RACES

Over time all races, or populations, change. Some small local populations have become extinct within recent times, possibly due to assimilation with a more dominant group, dramatic changes in the environment, or dwindling food sources. Other local populations have become greatly reduced in number. For example, before 1800 there were about 15,000 Aleuts living in the Aleutian Islands off the coast of Alaska. However, after the population came into contact with Russian explorers, the Aleuts contracted many unfamiliar diseases. By the mid-1800's their numbers had dwindled to a mere 2,500.

Some local populations have remained about the same size for thousands of years. This is true of the San of South Africa and for the aborigines of the central Australian desert. Still other local populations have grown tremendously in numbers. Such growth was particularly true of the people of north-

---

### BIOCHEMICAL VARIABLES USED IN HUMAN IDENTIFICATION

- The A-B-O blood group system, the M-N-S system, the Rh (Rhesus) system, and other systems of importance in blood transfusions
- The HLA (human leukocyte antigen) tissue factors used in tissue matching for transplants
- Unusual hemoglobins such as hemoglobin S (HbS), which is responsible for the sickle-cell disease
- The "secretor" factor—or the secretion in bodily fluids of the antigens characteristic of A, B, and AB blood groups
- Particular amino acids excreted in the urine; DNA sequences, also used in genetic fingerprinting by law enforcement agencies

---

### REASONS TO STUDY HUMAN RACES

- To trace the origins of the earliest humans
- To find out when and where the various geographic groupings first appeared
- To discover how long it took to develop the differences that can be seen and measured
- To understand the evolutionary processes involved, such as natural selection and the effects of disease
- To investigate the prehistoric and historic migrations that resulted in the present distribution of the races
- To measure the rate of ongoing evolution
- To assist physicians in the diagnosis of diseases, such as intolerance to milk sugar, or lactose
- To assist in human identification after a catastrophic disaster, such as an airplane crash, or in the identification of mysterious, isolated remains

## GEOGRAPHICAL RACES

The theory of geographical races is based on the premise that for hundreds of thousands of years, before long-distance travel became commonplace, various population groups evolved independently from one another, separated by such natural boundaries as mountains, oceans, and deserts. Over time each group developed distinctive characteristics suited to the group's particular environment.

| Classification | Geographical Origins |
|---|---|
| African | Africa south of the Sahara |
| American Indian | North and South America |
| Asian | Mainland Asia, Japan, Malaysia, Indochina, and Indonesia |
| Australian | The island continent of Australia |
| East Indian | The subcontinent of India, south of the Himalayas |
| European | Europe, European Russia, the Middle East, and North Africa |
| Melanesian | Papua New Guinea |
| Micronesian | The Micronesian islands of the western Pacific |
| Polynesian | The Pacific islands from New Zealand to Easter Island |

## PRESENT DISTRIBUTION OF POPULATIONS

The map below roughly reflects the present-day distribution of the geographical races.

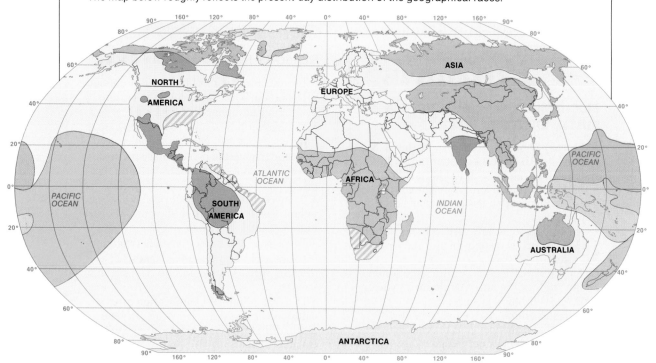

New populations can form wherever people of different geographical races come together to live within the same society. For example, two hundred years ago, the population of the Hawaiian islands was 100 percent Polynesian, but in today's increasingly international society, Hawaii contains similar numbers of Polynesians, Europeans, and Asians. These combinations have resulted in rising numbers of people born of mixed-race heritages.

western Europe, who colonized much of North America, Australia, and New Zealand. Important new foods brought from the Americas, particularly corn and potatoes, have been responsible for the increase in the number of people in other parts of the world.

### ▶ NEW POPULATIONS

Some new populations have come into being. Much of Central and South America are now made up of a new race that began forming at the time of Columbus' voyages to the Americas. These people, called Mestizos, are of combined European and American Indian ancestry. A population that combines West African and European ancestries has been developing in the United States since the 1800's. More recently a new population of mixed geographical origins—Asian, European, and Polynesian—has been forming in Hawaii. New populations continue to form, while others lose their separate nature.

In today's world, the concept of race has limited value. It does not account for the mixing of the world's populations, which is becoming common, nor does it allow for the natural changes that result from evolution.

### ▶ EXPLORING THE PAST

Scientists study native populations to find out where they came from originally. Through scientific detection work, for example, anthropologists have learned that the Navajo Indians of New Mexico originally came from Canada. They know this from studying their blood groups and by their general appearance. Anthropologists would like to know where the Pygmies of Africa came from and why they are so small in stature. The Ainu, who live in northern Japan, may be the last remnant of a local race that was there before the present-day Japanese came from the Asian mainland. Scientific expeditions try to recover and study ancient skeletons to learn more about our origins. As human beings, we want to understand the history of our own species—from the very first people to the changing groupings of populations that exist today.

STANLEY M. GARN
University of Michigan

See also ANTHROPOLOGY; EVOLUTION; GENETICS.

---

### Features Used to Identify Skeletal Remains

The following factors are examined by forensic anthropologists, or "bone detectives," whose findings are admissible as evidence in courts of law:

• Tooth size and shape and the number of cusps on the molar teeth;
• Skull shape and proportions;
• Nose width, projection of the cheekbones, and the size of the dental arch;
• Relative length of the long bones and the vertebral skeleton;
• Proportions of the finger bones;
• Size and proportions of the sacrum and the pelvis as a whole.

## RACHMANINOFF, SERGEI (1873–1943)

The Russian pianist, composer, and conductor Sergei Vasilievich Rachmaninoff was born on April 1, 1873, on his family's estate in Novgorod. He began to study piano with his mother at age 4, and when his family moved to St. Petersburg in 1882, he entered the music conservatory there. Three years later he transferred to the Moscow Conservatory, where he studied with many important Russian musicians. He completed his studies at the conservatory in 1892, receiving a gold medal in composition.

As a composer, Rachmaninoff gained world fame for his works for piano, notably the Prelude in C Sharp Minor (1892) and the Second Piano Concerto (1901). His works, with their flowing melodies and massive, stirring chords, are written in the tradition of such Russian romantic composers as Peter Ilyich Tchaikovsky. In addition to piano pieces, he composed symphonies and other orchestral works, operas, choral works, and songs.

Rachmaninoff was considered the best pianist of his day, with superb technique and a sensitive style. He toured extensively as a pianist and conductor and from 1904 to 1906 conducted opera at the Bolshoi Theater in Moscow. He left Russia after the revolution of 1917 and later settled permanently in the United States. He continued to give concerts and was one of the first pianists to make recordings. He wrote little music, however, producing only five major works between 1926 and 1940. They include *Rhapsody on a Theme of Paganini* (1934), for piano and orchestra, and the Third Symphony (1936). He died in Beverly Hills, California, on March 28, 1943.

Reviewed by KENNETH NOTT
Hartt School, University of Hartford

## RACINE, JEAN BAPTISTE (1639–1699)

The French dramatist Jean Baptiste Racine is famous for his ability to portray deep human emotions in a simple, classical style. Racine was born about December 21, 1639, at La Ferté-Milon. His parents died when he was a child, and he was brought up by his grandparents. When he was 10, he was sent to school in Beauvais. At 16 he began attending school at Port-Royal, a religious community. This school's strict form of Catholicism, known as Jansenism, influenced him strongly.

At Port-Royal, Racine read religious and philosophical works and gained a wide knowledge of Greek and Latin literature. Later, he studied philosophy and theology. In 1660, a poem he wrote in honor of Louis XIV won him favor at court, as well as the friendship of other writers. But when he began to write for the theater, he met with the disapproval of his former masters at Port-Royal.

Racine's first play, *La Thébaide (The Story of Thebes)* (1664), was produced by Molière. It was a momentary success, but it was *Andromaque* (1667) that made Racine famous. Over the next ten years, he wrote the great tragedies *Britannicus* (1669), *Bérénice* (1670), *Bajazet* (1672), *Mithridate* (1673), *Iphigénie* (1674), and *Phèdre* (1677).

In 1677, Racine retired from writing for the stage. That same year, he married Catherine de Romanet and began to devote more time to his duties at court. As the king's official historian, he accompanied the king and his armies to the Netherlands and Belgium.

The only plays Racine wrote after *Phèdre* were biblical dramas to be performed by the schoolgirls of Saint-Cyr. *Phèdre* is generally considered Racine's greatest tragedy. Like some of his other plays, it is based on characters in Greek mythology. All his plays show the destructive force of human passions, and all obey the classical rules for unity of action, place, and time. His style was to be much imitated throughout the following century.

Racine died on April 21, 1699.

Reviewed by WILLIAM D. HOWARTH
Author, *French Literature from
1600 to the Present*

# RACING

Each May some 250,000 people attend the Indianapolis 500 automobile race in Indianapolis, Indiana. Each year tens of thousands of runners around the world enter marathon races, and millions more watch eagerly to see who wins. Racing, in all its forms, has always been exciting to people, whether they take part or simply watch. People are interested in knowing who is the fastest runner, swimmer, cyclist, or skier; which horse, dog, plane, boat, or automobile is fastest.

Racing on foot may be the oldest form of sports competition. The earliest humans probably ran races. The footrace was a major sport at the ancient Greek Olympic Games. Winners were crowned with a laurel wreath and honored by the people. This sport was also popular at the Roman games. Today runners compete in track meets, cross-country races, and road races such as the marathon. Athletes even compete in walking races.

Probably every type of transportation has been used in races. In wintry climates people race on sleds, skis, and ice skates and in iceboats and snowmobiles. On water, people race canoes, rafts, rowboats, sailboats, motorboats, and so on. There are air races for planes, balloons, and gliders. On land, people race in automobiles, karts, and coaster cars and on skateboards, motorcycles, and roller skates. Bicycle racing is an Olympic event and an internationally popular sport.

Animal racing has attracted great interest for centuries. Horse racing has been traced to the Olympic Games of about 600 B.C. These were harness races, in which the horse pulled a chariot and driver. Horseback racing became popular somewhat later.

Dog racing was a spectator sport in ancient Egypt. Today it is particularly widespread in England. Greyhounds are the most common racing dogs. The main dog-racing event is the Waterloo Cup race at Liverpool, England.

Most races involve direct competition by the participants. They start at the same time from a starting line. The first to cross the finish line is the winner. But mass starts are dangerous in some racing, such as skiing and bobsledding. In these events competitors run the course individually. The person or team to complete the course in the least time is the winner.

Relay races are team races. Each team member races the same distance, except in track medley races. As one team member finishes, the next starts. This continues until the last team member completes the race.

Reviewed by NEIL AMDUR
*The New York Times*

See also AUTOMOBILE RACING; AVIATION; BALLOONS AND BALLOONING; BICYCLING; BOATS AND BOATING; BOBSLEDDING; HORSE RACING; ICEBOATING; ICE-SKATING; KARTING; MOTORCYCLES; OLYMPIC GAMES; ROLLER-SKATING; ROWING; SAILING; SKATEBOARDING; SKIING; SOAP BOX DERBY; SWIMMING; TRACK AND FIELD.

# RACISM

Racism is a specific kind of prejudice based on the belief that there are differences among the human races and that some are superior or inferior to others. Traditionally, races have been defined as distinct populations that have specific physical traits based on their geographic or ancestral origins. Racists believe that race not only determines a person's appearance but also that person's character, intelligence, and behavior.

Fanatical racists, such as the neo-Nazi "skinheads," routinely harass and promote violence against blacks and members of other racial groups.

Racism is one element in a wide range of prejudices that exist among different ethnic groups. Ethnic groups are defined as people of similar backgrounds, including their race, nationality, religion, language, and cultural heritage. People who believe that their own particular ethnic group is superior to others are called ethnocentric, or bigoted.

Racism is an extreme form of ethnocentrism, or bigotry. Racists think that they can judge a person based on his or her racial origins and are inclined to make false assumptions about an individual based on racial or ethnic stereotypes. Stereotypes attempt to define entire groups of people according to a narrow and usually uncomplimentary set of characteristics.

Racism often leads to discrimination, which is prejudice in action. For example, an employer might be prejudiced against a job applicant simply because that person has a different skin color. The prejudice becomes discrimination when the employer refuses to hire the applicant for that reason, even though the candidate might otherwise be qualified.

Sociologists (scientists who study social behavior) agree that racism is likely to flare up where two or more racial groups are forced to compete for what they perceive as limited resources or opportunities. Under such circumstances members of the stronger group, typically the majority group, might exclude other races to preserve their position of strength. They then justify their actions by stereotyping the less powerful group as naturally inferior.

Racist messages can be communicated among individuals in a society and also through literature, television, music, newspapers, and other media. Sometimes the messages are obvious and hateful, but often they are subtle and hard to detect. But once these false beliefs become rooted in people's minds and are passed down from generation to generation, they can become accepted as truth and therefore increasingly hard to overcome.

While some racists believe that their race is superior to others, there is no scientific evidence to support such theories. Although some physical differences among groups do exist, one group cannot be said to be genetically superior or inferior to another. In fact, the question of whether or not different races actually exist is under serious debate—especially in modern society, where the intermingling of the world's populations has become commonplace.

## History

Racism has been the root of some of the greatest injustices against humanity. In its most extreme form, racism has led to slavery and even genocide (the deliberate extermination of a targeted group of people).

Slavery is a system in which one group of people falls under the absolute domination of another group. The practice is probably as old as humankind itself. In ancient times, it was customary to make slaves out of prisoners of war. But it was not until the introduction of the African slave trade in the late 1400's that the buying and selling of human beings became a large-scale enterprise.

From the early 1500's until the mid-1800's, millions of Africans were enslaved in the Western Hemisphere, where they were forced to work on plantations and in mines, often under life-threatening conditions. Great numbers of Native Americans, Asians, and other non-whites also were exploited.

In the United States the enslavement of African-Americans was accepted at all levels of society. Scientists of the time maintained that blacks belonged to an inferior species and were therefore naturally subordinate to whites in both character and intelligence. Slave owners embraced the theory that slaves were not fully human; it helped them justify their sub-human treatment of them.

Organized racist groups developed soon after slavery was officially outlawed in the United States with the passage, in 1865, of the 13th Amendment to the Constitution. White supremacists formed terrorist groups, notably the Ku Klux Klan (KKK), that used violence and murder to prevent blacks from assuming equal status in the society.

Similar tactics of terror and dehumanization were used in Nazi Germany beginning in the 1930's, particularly against Jews. German leader Adolf Hitler claimed that Aryans—characterized as white Christians, especially those with fair features—made up the "master race," which was entitled to impose its will on all other "inferior" races. Hitler devised a plan, called the "Final Solution of the Jewish Question," by which he imprisoned Jews in concentration camps. By the time the camps were liberated in 1945, at the close of World War II, about 6 million Jews and other "non-Aryans" had been killed.

Racism certainly influenced American behavior during World War II. For years Asian immigrants had been seen as a "Yellow Peril," and when the nation went to war against Japan, the patriotism of Japanese-Americans immediately came under suspicion. Tens of thousands of Japanese-American citizens were ordered from their homes and placed in detention camps. Even though the United States also was at war with Germany and Italy, no German- or Italian-Americans were ever imprisoned.

### Racism Today

In the United States today racist attitudes and race discrimination persist despite the passage of social legislation intended to ensure equal treatment and the civil rights of all American citizens. Evidence demonstrates that in such fields of education, employment, and justice, minority groups still do not always experience equal advantages or opportunities. The tension caused by such inequalities, whether real or imagined, has been the underlying cause of several serious race riots.

Racism also persists in many other places throughout the world. In South Africa, for example, apartheid, the segregation of people according to race, was practiced by law until 1991, and multi-racial national general elections were not permitted until 1994. Segregation is still practiced unofficially, and equal rights are not guaranteed. Violence between the races remains widespread.

In other places throughout the world, growing numbers of young whites are joining organizations that encourage the revival of Nazi white-supremacist ideas. These self-described "skinheads" promote violent hate crimes against minorities. For example, race-related crimes have risen dramatically in Germany, where the numbers of foreign refugees seeking political asylum soared following the breakup of the communist countries in eastern Europe.

Members of the Ku Klux Klan, a white-supremacist society, conceal their identities and use such terrorist tactics as burning crosses to intimidate minorities.

Also of worldwide concern in eastern Europe is the recent campaign of attempted genocide in the war-ravaged republics that once belonged to the nation of Yugoslavia. For several years, Christian Serbs and Croats have pursued a policy of "ethnic cleansing" to rid the region of its Muslim population. Such episodes continually remind us of the atrocities that can result when intolerance and hatred are freely promoted within a society.

Reviewed by PATRICIA McKISSACK
FREDRICK McKISSACK
Authors, *Taking a Stand Against Racism and Racial Discrimination*

# RACKET SPORTS

Millions of people all over the world play a wide variety of racket (or racquet) sports for fun, exercise, and competition. Most of these sports come from a game that was invented in France during the Middle Ages (500–1450). This game was called **court tennis** because it was first played by monks in the monastery courtyards. Gradually, the game was adopted by kings and nobility and spread outside France.

Among the most popular racket sports, which are the subjects of separate articles in *The New Book of Knowledge*, are badminton, paddle tennis, table tennis (Ping-Pong), and tennis. Other racket sports may not be as familiar or as widely played, but they are enjoyed by many people throughout the world. These include squash, paddleball, racquetball, and platform tennis.

## ▶ SQUASH

Squash, or squash racquets, was invented in England during the mid-1800's by students attending an exclusive school called Harrow, located outside London.

They named the game "squash" because the first balls used, borrowed from a more difficult game called **hard racquets**, were punctured to make them softer and thus "squash" when hit against the court wall.

Squash arrived in the United States in 1882. The first court was built at St. Paul's School in Concord, New Hampshire. From there it spread to other schools, colleges, universities, and many private clubs.

**Equipment.** The racket weighs a little more than half a pound and is 27 inches (68.6 centimeters) long. Its hitting surface is strung with nylon or gut.

The ball is hollow. Its diameter is 1½ inches (3.8 centimeters). For years the ball was made of hard black rubber, and it was a rather dead ball. But in 1976, the "70+" ball was introduced to bring liveliness to the sport. This ball is slightly smaller, lighter, bouncier, and more like the "English" or "International" ball that is used in every country except the United States, Mexico, and parts of Canada.

**The Court.** The official four-wall American singles court is 32 feet (9.8 meters) long, 18½ feet (5.6 meters) wide, and 16 feet (4.9 meters) high at the front wall. Running along the lower part of the front wall is a sheet of metal 17 inches (43.2 centimeters) high. This sheet of metal, called a telltale, clangs when hit

Racket sports are fast-paced games played on walled courts. Most racket sports are played with a small racket and a rubber ball.

with a ball. Hitting the telltale is the same as hitting into the net on a tennis court. You lose the point.

There is also a doubles court on which two teams of two players compete. This court is 25 feet (7.6 meters) wide by 45 feet (13.7 meters) long.

**Rules and Play.** The object of squash is to hit the ball against the front wall so that it rebounds to an area in the court where the opposing player cannot return it to the front wall. The opposing player must hit the ball before it bounces twice on the floor. The basic idea is the same in racquetball and paddleball. The ball can hit many walls and still be in play, as long as the player returns it to the front wall before it bounces on the floor a second time.

To win a match, you must win three out of five games. Fifteen points usually wins a game. But if the score is tied at 13-all or 14-all, the game may be extended to a maximum of 18 points.

There are red lines on the floor and walls within which the ball must bounce to remain in play. If you hit outside these lines or into the telltale, you lose the point. If you interfere with your opponent's shot, a **let** is called, and the point has to be played over. If you get in the way of your opponent on purpose, you lose the point.

Points can be won whether or not you are serving. The player who wins the point is awarded the next serve. A player must serve from an area called a service box. The serve must hit the front wall above a service line. It must then rebound to a service area in the opposite rear of the court.

**▶ PADDLEBALL**

Paddleball is an outgrowth of handball, which was brought to the United States by Irish immigrants in the late 1880's. The one-wall variety is especially popular in New York City. When recreational parks were built in the 1930's, most of them included paddleball courts.

Four-wall paddleball was the creation of a physical education teacher at the University of Michigan in the 1930's. He wanted to keep his tennis team active during the winter months, so he made up a game employing a short paddle and a rubber ball to be played on the university's indoor four-wall handball courts.

**Equipment.** The official paddle is made of wood or a composite material. It is approximately 18 inches (46 centimeters) long and weighs about a pound. A leather thong is attached to the end of the handle, and it must be worn around the player's wrist at all times. There is no limit on the number or size of holes that may be drilled into the face of the paddle to reduce wind resistance. The same paddle is used for both one- and four-wall games.

The ball for four-wall paddleball is about 2 inches (5 centimeters) in diameter and is made of rubber. The one-wall ball is livelier and slightly smaller.

**The Court.** Like the four-wall racquetball court, the four-wall paddleball court is 20 feet (6.1 meters) wide and high and 40 feet (12.2 meters) long. The back wall, which is often constructed of tempered glass for spectator viewing, must be at least 12 feet (3.7 meters) in height. The walls are made of either cement blocks or plastic panels. The floor is usually made of wood.

The one-wall court is 20 feet wide and 34 feet (10.4 meters) long, with the front wall measuring 16 feet (4.9 meters) high. The court is often made entirely of concrete.

**Rules and Play.** The basic idea of paddleball is the same as that of squash. But in paddleball, the ball may hit the ceiling, and there is no telltale.

To win a match, you must win two out of three games. The first and second games are won by the first player who scores 21 points in each. If a third game is required to decide the match, an 11-point game is played. Only the person serving can score points.

In the one-wall version, the players are allowed to transfer the paddle from one hand to the other when making returns. Most one-wall paddleballers have learned to hit the ball equally well and hard using either hand.

There is one small difference in scoring between one-wall and four-wall paddleball. In one-wall, the winning side must win by a margin of at least two points. So, for example, final scores of 22-20 or 23-21 are not unusual in one-wall paddleball.

### ▶ RACQUETBALL

This very simple game is an offshoot of paddleball. It became one of the fastest-growing sports in the United States during the 1970's. Invented by a Connecticut tennis teacher in the 1940's, the sport was first played in community centers and other places that already had handball courts.

**Equipment.** The racquetball racket is made of either aluminum, fiberglass, carbon, or a combination of these materials. It is approximately 22 inches (55.9 centimeters) long and weighs about half a pound. A cord attached to the handle is looped around the player's wrist. The diameter of the rubber ball is 2¼ inches (5.7 centimeters).

**The Court.** Racquetball can be played on a one-, three-, or four-wall court. The four-wall court has the same dimensions and basic line markings as the court used in four-wall paddleball. Two players (singles) or four players (doubles) can play racquetball. A three-player version of the game, not played in tournaments, is called cutthroat.

**Rules and Play.** The basic idea of racquetball is the same as that of squash and paddleball. As in paddleball, the ball may hit the ceiling, there is no telltale, and you must win two out of three games to win a match. Each of the first two games is played to 15 points. If a third game is required to decide the match, an 11-point game is played. Only the person serving can score.

Because of the liveliness of the ball, power is the key to being an effective racquetball player. The hard-driven **kill shot**, or **roll-out**, which is hit just above the floor on the front wall, is frequently an outright winner.

### Four-Wall Racquetball and Paddleball Court

The courts used in four-wall racquetball and paddleball have the same dimensions and the same basic markings. Like other racket sports, these games can be played by two players (singles) or four players (doubles).

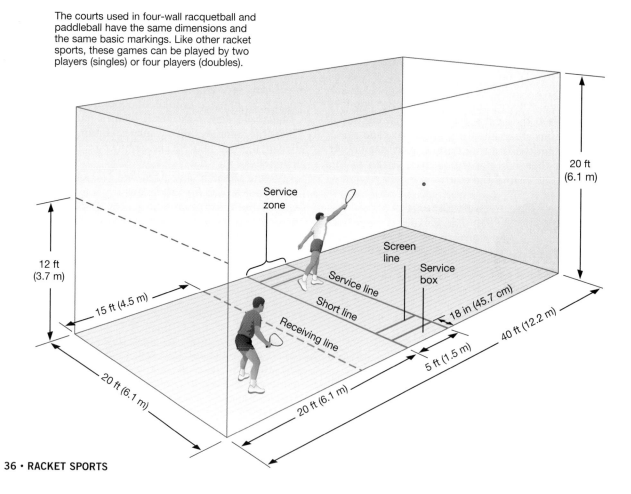

Platform tennis is played on a court that is raised off the ground—a platform—and surrounded by wire screening. Scoring is the same as in regular tennis.

### ▶ PLATFORM TENNIS

Platform tennis is a unique combination of tennis and wall games such as squash. The roots of this sport are to be found in Scarsdale, New York, where the first court was built in 1928 at a private home. It was constructed of wood and raised off the ground to enable outdoor play during the winter months. The sport quickly spread to country clubs that needed a cold-weather activity to stay open year-round.

**Equipment.** The oval-faced rackets contain many holes and are typically made of graphite or titanium. They are about 18 inches (45.7 centimeters) long and weigh about a pound. The ball is either yellow or orange and made of solid sponge rubber. It is about the same size as a tennis ball.

**The Court.** The overall playing court is about 30 feet (9.1 meters) wide and 60 feet (18.3 meters) long. The lines within which the ball must land are identical to badminton— 20 feet (6.1 meters) by 44 feet (13.4 meters). The framework surrounding the court is 12 feet (3.7 meters) high and has steel wire screening attached to it. The court, which is usually made of wood or aluminum, is divided in half by a net.

**Rules and Play.** Scoring is the same as in regular tennis, but only one serve is allowed. A tiebreaker set starts when each player has won six games.

The fundamental strokes for squash, racquetball, and paddleball are hit with a loose wrist. But the platform tennis stroke is very much like the more firm, locked-wrist motion of regular tennis. It is not necessary to hit the ball with great power. This is because of the shortness of the court, and because balls that are hit beyond the boundaries of the court may be returned after they have rebounded off the screens that surround the court.

DICK SQUIRES
Author, *The Other Racquet Sports*

See also HANDBALL.

Air traffic controllers monitor radar screens. Tracking the positions of airplanes is a primary use of radar, which detects and locates objects by means of radio waves.

## RADAR AND SONAR

Sometimes, when conditions are right, you can hear your own echo. If you shout "hello," the sound may bounce back at you from a large object. You then hear your own voice coming back. Your returning voice is called an echo. Radar and sonar are electronic devices that use the principle of an echo to detect and locate objects.

Both radar and sonar locate objects from the echo of a signal that is bounced off the object. Radar uses radio waves, which are a type of electromagnetic energy. Sonar uses the echo principle by sending out sound waves underwater or through the human body to locate objects. Sound waves are a type of acoustic energy. Because of the different type of energy used in radar and sonar, each has its own applications.

### ▶ RADAR

The word "radar" was formed from the first letters of the term "*ra*dio *d*etection *a*nd *r*anging." A radio wave is a type of electromagnetic radiation. (Microwaves, X-rays, and light waves are other types.) It is the fundamental part of this form of technology. "Detection," as used here, means finding an object or target by sending out a radio signal that will bounce back off the target as a radio echo. "Ranging" means measuring the distance to the target from the radar set (the device that sends out the radio signal and picks up the returning echo).

A true radar system uses radio waves. Another system, called optical radar or lidar (from the first letters of the term "*l*ight *d*etection *a*nd *r*anging"), is based on the same principle as radar but uses light waves.

### How Radar Works

Radar sets, also called radar systems, come in many different sizes, depending on the job they are expected to do. But all have four main parts—a transmitter, an antenna, a receiver, and an indicator (display screen). The transmitter produces the radio waves. When a radio wave strikes an object such as an airplane, part of the wave is reflected back to the radar set. The signal is detected by the antenna as a radio echo. The returning echo is sent to the receiver, where its strength is increased, or amplified. The echo is usually displayed as an image that can be seen on the indicator.

The usual type of indicator is the **plan position indicator**, or **PPI**. On the face of its large tube, the operator sees a map-like picture of the surrounding region. This picture looks as if it were made looking down at the area from high above the radar set. On the indicator, the echoes appear as bright spots, called **blips**. The blips show where land areas are located. Blips also show the position of targets, such as planes and ships. The radar operator can pick out these targets because they are moving, while the land areas are not.

A common type of radar is called pulse radar. This type of radar sends out radio waves in short bursts, or **pulses**. The distance to a target is determined by the time it takes the signal to reach the target and the echo to return. Radio signals travel at a known speed—about 186,000 miles (300,000 kilometers) per second, the speed of light. If the radio signal comes back in $\frac{1}{1,000}$ second, then the round trip is 186 miles (300 kilometers). The target must be half that far, or 93 miles (150 kilometers) away.

Pulsed transmission helps determine the distance more accurately. Why is this so? Imagine that you are about to shout across a canyon to make an echo. If you shout a long sentence, the first words will come back before you can finish. It would be impossible to hear the entire echo clearly because it would be mixed with your own speech. But if you shout a short word the echo comes back crisp and clear with no interference from the transmitter (you).

The location of the target in relation to the radar set is found in a different way. The radar antenna sends out radio pulses in a narrow beam, much like the beam of a flashlight. The antenna and its beam are rotated slowly through all possible directions, searching the entire horizon for targets. An echo is reflected from a ship or other object only if the narrow beam happens to strike it. The returning echoes are amplified by the receiver, then go to the indicator, which displays the range and direction of the target.

### Uses of Radar

Radar has both military and civilian uses. The most common civilian use is to help navigate ships and planes. Radar sets car-

ried on a ship or located at an airport pick up echoes from other ships and planes and help prevent collisions. On ships, they also pick up echoes from buoys in channels when the ships enter or leave port. Radar sets help commercial airplanes land when visibility is bad or in the event of mechanical failure.

Radar is also used in meteorology, including weather prediction. Weather forecasters use it, normally combined with lidar (optical radar), to study storms and locate hurricanes and blizzards. **Doppler radar** is based on the principle of the Doppler effect—that is, the frequency of a wave changes as the source of the wave moves toward or away from the receiver. By analyzing changes in the frequency of reflected radio waves, Doppler radar can track the movement of storms and the development of tornadoes. An improved Doppler radar system called Next-Generation Radar (NEXRAD) can predict weather more accurately and farther into the future.

Scientists use radar to track the migrations of birds and insects and to map distant planets. Because it can tell how fast and in which direction a target is moving, radar is used by police to locate speeding automobiles and control street traffic. Similar systems are used in tennis to measure the speed of serves and to call faults. Balloon-borne radar supports officials fighting drug trafficking. Surface-wave radar detects surface waves of the ocean to warn ships of icebergs and nearby vessels.

Historically, there have been two main military uses of radar: search radar and fire-

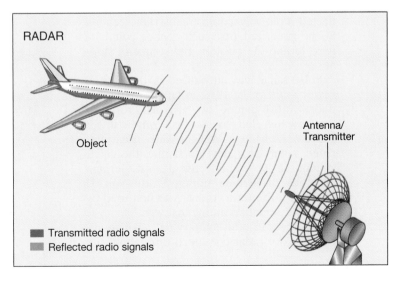

RADAR

Object

Antenna/
Transmitter

■ Transmitted radio signals
■ Reflected radio signals

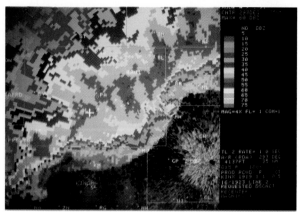

Doppler radar has improved the accuracy of weather forecasting. It uses changes in the frequency of reflected radio waves to track the movement of storms.

control radar. Search radar is the kind already discussed. It continually searches the horizon to find targets. Fire-control radar helps aim a gun or missile so that it will hit the target when fired and must be more accurate than search radar. The U.S. military has also developed specialized types of radar. For example, Miniature Synthetic Aperture Radar (MSAR) is used on aircraft to provide high-quality images in all kinds of weather.

### History of Radar

Radar technology began with experiments using radio waves in the laboratory of German physicist Heinrich Hertz in 1887. He discovered that these waves could be sent through many different materials but were reflected by others. In 1900, a radio pioneer, Nikola Tesla, noticed that large objects could produce reflected radio waves that are strong enough to be detected. He knew that reflected radio waves were really radio echoes. So he predicted that such echoes could be used to find the position and course of ships at sea.

Pulse radar was introduced in the United States in 1925. In 1935, radar was patented under British patent law partly as a result of the research led by Scottish physicist Sir Robert Alexander Watson-Watt. This patented radar later developed into the radar system that proved effective against German air raids on Britain during World War II (1939–45). The term "radar" was first used by U.S. Navy scientists during that war.

Advances in both military and civilian applications of radar continued throughout the 1900's. By the early 2000's, researchers were targeting their efforts at improving radar's range, quality, imaging, and size and reducing its cost.

### ▶ SONAR

The word "sonar" comes from the first letters of "sound navigation ranging." Sonar can detect and locate objects under the sea by echoes, much as porpoises and other marine animals navigate using their natural sonar systems.

### How Sonar Works

There are two types of sonar sets: active and passive. An active sonar set sends out sound pulses called **pings**, then receives the returning sound echo. Passive sonar sets receive sound echoes without transmitting their own sound signals.

In active sonar sets, the sound signals are very powerful compared with ordinary sounds. Most sonar sets send out sounds that are millions of times more powerful than a shout. Each ping lasts a fraction of a second.

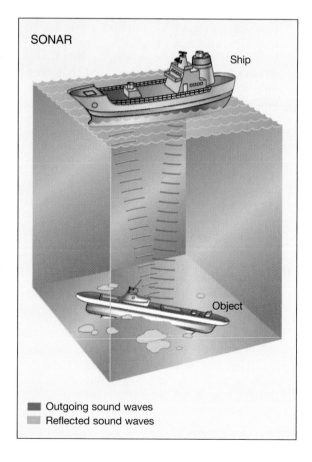

SONAR
Ship
Object
■ Outgoing sound waves
░ Reflected sound waves

Some sonar sets emit sounds you can hear. Other sonar signals are pitched so high that the human ear cannot hear them. These signals are called ultrasonic waves. ("Ultra" means "beyond," and "sonic" means "sound.") The sonar set has a special receiver that can pick up the returning echoes. The location of underwater objects can then be determined by the length of time that elapses between sending the signal and hearing the returning echo.

## Uses of Sonar

Sonar has many uses. Submarines use sonar to detect other vessels. Sonar is also used to measure the depth of water, by means of a device called a **Fathometer**. (One fathom equals 6 feet, or about 1.8 meters.) The Fathometer measures the time it takes for a sound pulse to reach the bottom of the sea and return to the ship. Fishing boats use Fathometers to locate schools of fish.

Oceanographers use sonar to map the contours of the ocean floor. Sound signals can also be sent into the mud or sand on the ocean floor and strike a layer of rock underneath. An echo then comes back, giving the distance to the rock layer.

The same principle is used in searching for oil on land. A sonar pulse is sent into the ground. Echoes come back from the different layers of soil and rock and tell geologists what kinds of soils and rocks are present. This helps them identify areas for drilling that are most likely to contain oil or gas. This subterranean mapping is called **seismic exploration**.

A special kind of sonar used in medicine is called **ultrasonography** or **echoscopy**. High-frequency sound waves produce different echoes when reflected by different body organs. Doctors can use these echoes to detect disease and to monitor the growth of an unborn child.

Extremely high-frequency sound waves are used in medicine and industry to clean many kinds of materials by shaking loose tiny particles of dirt or other matter.

## History of Sonar

It was nature itself that invented "sonic radar," or sonar, well before humans did. For example, bats fly in the dark with poor sight without hitting obstacles and locate prey by means of sound pulses humans cannot hear.

In 1906, American naval architect Lewis Nixon invented the first sonar-like listening device to detect icebergs. During World War I (1914–18), a need to detect submarines increased interest in sonar. French physicist Paul Langévin constructed the first sonar set to detect submarines in 1915. At first, these sonar sets could only "listen" to returning signals. By 1918, Britain and the United States

Members of a research team check their ship's sonar equipment. Sonar uses sound waves to determine ocean depth and locate undersea objects.

had built sonar sets that could send out, as well as receive, sound signals. The U.S. military began using the term "sonar" during World War II. As with radar, new military applications for sonar are constantly being developed. For example, in the early 2000's, the U.S. Navy introduced a sonar system to help clear military mines.

WILLIAM C. VERGARA
Bendix Corporation
Reviewed by KILI LAY
Science Writer

See also ECHO; NAVIGATION; RADIO ASTRONOMY; SOUND AND ULTRASONICS.

**RADAR ASTRONOMY.** See RADIO ASTRONOMY.

# RADIATION

Radiation is the emission of energy in the form of particles or waves. The particles associated with energy emissions are very small—so small that they have an unusual property: They may appear as waves, called **electromagnetic waves**.

An electromagnetic wave consists of two linked vibrations, an electric field and a magnetic field. The speed of these vibrations determines whether the emission is a radio wave, visible light, an X-ray, or some other form of **electromagnetic radiation**. All forms travel at the speed of light, about 186,000 miles (300,000 kilometers) per second, provided they are in a vacuum.

Much of the radiation we experience is due to the excess energy released when atoms or molecules change inside, with parts moving from higher to lower energy levels. Radiation may also come from the fusion of atoms or the decay of radioactive elements. These elements may occur naturally, or they may be artificially produced by scientists. The end result of all radiation energy transfer is heat. (See the article HEAT in Volume H.)

Radiation is found all around us, in various forms. Light, a form of electromagnetic radiation, is given off by the sun and is necessary for the survival of all living things. The sun and other stars also emit particle radiation in the form of cosmic rays. (See the article COSMIC RAYS in Volume C.) People have invented a wide array of uses for radiation. Electronic communication systems—including broadcast radio and television, two-way radios, cell phones, pagers, and wireless computer networks—rely on forms of electromagnetic radiation. Radiation energy enables us to cook our food and light our homes. Numerous everyday devices—remote controls, copy machines, and bar-code scanners, to name just a few—operate by means of radiation.

Doctors use X-rays, a penetrating form of radiation, to reveal inner parts of the body and diagnose disease. Other forms of radiation are used to detect and locate planes and other objects, read CD's and DVD's, and kill bacteria in foods. Radioactive elements are sources of great energy, which can be used to produce electricity. Scientists have harnessed the power of radiation for destructive purposes as well.

To understand radiation, it is necessary to understand the structure of the atom, where radiation begins.

Radiation is all around us and is used in many everyday appliances. Ovens that emit microwaves are used to heat food. Television operates by means of radiation (as does the remote that we click to change channels). Laser light, a special kind of light, is used to scan bar codes. Visible light itself is a form of radiation.

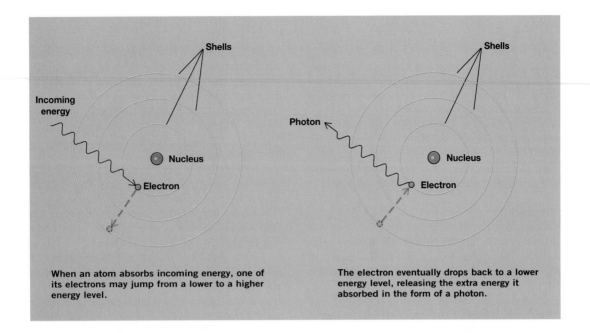

When an atom absorbs incoming energy, one of its electrons may jump from a lower to a higher energy level.

The electron eventually drops back to a lower energy level, releasing the extra energy it absorbed in the form of a photon.

▶ THE STRUCTURE OF ATOMS

Atoms are composed of three kinds of sub-atomic particles: neutrons, protons, and electrons. These particles are made up of even smaller particles called **quarks**. Scientists have found that each atom has a center, called the **nucleus**. The nucleus (plural nuclei) is composed of particles called **nucleons**. When electrically charged, nucleons are **protons**; and when electrically neutral, they are **neutrons**. A strong force holds the neutrons and protons together.

Each kind of atom also contains a particular number of **electrons**. Electrons are spaced around the nucleus in well-defined regions, called shells or energy levels. There may be several shells around the nucleus of an atom, and each shell may have one or more electrons. Electrons of higher energy are in outer shells, and those of lower energy are in shells closer to the nucleus. The electrons do not move around the nucleus in smooth circular paths, but more in the form of a cloud.

▶ ELECTROMAGNETIC RADIATION

Electromagnetic radiation results from a phenomenon known as electron jump. If an electron receives an input of energy or collides with another particle, it may become "excited" and jump out of its natural orbit to one of higher energy. But the electron will eventually fall back to its original orbit. As it does, the electron releases the extra energy it absorbed. That energy is emitted from the electron in the form of a quark called a **photon**. Photons are thought to be fundamental units of energy.

The energy of a photon's emission determines characteristics called its wavelength and frequency. The total possible range of radiation wavelengths and frequencies forms what is called the electromagnetic spectrum. When an atom absorbs outside energy, electrons may be forced out of their orbits over and over again very rapidly. And the atom releases photon energy very rapidly as radiation. The amount of energy that an atom can radiate is the same amount that it has absorbed. And, in electromagnetic radiation, there is only one speed for a photon, no matter what the frequency, wavelength, or intensity of the radiation: the speed of light.

Wavelength

When an electron drops back to its original orbit, waves of radiation are sent out. If the electron has fallen from an orbit near the original one, the waves will carry only a little energy. If the electron has fallen from a more distant orbit, the waves will carry more energy. We observe this greater energy as a change in the length of waves that an electron emits as a photon. The greater the electron's jump, the shorter the wave.

The length of a wave of radiation is the distance between the crest of one wave and the crest of the next. This is called the wavelength. For example, in the visible-light portion of the electromagnetic spectrum, color depends on wavelength. The wavelength of red light is longer than the wavelength of yellow light. Each color of light has a different wavelength. Therefore, each color is the result of a different-size electron jump. As a matter of fact, most forms of radiation are the result of the distances of electron jumps.

### Frequency

Scientists use another measurement, in addition to wavelength, to identify forms of radiation. It is called frequency. When you sit in front of a fire, you feel its heat waves and see its light waves. Both radiations reach you at the same time because both travel at the same speed. But the crests of the light waves are closer together than those of the heat waves—that is, the light waves are shorter. About 30 waves of light radiation reach you in the time it takes one wave of heat radiation to reach you. The number of waves that reach a particular spot in one second is called the frequency of the radiation.

We said that the frequency of the light waves is 30 times the frequency of the heat waves. We could also say that the wavelength of the heat waves is 30 times the wavelength of the light waves. When radio announcers say, "We broadcast on a frequency of 91.7 kilohertz," they mean that 91,700 waves, or vibrations, are reaching your radio each second. (The prefix "kilo" means 1,000, and "hertz" is a unit named after Heinrich Hertz, a German scientist.) To tune in this station, you turn the dial to the number 91.7. Radiation frequencies vary from very low to very high, just as wavelengths vary from very long to very short.

### The Electromagnetic Spectrum

The electromagnetic spectrum is a kind of chart or table used to list and identify the wavelengths of electromagnetic radiation. It is usually made with lines indicating every important radiation wavelength, from the longest waves to the shortest waves.

The range of radiation wavelengths is amazingly large. The longest wavelengths on the spectrum are radio waves. Some radio waves are hundreds or thousands of miles in length. Gamma rays, at the other end of the spectrum, have such short wavelengths that hundreds of millions of their waves could fit across your thumbnail. Similarly, the range of frequencies is from as low as thousands per second for radio waves up to million trillions per second for gamma rays!

The following descriptions of the kinds of radiation in the electromagnetic spectrum are in order of the longest wavelength and lowest frequencies to the shortest wavelengths and highest frequencies.

**Radio Waves.** Radio waves make up a very wide band of radiation and are used in many kinds of communication. Radio waves carry both radio and television signals, as well as signals to pagers, cellular telephones, and other communications devices. Radio waves are identified by their frequencies rather than their wavelengths. Star systems and interstellar clouds produce natural radio waves. (See the article RADIO in this volume.)

**Microwaves.** Radio waves that are shorter than approximately 12 inches (30 centimeters) are called microwaves. Like other radio waves, microwaves are used to carry telephone and other communications signals. They are also used in radar to detect aircraft and other objects. Their ability to heat certain

**THE ELECTROMAGNETIC SPECTRUM**
Electromagnetic waves appear in a very wide range of wavelengths and frequencies—so wide that it is impossible to illustrate to scale. But we can see from the illustration below that waves of increasing energy have shorter wavelengths (and greater frequencies). Radio waves, which have the lowest energy, have the longest wavelengths and the lowest frequencies. Gamma rays, which have the highest energy, have the shortest wavelengths and the highest frequencies. (The frequency scale shown with the spectrum below is in hertz.) For every wavelength, there is a corresponding photon, or light packet. For this reason, the illustration shows a photon at the start and end of every complete wave.

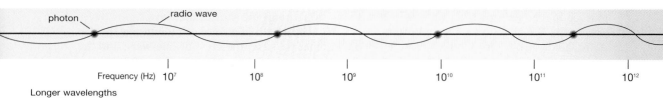

Radio Waves             Microwaves

photon     radio wave

Frequency (Hz)   $10^7$     $10^8$     $10^9$     $10^{10}$     $10^{11}$     $10^{12}$

Longer wavelengths
Lower frequencies
Lower energies

materials has led to many other uses, including microwave cooking. The Global Positioning System (GPS) depends on microwave transmission between satellites and a handheld instrument.

**Infrared Radiation.** The next band of radiation in the electromagnetic spectrum is infrared radiation. These waves are shorter in length and greater in frequency than microwaves. You cannot see infrared radiation, but you can feel it—it is heat radiation. Kitchen appliances such as toasters and electric broilers heat by infrared radiation. Night-vision goggles and cameras use infrared radiation to "see" objects in the dark and to monitor the health of trees and crops.

**Visible Light.** The human eye can detect waves in one small part of the electromagnetic spectrum. These are light rays, or visible radiation. We can see a thing only when light waves from it reach our eyes.

The wavelength of light waves is about halfway between the longest and the shortest wavelengths in the electromagnetic spectrum. Light waves make up only a tiny part of the spectrum, but there is a big variety of wavelengths among them. Light radiation such as that from the sun is composed of every color. When all the colors appear together, we see them as white light.

Each color has a different wavelength. Red light has the longest waves that we can see; about 13,000 of them cover a half inch of space. The second longest wavelength of light is the color orange, followed by yellow, green, and blue. Violet, the color with the shortest visible waves, has about 26,000 waves per half inch. The shadings of these colors have their own range of frequencies and wavelengths. They occur as a sequence of colors in the electromagnetic spectrum.

All electromagnetic radiation travels through empty space at the same speed. But when radiation passes through some substances—such as air, glass, or water—its speed is reduced slightly. When sunlight travels through drops of rainwater, the different wavelengths move at different speeds. As a result, the various wavelengths, or colors, travel in slightly different paths. You see these colors dispersed, or spread out, into a rainbowlike band. Scientists call this many-colored band the **visible light spectrum.** (For more information on visible light, see the article LIGHT in Volume L.)

**Ultraviolet Radiation.** Just past the shortest visible violet-light wavelengths are the radiations in the ultraviolet range. Ultraviolet rays are emitted by the sun and by certain types of electric lamps. Ultraviolet wavelengths range from just above those of violet light to 2.5 million waves per inch.

Ultraviolet rays are described as penetrating rays. Waves of radiation travel until they strike an object. Light waves are slowed down a little by glass or water and stopped by an opaque object (one that does not allow light to pass through). Shorter waves of radiation are more penetrating than the longer waves. The penetrating ultraviolet waves from the sun, for example, reach the nerves in our skin. Exposure to ultraviolet light darkens the skin, which prevents too much of this radiation from passing deeper into the body. Some ultraviolet radiation is good for you, but too much exposure can damage the body cells and should be avoided.

Only about half the ultraviolet rays from the sun reach the ground. Many of them are absorbed high up in the Earth's atmosphere. There, oxygen atoms absorb ultraviolet rays to form an unstable molecule of oxygen, called ozone. The ozone layer in the atmosphere acts somewhat like a blanket, keeping many of the ultraviolet rays from reaching the surface of the Earth. (See the article OZONE in Volume O.)

**X-Rays.** X-rays have a shorter wavelength than ultraviolet rays and are very penetrating. Some X-ray wavelengths are so short that 1,000 of them are not as long as a single ultraviolet wave.

X-rays are emitted from the sun but do not reach the surface of the Earth, because the

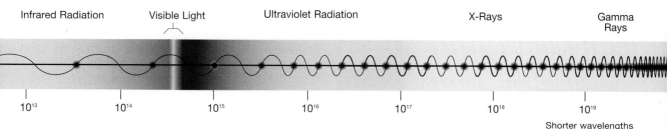

Infrared Radiation     Visible Light     Ultraviolet Radiation     X-Rays     Gamma Rays

$10^{13}$     $10^{14}$     $10^{15}$     $10^{16}$     $10^{17}$     $10^{18}$     $10^{19}$

Shorter wavelengths
Higher frequencies
Higher energies

atmosphere acts as a shield and does not allow them to get through. It is just as well that the atmosphere does this, for X-radiation is very penetrating. Too much of it can kill cells in the body and in time kill people. On the other hand, X-rays can be of great help when carefully used. Doctors use them to check internal parts of the body. Because X-rays can kill cells, they are sometimes used to destroy cancer cells. (See the article X-RAYS in Volume WXYZ.)

**Gamma Rays.** Gamma rays are bursts of photons emitted from the electrons of radioactive atoms and from atoms that are broken up in the sun and other stars. They are also produced in nuclear reactors. Gamma

Radioactivity can be extremely harmful. Properly controlled, however, it can be very useful in research, industry, and medicine.

rays are very short in wavelength, at least as short as the shortest X-rays.

▶ **RADIOACTIVE RADIATION**

Radioactive radiation is another form of radiation. It differs from other forms of radiation in the way it is generated. Radioactive rays are not produced by electron jumps. All radioactive radiation is emitted from radioactive atoms. Such atoms break down continually. As they break down, they radiate

particles of matter and energy. There are about 50 different atoms in nature that are radioactive. Scientists have created many more. Particles are emitted from nuclear reactions and travel as radioactive rays. Three are described here, but several more are known to exist.

**Alpha** particles are the nuclei of helium atoms and are composed of two neutrons and two protons. Their speed is about 10,000–20,000 miles (16,000–32,000 kilometers) per second. A thin sheet of paper can stop alpha particles. **Beta** particles are high-speed electrons that shoot out from radioactive atoms. They have a negative charge and can travel at speeds of 60,000–160,000 miles (96,000–256,000 kilometers) per second. A layer of thick aluminum can stop beta particles. **Gamma** rays are bursts of photons emitted from electrons and are included in the electromagnetic spectrum. They travel at the speed of light. Thick layers of concrete or lead are required to stop gamma rays.

Radioactive radiation is very penetrating. It can be extremely damaging to living things. Properly controlled, however, radioactivity has proved very useful in research, industry, and medicine. Scientists produce a reaction called **nuclear fission**, in which the nucleus of a heavy atom such as uranium is split, releasing a large amount of energy. In an opposite reaction, **nuclear fusion**, light atoms such as hydrogen are joined at high temperatures to form heavier atoms. This process, which powers the sun, releases a huge amount of energy. (See the articles NUCLEAR ENERGY in Volume N and RADIOACTIVE ELEMENTS in this volume.)

▶ **HISTORY**

Humans have studied radiation for thousands of years, particularly as it relates to light. Some ancient Greek philosophers thought that every visible object must emit a stream of light particles that allowed humans to see. This **particle theory** was accepted for many years because light appears to move in a straight line. Then, in the 1600's, Dutch scientist Christiaan Huygens demonstrated that under certain conditions light radiates, or spreads out. He proposed that light was actually a wave. The **wave theory** of light had become accepted by the 1800's.

Later, magnets were found to affect radiation. English scientist Michael Faraday discovered that light could be twisted if the beam was passed close to a magnet. In 1865, Scottish physicist James Clerk Maxwell suggested that light was made up of electromagnetic waves and predicted the existence of other electromagnetic waves traveling at the speed of light. In 1880, American physicist Albert Michelson developed an experiment that determined this speed. The existence of other forms of electromagnetic radiation was confirmed by the discovery of radio waves and X-rays toward the end of the 1800's.

In 1896, while investigating the recently discovered X-rays, French physicist Antoine Henri Becquerel discovered that uranium emitted radiation. Becquerel also demonstrated that the radiation emitted by uranium could be deflected by a magnetic field and must therefore consist of charged particles. Two other French scientists, Marie and Pierre Curie, discovered the radioactive elements polonium and radium. Madame Curie introduced the term "radioactivity," and the basic unit of radioactivity, the curie, is named in honor of the couple.

In 1911, British physicist Ernest Rutherford found that atomic particles consist primarily of empty space surrounding a well-defined core, called a nucleus. He also showed that radioactive elements undergo a process of decay. Rutherford was the first to artificially change one element into another. This unleashed incredible energy within the atom, which eventually would be harnessed for both beneficial and destructive purposes.

In 1900, German physicist Max Planck showed that radiation processes were electromagnetic in nature and proposed the **quantum theory**. This theory says that light energy is emitted in the form of tiny bundles, or quanta, of energy. ("Quanta" is the plural of "quantum.") In 1905, German-born physicist Albert Einstein proposed a photoelectric theory explaining that light consists of particles without mass; light is bundles of electromagnetic energy. Einstein also proposed a relationship for light and matter in his famous equation, $E = mc^2$ (energy is equal to mass times the speed of light squared).

Today scientists agree that light has a dual nature, part particle and part wave. The photon is now known to travel only at the speed of light but in a range of frequencies and wavelengths. The tiny quanta of energy are believed to be wave packets. The quantum theory explains the two kinds of results scientists observed in their research. In some experiments, light behaves as though it is made of waves. In others, light behaves as though it is made of small packets or particle energy.

The quantum theory is leading scientists to a fuller understanding of the nature of matter and of the many ways people can use radiation. Currently, scientists are investigating quarks, first named in 1964 by American physicist Murray Gell-Mann. Quark theory is helping them understand more about the nature of matter, energy, and radiation.

NORM THOMSON
Department of Science Education
University of Georgia

## WONDER QUESTION

### What is food irradiation?

Food irradiation is a process in which food is briefly exposed to a radiant energy source, such as gamma rays or electron beams, within a controlled facility. The purpose of this procedure is to kill bacteria and parasites that would lead to food-borne disease. Many foods—including some meats, seafood, fruits, vegetables, and spices—are irradiated. Studies have shown that irradiated food contains fewer disease-causing germs and is less likely to spoil. The food is not radioactive, and its nutritional value is basically the same. Some irradiated food may have a slightly different taste.

Irradiated food should be stored, handled, and cooked in the same manner as ordinary food. A warning label and an internationally recognized symbol, known as the **radura** (*right*), are included on the packaging to indicate that the food has been irradiated. In the United States, food irradiation is regulated by the Food and Drug Administration (FDA) and other agencies.

# RADIATION BELTS

High above the Earth's atmosphere is a large region of invisible radiation particles. Most of these particles occur in two belts, one inside the other, which circle the Earth at the equator. They are called radiation belts. The belts are thickest above the equator and become thinner as they extend above the Earth's North and South poles.

The radiation in these belts consists of electrically charged particles—mostly protons and electrons, which are usually found as parts of atoms. These protons (positively charged) and electrons (negatively charged) come from different sources, including cosmic rays and the sun.

Most radiation particles have a great deal of energy and move very fast. High-energy radiation particles can be a hazard to space travel because they can cause radiation sickness. Spacecraft traveling through zones of such particles must be shielded against them.

▶ **DISCOVERY OF RADIATION BELTS**

In the late 1950's, a team of American scientists, headed by James A. Van Allen, made a special study of **cosmic rays**, which are high-energy radiation particles that move through space at a high rate of speed. Some come from the sun, while others are released into space when a star destroys itself in a gigantic explosion called a **supernova**.

In 1958, data sent back to Earth from the space satellite *Explorer I* showed very few cosmic rays at the high altitudes where satellites were orbiting the Earth. Van Allen's team suspected that there was so much radiation at these altitudes that the satellite's Geiger counter—a device that records the number of radiation particles that enter it—failed to work properly. Data obtained by subsequent satellites and space probes confirmed their suspicions. Specially designed radiation counters in these spacecraft showed that the Earth is surrounded by two regions of extremely powerful radiation that must contain particles in addition to those that make up cosmic rays. These two areas are known as the **Van Allen belts**.

The lower edge of the inner Van Allen belt is about 400 miles (644 kilometers) above the Earth. At its thickest, over the equator, it reaches a height of about 3,000 miles (4,830 kilometers). The strongest radiation is at a height of about 2,000 miles (3,220 kilometers). The inner belt is much thinner at the poles and consists mainly of particles created when cosmic rays from space collide with atoms in the upper fringes of the Earth's atmosphere.

The outer Van Allen belt extends from about 8,000 to 12,000 miles (12,880 to 19,320 kilometers) above the equator. The outer belt is also much thinner at the poles. Most of the particles in the outer belt come from the sun. These charged particles, chiefly electrons and protons, stream off the sun continuously and form what is known as the **solar wind**. **Solar flares**, great eruptions of energy that occur on the surface of the sun, contribute to and enhance the solar wind by unleashing enormous numbers of charged particles into space at speeds of 1 million miles (1.6 million kilometers) per hour or more.

▶ **EARTH'S MAGNETIC FIELD**

The Van Allen belts exist because the Earth has a magnetic field. It is invisible, but you can observe its shape. Place a bar-shaped magnet with a sheet of paper on top of it on a flat surface. Sprinkle iron filings on top of the paper. The iron filings, acting like little magnets, will line up along the bar's magnetic field—along curved lines, from one pole of the magnet to the other.

The Earth's magnetic field is generated by its molten iron core and its rotation, which together have the same effect as a large bar magnet buried inside the planet. So the Earth's magnetic field lines loop around the Earth, emerging from one magnetic pole and

**The Earth is surrounded by two regions of radiation called the Van Allen belts. They are formed by charged particles trapped in the Earth's magnetic field.**

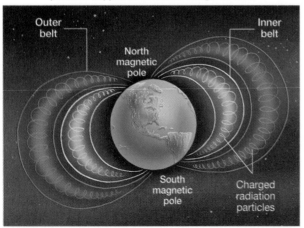

Outer belt

Inner belt

North magnetic pole

South magnetic pole

Charged radiation particles

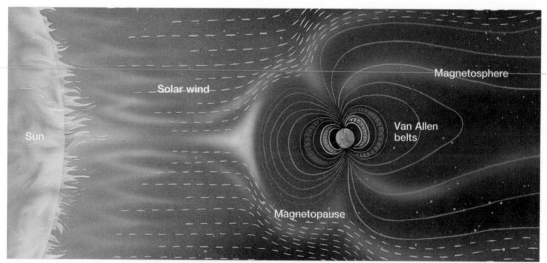

The Van Allen belts lie within the magnetosphere. The shape of this region is affected by the strong solar wind blowing against its outer boundary, called the magnetopause.

re-entering the planet at the other magnetic pole, just like the magnetic field lines of a bar magnet. The poles of the Earth's magnetic field do not fall exactly where its North and South poles are located geographically because the iron core is not exactly aligned with the Earth's axis of rotation.

When a charged particle encounters a magnetic field, its path of motion is bent and it is forced to follow a spiral or corkscrew path along the magnetic field's lines of force. In this way, charged particles from space and the Earth's upper atmosphere become trapped, spiraling rapidly back and forth between the magnetic poles along the Earth's magnetic lines of force. Radiation particles trapped this way are what form the Van Allen belts.

The Van Allen radiation belts lie within a much larger region of weaker radiation that surrounds most of the Earth. This region, known as the **magnetosphere**, extends outward for tens of thousands of miles. It consists of low-speed electrons and protons, and its shape is also determined by the Earth's magnetic field. The solar wind, however, is so strong it can distort the shape of the magnetosphere. The solar wind blows against the magnetosphere's outer boundary, called the **magnetopause**, pushing the magnetosphere nearer to the Earth on its sunlit side. On the dark side of the Earth, the magnetosphere trails off into space.

The lower edge of the magnetosphere comes to within a few hundred miles of the surface of the Earth. On the sunlit side of the Earth, it extends to a height of about 30,000 to 40,000 miles (48,300 to 64,400 kilometers), depending on the strength of the solar wind. The magnetosphere rises even higher above the dark side of the Earth.

Other planets in the solar system, notably Jupiter, Saturn, Uranus, and Neptune, also have radiation belts and magnetospheres.

### ▶ AURORAS

If the charged particles released by solar flares happen to flow in the direction of the Earth, they ultimately encounter the magnetosphere and are forced to spiral along its magnetic lines of force toward the Earth's magnetic poles. When the particles collide with the Earth's upper atmosphere, they create streamers of light called auroras. Auroras appear in about an eleven-year cycle known as the sunspot cycle, and they depend on the frequency and size of flares on the sun. The auroras seen in the sky near the North Pole are known as aurora borealis (northern lights). Those seen near the South Pole are known as aurora australis (southern lights). Auroras have also been observed in the upper atmospheres around Jupiter and Saturn's polar regions.

WILLIAM A. GUTSCH, JR.
President, The Challenger Center for
Space Science Education

See also COSMIC RAYS; EARTH; IONS AND IONIZATION; MAGNETS AND MAGNETISM; RADIATION; SPACE EXPLORATION AND TRAVEL (Danger from Radiation).

# RADIO

If you were to see someone wearing earphones dancing down the street, you would not consider it unusual. If you were riding in a speeding car on a turnpike and wanted to hear the news, a weather report, or the baseball scores, you would merely turn a knob or press a button or two. And if you wanted to get up early to study for a test in school, you would simply press some buttons and go to sleep that night, confident that you would be awakened on time by soft music the next morning.

Radio is a part of everyday life. Personal radios, car stereos, and clock radios are just some of the many kinds of radio receivers we use. Since its invention just over 100 years ago, radio has become one of our most popular and reliable forms of communication.

Radio is an electronic technology that enables communication between two points without connecting wires or cables. (Before radio, telephone and telegraph communication required a wire to carry the message between sender and receiver.) Radio waves can carry a signal representing sounds or other information along the ground or through air or outer space. These signals travel at the speed of light, so messages can reach any place in the world in about a second.

Communicating by radio involves three steps: 1) converting, or changing, sound or other information into an electrical signal; 2) transmitting the signal; and 3) receiving the signal. New technologies, such as digital signals and the use of satellites in radio transmission, have not changed these basic steps.

Radio communication's most familiar form is broadcast radio. In addition, radio has important uses in industry, transportation, and public safety. It is also used in communications networks, national defense, information processing, space travel and exploration, and many other areas.

▶ USES OF RADIO

Broadcast radio is designed to reach large numbers of people. Programming originates in a broadcast studio and is picked up by ordinary radio receivers—home stereo systems, car stereos, pocket radios, and others. Radio broadcasts provide many different kinds of information and entertainment for the public. A person can listen to recorded music, news reports, weather forecasts, sporting events, talk shows, speeches and interviews, educational programs, and even radio dramas.

In addition to broadcasting, radio is used in two-way communication. Police and fire departments as well as ambulance and taxi

companies use two-way radios to dispatch, or send out, vehicles and to stay in contact with them. Farmers, ranchers, hunters, campers, soldiers in combat, and others use walkie-talkies (portable two-way radios) to communicate and work together. Motorists, particularly truckers, use citizens band (CB) radios to alert one another to road hazards or traffic tie-ups. Airplane pilots use two-way radio to talk with other pilots and ground traffic controllers, as do astronauts in space to talk with their control stations on Earth and to other astronauts.

Paging systems are a form of one-way radio used by doctors, government officials, and others who need to be reached quickly. After receiving a paging signal from a small monitor, the person telephones his or her office to receive messages.

Radio is also important in communication systems such as telephone and telegraph. Although telephone networks rely on wires and cables, they also make use of radio. A cordless phone uses radio waves to communicate with its base. And when you talk long-distance on the telephone, your voice may be transmitted by radio waves over much of the distance. Some calls are sent by radio to relay satellites.

Radio is a key link in cellular telephone systems. Radio towers send and receive signals from cell phones. A computer tracks the strength of a cell phone's signal and, if the signal weakens, switches the phone to another tower. This allows callers to travel long distances without losing cell-phone reception.

Radio has many uses beyond voice transmission. Its waves can carry other kinds of information and signals. For example, radio waves carry guidance and control signals from computers on Earth to unmanned spaceships in outer space. These signals keep a spacecraft on course and help it perform maneuvers. Signals emitted by remote-control radio devices operate railroad switching systems and fly planes and rockets. In many homes, hand-held radio remote controls operate televisions, garage doors, and other devices. Radio signals are used to control model planes and toy race cars, too.

Radio plays an increasingly important role in computer networks. In a wireless computer network, computers use radio signals to send information to each other, to control peripherals such as printers, and to access the Internet. The heart of such a network is a base station with a two-way radio and a link to a high-speed Internet connection. Computers equipped to send and receive radio signals can access the network as long as they are within range of the base station.

Radio is used in the navigation system known as the Global Positioning System (GPS). In GPS, satellites above Earth beam down radio signals that help people determine their precise location. Radar, important for defense as well as air and sea navigation, is also a form of radio. (See RADAR AND SONAR in this volume.)

Certain kinds of telescopes can detect radio waves in outer space. These radio telescopes are used to study distant galaxies and are an important part of space research. (See RADIO ASTRONOMY in this volume.)

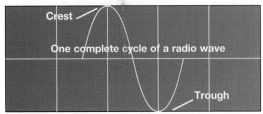

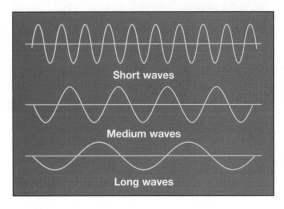

*Above:* Each radio wave has a high point (crest) and a low point (trough). The number of complete waves, or cycles, transmitted in one second is the wave's frequency. *Right:* Short waves have a high frequency, while longer waves have lower frequencies.

## ▶ HOW RADIO WORKS

To understand how radio works, it is necessary to know what radio waves are and how they behave.

### Radio Waves

Radio waves are electromagnetic. They are created when an electrical current flows through a metal wire or rod (the transmitting antenna). When they reach a corresponding receiving antenna, the radio waves produce a second electrical current that is changed into the sound you hear.

Radio waves travel in all directions from their source, like the ripples of water that form when a pebble is dropped into a pond. The electromagnetic waves travel best through air and outer space but can also penetrate the ground and water. Radio waves can neither be seen nor felt, and the sound or information that the waves carry can be recovered only with a radio receiver.

Each radio wave has a high point called a **crest** and a low point called a **trough**. The wave's strength, known as its **amplitude**, is determined by its height from trough to crest.

The distance from one crest to the next is the **wavelength**. If the wavelength is short, the crests are close together. If the wavelength is long, the crests are farther apart.

Radio waves are invisible, but their lengths can be measured with scientific instruments and detected by radio receivers. Radio waves may be measured in units as small as millimeters and as large as kilometers.

**Frequency**, a basic term in radio, is the number of cycles, or complete waves, transmitted or broadcast in one second. Frequencies may vary from a few cycles per second to millions of cycles per second.

All electromagnetic waves travel at the same speed—about 186,000 miles (300,000 kilometers) per second, the speed of light. This means that the higher the frequency, the shorter the wavelength. In high- and very-high-frequency broadcasts, the crests follow each other quickly. Many thousands or millions of cycles are completed in one second.

Although they move at the same speed as high-frequency waves, low-frequency waves

## HOW RADIO SIGNALS REACH US

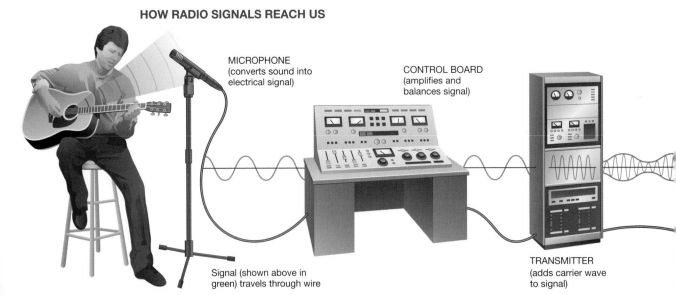

MICROPHONE (converts sound into electrical signal)

CONTROL BOARD (amplifies and balances signal)

TRANSMITTER (adds carrier wave to signal)

Signal (shown above in green) travels through wire

follow each other more slowly. For this reason, their frequency is lower. One way to remember this is that it takes more time to transmit ten long waves (low frequency) than it does to transmit ten short waves (high frequency).

Both low- and high-frequency waves are measured in **kilohertz** (usually written as kHz), or thousands of cycles per second. Very-high-frequency waves are measured in **megahertz** (MHz), or millions of cycles per second.

On the AM band of your radio you will find the numbers 540, 800, and so on up to 1600. Each number refers to a frequency measured in kilohertz. On the FM band, which uses very-high-frequency waves, the numbers run from about 88 to 108. These are frequencies measured in megahertz. Each U.S. radio station has a frequency assigned to it by the government, and it broadcasts only at that frequency.

### How Radio Signals Are Transmitted

A radio transmitter produces electromagnetic waves that are sent out in all directions by an antenna. In broadcast radio the transmitter may be located at the radio station. More often it is located next to one or more towers that make up the station's antenna. These towers are normally in rural areas where they are free from disturbance by static usually found in large cities.

The transmitter is connected by cable to the radio station's headquarters, which house the sound studio. In the studio, sounds come from microphones, computers, compact disc players, satellite feeds, and other audio devices. These feed into a control board, where a technician makes adjustments necessary to provide a strong, clear signal.

For a remote broadcast, which takes place outside the radio studio—such as a baseball game—the announcements and other sounds on the site are relayed back to the radio station by telephone. The broadcast is then sent as usual to the transmitter and antenna. Sometimes radio waves provide the link between the remote location and the radio station.

The next step involves the radio transmitter, which uses a powerful electrical current to produce the **carrier wave**. This is the electromagnetic wave at the specific frequency assigned to the station.

The transmitter combines the electrical current from the studio microphone with the carrier wave to produce the broadcast signal. The transmitter sends these signals to the transmitting antenna, which sends them out in all directions.

### How Radio Signals Are Received

The air around you is filled at all times with radio waves. Your radio receiver picks up these waves and turns them back into sound waves. How does it do this?

Every receiver has four basic units: the antenna, tuner, amplifier, and loudspeaker. Depending on the type of radio, you can see parts of some of these units. For example, car radio antennas are visible, usually near the driver's window or embedded in the glass of the windshield. If you have a personal radio, the antenna may be inside the metal band that connects the two earphones. Some radios have internal antennas hidden from view.

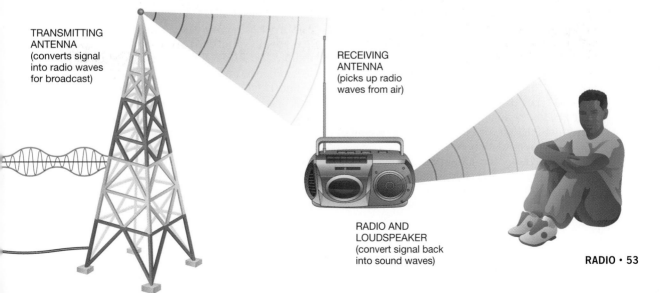

TRANSMITTING ANTENNA (converts signal into radio waves for broadcast)

RECEIVING ANTENNA (picks up radio waves from air)

RADIO AND LOUDSPEAKER (convert signal back into sound waves)

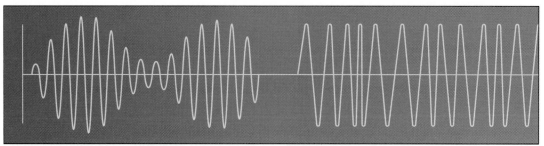

In AM radio, the amplitude (height) of the wave is modulated (changed) to determine the sound being broadcast. In FM radio, the amplitude remains constant, but the frequency is changed.

The antenna picks up radio waves from the air and converts them into a weak electrical current. This current represents the original sound picked up by the studio microphone.

On your radio, look for a large knob or buttons marked Tuning. These connect to the receiver's tuner circuitry. The tuner's job is to pick up the frequency of the station you select and to block the frequencies of other stations. It also separates the sound signal sent out of the radio studio from the carrier wave added by the transmitter.

You cannot see the third unit, the amplifier, because it is inside the radio. It strengthens the electrical current from the tuner so that the sound signal is strong enough to activate the loudspeaker.

The loudspeaker, which may be visible in some radios, fulfills the final step in receiving radio signals by changing the electrical signal back into sound waves. These sound waves are exact copies of those originally produced in the broadcast studio or at the remote broadcasting site.

### AM and FM

Before radio signals are broadcast, electrical currents that represent sounds are combined with the radio station's carrier waves through a process called modulation. In this process the pattern of the carrier is modulated, or changed. The modulation determines the exact sounds you hear from your radio.

Two types of modulation are used in standard radio broadcasting. One is called **amplitude modulation**, or AM. The other is called **frequency modulation**, or FM.

In AM radio, the amplitude, or height, of the carrier wave determines the properties of the broadcast sound. The rate of amplitude change (the number of times per second the carrier waves increase or decrease in height) determines the sound being broadcast.

In FM radio, slight changes in the frequency of the carrier wave determine the properties of the broadcast sound. The rate of frequency change determines the sound being broadcast. (Generally, the changes in frequency used to modulate the FM sound are small relative to the very high frequency of the carrier wave itself.)

AM radio is well suited for long-distance transmissions but is often disturbed by static. FM radio will not transmit as far, but it produces a clear sound.

A radio program's signal is transmitted in either AM or FM. Receivers have buttons or switches that select between AM and FM.

### Shortwave Radio

Shortwave radio can send signals long distances—even over oceans and to other countries—by bouncing them off the ionosphere, an atmospheric layer above the clouds. The name "shortwave" comes from the short lengths of the waves. They are 33 to 262 feet (10 to 80 meters) in length and have high frequencies of 3 to 30 MHz.

To listen to shortwave broadcasts, you must have a radio that can receive the signals. With a shortwave radio, you can hear music, news, and a wide variety of sounds and signals from around the world. Spies have used shortwave to send coded messages.

Shortwave radio was invented in the 1920's and became popular around the world in the late 1930's. Today shortwave radio in the United States is used mostly by hobbyists. In other countries, shortwave is more commonly listened to, and it provides news from international broadcasters such as the British Broadcasting Corporation or Voice of America, a news service that is part of the U.S. government. In 2002, it was estimated that 600 million shortwave receivers were in use.

Shortwave transmission is also used to transmit telephone and telegraph communications over long distances and to communicate with ships at sea and aircraft.

### Digital Radio

In the 1990's the radio industry began to adopt a new broadcasting technology called digital radio. Traditional broadcasts use **analog signals**, which are similar, or analogous, to the sounds they represent. **Digital signals** represent the original sounds in strings of 1's and 0's. This same digital code is used in compact discs and computers. In digital radio, sound waves are changed into digital code before they are combined with the carrier wave and sent through the air.

Digital broadcasting produces clearer sound. A digital FM signal sounds almost as good as a compact disc, and a digital AM signal sounds as good as an analog FM signal. Digital signals are less likely to be damaged by interference from other stations.

Some countries, such as Canada and the United Kingdom, have introduced digital radio broadcasts on frequencies that are separate from the AM and FM bands. In the United Kingdom, for example, digital stations broadcast on the frequencies between 217.5 MHz and 230 MHz. In the United States, however, digital signals are sent on the FM band, along with the analog FM signals.

Digital radio offers listeners and broadcasters new ways to use radio. Because many kinds of information can be put in digital code, stations can send more than just sound to your radio. Short text messages can appear on your radio to tell you what song is playing, what the weather will be like, or the name of the station. And in the future you might even be able to press a button on your radio that would let you buy the compact disc the station is playing.

Digital broadcast technology lets stations transmit more information than they can with analog signals. Some stations in the United States, especially noncommercial stations, want to use digital radio to broadcast more than one channel of programming at the same time. Listeners with digital radios would be able to tune to a station, then press a button on their radio that would switch to a sec-

ond channel broadcast by that station. This way, listeners might be able to hear whole new channels full of music, news, or even shows in other languages.

### ▶ THE RADIO INDUSTRY

Thousands of radio stations broadcast today in the United States on AM and FM. There are two kinds of stations: commercial and noncommercial.

The majority of stations are commercial, which means they make money by selling advertising. These stations are concerned mainly with airing programming that will be popular with as many listeners as possible so that businesses and manufacturers will want to buy ads on the station.

Noncommercial stations are not allowed to sell advertising and must make money by other means. There are several different kinds of noncommercial stations. Some

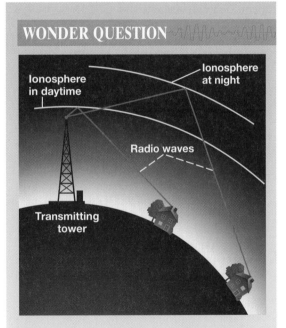

**WONDER QUESTION**

Ionosphere in daytime

Ionosphere at night

Radio waves

Transmitting tower

### Why can you hear radio stations from farther away at night?

AM radio stations can broadcast farther at night because they bounce their signals off the ionosphere, a layer of the atmosphere that acts as a sort of electronic "mirror" and reflects radio waves back to the ground. The ionosphere is higher at night than during the day. Radio waves thus travel farther before hitting the ionosphere and are bounced back to a point that is farther from their source.

## Radio Station Operations

A radio broadcasting station is an exciting place. Programs must be broadcast precisely on schedule. To make this possible, the people who work in the station must be alert and observant. These people are vitally concerned with the world around them and may work closely with celebrities and other people who make the news.

A radio broadcasting station has three major departments: the program department, the technical department, and the business department. Radio stations employ varying numbers of people. In small towns, stations with weak signals of a few hundred or even a few thousand watts may have only a few employees. One person may

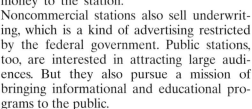

broadcast religious music and talk programming. Others are owned by colleges and high schools and are used to teach students how to run a radio station. Still others, called public stations, broadcast music and local and national news. These stations ask listeners to donate money to the station. Noncommercial stations also sell underwriting, which is a kind of advertising restricted by the federal government. Public stations, too, are interested in attracting large audiences. But they also pursue a mission of bringing informational and educational programs to the public.

Producing programs is expensive. Many stations, both commercial and noncommercial, get programs from **networks**. Networks are companies that produce programs and send them to stations around the country. This lets stations air shows that they might not be able to produce on their own. And listeners like being able to go from city to city and still hear their favorite shows.

Some networks own stations. Others do not. Two big networks that provide programming to commercial stations are ABC Radio Network and Westwood One. National Public Radio, which does not own stations, is the biggest provider of programming to public radio stations.

work in several departments. In large metropolitan areas, stations with strong signals of 50,000 watts or more usually have large staffs. For example, more people may work in the news department of a major New York City station than work in all departments of a small-town station.

The program department decides what to broadcast and when to broadcast it. It includes announcers and disc jockeys. People who write and schedule advertisements to air at specific times each day make up a subdepartment called traffic.

The technical, or engineering, department is responsible for ensuring that the announcer's words get from the studio to the transmitter and then to your radio. It is responsible for seeing that the station broadcasts on the frequency assigned to it.

Each station has at least one control room. Its most important piece of equipment is the control board. This board takes sounds and input from a variety of sources, including computers, microphones, and compact disc players. The engineer must hit the right switches at the right times so that continuous sound—voice or music—travels from the control board to the transmitter.

The business department includes accountants who keep the station's books in order and pay the bills. It also includes salespeople who sell airtime on the station for advertisements. At larger stations, some advertising is sold nationally by the companies that own them.

### Types of Programming

Radio stations air a wide variety of programming. With a few exceptions, each station specializes in a particular kind of music or news. These areas of specialization are called **formats**. In some cases, large companies own stations all around the country and program them with formats that are similar from city to city.

Most FM stations take advantage of FM's superior sound quality and play music. The songs music stations play—including pop, rock, jazz, classical, and country—may come from compact discs, records, tapes, or computer files.

AM stations and some on the FM band, particularly public radio stations, specialize in news. News comes into a radio station from many sources. Like newspapers, radio stations have reporters who cover and write local news. National and international news from networks and press agencies is received through the Internet. Reporters might also consult local newspapers for coverage, rewriting major stories of the day. Some AM stations focus on sports reporting and the broadcast of sporting events.

Writing news for broadcast is different from writing news that will be printed. Reporters must be careful to write clearly, since their listeners will not be able to review what they have said the way a newspaper reader can reread part of an article. But radio has an immediacy that newspapers cannot match. The reporter can interview people to give the listener a firsthand account of what has happened. Sometimes reporters are even able to use sounds—sirens blaring, birds chirping, or the hubbub of a crowd—to make listeners feel as if they are with the reporter on the scene. The radio news story can be used on more than one broadcast and can be changed quickly as events develop.

The radio industry offers many possible careers. On-air jobs, such as reporting or announcing music, require a good voice and quick thinking. Behind the scenes, stations need engineers, managers, producers, and advertising salespeople to run smoothly.

Some jobs, such as engineer positions, require specialized training and knowledge of technology. Reporters might benefit from education at a journalism school or from experience writing for newspapers. Most colleges have speech communication departments that teach public speaking and prepare students for radio careers.

▶ **REGULATION OF RADIO**

Even when radio was in its infancy, people realized its use needed to be controlled. Radio waves do not follow boundary lines. If two nearby stations transmit on the same frequency, they can interfere with each other. Neither broadcast can be heard clearly.

In 1909 a central bureau, administered by the International Telegraph Union, was formed in Bern, Switzerland. The bureau kept a list of the frequencies being used so that new stations could choose unused frequencies. As radio grew, the problems also grew. Today the bureau, now called the International Telecommunication Union, is a specialized agency of the United Nations.

By international agreement, every station has identifying call letters. With a few exceptions, call letters of commercial broadcast stations in the United States west of the Mississippi River begin with a K. Those east

## WONDER QUESTION

### What is static?

Static is a crackling, hissing, or crashing noise that interferes with radio reception. Static often comes from electrical disturbances in the atmosphere such as lightning during a thunderstorm. Anything from combing your hair to using an electric shaver or any other device with an electric motor may produce static. Static can also be caused by radio stations transmitting on frequencies close to the frequency of the station you are listening to.

The 1920's saw technological advances and the rise of networks. By about 1930, most American households were relying on radio as a source of news and entertainment.

of the Mississippi generally begin with W. But the first commercial radio station, KDKA in Pittsburgh, picked its call letters before this policy was established and has been allowed to keep K as its initial letter. Call letters for all Canadian stations begin with a C.

In the United States, the Federal Communications Commission (FCC), which is part of the federal government, regulates radio and television broadcasting, as well as other technologies that use electronic frequencies. The FCC assigns frequencies to stations so that their signals will not interfere with each other. It may let two stations broadcast on the same frequency provided that they are geographically far enough apart.

People who wish to start a radio station must apply to the FCC for a broadcast license. They may have to participate in auctions, bidding against other potential broadcasters who want to start a station on the same frequency. The FCC awards licenses and reviews them periodically.

### ▶ THE HISTORY OF RADIO

The development of radio was a long process that included many steps and involved many people from several countries. According to Vladimir K. Zworykin, a 20th-century electronics and television pioneer, technological developments such as radio resemble the climbing of a ladder. Each person's contribution enables other engineers to progress one step higher.

### Early History

Scottish physicist James Clerk Maxwell predicted the existence of radio waves mathematically in 1864, long before their discovery. In 1888, German scientist Heinrich Hertz demonstrated that radio waves exist and travel through space. To honor his discovery, radio engineers use his name in identifying the frequency of radio waves.

Hertz never communicated by radio. Guglielmo Marconi, an Italian physicist working in England, is considered the found-

er of radio communications. In 1901 he succeeded, on his first try, in sending and receiving messages across the Atlantic Ocean— between England and Canada. Marconi's radio really was a wireless telegraph, sending only dots and dashes.

In 1904 an English physicist, John A. Fleming, developed the first electronic vacuum tube, a device that made it possible to send sounds—speech and music—by radio. American Lee DeForest improved on Fleming's two-part tube (a **diode**) in 1906. He added a control unit called a grid to the tube, making it a **triode**. DeForest's triode made it possible to use a stronger loudspeaker in the radio so that more than one person could listen to a program. (Until this time, radios had a tiny loudspeaker that had to be held to the ear.)

At first, Marconi's wireless was used for signaling to ships at sea. The first voice and music radio broadcast was on Christmas Eve, 1906. Ship radio operators were surprised to hear a man speaking, a woman singing, and "O Holy Night" played on the violin. Next came the words, "If you have heard this program, write to R. A. Fessenden at Brant Rock, Massachusetts."

Fourteen years after Fessenden's experiment, an engineer at the Westinghouse Electric Corporation, Frank Conrad, began a series of voice broadcasts. The response was enthusiastic, and many radio sets were sold. Westinghouse decided to build a broadcasting station in Pittsburgh, Pennsylvania. The station was KDKA. Radio broadcasting had begun.

At first, broadcast radio was thought of mostly as a means of conveying information. But David Sarnoff, who started work as a messenger boy for the Marconi Wireless Company, came up with the idea in 1915 of radio as a "music box for the home." In time the Marconi Company became the Radio Corporation of America (RCA), and Sarnoff was president and chairman of the board for many years. RCA was instrumental in establishing networks that supplied programs to stations throughout the United States. Networks allowed stations to share the cost of programs.

The first round-the-world radio broadcast was made in 1930 with radio towers carrying the signal from one point to the next. Following this achievement, the new "wireless wonder," as radio was nicknamed, began to flourish as both a news medium and a source of entertainment.

### Networks and Programs

Radio pioneers created networks as a means of putting programs before the nation and drumming up support from advertisers. Sarnoff gave birth to the idea of a network early on, and in 1926 his RCA became half-

---

### THE GOLDEN AGE OF RADIO

Network radio was the major source of music, comedy, drama, sports, and news for many families from about 1930 to the late 1940's. The period came to be known as the Golden Age of Radio.

In the 1930's, during the Great Depression, U.S. president Franklin D. Roosevelt began his famous radio "fireside chats" to explain his New Deal policies and to rally Americans behind his plans. As Adolf Hitler rose to power in Germany before World War II, people all over the world turned to radio for developments.

For entertainment, the radio networks in the 1930's offered a variety of programs, including dramas, mysteries, comedies, thrillers, quiz shows, and historical documentaries. Great comedians who became famous on radio included Bob Hope, Jack Benny, and the husband-and-wife team of George Burns and Gracie Allen. Favorite radio comedy shows included *Amos 'n' Andy* and *Fibber McGee and Molly*. Adventure dramas such as *Buck Rogers*, *The Lone Ranger*, and *The Green Hornet* were popular. Radio also launched daytime dramas, called soap operas because detergent companies advertised on these programs to reach women at home.

Like all the other shows, radio dramas were performed live in the studio. Actors read their lines into microphones, and "sound men" added background noises—the sounds of galloping horses, gunshots, and so on—to make the show realistic. A 1938 radio adaptation of the science-fiction story *War of the Worlds*, presented by Orson Welles's Mercury Theatre, was so realistic that many people believed Earth had been invaded by Martians.

The coming of television signaled the end of the Golden Age of Radio. As early as 1948, TV began to take away radio's big advertisers, big shows, and big stars. Radio did continue to provide important news and information. But to entertain listeners, radio depended mostly on disc jockeys spinning phonograph records.

Radio dramas were performed live in the studio. Actors read their lines into microphones, and sound effects provided a realistic touch.

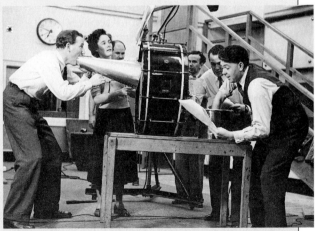

---

As drama and comedy programs migrated to television, radio again began to showcase music. By the 1960's, disc jockeys had become the stars of the airwaves.

owner of the first network, the National Broadcasting Corporation. NBC distributed its shows to two networks called Red and Blue. The first coast-to-coast program to air on a radio network was the Rose Bowl football game played on January 1, 1927.

NBC's main competitor, the Columbia Broadcasting System, also emerged in 1926. In 1928 it had 47 affiliate stations. A third network, which competed with NBC and CBS, was the Mutual Broadcasting System, founded in 1934. It owned no stations and only produced programs.

Before 1920, broadcasters aimed their programs primarily at narrow audiences. Announcers at local stations were often volunteers. Music was the dominant radio entertainment in the 1920's, but listeners also tuned in to sports and religious services on Sundays. In the late 1920's, drama and comedy programs became increasingly popular. Performers with roots in vaudeville moved to radio and found wide and eager audiences. Their shows and a variety of other programs ushered in radio's Golden Age.

Drama began to wane in the 1950's as television became more popular, and music regained its former standing as radio's main offering. Top 40, a format that features a limited selection of songs played repeatedly, began in 1949 and caught on during the 1950's. Disc jockeys became stars of the airwaves. Between records they announced the newest hit tunes, the weather, and the time of

day, and talked about whatever else came to mind. Some stations turned most of their attention to young listeners who wanted to hear rock and roll, country and western, and other popular music forms. In fact, a disc jockey, Alan Freed, is widely credited with coining the term "rock and roll."

Other stations specialized in classical music. Some stations, especially in large cities, began providing programs in foreign languages. In the 1970's, stations that broadcast only news and weather became popular. Sports events and call-in talk shows (in which people at home phone in their questions or comments and are heard on the air) have also helped radio continue to prosper.

### The Impact of Technology

Improvements in radio technology brought about major changes in broadcasting. Originally everything broadcast by a radio station was live, including the network programs. (A live broadcast is one transmitted at the time of production, such as a radio play in which actors read their lines into a microphone.)

As recording technology improved, tapes and records gradually replaced much of the live broadcasting. In early radio, for example, each commercial had to be read or performed live. Today stations receive programs via the Internet or in other electronic media. Live broadcasting is still common for sports, news reporting, and talk shows.

The development of the transistor spurred other important changes. First made at Bell Telephone Laboratories in 1948, the transistor is a small device that replaced tubes in radios. Transistors are smaller, lighter, and more reliable. They last longer and require less power than tubes. Also, they rarely burn out.

Because transistors require much less power than electron tubes, it became possible to build small, lightweight, battery-powered portable radios. People could easily carry these radios almost anywhere. Their low cost made it possible for people in developing countries to own radios.

An American engineer, Edwin H. Armstrong, invented and developed FM radio. Stereophonic sound, also known as stereo, was a big boost for FM. A stereo system features two speakers. The sound from the left half of an orchestra, for example, comes through the left loudspeaker. The sound from the right half of the orchestra comes through the right loudspeaker.

Music grew steadily on the FM dial. It got a boost in 1965 when the FCC forced some stations that owned both FM and AM stations to begin offering programming on FM not already airing on AM. As FM technology improved, the number of commercial FM stations in the United States and Canada grew rapidly—from fewer than 600 stations in 1950 to about 4,500 in the early 1980's. Commercial AM stations increased from roughly 2,000 to about 5,000 during the same period. Since then, FM stations have far outpaced AM stations in growth. As of 2003, more than 8,000 FM stations were broadcasting, compared with almost 5,000 AM stations.

## INTERNET RADIO

Beginning in the mid-1990's, radio broadcasters and users of personal computers started a new kind of broadcasting called Internet radio. Internet radio is not technically radio because its signals travel through the Internet rather than over the air. But it is much like radio. With a computer and a connection to the Internet, you can hear an almost endless variety of music, news, and other programming from all over the world.

Some Internet radio stations are simply AM or FM radio stations that are also sending a version of their signal to your computer. This is called **simulcasting**. Others are run by people with only a computer and no radio equipment, studios, or broadcast tower at all.

Internet radio works somewhat like digital radio. Sound sent over the Internet must first be **encoded**, or changed into digital code that a computer can understand. After the sound is encoded it is sent, or **streamed**, through the Internet. Your computer then decodes the signal and reproduces the sound.

▶**CURRENT AND FUTURE TRENDS**

The ability to transmit data in digital form, along with the arrival of the Internet, has dramatically changed the radio industry. Stations can now receive information from around the world much more quickly than before. With digital audio, they can also get programs and news reports in the form of computer files. For listeners, digital technology provides crisper and richer broadcasts.

Satellite radio, an alternative to broadcast radio, uses digital signals beamed from satellites. It is popular for cars because the signal does not fade as you drive.

Satellite radio service is another development. In this service, digital signals are beamed from satellites above the Earth to radios equipped with small satellite receivers. Two companies, XM Radio and Sirius Satellite Radio, offer this service in North America. Each features more than 100 channels of music and news, much of which cannot be heard on AM and FM radio stations. Unlike a broadcast signal, which fades or breaks up as you move away from the source, the satellite signal remains strong. You can drive coast to coast without retuning a satellite car radio. The sound quality is high—comparable to that of a compact disc—and the channels carry little or no advertising. Satellite radio listeners pay a monthly subscription fee.

In the future you may be able to listen to radio over a cell phone. Before this is possible, however, cell phones will have to be able to receive more digital information to support higher audio quality.

R. Peter Strauss
Chairman WMCA, New York, N.Y.
Reviewed by Michael Janssen
Associate Editor, *Current*

An amateur radio operator, or "ham," talks with other hams. Ham operators usually communicate over shortwave radio bands or frequencies.

## RADIO, AMATEUR

Amateur or "ham" radio is a two-way form of communication that allows people to transmit signals on specific radio bands or frequencies, usually shortwave. Amateur radio operators are called hams.

Ham radio is a popular hobby. There are more than 1 million operators worldwide, with approximately 680,000 in the United States. Many hams broadcast from their homes, vehicles, and other locations. They communicate by voice, computer (digital) signals, and international Morse code (a signaling code that uses dashes and dots).

The basic ham equipment includes a transmitter, a receiver, and an antenna. This can be purchased or built from a kit. The cost can range from about one hundred dollars to thousands, depending on the type of equipment. Many hams use small handheld units called handi-talkies or HT's, which look like cell phones.

People become hams for many reasons. Some enjoy just talking to each other, sharing personal experiences or discussing everyday events. Others play chess by radio. Hams enjoy communicating with nearby hams as well as with those from other parts of the world. Some use their radios to retransmit messages. This is known as handling traffic. There are only two restrictions—amateur radio may not be used to transact business or make money, and it cannot be broadcast to the public.

Most ham radio operators like to experiment. They may try all kinds of communication methods, including solar-powered radios, laser beams, satellites, and computers. Some inventions have been developed to enable people with disabilities to use ham equipment—for example, patterns of raised dots on receiver buttons that can be "read" by touch. Some people use their equipment to track satellites or to control model aircraft. Pictures from distant planets have been transmitted over ham television, which uses cameras to send images via the ham frequency.

Many hams use their skills to help the public. When an earthquake or other disaster strikes and normal means of communication are not working, ham radio operators step in to provide lifesaving communications and get help. These hams are trained for emergency communications and are members of ARES—the Amateur Radio Emergency Service. Police, firefighters, rescue services, and other government groups work closely with hams during these times.

▶ HOW TO BECOME A HAM

Anyone can become a ham, regardless of age or experience. Hams include Boy Scouts and Girl Scouts, doctors, nurses, truck drivers, teachers, lawyers, pilots, and even astronauts. The International Space Station has a complete amateur radio station on board, and most of the astronauts are hams. From the

### INTERNATIONAL MORSE CODE

| A | .- | K | -.- | U | ..- |
|---|---|---|---|---|---|
| B | -... | L | .-.. | V | ...- |
| C | -.-. | M | -- | W | .-- |
| D | -.. | N | -. | X | -..- |
| E | . | O | --- | Y | -.-- |
| F | ..-. | P | .--. | Z | --.. |
| G | --. | Q | --.- | Period (.) | .-.-.- |
| H | .... | R | .-. | Comma (,) | --..-- |
| I | .. | S | ... | Query (?) | ..--.. |
| J | .--- | T | - | Error | ........ |

ISS, they talk to students in schools and to other hams when possible.

A license is required to become a ham operator in the United States. Licenses are issued by the Federal Communications Commission (FCC), which regulates radio and television broadcasting, as well as other technologies that use electronic frequencies. The FCC assigns each ham operator his or her own station call letters (for example, K3UFG). The first letter indicates the ham's country (all call letters for U.S. hams begin with W, A, N, or K), and the number indicates the geographical region. The letters after the number are unique for that station.

There are several types of license classes—Technician, General, and Amateur Extra. Each one requires a better understanding of radio technology than the previous level. However, with each new license class comes additional privileges, such as being able to transmit and receive over a wider range of frequencies.

To obtain a beginner's (Technician) license, applicants must pass a short written examination that covers basic operating regulations and simple radio theory. For advanced licenses, applicants must pass longer and more difficult tests and know Morse code.

Licensing information is available through the FCC and through local and international radio clubs. Many hams belong to these clubs, which also hold meetings, contests, and other activities so that members can exchange ideas and learn about the latest changes in this field. In the United States, there are more than 2,000 clubs.

## ▶ HISTORY OF HAM RADIO

Amateur radio can be traced to the development of wireless telegraphy in the 1890's by Guglielmo Marconi of Italy. It quickly became popular, and many people were soon

## AMATEUR ABBREVIATIONS

| | | | |
|---|---|---|---|
| ABT | About | HI | Laughter |
| AGN | Again | HP | Hope |
| ANI | Any | HR | Here; Hear |
| BCNU | I'll be seeing you | HRD | Heard |
| BK | Break | HV | Have |
| BTR | Better | HW | How |
| CRD | Card | NIL | Nothing |
| CU | See you | NR | Number |
| CUD | Could | NW | Now |
| DX | Distance | OP | Operator |
| ES | And | PSE | Please |
| FB | Fine business | RCVD | Received |
| FER | For | RPT | Repeat/Report |
| FM | From | RX | Receive(r) |
| GA | Good afternoon; Go ahead | SN | Soon |
| | | TNX | Thanks |
| GE | Good evening | TU | Thank you |
| GM | Good morning | TX | Transmitter |
| GN | Good night | WX | Weather |
| GUD | Good | 73 | Best regards |
| HAM | Amateur | 88 | Love and kisses |

Hams trained for emergencies can help the public when normal means of communications are disrupted. This ham speaks with cyclone-relief workers in remote areas of India.

sending and receiving messages through the air. The U.S. government began licensing amateur radio operators in 1912.

By 1914, there were thousands of amateur radio operators in the United States. Hiram Percy Maxim, a leading Hartford, Connecticut, inventor and industrialist, saw the need for an organization to band together this fledgling group of radio experimenters. In May 1914 he founded the American Radio Relay League (ARRL).

Today ARRL is the largest group of radio amateurs in the United States, with approximately 160,000 members. A nonprofit organization, it represents U.S. radio amateurs in legislative matters and also oversees the U.S. delegation of the International Amateur Radio Union, which is made up of similar societies in 150 countries.

DAN MILLER
American Radio Relay League

See also RADIO.

# RADIOACTIVE ELEMENTS

All elements are made up of atoms—the basic units, or building blocks, of matter. Atoms of unstable forms of certain elements decay (break down) and radiate (give off) energy or subatomic particles. Elements that spontaneously decay and radiate energy or particles in this way are called radioactive. To understand radioactivity, it is necessary to understand the structure of atoms and how this decay occurs.

### ▶ THE ATOMIC NUCLEUS

Each atom has a center, called the **nucleus**. The nucleus (plural nuclei) is composed of particles called **nucleons**. Positively charged nucleons are called **protons**; those with no charge (neutral) are called **neutrons**. Negatively charged particles called **electrons** orbit the nucleus at different energy levels.

A strong force holds the neutrons and protons together. Because protons have a positive charge, they repel each other, so neutrons help maintain the stability of the nucleus. The more protons there are in a nucleus, the more neutrons are needed. Extra neutrons are required for heavy elements. However, it is the protons that hold the negatively charged electrons in their orbits.

The number of protons in the nucleus of an atom, known as the atomic number, determines the element the nucleus belongs to. For example, all helium atoms have two protons in the nucleus, and all uranium atoms have 92 protons in the nucleus. But atoms of the same element may have different numbers of neutrons. Different forms of the same element with different numbers of neutrons are called **isotopes** of that element.

In general, the stability of a nucleus is determined by its ratio of neutrons to protons. Unstable isotopes spontaneously decay, releasing particles or energy, and subsequently become more stable. A lone neutron is unstable and will decay spontaneously into a proton and an electron. All natural elements with atomic numbers of 84 and higher decay in one way or another—thus, all these elements change into another element (a process called **transmutation**) and are radioactive. Scientists have also artificially produced several radioactive elements.

Each radioactive isotope decays at a certain constant rate. The rate at which a radioactive element breaks down is called its **half-life**. The half-life of an element is the time it takes for half its atoms to break down. One isotope of uranium (uranium-238) has a half-life of 4.5 billion years. This means it takes 4.5 billion years for half the atoms in a uranium sample to break down. It would take another 4.5 billion years for half the remaining atoms to break down, and so on. Other elements have much shorter half-lives.

### ▶ THREE KINDS OF RAYS

All radioactive decay involves the emission of some particle or radiation. Elements or atoms radiate three distinct types of particles

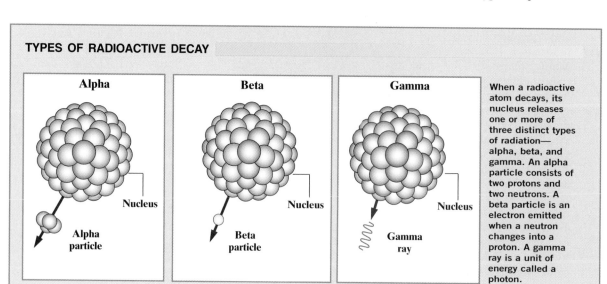

**TYPES OF RADIOACTIVE DECAY**

Alpha — Nucleus — Alpha particle

Beta — Nucleus — Beta particle

Gamma — Nucleus — Gamma ray

When a radioactive atom decays, its nucleus releases one or more of three distinct types of radiation—alpha, beta, and gamma. An alpha particle consists of two protons and two neutrons. A beta particle is an electron emitted when a neutron changes into a proton. A gamma ray is a unit of energy called a photon.

in streams, called rays. In heavy atoms, such as those of uranium, the nuclei decay easily and radiate particles much smaller than the atoms themselves. Some of these particles are fairly heavy. They are called **alpha particles** and are radiated in streams called alpha rays. Each alpha particle consists of two protons and two neutrons; each is identical to the nucleus of a helium atom. Other particles are very light. They are called **beta particles** and are radiated in streams called beta rays. A beta particle is an electron that is emitted when a neutron is transformed into a proton.

Finally, there are radiations that are made up of **gamma rays**. Gamma rays are a form of electromagnetic radiation and consist of very short waves similar to X-rays. A gamma ray is a **photon**, a fundamental unit of energy emitted when an excited electron jumps to an orbit of lower energy. For more information, see the article RADIATION in this volume.

When alpha, beta, and gamma rays are given off by nuclei of uranium and thorium atoms, for example, the nature of the atoms themselves is changed. These atoms are no longer atoms of uranium or thorium, but atoms of other elements. These other elements are also radioactive and break down further. After many such changes the atoms become those of lead, an element that is not radioactive. No radiations are given off, and no further changes occur.

▶ **USES OF RADIOACTIVE ELEMENTS**

The rate at which radioactive elements break down helps scientists determine the age of ancient artifacts. Such radiometric dating can also help estimate the age of the Earth itself. For more information, see the article RADIOMETRIC DATING in this volume.

Particles given off by radioactive elements can be used as tiny bullets with which to penetrate other atoms. Scientists use these atom-smashing particles to rearrange the nuclei of atoms. The nuclei can be broken down into simpler nuclei or built up into more complicated ones. In this way, scientists can form new elements with atoms that are even more complicated than those of uranium. Some of these elements, such as neptunium, exist in nature only in very small quantities. Others, such as americium, are not found in nature at all. All are radioactive and have very short half-lives.

| RADIOACTIVE ELEMENTS (BY ATOMIC NUMBER) | | | |
|---|---|---|---|
| Element | Atomic Number | Element | Atomic Number |
| Technetium (Tc) | 43 | Einsteinium (Es) | 99 |
| Promethium (Pm) | 61 | Fermium (Fm) | 100 |
| Polonium (Po) | 84 | Mendelevium (Md) | 101 |
| Astatine (At) | 85 | Nobelium (No) | 102 |
| Radon (Rn) | 86 | Lawrencium (Lr) | 103 |
| Francium (Fr) | 87 | Rutherfordium (Rf) | 104 |
| Radium (Ra) | 88 | Dubnium (Db) | 105 |
| Actinium (Ac) | 89 | Seaborgium (Sg) | 106 |
| Thorium (Th) | 90 | Bohrium (Bh) | 107 |
| Protactinium (Pa) | 91 | Hassium (Hs) | 108 |
| Uranium (U) | 92 | Meitnerium (Mt) | 109 |
| Neptunium (Np) | 93 | Unnnilium (Uun) | 110 |
| Plutonium (Pu) | 94 | Unununium (Uuu) | 111 |
| Americium (Am) | 95 | Ununbium (Uub) | 112 |
| Curium (Cm) | 96 | Ununquadium (Uuq) | 114 |
| Berkelium (Bk) | 97 | Ununhexium (Uuh) | 116 |
| Californium (Cf) | 98 | | |

By bombarding atoms with neutrons and other particles, scientists can produce radioactive isotopes for all the elements. The isotopes are inexpensive and very useful in scientific research. Scientists can also replace ordinary atoms in chemical compounds with radioactive atoms. Using special instruments, such as Geiger counters, scientists can follow the particles these tracer atoms leave behind. In this way, they can learn much about the details of chemical changes.

Radiation is used to sterilize foods and surgical instruments, killing bacteria without altering the food or instruments. Because it can also kill cancer cells, radiation is sometimes used as a cancer treatment. On the other hand, radiation can be very harmful; a person receiving a very large dose would become sick or die.

Radioactive elements are sources of great energy. When an atom of uranium is bombarded with a neutron, its nucleus is split. The energy released can be concentrated into a very powerful and destructive nuclear bomb. It can be used for peaceful purposes, too: For example, nuclear power stations have produced electricity for households and industry for many years. For more information, see the article NUCLEAR ENERGY in Volume N.

NORM THOMSON
Department of Science Education
University of Georgia

See also ATOMS; ELEMENTS, CHEMICAL.

# RADIO ASTRONOMY

When you look at a clear night sky, you can see the stars because they give off, or emit, light that reaches your eyes across the vast distances of space. Visible light is a form of energy called **electromagnetic radiation**. Besides visible light, many objects in space emit other kinds of electromagnetic radiation, some of it in the form of radio waves. Radio astronomy is the study of radio waves given off by celestial objects.

Electromagnetic radiation flows in waves like waves of water: Each wave has a high point called the crest. The distance from one crest to the next in a series of waves is called the **wavelength**. Light waves have very short wavelengths, about several millionths of an inch long. The wavelengths of radio waves, in contrast, can be many yards long.

In optical astronomy, scientists use optical telescopes to study objects in space by collecting and analyzing light from these objects. In radio astronomy, scientists study objects in space by collecting and analyzing the radio waves these objects give off. The types of telescopes radio astronomers use for this purpose are called **radio telescopes**.

▶ **RADIO TELESCOPES**

Radio telescopes are very valuable instruments. Using them, astronomers are learning facts about the universe that were not known before. Thus, radio astronomy has become an important part of the study of outer space.

High up in the Earth's atmosphere are layers of air that are electrified. These layers of air, called the **ionosphere**, act like a mirror to most radio waves and reflect them. Some radio waves, however, are able to pass through the ionosphere. Radio telescopes can observe only those radio waves that do pass through.

Many of the radio waves from outer space that are studied by radio astronomers are very short compared with the wavelengths used in radio and television broadcasting. Special antennas and electronic radio re-

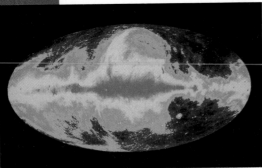

Radio telescopes, such as those of the Very Large Array (*far left*) and the Arecibo Observatory (*below*), collect radio waves from space and convert them into images called radiographs, such as this image of the Milky Way (*left*).

ceivers connected to radio telescopes are used to receive these short radio waves from outer space.

The radio telescope receives the shortwave radio radiation only if the telescope's antenna, or **reflector**, points in the direction from which the waves are coming. This fact is a great help to astronomers. They can point the radio telescope at the part of the sky they want to study and be sure that they are receiving radiation from that area only.

The reflector of most radio telescopes is shaped like a large bowl or dish and is covered with thin metal plating or a screen-like netting of metal. The reflector collects and focuses radio waves just as the mirror in a reflecting optical telescope collects and focuses waves of visible light. At the point of focus, the waves are collected by a device called the **feed**, which converts the waves into electrical signals and sends them to the radio **receiver**. The receiver amplifies, or magnifies, the signal because the radio waves collected by the reflector are often very weak after spreading out through billions of miles of space.

Some radio telescopes are fitted on a movable stand, or mounting, so that they can be pointed to almost any part of the sky. In large radio telescopes with stationary reflectors, the feed can be moved so the telescope can receive

radio signals from different parts of the sky. The size of the reflector is important because larger reflectors can detect signals from a greater distance and in greater detail.

The largest radio telescope in the world, located near Arecibo, Puerto Rico, has a reflector that measures 1,000 feet (305 meters) across. However, even a dish this size is limited in the detail it can detect from celestial objects. For instance, a radio telescope several hundred feet across can create a radio image of an object that is no clearer than an image obtained with a small, portable optical telescope. To overcome this obstacle, radio astronomers link two or more radio telescopes together to form a network, or array, known as an **interferometer**. An example is the Very Large Array (VLA) in New Mexico. The VLA consists of 27 individual radio tele-

Radio astronomers use computers to examine and store data collected by radio telescopes. This data can then be sent to astronomers working at other locations.

scopes, each with an antenna about 80 feet (24 meters) across, spread across almost 26 miles (42 kilometers) of desert. With all the antennas pointed at the same object in the sky, the radio waves received by each can be combined to produce a highly detailed image that is the equivalent of an image obtained by a single antenna measuring 26 miles across. This is known as the **baseline** of the array.

Other interferometers include the Multi-Element Radio Linked Interferometer Network (MERLIN), which consists of six radio telescopes spread out across more than 125 miles (200 kilometers) of countryside in Great Britain; and the Very Long Baseline Array (VLBA), which includes ten 82-foot (25-meter)-diameter telescopes covering a distance of about 5,000 miles (8,050 kilome-

ters), from New Hampshire to Washington State and from the Virgin Islands to Hawaii. Recently, both the United States and Japan have experimented with combining radio telescope networks on the surface of the Earth with radio-receiving satellites in space, forming one radio telescope with an immense baseline.

Data received by radio telescopes can be examined in real time or recorded for later study and analysis. This data can be translated into streams of numbers or lines on a graph. It can also be used to make images called **radiographs** of objects in space. In either case, the images and other data can be stored indefinitely and even shared with astronomers around the world via the Internet.

**Advantages of Radio Telescopes.** Radio waves of many wavelengths can pass directly through clouds or fog in the Earth's atmosphere that typically block the visible light emitted by objects in space. And they can be detected even on bright, sunny days. Thus, while astronomers using optical telescopes can usually observe the heavens only on clear, dark nights, radio astronomers can usually gather data day or night, in nearly any kind of weather. This is especially true for radio telescopes designed to receive radio waves with relatively long wavelengths (several inches or centimeters).

Observatories for optical telescopes are built on high ground or mountains, above the thicker, dustier air near the ground and away from city lights. Radio telescopes do not have to be located on mountain peaks. But they must be far removed from cars, heavy machinery, and other sources of artificial radio waves, which can interfere or jam the much weaker radio waves coming from objects in space. Because of this, radio telescopes are often located in isolated areas such as deserts or valleys. Radio telescopes designed to detect radio waves with short wavelengths are typically located in high and dry places to limit the effects of water vapor in the atmosphere, which absorbs short-wavelength radio waves.

Radio telescopes have another advantage over optical telescopes. In many places far out in space, there are giant clouds of dust and gases. Light waves cannot get through these, and astronomers using optical telescopes cannot see what lies behind the clouds. However, radio waves can pass through the dust and gases, so radio astronomers can explore parts of space that optical astronomers cannot.

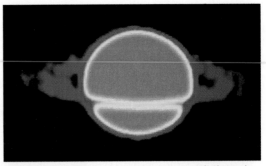

*Above:* All the planets in our solar system emit thermal radio radiation. This radio image of Saturn shows the relative coolness of the planet's rings in contrast to its atmosphere. *Below:* This radiograph of the sun during a total eclipse reveals details in the sun's outer atmosphere, or corona, which emits long-wavelength radio waves.

### ▶ OBSERVING THE RADIO UNIVERSE

Celestial objects produce two kinds of radio radiation—thermal radiation and nonthermal radiation. The amount of thermal radio radiation an object gives off depends on its temperature: the hotter the object, the more thermal radiation it gives off. Therefore, measuring the thermal radiation an object emits can determine the object's temperature. Thermal radio radiation is emitted from the sun and the planets and from clouds of hydrogen gas that surround some of the very hottest stars. Nonthermal radio radiation is created primarily when charged particles (mostly electrons) move rapidly within a magnetic field. The more numerous the charged particles, and the stronger the magnetic field, the stronger nonthermal radiation is generated. A variety of objects in space—clouds of gas, pulsars, and quasars—give off nonthermal radiation. Some objects emit both thermal and nonthermal radio radiation, including the sun (as well as many other stars) and galaxies. Observations of both kinds of radio radiation have provided immense amounts of information on all kinds of objects in space.

**The Sun.** An image of the sun taken in visible light shows its bright surface, or **photosphere**, marked in various places with darker, cooler regions called **sunspots**. In contrast, an image of the sun taken with short-wavelength radio waves reveals that the areas directly above the darker sunspots are actually aglow with radio radiation. These regions have strong magnetic fields in which charged particles from the sun's lower atmosphere are spiraling rapidly.

The sun's outer atmosphere, or **corona**, is usually too faint to be seen in visible light except during a total solar eclipse (when the moon completely blocks out the sun), but it emits long-wavelength radio waves. Using radio telescopes, astronomers can study the corona at any time and observe how eruptions, or flares, on the sun's surface or in its lower atmosphere blow holes in the corona and blast solar particles far out into space.

**The Planets.** All the planets in our solar system emit thermal radio radiation because they are heated to varying degrees by the sun. Radio telescopes can detect this energy and establish each planet's temperature.

Jupiter, Saturn, Uranus, and Neptune also emit nonthermal radiation, in part because charged particles streaming from the sun, called the **solar wind**, interact with the planets' magnetic fields. Jupiter also displays bursts of nonthermal radio emissions caused by the interaction between its large inner moon, Io, and its magnetic field. In addition, Jupiter has been found to have Van Allen Belts—regions of powerful radiation particles trapped in the planet's magnetic field—just like those of Earth.

**Stars.** Stars also emit radio waves, and one of the most significant discoveries of radio astronomy was the existence of a strange kind of star. In 1967, a star was discovered that was regularly emitting powerful pulses of nonthermal radio radiation. This pulsing star, called a **pulsar**, was actually the core of a star that had exploded. When a star runs out of its nuclear fuel, it blows much of its atmosphere off into space in a violent explosion called a **supernova**. As the atmosphere is blasted away, the star's core rapidly collapses in on itself. If the star was highly massive, this core would become a black hole. But the core of a less massive star collapses into a small, very dense, and rapidly rotating pulsar. As the pulsar spins on its axis, it emits radio waves that sweep through space like the beams of light from a lighthouse. Many other pulsars have since been discovered, and studying their radio waves has helped as-

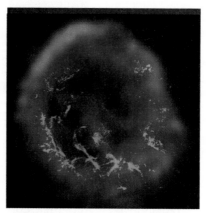

Radiation from a supernova remnant remains detectable for millions of years, long after it can be seen in visible light.

tronomers better understand the evolution of stars.

The material shed by supernovas includes the gas and dust of its atmosphere as well as huge amounts of light, radio, and other kinds of radiation. Over thousands of years, these supernova remnants continue to spread outward from the star's core and eventually become too faint to be seen in visible light. Their radio radiation, however, remains detectable for millions of years. Radio telescopes have revealed many supernova remnants, giving astronomers the opportunity

---

## RADIO ASTRONOMY AND THE SEARCH FOR EXTRATERRESTRIAL INTELLIGENCE

In 1959, the physicists Philip Morrison of the United States and Giuseppe Cocconi of Italy proposed using radio telescopes to search for artificially generated radio signals sent into space by intelligent beings living on other worlds. The reasoning was that since human beings have had the technology to transmit radio waves into space for many years (through radio and television broadcasts and radar), alien civilizations may have been doing the same—maybe for thousands of years or longer.

In 1960, the American radio astronomer Frank Drake conducted the first experiment to search for these signals using a radio telescope. These early searches were aimed at only two stars and focused on only one frequency. Since then, astronomers have used a variety of radio telescopes to scan millions of stars in billions of frequencies in a worldwide program now known as SETI—the *s*earch for *e*xtra*t*errestrial *i*ntelligence.

The first large-scale use of radio telescopes for SETI was Project Phoenix, run by the SETI Institute in California. A nine-year program that ended in 2004, Project Phoenix used the 1,000-foot (305-meter) radio telescope in Arecibo, Puerto Rico, to

"listen" for signals from about 800 stars like our sun. Another project, called SETI@home, began in 1999 and provides amateur astronomers worldwide the opportunity to participate in the search for extraterrestrial radio signals. Data collected from the Arecibo telescope are broken down into small pieces of information, which are sent over the Internet to people's personal computers. By combining thousands of computers in this way, researchers can analyze huge amounts of data much more quickly than they could using just one computer.

The SETI Institute, together with the University of California, Berkeley, is currently constructing the Allen Telescope Array to succeed Project Phoenix. This array will consist of 350 separate radio telescopes, each about 20 feet (6 meters) in diameter, which will have the equivalent sensitivity of a single 328-foot (100-meter) telescope and be able to study 100,000 more stars than the Phoenix Project. Unlike other telescopes or arrays, which are used for many other kinds of astronomical research, the Allen Telescope Array will be used exclusively to search for alien radio transmissions.

So far, no artificial radio signals have been discovered. But as the searches become more thorough and the telescopes more sensitive, it may only be a matter of time.

to study how the remains of old stars may lead to the formation of new planets and perhaps even life.

**Galaxies.** Galaxies that emit enormous amounts of radio radiation are called **radio galaxies**, and observations with radio telescopes have revealed that these galaxies are far larger and more violent than they appear in visible light through optical telescopes. Some of these galaxies emit radio radiation in a spherical region, or halo, that surrounds them and extends far beyond their visible-light borders. Other radio galaxies generate very intense radio radiation from a relatively tiny region at their cores, and this radiation can be more powerful than all the forms of radiation generated by our own galaxy, the Milky Way, combined. Still other radio galaxies have been found to have immense jets of material racing outward from their centers at close to the speed of light and are surrounded by huge clouds, or lobes, of charged particles so large that they dwarf the galaxy as seen in visible light. Lying at the center of radio galaxies are black holes millions or billions of times more massive than the sun. Matter falling in toward the black holes at very high speeds is heated to tremendous temperatures, and it is this heat that generates the radio energy.

Similarly, radio telescopes are used to penetrate the thick bands of dust that lie between the Earth and the center of the Milky Way galaxy. Astronomers have determined that our galaxy is shaped like a giant pinwheel slowly spinning around its center. Measuring the motion of stars and gas around this center has also revealed the presence of a black hole at the Milky Way's core. This black hole is about 3 million times as massive as the sun.

**Interstellar Space.** The space between the stars, or interstellar space, is not as empty as it looks; it is actually sprinkled with clouds of gas and dust that are often invisible to optical telescopes. Radio telescopes are used to obtain and analyze this material's spectra in the radio portion of the spectrum (just as optical

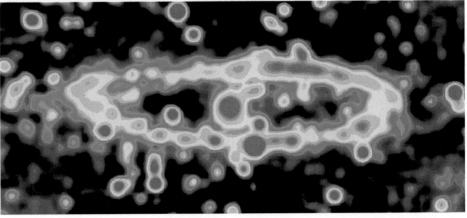

In visible light, features of the Andromeda galaxy (*above*) are obscured by dust and gas. Because radio waves can penetrate these materials, a radio image (*right*) can reveal valuable details about the galaxy's stars and structure.

## What was "Jansky's merry-go-round"?

"Jansky's merry-go-round" was the name given to an antenna built by the American radio engineer Karl Jansky in 1931–32. Asked by his employer to search for the sources of static that were interfering with transatlantic radio telephone service, Jansky built the antenna to detect radio waves with wavelengths of about 49 feet (15 meters). The antenna was mounted on wheels from a Model-T Ford automobile so it could rotate about its axis—just like a merry-go-round—to receive radio waves from any direction. With this simple apparatus, Jansky detected three sources of radio waves—near and distant thunderstorms, and another mysterious source that produced a constant background hiss. He determined that the intensity of the hiss peaked about every 24 hours, and this peak corresponded to a particular part of the sky. Jansky soon realized that the hissing static was in fact radio waves emitted by the Milky Way Galaxy. With this discovery, "Jansky's merry-go-round" became the world's first radio telescope.

telescopes are used to obtain and analyze spectra in the visible part of the spectrum). Studies have shown that this interstellar matter includes not only simple elements such as hydrogen but also more complex molecules such as water, alcohol, formaldehyde, and ethane. These and other molecules discovered in space are believed to be important for the development of life, so this discovery has suggested to scientists that the "recipe" for life may be abundant across the Milky Way and even across vast portions of the universe.

**The Universe.** When Edwin Hubble discovered in the 1920's that most galaxies were moving away from the Earth and each other, it led to the theory that the universe had begun as a very dense, very hot object that burst into existence long ago and was still expanding outward today. However, there was no direct evidence for this explosion, which came to be called the **Big Bang**.

This evidence was discovered in the 1960's, when scientists experimenting with a highly sensitive antenna for use with communication satellites discovered faint radio waves emanating from all parts of the sky. Scientists realized that these waves were the cooled remains of the intensely hot radiation generated when the Big Bang occurred billions of years ago.

### ▶ OTHER USES OF RADIO TELESCOPES

Although radio telescopes are used primarily to receive radio waves emitted from space, they have also been used to send radio waves into space. A special transmitter attached to a radio telescope produces radio waves, and the antenna sends them out into space. If a celestial object is relatively nearby, the waves hit it and are reflected back to the antenna, where they are amplified by the receiver. This is called **radar astronomy**. Astronomers used this technique to establish the distances of the moon and Venus from the Earth, as well as to create a crude map of Venus' surface, which is always hidden by clouds. More recently, space probes orbiting Venus have used radar to create much more detailed maps of the planet's surface. Radars have also been carried into orbit by the space shuttles, where they have been turned back down toward the Earth and revealed vast underground rivers and even hidden archaeological sites.

The National Aeronautics and Space Administration (NASA) uses a network of 15 radio telescopes, called the Deep Space Network (DSN), to communicate with space probes throughout the solar system. These telescopes, with dishes measuring up to 230 feet (70 meters) in diameter, are located in California, Spain, and Australia. They are used to send instructions to the space probes as well as receive data and images from them.

Radio telescopes are also instrumental in the search for extraterrestrial intelligence. For more information, see the feature accompanying this article.

### ▶ HISTORY

In 1931 and 1932, an American radio engineer, Karl Jansky, was trying to learn what caused hissing and crackling noises that were interfering with radio telephone calls. He dis-

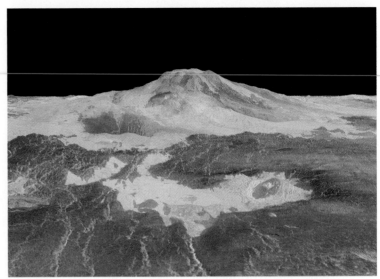

This image of Venus' surface was created by an orbiting space probe that bounced radio waves off the planet, a technique called radar astronomy.

covered that the crackling sounds were caused by radio waves given off by thunderstorms. But he still heard the faint hissing sound even when there were no thunderstorms. Noticing that the strength of the hiss varied each day in the same amount of time it takes the Earth to rotate relative to the stars, Jansky concluded that the sounds must be caused by radio waves that came from outer space. He noticed that the strongest hissing seemed to come from the center of the Milky Way galaxy, near the stars of the constellation Sagittarius.

Jansky told others about his results, but for several years only Grote Reber, a radio engineer, followed them up with additional research. Reber built a radio telescope to study the strange hissing sounds from space. After many years of work, he was able to prove that Jansky was correct. Radio waves were coming from the Milky Way. The science of radio astronomy had begun. After World War II, research in the field of radio astronomy increased dramatically. The result has been a tremendous increase in our knowledge of the universe.

COLIN A. RONAN
Fellow, Royal Astronomical Society
Revised by WILLIAM A. GUTSCH, JR.
President, The Challenger Center for
Space Science Education

See also ASTRONOMY; ELECTRONICS; OBSERVATORIES; PULSARS; QUASARS; RADAR AND SONAR; RADIATION; RADIO; SATELLITES, ARTIFICIAL; SPACE PROBES; TELESCOPES.

# RADIOMETRIC DATING

Radiometric dating is a method used to determine the ages of objects by analyzing the amounts of radioactive elements they contain. Uranium and thorium, as well as three other radioactive elements, are used to date rocks. To determine the age of things that were once part of living organisms, scientists use another radioactive element, carbon-14.

To understand how radiometric dating works, it is necessary to know what radioactive elements are and how they behave.

## ▶ RADIOACTIVE ELEMENTS

All elements are made up of atoms—the basic units, or building blocks, of matter. Atoms of unstable forms, or **isotopes**, of certain elements decay (break down) and radiate (give off) energy and subatomic particles. The term "radioactivity" is used to describe this process. When radioactive atoms decay, the atoms themselves are changed, forming atoms of more stable elements called daughter isotopes. Atoms of uranium and thorium, for example, decay and eventually form atoms of different forms of lead. Using an instrument called a **mass spectrometer**, scientists can separate and measure parent and daughter isotopes in a sample material.

Each radioactive element decays at a certain rate. The rate at which the element decays is termed its **half-life**, which can be defined as the time it takes for half the element's atoms to break down.

Most rocks and minerals contain atoms of one or more radioactive elements. For example, much of the thorium and uranium that was present when the Earth first formed is still present in the Earth's rocks. Knowing the half-life of a given radioactive element enables scientists to determine the age of the mineral containing it.

Thorium has a half-life of 14 billion years. It would take 14 billion years for just half the atoms in a given amount of thorium to break down. It would take another 14 billion years for half the remaining atoms to break down, and so on. Uranium has a shorter half-life than thorium. There are three naturally occurring isotopes of uranium. Two—uranium-238, with a half-life of 4.5 billion years, and uranium-235, with a half-life of 704 million years—are commonly used for dating rocks.

The rock layers of the Grand Canyon provide a glimpse of the Earth's long history. Using radiometric dating, scientists have estimated the age of the Earth itself.

## ▶ DATING THE EARTH'S ROCKS

When the Earth was first forming, there were no solid rocks. Uranium and thorium atoms moved about freely in the hot, molten Earth. When solid rocks formed, thorium and uranium atoms were imprisoned within the rocks. Many of the thorium and uranium atoms contained within the rocks remain there today. Some of them, however, have since become atoms of lead. This lead has also remained within the rocks along with the thorium and uranium.

To determine the age of a rock that contains thorium, scientists measure the amount of thorium now present in the rock. They also measure the amount of lead the rock contains. They know the rate at which thorium breaks down to form lead. They can therefore calculate how long it took the lead to form from the thorium.

Suppose, for example, that when a rock first became solid it contained about a pound of thorium. At the end of a year a small amount of lead—about a billionth of an ounce—would have formed. At the end of 1 billion years, about an ounce of lead would have formed.

Scientists can also date rocks by comparing the amount of uranium in the rocks with the amount of lead formed from the uranium. This is somewhat more complicated, for each of the three kinds of uranium breaks down at a different rate. And rocks may also contain some lead that did not come from the breakdown of thorium or uranium. Scientists are able to distinguish ordinary lead from lead that came from radioactive elements by analyzing its atomic structure.

In addition to uranium and thorium, three other radioactive elements—rubidium-87, potassium-40, and samarium-147—can be used in dating rocks. Each element has certain advantages. Rubidium-87 is especially useful for dating very old rocks. It has a half-life of 48.8 billion years. Potassium-40, which decays into argon-40, has the advantage of being found in almost all rocks. It has a half-life of 1.25 billion years, but it can be used to date rocks as young as a few thousand years as well as the oldest rocks known. Another advantage of using the **potassium-argon method** is that the amounts of these isotopes can be measured quite accurately, even in very small amounts. Samarium-147 may be preferred for rocks that have very little potassium and rubidium. The parent isotopes and corresponding daughter isotopes most commonly used to determine the ages of ancient rocks are given in the table accompanying this article.

Dating rocks using isotopes as timekeepers may seem simple, but the laboratory procedures are complex. Measuring very small amounts of isotopes is difficult. Thus, when reporting data, scientists often consider uncertainty. They state this uncertainty in terms

A researcher uses a mass spectrometer to determine the age of a rock sample. Uranium and several other types of radioactive elements can be used in dating rocks.

of plus (+) or minus (–) a number of years. And when possible, two or more methods of analysis are used on the same rock sample to support results.

Using these methods, scientists have dated many kinds of rocks. Samples of volcanic materials found in Kenya helped date the fossil remains of an early human at 6.2 million years. Samples from rock outcrops in southwestern Minnesota have been dated at 3.6 billion years and are thought to be among the oldest rocks in North America. Using radiometric dating, scientists can even estimate the age of the Earth itself—it is believed to be about 4.5 billion years old. Moon rock samples have been dated at 4.2 billion years.

▶ DATING ANCIENT ARTIFACTS

All living things contain carbon. They also contain small amounts of carbon-14, a radioactive isotope of carbon. Using carbon-14, scientists can determine the age of wood and

## RADIOACTIVE ELEMENTS COMMONLY USED IN RADIOMETRIC DATING

| Parent Isotope | Stable Daughter Isotope | Half-Life Values |
|----------------|-------------------------|------------------|
| Uranium-238 | Lead-206 | 4.5 billion years |
| Uranium-235 | Lead-207 | 704 million years |
| Thorium-232 | Lead-208 | 14.0 billion years |
| Rubidium-87 | Strontium-87 | 48.8 billion years |
| Potassium-40 | Argon-40 | 1.25 billion years |
| Samarium-147 | Neodynium-143 | 106 billion years |

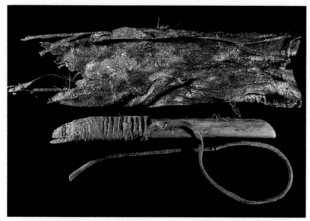

Radiocarbon dating can date objects, such as leather, wood, and bone, that were once part of a living organism. These artifacts date from A.D. 1415 to 1445.

clothing—in fact, anything that once contained or was part of a living organism. Dating an object by means of carbon-14 is called **radiocarbon dating**.

Carbon-14 is formed by cosmic rays—high-energy protons that bombard the Earth. These protons smash into atoms and molecules that make up our atmosphere. The atmosphere contains large amounts of nitrogen. Sometimes an activated neutron, formed through cosmic radiation, collides with a nitrogen-14 atom, producing a radioactive carbon-14 atom. Carbon-14 decays back to nitrogen.

As cosmic rays continually bombard the Earth, new carbon-14 is formed at a rate that just balances the breakdown of old carbon-14. This means there is a steady level of carbon-14 in the air, although fluctuations are known to have occurred over time. The carbon-14 combines with the oxygen of the air, forming carbon dioxide. Plants constantly absorb carbon dioxide, using it to make the food that builds and maintains plant tissues. The carbon dioxide used by plants contains small amounts of carbon-14. Therefore, every cell of a living plant contains a small amount of carbon-14. Because animals feed on plants or on other animals that live on plants, their bodies also contain small amounts of carbon-14. As the carbon-14 breaks down in the tissues of plants and animals, new supplies of carbon-14 are taken in.

When an animal or plant dies, it no longer takes in carbon-14. The carbon-14 that is in the tissues, however, continues breaking down at a steady rate. This rate is determined by the half-life of carbon-14—about 5,730 years. This means that about 5,730 years after a plant or animal dies, half the carbon-14 atoms present at the time of death are left. After 11,460 years, one-quarter of the original carbon-14 atoms are left. After 17,190 years, the carbon-14 atoms are about an eighth of the original amount, and so on. Because carbon-14 breaks down at this steady rate, scientists can determine the age of objects containing carbon-14.

One of the major technological advances in radiometric dating is the development of instruments that measure amounts of gases. One technique, called **accelerator mass spectrometry** (AMS), combines a particle accelerator with a mass spectrometer to measure nuclear particle emissions. A sample is heated or burned to release various gases, including carbon dioxide. The carbon or the carbon dioxide contains a few carbon-14 atoms. AMS techniques have extended the range of radiocarbon dating back to 100,000 years and are 1,000 to 10,000 times more sensitive than waiting for and measuring natural decay.

Because levels of carbon-14 in the air have varied considerably over time, scientists often check the accuracy of radiocarbon dates by comparing them with the annual growth rings of trees. (Ring widths vary according to weather patterns, and tree-ring records from very old trees such as redwoods and bristlecone pines are a very reliable dating method.)

Radiocarbon dating has enabled scientists to date the remains of mammoths and other animals that became extinct thousands of years ago. It has also provided valuable information on the history of early humans. Archaeologists have used it to analyze charcoal, wood, pottery, cloth, bones, and other remains from ancient sites and to determine the ages of wall and rock paintings. Radiocarbon dating is used in many other fields besides archaeology, including oceanography, geology, atmospheric science, forensics, and biomedicine.

NORM THOMSON
Department of Science Education
University of Georgia

See also ATOMS; RADIATION; RADIOACTIVE ELEMENTS.

**RADON.** See ELEMENTS, CHEMICAL; NEON AND OTHER NOBLE GASES.

**RAGTIME.** See JAZZ.

# RAILROADS

Quite often, people see trains only while waiting for them to pass at railroad crossings. But railroads have touched each of our lives in some way. Nearly everything in our homes—from the cars in our driveways, to the lumber from which our homes were built, to the food we eat—was shipped at some point by rail.

Railroads around the world are bigger, more efficient, and faster than ever before. Trains have always moved larger and heavier loads than any other form of commercial land transportation. North American railroads continue to set new records for amounts of freight they carry. Railroads also play an important role in the movement of people. In Europe, the passenger train is a popular way to travel. The high-speed railroads of France and Japan—capable of speeds greater than 200 miles (322 kilometers) per hour—have served as models for new rail systems in the rest of the world.

### ▶ WHAT IS A RAILROAD?

Simply, a railroad is a system in which vehicles with **flanged wheels** (a wheel with a projecting rim, or flange, to guide it along a track) travel over iron or steel rails. Most commonly, a locomotive pulls freight cars and/or passenger cars (together referred to as **rolling stock**) over these rails from one location to another. A railroad system is made up of several different components, including tracks, locomotives, and cars for transporting passengers and goods.

### ▶ TRACK

The most basic component of any railroad is the track. Proper track construction is essential to safe operation of the railroad. A good track consists of two securely anchored, parallel steel rails. Because of a train's weight, the track must be laid on firm, level, and well-drained ground.

Historically, rails were manufactured in 39½-foot (12-meter) lengths to fit the typical 40-foot rail car. These rails were joined end to end, but they were separated by a small gap between the ends of the rails. This gap al-

In every part of the world, railroads are an important means of transporting goods and passengers to nearby destinations or faraway places.

lowed the steel to expand with heat. If there were no gaps to allow for this expansion, the hot summer sun might expand the rails so much that they would push against each other and buckle. Steel train wheels rolling over these joints created the familiar clickity-clack sounds associated with railroads.

This type of jointed rail system is still used today, mostly on older lines. The rails are joined by a sandwichlike assembly of steel pieces called **angle bars**. With one angle bar on each side of the rails, the whole arrangement is held together by bolts that go through holes in the angle bars and the rails.

Today new rails are delivered in 1,500-foot (460-meter) lengths. The ends of these rails

## Why does the standard gauge measure 4 feet 8½ inches (1.4 meters)?

The source of the peculiar width known as standard gauge is said to have come from the ruts in the roads left by Roman chariots, but that legend has never been proven.

Railroads were born in England, and the greatest of the early English railroad builders was George Stephenson. When Stephenson was called upon to build the Stockton & Darlington, he made its gauge 4 feet 8 inches (1.4 meters), the same as that of the tracks of the railroad at the coal mine where he had formerly worked. Later he added another ½ inch (1.3 centimeters) to reduce binding of the wheels by the rails. Stephenson used this 4-foot-8½-inch (1.4-meter) gauge on all the other railroads he built, and he built more than anyone else in England.

Early railroad companies in the United States and other countries bought English locomotives and laid their tracks to fit the locomotives' wheels. In this way the Stephenson standard gauge became the most common in the world.

are welded together to form a continuous welded rail, which gives a quieter ride by reducing the clicking of the wheels.

Rails are fastened to **crossties**, or **ties**, which support the track and hold it together. Crossties also keep the rails parallel and separated at a specific distance, called the **gauge**. A flat steel **tie plate**, typically spiked to the tie, spreads the weight of a passing train over the crosstie. Rails are fastened to the tie plate by either spikes or special fasteners called **spring clips**.

For many years crossties were made only of wood treated with creosote (a preservative). However, the spring clip and other modern developments have made concrete and steel crossties practical and even desirable for some uses.

Ties made from an African wood called Azobe are becoming popular in many countries around the world. This wood is very dense and requires no preservative treatment. Concrete ties are very heavy and expensive, but they last a long time and hold tracks firmly. Steel crossties also hold rails firmly, but their biggest advantage is their low height, which makes them useful for low-clearance environments such as tunnels and under bridges.

Most of the world, including the United States, uses a standard gauge of 4 feet 8½ inches (1.4 meters). However, gauges around the world range from 2 feet (0.6 meter) to 5 feet 3 inches (1.6 meters). Some amusement parks operate 12-inch (30-centimeter)- or 15-inch (38-centimeter)-gauge railways, and some industries operate gauges as wide as 7 feet (2 meters). Some railroads in the United States run on narrow gauges, most commonly 3 feet (0.9 meter), but these are tourist lines that are not considered part of interstate commerce. Most narrow-gauge lines have disappeared from the United States, but narrow gauge remains important in Latin America, Asia, and Africa.

Some trolley and commuter railroads in American cities use wider gauges than the standard gauge, mostly as a way to prevent freight equipment from using those railroad systems.

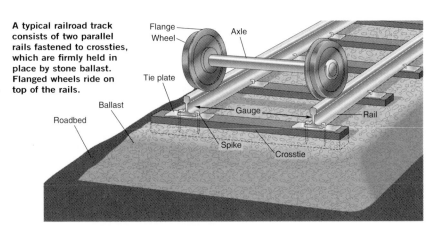

A typical railroad track consists of two parallel rails fastened to crossties, which are firmly held in place by stone ballast. Flanged wheels ride on top of the rails.

Crossties sit in a layer of crushed stone or fractured rock called **ballast**. Ballast serves several important purposes. The ballast's jagged edges interlock and form a sturdy, cushioned base for the crossties and track. Ballast also allows water to drain away from the track freely, and it helps control the growth of grass and weeds. Good drainage is one of the most important aspects of track structure. Track workers refer to the ballast between the rails and crossties as **crib ballast**. Ballast outside the rail is called **shoulder ballast**.

Rugged terrain poses a challenge to railroad designers, who strive for the straightest and most level track possible. Two solutions, although complex and expensive, include building bridges over deep valleys (*left*) and boring tunnels through mountains (*above*).

A railroad is built on carefully prepared ground called the **roadbed**. The first step in any track construction project is preparing the roadbed. Earth-moving machines form this smooth, flat, and hard-packed bed. The dirt surface is covered with a layer of small stone. Over time, and with the weight and vibration of passing trains, this stone becomes firmly embedded into the roadbed.

After the rails and ties are laid and assembled on top of the roadbed, stone ballast is dumped, or "flooded," into the new track structure. Specialized machinery then rolls, smooths, and aligns the ballast. At this point, trains are permitted to pass slowly over the area to help settle the roadbed. Then the machinery returns to do a final surfacing.

Trains cannot climb steep slopes, or **grades**, so the roadbed must be as level as possible. Since very few places in the world are naturally level for long distances, level roadbeds must be designed and constructed. It takes considerable time and effort to build a level roadbed—low spots must be filled and high spots must be dug away. If a hill is too high for a cut, railroad builders may tunnel through the hill or else run the roadbed around it. Very deep valleys may be crossed or spanned by bridges rather than by filled embankments.

Sometimes it is too costly to build a perfectly level roadbed. Therefore, most railroad tracks have a slight grade. The grade is measured by the rate the tracks climb or fall. A rise or fall of 2 feet (0.6 meter) for every hundred feet (30 meters) of track is called a 2-percent grade, quite a steep grade in railroad building. Most mainline tracks in the United States have grades no steeper than 1 percent. In some areas, however, it is impossible to avoid steep grades. In Switzerland, for example, some railroads have grades of 7 percent. This is just about as steep a grade as a train can climb without a rack and pinion. (A cog, or rack, railroad uses a toothed cog wheel on the locomotive that meshes into a ladderlike rack rail. The rack rail is mounted between the outer rails. Certain types of cog railroads can climb grades of up to 38 percent.)

Curves also are unavoidable, but railroad builders keep them as gentle as possible. Sharp curves are dangerous because they may cause a speeding train to leave the track, or derail. Therefore, curved tracks are often banked, or inclined, to permit higher track speeds.

### ▶ LOCOMOTIVES

There are many kinds of locomotives, large and small, designed for different jobs. Some locomotives are specially designed to pull passenger trains at high speeds. Others are built to haul mile-long freight trains. Still others are designed for rail yard switching duty. Locomotives are discussed more fully in the article LOCOMOTIVES in Volume L.

A locomotive is actually a power plant on wheels. Locomotives use various types of energy to pull their loads. In the **diesel locomotive**, also known as the diesel-electric locomotive, a powerful diesel engine works with electric traction motors to drive the wheels. Diesel locomotives are the most common types of locomotives and are capable of pulling the largest loads.

For more than 100 years, steam was the chief source of rail power all over the world. **Steam locomotives** are now used mainly for recreational railroading in many parts of the world. They typically provide power for main-line passenger excursions, as well as tourist and scenic rail trips. In many countries steam locomotives are being restored and preserved in museums. In Europe, South Africa, and Russia, several historically important steam locomotives are kept operational for special occasions. China still uses

Steam locomotives (*top*), which served the birth and growth of railroads, provide mainly recreational service today. Powerful diesel locomotives (*above*) move more trains than any other type. Electric locomotives (*right*) are commonly used in urban areas and also to propel the world's fastest trains.

Tall, wraparound windows are found atop a double-deck Amtrak Viewliner. The expanse of glass and outward facing seats treat passengers to a commanding view.

Hungry passengers traveling by long-distance train can make their way to the dining car for breakfast, lunch, or dinner. Food is prepared in the dining car's small kitchen.

steam locomotives to transport freight in the northern regions of the country.

Today the diesel locomotive has taken the place of the steam locomotive in many countries, and only a few steam locomotives remain in service. Diesel locomotives are more costly than steam locomotives, but diesels have many advantages. They are cheaper to run, they get much more energy out of their fuel, they cause less wear and tear on the tracks, and above all, they need far less maintenance than steam locomotives. The average steam locomotive spends a great deal of time in the shop for servicing and repairs.

**Electric locomotives** are most often used to pull high-speed passenger trains. In several countries around the world, including China, electric locomotives also are widely used for transporting freight.

Electric locomotives came into use in the late 1800's, but because of the high cost of electrifying a railroad, they never rivaled steam or diesel power. However, Switzerland and a few other countries that are poor in coal and oil but rich in hydroelectric power depend mostly on electric locomotives. Electric locomotives are also well suited for work in and near cities, because they create no exhaust fumes.

▶ PASSENGER SERVICE

Millions of people ride railroads each year, either for recreation or as their primary mode of transportation. Amtrak, a nation-wide passenger rail system in the United States, carries more than 20 million people each year. And more than 1 million people in the United States commute to work by rail every day. Tourist railroads, too, are approaching 1 million riders each year.

Commuter trains carry people from the suburbs to nearby city business and shopping centers. These trains have only passenger cars.

Commuter railroad operations are normally funded by the state in which they operate and are regulated by the Department of Transportation. The largest commuter rail systems include Chicago's Metra system, New Jersey's NJ Transit, and New York's MTA Metro-North Railroad. The New Jersey and New York systems bring people to jobs in and around New York City.

Subway systems and surface trolleys—known as light rail systems—are being built or expanded every year in major cities. The largest American subway system is New York City Transit. With a fleet of 6,000 passenger cars, it moves 1.1 billion people each year.

### Passenger Cars

A **coach** is the most common type of passenger car. Commuter coaches usually seat 80–125 passengers. On some lines, commuter coaches are double-deck. Long-distance coaches usually have larger, more comfortable seats, resulting in fewer seats per car—often around 50.

A **dining car** is a restaurant on wheels, where passengers can get breakfast, lunch, or dinner. Meals are prepared in a small onboard kitchen. Commuter railroads do not offer food service.

**Sleeping cars** are equipped with small hotel-like rooms where passengers can sleep during long train trips. Usually the seats in a room convert to beds for sleeping. Some bedrooms may be equipped with toilets and shower stalls.

Double-deck **observation cars** feature large windows on the top deck that extend up into the ceiling, providing passengers with an excellent view of passing scenery.

Some railroads use **mail handling cars** to carry bulk mail (mail in bags or other containers) and express, or time-sensitive, freight. These cars are typically found near the front of a passenger train. Until 1972, most intercity trains had an on-board post office where mail was sorted and distributed along a rail line.

**Baggage cars**, used on long-distance passenger trains, carry passengers' luggage. On many railroads today, baggage cars also carry mail and packages.

### ▶ FREIGHT SERVICE

American freight railroads are the largest, busiest, and most profitable in the world. Like all other freight railroads around the world, they move goods in various types of freight cars.

### Freight Cars

Freight cars are simply railroad cars that carry loads. The type of load to be carried determines the freight car design. For example, there are boxcars for general freight, tank cars for liquids, hopper cars for coal and sand, flatcars for containerized freight, lumber, steel beams, and bulky equipment, and rack cars for automobiles. As railroading becomes more standardized, the industry is settling on a few types of freight cars.

The **boxcar** is the most important type of freight car. There are more boxcars than any other kind of railroad car. A boxcar is an enclosed metal car with a big sliding door on each side for loading and unloading freight. Boxcars are widely used because they protect their contents from the weather and vandals, and they lend themselves well to the stacking of boxed merchandise. They carry grain, flour, canned goods, clothing, shoes, refrigerators, stoves, and other cargo that must be protected from the weather.

Freight cars vary in size and shape, depending on the goods to be carried. Specialized flatcars (*below*) transport piggyback containers. Boxcars (*bottom*) enclose and protect freight. Tank cars (*right*) carry liquids of all kinds, from milk to dangerous chemicals.

**Hopper cars** are open-topped, bathtub-shaped freight cars that are filled from the top and emptied from the bottom through hoppers, or chutes. Coal, sand, crushed stone, wood chips, and broken (recycled) glass are some materials shipped in hoppers. **Covered hoppers** carry powdered or granular materials that must be protected from the weather, like raw plastic (in pellet form), cement, flour, sugar, and grain. Hopper cars are unloaded from elevated ramps. The loads fall down into storage bins underneath the ramps.

The **flatcar** is an open platform on which almost anything can be carried. Flatcars are useful for handling odd and oversized loads that may not fit in boxcars, such as farm equipment, structural steel beams, and even small locomotives. Special flatcars with a sunken center, called well-type flatcars, are used for moving very large pieces of equipment, such as giant transformers for electric power plants, that would otherwise stand too tall to pass under bridges and tunnels. Other flatcars equipped with multi-level racks carry cars and trucks.

An important use of flatcars is in "piggy-back" freight service. Highway truck trailers are loaded on flatcars and sent by rail to distant points. In this way a long haul over a crowded highway is avoided. At their final railway destinations, the trailers are unloaded from the flatcars for hauling to customer factories or warehouses by truck. Piggyback freight traffic is the fastest-growing segment of the United States rail industry.

**Gondolas** are open-topped flatcars with low sides and ends. They carry loose or bulky materials, such as structural steel shapes, bundles of coiled steel or wire items, rail, scrap metal, and railroad wheels. Gondolas also carry **containers**, big waterproof and fireproof boxes of steel that hold up to 5 or 6 tons of freight. Containers are widely used for shipments of freight that do not take up a whole carload.

## BRAKING IMPROVEMENTS MEAN SHORTER, SAFER STOPS

A heavy freight train traveling at 60 miles (97 kilometers) per hour can require as much as 1 mile (1.6 kilometers) of track to stop. Shortening this distance is an important railroad safety issue. New developments in brake technology have cut this distance significantly.

Early trains were equipped with tread brakes that were activated by turning a wheel mounted on an upright staff (known as a brake wheel). A brake wheel was located on each freight and passenger car. On freight trains, brakemen rode the roofs of the cars and turned the brake wheels as commanded by the engineer's locomotive whistle. One brakeman was responsible for five or more cars, and most trains had at least three brakemen riding the rooftops. It was dangerous work, and often trains would arrive at a destination with fewer brakemen than they started with.

All that changed in 1869 when George Westinghouse devised a practical air brake. Westinghouse developed a system that piped compressed air from an air pump on the locomotive to all the train's brakes at the same time—no more jumping from car to car to set individual brakes. The air-brake system was refined over the next hundred years, but it was not drastically changed until the mid-1990's with the introduction of electro-pneumatic braking.

When standard air brakes are applied, there is a slight delay before they start working. Electro-pneumatic braking eliminates this delay; any or all of the train's brakes can be activated simultaneously from the locomotive. Electro-pneumatic braking systems have been shown to reduce stopping distances of long trains from more than a mile to just a few hundred feet.

are not touched from the time they are loaded until they reach their destination.

Specialized "bathtub" gondolas, with their taller sides and round bottoms, are specifically designed to carry coal. These cars are unloaded by a rotary dumper that physically tips the car upside down.

**Tank cars** are steel tanks on wheels. They carry all sorts of liquids: oil, gasoline, liquid soaps, acids and other chemicals, wine, milk, and orange juice, for example. Tankers that carry chemicals and food products are lined with glass or porcelain. Some tank cars are insulated for the transportation of items that need to be kept cold during shipment. Specially reinforced tank cars carry gases under high pressure. Other tank cars carry powdered materials.

**Refrigerator cars** look like boxcars, but they are insulated and carry cooling machinery to keep goods cold. Meat, dairy products, orange juice, and frozen foods are examples of goods carried in refrigerator cars.

**Stock cars**, also similar to boxcars, are designed to carry farm animals, usually cows or pigs. The car sides have plenty of air holes so the animals can breathe. Stock cars are not widely used since stops for water and food must be figured into the railroad's schedule.

The **caboose**, while not a freight car, represents a passing era in railroading. Traditionally the caboose was painted red, had a raised roof section called a cupola, and was the last car on every train. It was where the brakeman or conductor would keep watch on the train and fill out and file paperwork. As railroads began operating more efficiently in the 1980's and 1990's, the caboose was almost eliminated from freight service. However, several major railroads in the United States put cabooses back in service on freight lines for safety reasons. Often these trains must run in reverse for great distances, and the caboose provides a place where a worker can safely guide the train instead of hanging on to a freight car.

These standardized containers are designed to be shipped through an efficient combination of road and rail transport. They can be loaded onto specially built tractor-trailer trucks for over-the-road hauling, and they can be piggybacked onto railroad flatcars—with or without the wheeled trailer frame. Containers are easily transferred between railroad cars and trucks for door-to-door delivery. Containers also cut the cost of freight handling since the goods inside them

### ▶ FREIGHT OPERATIONS AND YARDS

Freight trains begin and end their runs in **classification yards**, where the trains are broken up and the cars are rearranged into new trains according to their destinations. These yards are made up of groups of tracks connected by switches. Each track splits up into a

Giant freight-yard cranes transfer loaded containers between trains and trucks or, in shipyards, between trains and freight ships.

number of sidings (side tracks), like the trunk and branches of a tree. Classification yards, also called switching yards, are usually located in major cities, at junctions with other railroads, or at division points (places where large segments of railroad come together).

When a train arrives with cars to be sorted, the locomotive is uncoupled, or disconnected, and a switching engine pushes the cars to the top of a slope called the **hump**. The cars are uncoupled and allowed to run down the slope to the classification tracks. An operator in a control tower controls the switches so that each car goes onto the correct track. The speed of the rolling cars is controlled by devices called **car retarders**, which squeeze the wheels against the rails. The operator in the control tower works the car retarders from a control panel. A list indicates where each car is to go, and the operator stops the cars when they have reached their assigned spots. Before car retarders came into use, a worker had to ride each car and stop it with the hand brake.

Computerized equipment makes it possible for a single operator in a control tower to monitor and run a whole freight yard from a central control panel.

Today an important yard operation involves the transfer of containerized freight from trucks to trains and from trains to trucks. A similar procedure is used in large shipping yards where containers are transferred to and from trains and large, oceangoing freight ships.

▶ SIGNALS

Just as traffic lights help control the safe flow of automobile traffic, railroad signal systems help keep trains from running into one another. These complex systems provide valuable information to the conductor, such as where trains are located and how the tracks and switches are aligned.

On almost every railroad, a green signal means go, indicating that the track is clear. A yellow signal warns of a train ahead and tells the engineer to approach at restricted speed. A red signal tells the engineer to stop the train—the line is not clear. Combinations of

From a dispatch center, operators control the flow of several trains by monitoring their positions and electronically changing signals along the tracks. Lights on the board show train locations and signal status.

red, green, and yellow signals convey other specific information to a train crew.

The earliest railroad signal systems were used in New Jersey in the mid-1800's. Today some systems use satellites to monitor train positions. A few railroads use cab signals, a system that detects signals and displays them in the locomotive's cab. This type of display is more easily seen than typical signals, which are located either above or alongside the track.

Train movements are also controlled by a dispatcher. Some of today's largest railroads are served by a team of centrally located dispatchers who use satellites and radio transmitters to watch and talk to any train on the railroad. Other satellite-based systems even permit mechanics to monitor the condition of locomotives and warn the crew of developing problems.

## ▶ RAILROAD WORKERS

As railroading becomes more efficient, fewer employees are required to do the same

The Civil War was the first American conflict in which railroads played an important part. They moved troops and war supplies, such as this large cannon.

amount of work. However, to operate safely, railroads still require many workers.

During the steam era, a typical train crew consisted of five men: an engineer, a fireman, a conductor, and two brakemen—one assigned to the front of the train and the other to the rear. Today train crews consist of two

or three people, depending on the train's assignments. A local train with a lot of switching is generally assigned a crew of three—an engineer, a conductor, and a brakeman. Long-distance trains with little work along the route do not have a brakeman.

In a typical train crew, the conductor directs operations and oversees the work to be done. The conductor also keeps track of which cars are set out and picked up and files the paperwork when the job is finished. The brakeman handles most of the coupling and uncoupling of cars and the throwing of switches. In addition to operating the locomotive, the engineer must follow all safety rules and stay up-to-date with any changes, improvements, and company bulletins. Train crews are union employees governed by the United Transportation Union (UTU) and the Brotherhood of Locomotive Engineers (BLE), which protect the wages and working conditions of the employee.

## ▶ HISTORY

Although the railroad industry was born in the 1800's, the idea of tracks is much older. The ancient Egyptians used hard, smooth tracklike guideways to transport the stones for the great pyramids, and the Romans built hard-surfaced guideways for chariots. The first recorded instance of rails used on roadways occurred in England in 1630. There, a system made up of crude plank railways and horse-drawn wagons was built to transport coal from the mines near Newcastle, England. Horses could pull a loaded coal wagon much more easily along the smooth, firm tracks than over the muddy, bumpy, hole-filled roads of the time. Soon many roads around the English coal mines were turned into these types of railways.

While various written accounts exist of rail-like systems during the 1700's, iron rails with outside ledges were first cast in England in 1776. The purpose of the ledge was to keep the smooth wagon wheels on the rail. Due to dirt buildup on the rails, however, the ledges were not effective in holding the wagon wheels in place. In 1785, William Jessop (1745–1814), a civil engineer, invented the first metal rails for flanged wagon wheels to travel upon. In 1801, Jessop found that with flanges on both sides of the wheels, "ten

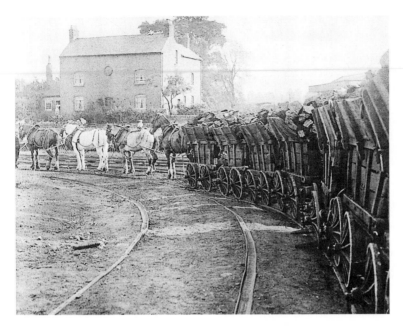

Before steam power replaced horse power, crude English mining railroads consisted of horse- or mule-drawn wagons, the wheels of which rode along channel-like rails.

horses could do the work that had employed four hundred on common roads." Rails were wider at the top than at the bottom until 1820, when machinery was invented to roll iron into a shape more like today's rails.

### Invention and Use of Steam Locomotives

Richard Trevithick (1771–1833), a successful English mining engineer, invented the steam locomotive. In 1804 he built a small locomotive that pulled a string of loaded cars on a mine railway in Wales.

In 1814, George Stephenson (1781–1848), an English engineer, constructed a noisy single-cylinder engine he called *Blucher*. He tried to quiet the engine by directing the exhaust up *Blucher*'s chimney, or stack. Sending the cylinder exhaust up the stack creates a vacuum in the boiler that forces air through the fire, which improves combustion. The faster a locomotive ran, the hotter the fire. That discovery was a very important step in the invention of a successful steam locomotive.

In 1825, Stephenson's *Locomotion* became the first steam locomotive to pull a passenger train. The success of his locomotive *Rocket*, in 1829, marked what many consider the beginning of the modern railroad.

### Early American Railroads

In spite of these acknowledged firsts in England, there are earlier reports of steam locomotives in America. Colonel John Stevens (1749–1838), an amateur inventor and wealthy landowner, built an experimental locomotive in 1825 that he operated on a circular track on his Hoboken, New Jersey, estate. Stevens, trying to promote the use of steam locomotion on railways, said, "I can see nothing to hinder a steam engine moving with a velocity of 100 miles (160 kilometers) per hour."

Before that, in the 1780's, John Fitch (1749–1838) invented a model of a steam locomotive that he showed to George Washington and his cabinet in Philadelphia. The 2-foot (0.6-meter) model had a boiler mounted sideways and flanges on the outsides of its wheels. This locomotive is preserved at the Ohio State Historical Society Museum in Columbus, Ohio.

The first railroad to open for business in the United States was the Granite Railway Company in Quincy, Massachusetts. The 3-mile (4.8-kilometer)-long track, completed in 1827, was made of wooden rails covered with strap iron. Its horse-drawn cars carried blocks of granite for the Bunker Hill Monument.

The second U.S. railroad, also completed in 1827, was a 9-mile (14.5-kilometer)-long Pennsylvania coal line that ran from the mines in Mauch Chunk (a town known as Jim Thorpe today) to the Lehigh River. Cars loaded with coal rolled downhill to the river, and the empty cars were pulled back up to the mines by mules or horses.

Horatio Allen (1802–90), a young engineer working for the Delaware & Hudson Canal Company, believed that mechanical power was a better method of moving freight. He imported four English-built locomotives for a railroad being constructed between Honesdale and Carbondale, Pennsylvania. The first of these, the *Stourbridge Lion*, arrived in New York City during May 1829. The engine performed beautifully, but it was too heavy for

George Stephenson

George Pullman

Consult the Index to find more information in *The New Book of Knowledge* about the following people associated with the railroad industry: Peter Cooper (1791–1883), Cornelius Vanderbilt (1794–1877), Leland Stanford (1824–93), George Westinghouse (1846–1914), Eugene V. Debs (1855–1926), Edward H. Harriman (1848–1909), and A. Philip Randolph (1889–1979).

**George Stephenson** (1781–1848), English engineer and inventor, was born in Wylam, England. Stephenson helped develop the steam locomotive in the early 1800's. In 1825, Stephenson's *Locomotion* was the first steam locomotive to pull a passenger train. He also helped construct the Stockton & Darlington Railway, the first railroad open to the public. Stephenson's locomotive *Rocket* won the prize for best locomotive design in a contest held in 1829; its success marked the beginning of the modern railroad.

**Matthias William Baldwin** (1795–1866), an industrialist and philanthropist, was born in Elizabethtown, New Jersey. In the 1830's, Baldwin designed and built *Old Ironsides*, a locomotive made of iron and wood that set speed records for its time. In 1832 he founded the Baldwin Locomotive Works, and in 1842 he patented a design that allowed railroad cars to go around curves.

**George Mortimer Pullman** (1831–97), born in Brockton, New York, dominated the railroad sleeping-car industry beginning in the late 1850's, when long-distance train travel became common-place. For more than half a century, Pullman cars were the most luxurious in the United States. In 1894, labor leader Eugene V. Debs led American Railway Union (ARU) members in a strike against the Pullman Company to protest pay cuts. The **Pullman Strike** touched off a nationwide railroad strike that required the intervention of federal troops because it affected the mail service. Debs was arrested and sent to prison for six months.

**Jason (Jay) Gould** (1836–92), born in Roxbury, New York, was a successful railroad tycoon and one of the most notorious "robber barons" of the late 1800's. As a director of the Erie Railroad (1867–68), Gould made a fortune issuing illegal stocks and bribing legislators. In his lifetime he also controlled the Missouri Pacific, Texas & Pacific, St. Louis Southwestern, and International & Great Northern railroads as well as the New York Elevated Railways, the Western Union Telegraph Company, and the New York *World* newspaper.

**James Jerome Hill** (1838–1916), a brilliant businessman and financier known as the Empire Builder, was born near Rockwood, Ontario, Canada. After establishing himself in St. Paul, Minnesota, Hill rescued the St. Paul & Pacific Railway from bankruptcy. From it he developed the Great Northern Railroad in 1893 that ran from Minnesota to Washington State. He also cofounded the transcontinental Canadian Pacific Railway in 1885.

**Casey (John Luther) Jones** (1863–1900), born in Fulton County, Kentucky, was a railroad engineer for the Illinois Central Railroad. On April 30, 1900, while running the *Cannonball Express* from Memphis, Tennessee, to Canton, Mississippi, Casey saw two trains blocking his track. To minimize the inevitable collision, he remained at his post to slow the train down as much as possible. He died with his hand on the brake, having saved the lives of everyone else on the train. Many ballads were written to celebrate his heroism.

Casey Jones

James Hill

the flimsy tracks. Although it could not be used in regular service, the *Stourbridge Lion* was the first real locomotive to operate on a North American railroad.

In 1830 the Baltimore & Ohio (B&O) Railroad opened its first 13-mile (21-kilometer) section of track in Maryland between downtown Baltimore and Ellicott's Mills. The B&O was the first railroad built for commerce rather than simply for mining or industry. It was feared that the many sharp curves on this new line would cause a large steam locomotive to derail.

To prove that steam could be used successfully, Peter Cooper (1791–1883), a manufacturer, designed and built a small locomotive he called *Tom Thumb*, which ran on the initial B&O section in 1830. Cooper's *Tom Thumb* is regarded as the first successful locomotive built in America. Also in 1830 the South Carolina Railroad's locomotive, *Best Friend of Charleston*, became the first locomotive built in America to pull a passenger train in the United States.

### Expansion of American Railroads

In the following years, many small railroads were constructed across America. The developments and innovations that resulted from these railroads helped advance railway technology. By the 1840's, America was building the biggest and best locomotives in the world.

To encourage the building of railroads in the unsettled lands of the West, President Millard Fillmore in 1850 signed the first of a series of land-grant acts. These acts granted railroads large areas of land on and along the rights-of-way. The railroads expected to sell or give the land to settlers and then earn more money by hauling their products to market. In return, the railroads agreed to carry government traffic at reduced rates. By the time the agreements ended in 1946, the railroads that had received land grants had paid back to the government many times the value of the land.

As railways expanded, the issue of track gauge (the width between the rails) became more urgent. If every railroad had its own gauge—and none of the gauges matched—the establishment of a national rail system for use by all railroads would be impossible.

The Civil War halted expansion temporarily, but construction of the first American transcontinental line began even before the fighting ended. Hard-driving construction crews of the Union Pacific pushed west over the Great Plains from the Missouri River, while the crews of the Central Pacific hacked their way through the rugged Sierra Nevada range. The two lines met at Promontory Summit, Utah, on May 10, 1869. That single event reduced the typical six-month cross-country journey to about five days. By 1900, seven rail lines crossed the United States from Chicago to the Pacific Ocean.

The 1860's also saw important advances in railroad safety. In 1863, steel rails began to come into use. Because steel is much stronger than plain iron, steel rails enabled trains to carry heavier loads at higher speeds than ever before, while reducing the danger of rail breakage. In 1868, Eli H. Janney (1831–1912), an inventor, patented an automatic knuckle coupler—the kind that is still used today on

America's first transcontinental railroad, finished at a ceremony held on May 10, 1869, opened western regions to new settlement and expanded trade.

railroad cars. In 1869, George Westinghouse (1846–1914), inventor and manufacturer, patented the first practical air-brake system.

The spread of railroads was also responsible for the establishment of standard time zones in 1883. Before then, each community kept its own time, based on the sun's position in the sky. This meant that no two nearby towns had quite the same time, making it difficult to coordinate railroad timetables. Standard time made things much simpler for travelers. Just a few years later, in 1886, the railroad companies finally agreed on a standard track gauge of 4 feet $8\frac{1}{2}$ inches (1.4 meters), which allowed the formation of a unified national rail system.

With a national rail system in place, the Industrial Revolution turned America into a mobile and agile society with almost unmatched industrial strength. However, the years of rapid rail expansion were also years of extensive corruption and rate discrimination within the railroad industry.

In the late 1800's, corruption was particularly evident in the form of inflated railroad construction costs. Also during this time, railroad shippers in all parts of the nation complained about freight rates that were very changeable and excessively high. They also complained about discrimination that favored big shipping customers, many of whom were charged lower rates.

The high freight rates especially angered farmers, who saw their earnings steadily drop because it became so expensive to transport their crops to market. Farmers pressured the federal government to create, in 1877, the Interstate Commerce Commission, which would regulate the rates that railroads could charge.

At the time of America's entry (1917) into World War I (1914–18), the government formed the United States Railway Administration (USRA), which managed the nation's major railroads and suppliers. Standard locomotive and freight car designs were established to replace the aging railroad equipment in service. By the war's end, the rail industry had been significantly improved by the USRA.

In the early 1900's, new methods of transportation threatened the dominance of the railroads: electric inter-urban railways (lines that connected neighboring towns); thousands of private automobiles; intercity buses; larger trucks; airplanes carrying mail, passengers, and high-priority freight; and a growing network of pipelines.

A nationwide rail strike by railroad workers took place in 1922. The American railroad industry was no stranger to smaller-scale strikes. A series of destructive and sometimes bloody strikes started in 1877. Generally, workers went on strike to protest low wages and poor and unsafe working conditions. For more information on the American labor movement, see the article LABOR MOVEMENT in Volume L.

During World War II (1939–45), locomotive and rolling stock builders were forced to shift production to guns, ships, and planes. The railroads themselves were heavily involved in the transport of troops and war materials. By the end of the war, America's railroad system was worn out. Locomotives, rolling stock, and track had been pushed to their limits, and maintenance was secondary to moving war-related traffic.

Advances during the postwar years included diesel locomotives and roller bearings for freight and passenger cars. But as America's passion for the automobile grew, large-scale government funding was directed toward highway projects. As more people traveled by car, railroad passenger service declined. This trend continued through the 1960's, a time when many passenger lines lost money or were eliminated altogether.

The government stepped in during the 1970's to help the ailing American railroad industry. Amtrak, a government-funded passenger railroad, was established in 1972 to operate passenger trains on tracks owned by freight railroads. Later, the government formed Conrail, a giant merger of seven financially weakened railroads. Under careful leadership, Conrail turned around and became a financially independent and powerful railroad by 1982.

Today railroading is strong—traffic is booming and profits are high. Increasing competition from air-freight companies and trucking companies has forced railroads to focus on customer service and on-time scheduling. Cross-country double-stack container trains and trailer-on-flat-car traffic dominate the rail scene. Pioneering methods such as Iron Highway and RoadRailer allow truck trailers to be easily loaded and transported by rail.

The future of railroads seems bright. Light rail systems, similar to the old trolley lines, are being built as "intercity people movers" in almost every metropolitan area. Tourist lines, scenic railroads, and railroad museum lines are being used by more people than ever before—and many rival the best operations anywhere in the world. As roadways have become increasingly crowded, more and more people choose to park their cars and turn to the convenience of mass transit. With continuing advances made possible by new technology, railroads will be better equipped to compete successfully in the world transportation picture.

MICHAEL J. DEL VECCHIO
Historian and Transportation Consultant

See also LOCOMOTIVES; TRANSPORTATION.

# RAILROADS, MODEL

How would you like to pull back the throttle on a huge steam or diesel locomotive and feel the giant come to life, easily pulling as many as 200 loaded freight cars? Or how would you like to be close to a railroad right-of-way along which roaring expresses speed in the night, bound for destinations perhaps hundreds or thousands of miles away? Few people have the chance to run a real railroad, but most of us can still enjoy the thrills of model railroading. If you're old enough and interested enough to read this article, you're also old enough to build a model railroad system that copies the operation of a real railroad, perhaps the one that passes close to your own home.

## ▶ GETTING STARTED

Many people who own train sets run their equipment on the floor, often only during the Christmas holiday season. The very first rule of building a real model railroad system is to build your railroad on a table or wooden platform. When your train layout is on a table, you can leave it up all year long in your room or in the basement, attic, or garage. If you live in an apartment where there isn't enough room for a year-round table, build your railroad on a large wooden panel on rollers so that it can be stored under the bed.

The size of a model railroad system depends on how much space is available. An excellent starting size for the small-size HO gauge or TT gauge trains is 4 feet by 8 feet, which also happens to be the standard size in which ¾-inch plywood sheets are sold at lumberyards. For O gauge, O-27 gauge, or S gauge trains, a model railroad system can be somewhat larger, perhaps 6 feet by 8 feet. A 6- by 8-foot table can be made by joining two pieces of plywood measuring 4 feet by 6 feet. If the lumberyard doesn't have this size sheet in stock, the plywood can be cut to order.

Most of the big model railroad club layouts are built to a height of 40 to 42 inches. This height is fine for grown-ups but too high for most boys and girls. It's hard to work on a high table. Your table should be about 2 or 3 feet off the ground. You can use two carpenter's sawhorses as legs or make some wooden or pipe legs.

## ▶ GETTING EQUIPMENT

There are hundreds of companies that make fine model railroad equipment. Most of the cars and locomotives available are closely modeled after those found on actual railroads.

At Christmastime it is possible to buy model railroad equipment in almost any department store as well as in toy stores and supermarkets. There are also special stores called hobby shops that sell model railroad equipment all year long. Hobby shops carry extra tracks, cars, and new locomotives and all kinds of electrical gadgets to make your trains run better, in addition to various kinds of buildings and accessory items.

The hobby shop dealer is usually able to answer technical questions. He can help you make your railroad better.

## ▶ A TRACK DESIGN

A real railroad usually runs between two major cities, such as New York and Chicago, Montreal and Toronto, or London and Edinburgh. The run from New York to Chicago is about 1,000 miles. This is far too long a run to model in miniature. Even if you could run track in a straight line in your home, such a length of track could measure at the most about 50 feet. A length of track 50 feet long in O gauge approximates only about one half mile of real railroad. In HO gauge, 50 feet is not quite a full mile. Therefore an HO train traveling at a scale speed of 60 miles an hour would travel the 50 feet of track in 1 minute. That's not a very long run, is it?

To make our model railroad run longer, the railroad line is twisted into curves and grades, and then the two ends are connected. The trains can then run continuously over the same track, and you can pretend that the several stations on your railroad represent many stations. Then you can run your trains as long as you like.

A good layout is perhaps the most important single thing to consider when planning a model railroad. It is possible to have both simple and complicated layouts for both large and small railroads.

In choosing a model railroad layout, you must decide whether to have a giant transcontinental empire or a smaller branch-line type of railroad. Many modelers find that the smaller line is more fun to model and operate. You will need enough sidings and yards to store extra equipment. You will also need a passenger terminal and an engine terminal.

Fortunately in model railroading you don't need everything at once. You can start with a single loop of track and add switches, sidings, and branches as you progress. You never grow out of your model railroad equipment unless you decide to change to a different-size gauge. Even the smallest switching locomotive, which may have been your first locomotive, will continue to be important as your railroad grows.

### ▶ SCENERY

Scenery will add to the realism of your model railroad. Plastic, wood, and cardboard buildings in easy-to-assemble form are readily available from hobby dealers everywhere. Many modelers prefer to make their own from wood and cardboard, following construction plans to be found in the various model railroad magazines published in the United States and other countries.

Mountains and hills are also easy to make. Old wire screen tacked to a simple wooden framework forms the base on which you can smear a thin coating of plaster or any of the several prepared scenic mixes. Many modelers find papier-mâché to be a handy and economical scenic material.

When they are dry, paint your mountains and hills with such earthy-looking colors as burnt umber or sienna. Avoid shiny enamel paints and very bright colors. Scenery should be subdued and lifelike. After painting the scenery, add trees and shrubs and sprinkle imitation grass material in likely places. Add more life to your railroad by clipping colored ads from magazines for use as store names, billboards, and posters.

### ▶ LOCOMOTIVES

It wasn't very long ago that the steam locomotive did almost all the hauling of freight and passenger trains. In a few areas where traffic was very heavy and in certain mountain areas, electric locomotives were also used. Steam locomotives are still used by many railroads throughout the world, and many model railroad fans still prefer to collect these.

Recently the diesel has replaced the steam locomotive in many areas. Although the diesel lacks the variety offered by the steam locomotive, it is more colorful. Most model railroads operate both steam and diesel "locos."

You may prefer an old-time railroad layout. If so, you will want only steam locomotives and old-fashioned railway cars.

The modeler will want to have among his locomotives at least the following: (1) a switching locomotive, (2) a small freight locomotive, (3) a local passenger locomotive, (4) a large freight locomotive, and (5) a fast passenger express locomotive. A railroad can use some locomotives for almost any type of service. For example, a GP-9-type general-purpose locomotive, available in HO, S, or O gauge, can be used for switching, passenger, or freight service.

Every layout should have a variety of freight cars, and no layout can have too many. Some hobbyists like to have a number of coal-hopper cars and several refrigerator cars. As president of your own model railroad, run it as you like.

For your passenger trains you will want several coaches and a Pullman, a diner, a baggage car, a mail car, and an observation car. These can be combined to make up almost any type of passenger train, from a local commuter to a speeding express.

### ▶ OPERATION AND FUN

The fun in model railroading comes from operating your railroad as much as possible like a real railroad. Get an actual railroad timetable and adapt it to your own model railroad. Make up names for your trains, and let them go by real timetable schedules. Such operations can become so involved that you will need the help of your friends to keep the railroad operating on schedule. Your friends can become yardmasters, towermen, station agents, and dispatchers.

You may enjoy starting your own model-railroad club. By pooling equipment, resources, and skills, you can build a much finer layout than you would have had if you built your own railroad without outside help.

HAROLD H. CARSTENS
Publisher
*Railroad Model Craftsman* magazine

# RAIN, SNOW, SLEET, AND HAIL

Any liquid or solid particle of water that falls from the atmosphere to the ground is a form of **precipitation**. Precipitation is part of a complex water cycle in which water is continuously recycled from the Earth's surface into the atmosphere and back to the surface again. Rain, snow, sleet, and hail are all forms of precipitation.

In addition to precipitation, the water cycle consists of three other basic processes: evaporation, condensation, and accumulation. Moisture gets into the atmosphere by **evaporation**, a process in which a liquid changes into a gas. Water, like other liquids, is made up of tiny particles called molecules. These water molecules are continually changing into **water vapor**—a gas that mixes with air and rises into the atmosphere. The rate of evaporation depends on such factors as the dryness and warmth of the air, the amount of wind, and the warmth of the water. The drier and warmer the air, the greater the evaporation. This is also true when it is windier and when the water is warmer. Everyone has experienced evaporation in various situations. For example, as you lie in the sun or wind after swimming, the moisture on your body disappears and your bathing suit becomes dry. This occurs as a result of evaporation. Evaporation also causes puddles to disappear and wet clothes to dry while they are hanging on a clothesline.

**Condensation** is the process in which water vapor changes back into a liquid. Condensation occurs when the air becomes saturated with water vapor. When this happens, some of the water vapor changes into water droplets. For example, after you take a hot shower, you will notice that water droplets have formed on the mirror in the bathroom. This occurs because the air in the bathroom has become saturated with water vapor. The warmer the air, the more water vapor it can hold. Therefore, condensation is more likely to occur when air cools. You can observe this on a hot, humid day when water droplets form on the outside of a glass of ice water. This condensation occurs because the air around the glass is cooled by the ice inside it.

When water droplets condense in the atmosphere, they form clouds. As the droplets become larger and heavier, they may start to

A rainy day in the city. Rainfall like this happens when the water vapor in the clouds in our atmosphere condenses and falls to Earth as water droplets.

fall from these clouds and drop toward the Earth. Sometimes they evaporate before reaching the ground. At other times, the droplets fall to the ground as precipitation. The process of **accumulation** occurs as this precipitation builds up in puddles, rivers, lakes, oceans, and other bodies of water. Precipitation is also stored in glaciers and polar ice caps. As the water that accumulates begins to evaporate, the water cycle begins again.

## ▶ RAIN

The surface waters of the Earth are constantly evaporating, changing into water vapor that mixes with air and is carried high into the atmosphere by winds and air currents. The temperature and pressure of the atmosphere decrease with altitude, so the air cools as it rises. Eventually, this cooling causes the water vapor in the air to condense. As it condenses, tiny droplets of water form around tiny airborne particles of matter called **condensation nuclei**, which include dust, solid particles in smoke, tiny crystals of sea salt, and volcanic ash.

Clouds are collections of enormous numbers of tiny water droplets. The droplets are so small and light that rising currents of air often keep many of them aloft. When small droplets fall toward the surface of the Earth, many of them evaporate before they can reach the ground. The droplets that remain suspended in the atmosphere because of air currents grow larger and heavier as a result of **coalescence**. This is a process in which water droplets collide with one another and in the process form larger droplets. When enough water droplets form and grow too heavy for rising air currents to keep them aloft, they fall to the ground as rain. The falling droplets of rain often collide with each other as well to form even larger raindrops. Depending on such factors as temperature, winds, and the thickness of clouds, raindrops can occur in various sizes. Small raindrops less than 2/100 inch (0.05 centimeter) in diameter that fall close together are called **drizzle**.

Under certain conditions, water droplets in clouds freeze because of low temperatures. However, if the temperature of the air at the bottom of a cloud or beneath a cloud is above the freezing point of 32°F (0°C), the frozen particles melt into raindrops as they fall to the Earth.

▶ SNOW

Like rain, snow begins as water vapor in a cloud. Depending on the temperature in the cloud and the types of condensation nuclei there, this water vapor changes either to all ice crystals or to a mixture of ice crystals and water droplets. Even at temperatures as low as –40°F (–40°C), liquid water can be present in clouds. This water is said to be **supercooled**. Supercooled droplets remain liquid until they bump into ice crystals, at which point they freeze.

When a cloud is very cold, water vapor may change directly from a gas into solid crystals of ice rather than into droplets of water that freeze. This process in which a gas changes directly into a solid is called **sublimation**. At

In cold weather, water vapor in the atmosphere changes into tiny ice crystals. As they fall to the ground, these crystals join together to form snowflakes, like the ones falling on this snowy day in the country.

temperatures below freezing, ice crystals may form around tiny particles of matter, just as water droplets are formed. Sometimes, ice crystals and water droplets form together. When this happens, the ice crystals quickly grow larger because water vapor is changed

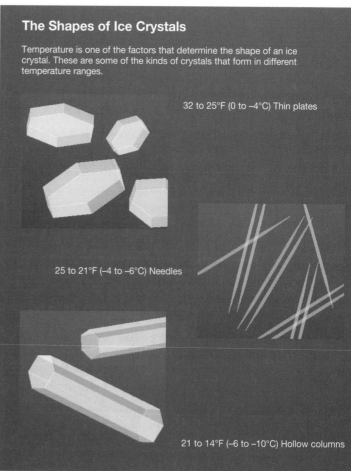

### The Shapes of Ice Crystals

Temperature is one of the factors that determine the shape of an ice crystal. These are some of the kinds of crystals that form in different temperature ranges.

32 to 25°F (0 to –4°C) Thin plates

25 to 21°F (–4 to –6°C) Needles

21 to 14°F (–6 to –10°C) Hollow columns

When rain falls through a very cold layer of air near the ground, it sometimes freezes on contact with a surface. Such a rainfall has frozen on these flower seeds and tree branches.

more easily to ice than to water. This is due to differences in the pressure of water vapor when it is over water or ice.

As ice crystals fall and move around, they collide with each other and stick together in a process known as **aggregation**. This is the process that forms large snowflakes. Each snowflake is made up of a number of ice crystals. The shapes of these ice crystals depend on the temperature in the cloud where they are formed. The shapes include hollow columns, thin plates, needles, six-pointed stars, and branchlike forms known as dendrites. Since snow often falls from different parts of a cloud and from areas with different temperatures, it is not unusual for the cloud to have a mixture of various types of ice crystals.

As snow nears the ground, it sometimes melts and falls as rain. This generally occurs when the air temperature is above freezing.

## ▶ SLEET

Sometimes falling rain passes through a layer of air in which the temperature is below freezing. When this happens, the rain freezes into small, round pieces of ice known as sleet. Sleet can fall and reach the ground even if the temperature at ground level is slightly above freezing. Although sleet typically has a diameter of only 2/100 inch (0.05 centimeter) or less, it can sometimes accumulate to depths of several inches on the ground.

If rain falls through a thin layer of freezing air near the ground, or if the ground or objects there are below freezing, the rain can freeze on contact. This is called freezing rain, or **glaze**. If drizzle is falling and freezes, it is called freezing drizzle. Sleet, glaze, and freezing drizzle

14 to 10°F (–10 to –12°C) Six-pointed star

10 to 3°F (–12 to –16°C) Dendrites

3 to –8°F (–16 to –22°C) Six-pointed star

Below –8°F (–22°C) Hollow columns

can cause very dangerous conditions. For example, driving is often extremely hazardous, and significant amounts of freezing rain can damage trees and power lines.

## ▶ HAIL

Sometimes small balls of ice, called **graupel**, form in the atmosphere when supercooled water freezes upon contact with ice crystals in clouds. As additional water freezes on the graupel, they may grow into larger balls of ice known as hail or hailstones.

Hail generally forms in large, violent thunderstorms with strong currents of rapidly rising air. These currents of air carry graupel high into the atmosphere, where layers of water freeze on them to produce hailstones, which may then fall thousands of feet to the ground or be carried up again on strong air currents. If the hailstones are carried up and down several times, they may collect several layers of frozen water. They can also remain suspended within a cloud, allowing layers of water to collect and freeze on them.

When a large hailstone is sliced open, it will often contain several cloudy and clear layers. These different layers are believed to be the result of variations in temperature and the amount of water present while the hailstone was being formed. For example, water that freezes quickly tends to be cloudy, while water that freezes slowly is clear.

Hailstones come in many shapes and sizes. Small hailstones usually have round or flattened ends. Large hailstones often have spikes or are oddly shaped, which is probably due to the rapid changes the hail experiences while being blown about in the atmosphere.

While an average hailstone is about the size of a pea, hail can grow to the size of a baseball or even larger. The speeds of the rising air currents in a thunderstorm are among the factors that determine the size of hailstones. Air currents moving at about 22 miles (35 kilometers) per hour produce hailstones about 1/2 inch (1.3 centimeters) in diameter. At a speed of about 37 miles (60 kilometers) per hour, hailstones about 3/4 inch (2 centimeters) are formed. The size increases to about 1 3/4 inches (4.5 centimeters) at 56 miles (90 kilometers) per hour and to about 3 inches (7.6 centimeters) at 100 miles (160 kilometers) per hour. One of the largest hailstones ever recorded fell in Coffeyville, Kansas, in September 1970. It measured more than 5 1/2 inches (14 centimeters) in diameter.

## ▶ MEASURING PRECIPITATION

Rain is measured with a rain gauge, which is often simply a hollow tube with a vertical measuring scale on its side. The size of the tube and the length of the vertical scale may vary, allowing the measurement of widely differing amounts of rain. Many rain gauges have a partial cover to help lessen the amount of evaporation that may occur between the time of rainfall and the time of measurement.

Snow can be measured by using a ruler and sticking it through the snow until it touches the ground. However, since wind causes snow to drift to varying depths, it is often difficult to get an accurate mea-

Hailstones start to form when strong currents of air carry small pieces of ice high into the atmosphere. After many layers of water freeze on them, they become heavy enough to fall to the ground (*left*). A large hailstone (*above far left*) is usually made up of several layers. Small ones (*above left*) often have round or flattened ends.

sure with this method. Several measurements often must be taken within an area, and the numbers are then averaged.

The liquid equivalent of snow can be determined by filling a rain gauge with snow. When the column of snow in the gauge melts, the amount of water can then be measured. The ratio of snow to liquid varies depending on the consistency of the snow. Typically, 10 inches (25.4 centimeters) of snow will equal about 1 inch (2.54 centimeters) of water. However, with a dry, powdery snow, it takes about 12 inches (30 centimeters) of snow to equal 1 inch (2.54 centimeters) of water. The wetter the snow, the lower the snow-to-liquid ratio.

Rain gauges, like this simple glass one (*above*) and this precision metal instrument being checked by a U.S. National Park ranger (*inset*), are used to collect and measure rainfall. These measurements can be taken to monitor and compare rainfall levels and patterns anywhere in the world.

▶ GLOBAL PRECIPITATION PATTERNS

The amount of precipitation that falls in a particular place depends on a number of factors, including temperature, wind patterns, proximity to oceans or other large bodies of water, and the presence of mountains. Some parts of the Earth receive more rain than others. For example, many areas along and near the equator have very heavy rainfall, while the polar regions and certain areas near the tropics of Cancer and Capricorn typically receive very little rain. Along the equator, currents of hot air absorb large amounts of water vapor that evaporates from the surface of the oceans. As this moisture-laden air rises to colder areas of the atmosphere, much of the water vapor condenses and falls to the surface. The polar regions receive little rainfall because the air is so cold that it cannot hold much water vapor. In many desert regions, the air is so hot and dry that rain rarely ever forms.

In addition to large-scale precipitation patterns, variations on a smaller scale can occur over the course of many years or in particular places. The most dramatic small-scale variations occur in and near mountain ranges. A great deal of rain typically falls on the windward side of coastal mountains, which is the side facing oncoming winds. As moisture-laden air blows inland from the ocean, it sweeps up the slopes of these mountains, cooling as it rises. The cooling of the moist air causes the water vapor in the air to condense and fall either as rain or as snow. Meanwhile, the leeward side of the mountains, which is the side facing away from the wind, receives little rain or snow because most of it has already fallen on the other side. In 1982, winter storms along the coast of central California dropped up to 24 inches (610 millimeters) of rain on the windward slopes of the coastal mountains there. The leeward side of the mountains received only a few inches.

Similar variations in precipitation sometimes occur near large lakes. For example, the so-called lake effect often results in snowfalls of several feet within a short period of time around the Great Lakes during the winter. The snow generally falls only in narrow strips along the lakes. Locations that are only a few miles away may not receive any snow at all.

H. MICHAEL MOGIL
Meteorologist, How the Weatherworks
See also CLOUDS; WEATHER.

## WONDER QUESTION

### What is the shape of a falling raindrop?

Small droplets of water within a rain cloud are round in shape. These small drops of water join, forming larger drops called raindrops. When raindrops fall through the air, they flatten out. As a result, a raindrop is shaped much like a hamburger bun. A raindrop is not shaped like a pear, as is commonly thought.

# RAINBOW

A rainbow is a beautiful band of colors that is sometimes seen in the sky. Often in the form of an arc or half circle, rainbows can be seen in various places when the sun is behind you—in the sky just after it rains, in the mist of a waterfall, even in the spray from a lawn sprinkler. Rainbows cannot be seen on cloudy days or when the air is very dry because sunlight and drops of moisture in the air are needed to form them.

Rainbows get their colors from sunlight. Light from the sun is a form of energy that travels through space like waves. Although we usually see sunlight as white light, it is actually made up of a combination of colors, with each color having a different wavelength. Under certain circumstances, our eyes can see each wavelength of color in sunlight separately. When sunlight strikes the outer surface of a drop of water such as a raindrop, for example, the drop acts like a prism, and the sunlight is refracted, or bent in another direction. Each wavelength in sunlight bends at a different angle, causing the light to separate into separate rays of color. These rays of color then strike the inner back surface of the water drop, which acts like a mirror and reflects the light back in the direction from which it came, back toward the sun. (This is why the sun must be behind you to see a rainbow.) When this process occurs in billions of water drops, it creates a multicolored arc—a rainbow—in the sky.

For the process to work, the sunlight must also strike the water drops at certain angles. The angle made by the sun, the inner back surfaces of the water drops, and our eyes should be less than 42 degrees. This configuration allows the internal reflection within the water drops to be directed back toward our eyes.

As sunlight strikes the outer surface of a raindrop, the raindrop acts like a prism (*left*), bending each wavelength in the sun's light at a different angle and producing a spectrum of colors that is then reflected back toward the sun. In a rainfall, when this is happening in millions of raindrops, a beautiful rainbow can appear in the sky (*above*).

If the rays of color are reflected only once within water drops, a bright rainbow called a primary rainbow is formed. Its colors are always arranged in the same order. Beginning at the outer part, or top, of the rainbow, the colors are red, orange, yellow, green, blue, indigo (dark blue), and violet. Sometimes the rays of color striking water drops are reflected twice within the drops. When this happens, a double rainbow is formed. The second rainbow is usually fainter than the primary rainbow, and its colors appear in reverse order.

H. MICHAEL MOGIL
Meteorologist, How the Weatherworks
See also COLOR; LENSES; LIGHT.

**RAINEY, JOSEPH HAYNE.** See UNITED STATES, CONGRESS OF THE (Profiles: House Representatives).

# RAIN FORESTS

Rain forests are lush with plants and filled with the sounds of insects, birds, and chattering animals. They are called rain forests because they receive more than 2½ inches (60 millimeters) of rain per month, making the air inside the forests very humid. Tall trees form covers of vegetation that capture water from the air. A person living in the forest might see bats, monkeys, and birds such as toucans, hornbills, and parrots. A person might also see flying squirrels flattening their bodies and gliding through the air or snakes slithering on the ground.

Tropical rain forests are found close to the equator from the Brazilian Amazon and Central America to Southeast Asia, Northeast Australia, and Equatorial Africa. In tropical rain forests, the average annual temperature is 77°F (25°C). Rain forests farther away from the equator are called temperate rain forests because they are cooler and experience less rainfall than tropical forests. Temperate rain forests can be found in the Pacific Northwest of the United States, Southeast Australia, New Zealand, and Chile.

## Life in the Rain Forests

Different layers of trees and plants grow in rain forests. The tallest trees are called **emergents** because they emerge above the rest of the forest. These emergents form a thick layer of leaves called a **canopy**, which allows little light to reach the forest floor. Plants growing beneath the emergents have large leaves to capture flecks of light passing through the canopy.

A shallow dig into a tropical rain forest floor reveals bright red and yellow soils. Soils with these colors are high in clay and low in vital nutrients. To survive in such conditions, some plants depend on cooperative relationships with fungi, which attach to plant roots. These fungi-plant associations help plants acquire nutrients from the soil. Other plants have roots that crawl out of the ground, capturing nutrients being washed down tree trunks during rains. Plants can also form deep carpets of roots on top of the soil to catch nutrients before they go into the ground.

It can be difficult to walk through rain forests because of the abundant plant growth. In the tropics, machetes are useful for cutting

Tall trees emerge from a rain forest in Costa Rica (*above*). A researcher studies the forest canopy from a gondola hanging from a giant crane (*right*).

through thick vines hanging down from the canopy or plants creeping up tree trunks.

However, if a visitor were to see the rain forest only from the ground, he or she would miss a sense of the distinct living community in the forest canopy. Some animals and plants live their whole life in the canopy, never touching the ground. Other canopy-dwellers, such as sloths, crawl down tree trunks only occasionally. Some plants, such as the strangling fig, begin their life in the canopy by growing on the branches of other trees. The strangling fig's thick roots eventually wind around its host tree and kill it.

Rain forest plants have developed many sophisticated methods to keep animals from eating their leaves, stems, or bark. The animals are often hindered by toxic compounds,

A worker in Paraguay burns part of a forest to clear land for farming. Such burning threatens many rain forests worldwide.

called alkaloids, that can either inhibit digestion or kill the animals. Some plants have developed other defenses, such as spines, to discourage vines and other climbing plants from crawling up their trunks.

### The Importance of Rain Forests

Rain forests are important because they contain the highest diversity of plant, animal, and insect species in the world.

Rain forests are also important because they affect Earth's climate. Rain forests stabilize the climate by keeping temperatures from rising. The forest plants do this by absorbing carbon dioxide, a gas in the atmosphere that traps the sun's heat and warms the world. Rain forests also stabilize the climate by controlling rainfall patterns. Because rain forests capture water from the atmosphere, the loss of these forests in some areas has turned them into grasslands or deserts.

Loss of rain forests affects people all over the world in many ways. For example, the cutting down of rain forests can trigger the growth of insect populations, such as mosquitoes, which can carry malaria and other diseases deadly to humans. Habitat loss can also force diseased animals to move closer to human communities. Monkeys carrying the fatal Ebola virus are a danger to people living in some African rain forest areas.

**Uses of Rain Forests.** Native people living in rain forests have traditionally depended on forest resources for all aspects of life, ranging from food and shelter to medicine. Many of these resources are also harvested and used in products exported to countries around the world.

Rain forests are a source of many agricultural crops and houseplants. The cacao plant is used to make chocolate, and the chicle plant is used in chewing gum. Other rain forest crops include coffee plants, rubber plants, and cinnamon. Rain forests also provide many medicines. Chemicals that plants produce to protect themselves have been extracted and used as treatments for disease. Extracts from one rain forest plant, the cinchona, have been used for hundreds of years to treat malaria.

Deadly fluids from some animals, such as frogs, have been used by native people on arrow tips for hunting. Cassava, a starchy root, has been a major agricultural crop. It can be dangerous if not prepared properly, since the roots have high concentrations of cyanide.

### Threats to Rain Forests

Today, native people's lives are changing rapidly, and traditional knowledge of how to live in rain forests is being lost. However, the threat to rain forests does not stem simply from a change in the native people's lives. Increasing demands are being made on rain forest resources from people all over the world. Rain forests are being cleared to mine minerals and metals, ranchers are converting forests to grasslands for grazing cattle, and timber companies are harvesting valuable tree species. Even tourists can pose a threat to tropical rain forests. Visitors often pay to stay in huts with thatched roofs, resulting in the overharvesting of the palms used for thatch. Plants sold as medicines or spices are also being overharvested, and animals are being killed for their skins or sold as exotic pets.

Many attempts are now being made to protect rain forests. Some rain forest products carry a "green" label showing that they were produced using methods that sustain rather than destroy the forests. Other attempts include restoring degraded forests so that they can return to their original condition.

KRISTIINA VOGT
Professor of Ecosystem Ecology
B. BROOKE A. PARRY
Research Assistant, School of Forestry and
Environmental Studies, Yale University

See also BIOMES; CLIMATE; JUNGLES.

**RALEIGH.** See NORTH CAROLINA (Cities).

## RALEIGH, SIR WALTER (1554?–1618)

Sir Walter Raleigh was the most varied in his genius and talents of all the great men of the age of Elizabeth I. He was soldier and sailor, courtier, poet, colonizer, historian, and scientist.

Raleigh was born about 1554 near Budleigh Salterton in Devonshire, England, within sight and sound of the sea. This turned his thoughts to adventure and travel from his earliest days. As a youth he fought in the wars in France, and for a time he attended Oriel College, Oxford. With no money but a great deal of pride, he next went soldiering in Ireland. Having views on Irish policy as on everything else—for he was very much a man of ideas—Raleigh got the chance of presenting them at the English court. There he won the favor of Queen Elizabeth I with his brilliance, eloquence, and good looks. He was made captain of her Guard, knighted, and given various posts in the government. The Queen turned him into a good servant of the state, and he was always a hard worker, full of plans at home and abroad.

The money that came to him from the Queen's favor Raleigh used in planting settlements in America. He sent out the first colony in 1585. It was a group of about 100 men, who lived on Roanoke Island, off the coast of North Carolina, for a year. This was the first English colony to gather experience of life in the New World—all the later colonies flowed from this first attempt. Much of our early knowledge of the Indians, the plant and animal life, and the geography of America we owe to Raleigh's efforts. In 1587 he sent out a second colony of over 100 persons, but all these were lost in the trackless forest of the mainland. Raleigh had spent a fortune on these efforts. Discouraged, he now gave up active colonization in America.

He transferred his attentions to southern Ireland, where he also hoped to establish English colonies. His friendship there with the poet Edmund Spenser (1552?–99), then writing his *Faerie Queene,* was more successful. Raleigh himself was one of the leading poets of the age, though he did not write much in quantity. His best-known lines are from a poem known as "The Nymph's Reply to the Shepherd," written in reply to Christopher Marlowe's (1564–93) famous lyric "Come live with me and be my love":

> If all the world and love were young,
> And truth in every shepherd's tongue,
> These pretty pleasures might me move,
> To live with thee and be thy love.

Raleigh's longest poem, "Book of the Ocean to Cynthia," was unfinished. It tells the story of his devotion to the Queen and its ups and downs. In 1592 he lost Elizabeth's favor by his secret marriage to one of her ladies-in-waiting, Elizabeth Throckmorton. He was exiled from court for some years. In 1595 he made his first voyage to Guiana in South America, where he hoped to find gold. Spain claimed Guiana, but Raleigh hoped to interest England in it. To this purpose he wrote a celebrated book, the *Discovery of Guiana.* Queen Elizabeth was not interested. But in 1596, during the war with Spain, Raleigh played a leading part in the capture of the Spanish city of Cadiz and thus recovered the Queen's favor.

On Elizabeth's death in 1603, King James I came to the throne. James was a personal enemy of Raleigh, who was accused of entering into a conspiracy against him. For this Raleigh was condemned to death. Though the sentence was suspended, he spent most of the rest of his life in the Tower of London.

There he wrote his great *History of the World* and made experiments in chemistry. But his mind remained fixed on Guiana. In 1616 he was allowed out of prison to lead a voyage there. Instead of finding gold he clashed with the Spaniards, and his elder·son, who had accompanied him, was killed. To satisfy Spain, Raleigh was executed on October 29, 1618. There was a great outcry against this. Public opinion in England turned against King James, and Raleigh died a popular hero.

Raleigh's efforts bore fruit after his death. He introduced the potato from the New World into Ireland. He was the first patron of smoking tobacco and made the habit popular; it was this that first set Virginia on its feet. In his eloquent prose and poetry Raleigh still lives in English literature, his name a household word in the English-speaking world.

A. L. ROWSE
Author, *Sir Walter Raleigh*

# RANCH LIFE

To many people, ranching brings to mind images of the Old West, with cowboys, sagebrush, wide-open spaces, and herds of cattle stampeding through the dust. While the Old West is long gone, there are many aspects of ranch life that remain the same. For instance, most ranches are still run by the families who live on them, although some are now owned by large corporations.

Ranching is one of the world's oldest industries. Its origins can be traced to the beginning of civilized life, when people began keeping herds of cattle. These people were called nomads because they moved their herds from place to place, looking for fresh grass and water. Later, as people began to settle in places where food and water were plentiful, they built huts for themselves and shelters and yards for their animals. They put up fences to keep their cattle from straying. These were the first ranches.

Since then, ranching has become a huge industry. Much of the meat we eat today comes from cattle raised on ranches. Cattle also provide by-products. These include gelatin for desserts, hides for leather, and fats for toothpaste, crayons, and other products.

Like other kinds of farming, ranching has many challenges. Some animals may become sick and die, for instance, or their food supply may be destroyed by excessive rain or drought. Also, ranches can be very isolated. Ranch families are usually miles away from other people or towns, although technology such as the Internet may bring the outside world into their homes. But despite these difficulties, most ranchers enjoy working with the animals, coexisting with wildlife, and being close to the land.

▶ **COWBOYS**

In the United States, ranch life has always centered on cowboys. They have a rich history, and stories and legends about them abound. To many, they are a symbol of the American West. People think of cowboys as free and independent people, unafraid to battle wild broncos or

*Top:* Although ranch life can be challenging, many ranchers enjoy working with animals and being outdoors. *Left:* Ranching has become a huge industry over the years, and while many ranches are still owned and operated by families, others are now run by large corporations. In addition to meat, cattle also provide a number of by-products.

angry steers, living close to nature under big skies and bright stars.

These days there are far fewer cowboys than there once were, and they no longer live as they did. But their hold on the imagination is still strong. Old-time cowboys are the heroes of many books, movies, legends, and songs. They are to Americans what knights and nobles were to Europeans—national heroes and a treasured part of the nation's past.

The American cowboy first appeared in Texas in the 1830's. Soon ranches spread from Texas through the Southwest to the Rocky Mountains, and cowboys were working in almost every part of the West.

Cowboys' lives centered on the roundup and the cattle drive. Twice a year they rounded up the cattle, branded the new crop of calves, and separated the beef cattle from the rest of the herd. Then they took the steers that were to be sold and drove them over many miles of open country to the nearest railroad terminal. From there the cattle were shipped to slaughterhouses and packing plants. Almost all of these facilities were in the East, where most Americans lived at the time.

In the 1800's, railroads were few and far between. Driving the cattle was a long, hard job, with constant danger from Indians and cattle thieves. The cowboys rose before dawn to start the cattle moving. They drove them all day through the heat or dust or wind and dozed around campfires at night, alert for trouble or for cattle that had strayed from the herd. They were often on horseback 15 hours a day.

Cowboys had to be resourceful and strong. They had to be skilled horsemen and handy with a lariat (a rope or lasso) and a gun. Their distinctive clothing was designed for protection. The wide-brimmed hat was worn to shield them from the sun and dust and to shed the rain; chaps protected their legs from cactus and tumbleweed; the gun and holster provided protection against rustlers, Indian attacks, and wild animals.

Today, because of competition from better-paying jobs in urban areas, there is a shortage of cowboys. Good cowboys and cowgirls are in high demand for their specialized skills. They must be able to spot sick cows and to

The American cowboy, hero of many books, legends, movies, and songs, first appeared in Texas in the 1830's.

dehorn steers so the cattle do not hurt each other. They must be able to rope and brand calves, administer medicine, and ride miles a day.

▶ RANCHING TODAY

Ranches currently exist in many parts of the world, including the United States, Australia, Canada, Mexico, and South America. Argentina, in the southern part of South America, is one of the greatest ranching countries in the world and is noted for its excellent beef. Great herds roam the Pampas of eastern Argentina, and the cowboys, called gauchos, are as famous as the American cowboys of the Old West.

Most ranches are located in flat, open country where there is plenty of grass for grazing. Often, this kind of country is too high, too rugged, too dry, or too wet to grow crops. Grazing cattle there is a way to produce food from that area.

A ranch can have 500,000 acres (200,000 hectares) of land or as little as 100 acres (40 hectares), depending on the climate and the size of the herd. In dry climates, cattle need more land to graze because there is less grass. In wetter climates, cattle can get the grass they need from a smaller area. In the American West and Southwest, the federal government owns many thousands of acres of land. Ranchers sometimes lease this land to feed their herds. Not all cattle spend their days grazing, however. Some are also placed in feed yards and given a corn-based mixture that helps them gain weight and produce more meat.

To check on their herds, ranchers often use all-terrain vehicles and pickup trucks. However, horses are still used as well. Many ranchers raise their own horses, which are specially trained to work with livestock. They are trained for roping calves and rounding up the herd. Quarter horses are commonly used on ranches because of their agility and speed.

Despite its rewards, ranching is a 24-hour-a-day, 365-day-a-year job. In a ranch family, everyone pitches in to help. Sometimes families also must hire outside help or depend on friends for such tasks as winter feeding, branding, and calving.

*Left:* Good cowboys and cowgirls are in high demand for their specialized skills, which include roping and branding cattle.
*Below left:* Although some ranchers now use ear tags to identify their cattle, many still use the branding iron. This creates a permanent mark that identifies the animal and discourages cattle thieves.
*Below:* Each ranch has its own unique brand mark, which can be a sign, a picture, a design, or the owner's initials.

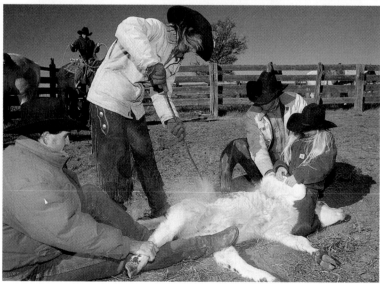

The rancher's goal is to produce the healthiest, most efficient animal possible. There are more than 80 different types of cattle, which can be bred in various combinations. By breeding certain cows with certain bulls, for example, a rancher can produce desired traits in the offspring, such as leaner meat or an animal that can survive well in a hot, arid climate.

Calves are born in the spring and fall. If the weather is cold or snowy, the rancher must make sure that the cows can calve (give birth) in a warm, dry place so that their babies do not get sick. During calving season, the entire family usually helps watch over the cows, which often calve at night.

After the calves are born, children of ranchers frequently help bottle feed them to help them grow, or to provide milk when the mother cannot. Once the calves have grown, some are used for breeding purposes, while others are used to produce meat.

When summer comes, the cattle are turned out to graze the range or forest land. In the meantime, ranchers grow and harvest crops such as hay that will feed their livestock in the winter. In the fall, ranchers gather to round up the cattle. Roundups are community events that families look forward to all year. They usually take all day or longer, depending on the size of the ranch.

### Branding

Branding began in the early days when cattle roamed the open range and belonged to anyone who could catch them. Many ranchers in the 1800's got their start by catching and branding these cattle, putting a fence around them, and letting them breed. Branding is still common.

Ranchers brand their cattle with a unique mark that identifies their animals and discourages cattle thieves. The brand mark of the ranch is burned with a hot iron into the side, hip, or back of each calf. Each ranch has a different brand mark, and some of them have very strange and interesting shapes. They can be signs, pictures, or the initials of the owner's name.

Today, instead of branding their cattle, some ranchers place a tag through the cow's ear. In addition to providing owner identification, these tags can be used to keep track of breeding records and to determine which

Computers and other new technologies have brought about many improvements in the ranching industry and have boosted productivity.

calves are going to market and which are being kept on the ranch. Some ranchers also use special electronic transmitting and receiving devices called transponders. Transponders enable the ranchers to "read" the information on the ear tag. By keeping track of the information in computers, ranchers can quickly access breeding and vaccination records and other important information that helps them make business decisions.

### Sheep Ranching

Some ranchers just raise cattle while others raise a variety of livestock, including sheep. Sheep, which eat grass and plants, are mostly raised in arid to semiarid regions. In the United States, the biggest sheep ranches are primarily in Texas, California, Wyoming, and Colorado.

Sheep produce meat, wool, and lanolin. In the spring, sheep are sheared for their wool. Removing the wool in one piece produces a fleece. Ranchers must keep watchful eyes on their sheep so they are not attacked by coyotes, dogs, or mountain lions.

### ▶ SUCCESSFUL RANCHING

To be successful, ranchers must be diligent, work hard, and make sure there is enough grass for the cattle to eat. And because the costs involved in raising cattle are high (including feed, vaccinations, and transportation to market), ranchers must be familiar with good management practices. This enables them to make a profit when it is time to market the cattle. Ranchers must also be familiar with conservation methods that protect and preserve the land as well as the wildlife that also use the land.

In addition, ranchers must stay informed as new developments occur in their industry. Although ranchers today face as many challenges as they always have, new technology has brought about many improvements. It has enabled them to grow better, more nutritious grass for their livestock and has pro-vided medicines that keep the livestock healthier. Taking advantage of these and other advances is important for all ranchers. To compete in a global market, they must use all available means to produce better beef as economically as possible.

ROBERT C. WELLS
King Ranch, Inc.
Reviewed by BECKY L. LANDA
Assistant Editor, *National Cattlemen*

See also COWBOYS.

---

**RANDOLPH, A. PHILIP.**  See LABOR MOVEMENT (Profiles).

**RANKIN, JEANNETTE.**  See UNITED STATES, CONGRESS OF THE (Profiles: House Representatives).

## RAPHAEL (1483–1520)

Raphael was one of the greatest artists of the Renaissance. His full name was Raffaello Sanzio. Raphael was born in the small town of Urbino, Italy, on April 6, 1483. His father, who was a court painter and a poet, taught Raphael to paint.

By the time Raphael was 12, both his parents had died. Soon after, he was working in Perugia, in the shop of the painter Pietro Perugino. Raphael's early works, many painted for churches in the area, were influenced by his master's sweet but conservative style.

In 1504, Raphael went to Florence, then the center of the classical style of the Italian Renaissance. It was an exciting time to be there. Leonardo da Vinci was painting the *Mona Lisa*, and Michelangelo had just completed the statue *David*. Leonardo's color techniques and Michelangelo's forceful figures had a lasting effect on Raphael. His most impressive works from this period are a series of gentle yet strong figures of the Madonna and Child, painted in jewel-like colors.

Pope Julius II heard of the brilliant work of Raphael and summoned him to Rome in 1508. By that time, Rome had become the art center of the Renaissance. Michelangelo was painting the ceiling of the Sistine Chapel, and Leonardo would come to Rome in 1513. The Pope had frescoes by older painters destroyed so that Raphael could decorate entire Stanze (rooms) in the Vatican Palace. Raphael's work in the Stanze was done from 1509 to 1517. It shows a number of religious, mythological, and historical scenes. He was also asked to decorate a great loggia (porch) in the Vatican.

In 1514, Raphael was made chief architect of the rebuilding of St. Peter's Basilica. A year later, he became guardian of the ancient ruins of Rome. He was also asked to design ten large tapestries for the Sistine Chapel. These tapestries represent the story of Saint Peter and Saint Paul. Raphael also painted and designed for private patrons during this time. To accomplish all his commissions, he had to have more and more help from his students. But in spite of their help, he was overworked. He died of a fever in Rome on April 6, 1520, at the age of 37.

Reviewed by S. J. FREEDBERG
Harvard University

The roundness and softness of the design add to the beauty of the *Madonna della Sedia (Madonna of the Chair)* (1514–15).

# RATIO AND PROPORTION

A ratio is a comparison of two or more quantities. A proportion is an equation stating that two ratios are equal.

**Ratio.** To show the comparison of two or more quantities, a ratio can be written in different ways, as a to b, $\frac{a}{b}$, or a:b. You can use a ratio, for example, to compare the number of girls to the number of boys in a school club. If out of 7 members there are 3 girls and 4 boys, you can write this ratio: 3 to 4, $\frac{3}{4}$, or 3:4. Each way shows that for every 3 girls in the club, there are 4 boys.

A ratio does not always tell you the total number of items in a group because ratios with equivalent, or equal, values can be expressed in more than one way. For example, if there are 35 members in a club—15 girls and 20 boys—the ratio may be stated as 15:20 or $\frac{15}{20}$. But $\frac{15}{20}$ is equivalent, or equal to, $\frac{3}{4}$, and this ratio may also be expressed as 3:4 or $\frac{3}{4}$. The ratio with the lowest terms is often the one used because it is easier to work with.

When you write a ratio, the order of the numbers is important. The first quantity in the comparison must be first in the ratio. A teacher-to-pupil ratio of 1 to 20, 1 teacher to 20 students, is very different from a teacher-to-pupil ratio of 20 to 1, 20 teachers to 1 student.

Ratios occur in many situations. If you are using a can of frozen orange juice that calls for 3 cans of water for 1 can of concentrate, no matter how much you make, the ratio of water to concentrate should always be 3:1. Rates, such as speed, are also a type of ratio. The speed of a car is the ratio of the distance it travels to the time it takes the car to travel that distance. If it travels 50 miles in 1 hour, the ratio is 50:1, or 50 miles per hour.

**Proportion.** A proportion—an equation, or mathematical sentence, stating that two ratios are equal—can also be written in more than one way. The example used earlier, $\frac{3}{4} = \frac{15}{20}$, is a proportion. This proportion can also be written using the symbol ::, as in 3:4 :: 15:20. This is read "3 is to 4 as 15 is to 20."

Proportions have a special property. The cross products, or the products of the numbers that are diagonally opposite each other in the equation, are equal. In the proportion $\frac{3}{4} = \frac{15}{20}$, arrows show the cross products:

$$\frac{3}{4} \diagdown \frac{15}{12}$$

When you multiply each pair of diagonal numbers, you will find that the products are equal, 3 x 20 = 4 x 15, or 60 = 60.

The concept of proportions is useful in solving problems. If you know three of the numbers in a proportion, you will be able to find the fourth number. Consider the equation $\frac{8}{10} = \frac{\square}{55}$, in which $\square$ stands for the unknown number. Set up the cross product equation. Multiply the first pair of numbers (8 x 55) and divide the answer by the number 10 from the second pair:

$$8 \times 55 = \square \times 10$$
$$440 \div 10 = \square$$
$$44 = \square$$

The proportion is $\frac{8}{10} = \frac{44}{55}$.

One application of proportions is in enlarging or shrinking similar geometric figures, which are exactly the same shape but not the same size. Look at the triangles below.

**Figure 1. Similar triangles**

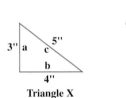

Triangle X          Triangle Y

As you can see, Triangle **X** has sides that measure 3 inches, 4 inches, and 5 inches. To make Triangle **Y** the same shape but twice as large, you must keep each side of Triangle **Y** in proportion to the corresponding side of Triangle **X**. Side **A** must be in proportion to side **a**, and sides **B** to **b** and **C** to **c**. To do this, multiply each side of Triangle **X** by the same number, **2**. Corresponding sides of Triangle **Y** must then be 6 inches, 8 inches, and 10 inches. Comparing the sides of both triangles gives the proportion $\frac{3}{6} = \frac{4}{8} = \frac{5}{10}$.

ERICA DAKIN VOOLICH
Mathematics Teacher
Solomon Schechter Day School

See also NUMBERS AND NUMBER SYSTEMS; PERCENTAGE.

**RATIONAL NUMBERS.** See NUMBERS AND NUMBER SYSTEMS.

**RAWLINGS, MARJORIE KINNAN.** See FLORIDA (Famous People).

**RAYBURN, SAMUEL T.** See UNITED STATES, CONGRESS OF THE (Profiles: Speakers of the House).

# READING

Reading, simply understood, is getting meaning from symbols that represent the language we speak. Among all living creatures, only human beings have learned to write and to read. People have learned to put their thoughts into symbols—marks, pictures, and letters—so that others can derive meaning and understanding from them through the act of reading.

Prehistoric people carved or painted hieroglyphics, or picture writing, on stones and walls to relate stories and record events. Centuries later letter alphabets were invented to form words. In the 1400's the printing press made books and newspapers available to all. Today computers make it easy for us to locate and read information on just about any subject. The process of learning to read has not changed, however, since the first crude markings on cave walls.

Long before they go to school, children can learn that reading is fun. Parents understand that reading aloud develops their child's language and reading skills.

### ▶ PARENTAL INFLUENCE ON LEARNING TO READ

Children learn to speak by listening to the talk of parents and others around them. They can learn to read in much the same way. Young children can begin to learn to read by listening to a parent read aloud while looking at the print being read. Research has demonstrated that reading aloud with children is the most important activity parents or other caregivers can provide to ensure that children will be successful readers.

Other home activities are also highly effective in developing language and reading skills. Parents serve as good reading models when children observe them reading regularly for information as well as for their own enjoyment. Talking with children on a regular basis and listening to their contributions courteously and responsively expand their vocabulary and concept development. Children learn to develop language by starting with simple concepts, such as hot and cold, and going to more abstract concepts, such as circle and square. Providing opportunities for children to participate in writing letters or other forms of writing also helps them develop key language skills and learn the value of print.

The very best ways for children to learn to speak, to listen, to write, and ultimately to read are to do these language activities often, and in a pleasant atmosphere.

### ▶ PRE-SCHOOL LANGUAGE PROGRAMS

Public or private pre-school programs offer activities that range from those with academic objectives to those encouraging play activities alone. Parents should ask very specific questions about the type and frequency of language development activities in the pre-school program. Some programs may be too skill-oriented for some children. Others may be too general for the child who needs to improve readiness language abilities. Since every child is different, it is important to choose the right program for each child.

If a child does not seem to be acquiring language in a normal and timely manner, advice should be sought and pre-school officials should be consulted about the availability of special language development services.

### ▶ KINDERGARTEN READING READINESS PROGRAMS

Kindergarten programs in the United States have many similar characteristics. Almost all, for example, stress wholesome personal and social development and general oral language growth. Pre-reading activities may include listening to and talking about stories and engaging in repetitive pattern rhymes, songs, and word games on a daily basis. By the middle of the school year, most kindergarten programs become more academic, and specific reading readiness skills are emphasized.

Research indicates that there are three reading readiness skills that are essential for reading success. These skills are taught in many kindergarten classrooms, and children who have had an enriched home language environment will have little difficulty learning them. The reading readiness skills are phoneme knowledge, letter name knowledge, and sound-symbol relationships.

**Phoneme Knowledge.** Phonemes are small units of sound. Children learn, for instance, that words such as "boy" and "ball" begin with the same sound but that "hat" and "toy" do not. They also come to know that there are three sounds in the word "cat." This pre-reading skill can begin to be learned at home as parents talk, sing, and play word games with their children. Youngsters may learn to clap along as songs are sung and to recognize rhyming words in nursery rhymes or other poems.

**Letter Name Knowledge.** Learning to identify letters by name is another important skill. Children should be able to look at the single letter *b*, for instance, and say its name. Parents who talk about letters in signs, ads, and on grocery items, and who also ask children to pick out letters themselves, give children a big advantage in learning to read.

**Sound-Symbol Relationships.** When children can associate the sound they hear in a word with the symbol, or letter, that represents that sound, they are learning sound-symbol relationships. For instance, children may know that the first sound they hear in the word "dog" is represented by the letter *d*.

Parents can help by talking about letters and the sounds they make and by pointing out how letters put together become words.

Ideally, through the experiences provided by kindergarten teachers and parents, children will become competent with these three essential readiness skills prior to formal reading programs in the first grade.

Teachers can encourage students to become successful readers by promoting participation in small group discussions.

▶ **BEGINNING READING**

In the 1990's, there were four dominant reading curriculum programs used in primary grade reading programs in the United States and elsewhere in the world where English is the language of instruction. These programs are most often referred to as literature based, code emphasis, whole language, and eclectic reading curricula.

**Literature Based Programs.** Reading textbooks, or readers, containing stories of literary quality with high appeal for children are the core of these programs. They are written for specific grade levels. Selected vocabulary from each story is studied, and students learn a variety of reading skills as well. These include word recognition skills, comprehension development, study and reference skills, and literary appreciation.

**Code Emphasis Programs.** Readers in these programs are also written for specific grade levels. The focus of student attention in these readers, however, is on phonics. Phonics is the intensive study of sounds, letters, and word elements such as consonant blends—*br, bl, th*—and vowel combinations—*ou, oo, ea*. These programs are very structured. Children often learn to sound out individual words in isolation. Then they read stories that include examples of the same or similar words.

**Whole Language Programs.** Whole language programs have been growing in popularity since the mid-1980's. Usually they do not have a designated grade level content, nor do they necessarily have a specific curriculum. Instead of readers, library books or trade books, often called natural language books, are selected by students and teachers

to be used for reading and classroom discussion. Studying "theme clusters" is a typical whole language classroom activity. While studying a theme on rivers, for example, students may pursue related topics in the context of mathematics, science, social studies, health, and reading. Specific reading skills are learned as the need arises on an individual or small group basis.

**Eclectic Reading Programs.** These programs use materials and methods selected from various sources. An eclectic program might include some features of any or all of the three programs described above. Most primary grade teachers use components of many different curriculum approaches on a day-to-day instructional basis.

As you can see, there are wide variations in how children learn to read in schools today. All children can learn to read if attention is paid to their individual differences and academic needs. Parents who have been active in their children's language development at home need not be anxious about the particular reading program used in their child's school. Unless there is some other problem, their child will most likely become a successful reader. If parents have not been able to be involved in home language activities such as those already described, then more structured first-grade reading programs may be necessary to ensure early reading success.

Parents who are concerned about a child's reading progress should openly discuss their anxieties with teachers. The earlier the problem is addressed, the more likely it will be resolved satisfactorily.

### ▶ DEVELOPING READING FLUENCY

To be successful in school and in later life, children need to become fluent readers. Fluency means reading with speed and accuracy. The most effective and efficient way to acquire this advanced reading skill is for a youngster to read as much and as often as practicable.

As children progress through the upper elementary grades, parents can help them develop reading fluency. Listening to youngsters read from their favorite books and then discussing what they have read, and urging children to use books to plan trips and to learn about other topics in which they are interested are all excellent means of helping bring about fluency.

The school also has a critical influence on fluency development. Teachers who read often to their students and who are themselves well-read will encourage the development of fluency in their students. In many classrooms, teachers promote student participation in literature circles. Students are motivated to read longer "chapter books" and are provided with opportunities to share thoughts and feelings about what they have read with their peers. Many teachers stress the importance of the daily reading of books for curriculum content knowledge as well as for developing individual pupil interests.

In some schools there has been a movement away from the use of school textbooks in mathematics, social studies, science, and other subjects. Instead, there is greater emphasis on hands-on curriculum materials, such as geoboards and magnets, as well as on the use of computers, CD-ROM's, and other technologies. These are all sound and effective learning activities. Secondary schools, however, still rely heavily on subject-area textbooks. It is important, therefore, that elementary students develop fluency in content-area reading as well.

Youngsters who regularly read books and other materials related to their personal, school, and other interests are most likely to develop full reading fluency. By reading and reflecting on all types of books, they will develop indispensable critical thinking skills. Such skills include being able to discern an author's purpose, to understand a character's motivation, to recognize biased writing, and to evaluate the worth of what is read.

### ▶ SPECIAL SCHOOL READING PROGRAMS

For a variety of reasons, some children do not become successful readers. There are a number of special school reading programs to assist pupils who are having trouble learning to read. Most of these programs attempt to individualize instruction as much as possible. Staff teachers and psychologists use various tests to diagnose a student's specific problems. Then a program of instruction is planned and implemented to meet the specific needs of that student.

Computers offer students an opportunity to develop their reading skills through a variety of learning activities in various subject areas.

Special reading programs may include early intervention, Reading Recovery, and all-day kindergarten language development. State and federal programs including learning disabilities programs and Chapter I services are found in almost all elementary and middle schools. Some private schools and academies provide individual tutoring and small group remedial reading services.

For children who are having difficulty learning to read, special efforts must be undertaken early enough to ensure success, and these efforts must continue to be made as long as such children are in school. It is especially important for these children to develop self-esteem and a sense of personal worth and social value. At each and every step toward progress, parents and teachers should be encouraging and highly supportive of struggling youngsters.

### ▶ ASSESSING READING PROGRESS

Standardized reading tests and other language evaluations are commonly administered in schools. Federally mandated tests known as the National Assessment of Educational Progress are administered every four years, and many states require their own tests at various grade levels. The results of these tests are most often used to determine the general progress of all students in the schools. When properly interpreted, however, they can be useful in assessing individual pupil progress in reading.

Currently most schools and classroom teachers also use alternative assessments called authentic, or portfolio, assessments. Authentic assessments often use a method other than a written test to evaluate individual student progress. Authentic reading assessments, for example, may be in the form of audio tapes of pupils reading aloud at specific points during the academic year.

Parents should ask to be informed regularly about their children's reading progress as measured by tests or portfolios, or by individual pupil journals in which students reflect on their own progress. Reading test results, however,

should not cause parents or teachers to make permanent judgments about children. At their best they provide temporary glimpses of current reading and language performance.

### ▶ DEVELOPING LIFELONG READERS

We learn to read at home and in school. We become fluent readers through positive home influences, supportive schools and teachers, and wise personal choices. The third and highest level of reading proficiency, literacy, is vital to an individual's intellectual and emotional development and to one's ability to make positive contributions to society. Although there are dozens of different definitions of literacy, it is defined here as the intellectual, emotional, ethical, and at times spiritual response to what is read.

To attain the proficiencies and attitudes necessary for lifetime literacy, youngsters should have home and school experiences in reading, reflecting on and discussing a wide variety of literary genres, including biography, fiction, poetry, plays, essays, and nonfiction. The more young people read and expand their interest in books of literary worth, the likelier they are to achieve literacy.

If ours is to be a literate society, we should all read widely throughout our lives in order to obtain information, acquire knowledge, and recognize wisdom. All human progress has to a significant degree depended on our ability to read.

JOHN C. MANNING
University of Minnesota

See also CALDECOTT AND NEWBERY MEDALS; CHILDREN'S LITERATURE; PHONICS.

# RONALD WILSON REAGAN (1911–2004)

40th President of the United States

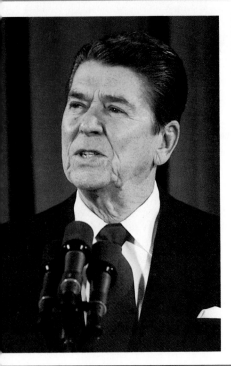

## FACTS ABOUT REAGAN

Birthplace: Tampico, Illinois
Religion: Christian Church
College Attended: Eureka College, Eureka, Illinois
Occupation: Radio announcer, actor, union official
Married: Jane Wyman (divorced 1948); Nancy Davis
Children: Maureen, Michael, Patricia Ann (Patti), Ronald Prescott (Ron)
Political Party: Republican
Office Held Before Becoming President: Governor of California
President Who Preceded Him: James Earl (Jimmy) Carter, Jr.
Age on Becoming President: 69
Years in the Presidency: 1981–1989
Vice President: George Bush
President Who Succeeded Him: George Bush
Age at Death: 93
Burial Place: Simi Valley, California

## DURING REAGAN'S PRESIDENCY

Sandra Day O'Connor became the first woman justice on the U.S. Supreme Court (1981). Some 240 U.S. Marines, part of a peacekeeping force in Lebanon, were killed by a terrorist bomb (1983). U.S. troops were sent to Grenada (1983) to prevent a Cuban attempt to take over that Caribbean island nation. The space shuttle *Challenger* exploded soon after launching (1986), in the worst disaster of the U.S. space program. *Below:* The president and Soviet leader Mikhail Gorbachev signed a historic treaty (1987) banning intermediate-range nuclear forces (INF). *Above:* Congress approved a new cabinet post (1988), the Department of Veterans Affairs.

**REAGAN, RONALD WILSON.** The life of Ronald Wilson Reagan is a story of unlikely successes. Born into a poor family, he came of age during the hard economic times of the Great Depression of the 1930's. Yet he was able to achieve great success in two quite different fields—as an actor and in politics. Reagan's political career began when, in 1964, after his acting career had ended, he was elected governor of California. He then twice sought—and twice failed to gain—the Republican nomination for the presidency, before winning the nomination and the election in 1980. At the age of 69, he was the oldest person ever to become president of the United States.

### ► EARLY YEARS

Reagan was born in Tampico, Illinois, on February 6, 1911. His father, John Edward Reagan, who was of Irish-American ancestry, earned his living as a shoe salesman. His mother, Nelle Wilson Reagan, was of English and Scottish ancestry. Neither of his parents had more than an elementary school education. Ronald, nicknamed Dutch, had an older brother, Neil.

Reagan's father often moved the family around the state searching for better-paying jobs. But life in the small towns of Illinois was pleasant. "My existence turned into one of those rare Huck Finn–Tom Sawyer idylls," Reagan recalled in his autobiography, *Where's the Rest of Me?* "Those were the days when I learned the riches of rags."

Dixon, a small town to which the family moved when he was 9, was the place where Reagan got most of his schooling. He was not an outstanding student. But his interests in drama, sports, and politics began early. His mother gave dramatic readings before clubs and in prisons and hospitals, and he was first exposed to acting before he started school. He began to play football—one of the great loves of his life—before he was 10 years old, in neighborhood games.

"There was no field; no lines, no goal. Simply grass, the ball, and a mob of excited youngsters," he later wrote. "Those were the happiest times of my life." Reagan graduated from that kind of football to action as a guard and end on the Dixon High School team. He also participated in basketball and track, acted in school plays, and was president of the student body. During most of his high school and college summers, he worked as a lifeguard at a summer resort near Dixon.

After his high school graduation in 1928, Reagan enrolled at Eureka College, a small college in Eureka, Illinois. He majored in economics; joined the college football, track, and swimming teams; and acted in school plays. He washed dishes at his fraternity house and saved money from summer jobs to help pay his expenses. His grades were not exceptional. But he earned acceptable marks through "quick studies" before tests. He also served for one year as president of the student body.

As a freshman, Reagan took part in a student strike that resulted in the resignation of the college president, who had proposed cutting back the curriculum and the teaching staff because of a shortage of funds. Reagan made the main speech at a rally that won support for the strike from nearly all the students. He later said that he learned then what it was like to succeed with an audience. His skill with audiences was to be a major factor in his successes in later life.

▶ **HIS ACTING CAREER**

Reagan earned a B.A. degree from Eureka in 1932, at a time when the Depression had left many people without jobs. He spent one last summer as a lifeguard. Then he set out to obtain a job as a radio announcer. He won a tryout for a job announcing football games at WOC in Davenport, Iowa, not far from Dixon. His tryout consisted of making up a play-by-play broadcast for an imaginary football game. He did well enough, and he was signed on. That job led to work at WOC's larger affiliate, WHO in Des Moines. By the time he was 25, he was one of the top sports broadcasters in the Middle West.

In 1937, Reagan traveled with the Chicago Cubs to their spring training camp near Los Angeles, California. While there, he managed to obtain a screen test from Warner Brothers, and he was offered an acting contract. He quickly accepted. Reagan's movie career spanned more than 20 years and over 50 movies. His most successful roles were in *Knute Rockne—All American* in 1940 and in *King's Row* in 1941. In *Knute Rockne,* Reagan played star halfback George Gipp, who died imploring his coach to have his teammates "win one for the Gipper."

In 1942, during World War II, Reagan entered the Army as a second lieutenant. He was disqualified for combat duty because of poor eyesight, and he spent the next four years making military training films. He then re-

Ronald Reagan as a young child (*right foreground*), with his parents and his older brother, Neil.

In the movie *Knute Rockne—All American*, Reagan drew on his love of football to play star halfback George Gipp.

As governor of California, Reagan signs a bill into law. Members of the state legislature look on.

turned to acting. After his Army experiences, Reagan, then a Democrat, became more politically conservative. He served as president of the Screen Actor's Guild from 1947 to 1952. He later appeared on television as the host of "General Electric Theater" and "Death Valley Days." Reagan had married Jane Wyman, an actress, in 1940. They had a daughter, Maureen, and an adopted son, Michael. The marriage ended in divorce in 1948. In 1952, Reagan married another actress, Nancy Davis. They had two children, Patricia (Patti) and Ronald (Ron).

▶ GOVERNOR OF CALIFORNIA

Reagan's entry into politics was helped by a speech he gave in 1964 that brought him to the attention of powerful Republicans. They urged him to run for governor of California.

In the 1966 election, Reagan faced Edmund G. (Pat) Brown, who had been a popular Democratic governor for eight years. Reagan was critical of state government spending and welfare payments that he believed were too high. He won the election by nearly 1 million votes. Four years later, Reagan easily won re-election. He served as governor until 1975.

▶ THE ROAD TO THE PRESIDENCY

Reagan first sought the Republican presidential nomination in 1968 but lost to Richard M. Nixon. In 1976, Reagan narrowly lost the nomination to President Gerald R. Ford.

**The 1980 Campaign.** Reagan immediately began his campaign for the 1980 nomination. In the primary contests, he called on his skills as a speaker to win support. His views seemed to reflect growing conservatism in the country, and he won the nomination easily. His nearest opponent, George Bush, was chosen as his vice presidential running mate.

In the election campaign, Reagan favored reducing total government spending while increasing the amount spent on defense. He also supported large tax cuts and state or local control of programs such as welfare. And he felt that the United States should take firmer stands against Communism.

In the election, Reagan overwhelmingly defeated the Democratic candidate, President Jimmy Carter, running for re-election. Reagan won 489 electoral votes to Carter's 49.

**His First Term.** Reagan's presidency began dramatically in 1981. Minutes after he was sworn in, Iran released 52 Americans who had been held hostage for more than 14 months during the Carter administration. Then, in March, Reagan was shot in Washington, D.C., by John W. Hinckley, Jr. But Reagan soon recovered.

**Domestic Issues.** Congress passed Reagan's requests for cuts in taxes and in some government programs. He also won increased funds for defense. By 1982, however, the country was in an economic recession. The economy improved in 1983. But the increased defense spending and tax cut had led to a record budget deficit. Democrats attacked Reagan for cutting social welfare programs and called for reduced defense spending and a tax increase in order to lower the deficit.

Reagan's appointment in 1981 of Sandra Day O'Connor as the first woman justice of the U.S. Supreme Court was a popular one. But the administration's support for prayer in the public schools and its opposition to abortion aroused much controversy.

| IMPORTANT DATES IN THE LIFE OF RONALD WILSON REAGAN | |
| --- | --- |
| 1911 | Born in Tampico, Illinois, February 6. |
| 1932 | Graduated from Eureka College, Eureka, Illinois. |
| 1937 | Acted in his first film, Love Is on the Air. |
| 1942–1946 | Served in the United States Army. |
| 1947–1952 | Served as president of the Screen Actors Guild. |
| 1967–1975 | Served as governor of California. |
| 1981–1989 | 40th president of the United States. |
| 2004 | Died in Los Angeles, June 5. |

The Reagan family gathers to celebrate the president's 1984 re-election. From left are daughters Patti and Maureen and their husbands; son Ron and his wife; Nancy and Ronald Reagan; and the president's brother, Neil Reagan. Eldest son Michael is absent.

**Foreign Affairs.** In 1983, Reagan sent U.S. Marines to Lebanon as part of a peacekeeping force. The Marines were recalled in 1984, after some 240 had been killed in a terrorist attack. Reagan also sent U.S. troops to Grenada in 1983, to prevent what the administration saw as a Cuban attempt to take over the Caribbean island nation. The president denounced the left-wing Sandinista government of Nicaragua as a threat to peace in Central America, and he repeatedly sought military aid for the anti-Sandinista guerrillas, known as contras.

**The 1984 Election.** At the Republican National Convention in Dallas, Reagan and Vice President Bush were easily renominated. Their Democratic opponents were former vice president Walter F. Mondale and Congresswoman Geraldine A. Ferraro. Reagan won a sweeping victory, receiving 525 electoral votes to 13 for Mondale.

**Second Term: Domestic Issues.** Reagan underwent successful surgery for cancer in 1985. His call for extensive changes in the federal income tax laws helped bring about passage of the Tax Reform Act of 1986. Congress also passed a major immigration bill that year. Reagan made two Supreme Court appointments in 1986—Associate Justice William Rehnquist as U.S. Chief Justice and Antonin Scalia as an associate justice. Nominees Robert Bork and Douglas Ginsburg failed to win a Supreme Court seat in 1987. A third nominee, Anthony Kennedy, won approval.

A stock market crash in 1987 raised questions about the nation's economic health. A new bill to balance the federal budget became law in 1987, but the huge deficit continued to trouble the government. In 1988, Congress approved a new cabinet post, the Department of Veterans Affairs, and the Senate approved a free-trade pact with Canada.

**Foreign Affairs.** Reagan ordered the bombing of military targets in Libya in 1986 in retaliation for its role in international terrorism. His policy of reflagging (flying the U.S. flag on) Kuwaiti oil tankers and providing them with a U.S. naval escort in the Persian Gulf led to clashes with Iran in 1987. The president's greatest diplomatic achievement was the 1987 treaty with the Soviet Union banning intermediate-range nuclear forces (INF), approved by the Senate in 1988.

The Iran-Contra Affair proved embarrassing to the administration. Congressional hearings in 1987 revealed that presidential aides had acted illegally by selling weapons to Iran and diverting the money to Nicaraguan rebels. For more information, see IRAN-CONTRA AFFAIR in Volume I.

**Retirement.** Reagan left the White House in January 1989 and was succeeded as president by his former vice president, George Bush. In 1994 it was revealed that Reagan was suffering from Alzheimer's disease. He died on June 5, 2004, at the age of 93.

JAMES O. BELL
*Los Angeles Times*

*Top left and right:* Examples of residential real estate include single family homes and cooperative apartments (apartments owned by corporations). *Above:* A real estate agent shows a client commercial space for lease.

# REAL ESTATE

Real estate (also called real property) is land and everything attached to it. This includes minerals that may lie beneath the surface (such as coal or iron); trees, crops, and other vegetation; and any buildings on it. Real estate is also the term used for businesses involved in buying and selling property.

Nearly one-third of the total wealth in the United States is represented by real estate. It is continually bought and sold by individuals, organizations, and businesses. Real estate is also traded, given away, or left to heirs upon the owner's death. However the property changes hands, the new owner usually has the same rights the former owner had.

These rights, called property rights, are protected by law. Property rights ensure that no one can use land without the owner's consent, although some property may have an **easement**, which allows it to be used for specific, limited purposes. For example, a power company may have an easement that allows

it access to power lines on the property. The government may take land from an owner under its right of **eminent domain** if the land is needed for something, such as a highway, that benefits the public. In such cases, the owner must be fairly paid for the property.

Real estate may not be transferred from one owner to another without a written agreement. There are two types of documents connected with this: a **lease** and a **deed** (also called a **title**). A lease is a contract between a property owner and tenant (one who uses the property). It contains the terms agreed upon by both, such as the amount of rent the tenant will pay and the length of time the property will be used. A deed shows that the landowner legally owns the property. When someone buys a piece of real estate, he or she receives a deed to the property from the previous owner.

A person who acts as the intermediary in the sale and purchase of property is called a real estate **broker**. When a home or other building is to be constructed, the broker—or real estate agent working for the broker—finds the proper site and handles its purchase. The broker (or a lawyer) also conducts a title search to be sure that no one except the seller has any claim to the property. He or she may help arrange for a **mortgage** from a bank or mortgage broker so the client can obtain the money to buy the property. A mortgage is a legal agreement by which a

person borrows money for the purchase of property and promises to pay it back. Under the terms of the mortgage, the lender can take over the property if the money is not repaid.

Real estate professionals usually specialize in specific types of real estate such as industrial properties or property management. Industrial property specialists typically obtain land and buildings for manufacturing plants. They bring in new businesses and factories, which provide jobs for people in the area. A broker or agent who specializes in property management collects rents on land or buildings, supervises the property's maintenance, and keeps the accounts and tax records.

Most real estate professionals specialize in residential real estate, which is usually land with houses or condominiums. When a person decides to sell a home, the broker or agent helps set a price and find a buyer. A description of the property is then added to a database called a Multiple Listing Service (MLS), which is shared with other brokers and agents. This information is also posted on the Internet.

The broker or agent usually shows prospective buyers the property, then acts as the go-between for the owner and buyer to work out a purchase agreement. For these services he or she is paid a commission, which is generally a percentage of the money involved in the sale or lease of the property.

Real estate professionals must be familiar with property and zoning, economics, insurance, finance, and general business practices. To become an agent or broker, one must pass a state examination and get a license. Brokers, who have more training than agents, must also first work as agents for a certain period. Training is available at many colleges and universities, which offer real estate courses and degrees. Many real estate firms also offer training to their agents to meet continuing education requirements.

The largest professional real estate organization in the United States is the National Association of Realtors (NAR), with approximately 1 million members. NAR members, called Realtors, pledge to follow a strict code of ethics and uphold certain standards of practice.

Reviewed by WALTER MOLONY
National Association of Realtors

## SOME TERMS USED IN REAL ESTATE

**Amortization:** The paying off of a debt, usually in periodic installments.

**Assessed value:** The value set on a piece of property by the local government for the purposes of taxation. Assessed value is different from **market value**, which is the price the property would sell for.

**Broker:** A real estate professional who handles the sale and purchase of property. Most real estate professionals are real estate agents, who work for brokers.

**Commercial property:** Property reserved by law for business use.

**Commission:** The fee paid to real estate brokers or agents for their services. It is a percentage of the money involved in a sale or lease of property.

**Deed:** A written document that is proof of the ownership of a piece of property.

**Escrow:** Money or other assets that are held by a third person until certain conditions in a written agreement between two parties are fulfilled.

**Lease:** A legal contract between a property owner and a person who uses the property. It states the terms under which the property is to be used, how much rent is to be paid, and how long the property is to be used.

**Mortgage:** A legal document by which a person borrows money for the purchase of property and promises to pay it back. If the money is not repaid, the lender can take over the property.

**Realtor:** A real estate broker or agent who is a member of the National Association of Realtors.

**Residential property:** Property reserved for homes.

**Title search:** An investigation of records to make certain there are no claims against a piece of property.

**Tract:** A defined area of land or water.

**Zoning:** The method by which a local government divides its area into residential, commercial, and industrial property.

# REALISM

In general, realism in art and literature refers to the attempt to represent familiar and everyday people and situations in an accurate, unidealized manner. More specifically, the term "realism" refers to a literary and artistic movement of the late 1800's and early 1900's. This movement was a reaction against romanticism, an earlier movement that presented the world in much more idealized terms.

▶ **REALISM IN LITERATURE**

Almost every work of literature has some degree of realism because it is important for readers to recognize and identify with the characters and the world they inhabit. But realism as a distinct style and literary movement dates back to France in the early 1800's, when authors began writing works that possessed several unique characteristics: The stories, or plots, were simple and were secondary to the characters; the characters tended to be from the lower or middle class and spoke as people really did, not in poetic language; and the author's voice, such as in comments or asides, was rarely—if ever—heard. Honoré de Balzac led the way with his masterwork, *The Human Comedy* (1824–47). In this series of novels and stories, the lives of every class of people come alive on the pages through long, lively descriptions. His plots, however, retained the romantic quality of melodrama. Gustave Flaubert's *Madame Bovary* (1857) was the first major work to fully embrace the realist style. Its frank, true-to-life portrayal of a woman seeking to escape her boring life through romantic involvements was shocking to readers of its day.

Great realist works in English literature include George Eliot's *Middlemarch* (1871–72) and the novels of Thomas Hardy. In the United States, realism was a popular style from the mid-1800's to about 1900. Among its practitioners were William Dean Howells (*The Rise of Silas Lapham*, 1885) and Henry James (*The Ambassadors*, 1903). Great Russian works of realism include Ivan Turgenev's *Fathers and Sons* (1862) and Leo Tolstoi's *War and Peace* (1869).

Realist drama is best represented by Norway's Henrik Ibsen (*A Doll's House*, 1879), England's George Bernard Shaw

French novelist Gustave Flaubert was the first author to fully embrace the realist style, in his classic work *Madame Bovary* (1857).

(*Pygmalion*, 1912), and Russia's Anton Chekhov (*The Cherry Orchard*, 1904).

A literary movement related to realism was **naturalism**. Naturalist authors also wrote about common people and everyday situations, but they studied human beings and their behavior with the objectivity of scientists. The characters in these stories are controlled by their heredity, environment, instincts, and passions, and they live in a natural world that is indifferent to their plights. Leading naturalists included the French novelist Émile Zola (*Germinal*, 1885) and the Americans Stephen Crane (*Maggie: A Girl of the Streets*, 1893) and Theodore Dreiser (*Sister Carrie*, 1900).

▶ **REALISM IN ART**

The realist movement in art also originated in France during the 1800's. The realists wanted to break away from the formal artistic styles and subjects of the past by creating objective, unemotional works that were unadorned with imaginative flourishes. Their works typically portrayed ordinary, or working-class, people (as opposed to heroic, historic, biblical, or royal figures) and scenes of traditional life, such as rural landscapes with farmers herding oxen or harvesting grain. The realists sought to honor what they felt was the noble dignity of humble people leading simple lives.

Realist artists created unsentimental paintings portraying ordinary people in everyday scenes. *Right: The Winnowers* (1855), by the leading French realist Gustave Courbet. *Below: Addie* (1899), by American realist Thomas Eakins.

The realists were led by Gustave Courbet, whose *The Burial at Ornans* (1849) and other works were large-scale, unsentimental paintings of common people in everyday scenes. Other realists included the social and political satirist Honoré Daumier (*The Washerwoman*, 1863) and Jean François Millet (*The Gleaners*, 1857). American realists included the painters Thomas Eakins (*The Gross Clinic*, 1875) and Winslow Homer (*Snap the Whip*, 1872) and, later, Grant Wood (*American Gothic*, 1930) and Edward Hopper (*Nighthawks*, 1942). Modern artists have taken realism to new heights, creating paintings so detailed and so realistic that they appear to be photographs and sculptures of human figures so lifelike that they are mistaken for real people. This kind of realism is often called **photorealism** or **superrealism**.

Two offshoots of the realist movement were the **Barbizon School** and the **Ashcan School**. The Barbizon School, which arose in the 1840's and 1850's, was a group of French landscape painters working in the town of Barbizon, who painted outdoors and at-tempted to faithfully depict the fleeting qualities of nature. The Ashcan School flourished during the late 1800's and early 1900's in the United States. Its artists, such as Robert Henri (*West 57th Street, New York*, 1902), painted gritty scenes of city life, such as alleyways and industrial centers.

Realism has a long history in the visual arts. In ancient Greece during the Hellenistic era (323–146 B.C.), sculptors began depicting people as they really appeared instead of how they should appear according to the Greek concept of the ideal human form. But the realist movement in art grew out of a desire during the Middle Ages (500–1450) to depart from the flat, formal, and stylized art that was popular at the time. The Italian artist Giotto di Bondone, in works such as *Madonna and Child* (early 1300's), led the way by painting biblical figures as emotional and lifelike as everyday people. The artists of this time also improved the depiction of reality by introducing perspective into their works and more realistic human forms based on detailed anatomical studies.

**RECESSIONS.** See DEPRESSIONS AND RECESSIONS.

# RECONSTRUCTION PERIOD

In United States history, the term Reconstruction has two meanings. One refers to the process of readmitting the Confederate states to the Union following their defeat in the Civil War (1861–65). The other refers to the postwar period in which millions of slaves were reabsorbed into Southern communities as free men and women.

▶ **BACKGROUND**

In 1860, Abraham Lincoln, the Republican candidate for the presidency, campaigned on the position that slavery should not be extended into new U.S. territories. This policy was contrary to the wishes of most Democrats in the South, where slavery had long been in practice. When Lincoln won the election, pro-slavery states in the South began to secede (withdraw) from the Union. They formed a new (but unrecognized) country called the Confederate States of America, and a civil war soon began.

The Civil War ended in 1865, when the Union states in the North defeated the Confederate states in the South. But the Southern states were not automatically restored to their former place in the nation. The states that had seceded would have to meet certain conditions before they would be taken back into the Union.

▶ **LINCOLN'S PLANS FOR RECONSTRUCTION**

In the last 18 months of his life, Lincoln gave much thought as to how the Union should be restored. On December 8, 1863, he presented his ideas for the first time when he issued the Proclamation of Amnesty and Reconstruction. Within its provisions, Lincoln proposed a general **amnesty** (official pardon) to all Confederates—except high army officers and officials—who would swear to support the federal government and the Constitution of the United States.

Lincoln's proclamation was not well received in Congress. Many members believed that Congress, not the president, should lay down the terms of reunion. Many also wanted to impose much harsher measures on the South. These members came to be known as **Radical Republicans**. Chief among them was Thaddeus Stevens, Republican congressman from Pennsylvania.

▶ **CONGRESSIONAL PLANS FOR RECONSTRUCTION**

By July 1864, while the war was still in progress, Congress had worked out its own plan of Reconstruction. This plan, set forth in what was called the Wade-Davis bill, required that a majority of voters in any state that had seceded must take an oath to support the Constitution. (In contrast, Lincoln had proposed 10 percent of voters.) The bill also imposed much stricter qualifications on voters. Both houses passed the bill, and it was presented to Lincoln on the last day of the session. But he kept it from becoming law by not signing it.

Four Southern states organized governments under Lincoln's plan of Reconstruction. But Congress, which is the final judge of the qualifications of its members, refused to receive their representatives and senators. Thus the political problem still existed when Andrew Johnson succeeded as president on April 15, 1865, following the assassination of President Lincoln.

The Radical Republicans believed that Johnson would be much harder on the former Confederate states than Lincoln had planned to be. Many were surprised, therefore, when the new president, on May 29, 1865, issued a proclamation much like Lincoln's proclamation of December 8, 1863. On the same day, in a proclamation relating to a new government for North Carolina, Johnson avoided any numerical requirement concerning the number of voters and gave the right to vote to the loyal "portion of the people." Within six weeks the president had issued similar proclamations for six other former Confederate states.

**The South's Response.** Under these proclamations, Southern states set up their own governments and agreed to meet some of the conditions President Johnson had laid down. They canceled their ordinances (laws) of secession, refused to pay the bonds they had issued to raise money during the war, and did away with slavery. But they would not admit regret for having left the Union. Instead, they elected to office many high officials of the former Confederate government and military. They refused to give African Americans, most of whom were former slaves, the right to vote. Both Lincoln and Johnson had urged that qualified blacks and those who had fought for the Union be given this right. In-

*Above:* U.S. senator Thaddeus Stevens and other Radical Republicans fought to raise the postwar status of African Americans. *Right:* The Freedmen's Bureau, a government agency, helped former slaves adjust to freedom.

stead, the Southern states passed laws, known as **Black Codes**, that were intended to keep blacks in a lower position. The South had been forced to free the slaves—but Southerners had no intention of making black people equal to white people.

**Civil Rights and the Freedmen's Bureau.** The South's refusal to act like a defeated enemy angered the Republican majority in Congress. When Southern senators and representatives arrived for the new session in December 1865, they were refused their seats. In April 1866 the Republicans passed a civil rights bill, making citizens of "all persons born in the United States …of every race and color," whether or not they had been slaves. Blacks were to have the same rights to property that white people enjoyed. President Johnson vetoed the bill, believing each state should make its own decision. But Congress passed the bill over his veto.

On July 16, Congress passed another bill over the president's veto to extend the duration of the Freedmen's Bureau, which was first created on March 3, 1865. (Various acts of Congress would continue it until 1872.) The purpose of the bureau was to aid freed slaves by furnishing supplies and medicines, setting up schools, and seeing that blacks were treated fairly by their former owners. The bureau accomplished much, but the South looked on it almost as a tool of a foreign government.

**The 14th Amendment.** So far, the Radical Republicans had shaped Reconstruction as they wanted it. But they knew that laws could be reversed by the courts. Therefore, they set out to amend the U.S. Constitution, whose provisions the courts were sworn to uphold.

By June 13, 1866, both houses had passed the 14th Amendment. The first section defined citizenship to include blacks and entitled them to equal protection of the law. The second section proposed, in effect, to reduce the number of representatives in Congress from any state that did not allow blacks to vote. The third section made former Confederates ineligible to hold many federal offices. The fourth made it unconstitutional for the United States or any state to pay the Confederacy's debt or to pay anyone for freed slaves. The amendment was ratified (approved) in 1868.

▶ **PRESIDENT JOHNSON CLASHES WITH CONGRESS**

By the summer of 1866, relations between the president and Congress had come close to the breaking point. The Radical Republicans wanted to end the power of the Southern aristocracy and the Democratic Party in the South. Their goals were to give blacks the vote and legal equality with white people. The president, himself a Southerner, sympathized with the South even though he despised the old, wealthy planter class. He also believed firmly in states' rights. He insisted that the South should be left alone to deal with blacks and that the president, rather than Congress, should decide when and how the Southern states should be readmitted to the Union. But Johnson was not tactful, and he was unable to compromise with those who did not agree with him

In the late summer of 1866, Johnson decided to go beyond Congress and appeal directly to the people. He spoke in the principal cities of the East and Midwest in support of his policies. But his bad temper and loose statements made him more enemies than friends.

Feeling stronger than ever, Johnson's opponents in Congress now decided to pass their own Reconstruction legislation. In March 1867, the First and Second (or Supplementary) Reconstruction Acts divided the former Confederate states that had not ratified the 14th Amendment into five military districts. Each district was to be administered by an army officer in command of enough troops to keep the peace while making sure blacks were allowed to vote. The representatives and senators of each of these states would not be seated in Congress—and the state would not be reaccepted into the Union—until a majority of a state's voters had framed a state constitution that Congress would accept. In addition, the state would have to ratify the 14th Amendment.

Johnson refused to approve the congressional Reconstruction plan on the grounds that it trespassed on states' rights. But it, too, was passed over the president's veto. Johnson and the Radical Republicans were now openly at war.

**The House Impeaches the President.** In 1867 the Republicans passed the Tenure of Office Act, forbidding the president to dismiss cabinet members and lesser government officials without the consent of the Senate. When Johnson dismissed his secretary of war, Edwin M. Stanton, without the Senate's consent, the Radicals decided to act. On February 24, 1868, the House of Representatives adopted a resolution to impeach President Johnson, charging him with "high crimes and misdemeanors in office." Actually, the chief reason for impeachment was that Johnson had blocked all of Congress' efforts to pass laws to reconstruct the South. After a trial before the Senate, the vote stood 35 to 19, one vote short of the two-thirds majority needed to find Johnson guilty.

▶ **RESTORING THE UNION**

Meanwhile, the Reconstruction Acts of 1867 and several similar bills had gone into effect. With soldiers keeping watch at the polls, clerks registered blacks as well as eligible whites. In the ten states of the former Confederacy, 1,330,000 voters were enrolled. Of these, 703,000 were blacks. The new voters elected delegates, among them many blacks, to the conventions that would frame new state constitutions.

The new state governments quickly approved the 14th Amendment, a necessary measure to be readmitted to the Union. By midsummer 1868, seven states had acted and were back in good standing. The remaining four—Virginia, Texas, Georgia, and Mississippi—were readmitted in 1870.

Between 1870 and 1881, 16 blacks were elected to Congress from Southern states. Many others sat in the state legislatures. Although they never controlled any state government, they were accused of lacking responsibility, spending too much money, and being dishonest. The mere fact that they held public office angered many whites, some of whom turned to violence in hopes of

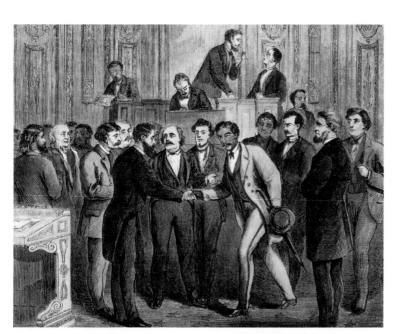

In 1868, John Willis Menard, a Republican from Louisiana, was the first African American to be elected to Congress.

## What were scalawags and carpetbaggers?

Scalawags and carpetbaggers were names given to white people in the South who supported blacks in government during the Reconstruction period that followed the Civil War.

Scalawags were generally poor Southern whites who supported the northern Radical Republicans in order to gain opportunities while the South was being rebuilt.

Carpetbaggers—named for travel bags made of carpet materials—were Northern white Republicans who went to the South, usually for political and economic gain. Carpetbaggers would try to win the blacks' support, promising them such riches as "forty acres and a mule" in exchange for their vote. Even today, people who are active in the politics of a city or state from which they did not originate are called carpetbaggers.

An 1872 cartoon from *Puck* magazine shows a carpetbagger (depicted as U.S. president Ulysses S. Grant) burdening the lives of the innocent in the postwar South.

keeping the freed slaves from enjoying their new rights.

**The Rise of the Ku Klux Klan.** The most notorious white-supremacist group that set about "putting the blacks in their place" was the Ku Klux Klan. Founded in 1866, this secret society soon spread throughout the South. The members—masked, clothed in white robes, riding only at night—singled out blacks who had displeased the old ruling class. They enforced their will through fear—with threats, whippings, and even lynchings (mob killings).

**The 15th Amendment.** One of the reasons whites used violence against blacks was to prevent them from exercising their right to vote. In order to protect this right, Congress passed the 15th Amendment, which was ratified in 1870. It guaranteed all citizens, including blacks, the right to vote.

▶ **THE END OF RECONSTRUCTION**

By 1870, with all the Southern states back in the Union, the North began to have a change of heart. Several of the Radical Republicans had died. Others were losing interest in the black cause and in reform. In the

South, many of the old leaders were being pardoned and given the right to vote again. State by state, Southern Democrats retook control over their governments. In 1877 the last federal troops withdrew from the South. Reconstruction had ended.

According to law, the South had been reconstructed. Secession was dead, the Union was restored, and slavery was ended. But in fact, it had not been reconstructed. After a few years, blacks saw their right to vote restricted, and increasingly they were kept out of office by economic power, fear, court decisions, and other means. Even more than that, the so-called Jim Crow laws were enacted to ensure that blacks could not travel in the same railroad cars, eat in the same restaurants, or sleep in the same hotels as white people. Black people had been given freedom. But equality would take another century to achieve.

PAUL M. ANGLE
Author, *The Lincoln Reader*

See also AFRICAN AMERICANS (Rural Emancipation Era: 1865–1915); CIVIL WAR, UNITED STATES; IMPEACHMENT; JIM CROW LAWS; JOHNSON, ANDREW; LINCOLN, ABRAHAM; RACISM; SEGREGATION; UNITED STATES, HISTORY OF THE (The Post-Civil War Period).

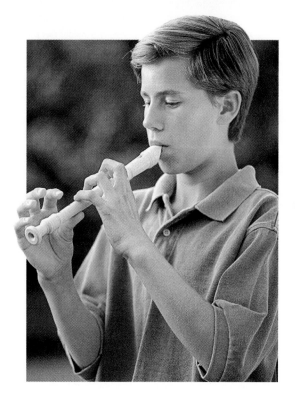

# RECORDER

The recorder is a woodwind instrument. Made of plastic or wood, it has seven finger-holes and one thumb-hole. The thumb-hole is on the opposite side of the instrument from the other holes. This is kept covered by the left thumb, except when you want the higher notes. Then you uncover it by letting the thumb drop away slightly from the hole, or half uncover it by bending the thumb.

To play the recorder you blow into the mouthpiece and cover the holes in various combinations. A variety of tonguing patterns, or **articulations**, allow you to "shape" musical phrases. You do not lift your fingers in the same order as the notes of the scale.

The recorder is a member of the fipple flute family. This type of instrument has a whistle-type mouthpiece set in one end of a vertically held pipe. The fipple, also known as the block, partially blocks the mouthpiece, leaving a narrow windway through which the player's airstream flows. This airstream flows across a sharp edge and into the instrument, creating the clear and sweet tone we recognize as the recorder.

Before the sound vibrations travel to your ear as distinct pitches, they must pass through the instrument. Finger holes are spaced along the recorder. When you cover all the holes with your fingers, the sound vibrations must pass down the full length of the instrument before escaping into the air. This gives the lowest note. When you take your fingers off certain holes, the sound vibrations can escape without passing down so much of the instrument. This gives higher notes.

## ▶ TYPES OF RECORDERS

Five sizes of recorder are in common use today. The smallest and highest is the sopranino. Then come the soprano, the alto (or treble), and the tenor. The largest and lowest is the bass. Its notes are written in the bass clef, but it sounds an octave higher, as do recorders in general.

Since these recorders have the same basic fingering, a player can soon learn to play all sizes. It is chiefly a matter of how wide the player stretches his or her fingers. A good stretch is needed for the tenor and bass recorders. The easiest sizes on which to start are probably the soprano and the alto.

## ▶ HISTORY

The recorder is one of the most ancient of instruments. Even the most primitive societies had some form of it. Images of instruments that could be recorders can be seen in artwork from as early as the 1200's, although it is impossible to tell if they have a thumb-hole. One of the earliest surviving instruments that can officially be called a recorder was found in Holland and dates from the late 1300's to early 1400's.

In the 1500's and 1600's the recorder became popular for **consorts** (a group of instruments played in concert), either with other recorders or with different types of instruments. The most common grouping of recorders during the Renaissance period was one or two altos, two tenors, and a bass.

In the 1600's and 1700's, composers began writing more music for soloists. Claudio Monteverdi used recorders in his operas. Henry Purcell, François Couperin, Johann Sebastian Bach, and George Frederick Handel all composed for the recorder. So did Georg Philipp Telemann, one of the most prolific composers for recorder in the baroque era, whose music was even more popular than Bach's during their lifetimes.

The recorder itself was almost forgotten for more than a century after Bach and Handel. The transverse flute had a wider range than the recorder and could be better heard in the orchestras that were developing in the 1700's. Though the recorder never died out, composers stopped writing for it in favor of the orchestral instruments such as the flute and oboe.

The great pioneer who revived the recorder in modern times was Arnold Dolmetsch. He felt that early music should be played on the instruments it was written for and began giving "historical concerts" in 1891 using recorders, viols, lutes, and harpsichords.

The recorder is now as popular as it ever was. Since the arrival of molds for the mass production of plastic recorders in the 1940's, the instrument has been an ideal tool for children in school music programs, as well as adult beginners. The American Recorder Society has local chapters across the United States for amateur players, including several Junior Recorder Societies for children.

Reviewed by LETITIA W. BERLIN
American Recorder Society

**See For Yourself**

## How to Play the Recorder

The recorder is not at all hard to learn. These tips will help you become a better player.

1. The finger or thumb must completely cover its hole. Any leak of air will spoil the note. When air escapes, try finger by finger (from the bottom upward) until you find one that is not covering properly. You do not have to press hard. Light but firm fingering gives the best results. Let your fingers move comfortably.

2. Maintain good posture and hand position. Sitting or standing in an upright but relaxed position makes it easier for you to breathe properly, which gives the notes a strong tone. If you find yourself gripping the recorder—a common mistake—consider putting a movable thumb rest on the middle joint so that your right thumb will not slide up the back of the instrument.

3. Use your tongue to separate notes you do not want to slur together. Tonguing interrupts the breath between one note and the next. The standard method of tonguing is to put your tongue behind your teeth and quickly take it away again. Keep your tongue and fingers well in step with one another by thinking of your movements a little ahead of the music.

4. Listen all the time to be sure you are in tune. You can lower the pitch a little by relaxing the breath or raise it by stressing the breath. The most important point of good recorder playing is keeping in tune.

5. Let your breath flow into the recorder in a deep and steady stream. This is the secret of making a beautiful tone. Take a breath before you start and a new breath whenever there is a rest in the music or a break in the phrasing. Learn to determine how much air you need for each phrase so that you do not take in too much or too little.

6. Practice this blowing exercise: play a long, *mezzo forte* (medium loud) tone on any note, keeping the tone straight and your throat open and relaxed. Now play the same tone at a *piano* (soft) dynamic. Try different pitches each day. Notice how much air each fingering can take at *mezzo forte* before the recorder squeaks, and how little air a *piano* tone needs before it wobbles or disappears.

A fingering chart for the C-major scale on a soprano recorder. Black means covered; white means uncovered. Many simple melodies can be played using only these notes.

| | | C | D | E | F | G | A | B | C |
|---|---|---|---|---|---|---|---|---|---|
| left hand | THUMB | ● | ● | ● | ● | ● | ● | ● | ● |
| | 1st FINGER | ● | ● | ● | ● | ● | ● | ● | ○ |
| | 2nd FINGER | ● | ● | ● | ● | ● | ● | ○ | ● |
| | 3rd FINGER | ● | ● | ● | ● | ● | ○ | ○ | ○ |
| right hand | 1st FINGER | ● | ● | ● | ● | ○ | ○ | ○ | ○ |
| | 2nd FINGER | ● | ● | ● | ○ | ○ | ○ | ○ | ○ |
| | 3rd FINGER | ● | ● | ○ | ● | ○ | ○ | ○ | ○ |
| | 4th FINGER | ● | ○ | ○ | ● | ○ | ○ | ○ | ○ |

# RECORDING INDUSTRY

The recording industry is based on the manufacture and distribution of sound recordings, primarily music. It is made up of hundreds of businesses in the United States and around the world, which together sell more than $10 billion worth of music a year. The industry's development has been determined by the constantly evolving technologies of storing and transmitting sound—from the phonograph discs of the late 1800's to today's compact discs and digital music files. (For information on recording technology, see the article SOUND RECORDING in Volume S.)

Music is the mainstay of the recording industry. CD's offer consumers high-quality sound, while tiny digital players can hold thousands of music files.

▶ BEGINNINGS

When American inventor Thomas Edison introduced the phonograph in 1877, he intended it as a means of capturing and playing back speech, to be used for business dictation. But by 1890, listeners were lining up to hear music from coin-operated phonographs, and soon Edison was selling phonographs and musical recordings for home use.

Edison's mechanical device made recordings one at a time on metal cylinders wrapped in tin foil. (See the article PHONOGRAPH in Volume P.) But with rising consumer interest in recorded music, manufacturers began looking for ways to mass-produce sound recordings. The gramophone, which had been introduced by German-born inventor Emile Berliner in 1887, used a flat disc instead of a cylinder. Discs were more durable and far easier to copy than cylinders. They also took up less storage space, provided room for printed labels, and could be made in larger sizes that held four minutes of music to the cylinder's two. Within a few years, record manufacturers doubled the discs' capacity again by recording music on both sides. By 1913, even Edison's company had begun producing discs, and cylinders were gradually phased out. As the library of available recordings grew and prices dropped, recorded music became one of the world's most popular forms of entertainment.

▶ ELECTRICAL RECORDING

The introduction of the microphone in 1925 greatly improved the quality of recordings and ushered in the era of electrical recording. Now recording engineers could capture a wider range of

## RECORDING INDUSTRY HIGHLIGHTS

**1877** Thomas Edison invents the phonograph.

**1895** First gramophones are sold.

**1930** The Golden Age of Radio begins.

**Mid-1930's** Introduction of the jukebox spurs record sales.

sound. And the best new phonographs, using amplifiers and speakers, could reproduce the sound better than earlier acoustic (nonelectric) phonographs could.

But the record industry faced rough times ahead. Since the early 1920's, the phonograph had been forced to compete with the radio for listeners' attention. With the economic collapse of the Great Depression of the 1930's, consumers stopped buying phonographs and records. Instead, they enjoyed the free entertainment delivered to their homes through radio. The record industry crashed. Victor, one of the earliest record companies, was sold to the Radio Corporation of America (RCA).

By 1933, however, record sales recovered, due mainly to the introduction of the jukebox (coin-operated phonograph). After a slowdown during World War II (1939–45), the record industry boomed again thanks to new technical developments.

**Magnetic Tape.** First developed in the 1930's, magnetic tape was widely adopted after World War II for making master recordings from which records were made. Tape recordings could be made far longer than the four-minute phonograph discs and could be cut and spliced for editing. The reel-to-reel format became the standard for professional recording, and a broad range of music became available. Because tape did not scratch or break like records, some thought that reel-to-reel tape players might replace home phonographs. But consumers found the tapes cumbersome and inconvenient to use, and the format did not catch on in the home.

**LP's and 45's.** In 1948, Columbia Records introduced phonograph records made of shatterproof vinyl that turned at 33⅓ revolutions per minute (rpm) and played for more than 20 minutes per side. These were great improvements over the shorter, less durable 78-rpm discs in use at the time. This new LP, or long-playing, format was soon adopted by every record company except RCA Victor, which brought out the competing 45-rpm discs in 1949. By 1950, the LP had been adopted for long works and for album-length collections, but the 45-rpm system became universal for short popular songs, or singles. The production of 78's had all but ended by the mid-1950's.

The stage was set for a boom in record and phonograph sales. The new records cost less and were more convenient to store. And radio fueled record sales: Having lost most of its comedy and drama programs to television, it showcased records because they provided low-cost programming. Consumers—especially teenagers—eagerly purchased recordings of songs made popular on the radio, and record sales skyrocketed.

**Stereo.** Stereo was a new technology that gave listeners a reason to buy new versions of recordings they already owned. Using two signal channels and two speakers, stereo created a realistic sound that was more like live music. At first, stereo was available only on tape, leading some to think tape would take over from the phonograph despite the inconvenience of having to thread tapes from one reel to another. However, stereo LP's appeared by 1958.

**Cassette Tapes.** In the 1950's and 1960's, many attempts were made to eliminate the inconvenience of tape by enclosing tape and reels in a package. One system, using stereo eight-track cartridges, was installed in many American cars. But the cartridges were bulky and often jammed. They were replaced by a rival format, stereo cassette tapes, which were more compact and dependable.

Cassette tapes made music portable. Cassette players were developed for cars in the 1970's, followed by battery-powered tape

**Mid-1940's** Reel-to-reel tape is introduced for home and professional use.

**Mid-1950's** LP's and 45's replace 78's.

**Mid-1960's** Cassette tapes make music portable.

**1982** The digital compact disc (CD) is launched.

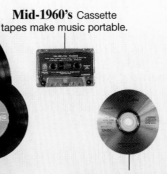

**Mid-1990's** Internet technology leads to digital music players.

A young woman downloads songs from an online music store to her digital music player. Such online sites offer numerous services, including creating and sharing playlists.

players—including boom boxes and tiny Walkman headphone units—that could go anywhere. By 1983 the cassette had replaced the LP as the most popular medium for recorded music.

### ▶ DIGITAL RECORDING

The compact disc (CD), launched in 1982, eventually replaced both the LP and the cassette. Because they are recorded digitally, CD's have none of the phonograph record's surface noise, and because they are "read" by laser light and not touched by a needle, they do not wear out. Now, instead of LP's for high-quality home listening and cassettes for listening on the go, a single format could be used for both. The many advantages of the CD propelled another boom in recorded music sales. Whereas the first ten years of the LP had roughly doubled sales, the first ten years of the CD nearly tripled them.

Despite this growth, the recording industry feared what it called "piracy," the unauthorized copying of commercial recordings. This worry had first arisen when home tape recorders appeared in the 1950's. Copying did occur but did not significantly affect record sales. When cassettes surpassed LP's in the early 1980's, the industry again worried that its sales would fall victim to home copying; instead, it found that listeners were happy to buy music on prerecorded cassettes. Now, however, the piracy issue returned with the emergence of CD recorders, which could copy CD's perfectly. By the late 1990's, CD-ROM "burners" in home computers and stand-alone CD recorders for use in stereo systems had become affordable, and copying CD's became very popular.

Perhaps the greatest threat to the recording industry came from the Internet. The mid-1990's saw the development of MP3, a software format that compresses digital music files into sizes small enough to be sent rapidly over the Internet. Music posted online could now be easily downloaded to computers and digital music players and shared among users. Some musicians who felt unfairly treated by recording companies welcomed the opportunity to distribute their music directly to the public.

Soon music files were widely available from illegal commercial Web sites and traded using file-sharing programs such as Napster. The recording industry responded by suing the sites and their customers. At the same time they began to set up online music stores, often in partnership with computer companies, where recordings can be purchased and downloaded legally. These sites offer an increasing number of services. Customers may be able to buy individual songs, create and share playlists, and burn CD's. Some services offer unlimited "streaming" of music for monthly subscription fees.

### ▶ THE FUTURE

Despite all its fears of lost sales, the recording industry continued to prosper (2000 was its most successful year ever). In the early 2000's, two new disc formats—SACD (Super Audio CD) and DVD-Audio—offered consumers music with sound quality surpassing that of standard CD's. But with the enormous popularity of digital music players such as the iPod, which can hold thousands of songs, downloading music may be the wave of the future. As always, the recording industry will evolve as the technology changes. It may shift away from the manufacture and distribution of physical recordings to the transmission and distribution of music as data. And the pace of change continues to accelerate.

IVAN BERGER
Contributing Editor
*Sound and Vision* magazine

# RECYCLING

Recycling is the process of turning used products into raw materials that can be used to make new products. Its purpose is to conserve natural resources, including clean water and air.

It does this in several ways. First, it reduces the need for new raw materials and reduces the environmental damage done by mining, logging, and other industries. Second, recycling generally takes less energy than the extraction and processing of raw materials, and produces less air and water pollution. Finally, recycling decreases the amount of waste that is sent to landfills or incinerators.

A girl sets out newspapers to be recycled. Recycling paper helps conserve trees, a valuable natural resource.

Most communities in the United States and Canada have recycling programs, as do many other countries. In cities and suburbs, curbside recycling collection is common. People separate their recyclables from their trash and set them out at the curb for collection. In smaller towns and rural areas, where people often must take their own trash to a local dump or other facility, recycling collection bins are provided at the same disposal site. To encourage recycling, some communities charge residents by the bag or can for trash collection, while offering free recycling.

The items most frequently collected by municipal recycling programs are paper and cardboard; steel cans and aluminum cans; glass containers and plastic containers; and yard waste. Other recycling efforts recover used motor oil, tires, car batteries, printer cartridges, and building materials.

Some U.S. states and most Canadian provinces have beverage container redemption laws, often called bottle bills. These laws were designed to reduce beverage container litter, as well as to promote recycling. Customers pay a deposit on each beverage container when they buy it and receive a refund when they return the empty container.

Once the recyclables are collected, they have to be turned back into useful materials. Metals are melted down, purified, and reused. Glass must be sorted by color before it is crushed and melted; the savings in energy and money is less from recycling glass than for metals.

Plastics, too, must be sorted before recycling in order to produce a high-value product; in practice, this means that only the most common types of plastic are recycled in large quantities. They can be ground into chips or powder, melted, and re-molded. Recycled mixtures of different plastics produce lower-value products, such as plastic lumber. Plastic lumber is used for outdoor products such as playground structures and fences because it will not splinter or rot.

Paper recycling is one of the most important, and complicated, recycling processes. To begin the process, used paper is combined with water to form a wet, fibrous mixture that can be substituted for wood pulp in the production of paper. Then the fibers are drawn out into sheets, which are stretched, pressed, and dried. By replacing much of the wood fiber required, paper recycling can greatly reduce the amount of wood needed by the paper industry. (To learn more, see the Wonder Question, How is paper recycled? in the article PAPER.)

People have always reused and recycled waste materials. Composting, for example, is a common form of recycling. Many materials were recycled during World War II (1939–45) to help the war effort. However, the emphasis on recycling household waste, as we know it today, emerged in the 1970's at a time of growing awareness of environmental problems. Recycling centers opened around the country, followed by recycling programs in cities and towns.

FRANK ACKERMAN
Author, *Why Do We Recycle? Markets, Values, and Public Policy*

**RED CLOUD.** See INDIANS, AMERICAN (Profiles).

# RED CROSS

In 1859, a Swiss traveler named Henri Dunant (1828–1910) was passing through northern Italy. He arrived at the town of Solferino the day after a fierce battle had taken place. Austrian troops under the command of Emperor Francis Joseph I had fought French and Italian troops led by Napoleon III. Thousands of dead and wounded lay on the battlefield, receiving no attention. Dunant and a group of volunteers quickly set up emergency hospitals, where they took care of the wounded soldiers from both armies.

Back in his native city of Geneva, Dunant could not forget the picture of the wounded men left to die on the battlefield for lack of medical assistance. Three years after the experience, he published a book. In it he outlined his idea for the formation of a neutral organization of volunteers in every country, who would be trained and ready to help the wounded in time of war.

Public interest in Dunant's book resulted in the appointment of a Committee of Five, of which Dunant was a member. The committee's job was to study ways of achieving Dunant's dream. The outcome of its work was the founding of the Red Cross in 1863. Today the Red Cross in an international movement, joining people in more than 170 countries in service to people in need.

### A New Idea in Service

The Red Cross is made up of national Red Cross and Red Crescent societies throughout the world and, in Israel, the Magen David Adom. In most countries its symbol is a simple red cross on a white background. Nearly all Muslim countries use a red crescent (quarter-moon shape) symbol.

The Red Cross performs its services through the national societies, the International Federation of Red Cross and Red Crescent Societies, and the International Committee of the Red Cross. There is no single program for Red Cross activity or organization. Each of the national societies is independent and bases its program on the particular needs of its nation's people.

The International Federation of Red Cross and Red Crescent Societies is an organization through which the individual societies help one another. It acts as a clearinghouse for Red Cross information from all parts of the world. It sends its specialists to national societies everywhere to help them establish new services or improve old ones. When an emergency arises that is too big for one Red Cross society to handle by itself, the federation can call in help from other societies.

With this kind of worldwide cooperation, Red Cross societies have been able to bring help to millions of people, including displaced persons, refugees, and victims of floods, fires, earthquakes, and other disasters.

The International Committee of the Red Cross, another international organization, is the successor to the original Committee of Five. The International Committee continues to guard Red Cross ideals and to give help during wars and other conflicts. It acts whenever a neutral group is needed. The work of the Red Cross in wartime is carried out under four international treaties called the Geneva Conventions, or Red Cross treaties. Under the terms of the treaties, the life and dignity of a helpless person must be respected, regardless of race, nationality, political allegiance, or station in life. The treaties protect the war-wounded, prisoners of war, civilian populations of occupied countries, and military hospitals and their staffs and supplies.

### Red Cross Services

Over the last 100 years the Red Cross has changed from an organization with a program of wartime services alone to one that serves at all times. In some European countries the Red Cross owns and operates hospitals and clinics that serve as nurse-training centers. It also helps to train community public-health workers. Part of the daily work of Red Cross societies in the new African and Asian nations is to educate people to good habits of health and hygiene. In Canada, the Red Cross Society has programs for children and adults that include water safety, first aid, and general health care.

A large number of societies have, or take part in, blood service programs. Blood is collected from volunteers, processed, and distributed to civilian and military hospitals and doctors. Most Red Cross societies have Junior Red Cross branches and disaster-relief programs. The disaster-relief program is a broad one, covering community preparedness, emergency relief activities, and finally the care of the disaster victims until they are able to care for themselves. Several countries have trained Red Cross ambulance corps.

All Red Cross societies take part in an international search in order to bring together members of families who have become separated or have been lost to one another through wars or other disasters.

## American Red Cross

The American Red Cross is a private voluntary organization supported mostly by contributions from the public. It was founded in 1881 largely through the efforts of a former New England schoolteacher, Clara Barton, who had worked voluntarily among the Civil War wounded. It was first chartered by Congress in 1900. The second charter, still in force, was granted in 1905. Under the charter the Red Cross is required to serve members of the Armed Forces and their families. The organization must also carry on a disaster preparedness and relief program. In addition, the Red Cross must provide assistance in carrying out the terms of the Geneva Conventions whenever such assistance is requested by a government.

Other Red Cross activities include collecting and processing blood from volunteer donors (people who give blood) and maintaining a reserve of nurses, who volunteer their services during emergencies. The Red Cross gives courses in home nursing and preparation for parenthood. It trains volunteers for service in Red Cross chapters, hospitals, clinics, and other agencies. It gives training in first aid and in swimming, boating, and other water skills. It takes part in international Red Cross training conferences and arranges study visits to the United States for officials from other Red Cross societies all over the world.

## Young People Are a Red Cross Strength

Most of the more than 170 Red Cross and Red Crescent societies have child and youth memberships, called Junior Red Cross in most countries. The Junior Red Cross movement started during World War I, when educators asked the Red Cross for a program that would allow young people to help in the war effort. In the United States, the junior branch of the Red Cross is now called Youth Services. It is made up of young people of elementary and high school age. In Canada, the Junior Red

The Red Cross provides young people with helpful skills through courses on such topics as first aid care, accident prevention, and healthy living habits.

Cross was first organized in 1922. Today this branch of the Canadian organization is known as Red Cross Youth.

The aims of the Red Cross services for young people are the same throughout the world. They seek to give the youth of many countries an opportunity to serve others, to teach the ideals of giving service to those in need, to encourage understanding and compassion, and to give young people a greater knowledge of the world they live in.

The International Federation of Red Cross and Red Crescent Societies urges all national Red Cross societies to expand their service opportunities for young people, particularly those for teenagers.

Among the many projects carried out by young Red Cross members around the world has been the exchange of gift boxes. To promote friendship and understanding among children of all nations, young Red Cross members have also exchanged paintings done by students and exhibits relating to school and community life. Children in disaster areas particularly have been sent chests of classroom and recreational supplies.

AMERICAN RED CROSS

**RED SEA.** See OCEANS AND SEAS OF THE WORLD.

**REED, JOHN SILAS.** See OREGON (Famous People).

# REED, WALTER (1851–1902)

Yellow fever used to cause thousands of deaths a year. Although a tropical disease, it did not always stay in the tropics. Boston and New York both suffered epidemics of yellow fever. Philadelphia once lost a tenth of its population to the same disease.

In 1900 an epidemic of yellow fever broke out in Cuba. It struck the United States troops who were still stationed there as a result of the Spanish-American War. The United States Army sent a group of doctors to disease-ridden Cuba. Heading the group was Dr. Walter Reed, whose work led to the control of yellow fever.

Reed was born in Belroi, Virginia, in 1851. He received medical degrees from the University of Virginia and from Bellevue Medical College in New York City. After working as a public health doctor in Brooklyn and New York City, Reed joined the army in 1874 as an assistant surgeon.

After 15 years of duty in the western United States, Reed moved to Baltimore, Maryland. Returning to his studies, he specialized in epidemic diseases at Johns Hopkins University. Later, in Washington, D.C., he became a professor at the Army Medical College. Reed was dedicated to his work. A brilliant man, he soon ranked as one of the leading scientists in the United States. He was often sent by the government to investigate outbreaks of typhoid, yellow fever, and other diseases.

When he was sent to Cuba, Reed faced what seemed an impossible job. The hospitals were full of patients with high fevers and yellowish-colored skins—victims of yellow fever. Hundreds had died of the disease.

Reed decided to follow up a clue he had found in earlier work on the disease. Yellow fever, he suspected, was carried by a certain type of mosquito. He could test this idea by allowing some of these mosquitoes to bite yellow-fever patients. If the infected mosquitoes then gave the disease to healthy persons, his idea would be right.

Yellow fever seemed to affect only human beings. Reed knew that he would need human volunteers—persons who would be willing to risk catching the disease. One of his co-workers—Dr. James Carroll—volunteered in spite of the great danger. When bitten by an infected mosquito, Dr. Carroll fell ill with yellow fever. He recovered but remained in poor health for the rest of his life. Another of Reed's co-workers—Dr. Jesse W. Lazear—died of the fever after being bitten accidentally by an infected mosquito. Other brave men volunteered despite the risk.

Reed worked patiently. He set up many careful experiments that soon proved his theory. He showed that yellow fever was carried by a mosquito. The disease could therefore be wiped out by destroying the carrier mosquitoes.

Military forces set about exterminating the mosquitoes and destroying their breeding places. As a result, yellow fever was controlled in Cuba and was no longer a threat to the United States itself.

Although his work led to the control of yellow fever, Reed could not identify the germ of the disease itself. Other scientists later identified the cause as a virus—a particle so small that it cannot be seen under an ordinary microscope.

In 1901 Reed returned to Washington and his position as professor in the Army Medical College. He died the following year, after an attack of appendicitis. The army hospital in Washington, D.C., was later named in his honor.

DAVID C. KNIGHT
Author, science books for children

Dr. Walter Reed's brilliant research led to the control of the dreaded disease yellow fever.

# REFERENCE MATERIALS

Is there a person anywhere in the world who knows every fact about every subject? No. It is impossible for one person to know everything. Fortunately, there are encyclopedias, almanacs, dictionaries, and many other kinds of materials that provide information on almost any subject imaginable. We call these special sources of information reference materials because people refer to them to learn the answers to their questions.

## Using Reference Materials

Let us say your teacher asks you to write a report on India. You can find all the information you need by selecting the right reference materials. Sometimes you will get enough information from a single book. Usually, though, you need to use several books or different kinds of reference materials.

**Almanacs.** You can find many important facts about India by using an almanac. It will have the population of India, the number of cars, the most important businesses, and more. An almanac has up-to-date facts because a new edition is published every year.

**Encyclopedias.** An almanac is a good first reference book for your report. But to get a deeper understanding of India, you should refer to an encyclopedia. An encyclopedia will have an article on India that will give the history of the country and list important cultural achievements. It will tell how the people of India live and include biographies of India's most influential men and women. You might want to find out more about the great Indian leader Mohandas Gandhi. If there is no biography of Gandhi in your encyclopedia, look in the *Dictionary of National Biography*. Here you will find a biography of Gandhi along with many other biographies.

**Newspapers and Magazines.** To find out about current events in India you can read recent newspaper and magazine articles. The *Readers' Guide to Periodical Literature* lists articles from the most important magazines and newspapers published in the United States. Look up India and you will find references to many articles.

**Electronic Sources.** Reference materials can also be found by using computers. Several encyclopedias, including *The New Book of Knowledge*, are available either on CD-ROM or over the Internet. Many newspapers and other news organizations provide the latest news, as well as archives of previous events, on their Web sites. And the Internet itself has become a virtual reference "book" for information of all kinds, as businesses, organizations, and individuals create their own online "pages" to share their interests and knowledge with the world.

## Choosing the Right Reference Source

The Library of Congress, the largest library in the United States, has more than 70,000 reference books. Your local library does not have that many books, but all libraries have a good selection of reference materials. Your job is to find the right references for the information you need.

Do you want to know the location of Sri Lanka? Look in an atlas. Would you like to know what Abraham Lincoln said about slavery? Look for a book based on his life or one on the history of the United States. Do you need to find a well-known saying by a famous person? Try *Bartlett's Familiar Quotations*. Do you want information about violins? *The Concise Oxford Dictionary of Music* is a good source.

The more you know about reference materials, the easier it is to find information. Librarians are trained to know all about reference materials, and they can help you explore the reference section in your library.

PEGGY KAYE
Author, *Games for Learning*

See also ENCYCLOPEDIAS; LIBRARIES (How to Use Your Library); RESEARCH.

---

## LOOK IT UP!
### Taking the Right Steps

To find information, follow these steps:
1. Decide on the information you need.
2. Think of words that summarize the information. To find out about bees, you might think of "bees," "insects," and "honey."
3. Look up these words and others you think of in an encyclopedia.
4. Ask a librarian to suggest additional reference materials.
5. As you work, you may need more information. When that happens, start again with step one.

In 1521, Reformation leader Martin Luther was brought before the Diet of Worms to renounce his religious views. He declared, "I cannot and I will not retract anything, since it is neither safe nor right to go against conscience."

# REFORMATION

The Reformation was a religious movement that began in Europe in the early 1500's. It was an attempt to renew and reform the Roman Catholic Church of the Middle Ages by returning to the ideas expressed in the Bible's New Testament. Because the movement was also a serious protest against certain abuses of the church, it is often called the Protestant Reformation.

### ▶ THE RELIGIOUS PROTEST

The need for religious renewal within the church was expressed a century or more before the Reformation began. In England in the late 1300's, a group known as the Lollards, followers of the English religious reformer John Wycliffe (1330?–84), became highly critical of the power and wealth of the church. They preached a form of Christianity that emphasized poverty, ethical purity, and strong religious devotion. Their ideas spread to Bohemia (in the modern-day Czech Republic), where Jan Hus (1372?–1415) and his followers, the Hussites, preached against corruption in the church. Chief among their complaints was the church's practice of raising money by selling **indulgences**, official papal documents that promised forgiveness for sins. For these and other reasons, the protest against the church grew stronger.

Between 1414 and 1418, church leaders assembled at the Council of Constance. Their primary goal was to settle the so-called Western Schism (1378–1417), which had long divided the leadership of the church between two popes, one in Rome and another in Avignon, France. But they also gathered to condemn the beliefs of the reformers. The council declared Wycliffe a **heretic** (one who holds certain views that church authorities consider questionable or untrue). Although he had been dead some years, his body was dug up and burned. Hus was burned at the stake (1415).

### Lutheranism

The Reformation is said to have begun in Germany on October 31, 1517, when a university professor of theology named Martin Luther (1483–1546) publicly posted 95 theses in Wittenberg, inviting discussion on the sale of indulgences. In 1521, after a long series of debates with papal representatives, Luther was **excommunicated** (deprived of the sacraments and the rights of church membership) from the Catholic Church. That same year he was brought before the Holy Roman emperor, Charles V, at the Diet (Parliament) in the German city of Worms to defend his reformist beliefs.

Luther had come to believe that God was not a terrible Judge but a comforting Father.

He believed that salvation was assured by repentance and faith in God's love and mercy. Thus, much of the elaborate structure of the church—popes, priests, sacraments, indulgences, pilgrimages, and worship of saints—now seemed to Luther completely unnecessary. The individual believer, he declared, can be in direct contact with God through Jesus Christ.

In 1530, at a parliament assembled at Augsburg, Luther's followers presented a written statement to Holy Roman Emperor Charles V. Known as the Augsburg Confession, it tried to show similarities between Lutheranism and Roman Catholicism and to explain where Lutheran interpretations differed. Charles V rejected the Augsburg Confession, but even today it remains the primary statement of faith among Lutherans.

## Calvinism

The most successful organizer of Protestant thought and life was a French-born theologian, John Calvin (1509–64), who lived in Geneva, Switzerland. Calvin believed that God had predestined (determined in advance) salvation for some people, but that others were less fortunate and were lost or damned forever. Calvin's views were presented in his textbook on theology, *The Institutes of the Christian Religion* (1536–59), which had great influence on the later development of Reformation teachings. Calvinism spread to Germany, the Netherlands, Great Britain, and France, where followers became known as Huguenots. The Huguenots fought a series of French Wars of Religion until the Edict of Nantes granted them limited religious toleration in 1598.

## Presbyterianism

In the 1550's while living in Geneva, a Scotsman named John Knox (1513?–72) became closely associated with Calvin. Knox, a Protestant, had been exiled from England when the Catholic queen Mary I came to the throne. In 1559, a year after Mary's death, Knox returned to his native Scotland, bringing the Calvinistic, or Reformed, faith with him. In Scotland, the Reformation took the form of the Presbyterian Church. Later it spread to the United States, Canada, Australia, New Zealand, and other places Scottish people migrated.

## Anabaptism

In Zurich about 1525, another Swiss religious reformer, Huldreich Zwingli (1484–1531), started the Anabaptist (or rebaptizing) movement. Anabaptists believed that only adults could understand the meaning and responsibilities of being a good Christian. They argued, therefore, that children who had been baptized must be rebaptized to declare their faith. This belief was too radical even for most Protestants.

## Anglicanism and Puritanism

The Reformation in England was motivated at first more by politics than religion. Henry VIII (1491–1547) broke with the pope over the question of divorce and set himself

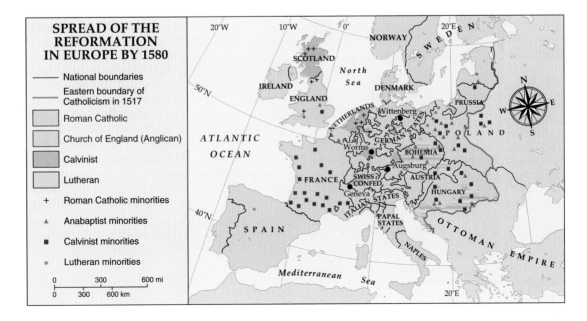

SPREAD OF THE REFORMATION IN EUROPE BY 1580

National boundaries
Eastern boundary of Catholicism in 1517
Roman Catholic
Church of England (Anglican)
Calvinist
Lutheran
+ Roman Catholic minorities
▲ Anabaptist minorities
■ Calvinist minorities
• Lutheran minorities

0   300   600 mi
0   300   600 km

up as the supreme head of the Church of England. Under Henry's son, Edward VI (1537–53), the classic English *Book of Common Prayer* was prepared. Ever since, it has bound together Anglicans the world over in a common way of worship. Under Henry's Catholic daughter, Mary I (1516–58), the Protestants were persecuted and exiled. But when Mary was succeeded by her Protestant half-sister, Elizabeth I (1533–1603), the Reformation was renewed and made secure.

During the reign of James I (1566–1625) the Bible was translated from Hebrew, Greek, Latin, and German manuscripts into an English version that

During the French Wars of Religion, the Huguenots avenged their persecution by destroying Catholic churches.

became known as the King James, or Authorized, Version. The work was begun by William Tyndale (1494?–1536) and completed by Miles Coverdale (1488?–1569).

After the English Civil War (1642–49), the Puritans, England's most active Protestant group, debated with leaders of the Church of England over such questions as the power of bishops. In 1689, the Toleration Act was passed, giving all religious faiths and institutions the legal right to exist.

The Puritan tradition of Protestantism spread into Scotland, where it merged with Knox's Presbyterian and Calvinistic views. Later it was brought to America. In New England the Puritans were variously known as Separatists, Independents, and Congregationalists.

In England in the 1700's, a clergyman named John Wesley split with the Church of England and began what is known as the Evangelical Revival with his preaching of the Bible in the streets and in open fields. This variety of Protestantism evolved into the Methodist Church, which grew rapidly in America and elsewhere.

▶ **THE CONTINUING REFORMATION**

One of the basic principles of the Reformation was that the Christian Church should continue reforming itself in its beliefs, practices, and organization. In the same way, it is a principle of Protestantism to protest not only against abuses of all kinds but even against its own errors and imperfections. Consequently, small groups of devout Protestants eventually formed their own independent churches in protest against the more highly organized churches such as the Lutheran, Reformed, and Anglican. Two such groups were the Mennonites (a sect of Anabaptists) and the Quakers (or members of the Society of Friends), both of whom stressed simplicity of life and doctrine. The Mennonites had a great influence on the development of the various modern Baptist churches. The Quakers became identified with nonviolence, pacifism, and aid to needy people.

HUGH T. KERR
Princeton Theological Seminary

See also BIBLE; CALVIN, JOHN; HUGUENOTS; HUS, JAN; KNOX, JOHN; LUTHER, MARTIN; PROTESTANTISM; PURITANS; QUAKERS; WESLEY, JOHN.

## WONDER QUESTION

### What was the Counter-Reformation?

The Counter-Reformation was a reform movement begun by the Catholic Church in the 1500's to address abuses within the church and to suppress the growth of the Protestant Reformation.

A milestone of the Counter-Reformation was the Council of Trent (1545–63), held in northern Italy in three separate stages under the leadership of three different popes. The Council started reforms in certain monastic orders and provided guidelines for the education of the clergy. In the area of religious doctrine, it directly opposed Protestantism by reaffirming such views as the necessity of the priesthood, the existence of the seven sacraments, and the sole right of the church to interpret the Bible.

# REFRIGERATION

Imagine a world without ice cream in the summer or fresh fruit in the winter. These treats may have been luxuries for our great-great-grandparents, who had to rely on natural ice to keep things cool. However, today we can enjoy virtually any food year-round, thanks to artificial refrigeration.

Refrigeration is not just used to keep food fresh. It is also used to keep air cool in buildings and vehicles, to preserve organs for life-saving transplant operations, and to store rocket fuel for space shuttles.

### ▶ HOW REFRIGERATION WORKS

Cold is simply the absence of heat. A refrigerator does not add cold to food; it removes heat. A refrigerator absorbs heat in one place and gives it off somewhere else.

Most refrigerators work on the principle that an evaporating liquid absorbs heat. When a liquid **evaporates** (changes to a gas), it absorbs a great deal of heat from the surrounding air and from nearby objects. If you have ever stood in a wet bathing suit when the wind was blowing, you have experienced cooling by evaporation.

The **refrigerant** (the substance that does the cooling in refrigerators) is normally a gas. But under high enough pressure, the refrigerant **condenses** (changes to a liquid) when cooled. When this happens, the refrigerant gives off heat. When the pressure is released, the refrigerant changes back to a gas. In doing so, it absorbs heat.

### The Compression System

Most household and commercial refrigerators use a cooling method called the compression system. The heart of this system is a motor-driven pump called a **compressor**. Refrigerant gas enters the compressor at low temperature and pressure and is compressed into a much smaller volume. As a result, the gas comes out of the compressor at a higher temperature and pressure.

The hot gas then flows into a long metal tube called the **condenser**.

As the compressor pumps more gas into the condenser, the pressure and temperature of the gas build up quickly. (You can see this principle at work when you pump up a bicycle tire or a basketball. After a few strokes, the barrel of the pump becomes hot to the touch.) In most refrigerators, a fan blows air over the condenser. At a certain point, the temperature of the gas trapped in the condenser becomes higher than the temperature of the air being blown over it. When this happens, the gas gives off heat to the surrounding air. As the gas cools, it condenses into a liquid, losing more heat in the process.

The liquid refrigerant then leaves the condenser and flows through a tube to a very narrow pipe called a **capillary tube** or a device called an **expansion valve**. Either device acts as a gatekeeper, preventing the refrigerant from passing through too freely. From here, the liquid refrigerant flows into a much wider tube called the **evaporator**, or cooling coil. In a home refrigerator this tube is built into the walls of the freezing compartment.

When the liquid refrigerant enters the evaporator, the refrigerant's pressure suddenly drops. As a result, the refrigerant turns back into a gas. This process absorbs heat and makes the evaporator—and the space around it—cold. The refrigerant gas then passes through a tube back to the compressor, where the cycle begins again.

### The Absorption System

Another method of refrigeration is the absorption system, which uses heat to produce a cooling effect. The absorption system is based on the fact that certain chemicals, normally gases, can dissolve very easily in water. As these gases are absorbed by the water, they release heat. When they bubble out of the water, they take heat with them and cool their surroundings. High temperatures drive the dissolved gases out of the water, just as

**THE REFRIGERATION CYCLE**

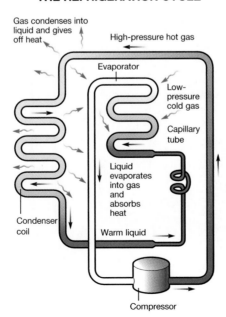

Gas condenses into liquid and gives off heat

High-pressure hot gas

Evaporator

Low-pressure cold gas

Capillary tube

Liquid evaporates into gas and absorbs heat

Condenser coil

Warm liquid

Compressor

soft drinks form more bubbles when they warm up.

Although less efficient than the compression system, the absorption system has some special advantages. Absorption systems can be designed with no solid moving parts. Most operate with very little noise. And they can operate on any source of high temperature heat, so that any fuel will provide refrigeration. In remote areas without electricity, this is the system of choice.

### The Air Cycle System

Jet aircraft use another cooling method known as the air cycle system. This air-conditioning system depends on the fact that expanding air absorbs heat. Expanding air does not absorb as much heat as evaporating liquid, but air-conditioning systems do not have to produce very low temperatures.

In the engine of a jet plane, air is pumped up to a high pressure before it enters the combustion chamber. Some of this compressed air is made to flow through a coil, where it is cooled. When the air is allowed to expand, it absorbs heat from the surroundings, which in turn become colder. This cooling effect is used to keep the cabin of the plane at a comfortable temperature for the passengers and crew.

### Dry Ice and Cryogenic Gases

Most gases can be turned into liquids if they are made cold enough. Some gases can even become solids when cooled. Carbon dioxide, which makes up part of the air we exhale, can form a very cold solid called dry ice. Unlike water ice, which melts into a liquid, dry ice sublimes (turns directly into a gas). This property makes dry ice ideal for cooling things without making them wet. Other gases, such as nitrogen, can form liquids that are even colder than dry ice. These so-called cryogenic gases are used in medical laboratories and hospitals. Cryogenic gases can preserve donated organs, which can save the lives of people who need heart transplants, for example.

### ▶ USES OF REFRIGERATION

The most familiar use of refrigeration is in refrigerators and freezers. Refrigerators have a freezing compartment, where ice-cube trays and frozen foods are kept. This compartment is colder than the rest of the refrigerator because the evaporator coils are built into its walls. A thermostat turns the machine on when the temperature gets too high and

**INSIDE A HOUSEHOLD REFRIGERATOR**

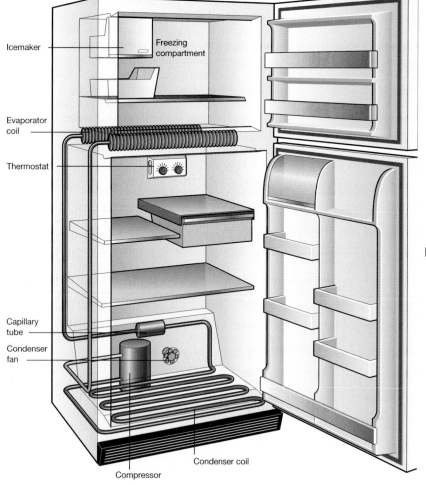

Icemaker

Freezing compartment

Evaporator coil

Thermostat

Capillary tube

Condenser fan

Condenser coil

Compressor

turns it off when the desired low temperature is reached.

All types of transportation equipment—trucks, railroad cars, and ships—that carry food are refrigerated to prevent spoilage. Some trucks use a large compression system to cool the space to be refrigerated. Liquid nitrogen is used in some trucks to keep fruits and vegetables cool over long distances.

Refrigerated warehouses are used for storing food and other perishable goods. Large refrigeration machines cool pipes containing brine (salt water). Brine can be made very cold without freezing. The cold brine is pumped through pipes that line the walls of the warehouse building. This produces a more even cooling than is possible by cooling the building directly from the evaporator.

Air conditioners are simply refrigeration machines with fans that circulate the cooled air through a room or building. A small home air conditioner, located in a window or an opening in the wall, cools one or two rooms. Air conditioning systems that cool big buildings may be as large as several rooms.

Refrigeration has many other uses. It is used in manufacturing rubber tires and some plastics and in treating certain metals. Refrigeration is also used to store two components of rocket fuel—oxygen and hydrogen. When these substances are cooled enough, they turn into liquids that take up only one-thousandth the space they would as gases. The liquid oxygen and hydrogen can then be stored in rockets. When the two liquids are mixed, the oxygen and hydrogen combine to form water, releasing the explosive energy that helps propel space shuttles into orbit.

▶ DEVELOPMENTS IN REFRIGERATION

For thousands of years people have used ice and snow to keep food cold and fresh. The Greeks and Romans, who lived in lands with hot summers, built snow cellars. These were underground rooms packed with snow brought from the mountains during the winter. The snow melted so slowly that food was kept cold all summer.

By the middle of the 1800's, scientists had learned a great deal about heat. Inventors began using this knowledge to develop refrigeration machines. The first such machine was patented in England in 1834 by Jacob Perkins, an American inventor. With the invention of these machines, it was no longer necessary to save ice from winter. Refrigeration could be artificially produced.

## Refrigeration and the Environment

One of the problems of artificial refrigeration has been the use of chemicals called chlorofluorocarbons (CFC's). These chemicals have been used widely as refrigerants and as propellants in spray cans. However, CFC's can escape into the air and reach the upper atmosphere, where they can destroy a layer of gas called ozone. Ozone acts as a shield that protects us from much of the sun's harmful ultraviolet rays. In the 1980's, scientists began noticing a potentially dangerous thinning of the ozone layer, particularly above Antarctica. Since then, countries have signed treaties pledging to phase out CFC's. Meanwhile, researchers are developing safer alternatives to replace these chemicals.

## New Technologies

Many new portable refrigerators use another method of cooling, called **thermoelectric refrigeration**. The system has no moving parts or chemical refrigerants. Instead, materials called semiconductors are used. A thermoelectric refrigeration device consists of a cold junction, made of one type of semiconductor material, and a hot junction, made of another type. When the device is connected to a circuit, electricity flows from the cold junction to the hot junction. Heat is absorbed from the surroundings, which become cooler.

Thermoelectric refrigerators are especially popular with campers. Traditional coolers need a constant supply of fresh ice to keep them cold. Thermoelectric refrigerators, on the other hand, can be operated simply by plugging them into a car's electric lighter.

Scientists are developing other new refrigeration technologies. **Magnetocaloric refrigerators**, for example, use powerful magnets and a material called gadolinium to cool things. Gadolinium changes temperature noticeably when placed in a strong magnetic field. Such a field can be used to cool a solid piece of gadolinium, which in turn can cool other things, such as water flowing around it.

ROBERT FOUNTAIN
Refrigeration Service Engineers Society

See also AIR CONDITIONING; LIQUID OXYGEN AND OTHER LIQUID GASES.

# REFUGEES

Imagine that you are standing alone with only the clothes on your back. You are in a strange place. You have been forced to leave home quickly because you were afraid someone would hurt you. You had to leave everything you own behind. You are tired, worried, lonely, and maybe hungry.

That is what it is like to be a refugee. Refugees are people who have had to flee from their homes to foreign countries. Usually they are escaping famine, danger, or persecution because of their race, religion, or political beliefs.

## ▶ A WORLDWIDE PROBLEM

Today it is estimated that there are nearly 26 million refugees. If one also counts the millions of people who have fled their homes but remain in their own countries, approximately 1 out of every 115 people in the world today is a refugee. Of any single country, Afghanistan has lost the largest number of people. From 1979 to 1989, more than 5 million Afghans fled to Pakistan and Iran to escape civil wars and invasions by the Soviet Union.

*Above:* In the late 1990's, thousands of Albanian refugees fled across the Adriatic Sea to find safety in Italy. Like many of the world's refugees, they left their homes to escape political turmoil and police brutality. *Left:* Refugee camps run by international agencies, such as the United Nations Children's Fund, help distribute food, clothing, and medicine to those displaced by war and other disasters.

Africa has one of the world's most serious refugee problems. Ethnic conflict and lack of freedom have combined with drought and famine to force millions from their homes. Many now live in camps in Tanzania, Sudan, Ethiopia, Uganda, and Kenya.

## ▶ HISTORY

The plight of refugees dates back to the beginning of human history. The word "refugee" was first used 300 years ago in reference to the Protestant Huguenots who fled Catholic rule in France. But the 1900's has become known as the "century of refugees."

In the early 1900's, persecution and changes in government forced countless numbers of Russians, Armenians, Jews, and others to leave their homes. With the rise of Fascist governments in Germany, Italy, and Spain in the 1930's, millions more were displaced. During World War II (1939–45), one in every eight Europeans became a refugee—including many Jews who escaped from Nazi Germany and thousands of children who were separated from their parents.

The flow of refugees did not end with World War II. In 1947, Great Britain's former Indian colonies were divided into two independent countries—India and Pakistan. Thousands of Hindus moved from Pakistan to India, while thousands of Muslims moved from India to Pakistan.

In 1948, when the nation of Israel was created from the territory of Palestine, Israel took in many of Europe's Jewish refugees. But when fighting broke out between Israelis and Arabs, thousands of Arabs lost their homes and lands. Today about 2.5 million Palestinian Arabs still live in refugee camps outside Israel, a situation that poses a major obstacle to lasting peace in the Middle East.

Several million Koreans who refused to live under Communist rule after World War

II fled to South Korea during the Korean War (1950–53). And as Communist governments took control in Eastern Europe, millions of East Europeans fled to the West. Later in the 1960's and 1970's, millions of people in Vietnam, Cambodia, and Laos risked their lives to escape Communist rule.

In the 1990's, ethnic conflict created a refugee population of about 9 million in what was once the Soviet Union. Later the breakup of Yugoslavia displaced at least another 2 million people.

The United States has always been a magnet for refugees from the Western Hemisphere. About 1 million Cubans have fled to the United States since Fidel Castro came to power in 1959. Thousands of Haitians have also sailed to the United States in tiny, overcrowded boats. Many people fleeing wars in Central America in the 1980's found refuge elsewhere in Latin America and in the United States.

▶ HELPING REFUGEES

Most refugees today are fleeing from one developing country to another. They usually need emergency help. Such help is provided by governments, international organizations, and voluntary groups.

**Refugee Camps.** Many refugees spend a long time in camps run by international and voluntary agencies. The camps try to provide shelter, food, and medical services. Conditions in such camps vary widely, but almost all are crowded. Children often suffer the most. They are less able than adults to endure illness and other hardships.

**Resettlement.** Refugee camps offer no long-term solutions. They can only provide temporary relief to those who have been displaced. Eventually the refugees must leave the camps to return to their homes or resettle in another country.

There is no best way to resettle refugees, but two basic procedures are generally followed. Some countries, such as Switzerland and Canada, keep refugees in special centers and gradually ease them into new ways of life. In contrast, countries such as the United States encourage refugees to go out on their own as quickly as possible. Volunteer agencies, church groups, and individuals (who act as sponsors) find housing, jobs, and other necessities for refugees.

The United States, like most countries, limits the number of foreigners who may enter the country to live. Since the Cold War ended following the fall of communism in the Soviet Union in the early 1990's, the United States and many other Western countries have been less willing to accept refugees who claim to be fleeing political persecution. This has increased the burden on international agencies trying to help the world's refugees.

Refugees who resettle far from their homes may encounter significant difficulties. Many must learn a new language and the ways of a different culture. They may often face resentment in their new communities. But in spite of such obstacles, many succeed in rebuilding their lives.

**Finding a Solution.** During World War II, several international agencies were set up to help refugees. Later, treaties and agreements between nations spelled out the rights of refugees and the duties of countries toward them.

The Office of the United Nations High Commissioner for Refugees (UNHCR) was created in 1950 to offer legal protection for refugees. This agency received the Nobel Peace Prize in 1954 and again in 1981 for its work.

The U.N. Children's Fund and the World Food Program support the UNHCR by providing emergency relief. More than 200 voluntary agencies, such as Catholic Relief Services and Save the Children, also help. Their tasks range from distributing clothing, food, and medicine to directing refugee camps.

The UNHCR and the other agencies need the help and support of governments to do their work. They can help ease the suffering of refugees, but they cannot stop the worldwide flood of homeless people. Refugees will continue to exist as long as there are wars, persecution, injustice, and poor economic and social conditions.

GIL LOESCHER
ANN LOESCHER
Coauthors, *The World's Refugees: A Test of Humanity*

See also IMMIGRATION.

**REGINA.** See SASKATCHEWAN (Cities).

**REHNQUIST, WILLIAM H.** See SUPREME COURT OF THE UNITED STATES (Profiles).

**REIGN OF TERROR.** See FRENCH REVOLUTION.

A reindeer pulls a sleigh in Lapland. Reindeer are native to Europe's far north, where they have been domesticated by Sami and other native peoples.

## REINDEER AND CARIBOU

It is spring on the Alaskan tundra, and a newborn caribou calf is just one hour old. Yet already it is strong enough to stand and follow its mother. Not far away, a wolf watches.

In northern Sweden, a man tends his reindeer herd. His shoes are made of reindeer leather, and his children drink reindeer milk. When they travel, reindeer pull their sled.

Reindeer and caribou are now classified as a single species. Caribou live in Alaska and Canada; reindeer live in Russia, Norway, Finland, and Sweden. Reindeer once lived in other parts of Europe, but those populations have been hunted to extinction.

Arctic peoples have hunted reindeer and caribou since prehistoric times. Nomadic groups followed the herds to get meat, skins for clothing, and bones for tools. About 200 years ago, reindeer were domesticated in parts of Scandinavia and Russia. Today some people still follow a traditional way of life based on reindeer herding.

**Characteristics of Reindeer and Caribou.** Caribou and reindeer are the only deer in which both males and females grow antlers. Scientists think having antlers helps females compete with males to find food.

Most reindeer and caribou are brown with white bellies and a white tail patch. But some in Greenland and eastern Canada are nearly white. Males are bigger than females. A typical male weighs about 300 pounds (135 kilograms), although the largest animals may weigh 700 pounds (315 kilograms) and stand almost 5 feet (1.5 meters) tall at the shoulder.

Reindeer and caribou have short legs and wide, flat hooves that help them walk in deep snow and across the spongy treeless plains known as the tundra. And they click when they walk! The sound is caused by a tendon that snaps against a bone in the foot.

Almost every plant that grows on the tundra is food for reindeer and caribou: new leaves, evergreen needles, even small twigs. They also have the unusual ability to digest lichens—these tiny organisms provide food for reindeer during the harsh winter months.

**Reindeer and Caribou and Their Young.** For most of the year, males and females stay in separate herds. But in the fall, when mating season begins, males and females come together, locating each other by means of a scent secreted from glands between the toes and around the anus. Males also call out, making a coughing sound. A single male defends a group of females, called a harem.

Pregnancy lasts for 228 days. Usually, all the calves are born within a five-day period. Their ability to stand and follow their mothers soon after birth helps protect the tiny calves from wolves and other predators.

**The Life of Reindeer and Caribou.** Reindeer and caribou live in herds of 10 to 1,000 animals. A few large herds on migration have 200,000 animals. Most herds migrate between the Arctic tundra in summer and woodland edges in the winter, traveling up to 600 miles (966 kilometers) each way.

In the summer, caribou and reindeer are tormented by mosquitoes and other biting insects. To get relief, they may stand in the middle of a snowfield, where insects are scarce.

Reindeer and caribou today are threatened because exploration for oil sometimes blocks their migration routes or destroys habitat. Some populations in Canada and the United States have been declared endangered.

CYNTHIA BERGER
Science Writer

**REINHARDT, DJANGO.** See JAZZ (Profiles).

# RELATIVITY

Most scientists believe that the universe is a very orderly place. They believe that all the forces and motions in it are regulated by a few rules, or laws of nature. These rules, when fully understood, explain and tie together many apparently unrelated things. For example, the rules explain the Earth's gravity, which pulls a well-hit baseball to the ground; the forces that keep an artificial satellite in orbit around the Earth or around a distant planet; the constant speed of light; and the way the planets and stars move in the sky.

The theory of relativity, first published by Albert Einstein in the early 1900's, is such a set of rules. It explains all the events mentioned above and many more. In addition, the theory of relativity has helped scientists predict many things about the universe that they cannot yet see or measure with telescopes or other instruments. The theory of relativity gives many clues to mysteries such as how the Earth, the planets, and the stars were formed and what will eventually happen to them billions of years from now.

Einstein was not the first scientist to try to pin down the basic laws of nature in words and mathematical equations. (Words and equations that define basic laws are called **theories**.) Throughout recorded history, many people have developed theories of the universe. Some had great value. They helped astronomers measure accurately the size of the Earth's orbit around the sun, for example. The theories gave practical ideas to inventors and engineers who designed weapons and machines.

But although many of these theories were accepted for a time, scientists usually found that the theories had two failings that ultimately proved to be fatal: (1) the theories ignored or failed to explain certain facts that did not fit the theory; and (2) as better scientific measuring equipment was built and new mathematical tools were developed, scientists determined that one or more of the key ideas in the theory proved to be wrong.

## ▶ THE PARTS OF RELATIVITY

There are two major parts to Einstein's theory. The first part, called the special theory of relativity, was published in 1905. The second part, called the general theory of relativity, was published in 1916. Both parts of the theory have been questioned and tested again and again by top scientists all over the world. While there have been some changes and modifications in these theories (several suggested by Einstein himself), his basic ideas now constitute one of the accepted explanations of how all forces and motions operate in the universe.

As is true with most creative basic research, Einstein's theory of relativity was developed with no practical reason in mind. As with all important scientific developments, however, relativity eventually came to affect almost everyone on Earth.

The most dramatic use of relativity was in atomic energy. The theory of relativity helped establish the scientific foundation for both the atomic and the hydrogen bombs. In fact, Einstein's famous letter to President Franklin D. Roosevelt in 1939—written after he emigrated from his native Germany and became a United States citizen—was instrumental in convincing the president that an atomic bomb could be built.

The theory of relativity has also played a vital role in **cosmology**, which is the study of the structure of the universe and what happens to bodies that move through space. The United States Apollo program that sent astronauts to the moon and all the other space exploration programs use many parts of the theory of relativity.

## ▶ EVOLUTION OF RELATIVITY

The best way to understand the theory of relativity is to follow part of the same train of thought that led Einstein to it. Like all scientists, Einstein based his new ideas on the work of many earlier researchers and thinkers all over the world. Even their errors often provided useful information.

His approach was what is usually called the scientific method. This can be thought of as a four-step process: (1) Study all the available facts and theories that are currently in use; (2) look for errors or inconsistencies—this search can be a mental process or a set of experiments or both; (3) if the old ideas do not work well, create a new hypothesis, or explanation; (4) test the new hypothesis in all possible ways, correcting it or abandoning it if it does not stand up. Einstein's genius was in step 3, where he created a new hypothesis that both corrected the errors of the older theories and explained many newly discovered facts. The theory also predicted phenomena, such as atomic energy, that were unknown before the theory was published.

Before the theory of relativity, the accepted laws of force and motion were developed by Sir Isaac Newton, the great English mathematician and philosopher. Through all the 1700's and most of the 1800's, Newton's laws of gravitation and motion were the foundations of physics and cosmology.

As scientists continued working in the mid-1800's, however, they began finding more and more situations that did not fit in with the Newtonian laws, which they had always accepted. By far the greatest problem concerned light. Scientists could not understand how light travels through space. As scientists experimented with light, they found that the only way they could understand how light traveled was to say that it was carried along in an invisible material. They called this material **luminiferous ether**. They assumed that the ether must exist all over the Earth and throughout the universe. By accepting the ether, the physicists could explain how light

energy traveled through space. Light, they said, traveled in the form of waves through the ether much as water waves travel through water.

There was one major difficulty with the ether, however. Its properties conflicted with the laws of mechanics.

▶ **THE MICHELSON-MORLEY EXPERIMENT**

The ether concept came under attack in the late 1800's. Scientists were becoming dissatisfied with it because they were unable to detect any ether. Finally, in 1887, two American physicists, Albert A. Michelson (1852–1931) and Edward W. Morley (1838–1923), devised an experiment to detect the invisible ether. The two reasoned that if ether filled the universe, the Earth must be passing through it very rapidly as it revolved around the sun each year. Therefore, if light traveled through the ether, it should be affected by the motion of the Earth through the ether.

An easy way to understand this experiment is to think of a boy standing on the shore of a stream, watching a boat out in the current. Suppose the current flows at 2 miles an hour and the boat moves at 20 miles an hour. If the boat heads downstream, it moves at 22 miles an hour (the speed of the current plus the speed of the boat). If the boat moves upstream, it travels at 18 miles an hour (the speed of the boat less the speed of the current). If the boat moves in some other direction it goes at some speed between 18 and 22 miles an hour.

In the Michelson-Morley experiment (see Figure 1), the Earth is the stream's bank, the ether is the water current, and light is used instead of the boat. In their experiment Michelson and Morley mounted a light source on the edge of a large platform. A mirror at the center of the platform split the light into two beams. One part of the beam traveled parallel to the Earth's motion through the ether. The other part traveled at right angles to the Earth's motion. A mirror arrangement on the edge of the platform reflected the

**Michelson-Morley Experiment**

**Figure 1.**
Experimenters used an interferometer to compare the speeds of light beams and found that light travels at the same speed regardless of the direction of travel.

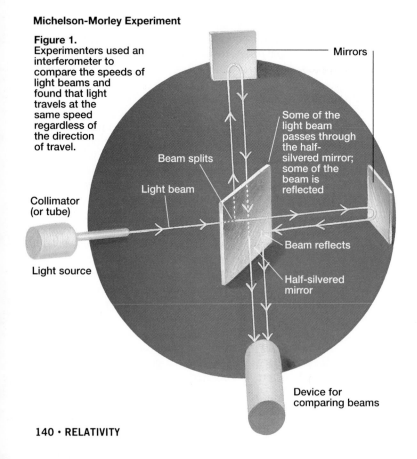

Mirrors

Some of the light beam passes through the half-silvered mirror; some of the beam is reflected

Beam splits

Light beam

Collimator (or tube)

Light source

Beam reflects

Half-silvered mirror

Device for comparing beams

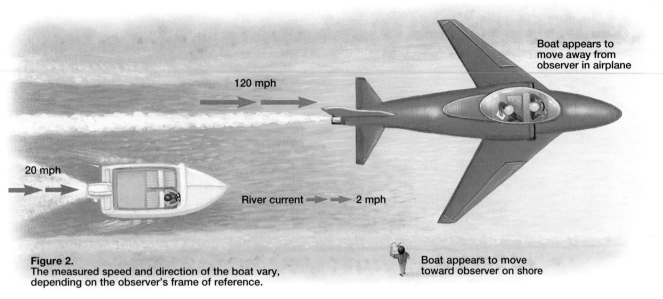

Boat appears to move away from observer in airplane

120 mph

20 mph

River current ➤ 2 mph

Boat appears to move toward observer on shore

**Figure 2.**
The measured speed and direction of the boat vary, depending on the observer's frame of reference.

light beams to a device that compared the arrival times of the beams. The experimenters expected to find a difference in the arrival times. The amazing result was that no matter in which directions the beams of light were aimed, they always bounced back at exactly the same instant. This convinced Michelson and Morley that the ether did not exist. The results of the Michelson-Morley experiment were checked repeatedly and they were confirmed by other scientists.

Since the ether concept was dead, scientists began searching for an alternative to it. Early in the 1900's Albert Einstein announced a new theory. It not only accounted for the motion of light but also explored the very nature of motion itself and of space and time.

### ▶ THE SPECIAL THEORY OF RELATIVITY

Einstein's theory of relativity provided a new framework for the old ideas about force, motion, and gravitation. Let us examine now the two parts of the theory of relativity to see how they changed many of science's major ideas about the whole physical world.

In creating the special theory of relativity, Einstein made two basic assumptions about the universe.

To understand the first assumption, think again about the boat in the stream and the boy on the bank observing and measuring its motion (see Figure 2). Assume that he can see nothing but the boat. If he can measure how far it is from him and can accurately figure its direction, he can make many calcula-

tions about its motion and other physical properties.

Now, suppose that there is another boy, flying overhead in a jet plane. He, too, is aware only of himself and the boat—he cannot see the movement of the stream or the banks of the river or the other boy, and he has no real information about the direction and speed of his plane. But he can measure the distance to the boat, figure its speed, and make a full set of calculations about it.

The point is that both boys, using the same laws of force and motion, will come up with different answers to questions about the movements of the boat and its physical properties. Each boy's measurements will take into account automatically, without his even being aware of it, his own position and motion. The position and motion determine his point of view. Technically, each point of view is called a **frame of reference**. The first assumption you can make, then, is that the same laws of force and motion hold true in different frames of reference. The second assumption is that the speed of light—186,272 miles per second—is the same in each frame of reference.

Using these assumptions, Einstein developed mathematical equations that describe the motion and speeds of any body of matter, from a tiny grain of sand to a planet or a star. When the speeds involved are those that scientists on the Earth were used to dealing with, the results of calculations with Einstein's equations were about the same as

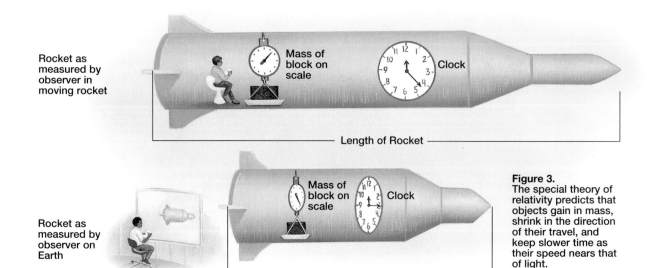

Rocket as measured by observer in moving rocket

Mass of block on scale

Clock

Length of Rocket

Rocket as measured by observer on Earth

Mass of block on scale

Clock

Length of Rocket

**Figure 3.**
The special theory of relativity predicts that objects gain in mass, shrink in the direction of their travel, and keep slower time as their speed nears that of light.

those obtained by using the Newtonian laws. This explains why Newton's laws were so useful and stood so long.

When the speeds involved approach the speed of light, however, the equations give many seemingly strange results. The many predictions made possible by these equations are difficult even to imagine. It is not necessary to understand the mathematics or all of the theory of relativity to appreciate how revolutionary these new ideas were when they were introduced and still are even today.

### Changes in Physical Properties

According to the special theory, all three of the fundamental quantities of mechanics—length, mass, and time—undergo surprising changes when things move at a speed near that of light. The length shrinks, the mass increases, and the passage of time slows down (see Figure 3).

As the speed of an object approaches that of light, the length of the object shrinks in the direction it is moving. But its width and depth (at right angles to the length) do not shrink at all. If the object is traveling at almost the speed of light, it will have almost no length in its direction of motion. Many experiments in laboratories have confirmed this shrinkage. The first experiments on changes in mass were made in 1909 by a physicist named A. Bucherer. He noted that beta particles, which are fast-moving electrons emitted by radioac-

tive substances, exhibited just the increase in mass predicted by the special theory. The time slowdown was demonstrated in the early 1920's by an American scientist named Herbert Ives (1882–1953).

The time-slowing idea has important implications for the world's growing space program. A clock, for example, that is traveling rapidly through space should slow down. This effect must be taken into account by navigation systems using atomic clocks in orbiting satellites. Much more dramatic, however, is the fact that an astronaut in a spaceship traveling near the speed of light would not age as fast as the people left behind on Earth. Another important finding of the special theory is that neither matter nor energy can move at a speed faster than the speed of light. The reason is that as the object moves close to the speed of light, its mass increases. The mass becomes infinitely great. Since there is no infinite force available to make the object go any faster, its speed levels off, and it approaches the speed of light as a limit.

The final major consequence of the special theory is the equivalence of mass and energy, shown by the famous formula $E = mc^2$. In this equation $E$ stands for energy, $m$ stands for mass, and $c$ represents the speed of light. The key point of the equation is that energy and mass are two forms of the same physical thing, and under the proper circumstances, can be changed from one form to the other.

This equivalence is one of the reasons it was possible to develop most of the uses of nuclear energy. In many of these reactions a material such as uranium 235 can develop great quantities of energy. In the case of an atomic bomb, the reaction is fast. In the case of a nuclear power station, the reaction is controlled and relatively slow.

### ▶ GENERAL THEORY OF RELATIVITY

The general theory of relativity, published eleven years after the special theory, attempts to explain within a single framework many of the laws of the physical universe. In fact, the special theory can be considered as a part of the general theory.

One of the key ideas in the general theory is that gravitation is a distortion of space. This concept of gravitation can be illustrated by thinking of space as a flat network of crossed rubber bands (see Figure 4). If a large stone is placed in the middle of the rubber bands, it produces a depression. Near the stone the rubber bands stretch from their flat surface, while farther away the surface of the bands very nearly retains its flat shape.

Just as the stone distorts the rubber bands, so does matter distort, or warp, space. This distortion of space is called gravitation.

If two large stones are placed close to each other on the rubber-band network, they will tend to move toward each other. The distortion of the rubber bands forces the two stones to move toward each other. Similarly, if two large objects in space are close to each other, they will tend to move (gravitate) toward each other. The distortion of space, or gravitation, forces the two objects to move toward each other. If space is not distorted, then the distance between the two points, measured along the rubber bands, will be a straight line. But this straight line becomes a curved line when matter is present, for matter distorts the space.

Is this strange picture anything like reality? Can the distortions of space predicted by the general theory be proved by experimentation and observation? Most scientists now answer "yes" to both questions. The following facts confirm the general theory of relativity:

1. The planet Mercury revolves around the sun in an elliptical orbit, as do all the planets. The point in the ellipse at which the planet is closest to the sun is called the perihelion. According to the general theory of relativity, the perihelion should rotate slowly around the sun because of the distortion of space by the sun. Careful observations by astronomers show that the motion of Mercury is almost exactly what is predicted by the general theory (see Figure 5).

2. Light from distant stars deviates slightly from a straight line as it passes close to the sun, according to the general theory. This already has been illustrated by taking photographs, during an eclipse of the sun, of stars that appear to be directly behind the edges of the sun. When the same stars were photographed later and the two photographs matched, the stars did not line up. The light from the stars had apparently been shifted while moving through the distorted space near the sun's surface (see Figure 6).

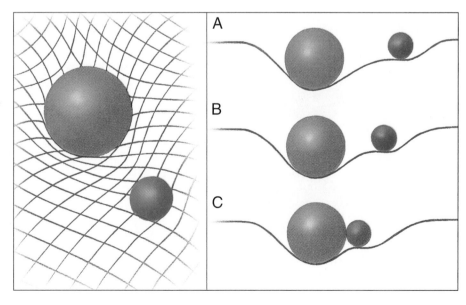

**Figure 4.**
The two objects distort the net (*right*), just as all objects distort the space they occupy. Figures A through C (*far right*) illustrate how this distortion causes bodies in space to gravitate, or move, toward one another.

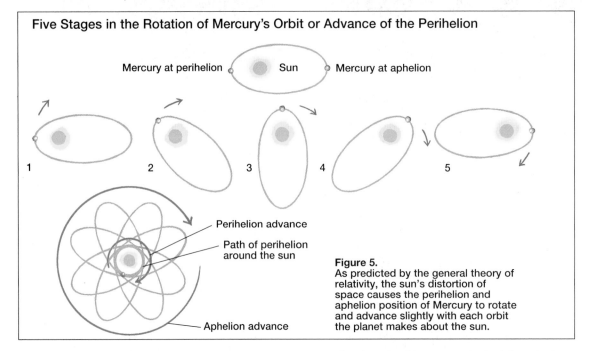

## Five Stages in the Rotation of Mercury's Orbit or Advance of the Perihelion

Mercury at perihelion    Sun    Mercury at aphelion

1    2    3    4    5

Perihelion advance

Path of perihelion around the sun

Aphelion advance

**Figure 5.**
As predicted by the general theory of relativity, the sun's distortion of space causes the perihelion and aphelion position of Mercury to rotate and advance slightly with each orbit the planet makes about the sun.

3. In a related effect, astronomers also have found galaxies that act as enormous "lenses," causing light from more distant galaxies to bend, and sometimes leading to multiple images of the same distant galaxy.

4. The general theory of relativity predicted that the frequency of light moving up or down in a gravitational field would be changed. This was verified in 1976 in an experiment that used light signals emitted by an atomic clock launched high above the Earth on a rocket.

5. The theory also predicted that a double-star system should radiate a form of energy called gravitational waves, and as a result of its reduced energy, it should slowly shrink in size. This shrinkage has been detected in a system known by the astronomical designation PSR 1913 + 16, which contains two dense objects known as neutron stars.

All these experiments indicate very strongly that the general theory of relativity presents a more accurate model of nature than any previous theory. Does this mean simply that Einstein was right and Newton was wrong? A "yes" answer would be an oversimplification. All physical theories are only approximations of nature. None is perfect. In this case, Einstein's is more accurate than Newton's and therefore will be used by scientists where needed, until it is eventually replaced with something better.

SERGE A. KORFF
New York University

Reviewed and Updated by CLIFFORD M. WILL
Washington University

ROBERT M. JONES
Associate Professor of Physics
University of Minnesota

See also EINSTEIN, ALBERT; ENERGY; GRAVITY AND GRAVITATION; LIGHT; MATTER; NEWTON, ISAAC; PHYSICS; PHYSICS, HISTORY OF; SCIENCE.

**RELIEF, PUBLIC.** See WELFARE, PUBLIC.

**Figure 6.**
Light bends as it passes through the sun's gravitational field, and the star appears to shift its position. This effect, seen during a solar eclipse, confirms the general relativity theory.

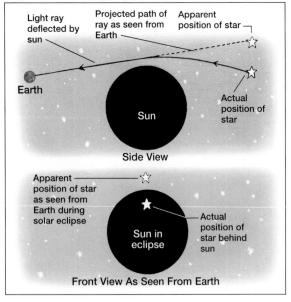

Light ray deflected by sun

Projected path of ray as seen from Earth

Apparent position of star

Earth

Actual position of star

Sun

**Side View**

Apparent position of star as seen from Earth during solar eclipse

Actual position of star behind sun

Sun in eclipse

**Front View As Seen From Earth**

# RELIGIONS OF THE WORLD

Religion means many different things to different people, but it is found to some degree in virtually every culture on Earth, past and present. Evidence suggests that it even existed in prehistoric times and that Neanderthals may have practiced religious rituals.

Today, religion takes thousands of different forms, some simple, others complex. Such diversity makes it hard to identify elements common to all faiths. But most contemporary scholars define religion by identifying a set of widely but not universally shared characteristics. These characteristics can include a collection of beliefs about what is ultimately important and real, a community of believers, images of a fulfilled human life, a set of rituals and practices (such as the Christian sacraments), authoritative texts (such as the Buddhist *Lotus Sutra*), and authoritative traditions (such as dress codes and dietary rules).

For many people, religion involves worship of one supreme being or deity. Other people worship many gods. Still others have a more general belief in a higher power or universal life force. Beliefs and practices generally include a moral code governing thoughts and actions. Almost always, this includes what many call the Golden Rule: Treat others as you would like to be treated.

Although beliefs vary widely, most religions share certain characteristics, including a community of believers, a set of rituals and practices, and authoritative texts. *Clockwise from left:* Muslim pilgrims pray in Mecca; Native Americans perform a ceremonial dance; a Jewish boy reads the Torah.

Not everyone who is religious belongs to an identifiable religion, however. Some simply believe in a divine power or have other spiritual beliefs that cannot be categorized. Also, there are some who have no religion at all. Current statistics indicate that at least one in ten people is nonreligious. People in this group often consider themselves atheists or agnostics. Atheists believe there is no God or supreme being. Agnostics believe it is not possible to know if these things exist.

▶ PURPOSE

Religion serves many purposes. On one level it unites those with similar goals and beliefs and requires them to behave in a way that benefits others, or at least those who share the same beliefs. These behaviors have traditionally helped people form communities, raise families, and live together more

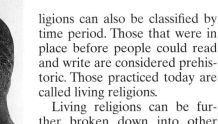

Like many ancient peoples, the Greeks and the Egyptians believed in multiple gods. *Above:* An Egyptian papyrus shows the falcon-headed god Horus approaching Osiris (seated). *Right:* Zeus was the chief god of the ancient Greeks.

harmoniously (thus ensuring survival). That is largely because in many countries and regions, there was just one religion; the religious diversity we see today did not exist. Everyone had the same faith, and the ruler was both a political and a religious leader. In some parts of the world, this is still the case.

On another level, religion can provide a sense of purpose, fulfillment, and inner peace. It gives many believers a sense of security. They feel that God or a higher power is watching over and protecting them, and that there is life—and greater happiness—after death. Religion can also be comforting to its followers during difficult times.

Despite these benefits, religion can have drawbacks. Some people are intolerant of those with different beliefs. This has led to countless wars, past and present, as well as violent clashes between groups and individuals.

▶ TYPES OF RELIGIONS

There are several ways to classify religions. One way is to group them according to their beliefs about God. For instance, followers of a religion can believe in one God (**monotheism**) or more than one God (**polytheism**). Re-

ligions can also be classified by time period. Those that were in place before people could read and write are considered prehistoric. Those practiced today are called living religions.

Living religions can be further broken down into other groups. Members of each group are related to each other because, for example, they all developed in the same part of the world or share some authoritative texts or beliefs. They may also be related because they revere some of the same ancient teachers or prophets or influenced each other over time.

One large group includes the faiths that originated in India and spread throughout the greater part of Asia. The most important in this group are Hinduism, Buddhism, Jainism, and Sikhism.

A second important group of related religions and belief systems originated in China and Japan. To a great extent they remained in the lands of their birth. These religions and belief systems are Confucianism, Taoism, and Shinto. To their followers they chart a way of life based on time-honored traditions, texts, and revered leaders.

Nearly one-third of the people in the world today are followers of religions in a third related group: Judaism, Christianity, and Islam. One of their bonds of kinship is monotheism.

All of these major religions can be further divided into subgroups such as branches, denominations, schools, movements, and sects.

▶ HISTORY

It is possible that religion started to develop as early humans tried to understand life's mysteries. They may have wondered, as many still do, how and why the world was created. They may have questioned the purpose of their existence, and tried to understand death. They may have also tried to strengthen the bonds uniting them by participating in rituals.

Because it is so difficult to find and interpret artifacts from our prehistoric ancestors, however, theories about their religious beliefs and practices are inconclusive. Still, there is considerable evidence to suggest that before the invention of writing, many groups of humans believed in male and female spirits who inhabited and controlled the natural world. Many also likely believed that their dead ancestors continued to exist as spirits. And many seemed to have worshiped or revered animals as totems, or symbols of their clan.

### Judaism

Probably the oldest of the world's living religions is Judaism, which began about 1800 B.C. in the Middle East. According to the Hebrew scriptures (what Christians call the Bible's Old Testament), the Lord (God) established a covenant (agreement) with a wandering herdsman named Abraham. In return for Abraham's loyalty and devotion, the Lord promised him land and numerous descendants. He also promised to bless all peoples through him and his descendants (who thus became God's chosen people). Approximately six centuries later, this covenant was honored and reaffirmed when God delivered the Jews and their leader Moses from slavery in Egypt. Jews believe that during this time Moses received the Ten Commandments,

Moses is a prominent figure in Judaism. Jews believe that God gave him the Ten Commandments—laws for moral and devout living.

which are God's laws for devout and moral living.

Although many consider these stories a blend of fact and legend, they indicate the importance to Jews of belief in one God. This is a God who loves them, demands faithfulness, and guides the course of history. Eventually the people settled into the land promised them and established a kingdom. They developed a rich religious life centered on sacrifices at the Temple in Jerusalem, then lost their land to foreign invaders.

After this, Jewish religious leaders (rabbis) helped Judaism shift its emphasis from sacrifices to prayerful gatherings in homes and synagogues. They also emphasized careful interpretation of God's laws and produced authoritative texts called the **Mishnah** and the **Talmud**.

Today there are about 14 million Jews worldwide. They are divided into numerous groups, though three are especially prominent: Orthodox, Conservative, and Reform.

### Christianity

Christianity emerged during the first century A.D. in Palestine, a province of the Roman Empire, as a sect within Judaism. It is based on the life and teachings of Jesus Christ, a Jewish religious teacher and reformer. Jesus emphasized the authority of

God and the importance of humans having complete trust in God, caring for the poor, and being sincere in all of their actions. The large crowds that gathered to hear Jesus brought him to the attention of the Roman authorities. Fearful that he was stirring up the populace against them, the Roman authorities had Jesus arrested, tried as a political criminal, and eventually crucified (executed by nailing to a cross).

After the crucifixion, Jesus' followers believed God had raised him from the dead. They began to spread his message throughout the Roman Empire. They believed that through Jesus, humans are forgiven by God and granted eternal life in God's fellowship.

From their beginnings, Christians have accepted the authority of the Hebrew scriptures. They eventually added to these texts their own sacred writings, called the New Testament, to form the Christian Bible. Christians believe they worship the same God as do Jews. Because of their belief in salvation through the risen Jesus Christ, however, they maintain that the one God exists in three divine persons: the Father, Son, and Holy Spirit. Traditionally Christians have believed that Jesus is the fully human incarnation of the divine Son.

In the centuries that followed, the Christian church grew tremendously. Christianity is now the world's largest religion, with about 2 billion followers.

## Islam

Islam began in the 600's in Arabia. It is based on what its followers, Muslims, believe are divine statements, or revelations, from Allah (God) to the prophet Mohammed. Muslims believe that Mohammed was the last of a line of prophets that include Abraham, Moses, and Jesus (whom they do not consider divine). They believe that the teachings of these prophets were sometimes misinterpreted or distorted by their followers until the appearance of Mohammed.

Muslims believe Allah revealed his will to Mohammed in a series of speeches. These speeches were eventually collected in the **Koran**, Islam's scripture. According to the Koran, there are five practices that Muslims must follow. These include at least one public profession of Islam's creed, the **Shahadah**: "There is no God but Allah; Mohammed is Allah's Prophet." Muslim practices also include praying five times a day, fasting during the day for a month each year, giving to charity, and traveling at least once to Mecca, the birthplace of Mohammed and Islam's holiest site.

Islam is currently the dominant religion in northern Africa and the Middle East, as well as in some South Asian countries: Pakistan, Bangladesh, Malaysia, and Indonesia. It has approximately 1 billion followers.

## Hinduism

Hinduism, the most complex of the major living religions, is the name given to a diverse set of beliefs and practices that originated among the inhabitants of India. Hinduism has no founder and no prophet. Its origins are not clearly established. Some Hindus believe that there

Christianity is the world's largest religion. It is based on the life and teachings of Jesus Christ, who lived in Palestine approximately 2,000 years ago.

are many gods and goddesses, some believe in one supreme god, and some believe that these divinities are symbols of an ultimate reality called **Brahman**.

Still, Hindus do agree on several key points. The first is that people have eternal selves that are trapped in a cycle of rebirths. When a person dies, he or she is reborn. The quality of the next life depends upon the person's **karma**, or actions, in previous lives. The law of karma rewards good actions and punishes the bad. Ultimately, a person with good karma will reach **moksha**, a state of happiness in which the eternal self is released from the cycle of rebirth and is therefore free of earthly cares and problems.

In addition, Hindus believe that karma determines which caste one is born into. Castes are rigid social divisions ranked according to religious purity that dictate a Hindu's social and religious obligations. Recent laws have made some aspects of the caste system illegal. Hindus also believe that there are many different ways to achieve moksha. Some practice disciplined meditation; others worship images of a deity to receive its blessings. Most Hindus also participate in certain rituals for important life transitions (marriage and death, for instance). There are approximately 900 million Hindus in the world today.

In this illustration from the *Gitagovinda*, a Hindu poem, Krishna (on left) is rejected by his consort Radha. Krishna is one of many Hindu deities.

## Buddhism

Buddhism is one of the most widespread and oldest religions. It was founded in India during the 500's B.C. and evolved as a reaction against the elaborate rituals and caste system of the ancient Indian Vedic religion.

Buddhism is based on the teachings of the historical Buddha, Siddhartha Gautama, a Hindu prince. Unlike some religious traditions (for example, Roman Catholic Christianity), Buddhism has no central authority. Nor is it based on belief in a supreme creator, although it does accept the existence of lesser deities. This religion centers instead on concepts known as the Three Jewels. They are the Buddha-jewel (the teacher), the **dharma** jewel (the Buddha's teachings), and the **sangha** jewel (religious community).

The most important Buddhist teachings are embodied in the Four Noble Truths. They consist of the following: Unenlightened life is suffering; the origin of suffering is ignorance and desire; suffering can be brought to an end in enlightenment and **nirvana**; and there is a path to the attainment of enlightenment and nirvana.

Buddhists believe that those who follow the Middle Way and the Eightfold Path can attain nirvana. Following the Middle Way means avoiding extremes of both desire and self-denial. The Eightfold Path outlines actions and ways of thinking that stress morality, compassion, and respect for others, as well as self-discipline and wisdom. Many Buddhists also believe that one can rely on the

caste system. But unlike the Buddha, Prince Vardhamana did not go on to teach moderation. He urged his followers to take the extreme path of asceticism, or self-denial. Vardhamana became known as Mahavira, the Great Hero. He was honored not because he had conquered others but because he had conquered himself. Jains revere Mahavira as a Jina (a perfected human being who has conquered bodily existence) as well as 23 other Jinas who came before him.

After Mahavira's death (from fasting), his teachings were gathered in many books. These became the sacred scriptures of the Jains. Most of them teach how to give up all worldly pleasures and how the educated person should live and behave. The sum of his teachings is given in one word: **ahimsa**. Ahimsa literally means "noninjury" or "nonviolence," and it implies a reverence for all life.

All Jains are vegetarians. Jains cannot take part in war. They cannot be butchers or engage in any work that might cause them to kill or injure any living thing. They cannot even be farmers, for in tilling the soil they might kill worms. Because of the limitations placed upon the Jains by their religion, many of them become teachers, merchants, or bankers.

Jains honor Mahavira and the other Jinas by attending festivals at temples, meditating on the ideal form of life the Jinas have achieved, and fasting. Jainism is found mostly in India and has about 4 million followers.

A procession of Buddhist monks files past a temple in Thailand. Buddhism is based on the teachings of the Buddha (*right*), a Hindu prince who was probably born in the 500's B.C.

power of spiritual beings called bodhisattvas and heavenly buddhas to help them reach nirvana.

Buddhism, which is divided into a number of schools, was the dominant religion of Asia before Communism, and there are still many Buddhists there. Buddhists are found in lesser numbers throughout the world. Estimates on the total number of Buddhists vary considerably and range from 230–500 million. An exact figure is hard to determine partly because no one knows how many Chinese are Buddhists.

### Jainism

Jainism also began in India, probably between 600 and 500 B.C. Another Hindu prince, Nataputta Vardhamana, began to preach what at first seemed to be the same reforms of Hinduism as those taught by the Buddha. He, too, accepted karma and believed in reincarnation. He, too, rejected the

### Sikhism

Sikhism was established in the 1500's. It arose in northwest India and what is now Pakistan as an alternative to Islam and Hinduism, which were considered too formal and ritualized. Even so, Sikhism is often described as a mixture of Hinduism and Islam. Sikhs, however, prefer to quote their founder Guru Nanak: "God is neither Hindu nor Muslim and the path that I follow is God's."

Sikhs believe in one God, who can be known through meditation. They believe that through devotion to God, primarily expressed in songs of praise, humans can overcome their ignorance of God and their sinful self-centeredness. Like Buddhists and Hindus, Sikhs believe in karma and reincarnation. Liberation from this cycle of rebirths occurs when one is united with God.

Sikhs revere a succession of nine human gurus who are considered spiritual successors of Guru Nanak. They also treasure *Adi Granth* ("original book"), which they regard as inspired by God and having the same authority as the gurus. They worship in temples and elsewhere and pray many times each day. There are about 23 million Sikhs worldwide.

## Confucianism

Confucianism is often regarded as more of a philosophy and system of ethics than a religion. It originated in China about 500 B.C. and profoundly influenced Chinese culture. Confucianism's founder was K'ung Ch'iu, also called Confucius, who became known as K'ung-fu-tzu (K'ung the Philosopher).

Confucius, a great teacher and sage, spent most of his life studying and reinterpreting ancient records, which he organized into the Four Books. To these he added a fifth book of his own, called *The Autumn and Spring Annals*. At his death he willed these books to his followers. Confucius' disciples added to his books selections from the master's sayings, known as the *Analects*.

Confucianism stresses the importance of living in harmony with others and adopting certain virtues. One of the most important is humaneness (**jen**), or a variation of the Golden Rule. This belief system also stresses appropriate actions for various circumstances (**li**), love of family, righteousness, honesty and responsibility, and meeting one's obligations to society.

Followers of Confucianism often also follow the teachings of Buddhism or Taoism—or both of these. For this reason, the exact number of Confucians is not known. But it is estimated that there are nearly 160 million. Most are in China.

## Taoism

Taoism, also from China, is a philosophical and religious system that originated sometime between the 300's and 200's B.C. It is traditionally traced back to Lao Tzu ("Old Philosopher"). Lao Tzu may have been a keeper of government archives. Taoist tradition holds that he was a contemporary of Confucius and that he wrote the 5,000-word *Tao-te ching*, or *Classic of Tao and Its Virtue*, also called the *Lao-tzu*. This work, which contains the basic Taoist teachings, has been one of China's most important books.

As Taoism developed, several themes became prominent. These themes center on the **Tao** (also spelled **Dao**), which is considered the source of everything in the universe. Tao also refers to the flowing energy and the natural order of the universe (reflected in the passage of seasons, for example). It has two complementary aspects, yin and yang (for example, dark and light or feminine and masculine). Being in harmony with the Tao requires a proper balance of these energies, which Taoists maintain comes naturally to humans when a simple, receptive approach to life is taken.

Taoists do not agree on the ultimate destiny of humans. Some believe that the pattern of energy that makes up our bodies and minds will dissolve and be redistributed among the different life forms. Others believe in life after death in one of several heavens or hells. Those Taoists who believe in life after death also believe in and worship numerous gods. These gods grant a happy afterlife to those who behave well, acknowledge their failings, and participate in religious festivals. The two most important of these festivals are chai and chiao. The first is intended to deliver souls from hell and the second is intended to win favor from the gods.

Taoism is found primarily in mainland China and Taiwan and has about 20 million followers. This religion is often practiced along with Buddhism and Confucianism.

## Shinto

The religion of Japan is best known by its Chinese name, Shinto, which means "The Way of the Gods." In Japanese it is called **Kami-no-michi**, which means the same thing. Shinto began many centuries ago, when the Japanese thought their islands were the only inhabited places on Earth. They believed in a number of nature gods and goddesses. Until recently they believed that their emperor was descended from these deities.

The most important sacred books of Shinto are *Kojiki* (*Record of Ancient Matters*) and the *Nihon-gi* (*Chronicles of Japan*). Assembled in

In Shinto, the religion of Japan, practitioners often visit public shrines, particularly during festivals. Shrines can be large or small, and each is unique. Some followers also have small shrines in their homes.

the early 700's, they are collections of myths of a time when the world was young and the gods mingled with the Japanese people.

The concept of **kami** is important in Shinto. Kami can be many things, including certain animals and objects, forces of nature, and spirits of the dead. They help connect humans to the wider social and natural world.

To follow the way of the kami is to embrace what is pure. This includes the virtues of sincerity, respect for others and nature, and gratitude toward one's elders and ancestors. It is also important to avoid impurities such as selfishness, dishonesty, disease, and death.

Followers of the kami way demonstrate their reverence for the kami both at home and at shrines. They celebrate numerous festivals throughout the year. These festivals have also contributed to a strong sense of national and ethnic identity among the Japanese. At times, Shinto has been the official religion of the country, but it is no longer. There are approximately 4 million Shintos in Japan.

### ▶ RELIGION TODAY

As always, religion continues to change, but technology has accelerated the process by allowing us to share an unprecedented amount of information. Also, people are no longer confined to isolated communities. These and other factors expose us to many different kinds of people and ideas, including those from different religious groups.

Especially in the United States, with its remarkable ethnic diversity, one is likely to have followers of different religions as neighbors, fellow students, co-workers, or friends. As a result, more people have learned about other faiths and have found that most share certain basic beliefs and values.

In addition, there has also been a shift in the way people view themselves in relation to society. The growing influence of contemporary Western culture on the rest of the world has resulted in a greater emphasis on individual freedom. This includes the right of the individual to choose his or her own faith—which may or may not be the faith of one's family or culture—or to refrain from participating in any organized religion.

At the same time, many organized religions have become more politically active and have encouraged greater social responsibility among followers on such issues as poverty, hunger, human rights, the environment, and world peace. Many organized religions have also sought to overcome long-held differences. A recent example of this is Pope John Paul's historic visit to a Syrian mosque in 2001. This was the first time a pope visited a Muslim house of worship.

Despite this, religious differences continue to exist, particularly among fundamentalist groups who are often intolerant of other faiths and ethnic groups. This continues to fuel conflict in many parts of the world, such as the Middle East and Northern Ireland.

Other trends today include the formation of new religions and belief systems. Examples include New Age ideologies and the Baha'i faith. New Age is a mixture of elements from various religious traditions, ancient practices, and belief systems. Baha'i, one of the fastest-growing religions in North America, is also a mixture of sorts. It considers all religions unified and humanity a single race.

W.T. DICKENS
Department of Religious Studies
University of Miami

See also BUDDHISM; CHRISTIANITY; CONFUCIUS; EASTERN ORTHODOX CHURCHES; HINDUISM; ISLAM; JEWS; JUDAISM; PROTESTANTISM; ROMAN CATHOLIC CHURCH; TEN COMMANDMENTS; and articles on different continents and countries.

# RELIGIOUS HOLIDAYS

Religious holidays have been celebrated throughout history. They involve feasts and festivals that serve many purposes. Our word "holiday" means "holy day." It is a time set aside as holy, sacred, or special.

All religions have holidays. Some occur according to the solar calendar. (The Gregorian calendar, which begins on January 1, is a well-known example of this type of calendar.) Others occur according to the lunar calendar, which is based on the phases of the moon.

Religious holidays are observed by people of many faiths, in many different ways. They can include special meals, such as the Jewish Passover Seder (*above left*), or rituals, such as the lighting of Advent candles by Christians (*bottom right*). Some holidays, such as the Hindu festival Holi (*above right*), are a time of great fun.

Holidays that fall at different times each solar year, such as Passover and Easter, are called movable holidays. Holidays that always fall on the same date on the solar calendar, such as Christmas and All Saints' Day, are called immovable holidays.

### ▶ WEEKLY HOLIDAYS

The first day of the week, Sunday, is a holy day for most Christians. It marks the day that Christ is believed to have risen from the dead. Churches hold services, and most people rest from their usual work. It is generally a legal holiday throughout the United States. The Jewish sabbath falls on Saturday. It begins at sunset on Friday and lasts until sunset on Saturday. Muslims keep Friday as their day for special community prayer services.

### ▶ SPRING AND SUMMER HOLIDAYS

Passover, or Pesah, is one of the most important holidays in Judaism. It is also called the Festival of Freedom because it celebrates the Exodus, God's delivery of the Israelites from slavery in ancient Egypt. It lasts seven or eight days, depending on one's location and tradition, and comes in March or April. Observant Jews refrain from any work on the first and last days of Passover, do not eat leavened bread, and follow specific rules for the preparation of all food.

Shavu'ot, or the Festival of Weeks, falls on the fiftieth day after the second day of Passover. For this reason, it is also known as Pentecost, from the Greek word for fiftieth, pentekoste. It is a time to give thanks for both the spring harvest and the Torah (which Jews believe was given to Moses by God on Mount Sinai).

The Jewish Arbor Day, Tu B'Shevat, is celebrated on the 15th day of the Hebrew month of Shevat. Shevat marks the beginning of spring in Israel and falls in January or February on the Gregorian calendar. It is celebrated by eating fruits and, particularly among the children of Israel, planting trees.

Easter is the most important movable feast of the Christian church. Its date, determined by the date of Passover, fixes the dates of the holidays connected with it—Lent, Shrove Tuesday, Ash Wednesday, Holy Thursday, Palm Sunday, and others.

Shrove Tuesday falls on the day before Ash Wednesday, which marks the beginning of Lent. The name comes from the practice of confessing and being absolved, or shriven, of one's sins before Lent. The day has many other names, including Mardi Gras. Mardi Gras is French for Fat Tuesday. This name came from the custom of housewives cleaning their cupboards of the fats, eggs, and other foods that are not eaten during the fast days that follow. They used up the forbidden ingredients in rich foods. Since Shrove Tuesday is the last day before the fast, it is a time for feasting and fun.

Pentecost takes place fifty days after Easter. It should not be confused with the Jewish holiday of the same name. In antiquity and the Middle Ages, many new Christians were baptized at Pentecost. They dressed in white clothing for the ceremony. For this reason the day came to be called White Sunday in England. It was later shortened to Whitsunday. Pentecost commemorates the coming of the Holy Spirit with its gift of faith to the apostles and disciples of Christ.

The Hindu fire festival, Holi, is celebrated in northern India during the full moon of late February or March. In Bengal the Holi festival honors Krishna, a Hindu god, and his destruction of evil forces. It is a time of great playfulness, when rules for proper behavior are set aside. Celebrants cheerfully spray one another with colored water and powders.

Caturmasya, which occurs in late July or early August, commemorates the four-month sleep of Vishnu, the Hindu god of social and cosmic order. During these four months, it is believed that demonic forces threatened to take over the world. Their defeat is celebrated during Navaratri, in the fall.

Buddhists in southeast Asia celebrate Wesak in April or May, which celebrates the birth, enlightenment, and death of the Buddha. This ancient and popular festival occurs during the full moon. Homes are decorated with lanterns, and the people go to the temples to pray. In Japan, this festival, called Obon, happens in July or August.

### ▶ FALL AND WINTER HOLIDAYS

The most sacred time of the year among Jews, the High Holy Days, begins with Rosh Hashanah, the New Year, and ends ten days later on Yom Kippur, the Day of Atonement. Rosh Hashanah is observed sometime between early September and October. Jews believe that during this period God remembers good and evil deeds and decides on rewards and punishment. This is a time to reflect on one's actions and to seek forgiveness from others and God. God's judgment is finalized on Yom Kippur. Those who observe Yom Kippur fast from sundown on the eve of Yom Kippur until sundown the next day.

The Jewish Feast of the Booths, or Sukkoth, follows Yom Kippur by five days. In many places children build small booths or huts of branches. This is in memory of the shelters in which the Jews lived during their years of wandering through the wilderness after the Exodus. The festival, which lasts nine or ten days, is also a thanksgiving for the fall harvest.

Hanukkah is an eight-day festival of lights celebrated by Jews in late November or De-

During Wesak, a holiday honoring the Buddha, many Buddhists burn joss sticks. It is believed that the smoke from these sticks sends messages to deceased relatives.

Muslims gather in front of a Pakistani mosque to celebrate Id al-Fitr. This holiday marks the end of the Muslim month of Ramadan, a period of purification and reflection.

cember. It commemorates the rededication of the Temple in Jerusalem by the Maccabees in 165 B.C.

The Feast of All Saints, November 1, also known as All Hallows or Hallowmas, is an important feast of the Roman Catholic Church. It honors all saints, particularly those who do not have a day of their own. All Souls' Day, November 2, is observed by the Roman Catholic Church. Masses are said for the souls of the faithful. Martinmas, on November 11, honors Saint Martin and is a harvest feast in many European countries. It was the Thanksgiving Day of the Middle Ages. Traditional foods such as roast goose are eaten.

The Feast of the Immaculate Conception, on December 8, is a time of great celebration in Spain. It is also Mother's Day in that country. The Day of Our Lady of Guadalupe, December 12, is Mexico's greatest religious holiday. It commemorates the Virgin Mary's appearance before a humble Mexican peasant. A church was built on the spot where she is believed to have appeared. Thousands of people visit the shrine of Our Lady of Guadalupe each year.

Advent (from the Latin adventus, meaning "a coming") is observed by Christian churches in honor of the coming of Christ. It covers a period that includes the four Sundays before Christmas. Christmas, which celebrates Christ's birth, is December 25.

Epiphany, on January 6, marks the end of the Twelve Days of Christmas.

Navaratri commemorates the defeat of the buffalo demon by the Hindu goddess Durga. This prepares the way for light to return at the winter solstice. This is celebrated in mid-November during Divali, the Hindu festival of lights. It is dedicated to Lakshmi, goddess of wealth, and is also the Hindu new year.

Among Muslims, there are several important holidays. Since they are based on the lunar calendar, the dates change each year. Ramadan, the ninth month of the Islamic year, is a time of purification and reflection. During this entire period, adult Muslims who are in good health must fast between sunrise and sunset. The last ten days of Ramadan, Laylat al-Qadr, are celebrated as the time that the prophet Mohammed is believed to have received his first revelation from God. Id al-Fitr is a period of feasting that marks the end of Ramadan. It is a day of merry-making that centers around one's close friends and family. Some Muslims also celebrate Mouloud, a nine-day period marking the birth of Mohammed. Mouloud includes many feasts, fairs, and pageants.

Reviewed by W. T. DICKENS
Department of Religious Studies
University of Miami

See also CALENDAR; CARNIVALS; CHRISTMAS; EASTER; HANUKKAH; HOLIDAYS; JUDAISM; PASSOVER; and PURIM.

# REMBRANDT (1606–1669)

The Dutch painter Rembrandt van Rijn was one of the greatest artists of the European baroque period. His paintings, drawings, and etchings cover a wide range of subjects—including portraits, landscapes, religious stories, and scenes of everyday life. His work displays a sympathetic understanding of human nature that continues to be admired today.

Rembrandt Harmenszoon van Rijn, one of seven children, was born in Leiden, Holland, on July 15, 1606. His father was a miller, and his mother was a baker's daughter. The simple, religious Harmenszoon family was called van Rijn ("of the Rhine") because the Rhine River flowed near their mill.

At 13, Rembrandt was enrolled in the University of Leiden. Soon after, he convinced his parents to allow him to study art with a local painter. After three years he went to Amsterdam to study with a noted artist, Pieter Lastman. Lastman had studied in Italy and had been influenced by the work of the Italian artist Caravaggio

*Self-Portrait* (1661–62)

(1573–1610). Though Rembrandt returned to Leiden after only six months, his stay in Amsterdam strongly affected his early style and subject matter.

Upon his return to Leiden, in 1625, Rembrandt shared a studio with a fellow artist, Jan Lievens. During his seven years in Leiden, Rembrandt painted ordinary people, including members of his own family. He also painted a number of self-portraits. He experimented with different techniques and was particularly interested in **chiaroscuro**—contrasts of light and dark.

About 1632 Rembrandt settled in Amsterdam, where there were more opportunities to paint portraits for rich patrons. In that year he painted his first group portrait, *The Anatomy Lesson of Dr. Tulp*, a picture of the Amsterdam Guild of Surgeons. His reputation established, he received many more commissions.

The next ten years were Rembrandt's happiest and most prosperous. In 1634 he married the beautiful and wealthy Saskia van Uijlenburgh. Rembrandt spent money extravagantly, buying fine clothes and jewels for Saskia and himself and purchasing a grand home that he filled with works of art. He worked long hours in his studio, producing paintings and teaching his many pupils.

The completion of the great group portrait known as *The Night Watch* in 1642 can be said to mark the end of Rembrandt's most successful period. That same year, Saskia died, leaving him with their infant son, Titus. At the same time, his style of portraiture was becoming less fashionable. Rembrandt began to paint more subjects of his own choosing, especially illustrations of Bible stories.

Earlier, Rembrandt had painted people in the midst of dramatic action. He had made them look like actors in a spotlight. Now he became more interested in people's inner feelings. The light in his paintings became a golden-brown haze surrounding the figures. His paintings, including his later self-portraits, reflected a deeper understanding of the human soul.

In 1656, despite the efforts of his son and of his devoted housekeeper, Hendrickje Stoffels, Rembrandt went bankrupt. He had to sell all his belongings and move to a poorer neighborhood. Yet Rembrandt's most creative period was the last ten years of his life. Though his popularity had declined, he continued to receive important commissions. One of these was perhaps his greatest group portrait, *The Syndics of the Cloth Merchants' Guild* (1661–62).

In 1663 Hendrickje died. Five years later Titus died. Old and in failing health, Rembrandt died the following year, on October 4, 1669, in Amsterdam.

Reviewed by Aaron H. Jacobsen
Author, *The Baroque Sketchbook*

**REMINGTON, FREDERIC.** See Wyoming (Famous People).

# RENAISSANCE

The word "renaissance" comes from the Latin *renasci*, which means "reborn." In European history, the Renaissance period saw a rebirth of interest in the learning and arts of ancient Greece and Rome. The Renaissance began in Italy about 1300, in the Late Middle Ages. It gradually developed in other European countries and ended about 1600.

The Renaissance saw a reawakening of the classical concern for wisdom and beauty. But it was also a time of discovery and growth. In these years, Europeans developed new scientific ideas and inventions, produced new literature and art, and discovered new lands and trade routes. They began to ask questions and think about the world in new ways.

These developments grew out of changes that took place late in the Middle Ages. Feudalism, which had structured society for much of the Middle Ages, began to break down. Society was no longer chiefly made up of feudal landlords and their vassals. The middle class, composed of merchants and artisans, became more important. Wealthy merchants and bankers began to play a major role in government. City-states and monarchies replaced feudal fiefdoms. People also began to take a more worldly view of life. They became less reliant on religion as the guiding force in their daily lives.

In his collection of scenes from the life of Pope Pius II, Italian painter Pinturicchio depicted court life in the city-state of Siena.

## ▶ THE RENAISSANCE BEGINS IN ITALY

The Renaissance originated in Italy for several reasons. The Italian peninsula juts into the Mediterranean Sea, which had long been the main trading route between Europe and the East. Italians traveled to foreign lands. Italian merchants and bankers did business all over Europe. Increasing trade brought great changes in European life. Cities grew, and wealth increased. The ruins of ancient Rome, a source of inspiration for the Renaissance, were in Italy. Italian scholars led the revival of interest in ancient learning. Artists from Italy set the fashions in painting, architecture, and sculpture. Italian explorers discovered new lands.

### Italian City-States

At the time of the Renaissance, Italy was not an independent nation with a unified government. It was divided into a number of in-dependent states that competed with each other for leadership. The Kingdom of the Two Sicilies in the south was the largest but also the poorest. In central Italy the pope ruled the city of Rome and a group of states called the Papal States. He was their **secular** (earthly) leader as well as their spiritual leader. Northern Italy was divided among several city-states, of which the most important were Venice, Milan, and Florence. Their rulers supported artists and scholars by commissioning buildings, monuments, statues, paintings, and other works. This system of **patronage** helped new ideas flourish.

**Venice.** Situated on the Adriatic Sea, the island city of Venice was an important port during the Renaissance. Spices and other products of the East passed through Venice on the way to other European cities. In theory Venice was a republic, whose government was headed by an official called the doge

Art and learning flourished in Florence, Italy, under the patronage of the ruling Medici family. This view shows Florence in 1480. The cathedral dome rises over the city center.

(duke). In fact it was an aristocracy, ruled by members of noble families. Surrounded by water, Venice was protected from the struggles of other Italian cities. Peaceful and wealthy, it devoted itself to the development of commerce and art.

**Milan.** Situated on the main trade routes that ran through the Alpine mountain passes, Milan profited from trade and also manufactured fine cloth and arms. The city had once been a republic, but in the 1300's a series of strong rulers, or despots, took over its government. Foremost among these were Gian Galeazzo Visconti, Francesco Sforza, and Ludovico Sforza.

**Florence.** Florence was an active city of merchants, craftsmen, artists, and scholars. Rich patrons employed architects to build fine homes, which they filled with paintings and statues. They paid for the building and decoration of churches and monasteries. They collected libraries and supported scholars. Noble families competed for glory as well as power. From this long struggle the Medici family emerged victorious in 1434. They ruled Florence with an iron hand. Lorenzo de' Medici, known as Lorenzo the Magnificent, brought the city to

a height of artistic glory achieved only by a few civilizations in history. Renaissance popes were great builders and patrons of the arts, and many gifted architects, painters, and sculptors were attracted to the papal court. When Leo X, a member of the Medici family, became pope in 1513, Rome replaced Florence as the center of Italian art.

▶ **THE SPREAD OF NEW IDEAS**

As trade between Italy and other parts of Europe increased, Italian culture and ideas spread. Scholars and artists traveled to Italy to study. Italian scholars and artists took positions in cities elsewhere in Europe. Warfare played a role in the spread of new ideas, too. In the late 1400's and early 1500's, armies from France and Spain made occasional raids into Italy. Soldiers returned home inspired by the beauty of Italian cities.

The development of printed books also helped spread new ideas during the Renaissance. Before the 1440's all copies of books had to be made by hand. The invention of printing

Printed books helped new ideas spread. This work by the scholar Erasmus was published in 1537.

with movable type, attributed to Johann Gutenberg, made it possible to produce many copies of a book at a time and thus spread interest in all types of learning.

As the Renaissance spread northward, it was reflected in different ways. Throughout Europe, however, the common threads were a revival of classical learning, advances in science, and a flowering of literature and the arts.

Geoffrey Chaucer, author of the *Canterbury Tales*, incorporated the major philosophical and artistic concerns of his age into his writings.

### THE HUMANISTS

The scholars who created the new interest in Greek and Roman antiquity were known as humanists. The word "humanism" comes from the Latin *humanitas*, meaning "culture." But it has also come to express the concern with human life that characterized the ancient Greeks and Romans.

Francesco Petrarch, one of the first humanists, wrote an imaginary conversation between himself and Saint Augustine, the great medieval church scholar. In it he examined whether a man should concern himself with this life or with the hope of heaven. Petrarch insisted that it was perfectly reasonable for men on Earth to seek the good things of this life and leave the glories of heaven until "we shall have arrived there." The humanists had little interest in theology (knowledge about God). Instead they studied history and read poetry that praised human deeds or expressed human feelings.

### A New Interest in Ancient Scholars

Petrarch revived the interest in ancient scholars. The humanists read how Rome became a great republic, as told by the historian Livy. They delighted in the poetry of Vergil, which told of ancient heroes. They read Cicero's letters and orations, filled with advice on how to conduct both private and public affairs. The early humanists also read Greek authors, for the Greeks had been the teachers of the Romans. Professors from Greek lands of the eastern Mediterranean were encouraged to come to Italy to teach.

The humanists modeled their works after those of the ancient authors. They copied the Latin of ancient times rather than the "new" style of Latin, called Vulgate, used during the Middle Ages. The humanists particularly admired Cicero, and they imitated his writings. Some of the humanists modeled their speeches after those once given in the Roman Senate. They tried to write letters like those of Cicero and to write histories as they imagined Livy would have written.

### Growth of National Literature

The humanists also wrote in the **vernacular**, the everyday language of the people. Many of these works remain classics of the first rank. Petrarch wrote sonnets in Italian, and his student Giovanni Boccaccio also wrote the *Decameron*, a collection of stories, in Italian. The Dutch scholar Desiderius Erasmus, in his *Praise of Folly*, poked fun at human follies, as did the French author

## WONDER QUESTION

### What is a Renaissance man?

A Renaissance man (or woman) is a person with many talents and accomplishments. This was an ideal of the Renaissance. Leonardo da Vinci is often named as the perfect example of a Renaissance man. He was a painter, sculptor, writer, architect, inventor, engineer, and even something of a scientist.

*Il cortegiano (The Courtier)*, a book by Baldassare Castiglione, describes the ideal Renaissance man. According to Castiglione, a true gentleman should be able to do many things. He should be witty. He should be skilled in arms and such vigorous sports as hunting, swimming, and wrestling. He should be a scholar, a writer, an orator, a poet, and a musician. The ideal tells much about the spirit of the Renaissance. It was an age when people believed in their ability to achieve great things.

**Giovanni Boccaccio** (1313–75), born in Paris, France, was a leading scholar and writer of the Italian Renaissance. He spent most of his life in Florence and, as a student of Petrarch's, helped lay the foundations of humanist thought. However, Boccaccio is best known for works written in Italian, especially the *Decameron*. It is a collection of 100 stories, supposedly told by a group of young people who fled Florence to escape the plague. The *Decameron* had a great influence on European literature.

**The Borgias** were a leading family in Renaissance Italy. Members of the family included political and church leaders who were involved in the wars and intrigues of the day, as well as patrons of the arts. Two Borgias became popes. **Alfonso de Borgia** (1378–1458) was elected Pope Calixtus III in 1455, and **Rodrigo Borgia** (1431?–1503) was elected Pope Alexander VI in 1492. Rodrigo's son **Cesare Borgia** (1475?–1507) gained a reputation for ruthlessness and treachery as he built a kingdom in central Italy. Rodrigo's daughter **Lucrezia Borgia** (1480–1519) was also involved in political intrigues. Her court at Ferrara was famous as a center for the arts.

Giovanni Boccaccio

Henry the Navigator

**Baldassare Castiglione** (1478–1529), born near Mantua, Italy, was a writer, courtier, and diplomat. Castiglione was a member of the ducal court of Urbino and also served the pope. He is best known for *Il cortegiano* (*The Courtier*), a book published in 1528 that describes the qualities of the ideal attendants of a royal court. Translated into several languages, it had a wide influence during the Renaissance.

**Henry the Navigator** (1394–1460), born in Oporto, Portugal, financed voyages of exploration and advanced the science of navigation. A Portuguese prince, Henry sponsored voyages to the Madeira Islands and along the western coast of Africa. His support led to the development of the ship known as the Portuguese car-

François Rabelais in his satirical tales about the giants Gargantua and Pantagruel. In Spain, Miguel de Cervantes Saavedra created *Don Quixote*, one of the most famous characters in literature. And in England, William Shakespeare, the outstanding dramatist of the Renaissance, wrote dozens of masterpieces, including *Hamlet* and *Macbeth*. To this day, many people still consider Shakespeare the greatest playwright in all of history.

### Religion and the Humanists

Some humanists thought that devotion to religion would increase if people studied the scriptures in the original languages. A few learned Hebrew and studied the Old Testament in its original language. Erasmus had an edition of the New Testament printed in its original Greek. He thought that a Christian should read and study "the philosophy of Christ" as a follower of Plato would study

Plato's books. In the 1500's humanist views on religion helped start the Protestant Reformation, led by Martin Luther of Germany and others who questioned the teachings of the Roman Catholic Church.

### ▶ ART AND MUSIC

Renaissance artists turned for inspiration to the classical world. They borrowed classical forms and used them in new and different ways. And where medieval artists had focused on religion, Renaissance artists looked to the broader world around them.

Renaissance architects used the domes, round arches, and columns of classical architecture to create a new Renaissance architecture. Painters and sculptors often drew their subject matter from Greek and Roman mythology. But although the subject matter was old, the way of painting was new. Painters wished to give their work the ap-

avel, improved maps, and better navigational instruments. His observatory, near Sagres, was a center for the study of astronomy and navigation.

**Niccolò Machiavelli** (1469–1527), born in Florence, Italy, is best known for his book *Il principe* (*The Prince*). Machiavelli was a statesman and diplomat who rose to high positions in Florence in the early 1500's, a time when the Medici family

was briefly out of power. In 1512, when the Medici family returned to power, Machiavelli was removed from office. He turned to writing. *The Prince* presents his view of how a ruler should acquire and hold power. He was the first to express the idea that power, not ethics, is the most important factor in politics.

**Marguerite of Navarre** (1492–1549), born at Angoulême, France, was one of the most influential women of the French Renaissance. Marguerite was the sister of the French king Francis I and the wife of Henry II of Navarre. She was a patron of the arts and supported some of the leading humanist scholars and religious reformers of her day. She was also an author. Among her best-known works is the *Heptameron*, modeled on Boccaccio's *Decameron*.

**Michel Eyquem de Montaigne** (1533–92), born near Bordeaux, France, was a writer whose works reflected the questioning spirit of the Renaissance. Born to a noble family, Montaigne was a judge, politician, and diplomat. But he spent much of his life studying and writing at the family estate east of Bordeaux. His *Essais* (1572–80) created the form known as the essay. In these short works, Montaigne

Niccolò Machiavelli

Marguerite of Navarre

Francesco Petrarch

questioned accepted customs and argued for greater tolerance.

**Andrea Palladio** (1508–80), born in Padua, Italy, was an architect whose designs for palaces and villas remain vitally influential. Buildings in the Palladian style featured pediments, porticos, columns, and other classical touches. They were generally symmetrical (having balanced proportions).

**Francesco Petrarch** (1304–74), born in Arezzo, Italy, was among the greatest scholars and poets of his day. Petrarch spent much of his time at the courts of various Italian cities. He was a leader in the revival of classical learning and in the school of thought known as humanism. Petrarch is best known today for his Italian sonnets, addressed to Laura, an idealized love whose true identity is unknown.

pearance of reality. They studied the interplay of light and shade, perspective (the illusion of depth), and the human body. Improvements in painting techniques allowed painters to work in new ways. For example, the Flemish painter Jan van Eyck discovered that painting with slow-drying oils instead of with quick-drying egg tempera permitted him to work more slowly and in greater detail.

Artists of the Renaissance painted worldly subjects, as well as religious ones. Their works included portraits of many powerful and wealthy patrons, including kings and princes. Sometimes an artist painted his patron in a mythological or even sacred scene. In *Adoration of the Magi*, Sandro Botticelli pictured Cosimo de' Medici as one of the wise men kneeling before the infant Jesus. The artist even included himself in the painting.

Music, like art, became more worldly during the Renaissance. It was written for the-

ater and court entertainment, as well as for the church. The development of the violin, the flute, and the organ gave rise to a demand for new musical forms. The most important of these were the opera and the oratorio, in which voices were accompanied by instruments. The madrigal, a form of nonreligious song usually unaccompanied by instruments, was also popular.

▶ **EXPLORATION AND SCIENCE**

The Renaissance was an age when Europeans made many discoveries about the physical world. European explorers found sea routes to Asia and lands unknown to them in the Western Hemisphere. Their voyages changed popular ideas about geography. This period saw developments in navigation (the compass and other navigational tools), warfare (the introduction of gunpowder), mining, trade, and commerce. Weights, measures, and coinage were standardized to meet the growing needs of bankers and merchants.

These changes, along with the growth of independent thought, encouraged the development of scientific ideas and method. Most people still clung to medieval ideas. But some scholars laid the foundations of modern scientific method by direct observation and experiment. There were advances in mathematics, physics, and other sciences, including medicine and astronomy.

Bombast von Hohenheim, a Swiss-born physician and philosopher who went by the name Paracelsus, studied diseases among his contemporaries. He held that the functions of the body are chemical in

In the 1500's, Danish astronomer Tycho Brahe measured the movements of the stars and planets.

nature and so can be treated by chemical processes. Belgian anatomist Andreas Vesalius, a lecturer at the University of Padua, insisted that surgery should be performed by skilled doctors trained in anatomy and not by barbers, as was usual up to that time. He dissected human bodies in his laboratory, and in 1543 he published the first complete treatise on human anatomy.

The same year, Nicolaus Copernicus, a Polish-born astronomer living in Italy, published his observations that laid the foundations for the modern study of astronomy. Copernicus rejected the theory of the ancient Greek astronomer Ptolemy, who believed that the sun and other heavenly bodies revolve around the Earth. He turned to other ancient writers and found that several ancient Greeks had stated that the Earth moved around the sun. Starting from this point, Copernicus went on to develop his own theory that the Earth and other planets move around the sun and that the Earth rotates on its own axis.

▶ **THE END OF THE RENAISSANCE**

By the end of the 1500's, the ideas introduced by the Renaissance were themselves being replaced by even newer ideas: The Roman Catholic Church had been split by the Protestant Reformation; artists had begun to adopt new styles; scholars were increasingly questioning traditional views and accepted beliefs. But the styles, ideas, and scientific advances that emerged in later years all were built on foundations laid during the Renaissance.

KENNETH S. COOPER
George Peabody College

See also EXPLORATION AND DISCOVERY; HUMANISM; ITALY, ART AND ARCHITECTURE OF; MEDICI; REFORMATION; RENAISSANCE ART AND ARCHITECTURE; RENAISSANCE MUSIC.

Surrounded by water, Venice, Italy, was an important port during the Renaissance. It became famous as a center of commerce and art.

Giotto painted the fresco *Meeting at the Golden Gate* about 100 years before the Renaissance. His natural portrayal of people and their emotions influenced the painters of the Renaissance.

# RENAISSANCE ART AND ARCHITECTURE

In the early 1400's a new movement in art and literature began in Italy. This movement was known as the Renaissance. It spread all over Europe, and its influence has been felt to this day. The spirit of the Renaissance affected not just the arts but all phases of life. As a result, the name of this artistic movement has been given to the whole period of history of the 15th and 16th centuries.

## ▶THE SPIRIT OF THE RENAISSANCE

The word "renaissance" means "rebirth" or "revival." In the 14th century many Italian scholars believed that the arts had been declining in quality for 1,000 years. They admired the art and writing of the Classical Age (400 B.C.–A.D. 400), the time of the Greek and Roman empires. To revive the glory and grandeur of the ancient past, these scholars eagerly studied classical literature, architecture, and sculpture.

But the Renaissance was much more than a rebirth of classical art. It was a rejection of the Middle Ages, which were just ending. During medieval times, the arts were concerned mainly with religion, with the life of the spirit, with the hereafter. Little importance was given to life on earth except as a preparation for the next world. But as the 15th century began, Italians were turning their attention to the world about them. People started to think more about secular, or nonreligious, matters. They began placing faith in their own qualities and their own importance. This new spirit was called **humanism**. Discipline, unquestioning faith, obedience to authority—these medieval virtues were no longer blindly accepted. People asked questions and wanted to find their own answers.

Artists were among the first affected by the new spirit of humanism. In their work they began to focus on human life on earth.

### ▶ THE EARLY RENAISSANCE IN FLORENCE

The spirit of humanism was expressed by the painter Giotto di Bondone (1267?–1337) a century before the Renaissance actually began. Giotto's religious pictures were painted with great sympathy for the human qualities of his subjects. Holy figures are shown in countryside settings, dressed in worn and commonplace clothing. Giotto's lovely paintings seem to have been created especially for the common people of his time. Never before in Christian art had viewers been reminded that the saints of their religion were peasants like them.

Soon after Giotto died, a terrible plague, followed by small but destructive wars, swept through Italy. Progress—including the progress of art—was slowed. At least 50 years passed before Giotto's ideas became popular. But then it became clear that Giotto had been the forerunner of Renaissance painting.

#### The First Generation

Early in the 15th century, Florence, where Giotto had worked, became the first great center of the Renaissance. There a group of young artists experimented with new techniques. The architect and sculptor Filippo Brunelleschi (1377?–1446) was a leader of the group.

Attempting to break with the Gothic traditions of building, Brunelleschi looked to classical architecture for inspiration. After studying Roman buildings, he developed a new approach to architecture. In 1421 he designed the first Renaissance building, the Ospedale degli Innocenti (Foundling Hospital) in Florence. The facade (front) of the building has a **colonnade**—a series of wide arches separated by slender Corinthian columns like those used in classical architecture. Between the arches are colored terra-cotta (hard-baked clay) medallions of babes in swaddling clothes made in the workshop of Luca della Robbia (1400?–82). Harmonious proportions distinguish Brunelleschi's architecture.

Brunelleschi devised a mathematical method for creating the illusion of depth on a flat surface. This method, called **perspective,** is based on the principle that objects appear smaller as they go farther into the background. It became a valuable tool to painters.

Brunelleschi was less successful as a sculptor than as an architect. In 1401 he competed with Lorenzo Ghiberti (1378–1455) for the commission to design a pair of bronze doors for the Baptistery of Florence Cathedral. The doors were to be carved in **relief** sculpture, in which the figures remain attached to a background. The subject chosen for the competition was the *Sacrifice of Abraham*. Ghiberti's design won.

Later, about 1435, Ghiberti designed reliefs for a second pair of doors for the cathedral. Impressed with the great beauty of the doors, Florentines called them the Gates of Paradise. A comparison of the two pairs of doors shows how the new ideas of the Renaissance influenced Ghiberti. In the earlier doors his designs are closer to the flat, patterned compositions of the Gothic style. The reliefs on the Gates of Paradise look much more realistic and are done in perspective. The human figures look more like classical sculptures.

Tommaso Guildi, nicknamed Masaccio (1401–28), was another member of the early Florentine group. He was one of the first painters to use perspective as a device to make his painting look more real. Masaccio went much further than Giotto in giving his subjects dignity and emotion. His compositions were always very simple, usually built up in geometric arrangements.

The most famous sculptor in the group was Donato di Niccolò di Betto Bardi, known as Donatello (1386?–1466). He studied human anatomy and classical sculpture. He was not content to follow formulas handed down from the Middle Ages. He and other Renaissance artists went directly to nature itself. Donatello's sculptures have a realism and freshness that came from his studies of live models.

#### The Second Generation

The revolution begun by Brunelleschi, Masaccio, and Donatello was continued in the second half of the 15th century. The Florentine architect Leon Battista Alberti (1404–72) followed Brunelleschi's example of imi-

The Foundling Hospital in Florence was designed by Brunelleschi in 1421.

tating the forms used in classical architecture. But Alberti's buildings are much heavier and actually closer in form to ancient Roman buildings than Brunelleschi's. St. Andrea, a church in Mantua begun in 1470, shows how Alberti took over the motif of the Roman triumphal arch and made it the main theme of the facade. A triumphal arch has three sections, with a large central opening. St. Andrea's facade is divided into three similar parts, with an enormous central archway forming a dramatic entrance to the church.

Many 15th-century Italian painters continued some of the Gothic traditions of painting

**Right: The Gates of Paradise (1435?), a pair of doors for the Baptistery of Florence Cathedral designed and executed by Lorenzo Ghiberti. Below: Isaac, Jacob, and Esau, one of the panels on the doors.**

The Expulsion from Paradise, painted by Masaccio about 1424. Church of the Carmine, Florence.

the Renaissance is that its new ideas did not immediately replace all the other traditions but took hold gradually.

Paolo Uccello (1397–1475) was one of a group of artists who were fascinated by perspective. His paintings of battle scenes contain crowds of figures arranged according to the rules of perspective. However, Uccello, like Fra Angelico, emphasized flat patterns and tiny details much as medieval artists had done.

Sandro Botticelli (1444?–1510), a masterful painter of graceful, rhythmic line, was another of those who combined the old and the new. For subject matter, Botticelli often turned to the myths of the ancient Greeks.

Piero della Francesca (1420?–92), from the town of Borgo San Sepolcro, in central Italy, went to Florence. There he became interested in perspective. When he returned to Umbria, he applied the knowledge that he had gained in perspective, lighting effects, and anatomy to his painting. Most of his pictures are constructed with the same precision as a work of architecture. Each form was simply drawn, with no unnecessary details. Piero used light and shadow to model his figures and to help give the illusion of depth.

Angel (1450?), by Fra Angelico. Louvre, Paris.

while also using such new discoveries as perspective. Fra Angelico (1400?–1455), a Dominican monk, was one of these painters. His work is a blend of the old and the new. His figures are rather flat, as in medieval painting. It was entirely natural for a monk, schooled in the medieval traditions of the Church, to continue using older methods. One of the important things to understand about

## THE HIGH RENAISSANCE IN ROME

In the 16th century the center for Renaissance artists shifted from Florence to Rome. Almost every great name in 16th-century art went to Rome either to work on some project for the popes or the nobility or just to see what was going on. It was a time of splendor, and it was called the High Renaissance.

The climax of church architecture in the High Renaissance was St. Peter's Basilica. It was built to replace an early Christian church on the same site. Donato Bramante (1444–1514) and Michelangelo Buonarroti (1475–1564) were the main architects, although their original plans were altered by others. The basic plan of 1506, by Bramante, called for a central-type building. Bramante's plan was not carried out, and the church was lengthened. Michelangelo designed the huge dome.

### Leonardo da Vinci

The climax of late 15th-century painting came in the work of Leonardo da Vinci (1452–1519). Leonardo studied painting in Florence, but he spent much of his life working in Milan. The last few years of his life were spent in France in the service of King Francis I.

Leonardo is the perfect example of the "Renaissance man" because he was interested in and well informed about a great many subjects: literature, science, mathematics, art—almost everything about man and nature. Like many artists of the time, he was a sculptor and an architect as well as a painter. His paintings, particularly *The Last Supper,* the *Mona Lisa,* and *The Madonna of the Rocks,* have made him famous. The unique way he handled light and shadow is his most unusual characteristic. Leonardo's remarkable ability to grasp and express the mysteries of man and nature made him one of the greatest of all painters.

### Raphael

The talented painter Raffaello Sanzio, known as Raphael (1483–1520), from

Detail from *The Battle of Constantine* (1465?), by Piero della Francesca. Church of San Francesco, Arezzo.

*The School of Athens* (1510–11), by Raphael. Stanza della Segnatura, Vatican.

*Ginevra de' Benci* (1474–78), by Leonardo.
National Gallery of Art, Washington, D.C.

*Madonna and Child* (1504?), by Michelangelo.
Bruges, Belgium.

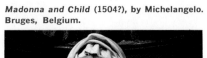

Urbino, was called to Rome by Pope Julius II. Many influences went into the formation of his beautiful style of painting. From his early training in Urbino he developed a feeling for spaciousness and open landscape. When he was 21 years old, he went to Florence, where he absorbed the achievements of the Florentines. From them, especially from Leonardo, he learned how to group figures in space. Michelangelo's influence can be seen in the twisting postures of his human figures.

Everything Raphael painted—especially his madonnas—has an air of serenity and dignity. His famous madonna painting, *La Belle Jardinière* ("The Beautiful Gardener"), painted in 1507, has an unusually pleasing composition. Raphael envisioned man as the ruler of his environment, not as its servant, a High Renaissance idea beautifully expressed in this painting.

### Michelangelo

One of the greatest 16th-century artists was Michelangelo Buonarroti (1475–1564). In sculpture, architecture, and painting he was so outstanding that he was called divine. He was born in Caprese, and as a young man moved to Florence, where he studied the works of Giotto, Masaccio, Donatello, and the Greeks and Romans. He became fascinated with the problems of representing the human body, and he devoted himself completely to mastering them.

In 1505 Michelangelo was called by Pope Julius II to Rome, where he was commissioned to work on a number of projects. The most important were the Pope's tomb, the decoration of the ceiling of the Sistine Chapel in the Vatican, and the new basilica of St. Peter's.

The Sistine ceiling, which took 4 years to paint under difficult conditions, is composed of hundreds of figures from the Old Testament. In all his representations of the human figure, whether in sculpture or in painting, Michelangelo strove for monumentality.

With the art of Michelangelo the High Renaissance came to its climax. His work, in fact, betrayed signs of a changing attitude in the art of the day. The twisted, tormented figures and the flattened space of his painting of *The Last Judgement,* for example, already displayed a new direction in European art.

### ▶ VENICE AND NORTHERN ITALY

Venice was the most important northern Italian city of the Renaissance. The Venetians lived a gay and luxurious life. Enjoying the benefits of an active trade with the east, they imported silks, jewels, slaves, and exotic foods. Close connections with Eastern art and a naturally colorful location inspired the Venetian painters to use bright color. They were influenced by the new "scientific" developments in Florentine art. But their use of anatomy and perspective was combined with their love of color and pageantry.

One of the most important north Italian painters was Andrea Mantegna (1431–1506). Born in Padua, a city not far from Venice, Mantegna introduced many Florentine characteristics into north Italian painting. He particularly admired the realism of Donatello's sculptures, and like Donatello, he studied ancient Roman art. He used perspective to create the effect of a stage on which his figures perform. Mantegna's scientific approach to painting is like Piero della Francesca's. His solid, sculptural figures are similar to Masaccio's.

The greatest of the 15th-century Venetian painters was Giovanni Bellini (1430?–1516). Mantegna's friendship with Bellini had a direct influence on Venetian painting. Bellini's rich, mellow color and warm lighting bring out the human qualities of his serene madonnas and saints. He was one of the first Italians to use oil paint on canvas.

### ▶ THE HIGH RENAISSANCE IN VENICE

Two of Giovanni Bellini's pupils became the most outstanding Venetian painters of the High Renaissance. They were Giorgione (1478?–1510) and Titian (1488?–1576), whose full name was Tiziano Vecelli. Giorgione's colorful and poetic pictures attracted a large following of artists known as Giorgionesque painters.

Titian began as a Giorgionesque painter but developed far beyond this style. He achieved such mastery in the handling of bright, warm color that he was considered to be the equal of Michelangelo. Titian's huge canvases are full of sweeping movement and rich color. In his late works figures and objects melt into a glow of light and color—a treatment of painting that seems very modern.

*Self Portrait* (1498), by Dürer. Prado, Madrid.

Andrea Palladio (1518–80) was the major north Italian architect of the period. The Villa Rotonda, begun in 1550 near Vicenza, a city near Venice, shows how closely Palladio followed Roman architecture, without becoming dry or too scholarly. Built as a country home, it has a symmetrical plan, with porches on all four sides that allow a full view of the countryside. Colonnades, resembling Greek temple fronts, surround a square building topped by a dome. The superb proportions of this and all Palladio's buildings make them very attractive.

▶ THE NORTHERN RENAISSANCE

Oil painting had become popular in Venice by the end of the 15th century. The Venetians learned a great deal from Flemish artists. The Flemish painter Jan van Eyck (1370?–1440?) is often given the credit for developing an important oil technique.

The Flemish and German styles of the early 15th century were completely different from the early Renaissance style of the Florentines. Instead of simple geometric arrangements of three-dimensional figures, as in Masaccio's paintings, the northern Europeans aimed at creating realistic pictures by rendering countless details—intricate floor patterns, drapery designs, and miniature landscapes. This intricate style of the north did not develop from a humanistic classical art (ancient Roman and Greek) but from the Gothic tradition of mysticism and tormented realism.

*The Harvesters* (1565), by Bruegel. Metropolitan Museum, New York.

### Flemish Painting

Van Eyck's *Madonna of the Canon van der Paele,* painted in 1436, is an excellent example of Flemish realism. All the details of the room—the patterned carpet, the armor of Saint George, the architecture—make this picture seem very real. There is no sign of the Italian sense of beauty here: the figures are not idealized. In the faces of the people can be seen the wrinkles and imperfections of real life.

One of the best-known Flemish artists of the second half of the 15th century was Hugo van der Goes (1440?–82). When the Florentine painters saw Hugo's work, they were impressed by its lifelike quality. This Flemish influence can be seen in later Florentine paintings. There were many such interchanges between Italy and Flanders in the course of the century. Gradually the hard outlines of the Flemish style became softer because of Italian influences, and by the middle of the 16th century the ideas of the Renaissance had been absorbed into Flemish art.

### German Painting

The German artist Albrecht Dürer (1471–1528) went to Italy, where he was impressed by the countryside and by the art he saw. While in Venice, he came to know and admire Giovanni Bellini. Bellini, in turn, admired Dürer's work. Dürer had been trained in the Gothic tradition of German art. He had learned to imitate nature accurately and painstakingly. He was a master in the use of sensitive line in drawings, woodcuts, engravings, and paintings.

As a result of his contact with Italian art, Dürer came to share many of the ideals of the Renaissance. He devoted himself to studies of anatomy, to the rules of proportion, perspective, composition, and to the effects of light and color. He passed on to German art all that he learned from the Italians.

### France: the School of Fontainebleau

Francis I, who reigned from 1515 to 1547, brought the Renaissance to France when he imported such artists as Leonardo da Vinci and Benvenuto Cellini (1500–71), a famous bronze-worker and goldsmith, to decorate his château (castle) at Fontainebleau. Other Italians who came were Giovanni Battista Rosso (1494–1540), Francesco Primaticcio (1504–70), and Niccolò dell'Abbate (1512?–71). They began a school of painting known as the School of Fontainebleau. The style of the school was an outgrowth of the Italian style of about 1520–50 known as mannerism. The term "mannerism" was intended as a criticism because the art was thought to have put too much stress on technique, or the "manner" in which it had been created.

French artists of the Fontainebleau School adopted the elegant and refined mannerism of Cellini and Primaticcio. Jean Goujon (1510?–68?), a French sculptor, did several fountain reliefs about 1548 that are clearly mannerist. They are long figures of graceful nymphs with their draperies clinging and swirling.

### ▶ THE END OF THE RENAISSANCE

During the second quarter of the 16th century, mannerism began to take hold in European art. This was the first truly international European style. Renaissance art had been typically Italian in style, but mannerism developed throughout Europe and combined many traditions. The art of northern painters such as Pieter Bruegel the Elder (1525?–69) and Dürer can be considered part of this school. So can the work of Michelangelo and Tintoretto and many other 16th-century Italian artists. The work of the French painters of Fontainebleau and that of El Greco in Spain is also part of the mannerist style.

Mannerism was both a reaction against and an outgrowth of the High Renaissance. It was typified by abnormally lengthened or distorted figures and the replacement of perspective with a flatter and less organized type of space.

By the end of the 16th century the High Renaissance in Italy had given way to late mannerism and the early baroque. But the discoveries and ideals of the Renaissance remained as a permanent heritage to all artists who came afterward. Perhaps the most important contribution of the Renaissance was its vision of man as beautiful, noble, and independent.

SARAH BRADFORD LANDAU
Department of Fine Arts
New York University

See also ARCHITECTURE; ITALY, ART AND ARCHITECTURE OF; PAINTING; SCULPTURE.

# RENAISSANCE MUSIC

The court of Burgundy was very important to the history of music during the first part of the 15th century. The patronage of the dukes of Burgundy, Philip the Good (1396–1467) and Charles the Bold (1443–77), brought about many new developments.

Guillaume Dufay (1400?–74) was a famous musician in the court of Philip the Good. He wrote compositions of many different kinds. Some of his pieces are known as *chansons,* the French for "songs." Chansons are songs for several voices or for a voice with two or more instruments. The songs often deal with love. Sometimes they were sung at festive court entertainments. The banquet hall was hung with splendid tapestries, the nobles were garbed in silk, and the air was scented with sweet perfume.

Dufay also wrote masses for use in the Roman Catholic Church. These masses were often based on a particular melody, which was used throughout. Such a tune was called in Latin a *cantus firmus* ("fixed melody"). A mass based on such a melody is called a *cantus firmus* mass. The melody might be drawn from the Gregorian chant, or it might be a popular tune, perhaps a love song, of the day. One tune Dufay used was called "If I Have a Pale Face." Another was called "The Armed Man." Today popular music is often used in religious services, such as weddings and folk masses.

Another important musician at the Burgundian court was Gilles Binchois (1400?–60). Like Dufay, he composed both sacred music and chansons.

## Flemish Composers

During the second half of the 15th century Flemish composers had the greatest influence on the art of music. Jean d'Ockeghem (1425?–95) wrote some excellent chansons, but his finest work is found in his masses. One remarkable mass is the *Missa Prolationum.* In this, every voice has a different time signature. Also, the two upper voices and the two lower voices are in strict canon. That is, one voice begins alone, and the other, coming in later, imitates it strictly throughout.

A little later came Jacob Obrecht (1452–1505). He was especially famous for his masses. In fact, more than two thirds of his works are in this form. One particularly beautiful mass is based on the tune "Maria Zart," an old German song honoring the Virgin Mary. He wrote love songs, too. Gustave Reese (1899–1977), a great authority on Renaissance music, said of Obrecht's music, "Its sheer loveliness makes him one of the greatest figures in a great generation."

But the peak of achievement was reached with Josquin des Prez (1450–1521). He was a great personality, a great teacher, and a great composer. A student of his wrote that Josquin "never gave a lecture on music or wrote a theoretical work, and yet he was able in a short time to form complete musicians, because he did not keep back his pupils with long and useless instructions, but taught them the rules in a few words, through practical application in the course of singing." After his death Cosimo Bartoli, in a book printed in Venice in 1567, compared him to the artist Michelangelo: " . . . as there has not thus far been anybody who in his compositions approaches Josquin, so Michelangelo, among all those who have been active in these his arts, is still alone and without a peer; both one and the other have opened the eyes of all those who delight in these arts or are to delight in them in the future."

Josquin wrote many fine chansons and a great deal of religious music, both masses and smaller works. A five-voiced *Miserere* (a setting of Psalm 51) is especially eloquent and powerful. His music is often very profound and serious, but he sometimes shows a delightful sense of humor. For a while he was master of the chapel music in the court of King Louis XII of France. He was asked to write a piece in which the King could perform. But the King had a very poor voice. So Josquin wrote a piece containing a part marked *vox regis* (the Latin for "the king's voice"). This consisted of just one note repeated all the way through. History does not tell us what the King thought of this joke.

An outstanding Flemish composer who lived at about the same time as Josquin was Heinrich Isaac (1450?–1517). After he became court composer to Emperor Maximilian I at Vienna, he often traveled to the beautiful little town of Innsbruck in the

Austrian Alps, where Maximilian had one of his several palaces. One day Isaac had to leave Innsbruck. He was so sad that he wrote a lovely song of parting, "Innsbruck, ich muss dich lassen" ("Innsbruck, I now must leave thee"). It became almost as popular as a folk song. It was turned into a chorale of the German Lutheran Church. The music is still used today in Episcopal hymnals, but the words have been changed to "Come see the place where Jesus lay."

In a lighter vein were the songs of Clément Janequin (1485?–1560?). This clever French composer delighted in musical tone painting. One of his most famous pieces is "Le Chant des Oiseaux" ("The Song of the Birds"), in which the voices imitate many different kinds of birdcalls. In another chanson, "La Bataille" ("The Battle"), he imitated the sounds of war: drumbeats, fanfares, and battle cries. No wonder that a poet friend of his wrote about him:

> If he with heavy chords motets compose,
> Or dare to reproduce alarms of battle,
> Or if in song he mimic women's prattle,
> Or imitate birds' voices in design,
> Good Janequin in all his music shows
> No mortal spirit—he is all divine.

### Madrigals

In a publication of 1530 the term "madrigal" is used probably for the first time in the 16th century. Madrigals of that period were vocal settings of Italian poems of high quality. As in the chansons, the verses often told of unrequited love. The emotions were intense, so the music, too, had to be very expressive. Philippe Verdelot (?–1550?), a Flemish composer who lived many years in Italy, may have been the first man to write madrigals of this kind. Others who composed madrigals at this time were Jacob Arcadelt (1505?–60?), Adrian Willaert (1490–1562), and Cypriano de Rore (1516–65). Luca Marenzio (1553–99) brought the madrigal to a high degree of sophistication. In the late 16th and early 17th century men such as Claudio Monteverdi (1567–1643) and Carlo Gesualdo (1560?–1613) were still writing very emotional and expressive madrigals.

This form was taken over in England at the end of the 16th century. Composers such as Thomas Morley (1557–1602), Thomas Weelkes (1575?–1623), and John Wilbye (1574–1638) wrote many beautiful madrigals to English texts. Some of these were very sad and doleful, but others were gay and dancelike.

### Ayres

Another popular vocal form in England was the ayre. The ayre was a song for solo voice with lute or viol accompaniment. Some of these songs were very serious and emotional. John Dowland (1562–1626) wrote a great many of this type. Other ayres were light and gay, such as Morley's "It Was a Lover and His Lass."

### Instrumental Music

In England at this time, instrumental music as well as vocal music was very popular. Some of the best composers of keyboard music were William Byrd (1543–1623), John Bull (1562?–1628), and Orlando Gibbons (1583–1625). Byrd was particularly famous in his own day. A contemporary, Father William Weston, referred to him as "the most celebrated musician and organist of the English nation." Although he was a loyal Catholic and wrote great music for the Roman Catholic Church, he also held important positions in the Church of England—a very unusual state of affairs. Of his lighter music for the virginal (a small rectangular instrument belonging to the harpsichord family), the pavanes and galliards are especially charming. (The pavane was a slow dance. The galliard, which usually followed it, was a faster dance that used the same theme in different meter.)

### Religious Music

Often considered the most typical Renaissance composer of sacred music is the Italian Giovanni Palestrina (1525?–94). Though he composed a number of different kinds of music, it was as a composer of masses that he particularly excelled. In fact, he was one of the greatest mass composers that ever lived. As many as 105 of his masses have survived—an amazing number. He is famous for the purity and serenity of his unaccompanied vocal music.

Two great contemporaries of Palestrina were the Fleming Roland de Lassus (1532–94) and the Spaniard Tomás Luis de Victoria (1549?–1611). Like Palestrina, Victoria is famed for his church music. Less serene than Palestrina's, it is filled with an ardent and intense mysticism. Lassus led a most varied career. When a young boy soprano, he was kidnapped three times because of the beauty of his voice. In later years he traveled a great deal, finally settling in Munich, Bavaria. He wrote many different kinds of music, ranging all the way from lively or tender chansons to the powerful and profound *Penitential Psalms* of 1565. A versatile, active person, he presents a vivid contrast to the more contemplative Palestrina.

For still another type of religious music, it is interesting to turn to the work of the Venetian composer Giovanni Gabrieli (1557–1612). A fine example of the brilliant piece for so-loists, double chorus, and brass ensemble (with one violin) *In ecclesiis benedicite Domino* ("Bless ye the Lord in His sanctuaries"). It glows with all the pomp and circumstance of the wealthy city of Venice, where it was written. He also wrote fine instrumental music.

The musical language of the Renaissance was spoken with many different accents. The people of Italy, France, the Netherlands, and England all had their own individual dialects. Yet underlying these differences was the spirit of newness—of rebirth. The composers themselves felt this spirit, and that is why the best of their music is still so vital today.

DIKA NEWLIN
Virginia Commonwealth University

## RENOIR, PIERRE AUGUSTE (1841–1919)

The painter Pierre Auguste Renoir was born in Limoges, France, on February 25, 1841. When he was 4, his family moved to Paris. As a boy, Renoir drew on the floor with chalk from his father's tailor shop. To stop his chalk from disappearing, his father gave the young artist pencils and paper.

At 13, Renoir became an apprentice in a porcelain factory, where he decorated plates for four years. Then he painted fans and blinds

**Renoir's style changed over the years, but he always exhibited a masterful use of light and color and a preference for painting human figures. (*Two Sisters*, 1910)**

and drew scenes on the walls of cafés. In 1862 he entered the Paris studio of Swiss artist Charles Gleyre (1808–74) to study art.

Renoir and his friends gradually found new ways of painting. They liked to show the fleeting changes of light on figures and landscapes by using small dabs of pure color. This kind of painting, called **impressionism,** was not popular, but he began to earn a little money from doing portraits. In 1879 his large picture of Madame Charpentier and her daughters was greatly admired.

About 1884, Renoir changed his technique somewhat and painted figures with careful outlines and harsh colors. In the 1890's he developed another style, using rich colors and flowing brushstrokes. Throughout his career Renoir liked to paint women and children. His wife, Aline, and their three sons were favorite later subjects. One of the sons, Jean, became a well-known filmmaker.

Because of Renoir's arthritis, the family moved to the warmer climate of southern France about 1902. But even in that climate he became so crippled that he could not leave his wheelchair. In spite of his suffering, Renoir never lost his love for life and painting. He painted a picture of flowers on the day he died—in Cagnes, December 3, 1919.

KIRSTEN H. POWELL
Middlebury College

The survival of all living things—animals, plants, and other organisms—depends on the ability of each species to produce offspring.

# REPRODUCTION

In the spring, poppy seeds sprout. Poppy plants burst into leaf. They flower and produce seeds. In the fall, with the coming of frost, the poppies die. But their seeds survive and sprout the following spring. A new generation of poppies replaces the one that has died. Poppy plants continue to exist.

Every kind of living creature, from tiny bacteria to enormous whales, makes new living things like itself. In other words, it **reproduces**. An individual plant or animal may fail to reproduce, but that does not hurt the individual. Nor does it hurt the species (kind) of animal or plant, so long as enough other individuals of that kind reproduce.

Among living creatures there are two main types of reproduction. In one type the new individuals, or young, come from a single parent. Bacteria, for example, grow to a certain size and then divide into two equal parts. Each new bacterium is a small copy of the parent. This type of reproduction is called **asexual reproduction**.

The other main type is called **sexual reproduction**. In this type, young are produced by two parents or from two different parts of the same parent. When two deer mate, for example, living material from both animals is joined, or fused. In time a fawn is born, looking like its parents but not exactly like either one.

Some living things can reproduce sexually at some times and asexually at others.

## ▶ASEXUAL REPRODUCTION

There are three main ways that living things reproduce asexually. They may divide like bacteria, they may form buds, or they may create spores. The simplest of these ways is dividing.

### Dividing

Bacteria, amoebas, and many other tiny one-celled creatures reproduce by dividing in half. Some larger creatures, too, may divide in half. This is true, for example, of a freshwater relative of the earthworm. The body of this worm slowly pinches in around the middle. Finally the body separates in two. The front end grows a hind end, while the hind end grows a front end.

New plants may grow from pieces of an older plant. For example, if you set a sweetpotato root (the part you eat) in water, the root will sprout leafy shoots and new roots. In time you will have a sweet-potato vine.

### Budding

A number of living things, such as yeasts, sponges, corals, and grasses, can reproduce by forming buds. Unlike flower or leaf buds, these buds develop into complete new individuals. The threadlike hydra will serve as an example. This is a tiny water animal related to corals and jellyfish.

Sometimes a hydra develops a bulge on its side. This bulge—which is a bud—slowly grows into a complete new animal just like the parent. The new hydra may separate from the parent and take up life on its own. Or it may remain attached to the parent and, in turn, produce buds. In some creatures entire colonies, or groups, may form this way, each individual a descendant of the one original parent.

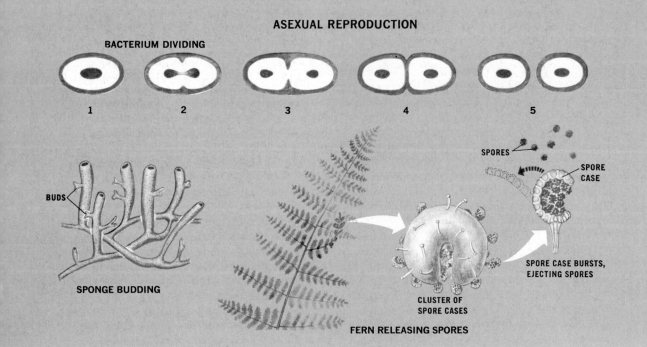

## ASEXUAL REPRODUCTION

**BACTERIUM DIVIDING**

1    2    3    4    5

BUDS

**SPONGE BUDDING**

SPORES

SPORE CASE

SPORE CASE BURSTS, EJECTING SPORES

CLUSTER OF SPORE CASES

**FERN RELEASING SPORES**

### Spores

Some plants reproduce by means of tiny specks of life called spores. You may have seen tiny black dots on the undersides of fern leaves. These dots are spore cases filled with spores. When the spores are ripe, they fall. Those that land on moist, cool ground sprout into tiny new plants.

Mosses and a number of other plants reproduce by forming spores. So do yeast cells and certain one-celled creatures.

### ▶ SEXUAL REPRODUCTION

Most creatures, even those that can reproduce asexually, reproduce by sexual means. For example, let us look again at the tiny hydra. A bud develops on the parent hydra. This time the bud does not develop into a complete new individual. This bud contains sperm if the hydra is a male or eggs if the hydra is a female. Eggs and sperm are special reproductive cells.

When the eggs or sperm are ripe, the bud bursts open and sheds its contents into the water. The eggs, as in all creatures, are bigger and rounder than the sperm. Eggs contain a food supply that will nourish the new individual as it develops. Unlike sperm, eggs have no means of moving about.

Hydra sperm, like those of most species, have thin, whiplike tails that enable them to swim toward an egg. A sperm is very much smaller than an egg. It lacks a food supply of its own.

Hydras produce many eggs or sperm in a single bud. Some of the sperm from the male hydras meet some of the eggs from the females. When a sperm fuses with an egg, the egg is said to be **fertilized**. A fertilized egg contains living material from two parents. It grows and develops into a new individual combining the traits of both parents.

Sexual reproduction in most creatures is more complicated than in the hydra. However, it involves the same basic steps. First, reproductive cells must form. In most species the two sexes are separate. Eggs are formed by females, and sperm are formed by males. Next, eggs must be fertilized. Sperm need a fluid in which to swim to the egg. If sperm are not shed into water, the body must produce the necessary fluid. Finally, some sort of food and protection for the developing egg must be provided until the young can care for itself.

### Care of Eggs Shed in Water

Hydras and many other animals shed their eggs and sperm directly into water. They do little if anything to ensure the survival of their offspring.

Many other animals have special ways of making sure that their eggs and sperm meet and that their fertilized eggs are protected.

## REPRODUCTION OF HYDRA

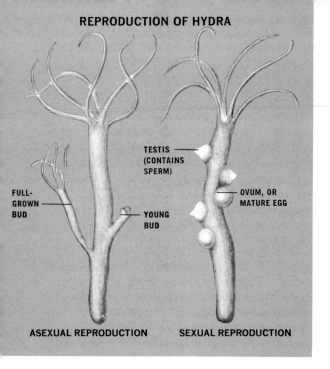

TESTIS
(CONTAINS
SPERM)

OVUM, OR
MATURE EGG

FULL-
GROWN
BUD

YOUNG
BUD

ASEXUAL REPRODUCTION          SEXUAL REPRODUCTION

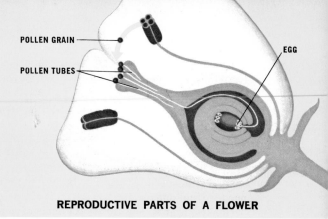

POLLEN GRAIN

POLLEN TUBES

EGG

**REPRODUCTIVE PARTS OF A FLOWER**

Sperm, contained in pollen grain, fertilizes egg.

A female trout, for example, makes a nest. She uses her tail fin to scrape a hollow in a stream bottom. There she sheds her eggs. The male swims along beside her and covers the eggs with sperm. The female then scrapes gravel over the fertilized eggs. This helps prevent enemies from eating the eggs.

The eggs of some water animals are protected with a thick jellylike coating. In such species the sperm fertilizes the eggs just as they leave the female's body and before the coating is formed. A male horseshoe crab, for example, clasps the female's shell and sheds his sperm directly over the eggs. The pair usually dig into the sand before depositing their eggs and sperm. As the mating pair withdraws, the sand drifts over the eggs, giving them extra protection.

In many lobsters, crabs, and shrimps, the male clasps the female and fertilizes the eggs as they are shed into the water. Frogs and toads mate in a similar fashion.

### Fertilization Inside the Body

In salamanders, which are related to frogs and toads, eggs are fertilized inside the female. The male courts his mate and then deposits one or more jellylike packets of sperm on the ground or the pond bottom. The female squats over a packet and draws it up into an opening beneath her tail. The sperm fertilize the eggs before the eggs are shed.

Male squids also produce packets of sperm. A male uses a special tip on one of his tentacles to place the packet inside the body covering of the female.

Snails, guppies, sharks, rays, some crabs, and other water animals also fertilize their eggs internally. In some the eggs remain inside the female until they hatch.

Among land animals, fertilization usually occurs internally. If eggs and sperm were shed directly onto the ground, they would soon dry out in the air. Moreover, the sperm would have no way of swimming toward the eggs unless dew or rainwater happened to be present.

Male spiders deposit their sperm in a drop of fluid. Then they place the drop of fluid in an opening on the body of the female. She later spins a cocoon in which she lays the fertilized eggs.

In most land creatures, however, fluid containing sperm is inserted directly from the body of the male into the body of the female. This is true of insects, reptiles, birds, and mammals, including man.

In seed plants, such as pine trees and daffodils, both eggs and sperm have heavy coatings that keep them from drying out. The sperm, contained in tiny pollen grains, may be transferred by wind or by insects to the female part of the flower. Although the sperm have no tails, they are carried down into the egg in a special pollen tube. The fertilized egg is protected inside a tough seed coat and by the fruit.

### Care of Eggs Fertilized Internally

Most insects lay their eggs in protected places where the newly hatched insects will find food. Insect eggs are very small and contain very little food. Insects hatch before they are fully developed, and most species pass through several stages before they look like their parents.

The eggs of both birds and reptiles are well supplied with yolk and protected by shells. With a large yolky egg the young develop into small copies of their parents before food is needed from outside.

Snakes, lizards, and turtles lay their eggs in holes in the ground, and many cover the nests with mud or sand. The eggs of some lizards and snakes remain inside the mother until the young hatch.

Most birds build nests of some sort and hatch the eggs with the warmth of their own bodies. The parents take turns feeding and guarding the young.

In most mammals the eggs are small and have little yolk. The developing individual gets the nourishment it needs from its mother's body. After birth the young suckle milk from the mother. The result is that the offspring are large before they have to fend for themselves.

Small mammals, such as mice and foxes, may have from two to a dozen or more offspring at a time. Few of these offspring manage to grow up. Large mammals, such as horses and elephants, usually have only one offspring at a time. The parents feed and guard the young for a long time. Each offspring has a good chance of growing to full size and of reproducing in turn.

Human beings usually produce babies one at a time. Their babies are helpless at birth. But they are so well taken care of that each has a better chance of growing up than any other kind of creature.

N. J. BERRILL<br>
McGill University

See also CELLS; EGGS AND EMBRYOS; FLOWERS; GENETICS; METAMORPHOSIS.

## HUMAN REPRODUCTION

One of the marvels of nature is the ability of living beings to reproduce themselves. Humans belong to the class of living beings known as mammals. All mammals reproduce by the mating of a male with a female of the same species. This is called sexual reproduction.

Unlike most other mammals, human beings have no special mating season. They are unique in having the ability to plan their reproduction. The mating of grown-up male and female humans marks the beginning of a family. A family is a very important feature of our civilization. A family must be planned with much thought and care, since the production of a new human life is a great privilege and even greater responsibility.

In the human as in other mammals, the body structure of the male and female is specially adapted for the part each has in mating. The male's contribution is the sex cell known as the sperm. The female's is the ovum, or egg. When the two sex cells combine, the process is called fertilization. The fertilized egg is the very beginning of a human life.

As boys grow into their teens, the parts of the body that have to do with reproduction grow and develop. The sex cells, or sperm, are contained in the testes, a pair of oval-shaped structures over an inch (2.5 centimeters) long. They are located in a pouch called the scrotum, under the penis, outside the body. The tubular-shaped penis serves as the passageway for urine and also for the sperm cell fluid.

In the female, the main parts of the body involved in reproduction are the uterus and the ovaries. The uterus is the womb or nesting place for the fertilized egg. The uterus is a small, hollow, pear-shaped organ located in the lower central part of the abdomen.

On both sides of the uterus is an ovary that contains the ova, or eggs. When a girl is reaching her teens, the ovaries become active. About once a month an ovary discharges an egg that reaches the uterus through a connecting tube on each side of the uterus. The egg is a tiny speck, hardly visible to the naked eye. Unless fertilized by a sperm, the egg dries up and is expelled about 2 weeks later from the uterus. The uterus throws off this dried-up egg mixed with some blood and mucus through the vagina and then out of the body. The vagina is a small tunnel-shaped structure that has an opening between the one for the urine and the one for the bowel movement. This discharge normally lasts from 3 to 7 days and occurs usually once a month. Known as menstruation, it is nature's cleansing process of the uterus. It starts at the period of development known as puberty and indicates that the body is maturing to make future reproduction possible.

In the mating process in humans, a small amount of special fluid containing sperm cells is deposited by the penis into the vagina. The sperm cells have a remarkable ability to travel rapidly up the vagina into the uterus. The tiny sperm cannot be seen by the naked eye. But under a microscope one sees the tiny tadpole-shaped cell with a long threadlike tail that acts as a propeller. If an egg has been discharged from the ovary about this time and is moving toward the uterus, the sperm and ovum unite, resulting in a fertilized egg.

In the uterus, this fertilized egg undergoes a series of changes. Within a month, it grows and develops into an embryo about a quarter inch long. As it continues to grow, it becomes the fetus, soon developing all the necessary organs—heart, lungs, brain, nervous and digestive systems. It obtains nourishment from the mother through the placenta, a disk-like structure, which connects the blood supply of the mother to the fetus through a ropy-looking cord from its belly button (navel). Every human being has a belly button, which is a reminder of how each of us began life.

In about nine months, the tiny fertilized egg has become a baby ready to leave the mother's body. The muscular uterus squeezes down, pushing the baby out through the vagina, which now has enlarged to become the birth canal. The baby is usually born head first and is expelled with the cord, which is then cut. Afterward the placenta, now called the afterbirth, is pushed out of the mother's body. The miracle of reproduction is now complete.

JEAN PAKTER, M.D., M.P.H.
Director, Bureau of Maternity Services
and Family Planning
New York City Department of Health

See also BODY, HUMAN; GENETICS.

---

# REPTILES

Crocodiles, lizards, snakes, and turtles are all reptiles. They are grouped together because they are alike in many ways, sharing many important features. Although other animals have some of these features, only reptiles have all of them.

Reptiles are vertebrates. This means that they have bodies supported by a framework of bone—the skeleton. A reptile's body is covered by dry, scaly skin. Most reptiles have four legs. Each foot ends in five clawed toes. All reptiles breathe air through their lungs.

A reptile's body temperature varies. Reptiles regulate their body temperatures in many ways: by changing their color to absorb or reflect heat; by moving to the shade when the sunlight is too hot; by retreating into a burrow when it is too hot or too cold above ground; and in other similar ways.

The eggs of most reptiles dry easily. Because of this the eggs must be laid in moist places in the earth or sand or in rotten wood. Young reptiles look much like their parents, although they may be colored differently.

### History of Reptiles

The first reptiles walked on the earth about 300 million years ago. These early creatures flourished and branched out—over millions of years—into many different kinds of animals. Scientists say that the first birds developed from certain of these reptiles. Other reptiles developed into the first mammals (animals that nurse their young on their milk).

Reptiles themselves developed along many separate lines. Huge dinosaurs, flying reptiles, and reptiles of the sea spread throughout the earth in great numbers. Today there are about 6,000 kinds of reptiles.

### Living Reptiles

There are four main groups of living reptiles.

The first group is made up of crocodiles, al-

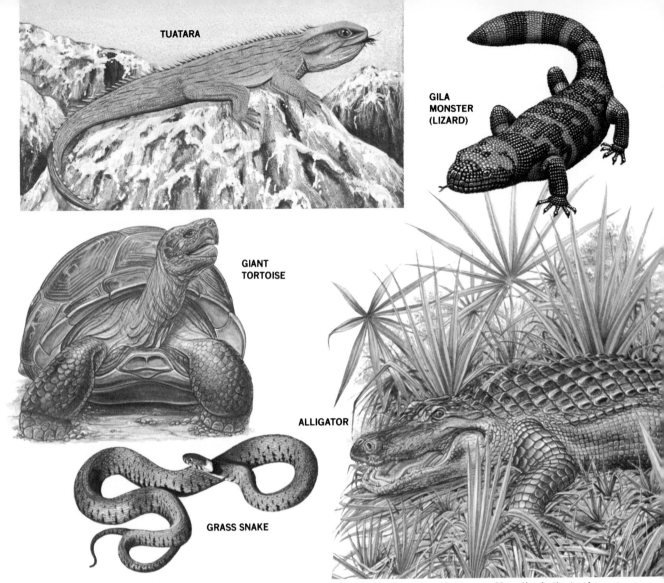

TUATARA

GILA MONSTER (LIZARD)

GIANT TORTOISE

ALLIGATOR

GRASS SNAKE

**Reptiles are cold-blooded and must warm themselves in the sun. Many live in the tropics.**

ligators, gavials, and caymans. These are the largest reptiles. Each has a long body, tough skin, strong jaws, and a powerful tail.

The second group is made up of turtles and tortoises. Many turtles have bodies that are almost entirely enclosed within a hard, two-layered shell. When threatened, many can withdraw completely into this shell.

The third group is made up of lizards and snakes. These animals are generally easy to tell apart. Snakes, for example, are legless and cannot close their eyes. Most lizards are four-legged and are able to shut their eyes.

The fourth group contains only one kind of animal—the tuatara. This creature looks somewhat like a lizard. The tuatara has three eyes, as do many lizards. The third eye, located on top of the head, is covered by a thin scale. It does not function as a normal eye, and scientists do not know what its function is. The tuatara can remain active at 52°F (11°C)—a temperature at which most reptiles move about slowly, if at all. The tuatara is the last remaining reptile of a group that was widespread in prehistoric times. Today it is found only on islands off the coast of New Zealand.

Reviewed by RICHARD G. ZWEIFEL
American Museum of Natural History

See also CROCODILES AND ALLIGATORS; DINOSAURS; LIZARDS; SNAKES; TURTLES.

**REPUBLICAN PARTY.** See POLITICAL PARTIES.

# RESEARCH

What is research? Research is the careful search for information. A person who carries out the careful search is a researcher.

## Who Does Research?

At one time or another, everyone is a researcher. For example, people who want to buy a new car do some research to decide which automobile is best for them. They read about different car models in magazines and go to car dealers to compare brakes, air bags, and other features. They compare prices, too. After making this careful investigation, they analyze the information and choose their car. They are researchers.

Doctors also do research. A doctor who knows about cells and cancer decides she wants to understand more about how cancer cells grow. By reading medical books and journals on the subject, she learns enough to develop a new idea about cancer growth. She does experiments to see if her ideas are correct. Someday her research may point the way to a cancer cure.

Imagine a historian who wants to know more about ancient Egypt. He must read books on the subject. He asks professors of ancient history to share their knowledge. He visits museums to study Egyptian art. By doing this research, he may develop new theories about how people lived in the past.

You and your brother may be researchers, too. Let us say your brother thinks Babe Ruth is the greatest baseball player of all time. You think Hank Aaron is better. The two of you will want to look through a book of baseball records and compare the two players' statistics. You might read books or magazine articles about them. After this research you may still disagree. But you have more information to back up your arguments.

## Basic and Applied Research

Some researchers simply want to increase their knowledge about a subject. The historian wants to know more about the past. You and your brother want to know more about baseball. The doctor wants to discover how cancer cells grow. This is called **basic research**.

Other researchers want to put what they learn to practical use. They plan to apply their research to meet practical needs. Research carried out with a practical goal in mind is called **applied research**.

Basic and applied researchers can work together. A doctor investigates how cancer cells grow. She does basic research. A drug company uses her research to develop new drugs. The drug company does applied research.

Basic and applied research can be carried out in two different ways. The research can be formal and scientific or it can be informal. A rocket scientist who wants to improve rocket fuel will conduct many experiments. If he makes a tiny mistake, his research is useless. If he is very careful, he may produce a better fuel. So step by step he slowly does his research. Careful scientific research is called formal research. A rocket scientist does formal research.

A car mechanic, on the other hand, may want to know which tool is best for fixing a motor. He calls other mechanics to ask their advice. He writes to car dealers to see which tool they recommend. Based on this research, he selects a tool. There is no reason for the mechanic to make a slow, detailed scientific study. If he goes too slowly, he will never get any motors fixed, which was the point of his research in the first place. Research that is not scientific is called informal research. A mechanic does informal research. Which kind of research is best? It depends on what type of question you want answered.

## What Does a Researcher Do?

A researcher usually begins to work by asking a question. The rocket scientist asks: Can I create better fuel? The doctor asks: How do cancer cells grow? The baseball fan asks: Who is the best baseball player? Research is what a researcher does to find an answer. Some researchers need to read books. Others may have to conduct scientific experiments. Researchers may work in libraries, laboratories, museums, stores, or even schools.

Suppose the superintendent of a school district wants to answer this question: What is the best way to teach reading? How can the superintendent answer this important question? First, she must find out what experts on the subject have to say. She begins by reading books they have written. It turns out that the experts disagree. The superintendent wants to know which experts are correct. She also wants to know how teachers in her school district feel about different methods of reading instruction. She surveys the teachers and learns that some of them prefer one method of instruction and some prefer other methods.

The superintendent decides to conduct an experiment during the school year. Different methods of teaching reading will be used in different classes to learn which methods do the most for the students in her district. After reading books, surveying teachers, and conducting a yearlong experiment, the superintendent will analyze all of her information. As a result of her research, she will decide which approach to reading she thinks is best for the students in her school district.

### Are Researchers Always Right?

If researchers are lucky, they are able to get all the necessary facts and information. But not all researchers are lucky. Sometimes they cannot find the information they need. Or they may discover that the information they gathered is incorrect. Naturally, it is impossible to make good use of faulty research.

Why do researchers sometimes fail to get the right answers? Are they careless in their work? Not always. Even careful researchers sometimes make mistakes. For instance, before a drug company begins to sell a new product, it conducts careful research to discover how the drug works. Researchers try to determine if the drug will have any bad effects on people. The company's researchers try to be as exact and scientifically accurate as possible. On occasion, however, they make mistakes and, even though they do careful research, they fail to discover some problem. If it is a small problem, the company can correct it and continue selling the drug. Sometimes, though, the problem is serious. In that case, the drug is a poor product and the company will have to remove it from stores.

### How Do Researchers Share Their Discoveries?

Let us say an astronomer wonders about the planet Pluto. What is Pluto really like? The astronomer starts a research project. He reads books about the planet. He looks through his telescope and studies satellite photographs. He analyzes all the information. He discovers facts about Pluto that no one ever knew before. What will the astronomer do with this new information? He will write a report about his findings and publish the report in a maga-

zine. If he has a lot of information, he may even write a book. Then other astronomers will read his writings when they want to know more about Pluto.

### Research and Reports for School

You may have already done a lot of informal research. What are your interests? Maybe you like whales. To discover more about them, you have read books on the giant mammals, visited aquariums, and watched nature shows about whales. Whenever you could, you searched for more information. You became a whale researcher. Your research was informal. You did not look for information in an exact, systematic, or scientific manner.

When you write a report for school, on the other hand, you must do formal research. You do not need to be as exact as a rocket scientist, but you must work carefully and systematically to get good results.

Each year in school, your teacher will probably assign one, two, or maybe more research projects. In January you may have to report on the life of Thomas Jefferson. In March you will have to know about sea turtles.

To complete each assignment, you must do two things. First you need to search for information. In other words, you must research the topic. Second, you have to prepare a report. The report is how you share your information with your teacher and classmates. Most often you will have to prepare a written report. But sometimes your teacher may ask you to give an oral report, put on a play, or prepare a visual display.

**Researching the Report.** What is the best way to begin your research? First, try to determine where you will get your information. You might read books, magazines, or the encyclopedia. You might visit a museum. Or you might interview an expert on the subject.

How will you remember what you learn? You should take notes. There are different systems of note taking. Here is one you can try. Get a package of index cards. As you read, think about the most important information on each page or in each paragraph. Write the most important facts or ideas on a card. Give each card a label.

Suppose you are doing research on Thomas Jefferson. You might label one card "Early life," another "Declaration of Independence," and a third "American leader."

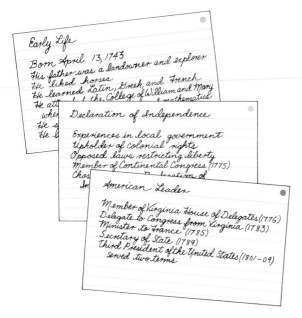

Early Life
Born April 13, 1743
His father was a landowner and explorer
He liked horses
He learned Latin, Greek, and French
He attended the College of William and Mary
when...
He s...
He l...

Declaration of Independence
Experiences in local government
Upholder of colonial rights
Opposed laws restricting liberty
Member of Continental Congress (1775)
Chos...
In...

American Leader
Member of Virginia House of Delegates (1776)
Delegate to Congress from Virginia (1783)
Minister to France (1785)
Secretary of State (1789)
Third President of the United States (1801-09)
Served two terms

It is important to remember where you obtained facts. To help you keep track of this information, prepare a special card for each book or magazine you read. On the card, write the author's name and the title of the book or the author's name, title of the article, and the magazine. Assign each book or magazine a color. Then place a colored dot that corresponds to the source of your information on every card you write.

**Writing the Report.** Once you have enough information, you can start writing the report. There are five stages in report writing. Stage one is writing an outline. Your report will have several paragraphs. The outline should show the main idea of each paragraph as well as the ideas you will use to tell about the main idea. Here is an outline for a report on Thomas Jefferson.

I.  Introduction
II.  Early life
    A.  Family life
    B.  Education
III.  Declaration of Independence
    A.  Why he wrote it
    B.  What it says
    C.  Why it is important
IV.  American leader
    A.  Secretary of State
    B.  Vice President
    C.  President
V.  Conclusion

Next comes stage two—writing a first draft. Go paragraph by paragraph. Look at your note cards when you need information. You may want to include some exact words from one of the books you used for your research. If you do, be sure to enclose these words in quotation marks and write a footnote. A footnote tells where you found the words. It is how you acknowledge, or give credit to, someone else's thinking.

Stage three is the editing and revising stage. Read your report carefully. As you read, look for problems. Ask yourself: Is each paragraph clear? Is each paragraph well organized? Have I left out important ideas? Make any changes you want. You may need to write a new draft in order to read all your changes. You may even have to edit and revise your new draft. Some writers compose many drafts before they are satisfied.

Stage four is the time to correct spelling and punctuation errors in your final draft. This is called "proofreading."

Finally, in stage five, copy your last draft, using your best handwriting or your most exact typing. When you are done, proofread it to make sure your report is perfect. This is the copy you will give to your teacher.

Some reports need a **bibliography**—a list of all the books and magazines you read for your report. The bibliographic form for books:

Bober, Natalie S. *Thomas Jefferson: Man on a Mountain.* New York: Atheneum, 1988.

Sandak, Cass R. *The Jeffersons.* New York: Macmillan Children's Book Group, 1992.

is a little different than the one for magazines:

Gardiner, Harry. "Young Thomas Jefferson." *Cobblestone,* vol. 10, no. 9 (September, 1989), 6–8.

Potratz, Jean K. "Thomas Jefferson, John Adams: Two Famous Friends." *Highlights for Children,* vol. 45, no. 7 (July–August, 1990), 32–33.

Arrange all the entries in alphabetical order by the author's name.

Now your report is finished. Through your research, you learned a lot of information. By writing a report, you found a good way to share your knowledge.

PEGGY KAYE
Author, *Games for Learning*

See also LIBRARIES; REFERENCE BOOKS.

# RESINS

There are two kinds of resins, natural and synthetic (man-made). Resins are used in paints, varnishes, printing inks, and plastics, to name only their most important uses. They have a wide range of hardness, color, flexibility, strength, and elasticity. Some are gummy and soft. Others are hard and rigid.

Natural resins come mostly from trees. When the bark of certain trees is injured, a thick, sticky material oozes out of the wound. This sticky material, which is sometimes called pitch, is made up of two parts, an oil and a resin. The oil gradually evaporates, leaving the resin. The resin itself is a mixture of materials. Each kind of tree makes its own resin, which is different from the resins of other trees. Many trees produce resins, but only a few are used commercially.

Most resins are gathered by cutting, or slashing, the bark of a tree and collecting the liquid in cups. After the liquid is collected, the oil is separated from the resin by distillation. Perhaps the best-known resin is rosin, which comes from certain pine trees. The oil that is separated from rosin is known as spirits of turpentine. Rosin is used in making printing inks, paper coatings, and varnishes. It is also used in some kinds of soap, in linoleum, and in flotation agents that separate valuable ores from worthless rock. Plain rosin is used to stop unwanted slipping. Baseball players use powdered rosin on their hands to get a better grip on the bat or on the ball. Boxers, ballet dancers, and tightrope walkers use rosin on their footgear to keep their feet from slipping. Violinists use it on their bows, so that the bows will "bite" the strings better.

Stumps of trees that have fallen or been cut down also produce resin. This resin may be obtained by grinding up the stumps and treating the wood chips with hot steam. This drives off the turpentine as a vapor. The resin remains in the wood chips and is dissolved out with a solvent, such as gasoline. The solvent is then distilled off, leaving the useful resin.

Under certain conditions the resin of ancient trees has been preserved and can still be found in the ground. Such resins are called fossil resins. They are much harder than other resins. Amber is the best-known fossil resin. It is often used in jewelry.

Many resins give off a pleasant odor when they are burned or heated. For this reason, resins have long been used for incense. Myrrh and frankincense (also called olibanum), two resins used in incense, are mentioned in both the Old Testament and the New Testament of the Bible. Resins were once thought to have curative properties and were often used as medicines. Very few resins are still used as medicines, but some are used in cough drops and cough syrups.

Certain resins contain dyes that were once very important, though now they have largely been replaced by less expensive man-made dyes. A reddish dye that has been used to color varnish for violins comes from a resin called dragon's blood. Turmeric, a resin used to season and color food, is the source of a yellow fabric dye that was once important.

Today the most important use of natural resins is in varnishes. Even in ancient times resins were used as coatings to preserve wood. At first, the resin was simply smeared on or melted on with a hot iron. The resin was then rubbed until a smooth, hard, shiny surface was formed. In Roman times, it was found that the resin could be dissolved in a solvent and painted onto a surface. The solvent evaporated, leaving a smooth, shiny film of resin. Varnishes are made in much the same way today. Other modern uses of natural resins are in the manufacture of printing inks, polishes, and coatings for paper.

Lac is a resin produced by the lac insect, which feeds on the sap of certain trees. These insects swarm twice a year. The lac that they secrete forms a thick layer over the twigs they feed on. The lac is collected by scraping it off the trees and drying it. It contains many impurities, such as twigs, bark, and the bodies of the insects. Most lac comes from India. Lac is the source of a red dye that was formerly important, and of shellac, which is purified lac. Shellac dissolved in alcohol is used in the same way as varnish. White shellac is bleached orange shellac.

## ▶ SYNTHETIC RESINS

Synthetic resins are made by man from chemicals containing carbon, hydrogen, and other substances. Some of them are similar chemically to natural resins; others are quite different. Because synthetic resins are less expensive and more uniform in quality, they have largely replaced natural resins for many uses.

One of the most important uses of synthetic resins is in plastics. Resins are the chief ingredients of plastics. The resin gives a plastic most of its qualities, such as strength, durability, and hardness.

Synthetic resins are also used in paints, varnishes and lacquers, and printing inks. Extremely strong adhesives are made from synthetic resins.

One unusual use for resins is in purifying water. Water is made hard by small amounts of metals, such as calcium, magnesium, and iron, dissolved in the water. These metals are present as electrically charged particles called ions. Ions are much too small to be seen, but they make themselves very noticeable. When soap is dissolved in hard water, the metal ions in the water combine with the soap and form a useless material called soap curd. Soap curd is what makes the familiar bathtub ring. Certain resins, called ion-exchange resins, can remove the metal ions that make the water hard. These resins are bristling with hydrogen ions. When hard water passes over the resin, the metal ions stick to the resin and hydrogen ions take their place. This makes the water become an acid. The water is then passed over another type of resin that takes out nonmetallic ions, such as those of chloride and sulfate, and gives off hydroxyl ions in exchange. A hydroxyl ion consists of one atom of hydrogen plus one atom of oxygen. It has a negative electric charge. (Hydrogen ions have a positive charge.) The hydroxyl ions combine with the hydrogen ions from the first resin to form pure water. Water treated by the ion-exchange process is very soft and contains hardly any impurities.

Ion-exchange resins can be made to pick certain kinds of metal ions out of a solution and let others pass by. This helps chemists find out what is in the solution.

The resins lose their ability to exchange ions after a while, but they can be "recharged" by soaking them in inexpensive chemicals.

▶ **GUMS**

Gums are hardened sticky juices from plants. Some plants form gums that are mixed with resins. Many different sorts of gums are found in nature. Many plant gums swell in water. Others dissolve in water, making a gluelike liquid.

Gum arabic comes from acacia trees. There are many varieties of acacia trees, and each may produce a different gum. Gum arabic dissolves in water, forming a sticky liquid. This gum is used in making candy and medicine and in printing designs on textiles. Some inks contain gum arabic to make the ink stick to paper or cloth. Most gum arabic comes from Africa.

Tragacanth gum is a yellowish powder. It comes from a shrub that grows in the Middle East. Tragacanth gum is used to make mixtures of oil and water called emulsions and to preserve food.

Agar, sometimes called agar-agar, is obtained from seaweeds that grow mostly in the Pacific and Indian oceans. When dried, agar is a light-brown flaky material. It swells and dissolves in hot water. Agar is used as a substitute for gelatin and for egg whites. Even sausage casing can be made from agar. One of agar's uses is in science. So that scientists can study bacteria easily, the bacteria are raised in small glass dishes of agar.

Chewing gum is made from chicle, the dried juice of sapodilla trees, which grow in Mexico, Central America, the West Indies, and parts of Africa. Chicle does not dissolve in water, but it does dissolve in many other liquids, such as kerosene and ether. The gum is purified by dissolving it and filtering out bark, insects, and other impurities. The liquid is then evaporated, leaving clean chicle. The chicle is mixed with sugar, starch, and flavoring to make chewing gum.

Gutta-percha is made from the milky juice of trees found chiefly in the Malay Peninsula. For many uses it has been replaced by less expensive synthetic resins. But it is still used for electrical insulation, especially to protect underwater cables.

Balata is a rubberlike gum from a tropical tree. The gum is treated with chemical solvents, and the part that dissolves is recovered and used with chicle to make chewing gum. The part that is left, called gutta balata, is used to make the coverings of golf balls.

ELBERT C. WEAVER
Phillips Academy (Andover, Mass.)

See also PLASTICS.

# RESTAURANTS

A restaurant is a public eating place. The word "restaurant" was first used in France in 1765. Because the word has been used for a long time, it has become the popular way to refer not only to a place where full meals are served but also to snack shops, drive-ins, cafeterias, hotel dining rooms, and cafés.

Historical records of restaurants go back many hundreds of years. In Egypt in 512 B.C. there was a public dining place where a single dish was offered—a combination of wildfowl, onions, and cereal. The first lunch for business people is said to have been prepared by a Roman innkeeper in 40 B.C. for ship agents who were too busy to go home.

During the Middle Ages, travelers could find meals as well as lodging at inns and taverns. Where there were no inns, monasteries and manor houses sometimes served food to travelers.

By 1650, England had coffeehouses, where people met to discuss politics and literary affairs. Customers of the coffeehouses were expected to drop coins into a box on which was written "To Insure Promptness." The initials of that phrase, T.I.P., are said to be the origin of the modern word "tipping."

The French tradition of fine restaurants began after the French Revolution of 1789. During the Revolution many aristocrats who were in hiding were said to have been fed in secret by their former servants. Other wealthy citizens were willing to pay a charge for these well-cooked meals. By the time the Revolution was over, many of the chefs had gained great reputations. They continued to serve meals to paying guests.

In Colonial America wayside taverns and inns, patterned after those in England, were the only public eating places. Many of the famous old inns—such as Raleigh Tavern in Williamsburg, Virginia, and Wayside Inn in Sudbury, Massachusetts—still exist.

The first restaurant in the United States that was not a part of an inn or a tavern was Delmonico's, opened in New York City in 1827. The demand for food service away from home grew, and many other restaurants were soon started.

The cafeteria, where the guest stands in a line and picks up food at a counter, was de-

**A chef at work in the kitchen of a French restaurant.**

veloped by John Kruger in Chicago. He had seen smorgasbord, a buffet meal offering many different dishes, served in Sweden and decided to design an eating place that served meals in a similar way.

As early as 1762, an innkeeper in America started curb service for people on horseback. A person could ride up to a window and be served without dismounting. This was the forerunner of the modern drive-in.

## ▶ TYPES OF RESTAURANT SERVICE

There are many kinds of eating places available to suit the needs and tastes of everyone. The following are some of the main types of restaurant service. Many of these may be found combined in one restaurant.

**Cafeteria and Buffet Service.** Cafeterias display their food selections. The customers pick up their food at a counter and carry it to individual tables to eat. There is usually a wide variety of food items. The prices are somewhat lower than they are in restaurants where the food is brought to the table and served to the customer. Cafeterias are popular not only because of the prices but also because a meal can be obtained quickly.

**Counter Service.** In some restaurants the customer eats at a counter. Many snack shops, luncheonettes, coffee shops, and sandwich-soda fountains have counters.

**Table Service.** In a great many restaurants the customers sit at tables and are served by a waiter or waitress. This type of service may be quite informal. But in many restaurants and hotel dining rooms, the atmosphere is formal. The floor is carpeted, the lights are dimmed, and the tables are covered with white linen.

**Fast-food Service.** Fast-food restaurants serve meals that can be prepared quickly, such as hamburgers. Customers may eat inside the restaurant or pick up and pay for the food at a drive-in window.

**Take-Out Service.** Some restaurants prepare food for customers to take away and eat somewhere else. Telephone orders are accepted, and delivery may be included. Take-out places specialize in such foods as chicken and pizza.

▶**STYLES OF COOKING**

Restaurants are classified according to the foods they serve, as well as according to the type of service they provide.

In general, restaurants prepare food according to typical national eating habits. In North America and most of Europe, this would mean a variety of appetizers, main dishes (entrées), vegetables, salads, and desserts or fruit. In Asian countries, soup, rice, and dishes to accompany rice are popular.

Some restaurants feature one general kind of food, such as seafood, steaks, pancakes, or sandwiches. The featured foods generally are the best-prepared dishes on the menu (the list of dishes served).

Some restaurants serve food of only one national origin. For example, a restaurant may serve only French, Greek, Chinese, Mexican, or Italian food. Restaurants that serve French or Chinese food are especially popular and may be found all over the world.

Some restaurants specialize even more and serve food typical of only one area of a country. Food typical of New England, the South, or Hawaii may be served in restaurants found in many parts of the United States. Similarly, there are restaurants specializing in foods from northern Italy and others that specialize in southern Italian dishes.

▶**BEHIND THE SCENES IN A RESTAURANT**

Restaurants and the companies that supply restaurants with food, linens, and other items employ large numbers of people in most countries of the world. In the United States, more than 8,000,000 people work in the food-service industry. About 250,000 new employees must enter the industry each year to meet the need for personnel at all levels. Before a meal can be served to a customer in a restaurant, there are many jobs that must be done.

**Planning Menus and Food Purchases.** The first decision concerns the food items to be served. In large eating places, preparing the menu is a full-time job.

Once the menu has been chosen, food must be bought in the amounts needed. It may be bought in quantities to last a week, a month, or even several months. It is difficult to predict the number of customers who will eat in a restaurant on any one day and what dishes they will choose.

**Storing and Preparing the Food.** When the food arrives at the restaurant, it must be stored. Freezers must be available for frozen foods. Other foods, such as meats, fruits, and vegetables, must be refrigerated.

Most foodstuffs need some preparation before the actual cooking is done. Vegetables and fruits must be cleaned and perhaps cut. Meats must be sectioned into the needed cuts for cooking. Sauces, too, are usually prepared ahead of time. The actual cooking of the food is done as close as possible to the time the customers arrive.

**Serving the Food.** Once the food is cooked, it must be kept tasty until it is served. Warm foods must be kept warm, and cold foods, cold.

When customers enter a restaurant, they usually are given a menu. They make a selection and give their order to a waitress or waiter, who serves the food

**Cleanup and Maintenance.** When the customers have finished their meal, the dishes must be removed, washed, and stacked for reuse. Crumbs must be swept up, spills must be wiped away, and everything must be freshened for the next customers.

Sanitation laws for restaurants differ from country to country. In the United States, the U.S. Food and Drug Administration has approved a uniform national plan for the training of food-service managers.

CHARLES H. SANDLER
National Institute
for the Foodservice Industry

The majority of retail stores were once clustered in downtown areas. Then suburban shopping centers gained popularity. The most recent trend is toward elaborate indoor malls.

# RETAIL STORES

Almost all the food we eat, the clothes we wear, and the things we need for our homes are bought in retail stores. Goods are gathered from all over the world and made available to us in retail stores.

There are many kinds of retail stores. A retail store may be a small shop run by one or two people or a large department store with hundreds of employees. The grocery, drugstore, bakery, and candy shop are all retail stores. Department stores are usually quite large and include almost every kind of merchandise a customer might want, such as clothing, furniture, toys, and cosmetics. Specialty stores usually sell only one type of merchandise, such as hardware, furniture, or clothing. Variety stores sell many kinds of low-priced goods—stationery, toilet articles, and housewares, for example. Discount stores offer merchandise at lower than usual prices. Discount stores are also called cut-rate or off-price stores. Supermarkets are retail stores that deal in food products, although many now include a large number of nonfood items. Many of these types of retail stores may belong to a "chain," or group of stores under the same ownership. Chain stores often have many branches in different cities.

Shopping centers or malls—clusters of stores—have become a familiar feature of the landscape across the United States and in other countries. In a mall, many stores are enclosed under one roof so that customers can shop with ease and comfort. In addition to department and chain stores, malls may contain offices, hotels, movie theaters, restaurants, and other services.

Retail stores of one kind or another are found in countries all over the world. But they are not all the same. In the United States, Canada, Western Europe, and Japan, department stores are quite common. In many Japanese department stores, the roof of the building is often a playground for children, with fishponds, merry-go-rounds, and slides.

Variety stores, formerly called dime stores, are common in many countries. But specialty stores and grocery stores are probably the most universal kinds of retail establishments. Supermarkets, first popular in the United States, Canada, and Great Britain, are now found around the world.

▶IMPORTANCE OF RETAILING

Retail stores buy goods in large quantities from producers and wholesalers and sell these goods in smaller quantities to consumers. It is in the retail store that the customer has the chance to examine the goods and say, "I don't like this," or "I'll take that." Thus the merchant learns what the public wants and needs.

The orders that retailers send to manufacturers reflect their knowledge of their customers' likes and dislikes. Naturally they order items that are in demand and do not order items they cannot sell. Manufacturers also want to sell as much as possible, so they make more of the popular items ordered by retailers. To make more of these items, they need more of the raw material from which these items are made. The producers of the raw material, in turn, produce more of it.

Retailing is one of the largest industries in the United States. There are nearly 1.6 million retail stores. This is 23 percent of all the country's businesses. More than 22 million people work in stores in the United States— about one out of every six workers.

## ▶ CAREERS IN RETAILING

There are many different kinds of jobs in retailing. You can be the all-around person who runs a local store, or you can work in any of the dozens of departments of a large store.

A large department store has more selling jobs than any other kind of job. But people also work as buyers of merchandise, advertising copywriters, accountants, interior designers, and human relations experts.

Retailing offers more executive opportunities than almost any other trade. It has a high proportion of executives, whereas in other industries there are often hundreds of people under one supervisor. In retailing, the road to success is not easy or short; but for the hardworking, interested person, retailing holds great rewards.

Reviewed by CHARLES A. BINDER
National Retail Merchants

See also DEPARTMENT STORES; SALES AND MARKETING; SUPERMARKETS.

# RETARDATION, MENTAL

No two people are exactly alike. We each develop at different rates and have our own unique characteristics. Most of these differences do not limit our ability to deal with the everyday tasks of life. In some cases, however, a person may develop so slowly or may fail to master so many basic skills that parents and professionals decide that the person would benefit from extra help. A decision about what type of challenges the person experiences must be made. This is called a diagnosis. One possible diagnosis is mental retardation.

## ▶ DIAGNOSIS

The diagnosis of mental retardation requires that a person meet three criteria. First, the person must be evaluated using a comprehensive test of intelligence. Such tests provide an IQ score that indicates how the person compares in intelligence to other people of the same age. Most people receive an IQ score near 100, which indicates average intelligence. A diagnosis of mental retardation requires that a person has an IQ of 70 or below. Second, the person must have challenges in adaptive behavior—the ability to succeed at the activities that are typical for most people his or her age, such as taking care of personal hygiene, communicating effectively, or mastering basic school or work tasks. Third, these challenges in intelligence and adaptive behavior must be apparent before the person reaches the age of 18. (A person who has problems that occurred after age 18 would receive a different diagnosis.)

## ▶ DIFFERENCES IN SEVERITY

Not all people with mental retardation are affected to the same degree or need the same amount of help. For this reason, professionals classify people with mental retardation according to whether they require intermittent (occasional), limited, extensive, or pervasive (constant or total) support. Those who are mildly affected by mental retardation may need help only when they are learning new skills or entering new settings. People with more severe mental retardation may require constant supervision and assistance.

## ▶ FREQUENCY OF OCCURRENCE

The exact number of people who have mental retardation is difficult to estimate, but it is probably between 1 and 2 percent of the population. The occurrence of mental retardation is 1½ to 2 times more frequent in males than in females. Although children with the most severe forms of mental retardation are typically identified at very young ages, often at birth, many children are not diagnosed until they are between 10 and 14 years old.

Children with mental retardation and their typically developing peers both benefit from friendships with each other.

▶ CAUSES OF MENTAL RETARDATION

Mental retardation has many causes, including genetic problems and environmental factors. Scientists have identified more than 750 genetic problems that cause mental retardation. The most common of these is **Down syndrome**, which is caused by the presence of an extra chromosome. The chromosomes in our body are made up of genes, which contain the chemical instructions for growth and development. Most people have 46 chromosomes in each of their cells. People with Down syndrome have 47 chromosomes. This gives them a distinctive physical appearance, including a small face and eyes that slant upward. The presence of the extra chromosome can also cause health problems, such as heart defects. Language is a special problem for these individuals, and their speech can be difficult to understand.

**Fragile X syndrome** is the second most common known genetic cause of mental retardation. In fragile X syndrome, people inherit a gene that fails to make the necessary chemical instructions for typical growth and development. This gene is on the X chromosome. Males have one X chromosome in each of their cells, whereas females have two X chromosomes. As a result, males with fragile X syndrome are more likely than females to receive a diagnosis of mental retardation because males do not have a healthy "backup" copy of the gene. Some females with fragile X syndrome may have mental retardation, while others have learning disabilities and still others are not affected at all.

A third genetic cause of mental retardation is **phenylketonuria (PKU)**. Children with PKU inherit a gene that causes problems with an enzyme that helps the body break down certain foods into the substances it needs to grow and develop. This leads to a buildup of chemicals that poison the body. If left untreated, children with PKU suffer the effects of this gradual poisoning and by middle childhood are diagnosed as having mental retardation.

Environmental factors can also cause mental retardation. Consuming alcohol, smoking, or using illegal drugs during pregnancy can hurt a developing baby. Alcohol use during pregnancy can hurt the fetus by causing **fetal alcohol syndrome (FAS)**. Children with FAS have a distinctive appearance, including a small head, widely spaced eyes, and thin lips. In addition to mental retardation, they can have severe emotional problems. Maternal infection with certain viruses, such as rubella, during early pregnancy can also lead to mental retardation.

Other environmental factors can cause mental retardation after birth. These include exposure to lead and other poisons in the environment. Although lead is no longer allowed to be present in products such as gasoline and paint, it can still be found in the environment, particularly in the paint on homes built before the early 1970's. Children can ingest this lead by eating peeling paint or by swallowing paint dust. Mental retardation can also be caused after birth by head trauma from an accident, by a stroke, and by serious diseases, such as meningitis and encephalitis.

### PREVENTION AND IDENTIFICATION

Many cases of mental retardation are preventable. For example, infants can be screened for PKU using a simple blood test. Infants who are found to have PKU can be put on a special diet that prevents the poisonous buildup that causes mental retardation. Good prenatal care, including monitoring of a pregnant woman's diet, can also help prevent mental retardation. Fetal alcohol syndrome can be prevented by avoiding the use of alcohol during pregnancy. Limiting exposure to lead and other environmental poisons and vaccinating children against certain diseases are additional preventive measures. Also, the use of bicycle helmets, car seats, and seat belts can reduce the risk of brain trauma from accidents that can lead to mental retardation.

There are also several tests that can determine if unborn children have genetic problems, such as Down syndrome or fragile X syndrome. Amniocentesis and chorionic villus sampling are two such techniques. Each test involves obtaining cells from the unborn baby and examining the genetic material of the cells.

### EDUCATION

For much of the 1900's, people with mental retardation were not treated very well. They were often locked away in institutions that did little more than keep them alive. That situation has changed dramatically, due in part to changes in society's attitudes and the passage of some important laws.

Public Law 94-142, the Education for All Handicapped Children Act, guarantees all children with special needs, including mental retardation, between the ages of 3 and 21, the right to an appropriate public education. This law is the basis for inclusion, which means that children with mental retardation or other special needs attend regular education classes for at least part of the school day. Students with mental retardation who attend regular education classes may do so with special assistance in the form of tutors or aides or with changes in the curriculum designed to overcome the students' challenges. Inclusion can have benefits for both students with mental retardation and those without mental retardation, who can learn patience and respect for individual differences.

Public Law 99-457 requires education, health, and social services for infants and toddlers with special needs and help for their parents. These early intervention services help ensure that young children with mental retardation start off on the right foot and that families develop the skills and resources they need to provide healthy, caring, and supportive homes for their children.

Public Law 93-112 helps people with mental retardation and other special needs prepare to finish school and live as productive and independent adults by assisting with job skills and finding employment. It also helps families arrange care for their adult children with mental retardation in their homes or in community-based housing rather than in hospitals and other institutions.

### FINDING AN IDENTITY

Most teenagers and young adults struggle to figure out who they are, what they want to be, and how to be independent from their parents. In short, they search for their identities. People with mental retardation also have a sense of identity and are influenced by the world around them. They can be aware of the challenges that keep them from doing the same things as other people their own age, such as having a driver's license or living independently. As a result, the person with mental retardation may experience frustration and sadness. Fortunately, with the help of parents, teachers, other professionals, and their typically developing peers, many individuals with mental retardation are able to graduate from high school, live away from their parents, have jobs, and start their own families.

LEONARD ABBEDUTO
MELISSA M. PAVETTO
Department of Educational Psychology
Waisman Center on Mental Retardation and
Human Development
University of Wisconsin-Madison

See also DOWN SYNDROME; MENTAL ILLNESS.

**REUTHER, WALTER P.** See LABOR MOVEMENT (Profiles).

**REVELS, HIRAM RHOADES.** See UNITED STATES, CONGRESS OF THE (Profiles: Senators).

## REVERE, PAUL (1735–1818)

Paul Revere, a silversmith and American Revolutionary patriot, was born in Boston, Massachusetts, on New Year's Day, 1735. His father, Apollos Rivoire, was born in France. Because Apollos Rivoire was a Huguenot (Protestant), his religious beliefs were not tolerated in France. In 1716, he emigrated to America. He served as an apprentice silversmith in Boston and then opened his own shop. To make his name easier to pronounce, Apollos Rivoire changed it to "Paul Revere."

His son, young Paul Revere, attended the North Writing (Grammar) School. There he learned to read well enough to understand a newspaper or book without difficulty. He also learned to write reasonably well. While in his early teens, he was taught his father's trade. Paul was 19 when his father died, and he took over the family business. In 1757, he married Sara Orne.

Revere was a skilled artisan, and he carried on a thriving business. He won a reputation as the leading silversmith in Boston and one of the best in America. Many examples of his work have been saved and can be seen in museums throughout the United States.

### ▶ REVOLUTIONARY PATRIOT

Revere was an influential figure among the artisans of Boston, and he took an active part in the events leading up to the Revolution. He joined the North End Caucus, a group of colonists organized to protect the rights of the American colonists against the actions of the British Government. He became friendly with such colonial leaders as James Otis, Dr. Joseph Warren (1741–75), Samuel and John Adams, and John Hancock. Along with the majority of other Massachusetts colonists, Revere protested the Stamp Act of 1765. This act placed a tax on newspapers, legal and business documents, and many other items. Later, he was asked by the Sons of Liberty, who led the opposition to the British, to make a silver punch bowl in honor of the members of the Massachusetts legislature who had defied the Stamp Act. Revere also made many engravings celebrating the exploits of Massachusetts patriots.

In 1773, Revere took part in what became known as the Boston Tea Party. Angered

---

The following excerpts are from Henry Wadsworth Longfellow's poem "Paul Revere's Ride." Note that in the second stanza Revere is incorrectly described as being "on the opposite shore."

### PAUL REVERE'S RIDE

Listen, my children, and you shall hear
Of the midnight ride of Paul Revere,
On the eighteenth of April, in Seventy-five;
Hardly a man is now alive
Who remembers that famous day and year.

He said to his friend, "If the British march
By land or sea from the town to-night,
Hang a lantern aloft in the belfry arch
Of the North Church tower as a signal light,—
One, if by land, and two, if by sea;
And I on the opposite shore will be,
Ready to ride and spread the alarm
Through every Middlesex village and farm,
For the country folk to be up and to arm."

. . .

So through the night rode Paul Revere;
And so through the night went his cry of alarm
To every Middlesex village and farm,—
A cry of defiance and not of fear,
A voice in the darkness, a knock at the door,
And a word that shall echo forevermore!
For, borne on the night-wind of the Past,
Through all our history, to the last,
In the hour of darkness and peril and need,
The people will waken and listen to hear
The hurrying hoof-beats of that steed,
And the midnight message of Paul Revere.

because the British Government had placed a tax on tea without the consent of the colonists, Revere and over 100 other patriots from Boston and neighboring towns disguised themselves as Indians. They boarded three British ships, loaded with tea, in Boston Harbor and dumped the tea chests overboard.

Revere served as a courier for the patriots' Committee of Safety. He also was appointed official courier from the Massachusetts Provincial Congress to the Continental Congress. Communications were poor, and the role of the courier on horseback was a vital one. Revere rode to New York and Philadelphia several times to carry news of important events. But his most famous ride took place on the night of April 18, 1775.

A group of patriots, fearing a clash with the British soldiers, had stored ammunition and other military supplies at Concord, Massachusetts, about 35 kilometers (22 miles) from Boston. But they began to suspect that the British military governor, General Thomas Gage (1721–87), was planning a secret raid on the supplies. On April 16, Revere was sent to warn John Hancock and Samuel Adams, who were at nearby Lexington.

Upon his return, Revere and other patriots arranged for a warning system to indicate the British plan of attack. If the British came by land, one lantern would be hung high in the steeple of Boston's North Church; if they came by sea, two lanterns would be placed there. The signal would be flashed to patriots waiting at Charlestown, Massachusetts, across the Charles River.

### ▶ REVERE'S RIDE

Revere knew the North Church well, for when he was 12, he and some friends had rung the bells for church services. On the night of April 18 he was summoned by Dr. Joseph Warren. The British were planning to cross the Charles River by boat and then march to Concord. Revere was told to give the signal—two lanterns—and to ride for Lexington, rousing the Minutemen. A second rider, William Dawes (1745–99), was dispatched by another route.

Revere alerted the church sexton, who lighted the lanterns. Meanwhile, Revere returned home, put on his riding boots, and headed for the river, where his boat was hid-

den. Two friends accompanied him. The boat's oars were wrapped with a woman's flannel petticoat to muffle their sound in the water. Cautiously, the three men rowed past the *Somerset,* a British man-of-war guarding the bay. Finally they reached Charlestown. The local patriots had seen the signal and had one of their best horses waiting.

The countryside was thick with British soldiers as Revere galloped off. He eluded two of them guarding the road to Cambridge. He entered Medford, alerted the Minutemen and, then, in his own words, "I alarumed [alarmed] almost every house till I got to Lexington." Dawes and another rider, Dr. Samuel Prescott (1751?–77), joined Revere in Lexington, and together they rode on to Concord. About halfway there, the three were stopped by British soldiers. In the chase that followed, Revere was captured. Dawes fell from his horse and escaped into the woods. Only Prescott rode on to Concord, where he alerted the patriots.

Later that night, Revere was released—without his horse. He walked back to Lexington, arriving just as the first shots of the Revolution were being fired.

During the war Revere was given a number of assignments. He made copper plates for printing money. He designed the seal of the state of Massachusetts. And he was sent to the Continental Congress in Philadelphia to arrange for the manufacture of gunpowder, which was badly needed. He then helped to set up a powder mill in Canton, Massachusetts. At the same time, he served in the Massachusetts militia, rising to the rank of lieutenant colonel.

### ▶ LATER YEARS

When the war ended in 1783, Revere returned to his work as a silversmith. He also set up a bell foundry and in 1792 cast the first church bell made in Massachusetts.

After his first wife died in 1773, Revere married Rachel Walker. He had 16 children, but many of them died in infancy.

Paul Revere died in Boston on May 10, 1818, at the age of 83. In tribute one newspaper declared: "Seldom has the tomb closed upon a life so honourable and useful."

CLARENCE L. VER STEEG
Author, *The American People: Their History*

*The Spirit of '76,* painted by Archibald M. Willard for the 100th anniversary of the Revolutionary War shows patriots rallying to the cause of American independence.

# Revolutionary War

April 19, 1775, marked the end of an era. On that day the first shots of the Revolutionary War were fired at Lexington, Massachusetts. Six and a half years later, on October 19, 1781, the British forces surrendered at Yorktown, Virginia. What had started as a fight for the rights of English people in the 13 colonies ended in the creation of an independent nation—the United States of America. This war is also called the American Revolution and the American War of Independence.

▶ **BACKGROUND OF THE REVOLUTION**

Life in the 13 colonies had been going on undisturbed by England for over 100 years. The great distance between the colonies and England was one reason for this. Another was the pressure of British involvement in wars on both the European and the American conti-

nents. During this period the colonists learned to manage their own affairs.

Life in the colonies differed in many ways from life in England. English visitors who went to the colonies found it difficult to understand the new way of life that the colonists were leading. The independent spirit and the attitude of the colonists toward the British Government were also puzzling to them. King George III did not understand the colonists, either. He was a well-meaning monarch, but he was shortsighted in his approach to the colonists and their problems.

The people who had journeyed to America from Europe had gone in search of the opportunity to lead a better life and earn a better living. Many had gone to escape the political and religious persecution that existed throughout Europe at that time. America was a land of opportunity. Restrictions existed in the colonies as they did in most countries then. But the colonists did not find them especially oppressive.

### Opposition to British Policies

British policy toward the 13 colonies changed abruptly in 1763 after the French and Indian War. As a result of winning this war, England was the dominant power on the North American continent. But the war had been an expensive one, and the English people were heavily taxed. And in addition to the war expenses, England now had a vast new territory to govern.

The British Government began to feel that the colonists should pay their share of the costs of the colonial administration, including the establishment of a postwar army. Because this army would protect the colonists, the British Government believed that the colonists should help pay for it. To reduce the possibility of further trouble on the western frontier, the British issued the Proclamation of 1763. This closed the lands west of the Allegheny Mountains to further settlement or colonization.

These measures angered the colonists. They felt that they were now being taxed unfairly and that their freedom of movement was being unjustly curtailed.

**Sugar Act.** In 1764 the Revenue, or Sugar, Act was passed by the British Parliament. The molasses trade between the colonies and the French and Spanish West Indies had been extremely profitable for the colonies. This act made the tax on molasses from the French and Spanish West Indies much higher than the tax on molasses from the British West Indies. It was hoped that the colonists would buy from the British islands or pay the tax. Customs officials were given more power to enforce the tax on molasses.

The colonists felt that these measures and those that followed violated their colonial charters and their rights as English subjects. They argued that they were being taxed by a parliament in which they had no representative. "No taxation without representation" was the cry that echoed throughout the colonies. The British Government, on the other hand, argued that the interests of English people everywhere were represented in Parlia-

Left: A typical British tax stamp, used after the passage of the Stamp Act in 1765. Right: A woodcut expressing colonial opposition to "the fatal stamp."

ment, whether they had a representative there or not. The colonists rejected this argument and said that their only legal allegiance was to George III and not to the Parliament.

**Quartering and Stamp Acts.** In 1765 the British prime minister, George Grenville, persuaded Parliament to pass the Stamp Act and the Quartering Act. The Quartering Act required colonial authorities to provide certain supplies for the British troops stationed in the colonies. The colonists were angered by this —especially by a provision of the act saying that under certain circumstances, they would have to quarter British soldiers in their homes.

The Stamp Act required the colonists to pay for stamps on all legal documents, business forms, and even newspapers. This stamp was really not so unusual. In fact, even today, legal documents, playing cards, and cigarettes must be stamped. But the colonists were not used to being taxed. They especially resented being taxed by a parliament that did not represent them.

The British Government never expected the storm of protest that the Stamp Act created in America. The Stamp Act was criticized in every colony. Royal agents attempting to enforce the act were beaten by angry colonists. A Bostonian named James Otis agitated strongly against the act. "Taxation without representation is tyranny!" he declared.

Boston became the center of colonial defiance of England's tax policies. A mob of Bostonians ransacked the home of Thomas Hutchinson, the royal lieutenant governor. Rioters burned the barge used by the royal tax collector. Tempers ran high in Boston, and discontent boiled up in each of the 13 colonies. Samuel Adams became the chief speaker against the British, and other Bostonians rallied around him. Adams found an able associate in John Hancock, a wealthy merchant.

Citizens' groups called the Sons of Liberty sprang up in all the colonies to protest the Stamp Act. By October, 1765, opposition to the tax served as the basis for a congress. The Stamp Act Congress, with delegates from nine colonies, met in New York. It was the first intercolonial meeting called for and arranged by the colonists themselves.

Among the speeches delivered, one suggested the new idea of colonial unity. Christopher Gadsden, a South Carolina merchant, proclaimed, "There ought to be no New England man, no New Yorker, known on the continent, but all of us Americans!"

If the delegates were not yet ready to accept that proposition, they displayed enough solidarity to draw up a Declaration of Rights. This declaration suggested to the King that the colonies could do their own taxing, since they were not represented in Parliament.

**Townshend Acts.** The Stamp Act proved unenforceable and was revoked after a year. But colonial jubilation over the repeal ended quickly when Parliament passed the Declaratory Act. This act said that Parliament had every right to tax the colonies. New, more hateful taxes were passed by Parliament in 1767. These were the Townshend Acts, named after Charles Townshend, the British chancellor of the exchequer. They placed a duty on many products brought into the colonies from England, particularly lead, glass, paint, paper, wine—and tea.

Colonial reaction to the Townshend Acts was furious, since the new law gave any officer of the King the right to search people's houses for taxable goods. To counter the Townshend Acts, non-importation agreements were reached among the colonial merchants. This meant that merchants agreed not to import any goods from England.

**Boston Massacre.** It became quite respectable, especially in busy Boston, to smuggle goods that were taxable under the Townshend Acts. In 1768, King George, annoyed by the widespread disobedience to the despised law in Boston, ordered 4,000 troops under General Thomas Gage to be sent there, along with a flotilla of warships. The Americans would be shown their place.

The Redcoats, or "Lobsterbacks" (as Bostonians nicknamed the British soldiers), received a cold welcome. Bostonians and soldiers brawled in taverns and on the streets.

Matters grew more tense, and serious violence seemed imminent. To prevent riots in the streets of Boston, British authorities shipped several battalions out of the city. They hoped that with fewer soldiers around, the situation might become calmer. But shifting a few hundred Redcoats did not pacify the Bostonians. They wanted all the soldiers to go.

Matters came to a head on March 5, 1770. Some boys taunted a British sentry walking his post at the Customs House on King Street. A group of local toughs gathered and began throwing snowballs at the sentry. The guard called for help. A squad of soldiers came with bayonets fixed on their loaded muskets. The crowd, which had swelled into a mob, grew ugly. Sticks, brickbats, and snowballs showered upon the troops.

Suddenly a British musket went off. Then a ragged volley raked the threatening mob. When the gunsmoke cleared, five civilians lay dead in the snow—among them, a free black laborer named Crispus Attucks. Several other Bostonians were wounded. The ugly affair was labeled the Boston Massacre.

**Committee of Correspondence.** In June, 1772, a royal revenue vessel, the *Gaspée,* was chasing smugglers near the coast of Rhode Island. The naval vessel ran aground in Narragansett Bay, and a band of citizens of Providence rowed out to the cutter and burned it. The British Government threatened to take the guilty colonists back to England for trial.

It was at this time (November, 1772) that Sam Adams proposed that the colonies form a committee of correspondence. In this way, people in each of the 13 colonies would

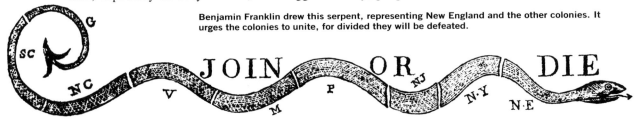

Benjamin Franklin drew this serpent, representing New England and the other colonies. It urges the colonies to unite, for divided they will be defeated.

JOIN OR DIE

be kept informed through letters of what was going on in the other colonies.

**Tea Act and Tea Party.** In 1770 the British prime minister, Lord North, repealed all the Townshend Act taxes except that on tea. Because of this tax the colonists refused to buy British tea. As a result the British East India Company was in financial trouble and asked Parliament for help. In 1773, Parliament passed the Tea Act. This act made it possible for the company to pay the Townshend tax and still charge a lower price than any other importer of tea was charging. But there was still a tax on the tea. To the Americans this was taxation without representation. Sam Adams called for an American boycott of tea. The Sons of Liberty enforced the boycott, often with violence against offenders.

On the night of December 16, 1773, there were three tea-laden cargo ships from England at anchor in Boston Harbor. Several hundred Bostonians, disguised as Indians, raided the vessels and dumped 342 cases of tea into the water. This event is known as the Boston Tea Party.

**Intolerable Acts.** The tea dumped into the harbor was very valuable, and the British reacted vigorously to this act of defiance. Lord North's government drew up the so-called Intolerable Acts (1774). One of these acts was the Boston Port Bill, which closed Boston Harbor to all shipping. Warships of the Royal Navy patrolled the harbor mouth. Boston was effectively blockaded, except for a narrow neck of land that connected the city to the mainland. The wealthy port faced both hunger and economic ruin.

This punishment was to continue until the citizens of Boston paid for the tea that had been dumped. To prevent mob violence, General Gage placed the city under martial law and brought in hundreds of troops.

The Bostonians proved more stubborn than the British. They refused to pay a cent. Word of Boston's plight was sent out to the other colonies through the Committees of Correspondence. The people of New York, Connecticut, Philadelphia, Baltimore, and Charleston rushed food and money to the surrounded, besieged, and beleaguered town. Every colony rallied to Boston's support.

### First Continental Congress

In September, 1774, the First Continental Congress was held at Philadelphia. All the colonies except Georgia were represented.

The Boston Tea Party was organized by a group of patriots to protest the Tea Act. Disguised as Indians, they boarded British ships and dumped their cargoes of tea overboard.

The delegates drew up a list of rights and grievances addressed to the people of Britain. At the same time they pledged support for Boston.

One of the most important accomplishments of this Congress was the Continental Association. This was an agreement among the colonies to refrain completely from importing or exporting British goods until Britain met their demands. But George III declared, "The die is now cast, the colonies must either submit or triumph. . . . There must always be one tax to keep up the right, and as such I approve of the Tea Duty."

The winter of 1774–75 brought growing discontent to Boston. The Port Bill had turned the once prosperous harbor into a desert. Ships lay rotting at anchor, commerce was at a standstill, and unemployment grew each day. In April, 1775, Parliament passed the **Restraining Act,** which forbade the colonists to trade with any country other than England and the islands of the British West Indies. It also barred the colonists from fishing in the waters off Newfoundland.

### Preparations for War

Recruits swelled the ranks of the Sons of Liberty. Flames of revolt were rising in Boston, but the British ignored the obvious military preparations of the Americans. Neither General Gage nor his officers could seriously consider "bumpkins, peasants, and illiterate plowboys" a threat.

General Gage mocked the Colonial militia, and he was fully convinced that the Port Bill would eventually humble Boston into submission. This viewpoint was supported not only in Boston but in every colony by persons called Tories, or Loyalists. These individuals remained faithful to King George III and considered the Patriots (those colonists who were critical of British rule) traitors and rebels. This bad feeling between Tories and Patriots was to cause much bloodshed in the coming years.

In February, 1775, General Gage began to take more seriously the military activities of the Patriot group called the Minutemen (because they were ready to take up arms at a minute's notice). His soldiers began looking for hidden weapons, and on several occasions they narrowly avoided clashes with the Minutemen.

### ▶ THE WAR BEGINS

The main American arms storehouse was at Concord, about 32 kilometers (20 miles), from Boston. To protect the guns, shot, and powder concealed there, the Americans decided that if any large British force was sent out of Boston, all available militia would assemble to block their route to Concord.

On April 18, 1775, rebel spies warned Dr. Joseph Warren, a leading Patriot, that Gage was ferrying troops across the Charles River for a swift march against Lexington and Concord. Warren sent Paul Revere and William Dawes to rouse the Minutemen. All that night, Revere and Dawes rode, in the words of Longfellow's poem, "through every Middlesex village and farm," spreading the alarm that the British were coming.

Patriots leaped from bed, grabbing their powder horns, cartridge boxes, and flintlocks. Then they dashed into the darkness to mobilize at pre-arranged places.

### Lexington and Concord

At dawn on April 19 the British column reached Lexington. Fewer than 100 Minutemen had gathered to face the Redcoats. The British commander, Major John Pitcairn, ordered his troops to spread out. Awed by the sight of so many soldiers, the Americans, under Captain John Parker, broke ranks and began to straggle away. Suddenly a shot rang out, and then others followed. Eight Americans fell dead. Ten others were wounded. The Revolutionary War had begun.

Later, at Concord, Minutemen drove the Redcoats from the town. From behind every rock, tree, and hill, men and boys blasted away at the British. The hated Lobsterbacks withdrew from Concord and retreated toward Boston. Their march was plagued almost every step of the way by American snipers.

Lexington and Concord unleashed a terrible storm over the 13 colonies. Patrick Henry of Virginia had voiced the sentiments of most Americans in March when he thundered, "I know not what course others may take, but as for me, give me liberty or give me death!" But the colonists were divided among themselves at the start of the war. Thousands still supported the Crown. Before long, neighbor fought neighbor in a bitter civil war between Loyalists and Patriots.

No one knows which side fired "the shot heard round the world" at the Battle of Lexington on April 19, 1775. It was the first shot of the Revolutionary War.

General Gage soon realized that what the Americans lacked in military skill they made up for in bravery and determination. He soon found himself in an unenviable position. Some 6,000 militiamen commanded by General Artemas Ward ringed Boston and kept Gage locked up inside the city. The only route open to the British was by sea.

Day by day, Ward's army grew more numerous as detachments marched in from Rhode Island, Connecticut, and Vermont (then known as the New Hampshire grants). Leaders who had some military training also joined the forces surrounding Gage. Israel Putnam, a veteran Indian fighter; John Stark, veteran of many frontier battles; and young Nathanael Greene were among the leaders.

The Americans did not sit still. On May 10, 1775, a detachment led jointly by Ethan Allen of Vermont and Benedict Arnold, who commanded a Connecticut militia company, surprised and captured the British stronghold of Fort Ticonderoga on the southern tip of Lake Champlain. Allen's "Green Mountain Boys" swarmed into the enemy fort with hardly a shot fired.

Left: A British private stationed at Fort Ticonderoga on Lake Champlain. Right: A private in the American forces that captured Ticonderoga in May, 1775.

The Battle of Bunker Hill really took place on Breed's Hill, near Boston. The Americans resisted several British charges before they ran out of ammunition and had to retreat.

### Bunker Hill

On June 17, 1775, a major clash took place between the Americans and the British. General Ward had some troops dig in on heights overlooking the British lines. The Patriots entrenched themselves on Breed's Hill next to Bunker Hill.

General Gage could not allow the Americans to hold a fortified position that dominated his. He held a meeting with three officers newly arrived from England—General Sir William Howe, General Sir Henry Clinton, and General John Burgoyne. They advised him to blast the Americans off the hill with artillery.

A furious bombardment by naval and field guns failed to dislodge the Yankees. Gage sent several regiments under General Howe to do the job. The British regulars started up Breed's Hill as though on parade. But their perfect alignment was shattered by a murderous volley from the Americans on the hilltop, who had been ordered by one of their commanders—William Prescott—''Don't fire until you see the whites of their eyes.''

Again and again the Redcoats tried to storm the crest, only to be beaten back. It was not until the Americans had run out of powder and shot that they yielded the position. Taking the hill cost the British many more dead and wounded than the Americans suffered, although among the fallen Patriots was Dr. Joseph Warren.

When the battle was over, a young British officer exclaimed, ''I can't believe it! Those bumpkins fought like Englishmen!'' ''Of course they did,'' another officer said. ''After all, they *are* Englishmen!''

### Second Continental Congress

At the very moment the fighting was raging on Breed's Hill, a less spectacular but more momentous event was taking place in Philadelphia, where the delegates to the Second Continental Congress were gathered.

A Massachusetts delegate had proposed to the Congress the formation of an army responsible to Congress and not to the colonial legislatures. This was a novel idea and a stirring one. With such an army in the field, the British would be facing not raw militia but a trained, disciplined force.

Such leading Rebels as John Hancock and John Adams thought that a Continental army would be a good thing. They argued in favor of the proposal, and Congress voted to create a regular army. Its 20,000 members would include those militia forces then serving against the British.

**Washington Takes Command.** Selecting a commander in chief for the new army called for much consideration. At last Congress chose a 43-year-old Virginian, a man of wealth and position named George Washington, a colonel in the Virginia militia. Washington had fought in the French and Indian War. He was a good organizer and a man of quiet strength, who inspired confidence.

The newly appointed commander in chief went to Boston and took over the Continental Army at Cambridge, Massachusetts, on July 2, 1775. The troops he inherited were disorganized and disorderly rather than a disciplined military group. But after Washington came, they began to behave in a more soldierly manner. He worked and drilled them relentlessly.

There was little action for the army around Boston that winter. The American forces had the British penned up in Boston, but Washington did not know how long he could keep them there. A rumor spread that reinforcements were on the way for General Howe, who had replaced Gage as commander at Boston. Washington knew that a determined assault by superior British forces would break his blockade lines. He needed cannon to bombard the British positions. Someone remembered that at Fort Ticonderoga there were heavy guns, and Washington's chief of artillery, Colonel Henry Knox, offered to bring this equipment from the captured British fort.

Knox had undertaken a difficult job. It was now November. Hauling the cannon overland in the dead of winter seemed impossible. But Henry Knox was a determined man. He gathered a party of volunteers and began the long haul from Ticonderoga to Boston after loading the guns on ox-drawn sleds.

### Defeat in Canada

Progress was slow and tedious, but the guns were dragged to Boston over ice-slick trains in bone-chilling cold. While Knox was making his painful way with the cannon, an American military expedition under the command of General Richard Montgomery captured Montreal in Canada in November, 1775. The colonists hoped to gain the aid of the French

Canadians and to prevent the British from using Canada as a base for attack. But the American adventure in Canada ended disastrously when an attempt to capture Quebec failed. Montgomery was killed during the fighting. And only a handful of survivors eventually stumbled back across the border under the leadership of Colonel Benedict Arnold, who assumed command after Montgomery's death. The Americans abandoned Montreal. Their dreams of conquest in Canada were over.

### ▶WAR IN THE EAST: 1776–77

But the fortunes of war turned for the Yankees in March, 1776. Henry Knox finally reached Boston with the cannon. Washington mounted the guns on Dorchester Heights. The fear of a devastating American bombardment was so great that General Howe evacuated Boston by sea on March 17, 1776. Some thought he was sailing for Halifax, Nova Scotia. But others, including Washington, believed that Howe intended to attack New York City by land and sea in a major effort to capture that great port.

The loss of New York and its fine harbor would be a stunning blow to the Americans. To forestall the possibility, Washington rushed troops there from Boston. His troops were set to work digging entrenchments and gun emplacements from one end of Manhattan Island to the other.

Washington had correctly guessed Howe's intentions. In June a British fleet of 130 warships arrived in New York Harbor. It was followed in July by another fleet carrying more Redcoats and Hessians (German soldiers hired by King George III to fight for England).

The British landed on Staten Island, ferried over to Brooklyn, and drove the outnumbered Americans from one defensive position to another. A succession of battles in Brooklyn, Long Island, Manhattan, and White Plains ended in American defeat. The major battle took place on Long Island on August 27, 1776. All Rebel resistance around New York City and Westchester County was broken. During this campaign, Captain Nathan Hale was executed by the British for crossing their lines to get information for Washington.

The British occupied New York in mid-September, 1776, while Washington, pursued by strong enemy forces under General Lord Cornwallis, retreated to Peekskill, New York. From there he crossed the Hudson River and began a long and grueling march through New Jersey. He crossed the Delaware River near Trenton and paused to rest his exhausted troops. At the time, Washington had only 5,000 soldiers. They were thinly clad, hungry, poorly armed, and disheartened. Never had the American cause been at such a low ebb.

## Declaration of Independence

The Second Continental Congress meeting in Philadelphia passed the Declaration of Independence on July 4, 1776. The motion for a declaration of independence had been made on June 7 by Richard Henry Lee of Virginia. Virginia's great leader Thomas Jefferson wrote the text of the Declaration of Independence. The Declaration gave a new dignity to the American cause. The Patriots were now fighting for their freedom as a nation—the United States of America.

In the winter of 1776 a bleak future seemed to stretch before the Americans. But all did not lose hope. A writer named Thomas Paine penned a stirring series of pamphlets called *The Crisis,* in which he wrote: "These are the times that try men's souls. The summer soldier and the sunshine patriot will, in this crisis, shrink from the service of their country; but he that stands it *now,* deserves the love and thanks of man and woman."

## Trenton and Princeton

George Washington was no "summer soldier," and the tattered soldiers he led were not "sunshine patriots." They longed to strike a blow at the enemy. The opportunity came on Christmas Eve, 1776. Scouts brought word to Washington that in Trenton, on the opposite shore of the Delaware River, 1,400 Hessians under Colonel Johann Rall were celebrating the holiday.

Washington decided to break up the party. On Christmas night his troops crossed the ice-choked Delaware during a sleet storm. Rugged former whalers from Marblehead, Massachusetts, handled the boats, which transported troops and cannon to the enemy side of the river. At daybreak the Americans were in position. They fell on the Hessians with such fury that Rall and most of his troops were killed.

General William Howe was furious over the Trenton affair. He ordered General Cornwallis to "run Washington into the ground." By January 2, 1777, Cornwallis had apparently succeeded. Washington's troops were surrounded in Trenton by 8,000 British regulars.

But the Americans slipped out of the British trap and escaped to Morristown, New Jersey, where the Continental army went into winter camp. Before encamping, Washington scored another triumph over the enemy at Princeton, New Jersey. There he suddenly turned on the pursuing British and scattered some of the

General Washington reviews his troops at their winter quarters at Valley Forge, Pennsylvania, in 1777. That winter was bitterly cold, and the army was short of supplies.

King's best troops in a sharp battle on January 3, 1777.

Somehow the American Army survived the grueling winter at Morristown. With the coming of spring, the army's spirits lifted. Congress had managed to purchase supplies in Europe. Guns, muskets, powder, shot, shoes, and clothing were distributed to the troops.

The British also stirred with the coming of good weather. A bold plan had been conceived to end the revolution at one stroke. General John Burgoyne was to strike south from Lake Champlain in an advance to Albany, New York, while General Howe was to head north from New York and join Burgoyne. This maneuver would take the Hudson Valley and probably end the war—if it was successful. But something went wrong. Instead of marching to Albany, Howe moved against the American capital at Philadelphia.

### Fighting in Pennsylvania

To counter this thrust, Washington brought his troops from Morristown into Bucks County, Pennsylvania, where he could interpose his forces between Howe and Philadelphia. While awaiting the enemy, Washington was joined by a young French nobleman who had volunteered to serve the American cause. He was the 19-year-old Marquis de Lafayette. Lafayette was assigned as an aide to Washington and did memorable service for the rest of the war.

Lafayette was one of many foreign volunteers who aided the Americans in their struggle for liberty. Others were Baron de Kalb, a German; Count Casimir Pulaski, a Pole; Thaddeus Kosciusko, another Pole; and Baron von Steuben, a Prussian officer, who drilled the Continentals and forged them into a disciplined army.

Howe sailed from New York. His fleet landed at a point about 80 kilometers (50 miles) south of Philadelphia, and the struggle for the American capital began. The Yankees fought bravely but were defeated at Brandywine Creek. The way to Philadelphia was open. On September 26, 1777, Howe took the city, and members of the Second Continental Congress fled to York, Pennsylvania.

Although he had been beaten, Washington struck back at the British in the battle of Germantown on October 4, 1777. Again the British triumphed, but the Americans fought so well that foreign military experts praised Washington's troops. "No army with such spirit is a defeated army," a French officer told the American commander in chief. "You will yet prevail."

### Articles of Confederation

On November 15, 1777, shortly after Germantown, the 13 colonies took a step that brought them much closer to unity as a nation. Congress adopted the Articles of Confederation, which had been drafted by a committee headed by John Dickinson of Pennsylvania. The Articles were regulations by which the colonies agreed to be ruled until the war ended. Their aim was to give Congress the necessary powers for winning the war. But the Articles did not go into effect until 1781, after all the colonies had ratified them.

In the field, Washington pulled back to Valley Forge, Pennsylvania, where he set up winter quarters only 32 kilometers (20 miles) from Philadelphia. His troops suffered agonies in the coldest weather in many years. The soldiers wrapped themselves in rags to keep warm. Disease spread through the camp. The army endured starvation, scurvy, and frostbite, while only a short distance away, the British lived in comfort and plenty.

But the ordeal of Valley Forge hardened the core of Yankee resistance. To that awful camp came the Prussian Baron von Steuben. He took the sick and hungry Americans and made them into first-class soldiers. An exacting drillmaster, von Steuben turned Washington's "band of scarecrows" into top-notch troops comparable to any army in the world. "Give them enough to eat and they'll whip the Lobsterbacks at will," von Steuben bragged.

### Saratoga Victory Brings France into the War

In July, 1777, General Burgoyne started southward from Lake Champlain and recaptured Ticonderoga on July 6. He knew that Howe was not marching to meet him. But he did not know that one of his units, a mixed force of Loyalists and Mohawk Indians under Colonel Barry St. Leger, would be beaten by Benedict Arnold on August 22, 1777. And Burgoyne did not expect the obstacles he would encounter on his way south when Patriots felled trees across the road.

Burgoyne continued his advance toward Albany. He sent a force of Hessians into Vermont. There, he heard, the Rebels had stored supplies of food and had many horses, both of which Burgoyne needed. His Hessians were defeated on August 16, 1777, at Bennington, Vermont, by the American general John Stark and a force of hardy Vermonters.

This setback did not deter Burgoyne. He pressed ahead to Bemis Heights, just north of Albany. On September 19, 1777, in the first battle of Freeman's Farm, he ran into an American army under General Horatio Gates. The brilliant work of Colonel Henry Dearborn and Virginia riflemen under Daniel Morgan brought an American victory.

Burgoyne dug in to await St. Leger while Gates surrounded him. At last the British general realized that help was not coming. On October 7, 1777, he tried to cut his way through the encircling Americans. The attempt failed in the second battle of Freeman's Farm, which saw Benedict Arnold emerge as the hero of the day.

Burgoyne resisted stubbornly until October 17, 1777, when he saw that further fighting was useless. He surrendered his 5,000 soldiers to General Gates at Saratoga. It was the turning point of the American Revolution. The great victory at Saratoga encouraged the Rebels and, even more important, brought France openly into the war as an American ally. Burgoyne's defeat convinced King Louis XVI of France that the British could be beaten. Before this, France had given the Rebels secret military aid on a large scale, but now France openly recognized the independence of the United States, and the two countries formed a military alliance.

▶ YEARS OF HOPE: 1778–81

Americans faced 1778 with new hope and courage. But the British were worried by France's entry into the hostilities. General Clinton, who had succeeded Howe at Philadelphia, believed that Howe had blundered by occupying that city. But Clinton could not change what had been done. The British Government was concerned that a French fleet might bottle Clinton up in Philadelphia. Clinton was ordered to ship some troops to defend the British West Indies against a French raid and to march the rest of them overland to New York. On June 18, 1778, Clinton began his withdrawal to New York. He was hampered by rains, clumsy supply wagons, and American raiders.

Washington decided to launch a full-scale attack on Clinton's troops, against the advice of his senior officer, Major General Charles Lee. But on June 28, when Lee learned that young Lafayette was to be given 6,000 troops for the attack, he insisted on leading it. A great battle erupted at Monmouth Court House, New Jersey. British regulars fell back, astounded by the disciplined tactics of von Steuben's trained men.

But General Lee did not prove up to the ability of the troops he led. He missed many opportunities to force out the enemy and ordered a withdrawal, which spread confusion in the American ranks. Washington angrily reversed Lee's order to retreat. Lee was later court-martialed for his conduct at Monmouth.

The battle ended at nightfall on June 28. Clinton retreated, but Washington's tired army could not pursue. Clinton reached New York in disorder. No one then knew that Monmouth was to be the last major battle in the north. Clinton stayed in New York City. The American forces crossed the Hudson River to New York from a point near Paramus, New Jersey, moving to White Plains, New York. For the rest of the war, only minor clashes took place in that region.

**The War in the West**

From the very beginning of the Revolution, a vicious side war was fought in the border territories beyond the Alleghenies and on the New York frontier. The British gave arms to bands of Indians, who raided pioneer settlements in Kentucky.

A frontiersman named George Rogers Clark recruited a force of hardy pioneers. They destroyed the main British centers, Kaskaskia and Cahokia, from which the hostile Indian raiders were supplied with arms. Clark also took Vincennes and other enemy posts in the Illinois country. In December, 1778, the British recaptured Vincennes. Clark mobilized his forces and led them through the bitterest cold, fording streams and pressing over frozen swampland, to complete an incredible march that covered 290 kilometers (180 miles) in 18 days.

Clark's tough pioneers fell on the British, recaptured Vincennes, and broke the enemy's hold on the huge tract known as the Northwest Territory. But even as Clark quieted the trouble in his territory, trouble exploded in the Mohawk Valley of upper New York State. It spread to the Wyoming Valley of eastern Pennsylvania. There the Loyalist colonel Sir John Butler led Loyalists and Indians on a raid through that fertile region. Butler and his force joined with the Mohawk Indian chief Joseph Brant and his Indian followers and later raided the rich Cherry Valley of New York state, leaving behind a trail of burned cabins and murdered settlers.

General Washington sent generals John Sullivan and James Clinton to deal with the Loyalists and Indians. The Patriot troops left a path of destruction through the Indian Territory, but the fighting continued through 1780 and 1781. The New York frontier had no peace until American troops under Colonel Marinus Willett defeated the main force of the enemy at Jerseyfield, New York, in December, 1781.

## The War at Sea

Great battles raged on land, but the war was also a war at sea almost from the beginning. The Americans had no navy to match the strength of British sea power. They therefore commissioned daring sea captains as privateers—sailors authorized by Congress to prey on British shipping. Such bold privateers as John Barry, Joshua Barney, and John Paul Jones carried out their commissions with outstanding success.

The most successful of the American naval heroes was John Paul Jones. He struck at the heart of the British Isles. In a daring raid in 1778, he actually landed at Whitehaven, a port on the Irish Sea. He and his crew captured a British sloop of war and looted the Earl of Selkirk's castle on St. Mary's Isle in Solway Firth.

Jones carried out his most famous feat on September 23, 1779, as captain of the *Bonhomme Richard,* a merchant ship converted to a warship. Although his ship was slow and clumsy, Jones attacked a British convoy off Flamborough Head in the North Sea. The mer-

The most famous Revolutionary naval hero was John Paul Jones. In 1779 his flagship, the *Bonhomme Richard (left),* won a moonlit battle with the British *Serapis.*

chant ships were escorted by a 50-gun man-of-war, the *Serapis*, which promptly engaged the *Bonhomme Richard*. In the furious fight that followed, the American ship was blasted to splinters but still managed to keep afloat. When the captain of the *Serapis* called on the Americans to surrender, Jones replied, "I have not yet begun to fight!" Eventually the *Serapis* was forced to surrender.

No national navy of any size opposed the traditional British rule of the seas, but the Americans sent out almost 2,000 privateers during the war. These vessels sank a number of royal merchant vessels and warships.

In an act of treason, Benedict Arnold (seated) passed critical information to the British major John André. Arnold's treachery was revealed when American troops captured André and found the papers in his stocking.

The balance of sea power shifted to the Americans when France entered the war as an ally. French ships played the decisive role in 1781 by keeping the British army under Cornwallis bottled up at Yorktown, Virginia, and repulsing a British relief expedition.

### War in the Hudson Valley

As the war dragged on, General Henry Clinton, the British commander in New York, decided to revive Burgoyne's old plan to overrun the Hudson Valley. His first blow in that operation was to take Stony Point, New York, a stronghold located a short distance south of West Point, in May, 1779.

West Point, which dominated the Hudson River, was powerfully defended. Clinton had to conquer that American fortress before the Hudson Valley could be made British. His scheme received a setback when the Yankees regained Stony Point in a daring night assault on July 15, 1779, led by General Anthony (Mad Anthony) Wayne.

**Benedict Arnold's Betrayal.** As a result of this American victory, Clinton changed his tactics. Instead of storming West Point, which would have meant great cost in soldiers and equipment, the wily British general sought an American traitor who could help him get it through stealth. Clinton found his man. He was Benedict Arnold, hero of Quebec and Saratoga and veteran of a dozen Revolutionary War battles. Arnold was Washington's favorite combat officer. The commander in chief regarded him with respect and affection, although Arnold was passed over for promotion by Congress several times.

After Arnold was wounded at Saratoga, he was made military commandant of Philadelphia, where he met and married a beautiful Loyalist, Peggy Shippen. Perhaps driven to desperation by his need for money or to revenge congressional slights, Arnold offered his services to the British. He negotiated with General Clinton through Major John André, the British general's adjutant.

In January, 1780, Arnold was relieved of duty in Philadelphia, and in August he was put in command of West Point. Arnold now had the plans of the fort, showing defensive positions and gun emplacements. Working through André, he made a deal with the enemy. A British sloop of war, the *Vulture*, sailed up the Hudson to a point where André and Arnold could meet. The papers were turned over, but André was caught by an American patrol while carrying the secret documents to New York. His capture exposed the treasonable plot. André was convicted and executed as a spy.

Arnold fled to the *Vulture* and went to New York. The British gave him a brigadier general's commission and a cash settlement. He served his former enemy with skill and daring, leading raids into his native Connecticut and on the Virginia coast.

### Who was Molly Pitcher?

Molly Pitcher was a heroine of the Revolutionary War. She won her nickname and her fame in 1778 at the Battle of Monmouth, New Jersey.

Molly was born Mary Ludwig on October 13, 1754, on a dairy farm near Trenton. Her father, John Ludwig, was a German immigrant. When Molly was 15, she went to Pennsylvania to work as a housemaid, and soon afterward she married John Hays.

John fought in the Revolution with the American artillery. Molly went to the army camp to take care of him. She cooked, sewed, and washed for John and the other soldiers.

The Battle of Monmouth started on June 28, a very hot day. All day long, Molly ran back and forth from a well, bringing water to the hot, thirsty fighters and helping the wounded. Seeing her, the soldiers cried thankfully, "Here comes Molly with her pitcher! Molly, bring the pitcher here." Soon they were just calling, "Molly! Pitcher!" And she won her battle name.

During the battle, Molly's husband was overcome by the heat and fell beside his cannon. Molly stepped up to the cannon and took his place. As long as the battle raged, Molly loaded and fired with the rest of the soldiers. Today there are monuments at Monmouth and at her grave, honoring her as a brave fighter.

Many years later, in 1822, the Pennsylvania General Assembly passed an act to give Molly a soldier's pension. Until she died in 1832, Molly received $40 a year from her grateful country, in honor of her services.

### War in the South

During the time that battles raged in Massachusetts, New York, New Jersey, and Pennsylvania, the war hardly touched the southern colonies. No large-scale fighting had taken place in the South since 1776, when a British attack on Charleston, South Carolina, had been driven back.

That situation changed in 1778. The British high command switched its strategy and decided to conquer the southern colonies, where Loyalist support was strong. In December, 1778, a mixed force of British, Hessian, and Loyalist troops captured the important seaport of Savannah, Georgia.

A combined French-American army made a belated attempt to recapture Savannah almost a year later (October 9, 1779), only to meet with disaster. After the defeat, French naval and military forces were withdrawn, and only a weak American army commanded by General Benjamin Lincoln remained.

**Carolina Campaigns.** General Henry Clinton rushed a powerful army from New York to invade the South and overwhelmed Charleston. On May 12, 1780, the Americans there surrendered, and the Redcoats marched into the city with bands playing and flags flying. After the fall of Charleston, those Rebels and their sympathizers who would not take an oath of allegiance to the crown were arrested.

In June, 1780, Clinton delegated the task of maintaining the British hold on the South to General Charles Cornwallis, who was not content just to hold his ground. He quickly smashed an American army marching to attack the British munitions store at Camden, South Carolina. This force had as its leader General Horatio Gates, the victor of Saratoga. Gates stumbled into a British trap at Camden on August 16, 1780, and his militia fled in a disgraceful manner. Only a few regiments of Continental regulars were left to face Cornwallis.

Some Carolinians engaged in partisan warfare. Francis Marion, a planter, conducted a guerrilla campaign against isolated British outposts and supply depots. Marion was soon nicknamed the Swamp Fox because he retreated into the swamps after each raid. Marion, together with Thomas Sumter and Andrew Pickens, kept Cornwallis off balance. The Americans also scored a victory over a Loyalist army at Kings Mountain, South Carolina, on October 7, 1780.

But it was not until December that real hope came to the South—in the form of General Nathanael Greene, who had replaced Gates. Greene inspired the discouraged remnants of the American army. He sent out a call for "men who love their homes, wives, and children ... and will fight to protect them." The men came to him. Lieu-

Consult the Index to find more information in *The New Book of Knowledge* about the following people associated with the Revolutionary War: American officers Ethan Allen, Benedict Arnold, George Clinton, Nathan Hale, John Paul Jones, Henry Lee, Francis Marion, and George Washington; political leaders John Adams, Samuel Adams, Benjamin Franklin, John Hancock, Patrick Henry, John Jay, Thomas Jefferson, Robert R. Livingston, Paul Revere, Thomas Paine, and James Otis; flag maker Betsy Ross; French officer Marquis de Lafayette; and the British spy John André.

*Washington Crossing the Delaware* by Emanuel Leutz

**Crispus Attucks** (1723?–70), a free black of mixed descent, was one of the first martyrs of the revolutionary movement. On March 5, 1770, while protesting in the streets of Boston against "taxation without representation," Attucks and a group of patriots were fired on by British soldiers. Attucks was among five patriots killed that day in what became known as the Boston Massacre.

**John Burgoyne** (1722–92), born in Lancashire, England, and known as Gentleman Johnny, was a major general of the British Army when the Revolutionary War began. In Canada he beat back the Americans at Trois-Rivières on June 8, 1776. The following year he recaptured Fort Ticonderoga in New York, previously taken by Ethan Allen. But Burgoyne's luck changed at Saratoga. Lacking promised reinforcements, he was defeated at the battles of Freeman's Farm and Bemis Heights, losses that forced his surrender on October 17, 1777. Burgoyne later served as commander in chief in Ireland. He retired from public service in 1783 and became a playwright.

**George Rogers Clark** (1752–1818), born near Charlottesville, Va., was a soldier and frontiersman who won three significant victories during the Revolutionary War. By beating back the British at Kaskaskia, Cahokia, and Vincennes in 1778–79, Clark was able to claim the Northwest Territory for the United States—an enormous region that today includes the states of Ohio, Indiana, Illinois, Michigan, and Wisconsin and part of Minnesota. His brother William was the co-leader of the Lewis and Clark Expedition (1804–06).

**Charles, Marquess Cornwallis** (1738–1805), born in London, took part in the first unsuccessful attack on Charleston, S.C., in the summer of 1776 and was defeated by George Washington's troops at Princeton, N.J. Cornwallis, a major general, later succeeded at the battles of Brandywine Creek and Ger-

tenant Colonel Henry ("Light Horse Harry") Lee brought in 300 well-equipped troopers. Colonel William Washington added another fine cavalry troop.

On January 17, 1781, American troops under the command of Brigadier General Daniel Morgan defeated the British in a cleverly fought battle at Cowpens, South Carolina. Then followed a series of engagements that weakened the guerrilla-plagued British. They were soon exhausted from chasing the elusive Americans.

Cornwallis then won a bruising battle with Greene at Guilford Courthouse, North Carolina on March 15, 1781. He retired to Wilmington to gather troops and supplies transported there by the Royal Navy.

With Cornwallis away, rebel activity broke out everywhere in South Carolina. Greene fought successive battles with the British until they were confined to the areas around Savannah and Charleston. It was only a matter of time before they would have to give up both cities. Meanwhile, events elsewhere were reaching a climax.

### Yorktown

Cornwallis marched into Yorktown, Virginia, and awaited his orders from Clinton. They never arrived. On September 5, 1781, a French fleet commanded by the Comte de Grasse defeated a Royal Navy squadron in Chesapeake Bay. This French victory ended the last chance Cornwallis had to save his army, which was already penned in at Yorktown by French and American troops. The Americans, led by Washington, and the French, under the Comte de Rochambeau, had marched to Yorktown, where they surrounded Cornwallis. For the first time in the war, it was the British, not the Americans, who were on short rations.

Cornwallis held out, even after he learned what had happened in Chesapeake Bay. Although the outcome was now certain, he fought on. The Yankees took British positions, and French warships kept up a merciless bombardment.

On October 9, Washington and Rochambeau brought up their heavy guns. A hundred mammoth cannons blasted the Redcoats for

mantown, north of Philadelphia, in the fall of 1777. Promoted to lieutenant general, Cornwallis was placed in charge of the Carolinas after the British finally took Charleston in May 1780. He later won the battles of Camden and Guilford Courthouse. Eventually Cornwallis invaded Virginia, proceeding as far as Yorktown. Surrounded by French and American troops, he was forced to surrender on October 19, 1781, thus ending the war. He later served as governor-general of India (1786–94 and 1805) and of Ireland (1797–1801).

**Horatio Gates** (1728?–1806), born in Maldon, England, had recently immigrated to America when he was placed in charge of the American forces in the north. In 1777 Major General Gates won a critical victory for the Americans at Saratoga. But in 1780, while commanding forces in the south, Gates suffered a major defeat at Camden, S.C., and was replaced by Nathanael Greene. After the war he retired to Manhattan Island, N.Y.

Charles, Marquess Cornwallis

Nathanael Greene

**Nathanael Greene** (1742–86) was born in what is now Warwick, R.I. Although a Quaker, and therefore unsympathetic to warfare, he joined the Continental Army in June 1775 and was made a brigadier general. Greene fought at Trenton and Brandywine Creek, north of Philadelphia, but he is best remembered for his brilliant campaigns in Georgia and the Carolinas. Greene's army forced General Cornwallis to retreat from those colonies, leading to his defeat at Yorktown. Many military historians regard Greene as the war's finest strategist. In gratitude for his contributions, Georgians gave Greene a generous land grant near Savannah, Ga.

**Jean Baptiste Donatien de Vimeur, Comte de Rochambeau** (1725–1807), born in Vendôme, France, was a French general who brought military aid to George Washington in the final years of the Revolutionary War. In 1781 he helped plan the successful and conclusive Battle of Yorktown. Imprisoned in 1793 during the French Revolution, he was later released and appointed Marshal of France, the nation's highest military rank.

**Friedrich Wilhelm Augustin, Baron von Steuben** (1730–94), born in Magdeburg, Prussia, was a veteran of the Seven Years' War (1756–63) and an aide-de-camp to King Frederick the Great. In 1778, a year after coming to America, George Washington appointed him inspector general of the Continental Army, responsible for training and drilling American troops at Valley Forge, Penn. Von Steuben also commanded some American forces at the battles of Monmouth and Yorktown. After the war he became a naturalized American citizen. Annual parades are still held in his honor.

eight days. Cornwallis finally asked for terms. Surrender negotiations lasted until October 19. On that morning the defeated British marched out of Yorktown. General Charles O'Hara, acting for Cornwallis, handed his sword over to General Benjamin Lincoln. The British band played a tune called "The World Turned Upside Down." Except for a few minor skirmishes in the South, the Revolutionary War in America was over.

When news of the surrender reached King George III, he wanted the British to keep on fighting. But the British government and the people were weary of the war. Lord North's Cabinet fell, and a new one was chosen to negotiate the peace.

▶ **PEACE**

Peace talks began in Paris in April, 1782. Congress ratified a preliminary treaty the following year. The final version was signed in Paris on September 3, 1783. John Adams, Benjamin Franklin, John Jay, and Henry Laurens were the American representatives. David Hartley represented the British side.

The treaty extended the western boundary of the United States from the Allegheny Mountains to the Mississippi River, the northern boundary to the Great Lakes, and the southern boundary to the 31st parallel. The treaty also provided that Congress would "recommend" to the states that they return property seized from the Loyalists (Tories) during the war.

### Results of the Revolution

The end of the Revolution brought complete independence to the 13 colonies, which combined to form the United States of America. The success of the war brought about the first break in the European colonial system and set in motion a chain of revolutions that has continued to this day. The firm establishment of republican government was finally secured in the United States in 1789 with the adoption of the Constitution.

IRVING WERSTEIN
Author, *1776: The Adventure of the American Revolution Told with Pictures*

See also DECLARATION OF INDEPENDENCE.

**REYE'S SYNDROME.** See DISEASES (Descriptions of Some Diseases).

# REYNOLDS, SIR JOSHUA (1723–1792)

One of England's great portrait painters, Joshua Reynolds was a well-educated, deep-thinking man who considered carefully every brush stroke. His learning included history, literature, and philosophy as well as art.

The son of the Reverend Samuel Reynolds, a schoolmaster, Joshua was born on July 16, 1723, in the town of Plympton Erle, not far from the port of Plymouth. He began drawing at an early age, and when he was 17, he studied portrait painting. From 1743 until 1749 he worked alone in London and in Devon. Then he went to Italy to study the masters of that country. Copying and analyzing the works of these great painters and working out his own methods, he became an expert artist.

In 1753, Reynolds settled in London and won quick success as a portrait painter. He had remarkable talent for capturing the character of his models, who included celebrities such as the writer Samuel Johnson. Reynolds painted portraits of women and children, too, with delicacy and taste.

As time passed, Reynolds became a friend of the most important people of his day. Before he was 40, he became deaf, but he did not allow his deafness to discourage him. He continued to lead a full social life and was increasingly sought after as a portraitist.

In 1768 the Royal Academy, a society that exhibited works of art and provided art instruction, was founded in London. Reynolds was made its first president, and in 1769 he received the honor of knighthood. Sir Joshua wrote a controversial series of essays on the principles of art for the students of the Royal Academy. These essays, called the *Discourses*, are still read and argued about today.

Sir Joshua was always willing to try something new. He was constantly experimenting with methods and materials. Unfortunately some of the paints he used have not lasted well. For example, the foreground of one of his best-known works, *The Age of Innocence*, has cracked. A visit to Holland and Flanders in 1781 affected his way of painting. He was especially influenced by the painter Rubens. Even though he was 58 and successful, he was

*Master Francis George Hare* (1788) is one of many charming and lifelike portraits of children painted by Sir Joshua Reynolds. It hangs in the Louvre.

willing to accept new influences and to change his own style. His fame grew, and in 1784 he was named painter to the king.

A good-natured, calm, and pleasant-mannered man, Sir Joshua was kind to young students at the Royal Academy. His powers of work were remarkable, and it is estimated that he painted over 2,000 portraits. Among those considered his best are *Nelly O'Brien* and *Mrs. Siddons as the Tragic Muse*.

In his last years, Sir Joshua's eyesight began to fail, and he eventually stopped painting. He died in London on February 23, 1792, and was buried in St. Paul's Cathedral.

HERBERT B. GRIMSDITCH
Fleetway Publications (London)

**RHEUMATIC FEVER.** See DISEASES (Descriptions of Some Diseases).
**RHINE RIVER.** See RIVERS.

# RHINOCEROSES

Rhinoceroses have huge, heavy bodies and one or two large horns above their nostrils. They usually move about slowly, paying little attention to their surroundings. They do not hunt other animals for food but eat only grass and other plants. Though usually quiet and retiring, they may become very fierce if cornered. They can charge at speeds of about 50 kilometers (30 miles) an hour. Then their strong, pointed horns and large size make them powerful and dangerous.

The smallest rhinoceros, the Sumatran, usually weighs less than 1 metric ton. At the shoulder, it may measure somewhat more than 1 meter high. The largest rhinoceros, the African white rhinoceros, weighs about three times more than the Sumatran and is about twice as high at the shoulder.

The great body of the rhinoceros rests on four short legs. Each foot has three toes. Rhinoceroses are hoofed animals and are related to horses.

The horns of some kinds of rhinoceroses are often very long—as long as 1 meter or sometimes more. The animal may have one or two horns, depending on the kind of rhinoceros. The horns are made up of closely packed masses of tough hairs. The rest of the body is usually hairless except for patches of hair about the ears and at the tip of the tail. Because the tough, thick skin has no sweat glands, rhinoceroses must cool themselves in baths of water, mud, dust, or ash.

Rhinoceroses usually travel alone, but they are sometimes found in small family groups. A female bears only one young at a time. The calf is born about 18 months after mating and remains with the mother for several years.

There are five different kinds of rhinoceroses living today. Two of these—the black rhinoceros and the white rhinoceros—are found in Africa. Both African kinds have two horns.

The other three kinds live in Asia. Indian and Javan rhinoceroses have one horn. (Females of the Javan kind usually lack horns.) Deep folds divide the skin of these Asian rhinoceroses into great shieldlike sections. The Sumatran rhinoceros has two horns, and its skin is not so deeply folded. Its body has a thin covering of short hair.

Reviewed by ROBERT M. McCLUNG
Author, science books for children

See also HOOFED MAMMALS.

**A white rhinoceros nurses her baby. Young rhinoceroses are called calves.**

# RHODE ISLAND

*Rhode Island's official name—the State of Rhode Island and Providence Plantations—comes from the names of the colony's two most important original settlements. Providence Plantations was founded in 1636 by the English clergyman Roger Williams, who sought a place where one could worship God freely. Williams believed that God's Providence had led him safely there, and so the place was named.*

*No one is certain of the origin of the name Rhode Island, which was what the colonists called today's Aquidneck Island. Some believe that it came from the Dutch word for "red," referring to the color of the island's rocky cliffs. Others say that early English settlers mistook Aquidneck Island for Block Island, which the early explorer Giovanni Verrazano had likened to the Greek island of Rhodes.*

*Rhode Island's official nickname, the Ocean State, emphasizes the importance of the Atlantic Ocean and Narragansett Bay to tourism and the state's economy. A former nickname, Little Rhody, is no longer used.*

State flag

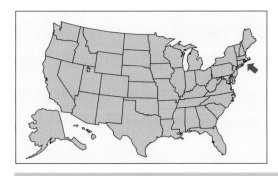

Rhode Island is the smallest of the fifty states. It is located in southern New England on the shores of the Atlantic Ocean and Narragansett Bay. Woodlands, forests, lakes, ponds, and hundreds of miles of coastline give the state a rural feeling. Yet Rhode Island is more densely populated than any other state but New Jersey.

Rhode Island was one of the original 13 colonies. Because the state is so small, generally unsuited for agriculture, and lacking in precious minerals or coal, Rhode Islanders have often resorted to enterprise and ingenuity to earn a living. In the 1800's, Rhode Island became America's first industrialized state, turning out a wide array of products, from steam engines to textiles and jewelry.

In the 1970's, manufacturing declined and the state began to lose population. Rhode Island's economy became increasingly based on services. Today health care, tourism, and education are among the leading industries.

As early as 1730, Newport became America's first summer resort, where planters from the West Indies and the South flocked to enjoy the climate. Later, during the Gilded Age (1865–1900), high society made Newport

the Queen of Resorts, with beaches, campgrounds, shore resorts, amusement parks, and the enormous summer mansions of many of the nation's richest families. The America's Cup Race was held in the waters off Newport from 1930 until the Cup was lost to Australia in 1983. But professional yachting remains a major sport in Newport, which has been called the Yachting Capital of the World.

## ▶ LAND

Rhode Island is the smallest state in the nation. Block Island Sound and the Atlantic Ocean form the southern boundary of the state.

### Land Regions

Rhode Island is made up of two land regions, the Seaboard Lowland and the New England Upland.

**The Seaboard Lowland**, also known as the Coastal Lowland, covers eastern Rhode Island. This area's rocky terrain resulted from a glacier that once covered the land. As the huge ice sheet melted, vast amounts of sand and gravel were deposited. Much of the Seaboard Lowland is now under Narragansett Bay.

Rhode Island's 36 islands are part of the Seaboard Lowland. The largest is Aquidneck

*Opposite page, clockwise from top left:* Yacht racing is popular in Rhode Island waters. Trinity Church is one of Newport's many historical buildings. Misquamicut State Park on Block Island Sound is a popular recreational spot.

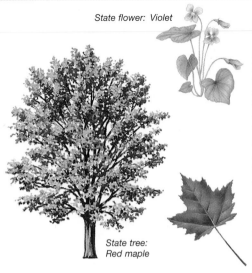

State flower: Violet

State tree:
Red maple

## FACTS AND FIGURES

**Location:** Eastern United States; bordered on the north by Massachusetts, on the east by Massachusetts and the Atlantic Ocean, on the south by Block Island Sound and the Atlantic Ocean, and on the west by Connecticut.

**Area:** 1,231 sq mi (3,189 km²); rank, 50th.

**Population:** 1,048,319 (2000 census); rank, 43rd.

**Elevation:** *Highest*—812 ft (247 m), at Jerimoth Hill in Providence County; *lowest*—sea level.

**Capital:** Providence.

**Statehood:** May 29, 1790; 13th state.

**State Motto:** *Hope.*

**State Song:** "Rhode Island."

**Nickname:** Ocean State.

**Abbreviations:** RI; R.I.

State bird:
Rhode Island Red

The rocky landscape east of the Sakonnet River in eastern Rhode Island is typical of the terrain in the Seaboard Lowland region.

there. Out in Long Island Sound is Block Island, which officially is the town of New Shoreham.

**The New England Upland** covers the northern and western parts of the state. The thin, rocky, acidic soil in this region made agriculture especially difficult for the early settlers. Today much of the land has returned to forest and woodlands.

### Rivers, Lakes, and Coastal Waters

Rhode Island has 40 miles (64 kilometers) of general coastline on the Atlantic Ocean and 384 miles (618 kilometers) of tidal shoreline, including the sounds and bays. The dominant physical feature of Rhode Island is Narragansett Bay, which divides the state nearly in two.

Except for the Pawcatuck River, which forms part of the border with Connecticut in the southwest, nearly all Rhode Island's rivers empty into Narragansett Bay. The two most important river systems that drain the state are the Blackstone and the Pawtuxet rivers. The Blackstone begins in Massachusetts and flows into Narragansett Bay at its northern point. The Pawtuxet drains the midsection of the state. Its upper branches were dammed to create the Scituate Reservoir, the source of drinking water for Providence and many other communities. The Scituate Reservoir, which is closed to all recreational and industrial uses, is the largest artificial lake in New England, covering an area greater than the city of Providence. Of Rhode Island's

Island, which contains the towns of Newport, Middletown, and Portsmouth. Off Aquidneck are a number of tiny islands with quaint names, such as Hog, Hen, Goat, and Gooseberry. Connected to Aquidneck by the Claiborne Pell Bridge is Conanicut Island, which is the town of Jamestown. Just to the north are Prudence and Patience islands. Both are populated, but one must go by boat to get

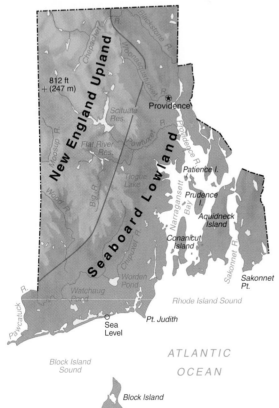

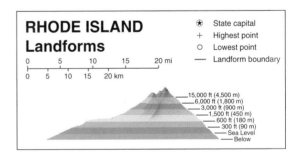

**RHODE ISLAND Landforms**

⊛ State capital
+ Highest point
○ Lowest point
— Landform boundary

The return of the woodlands brought back beavers, which had not been seen in Rhode Island since colonial times. The woods also support large numbers of woodchucks, skunks, opossums, and white-tailed deer. Wild turkeys have been successfully reintroduced. Peregrine falcons are known to nest on the ledges of tall buildings in Providence.

Rhode Island's waters are home to more than 200 species of fish and shellfish. Among the most abundant varieties are swordfish, tuna, marlin, and the local variety of clam, known as the quahog.

### Natural Resources

Rhode Island's greatest natural resource is Narragansett Bay, which has long provided a living to fishermen and clammers and a play-

*Left:* Wickford is one of several towns situated on beautiful Narragansett Bay. *Below:* The bluffs of Block Island overlook the Atlantic Ocean.

many natural ponds, Worden Pond in South Kingstown is the largest.

### Climate

Rhode Island experiences distinct seasons. Summers are warm, winters are cold, and spring and autumn are mild. In Warwick, temperatures average 29°F (−2°C) in January and 73°F (23°C) in July. The average annual precipitation is 46 inches (1,168 millimeters). Hurricanes and great coastal storms called northeasters can bring tremendous amounts of rain and other precipitation.

### Plant and Animal Life

By the end of the colonial era, most of Rhode Island had been deforested. But today about 60 percent of Rhode Island has returned to woodland. Oak, ash, hickory, maple, beech, birch, hemlock, cedar, pine, and flowering dogwoods are among the most common trees. Flowering plants and shrubs include violets, buttercups, lilies, goldenrods, wild roses, rhododendron, mountain laurel, and azaleas.

ground for vacationers. Except for sand, gravel, and some usable granite and limestone, Rhode Island's mineral resources are extremely limited. The rivers are shallow and filled with narrows and falls. During the Industrial Revolution, most rivers were diverted and dammed to provide power for the mills that sprang up along their banks.

In response to demands that the environment be protected and restored and that development be better controlled, Rhode Island created the Rhode Island Coastal Resources Management Council in 1971 and the Department of Environmental Management in 1977. In addition, vigorous environmental

tugal. Only 4 percent were African American. The Native American population was all but eliminated.

After 1830, industrialization and economic development attracted thousands of foreign immigrants. The first large non-English group to come were Irish escaping Ireland's great potato famine in the 1840's. According to the 1865 state census, foreign-born Irish constituted nearly 15 percent of Rhode Island's population. Other immigrants included substantial numbers of French Canadians, Germans, Swedes, Poles, Portuguese, Italians, Greeks, Armenians, and Russian Jews. In 1913 Providence became the fifth largest port of entry for immigrants in the nation. By the 1920's, Rhode Island had the highest percentage of immigrants in the United States, a distinction it maintained until the 1970's.

In recent decades, despite a weakened economy, Rhode Island has continued to attract new groups, including Southeast Asians, Hispanics, and Africans. Despite the influx of new peoples, 85 percent of all Rhode Islanders still trace their ancestry to Europe. More than 60 percent are Roman Catholic, the highest proportion of any state in the nation.

groups, such as Save the Bay and the Nature Conservancy, have played major roles in safeguarding and recovering Rhode Island's natural resources. The state also has an ambitious program to preserve farmland and green acres by purchasing development rights to farms around the state.

▶ PEOPLE

Until 1830 the great majority of Rhode Islanders were native-born Yankee descendants of British settlers. There were also small numbers of Scotch-Irish, French Huguenots, and Sephardic Jews from Spain and Por-

*Top:* Memorial Day and other national holidays are celebrated with parades throughout the state. *Right:* The Brown & Hopkins Country Store in Chepachet, which opened in 1809, claims to be the oldest continuously operated general store in the United States.

### Education

Rhode Island's first public school law was enacted in 1800, but only Providence and Smithfield tried to implement it. In 1845, the American educator Henry Barnard established the State Board of Education and

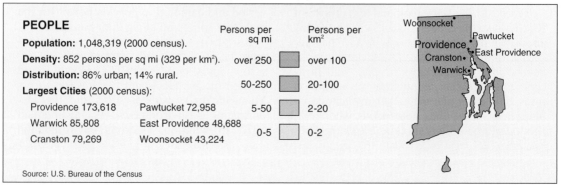

**PEOPLE**

**Population:** 1,048,319 (2000 census).

**Density:** 852 persons per sq mi (329 per km²).

**Distribution:** 86% urban; 14% rural.

**Largest Cities** (2000 census):

| | |
|---|---|
| Providence 173,618 | Pawtucket 72,958 |
| Warwick 85,808 | East Providence 48,688 |
| Cranston 79,269 | Woonsocket 43,224 |

| Persons per sq mi | Persons per km² |
|---|---|
| over 250 | over 100 |
| 50-250 | 20-100 |
| 5-50 | 2-20 |
| 0-5 | 0-2 |

Source: U.S. Bureau of the Census

became Rhode Island's first commissioner of education. Catholics created a parochial school system that educated about one-quarter of Rhode Island's schoolchildren. In 1961 the State Board of Education was replaced by the Rhode Island Department of Education.

Today higher education is one of Rhode Island's major industries. Each year its twelve colleges and universities produce twice as many college degrees as there are high school graduates in the state.

Brown University, in Providence, was founded by Baptists in 1764. An Ivy League school, it is the seventh oldest college in America. The Rhode Island School of Design, also in Providence, is one of America's leading art schools. Johnson and Wales University, also in Providence, has a national reputation for its culinary arts program. Roger Williams University, in Bristol, has the state's only law school. Other private institutions include Providence College in Providence, Salve Regina University in Newport, Bryant College in Smithfield, and the New England Institute of Technology, a two-year school in Warwick.

The public higher educational system includes the University of Rhode Island in Kingston, Rhode Island College in Providence, and the multicampus Community College of Rhode Island. In addition, advanced military strategy is taught at the U.S. Naval War College in Newport.

### Libraries, Museums, and the Arts

Newport's Redwood Library, founded as a private institution in 1747, is Rhode Island's oldest library. The Free Library Act of 1875, which provided funds to any library open to the public, helped establish public libraries in most Rhode Island towns.

In 1964 the State Department of Library Services was created to coordinate library resources in the state. Today nearly all public li-

*Above:* The Herreshoff Marine Museum in Bristol displays colonial ships and other maritime relics. *Left:* The Rhode Island School of Design Museum of Art in Providence features French and ancient Greek and Roman works of art.

braries are linked together in a system that allows residents to borrow books from any library. All of the colleges and universities have substantial libraries, especially Brown University, with nearly 3 million volumes. The Rhode Island Historical Society in Providence has a library and museum devoted to the state's history. The Newport Historical Society maintains a library and museum focusing on Newport's colorful past.

Rhode Island supports a wide array of museums. Providence features the Rhode Island School of Design Museum of Art, the Culinary Archives and Museum, the Jeweler's Museum, and the Roger Williams Park Museum of Natural History. Newport museums include the International Tennis Hall of Fame and Tennis Museum and the U.S. Naval War College Museum. Bristol is home to the Herreshoff Marine Museum. Pawtucket offers Slater Mill Historic Site, America's first textile mill. The state also maintains many outstanding historic buildings, including two Vanderbilt mansions in Newport—the Breakers and Marble House—and the John Brown House and the First Baptist Meeting House in Providence.

## PRODUCTS AND INDUSTRIES

**Manufacturing:** Jewelry and silverware, novelty items, toys, on-line lottery systems, wire and cable products, meteorology and navigation equipment, medical supplies and equipment.

**Agriculture:** Nursery, greenhouse, and turf products; dairy products; hogs; potatoes; poultry and eggs; berries; fish; lobster; quahogs (clams).

**Minerals:** Sand and gravel, stone.

**Services:** Wholesale and retail trade; finance, insurance, and real estate; business, social, and personal services; transportation, communication, and utilities; government.

*Gross state product is the total value of goods and services produced in a year.

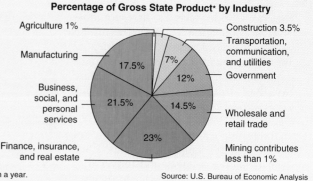

### Percentage of Gross State Product* by Industry

Agriculture 1%

Manufacturing — 17.5%

Business, social, and personal services — 21.5%

Finance, insurance, and real estate — 23%

7%

12%

14.5%

Construction 3.5%

Transportation, communication, and utilities

Government

Wholesale and retail trade

Mining contributes less than 1%

Source: U.S. Bureau of Economic Analysis

*Left:* Retail sales and other service industries make up the largest segment of Rhode Island's economy. *Below:* Toys are among the many products manufactured in the state.

Despite its small size, Rhode Island supports a substantial performing arts culture. The Rhode Island Philharmonic and Trinity Repertory Company head a list that includes the Ocean State Chamber Orchestra, Ocean State Light Opera Company, State Ballet of Rhode Island, Rhode Island Civic Chorale, Providence Civic Chorale, and Westerly Chorus. Many local communities have theater companies and choral groups, and some of the colleges have vigorous performing arts programs. In addition, the Newport Music Festival, Newport Jazz Festival, and Newport Folk Festival are internationally renowned.

### ▶ ECONOMY

Because Rhode Island is so small and has so few natural resources, its residents have always had to work energetically and ingeniously to secure a good living. Rapid industrialization in the 1800's reflected that effort. But in the 1900's, the state turned increasingly toward a service economy. At the beginning of the 1900's, 59 percent of the state's workers earned their living in manufacturing. By the mid-1990's the number had fallen to 16 percent. While that is still above the national average, the steep decline in manufacturing jobs has forced the state to diversify its economy.

### Services

The service sector now accounts for 78 percent of the state's employment. It includes tourism, health industries, advertising, banking, finance, insurance, education, government, transportation, communications, utilities, and wholesale and retail services. Health care services are the state's largest employer, followed by food and restaurant services.

### Manufacturing

In 1900, Rhode Island ranked as the nation's sixth largest industrial center. Textiles were its number one industry, employing 55 percent of the state's industrial workers. After World War I (1914–18), the industry began to leave New England. By the 1990's textiles accounted for fewer than 10 percent of the dwindling force of industrial workers in the state. Now only specialty textiles, such as lace and narrow braid, are made in Rhode Island.

Known as the Jewelry Capital of the World, Rhode Island is a leader in the production of costume jewelry, though employment has dramatically declined in recent decades. Other manufacturers produce electronic and office equipment, on-line lottery systems, medical equipment and supplies, toys, navigation and meteorological equipment, wire and wire products, machine tools, dies and molds, drugs and biomedical products, and liquid and aerosol products. Defense-related manufacturing, once a significant part of Rhode Island's economy, declined when the Cold War ended in the 1990's.

### Agriculture and Fishing

Agriculture contributes little to Rhode Island's economy. About 60 percent of the agricultural value comes from greenhouses and nurseries that produce flowers, plants, shrubs, and turf products. Seasonal crops, such as strawberries, blueberries, and corn, potatoes, and other vegetables, are raised for local markets. Dairy farms and apple orchards were once significant, but their numbers are decreasing.

Rhode Island's waters are home to more than 200 species of fish and shellfish. However, the stocks of many of the most desirable commercial fish, such as flounder, striped bass, cod, and mackerel, were severely depleted by overfishing in the 1970's and 1980's, resulting in sharp limitations on commercial fishing by the end of the century. The shellfish industry grows stronger as the cleanup of Narragansett Bay progresses.

### Mining and Construction

Mining and construction combined account for less than 3 percent of the gross state product (GSP) and employ less than 2 percent of the state's workforce. Except for sand and gravel pits and one limestone quarry, the state has no other mining locations. The construction and maintenance of roads, buildings, bridges, and the like account for most of the activity.

### Transportation

In Rhode Island's early days, waterways were the most important routes of transportation. Providence and Newport sent goods by sea to the West Indies, South America, Africa, and China. Foreign commerce through Rhode Island ports declined rapidly after the 1830's, when improvement of inland

Rhode Island's once prosperous commercial fishing industry went into decline due to overfishing in the latter half of the 1900's.

transportation made it easier for goods to be shipped from Boston, New York, and Philadelphia. Today most of Providence's seaport trade is coastal traffic, chiefly tankers carrying fuel oils and gasoline. Other important cargoes are coal, lumber, chemicals, and cement.

In the latter half of the 1800's, the railroad became the principal means of transportation in Rhode Island. But in the 1900's, trucks and buses slowly took over much of the passenger and freight business, and an extensive system of roads and highways was built. Today only one railroad line remains in operation: Amtrak stops in Rhode Island on its New York–Boston route.

Bridges and ferry services connect the islands to the mainland. The state's principal airport is the Theodore Francis Green Air-

# Places of Interest

The Breakers, in Newport

Roger Williams Park Zoo, in Providence

Touro Synagogue National Historic Site, in Newport

**Benefit Street**, in Providence, nicknamed the Mile of History, is a mile of restored colonial and Victorian houses. Notable landmarks include the Rhode Island School of Design, the Providence Preservation Society, the Old State House, the First Baptist Meeting House, the Providence Atheneum, the Stephen Hopkins House, the Nightingale-Brown House, and the John Brown House. Brown University, the Haffenraffer Museum, the Harbor Heritage Museum, and the Roger Williams National Memorial are located nearby.

**Block Island**, named for the Dutch sea captain Adriaen Block, became a

The International Tennis Hall of Fame and Tennis Museum, in Newport

resort in the late 1800's. It remains one of the most quaint and picturesque places in Rhode Island.

**Bristol** is the home of America's oldest Fourth of July parade. Places of interest include Linden Place, a Federal-style mansion built in 1810, and Blithewold mansion and gardens, built in 1907.

**Casey Farm**, built in Saunderstown around 1750, is a functioning colonial farm with an impressive collection of original furniture. During the Revolutionary War, a skirmish between foraging British sailors and American scouts took place here. A bullet hole in a door remains from the encounter.

**Clemence Irons House**, built in Johnston about 1680, is an outstanding example of early New England colonial architecture. It is maintained by the Society for the Preservation of New England Antiquities.

**Gilbert Stuart Birthplace**, in North Kingstown, was built in 1751. The famous painter was born there in 1755. The site has been restored with appropriate furnishings from the 1700's.

**John Brown House**, in Providence, was built in 1786. Today it is a museum and the headquarters of the Rhode Island Historical Society. President John Quincy Adams once described the house as "the most magnificent and elegant mansion that I have ever seen on this continent."

**Newport** is Rhode Island's primary tourist destination. Among its many attractions are extravagant mansions, including the Breakers and Marble House; the Cliff Walk; Ocean Drive; Touro Synagogue National Historic Site, the oldest synagogue in the United States; the International Tennis Hall of Fame and Tennis Museum; old Fort Adams; colonial houses; beaches; and museums, antique shops, and restaurants.

**Roger Williams Park Zoo**, in Roger Williams State Park in Providence, is America's third oldest zoo. Its modern design contains large areas that simulate the wild animals' habitats. The zoo has a breeding program for rare and endangered species.

**Slater Mill Historic Site**, in Pawtucket, is where the Industrial Revolution began in the United States. The site includes the original 1790 Slater Mill as well as the 1810 Wilkinson Mill. Historic textile machinery and a reconstructed 1820's waterwheel are displayed. The site also includes a 500-volume library of books on the history of textiles.

**State Recreation Areas.** Rhode Island has nearly two dozen state parks and hundreds of other attractions. For more information, contact the Economic Development Corporation, Tourism Division, One West Exchange Street, Providence, Rhode Island 02903.

Providence, the capital of Rhode Island and the state's largest city, is a seaport and center for business and manufacturing. Thomas Street (*below*) is lined with historic homes.

port, located in Warwick, near Providence. Deepwater seaports are found in Providence, Quonset, and Newport.

## Communication

The first newspaper in Rhode Island, the *Rhode Island Gazette*, was published in Newport in 1732 by James Franklin, a brother of Benjamin Franklin. Today Rhode Island's largest daily newspaper is the *Providence Journal-Bulletin*. Other dailies are published in Westerly, Pawtucket, Woonsocket, and Newport.

Rhode Island's first radio station was WJAR, founded in 1922. Today the state has 25 radio and 4 television stations. In addition, radio and television broadcasts from Boston reach most of the state, and Boston newspapers are widely circulated.

## ▶ CITIES

Seven of Rhode Island's nine largest cities are clustered around Providence, the largest city. About 80 percent of Rhode Island's population lives in this metropolitan area.

**Providence** is the capital of Rhode Island and one of the largest cities in New England. Settled on a site chosen by Roger Williams in 1636, Providence became the sole capital of Rhode Island in 1900.

For many years, Providence was mainly a seaport town. Although it remains an important port for coastal traffic, today it is chiefly a financial, business, and manufacturing center. Providence is also a cultural and educational center, with important museums, libraries, and art galleries and most of the state's institutions of higher education. The city is also well known for its many historical sites.

**Warwick**, the state's second largest city, is one of Rhode Island's four original settlements. Located on the western side of Narragansett Bay, Warwick is primarily a residential community. Its population grew rapidly in the mid-1900's but has stablilized in recent years. Warwick is also a popular resort area.

**Cranston**, a southern suburb of Providence, was originally part of Providence. It became a separate town in 1727. Today it is the third largest city in the state. Points of interest include the Pawtuxet Village historic district, which hosts the annual Gaspee Days celebration, and the Governor Sprague Mansion.

**Pawtucket**, north of Providence, is located at the falls of the Blackstone River. An important manufacturing center, Pawtucket has been called the cradle of the Industrial Revolution in America. The nation's first successful water-powered cotton-manufacturing machinery went into operation there, at Slater Mill, in 1790.

**Newport**, founded in 1639, was one of the original towns of Rhode Island and the principal seat of government for the colony. Oceanic commerce brought wealth and pros-

The Pawtuxet Rangers march in front of the state capitol in Providence to celebrate Heritage Days and Rhode Island's role in the Revolutionary War.

## INDEX TO RHODE ISLAND MAP

Counties in parentheses    ★ State Capital

perity to the city until the late 1700's, when the patterns of trade and commerce shifted to the mainland. Newport then became a resort area. Today it is Rhode Island's foremost tourist attraction.

## ▶ GOVERNMENT

Rhode Island was governed by its Great Charter of 1663 until a new state constitution was adopted in 1842. It remains in use today. Like most other state governments, Rhode Island's is made up of three branches—executive, legislative, and judicial.

The executive branch includes the governor, lieutenant governor, secretary of state, attorney general, and treasurer. They are all elected to 4-year terms.

The legislative branch is called the General Assembly, which is divided into a senate and a house of representatives. The members of the legislature serve 2-year terms.

The judicial branch is headed by the supreme court. Below it are the superior courts, district courts, family courts, probate courts, and municipal courts.

---

## GOVERNMENT

**State Government**
Governor: 4-year term
State senators: 50; 2-year terms
State representatives: 100; 2-year terms
Number of counties: 5

**Federal Government**
U.S. senators: 2
U.S. representatives: 2
Number of electoral votes: 4

For the name of the current governor, see STATE GOVERNMENTS in Volume S. For the names of current U.S. senators and representatives, see UNITED STATES, CONGRESS OF THE in Volume U-V.

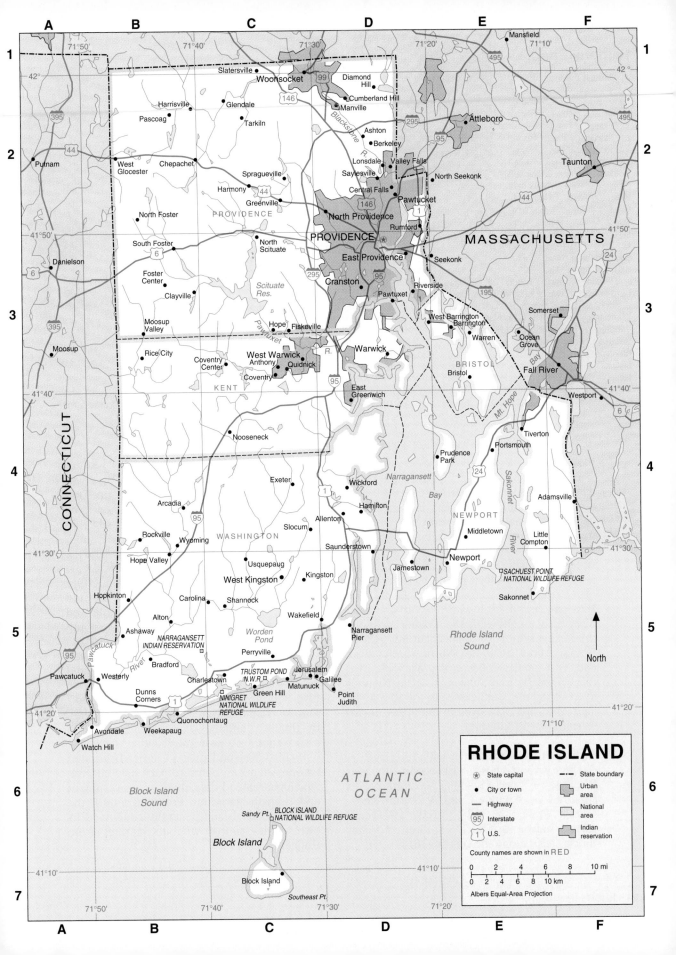

## Famous People

Consult the Index to find more information in *The New Book of Knowledge* about the following people who were either born in or are associated with Rhode Island: founder Roger Williams (1603?–83); Puritan outcast Anne Hutchinson (1591?–1643); Revolutionary War general Nathanael Greene (1742–86); naval officers Oliver Hazard Perry (1785–1819) and Matthew C. Perry (1794–1858); and educator and reformer Prudence Crandall (1803–90).

Roger Williams

**Nelson Wilmarth Aldrich** (1841–1915), born in Foster, was a leading Republican, serving as a U.S. senator from Rhode Island from 1881 to 1911. He was dubbed the General Manager of the United States because he wielded such power in the government. His Aldrich Plan (1911) served as the basis for the Federal Reserve Act of 1913, which established a central bank in the United States. His grandson, **Nelson Aldrich Rockefeller**

(1908–79), served as governor of New York (1959–73) and as vice president of the United States (1974–77).

**Edward Mitchell Bannister** (1828–1901), born in Nova Scotia, Canada, was the first African American to win a prize in a national art exhibition in the United States. His painting *Under the Oaks* won the highest prize at the 1876 Philadelphia Centennial Exposition. Bannister helped found the Providence Art Club in 1880, which became the Rhode Island School of Design.

**The Brown Brothers,** Nicholas, Joseph, John, and Moses, all born in Providence, were major figures in Rhode Island during the Revolutionary War period and after. **Nicholas** (1729–91), a leading merchant, helped establish the new College of Rhode Island, later named

Brown University, in Providence in 1770. **Joseph** (1733–85) ran Hope Furnace, a facility that made pig (crude) iron. Also an architect, Joseph designed University Hall at Brown University, the Meeting House of the First Baptist Church, and his brother's house, the John Brown House. **John** (1736–1803) was a leader in the Revolution in Rhode Island, supplying the Continental Army with clothing and munitions. His many commercial enterprises opened trade to India and China. A promoter of the slave trade, he was twice prosecuted by his brother Moses' abolition society. **Moses** (1738–1836), a merchant, manu-

George M. Cohan

▶ **HISTORY**

Evidence suggests that Native Americans came to Rhode Island at least 10,000 years ago. When European settlers arrived in the early 1630's, they found several tribes, including the powerful Narragansett Indians, who occupied approximately two-thirds of the state. The Narragansetts had captured Aquidneck Island and much of the territory north of present-day Providence from the Wampanoags, a tribe who lived to the east. They also fought with the Pequot to block their expansion from Connecticut into Rhode Island. About 1630 the Narragansetts took over two smaller tribes in the Warwick area, the Cowesetts and Shawomets. The Niantics lived along the southern coast of Rhode Island. The Nipmucks lived in the upper northwestern part of the state.

### Exploration and Early Settlement

The earliest-known European to see Rhode Island was Giovanni Verrazano, who explored the Atlantic Coast of North America for France in 1524. Nearly 100 years passed before a Dutch explorer, Adriaen Block, sailed along the coast in 1614.

Providence Plantations, Rhode Island's first permanent white settlement, was founded in 1636 by Roger Williams, an English clergyman who had been banished from the Massachusetts Bay Colony for his religious beliefs. Two Narragansett chiefs, Canonicus and Miantonomi, gave Williams land on which to build a colony and establish a government based on freedom of religion. Other religious exiles, particularly from the Puritan communities of Massachusetts, soon followed and established settlements in Portsmouth (1638), Newport (1639), and Warwick (1642).

As Rhode Island developed into a haven for religious "radicals," other New England colonists began calling it such names as "a hive of heretics" and "Rogues' Island." Rhode Islanders were constantly threatened by the surrounding colonies, which tried to assume authority over their lands.

In 1663, England's King Charles II granted Rhode Island an extraordinary new charter, which guaranteed the colony self-government and religious freedom. From then until the 1750's, Rhode Island generally conducted its own affairs almost without restraint from England.

facturer, and philanthropist, was the financial sponsor of Samuel Slater's mill. Moses led the movement that outlawed the slave trade and slavery in Rhode Island. He helped found what became the Moses Brown School.

**Ambrose Everett Burnside** (1824–81), born in Liberty, Indiana, became a successful businessman in Rhode Island before earning fame as a Civil War general. A veteran of the battles of First Bull Run (Manassas) and Antietam (Sharpsburg), Burnside was appointed to replace George McClellan as commander of the Army of the Potomac in October 1862. But after suffering a crushing defeat at Fredericksburg in December, he was relieved of his command. He later served as governor of Rhode Island (1866–69) and as a U.S. senator (1875–81). He is also remembered for the style of whiskers he wore, now known as sideburns.

**George M. Cohan** (1878–1942), an actor, playwright, producer, and songwriter, was born in Providence. Cohan composed more than 500 songs, most notably "Yankee Doodle Dandy," "Give My Regards to Broadway," and "Over

There," which became an unofficial anthem for U.S. soldiers fighting in World War I. He was awarded the Congressional Gold Medal in 1940.

**George Henry Corliss** (1817–88), born in Easton, New York, invented a mechanism that vastly improved the performance of steam engines, which greatly boosted Rhode Island's textile industry. The Corliss Steam Engine Company, founded in 1848, became the world's largest steam engine factory.

**Ida Lewis** (1842–1911), born in Newport, was keeper of the Lime Rock Lighthouse in Newport Harbor for nearly fifty years. She became famous for rescuing at least 17 people, including six soldiers, from drowning. Although Lewis had been the unofficial keeper of

Ida Lewis

the lighthouse since her father suffered a stroke in the late 1850's, the government did not make her position official until 1879, when she was also awarded a Congressional Gold Medal for her heroism.

**Gilbert Charles Stuart** (1755–1828), born in North Kingstown, became one of the best known of the early American portraitists. In 1775 he went to London to study under Benjamin West, a leading American artist living in England. After returning to the United States in 1793, Stuart painted portraits of George Washington, John Adams, Thomas Jefferson, and James Madison. His portraits of Washington, including the one that appears on the dollar bill, are the most famous.

### King Philip's War

In 1675, war broke out when the Wampanoag Indians attacked Plymouth Colony. The conflict was named for Metacomet, the Wampanoag chief whom the colonists called King Philip. Fighting eventually spread to Rhode Island, when a colonial army attacked a major Narragansett settlement in what became known as the Great Swamp Fight. In retaliation, the Narragansetts swept away white settlement from the western side of Rhode Island and burned the town of Providence. Nearly all of the settlers fled to the safety of Aquidneck Island.

The Narragansetts were defeated in 1676, and English settlers quickly spread across most of the colony. The Indians were left with only a fraction of their former lands.

### The Revolutionary War Period

After 1750, Rhode Island's status as a semi-independent colony conflicted with Britain's desire to take greater control over its American territories. Because Rhode Island had been free to do what it pleased for so long, it deeply resented new British rules and regulations. As a result, Rhode Islanders

reacted violently to the Stamp Act and Britain's efforts to press men to serve in the British navy and to regulate trade. A group of Providence men revolted in 1772 by burning a British customs ship, the *Gaspee*, when it ran aground off Warwick. When the Revolutionary War broke out in Massachusetts on April 19, 1775, Rhode Island sent militia units to help.

On May 4, 1776, the Rhode Island General Assembly repealed an oath of allegiance to King George III that had been required of officials since 1765. When the news of the Declaration of Independence arrived, Rhode Islanders welcomed it with cannon salutes and speeches.

Rhode Island suffered greatly in the war. From 1776 to 1779 the British occupied Newport and surrounding areas. Cut off from firewood, British soldiers cut down nearly all the trees on Aquidneck and Conanicut islands and tore down many shops and houses in Newport for fuel. The one effort to push the British out failed. The 1778 Battle of Rhode Island was mostly notable for the colony's newly formed black regiment that beat back three advances by the British. In October

In the early 1900's, before World War I, the textile industry employed more than half of Rhode Island's industrial workers.

1779 the British evacuated Newport to concentrate their forces in the South.

### Ratifying the Constitution

Although Rhode Island was eager to split from Great Britain, it was the last of the original 13 states to ratify the U.S. Constitution. Rhode Islanders were afraid to replace one powerful central government with a new one. They refused to send any delegates to the Constitutional Convention in Philadelphia in 1787, and they alone submitted the Constitution to a popular referendum, which overwhelmingly rejected ratification by a vote of 2,708 to 237. Eleven times the General Assembly refused to call a constitutional ratifying convention, and when Rhode Island finally ratified the Constitution on May 29, 1790, it attached 21 suggested amendments. By then George Washington had been president nearly two years.

Unlike every other state except Connecticut, Rhode Island refused to write itself a new constitution, choosing instead to keep the form of government outlined in its colonial charter. But in 1841 agitation to expand the vote and to reform the government finally erupted into an armed conflict, called the Dorr War. This led to the adoption of a new constitution in 1842.

### Leader of Industry

In 1790, America's Industrial Revolution began in Pawtucket when Samuel Slater started spinning cotton there with power-driven machines. By 1815 Rhode Island had 100 textile mills in 21 towns. From the 1820's to the 1920's, the production of cotton, wool, and lace products was Rhode Island's leading industry. Textile companies employed thousands of workers, making it a highly desirable destination for thousands of European immigrants. Other major industries also developed, including the production of machines and costume jewelry.

Industrial production was so advanced by the time the Civil War began in 1861 that Rhode Island became a major producer of cannons, rifles, bayonets, buckles, metal stirrups, uniforms, blankets, tents, boots, belts, harnesses, and other necessary war materials. In addition to its economic contribution, Rhode Island also supplied the Union Army with 24,000 troops.

By the end of the century, more than 1,500 factories were manufacturing everything from buttons to blackboards, mirrors to locomotives, hats to hydrants, silverware to cannons. Rhode Island also had more than two dozen auto and truck makers. The Alco, produced in Providence from 1909 to 1913, was one of the finest automobiles made in America before World War I.

### The 1900's

Rhode Island's economy peaked between the years 1890 and 1912. But the industrial powerhouse began to fade as the textile industry increasingly left New England for the South, where labor was cheaper. The decline of manufacturing was accompanied by labor unrest, particularly during the Great Depression of the 1930's. On several occasions, the governor had to call out the National Guard to put down strikes. To make matters worse, in 1938 a hurricane devastated the state and killed 258 people.

Since the end of World War II in 1945, Rhode Island's greatest struggle has been to establish a sound economy and achieve steady economic growth. The continuing loss of manufacturing jobs and slow development have made it difficult to keep up with costs of urban renewal, the repair of bridges, roads, and buildings, and the social needs of new immigrants. Increasingly, the state is becoming aware that its future is in its educational system, which must produce a new era of ingenuity and enterprise.

J. Stanley Lemons
Rhode Island College

## RHODES, CECIL (1853–1902)

Cecil John Rhodes was one of the great empire builders of the 1800's. Recognizing the vast natural wealth of Africa, he spent his life trying to create a union of African states under British rule, "from the Cape to Cairo."

Rhodes, one of twelve children, was born on July 5, 1853, in Bishop's Stortford, Hertfordshire, England. At the age of 17 he went to live with his oldest brother, Herbert, a cotton farmer in the British colony of Natal (now a province of South Africa). During the diamond rush of 1871, the brothers staked a claim in the Kimberly diamond fields. Almost overnight, Cecil Rhodes became a rich man.

At the age of 28, Rhodes became a member of the legislature of the British Cape Colony (now part of South Africa). In 1885 he convinced the British to take control of Bechuanaland (now Botswana). Rhodes then obtained mining rights from the Ndebele people in an area northeast of Bechuanaland.

This enabled him to form the British South Africa Company (B.S.A.C.), which was granted a charter to rule the area in 1889. The area (now Zimbabwe) was named Rhodesia.

Rhodes became prime minister of the Cape Colony in 1890. But in 1895 he was forced to resign over a scandal involving a plot to provoke an uprising in the neighboring Boer (Dutch-speaking) state of the Transvaal. Resulting hostilities contributed to the outbreak of the Second Boer War (1899–1902).

Rhodes died near Cape Town on March 26, 1902, at the age of 48. He left his home, Groote Schuur, to be used as a residence by future prime ministers of South Africa. The famous Rhodes scholarships—which provide funds for outstanding students from the British Commonwealth countries, the United States, and Germany to study at Oxford University—are supported by a grant set up by his will.

JOHN E. FLINT
Author, *Cecil Rhodes*

See also BOER WAR; SOUTH AFRICA; ZIMBABWE.

---

**RHODESIA.** See ZIMBABWE.

# RICE

When the Chinese greet one another, they do not say, "How do you do?" Instead they say, "Have you eaten your rice today?" This expression is used because rice is very important to the Chinese. It is important to many other people as well. Nearly half the population of the world lives partly or almost entirely on a rice diet. In most countries of Asia each person eats from 130 to 440 pounds (60 to 200 kilograms) of rice a year. In the United States, each person eats about 15 pounds (7 kilograms) of rice a year. In South America, the amount eaten a year is more than three times this much. Wheat is the only grain that is more important than rice as a food for human beings, and it is only slightly more important.

An advantage of rice is its high yield when it is cultivated properly. The average yield per acre is much higher than for wheat. Because of this high yield, rice has long been a symbol of fertility. Rice is thrown at a bride and groom after a wedding ceremony to wish them many children.

Rice probably originated in southern India, where it has been grown for thousands of years. From there it spread eastward into China before 3000 B.C. It then spread westward into Persia (Iran) and Egypt. Rice was not taken to North America until the 1600's. Today the leading rice producers are China, India, Indonesia, Bangladesh, Vietnam, Thailand, and Myanmar. In the United States rice is grown chiefly in Arkansas, California, Louisiana, Mississippi, and Texas.

### ▶ THE RICE PLANT

The rice plant belongs to the grass family. It has long, narrow leaves and several stems. At the top of each stem, a head of flowers

Nearly half the world's population lives partly or entirely on a rice diet. Rice (*above*) is grown in flooded fields called paddies (*right*).

forms. The grains, or seeds, develop from the flowers. Each head produces 50 to 150 grains of rice. Most rice plants grow 2 to 5 feet (60 to 150 centimeters) high. Rice is considered an annual plant. Most varieties take five or six months to ripen. But where the growing season is long enough, a second crop develops from the plants.

Rice thrives only where the weather is warm and the soil is wet. Most rice is **lowland rice**. It is grown on level land and is kept flooded in 4 to 8 inches (10 to 20 centimeters) of water for part or all of the growing season. **Upland rice** is grown in areas where the land is too rugged for flooding but where the rainfall is heavy enough so that flooding of the fields is not needed. Upland rice yields much less grain than lowland rice.

### ▶ GROWING AND HARVESTING RICE

In Asia and other parts of the world, rice seed is sown in seedbeds by hand. When the plants are 7 inches (18 centimeters) high or more, they are pulled from the bed, trimmed, and transplanted to a muddy field. The fields then are flooded. Later they are usually drained for weeding, which is done by hand. The fields are flooded again and are drained a short time before harvesting.

In the southern United States rice is usually seeded by a machine called a grain drill. The field is flooded when the plants are 6 to 8 inches (15 to 20 centimeters) high. In California and some other places, the seeds are scattered on flooded fields from airplanes. Weeds are controlled chiefly by chemical sprays.

Most of the world's rice is harvested by hand, using sickles and knives. The grains are knocked free from the straw by threshing. Threshing is done by machines that beat the rice heads or by animals that trample on them. In some countries rice is cut and threshed in one operation by machines.

### ▶ MILLING

The threshed grains of rice are called **rough rice** or **paddy rice**. (The word "paddy" is also used for the flooded field where rice is grown.) Rice in this rough state is still covered with coarse hulls that must be removed before the rice is cooked. Hulling may be done by machine in a rice mill, or the rice may be pounded by hand in a mortar.

Rice with the hulls removed is called **brown rice**. Brown rice is covered with a brownish outer skin called the bran. Most of the vitamins and minerals of the rice grain are stored in this bran. Although many people eat brown rice, most people prefer **white rice**—rice that has been milled to remove the bran.

Rice bran is removed by sending the rice kernels through a hulling machine that gently grinds the surface of each grain. In the milling process, the whole grains are separated from the broken grains, the flour, and the bran. Some rice is also scoured in a machine called a pearler. After milling, the rice kernels are white and have a polished surface. Since nutrients are lost in the milling process, white polished rice is often enriched by adding vitamins and minerals.

**Converted rice** is a slightly darker milled rice that has more B vitamins and minerals than ordinary polished rice. Before converted rice is milled, it is soaked in water that is just under the boiling point. Then it is steamed under pressure. This process is called **parboiling**. Vitamins from the bran soak into the grain during parboiling.

▶ RICE PRODUCTS

Rice is used in many ways. It supplies abundant food energy, but other foods are needed to provide a well-balanced diet. In North America, there are three classes of rice—long grain, medium grain, and short gain. All have the same food value. But long-grain rice tends to cook dry. Medium- and short-grain rice cook moist, yet firm.

Rice may be eaten boiled or baked or in the form of a breakfast cereal. Rice flour, a by-product of milling, is used to make bread, sugar, starch, face powder, and glue. Wine can be made by fermenting rice. Such wine is called sake in Japan, samshu in China, and ar-rack in India. Rice can also be used to make malt—an ingredient of beer.

Hulls and bran from milled rice can be fed to farm animals. Hulls are also used as animal bedding, packaging material, and fuel. In Asia, rice straw is used to make hats, baskets, mats, roof thatching, and paper.

▶ WILD RICE

The wild rice of North America is not really rice at all but a native grass. For many years it was an important food of Indians of the Great Lakes region. They gathered the harvest by slipping through the water in their light canoes. The stalks were tilted over the canoes, and the grains were gently knocked off with sticks. Because wild rice grows in water and is also harvested in water, it has never been grown in large quantities. Most of the wild rice produced in the United States today comes from Minnesota.

JOHN H. MARTIN
Oregon State University

See also GRAIN AND GRAIN PRODUCTS.

---

# RICE, CONDOLEEZZA (1954– )

In 2005, Condoleezza Rice succeeded Colin Powell as U.S. secretary of state. Rice had previously served as head of the National Security Council (NSC), advising President George W. Bush on national security and foreign policy matters. She was the first African American woman to hold the position of national security adviser and the first to become secretary of state.

Rice's unusual first name is a variation of *con dolcezza*, a musical direction that means "with sweetness." She was born on November 14, 1954, in Birmingham, Alabama. Condi, as her friends call her, was always an outstanding student and skipped the first and seventh grades. The family later moved to Colorado.

At 15, Rice entered the University of Denver. At first she planned to become a pianist, but she changed her major to political science and graduated with honors. Rice went on to earn a Ph.D. in international studies, with a focus on Eastern Europe and the Soviet Union. In 1981 she became an assistant professor at Stanford University. In 1989 she was hired to advise President George H.W. Bush, just as Communism was collapsing in Eastern Europe.

Rice returned to Stanford in 1991. Two years later she was named provost of the university. After six years, Rice left Stanford and became foreign policy adviser to George W. Bush during his 2000 presidential campaign. Rice was appointed national security adviser when Bush took office in 2001. She helped shape U.S. defense policy, including the response to the terrorist attacks of September 11, 2001, and the Iraq War.

As secretary of state, Rice concentrated on promoting democracy throughout the world. She declared all peoples should be able to express themselves freely and have an opportunity to participate in "free and fair elections."

Reviewed by SASHA PATTERSON
Rutgers, The State University of New Jersey

# RICHARD

Richard is an old Germanic name that means "strong ruler." Three kings of England have reigned (r.) under this name.

**Richard I** (1157–99) (r. 1189–99) is better known as Richard the Lion-Hearted. Born in Oxford on September 8, 1157, he was the third son of Henry II and Eleanor of Aquitaine. A brave soldier, he led the Third Crusade (1190–92) to the Holy Land. On his return in 1192, Richard was captured by his enemy, Duke Leopold of Austria. Leopold turned Richard over to the Holy Roman emperor, Henry VI, who released him in 1194 after an enormous ransom had been paid.

King Richard I of England was nicknamed *Coeur de Lion*, meaning the Lion-Hearted, for his courage in battle. He used his country's wealth to finance his overseas military expeditions and led the Third Crusade to the Holy Land, where he succeeded in capturing the port city of Acre.

Richard I was neglectful of his kingdom, spending only six months of his ten-year reign in England. During his absences, his ministers ruled in his place, while his brother John threatened to overthrow him.

Richard spent the last years of his life defending his French territories, Aquitaine and Normandy, against the French king, Philip Augustus. He was wounded by an arrow and died on April 6, 1199.

**Richard II** (1367–1400) (r. 1377–99), the son of Edward, the Black Prince, was born on January 6, 1367, in Bordeaux, France. Richard was only 10 when he succeeded his grandfather, Edward III, so his uncle, John of Gaunt, the Duke of Lancaster, effectively ruled the kingdom until he came of age.

The young King Richard displayed considerable courage in facing the rebels during the Peasants' Revolt in 1381. He later became a notable patron of art and culture, and his court circle included the great poet Geoffrey Chaucer. As he grew older, however, Richard became increasingly overbearing and sought to free himself of the barons' control.

In 1386 Parliament demanded the dismissal of Richard's friend, the Earl of Suffolk, as chancellor. Two years later the "Merciless Parliament" met, led by the king's leading opponents. Known as the Lords Appellant, these opponents had several of Richard's principal advisers executed on grounds of treason. For the next nine years, Richard ruled more moderately, but in 1397 he took his revenge. He had one of the appellants executed and three others sent into exile, including his cousin Henry Bolingbroke, John of Gaunt's son.

In 1399, while Richard was away in Ireland, the banished Bolingbroke invaded England with an army that met little resistance. When Richard returned from Ireland, he was imprisoned, and Bolingbroke took the throne as Henry IV. Richard died the following year, presumably murdered at Henry's command.

**Richard III** (1452–85) (r. 1483–85) seized power during the final years of the Wars of the Roses between the houses of York and Lancaster. Richard was born in Northamptonshire on October 2, 1452. As Duke of Gloucester, he loyally supported his brother, King Edward IV, and played a decisive role in helping Edward defeat the Lancastrians in the battles of Barnet and Tewkesbury (1471).

When Edward IV died in 1483, his young son succeeded him as Edward V. Richard feared that the young king's mother, Elizabeth Woodville, and her relatives would seize control, so he declared himself Lord Protector of his nephew. Soon afterwards, Edward V and his brother were declared illegitimate, and Richard was proclaimed king. (For more information, see the Wonder Question in the article ENGLAND, HISTORY OF in Volume E.)

Richard's short reign was troubled, and he lost the support of several of his closest allies. In 1485, Henry Tudor, a descendant of the House of Lancaster, successfully invaded Britain. Richard was killed at Bosworth Field on August 22, leading a desperate cavalry charge. Henry succeeded him as Henry VII.

CHARLES KIGHTLY
Contributor, *The Illustrated Dictionary of British History*

**RICHARDSON, HENRY HOBSON.** See LOUISIANA (Famous People).

# RICHELIEU, CARDINAL (1585–1642)

Armand Jean du Plessis, Duc de Richelieu, better known as Cardinal Richelieu, was one of the most important figures in French history. He strengthened the French monarchy during a period when it was weak and helped make France the leading power of Europe.

Born in Paris to a noble family on September 9, 1585, Richelieu at first planned a career in the army. Under pressure from his family, he agreed instead to enter the Roman Catholic Church. While barely in his 20's, he became Bishop of Luçon. Richelieu's abilities attracted the attention of Marie de Médicis, mother of the young King Louis XIII. She appointed Richelieu to an important post in the government.

Richelieu had great ambition as well as political genius. He was determined to become the most powerful man in France. In 1622 he was made a cardinal by the church. Two years later he was appointed the king's chief minister. In his climb to success, Richelieu made many enemies. Even Louis XIII came to dislike the crafty Richelieu. But the king knew that he could not rule without him, and Richelieu remained chief minister until his death 18 years later.

As chief minister (1624–42) under King Louis XIII, Cardinal Richelieu made France one of the most powerful countries in Europe.

The power of the French monarchy had been weakened during the sickly childhood of Louis XIII. Richelieu sought to restore the king's power and thus give France a strong, centralized government. He forced the Huguenots (French Protestants), who had controlled their own area of France, to yield to the king's authority. He also curbed the power of the great nobles, who had ruled parts of France almost as independent states. He reformed the finances of the country and appointed loyal and competent officials to serve the king.

In foreign affairs, Richelieu's goal was French security and the peace of Europe. He saw a threat to both in the powerful Habsburg family, whose members ruled Spain, Austria, and the Holy Roman Empire of German states. During the Thirty Years' War (1618–48), which began as a religious conflict between Catholics and Protestants, he allied France—a Catholic country—with the Protestant countries who opposed the ruling Habsburgs. As a result of the war, France emerged as the leading power in Europe.

Richelieu died on December 4, 1642. He did not live to see the end of the war and the rise to greatness of France under its next king, Louis XIV.

Reviewed by JEAN T. JOUGHIN
American University

---

## Did you know that...

in 1635, Cardinal Richelieu founded L'Académie Française (the French Academy), a society dedicated to preserving French language and culture? The society is made up of forty intellectuals (called the immortals), who are appointed for life. It is renowned for its *Dictionnaire*, first published in 1684, and its annual literary prize, awarded since 1914.

## RIEL, LOUIS (1844–1885)

Some western Canadians regard Louis Riel, founder of the Canadian province of Manitoba, as a hero; others see him as a traitor. Riel was born in the Red River colony near present-day Winnipeg on October 22, 1844. His father was a prominent métis (person of mixed Indian and European ancestry). Riel was schooled in St. Boniface and later studied for the priesthood in Montreal. He dropped out of college and studied law for a time before returning to Red River in 1868.

Riel came home at a critical time. In 1869 the government of Canada was preparing to absorb Red River into the new Dominion of Canada. The métis resented their treatment by Canada and feared they would lose their land. Under Riel's leadership, they resisted Canadian control in an uprising called the Red River Resistance. As head of a provisional government, Riel negotiated better terms for Manitoba's entry into Canada, enabling it to enter as a province rather than a territory and securing some protection for the French language. But Riel's role in the uprising, especially the execution of a Canadian named Thomas Scott, outraged many Canadians. In 1870, Riel fled Red River to avoid capture by the military and later went into exile in the United States. During this period he suffered increasingly from mental illness.

In 1884, while living in Montana, Riel was asked by the métis to return to what is now Saskatchewan and lead them in forcing Canada to recognize their land rights there. In March 1885, what was intended to be a peaceful movement developed into the North West Rebellion, largely as a result of Riel's strategy. The métis formed a provisional government and took up arms. This time Canada responded with armed force, quickly crushing the rebellion. Riel was tried for treason, convicted, and hanged in Regina, Saskatchewan, on November 16, 1885.

Riel's place in Canadian history remains controversial. In 1992 the Canadian Parliament recognized his contribution to the creation of Manitoba. In 2004 Canadian prime minister Paul Martin promised Native leaders he would explore ways of commemorating Riel's accomplishments.

J. R. MILLER
Canada Research Chair and Professor of History
University of Saskatchewan

---

**RIFLES.** See GUNS AND AMMUNITION.

**RIGHTS, BILL OF.** See BILL OF RIGHTS.

**RIIS, JACOB.** See NEW YORK CITY (Famous People).

**RINGLING, JOHN.** See FLORIDA (Famous People).

**RINGWORM.** See DISEASES (Descriptions of Some Diseases).

## RIO DE JANEIRO

Rio de Janeiro, Brazil's second largest city, is one of the most beautiful cities in the world. A bustling financial, tourist, and commercial center of nearly 6 million people, Rio (as it is often called) is also the home of the nation's leading cultural institutions.

Rio is an old city, but it is also one of the most modern in South America. Locked in by sea, mountains, and forests, Rio cannot expand horizontally and so is a city of tall buildings. The lowland adjoining the bay is divided into three zones. The southern zone is modern and stylish, though many old churches and other colonial structures contrast with the newer buildings. Avenida Atlântica, an avenue that runs along the

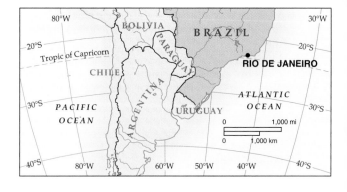

beaches, has many apartment buildings, hotels, theaters, and restaurants. The center zone is the commercial region and is marked by tall office buildings and crowded streets. It is

The statue *Christ the Redeemer* stands atop Corcovado Mountain, overlooking the city of Rio de Janeiro.

concentrated on Avenida Rio Branco and Avenida Presidente Vargas. In the northern zone, people live in more modest houses. On the hillsides, people live crowded together in poorly constructed housing, known as favelas.

**The City.** With so many beautiful beaches at their disposal, the Cariocas, as the residents of Rio are called, enjoy swimming, sailing, fishing, deep-sea diving, and volleyball. As in the rest of Brazil, the favorite sport is *futebol* (soccer), played at Maracanã Stadium, the largest stadium in the world. Carnival, celebrated for four days before Ash Wednesday, is Rio's liveliest festival. People come from all around the world to watch Rio's Carnival parade, held all night long on Sunday and Monday.

Rio's setting is one of the most attractive in the world. To the west are the Serra dos Orgãos (Organ Mountains), which give the city a magnificent background. To the east is Guanabara Bay, a deepwater inlet of the Atlantic Ocean. Pão de Açúcar (Sugarloaf Mountain), at the entrance to the bay, is a cone-shaped rock 1,296 feet (395 meters) high. Nearby is Corcovado, a sharp, rocky peak 2,310 feet (704 meters) high. Upon its summit rises the 125-foot (38-meter)-tall statue *Christ the Redeemer.*

Rio is world famous for its miles of golden beaches. The best known are Copacabana, Ipanema, Leblon, and Leme. The island of Paquetá, the Rodrigo de Freitas Lagoon, and Tijuca Forest add to Rio's natural beauty.

Rio is the educational and cultural center of Brazil. The Federal University of Rio de Janeiro (founded 1920) is located there. The city has many fine art galleries, theaters, and concert halls. Other attractions include the National Museum and National Library.

**Economic Activity.** Although Rio is not primarily an industrial city, many of its people are engaged in manufacturing food products, building materials, electrical equipment, and chemicals. Many of Brazil's imports and exports pass through Rio, since it is a major port on the Atlantic coast. Service industries, including banking and other financial businesses, tourism, and entertainment activities, dominate the city's economic life.

**History.** Before Europeans arrived in Rio, Tupi Indians lived in the area. In 1502 a Portuguese navigator led an expedition into Guanabara Bay. He thought the bay was the mouth of a big river, and because he found it on January 1 he called it Rio de Janeiro ("River of January"). In 1567 the Portuguese won a battle against French Huguenots who had settled in the region. The battle took place on January 20, the Feast of Saint Sebastian. To honor the saint as well as Dom Sebastião, king of Portugal, the victors called the city Saint Sebastian of Rio de Janeiro.

Rio's fine bay and favorable climate attracted many settlers. The city was made the capital of the Portuguese colony in 1763. When the French emperor Napoleon I invaded Spain and Portugal in 1808, the Portuguese king and court fled to Rio and made the city the capital of the entire Portuguese empire. In 1822, Brazil became an independent empire with Rio as its capital. In 1889, Rio became the capital of the newly formed republic of Brazil.

Because Rio was the national capital for so many years, its growth paralleled that of Brazil itself. The growth of the country and the desire for a more centrally located capital led the federal government to create a new capital city, Brasília, in 1960. Today Rio de Janeiro is the capital of Rio de Janeiro state.

Reviewed by IRENE FLUM GALVIN
Author, *Brazil: Many Voices, Many Faces*

# RIO GRANDE

The Rio Grande is the third longest river in the United States and the fifth longest in North America. Its basin drains an area of 182,215 square miles (293,366 square kilometers). From its headwaters in the Rocky Mountains of southwestern Colorado, the Rio Grande flows 1,885 miles (3,033 kilometers) across central New Mexico, through canyons in Big Bend National Park in southwestern Texas and northern Mexico, and east across the semi-tropical Tamaulipas plain before emptying into the Gulf of Mexico at Brownsville, Texas. Its name is derived from the Spanish words meaning "great river."

The Rio Grande's major tributaries are the Chama, in New Mexico; the Pecos, in Texas; and the Conchos, in Chihuahua, Mexico. There are many smaller, intermittent tributaries, activated by rainstorms or melting snow from mountains. Albuquerque, New Mexico; El Paso, Texas; and Ciudad Juárez, in Chihuahua, are the largest cities on the river.

For 1,200 miles (1,932 kilometers)—almost two-thirds of its length—the Rio Grande forms the international boundary between the United States and Mexico as it flows along the western and southwestern part of Texas. The border was designated in 1848 under the Treaty of Guadalupe Hidalgo, which concluded the Mexican War.

The rich history of the Rio Grande is well documented, beginning with early Pueblo Indian settlements and the arrival of Spanish explorers in the 1500's, as countless films, books, and songs have chronicled the river's past. But the river itself has been neglected. Along significant stretches, the quality of its water is degraded, the streamflow is diminished, and the river's banks and riverbed are choked with non-native plants. Demand for water from the Rio Grande exceeds what is available; this situation has created tension between people living upstream and those living downstream, as well as between the United States and Mexico—especially during periods of drought.

Upstream from the border, Native American communities and cities in New Mexico and Colorado and on the Conchos River in Chihuahua struggle with increasing local demand for water from the Rio Grande, while also trying to conserve enough for the nearly 8 million people who live downstream.

Still, the Rio Grande flows through areas of great natural beauty, sustains important wildlife habitats, and offers many recreational opportunities. In 1978, the U.S. government selected a 196-mile (316-kilometer) stretch in southwest Texas and designated it as the Rio Grande Wild and Scenic River; the upper 69 miles (111 kilometers) lie within Big Bend National Park.

Tyrus G. Fain
President
Rio Grande Institute

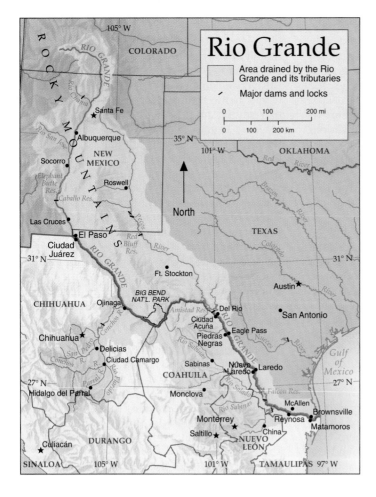

# RIVERA, DIEGO
(1886–1957)

Mexican artist Diego Rivera was the leader of an artistic and political movement (1923–30) that celebrated the native history and culture of Mexico with vast public murals.

Rivera was born on December 8, 1886, in the mining town of Guanajuato. At age 10 he entered the Academy of San Carlos, a noted art school in Mexico City, graduating with a fine arts degree in 1905.

When the Mexican Revolution began in 1910, Rivera went to live in Paris. His best-known work from this period is *Zapatista Landscape—The Guerrilla* (1915), a cubist portrait of the revolutionary hero Emiliano Zapata. Zapata is portrayed as a collection of geometric shapes—including his gun and parts of his hat, shawl, and face—floating in front of a realistic landscape of the Valley of Mexico.

After the Revolution ended in 1920, the new Mexican government asked Rivera to return and create murals that celebrated native history and culture. He painted ten major murals between 1923 and 1953, most of them frescoes (paintings on walls covered with wet plaster). His greatest Mexican mural, at Mexico City's Ministry of Education, consists of 134 panels depicting the history, festivals, and industries of Mexico. Between 1930 and 1935, Rivera painted seven murals in the United States. The most famous of these, the fresco cycle, or series, *Detroit Industry* (1932–33) at the Detroit Institute of Arts, celebrates factory workers.

Rivera married several times; one of his wives was Mexican artist Frida Kahlo. Rivera died in Mexico City on November 24, 1957.

LINDA BANK DOWNS
Author, *Diego Rivera:
The Detroit Industry Murals*

---

# RIVERS

A river is any natural stream of fresh water that flows in a channel. But what makes a river begin? Why do rivers flow in some places and not in others?

No place on the surface of the Earth is perfectly level. Wherever rain falls, some water evaporates, some seeps through the soil into the ground, and some rainwater remains on the surface. Once enough water collects on the surface, it begins to flow across the land, following the shortest and steepest way downhill. A river begins to form.

As water flows, it erodes (wears away) the land beneath it and begins to pick up and carry small particles of dirt and rocks. This starts the process of forming a stream channel. The steeper the slope, the more water comes together, and the more power it has to carry material and make the stream channel bigger.

## ▶ RIVER STRUCTURE

Rivers come in many sizes, shapes, and forms. Some flow lazily and very slowly. Others flow swiftly—sometimes fiercely. Little rivers that are narrow and not very deep are sometimes called streams, creeks, or brooks. The place where two rivers come together is called a **confluence**. Small rivers that join bigger rivers are called **tributaries**. A large river and all its tributaries form a **river system**.

The way a river flows depends on the slope of the land, the quantity of water in its chan-

> This article discusses the physical structure of rivers and their importance. It also includes descriptions of major rivers of the world. Information relating to rivers can be found in several other articles in this encyclopedia, including DAMS, EROSION, FLOODS, IRRIGATION, WATER POLLUTION, and WATERPOWER.

*Clockwise from right:* Ships sail on the Nile River, the longest river in the world. The Amazon River winds through dense rain forests and flows east across Brazil into the Atlantic Ocean. The Mekong River forms the vast Mekong Delta, an important rice-growing region in Vietnam.

nel, and the amount and type of material it carries (called its **load**). The beginning of a river is called its **source**. Every river flows through a **river valley**. Most of the time, the river only has water flowing through a small area of the valley, called the **riverbed** or **river channel**. The **riverbanks** are the sides of the river channel that separate it from the rest of the valley.

A **drainage basin**, or **watershed**, is the land area that is drained by a river and its tributaries. Drainage basins are separated from each other by high areas of land, such as mountain ridges. These heights, called **drainage divides**, or **watershed boundaries**, determine the slope of the land and which way the water will flow.

Many familiar land features are mainly the result of the never-ceasing work of rivers. Running water carves the landscape and deposits new features on the land. As water flows within a channel or riverbed, it carries sand, silt, pebbles, and gravel. The faster the water flows, even larger stones and boulders can be carried downstream.

The heavier materials are rolled along the bottom of the river, while the finer sands and silts are carried in suspension, meaning within the water itself. A stream may lose part of its carrying power because it lacks water or because its slope becomes more gentle. Then it flows more slowly and deposits the heaviest materials first.

▶ **RIVER DELTAS**

Where a river ends its flow is called the river's **mouth**. This is usually the place where the river flows into another river, a lake, or the sea. When a river reaches a lake or the sea, its flow slows down suddenly. It is no longer capable of carrying its load. Much of this is deposited as **sediment** at the mouth of the river to form a fanlike deposit called a

**delta**. Ocean waters carry away the material that does not get deposited on the delta. As a result, the seawater may be muddy for great distances along the coast as the silt (fine soil particles) is carried with the ocean currents.

Deltas may be very large, especially if more than one river empties into the sea in the same place. For example, the Netherlands is for the most part a large delta made by the Rhine, Meuse, and Schelde rivers. The location of a river mouth can also shift position along the edge of an ocean or sea. Much of coastal Louisiana was created by delta deposits from the Mississippi River as it shifted over time.

Delta soils tend to be fertile. In such countries as Egypt, Pakistan, and India, millions of people live on delta land. Almost the entire country of Bangladesh is located on the delta at the mouth of the Ganges River. People in these areas raise crops and build cities on deltas, though they know that every year may bring another flood. In arid (dry) regions, the delta plain may be the one place with fertile soil and enough water for farming.

Other rivers, such as the Hudson in New York and the Thames in England, have no deltas. Instead, they have **drowned mouths**. These are formed when, due to geology or climate, the sea level rises in relation to the

land and the lowest portions of the rivers are submerged by the sea. An **estuary** is the zone where fresh water from a river mixes with salt water. The size of an estuary varies depending on the tidal range at the river mouth. Estuaries can sometimes extend far up a river, away from the coast.

▶ **RIVER FLOW**

The amount of **precipitation** (the moisture that falls to the ground as rain, snow, hail, or sleet) determines the amount of water in any river. The amount of water also depends on underground springs. Water seeps and trickles underground after each shower or melting of ice and snow. It collects in cracks and crevices inside the Earth, and much of it finally reaches a river.

In places that are very dry, a river may disappear underground or evaporate into the air. Then the riverbed is dry and fills with water again only when it rains. Such rivers are called **intermittent** rivers or streams. In some countries (Algeria, Libya, Israel, and Saudi Arabia, for example), the beds of intermittent rivers are called **wadis**. In the southwestern United States, the same kind of dry riverbed is called an **arroyo**. In the western United States and Canada they are sometimes called **washes**. These intermittently dry streams are usually found in desert regions. Water may actually flow in these rivers only once every few decades.

## THE LONGEST RIVERS IN THE WORLD

| Name of river | Length of river | |
|---|---|---|
| | miles | kilometers |
| Nile | 4,160 | 6,693 |
| Amazon | 4,000 | 6,436 |
| Ob'-Irtysh | 3,461 | 5,569 |
| Yangtze (Chang) | 3,434 | 5,529 |
| Paraná | 3,030 | 4,875 |
| Yellow River (Huang He) | 2,903 | 4,671 |
| Amur | 2,705 | 4,352 |
| Lena | 2,700 | 4,347 |
| Congo | 2,700 | 4,347 |
| Mekong | 2,600 | 4,186 |
| Niger | 2,600 | 4,186 |
| Yenisey | 2,566 | 4,129 |
| Missouri | 2,466 | 3,968 |
| Mississippi | 2,357 | 3,792 |

Source: Webster's Geographical Dictionary

Some rivers have their sources in highlands or mountains where there is heavy precipitation. Sometimes these rivers cross vast desert regions. Despite the loss of water by evaporation from the hot desert sun, these rivers often have plenty of water to spill into the sea. They receive so much water at their source that they can cross hundreds of miles of desert without going dry. The Nile and the Colorado rivers are examples.

▶ RIVER FLOODS

If a river channel receives more water than it can hold, the water spills over onto the land on either side of the river. This is called a **flood**. As the river overflows, it deposits some of the heavier gravel and sand on the valley floor next to the river bank. This ridgelike deposit is called a **natural levee**. Then the overflowing water continues to spread over the valley floor beyond the levees and deposits the finer silt and sand.

Material that is deposited on land by rivers is called **alluvium**. The flat valley floor on either side of the river is called a **floodplain**.

Flood Control. People use the rich soils of the floodplain for growing crops. They often build cities and factories near a river and use the river for a water supply or for shipping cargo. When a river overflows its banks, serious damage may be done to artificial structures that are in the path of floodwaters. Sometimes artificial levees of stone or concrete are built on top of the natural levees to hold the river in its channel. Sometimes the water level is controlled by the construction of dams, which store water in reservoirs during high-water periods and release the stored water for use during times of low water.

▶ LIFE CYCLE OF A RIVER

Rivers can be classified in three ways—young, mature, and old. These names do not refer to the age of a river in years. Instead, they describe certain features in the appearance of a river.

A **young river** flows rapidly. Its bed is steep and irregular. Its flow is often interrupted by rapids and waterfalls. There are few tributaries. The valley through which a young river flows is often steep-sided. There is no broad floodplain nor any natural levees.

In a **mature river** most of the rapids and waterfalls have disappeared. Mature rivers flow more slowly than young rivers. The slope of the riverbed is gradual. The river valley is broad, and the mature river often meanders (winds) across a wide floodplain. Natural levees and swamps are sometimes present, and the river often has tributaries.

**Old rivers** meander slowly back and forth through broad, flat valleys and wide floodplains. The sides of the river valley are worn down to gentle

The Missouri River is the longest river in the United States. From its headwaters in Montana, the river cuts through mountains and prairies, eventually flowing into the Mississippi River.

slopes. An old river often creates a delta where it empties into the sea.

Some rivers that grew old over the ages have been rejuvenated (made young again) by uplifting of the Earth's crust. A river may be youthful at its source, be mature farther downriver, and end up as an old river at its mouth. The Mississippi is such a river.

## ▶ IMPORTANCE OF RIVERS

People have always used rivers for transportation. In the early history of many countries, rivers served people by providing water for growing crops. The ancient Egyptians used the waters of the Nile to aid in growing crops as early as 3400 B.C. The ancient Babylonians, Chinese, and American Indians all used river water for irrigation. People have often harnessed a river's waterpower to turn wheels and grind grain.

A map of any country shows at a glance that people like to live near rivers. Hundreds of cities throughout the world are built on the banks, floodplains, and deltas of rivers. Rivers not only provide water for home use, but furnish water for industry and supply sources of food and recreation.

**Commerce and Trade.** Some rivers provide natural transportation routes for the movement of large quantities of goods. River barges carry heavy cargoes on the Illinois, Mississippi, Ohio, and Hudson rivers. In Europe many rivers are crowded with barges moving from country to country.

Not all rivers are suitable for navigation. Some rivers do not have enough water year-round. Rivers in Europe, Asia, and North America may freeze in the winter. In other cases, waterfalls and rapids may prevent navigation.

Some large navigable rivers, such as the Mackenzie in Canada and the Lena, Ob', and Yenisey in Russian Siberia, flow northward into the Arctic Ocean, where there is little or no trade. Though they are navigable for part of the year, not much freight is shipped on these rivers. There are few cities or people to

carry on trade. Therefore, there is not much transportation. In the tropical rain forests of the Congo and Brazil there are also many navigable rivers but few people to use them. If these areas are developed, the rivers will be used in many ways.

**Boundaries.** Many rivers serve as boundaries between nations. Rivers that serve as partial international boundaries include the St. Lawrence, Yalu, and Rio Grande. Provincial and state boundaries also follow the courses of some rivers. Examples are the Ot-

A tugboat pushes barges on the Mississippi River. The river is a natural transportation route for the movement of heavy cargoes.

tawa in Canada, the Murray in Australia, the Ganges in India, and the Ohio and Mississippi in the United States.

**Sources of Power.** People have always used the force of falling river water to provide power. A river must have rapids or a waterfall to supply this energy. In the past, factories using waterpower had to be located near the rapids or falls. Since the development of electricity the pressure of the falling water is used to turn a turbine. This, in turn, runs electric generators. The electricity can be sent many miles over wires. It is no longer necessary for factories to be situated at the waterfalls.

If natural falls do not exist, dams are built to back up the water. Gates in the high dam are opened. As the river water rushes through the openings, it drops down to the river below the dam and turns the turbines that have been built there.

**Irrigation.** Much of the Earth's land is too dry to produce crops. People have therefore developed methods of using rivers to irrigate the soil.

Today rivers are used for large irrigation systems. Dams are constructed across rivers to store water. When water is needed for growing crops, the water in the reserve or reservoir is piped into fields. Electric generators supply power to pump water hundreds of miles through pipes. Dams conserve water that collects during rainy seasons.

**Water for Industrial Use.** Industries use vast quantities of water. Paper factories use much water to wash the wood and to mix the wood pulp into a mash that is pressed into paper. Iron and steel mills use enormous quantities

Rafters float down the Colorado River through the steep-sided gorges of Glen Canyon National Recreation Area.

of river water each day to cool and wash the various iron and steel pieces that are being formed.

Industries also use rivers as places to dump their waste materials. And people discharge the sewage and waste of their homes through pipes into the rivers nearest them. Today there are so many cities and people and industries that many rivers are badly polluted. Pollution kills fish and other animal life as well as harming aquatic plants. It destroys the

recreational value of rivers. Polluted rivers are a health hazard. If the polluted water is to be used for drinking or washing, it must be purified by chemical means in water-treatment plants near the rivers. This is an expensive process. Not all river water used by people today is purified.

**Sources of Food.** Rivers have long provided people with food in the form of fish. Millions of people in South America, Africa, and Asia fish for their food every day. In North America and Europe large industries are based on river fishing. The salmon industry is one example of a large river-fishing industry in Canada and the United States.

**Recreation.** Rivers are valuable for recreation. People camp and picnic near rivers. Rivers are used for swimming, boating, and water-skiing. State and national parks that have been created near rivers are favorite places for people to spend holidays and vacations and enjoy water sports.

▶ **SOME RIVERS OF THE WORLD**

**The Amazon River**, the most important river in South America, has the largest volume of any river in the world. Its drainage basin is 2,053,318 square miles (5,318,094 square kilometers). The Amazon is also the second longest river in the world. Its length is about 4,000 miles (6,436 kilometers), which includes 100 miles (160 kilometers) of the Marañón. See the article AMAZON RIVER.

**The Amur River** in northeast Asia rises in northern Mongolia and flows eastward, emptying into the Sea of Okhotsk. The river, about 2,705 miles (4,352 kilometers) in length, forms part of the border between Russia and China.

**The Brahmaputra River** of southern Asia rises in the Himalayas and empties into the Bay of Bengal. It is about 1,800 miles (2,900 kilometers) long. The delta formed by the Brahmaputra and Ganges rivers in Bangladesh is one of the world's largest.

**The Colorado River** rises in Rocky Mountain National Park and empties into the Gulf of

California. The Colorado is about 1,450 miles (2,350 kilometers) in length and drains areas in both the United States and Mexico.

**The Columbia River** rises in the Canadian Rockies in British Columbia. It is about 1,214 miles (1,953 kilometers) long and drains a basin in Canada and the United States. The Grand Coulee and the Bonneville dams on the Columbia supply water for irrigation and power and help to control floods.

**The Congo River**, the second longest river in Africa and one of the longest rivers in the world, is about 2,700 miles (4,350 kilometers) long. See the article CONGO RIVER.

The Danube is the second longest river in Europe. On its banks are four national capitals—Budapest (*above*), Vienna, Bratislava, and Belgrade.

**The Danube River**, the second longest river in Europe, is 1,771 miles (2,851 kilometers) long. It rises in the Black Forest of Germany and empties into the Black Sea. It flows through or borders nine countries. On its banks are four capitals—Vienna (Austria), Bratislava (Slovakia), Budapest (Hungary), and Belgrade (Serbia and Montenegro). The Danube is controlled by the countries bordering it. Each nation regulates its own uses of the river and its banks.

**The Delaware River** rises in the Catskill Mountains in southeastern New York. It is about 280 miles (451 kilometers) in length and empties into Delaware Bay. The river is used to produce hydroelectric power. The Delaware Aqueduct system is one of the sources of water for New York City.

**The Dnieper River**, the third longest river in Europe, rises in the Valdai Hills near Moscow, flows through Belarus and Ukraine, and empties into the Black Sea. It is 1,420 miles (2,285 kilometers) long. The river is an important source of hydroelectric power. Canals link the Dnieper to the Baltic Sea, forming a continuous north-south waterway.

**The Don River** rises in the central uplands of Russia. It flows for 1,224 miles (1,969 kilometers) and empties into the Sea of Azov, which connects with the Black Sea.

**The Ebro River** rises in the Cantabrian Mountains of northern Spain. It flows for about 565 miles (909 kilometers) before emptying into the Mediterranean Sea. It is the largest river entirely within Spain. The Ebro supplies much of Spain's hydroelectric power.

**The Elbe River** rises in the Sudetes, a mountain range between the Czech Republic and Poland. It flows across northern Germany and empties into the North Sea. The river is about 724 miles (1,165 kilometers) in length.

---

**Did you know that...**

many of the world's great civilizations arose on the floodplains of major rivers? The rich, fertile soil of floodplains is refertilized with nutrient-rich sediment every time a river floods, providing the perfect conditions for sustainable, permanent, and productive farming. Floodplains are also located right next to the river, which provides a constant supply of water and a means of transportation. These conditions allowed humans to settle permanently and provided enough food security to allow for the development of large civilizations.

Mesopotamia, considered the cradle of modern civilization, was built on the floodplain land between the Tigris and Euphrates rivers. This is where the modern-day city of Baghdad is located. The great Egyptian cities where the ancient pharaohs ruled are located in the Nile's floodplain. Before the United States was settled by Europeans, large Native American cities such as Cahokia were located in the floodplain where the Missouri and Mississippi Rivers join, and where the modern-day city of St. Louis is now located.

The **Ganges River**, the main river in India, is considered the most sacred river of Hinduism. See the article GANGES RIVER.

The **Garonne River** of southwestern France rises in the Pyrenees mountains of Spain and flows through the famous Bordeaux wine region. It is 357 miles (574 kilometers) long and empties into the Bay of Biscay.

The **Guadalquivir River** rises in the mountains of southern Spain and empties into the Atlantic Ocean. It irrigates olive groves and fruit orchards of the Andalusian plain. The cities of Córdoba and Seville are on its banks. It is 408 miles (656 kilometers) long, and only short portions are navigable.

large cotton and grain area.

The **Irrawaddy River**, one of Southeast Asia's major rivers, flows south through the length of Myanmar and empties into the Andaman Sea. It is about 1,300 miles (2,092 kilometers) in length and is navigable for small ships along part of its course. The Twante Canal links the river to the port city of Yangon

*Clockwise from right:* The Ganges River, the main river in northern India, is considered the most sacred river of Hinduism. Bear Mountain Bridge spans the Hudson River, which rises in New York's Adirondack Mountains and empties into upper New York Bay at New York City. The Lena River, a chief waterway of Siberia, is one of the longest rivers in the world. Canada's great Mackenzie River freezes in places as it flows northwest to the Arctic Ocean.

The **Hudson River** rises in the Adirondack Mountains of New York and empties into upper New York Bay at New York City. Part of the river forms a boundary between New York and northeastern New Jersey. It is 306 miles (492 kilometers) long. The New York State Barge Canal system links the Hudson to the Great Lakes and Lake Champlain. The Richelieu Canal connects it with the St. Lawrence River. The lower Hudson (the North River) is part of New York Harbor.

The **Indus River**, Pakistan's greatest river, rises in China (Tibet) and empties into the Arabian Sea. The Indus is about 1,800 miles (2,896 kilometers) in length. It irrigates a

(formerly Rangoon). The river's delta is one of the world's great rice-producing regions.

The **Jordan River**, the longest river of Israel and Jordan, flows from Syria and Lebanon to the Dead Sea. The river is mentioned in both the Old Testament and New Testament of the Bible. See the articles ISRAEL and JORDAN.

The **Lena River** in central Siberia is about 2,700 miles (4,347 kilometers) in length; it is one of the longest rivers in the world. It rises in the Baikal Range and empties into the Laptev Sea through a wide delta.

The **Liffey River** rises in the Wicklow Mountains of Ireland, flows through Dublin, and empties into Dublin Bay on the Irish Sea.

is about 2,635 miles (4,240 kilometers).

**The Magdalena River**, about 956 miles (1,538 kilometers) long, is Colombia's chief river. It rises in the mountains of southwestern Colombia and empties into the Caribbean Sea.

**The Manzanares** is the river of Madrid. It rises in the Sierra de Guadarrama in Spain and flows 50 miles (80 kilometers), emptying into the Jamara, an arm of the Tagus River. It is noted for the beautiful bridges that span it at Madrid.

**The Mekong River** rises in China and flows through Southeast Asia before emptying into the South China Sea. About 2,600 miles (4,186 kilometers) long, it is one of the longest rivers in Asia. The vast delta it forms in Vietnam is an important rice-growing region.

**The Meuse River** rises in eastern France. It flows for about 580 miles (933 kilometers) through France, Belgium, and the Netherlands and empties into the North Sea. The river forms part of the Dutch-Belgian border.

**The Mississippi River**, the second longest river in the United States, is about 2,357 miles (3,792 kilometers) long. See the article MISSISSIPPI RIVER.

Canals connect the 50-mile (81-kilometer) Liffey with the Shannon River, making a waterway across Ireland.

**The Loire**, the longest river in France, rises on Mont Gerbier de Jonc in southeastern France. It flows for about 634 miles (1,020 kilometers) and empties into the Atlantic Ocean. Only the lower Loire is navigable.

**The Mackenzie River** in northwestern Canada is Canada's greatest river and part of a large river system. The river is about 1,120 miles (1,800 kilometers) in length. It rises in Great Slave Lake and flows northward, emptying into the Beaufort Sea, an arm of the Arctic Ocean. The total length of the system

**The Missouri River** is the longest river in the United States. The river rises in southwestern Montana and flows about 2,466 miles (3,968 kilometers), eventually joining the Mississippi River. Including its longest tributaries, it flows 2,683 miles (4,317 kilometers). See the article MISSOURI RIVER.

**The Murray River**, the chief river of Australia, is 1,609 miles (2,589 kilometers) long. The Murray rises in the Australian Alps in New South Wales and empties into the Indian Ocean at Encounter Bay.

**The Niger River**, the third longest river in Africa, is about 2,600 miles (4,186 kilometers) long, with a drainage basin of about 584,000 square miles (1,513,000 square kilometers). Its waters irrigate an enormous area of West Africa. It empties into the Atlantic Ocean.

**The Nile River** is the longest river in the world. Located in northeast Africa, it is about 4,160 miles (6,693 kilometers) in length. See the article NILE RIVER.

**The Ob' River** rises in the Altai Mountains of Central Asia and empties into the Gulf of Ob, on the Kara Sea, part of the Arctic Ocean. It is about 2,287 miles (3,680 kilometers) long, and flows about 3,461 miles (5,569 kilometers) long with its tributary the Irtysh. Much of the river is navigable several months of the year. It is an important source of hydroelectric power.

**The Oder River** rises in the Oder Mountains of the Czech Republic, flows 567 miles (912 kilometers) through Poland, and empties into the Stettin Lagoon, an arm of the Baltic Sea.

**The Ohio River**, in the United States, rises at the junction of the Allegheny and Monongahela rivers at Pittsburgh, Pennsylvania. The river, about 975 miles (1,569 kilometers) long, is one of the chief tributaries of the Mississippi. See the article OHIO RIVER.

**The Orange River** in southern Africa is about 1,300 miles (2,090 kilometers) long. It rises in the Drakensberg range of South Africa and empties into the Atlantic Ocean. Diamond deposits are located near the river's mouth.

**The Orinoco River** is one of South America's greatest rivers and its third largest river system. It rises in the Serra Parima Mountains near the Venezuela-Brazil border and flows 1,281 miles (2,061 kilometers) across Venezuela to the Atlantic Ocean. Small vessels can navigate much of the river, but they are obstructed by rapids about 100 miles (161 kilometers) from its mouth. The mouth of the delta was sighted by Columbus in 1498.

**The Ottawa River** forms part of the boundary between the Canadian provinces of Quebec and Ontario. The river is about 696 miles (1,120 kilometers) long, rises in the Laurentian Plateau, and empties into the St. Lawrence River near Montreal.

**The Paraguay River** rises in Brazil and flows south to join the Paraná at the Argentine border. About 1,584 miles (2,549 kilometers) long, it is a chief means of transportation.

**The Paraná River**, about 3,030 miles (4,875 kilometers) long, is the second longest river in South America. It rises in southeastern Brazil and empties into the Río de la Plata near Buenos Aires in Argentina. It drains a vast area. The river forms part of the Río de la Plata estuary.

**The Platte River** is formed by the joining of the South Platte and the longer North Platte rivers, which rise in the Colorado Rockies. The Platte River is about 310 miles (499 kilometers) long, flowing for its entire length in Nebraska. It joins the Missouri River at Plattsmouth. It supplies hydroelectric power and water for irrigation, but the river is too shallow for navigation.

Boats transport goods along the Niger River, Africa's third longest river. Its waters irrigate an enormous area of West Africa.

The Rio Grande flows through deep canyons in Big Bend National Park. The river forms most of the U.S.-Mexico boundary.

**The Po River**, Italy's longest river, rises in the Italian Alps and flows eastward about 405 miles (652 kilometers) to the Adriatic Sea. The Po is navigable for small boats for much of its length. The river irrigates crops in the Lombard fields and provides hydroelectric power for Italy's leading industrial area.

**The Potomac River** rises near Cumberland, Maryland, flows for 287 miles (462 kilometers), and empties into Chesapeake Bay. Just above Washington, D.C., are the Great Falls of the Potomac.

**The Red River** in Vietnam rises in China and empties into the Gulf of Tonkin. It is about 500 miles (805 kilometers) long. Its red color is due to iron oxide in the silt the river carries. The Red River ends in a great delta below Hanoi. The delta was an important rice-producing area. Dikes for flood control line the channels of the delta.

**The Rhine River** rises in the Swiss Alps. It flows 820 miles (1,319 kilometers) through Switzerland, Germany, and the Netherlands and empties into the North Sea. The Rhine flows along the Swiss-Austrian, Swiss-German, and French-German borders. Below Bonn the river passes through the Ruhr iron and coal district. Economically, it is the most important river of western Europe.

**The Rhône River** rises in the Swiss Alps. It flows for 505 miles (813 kilometers), passes through France, and empties into the Mediterranean Sea. The Rhône supplies hydroelectric power and irrigates vineyards and olive groves.

**The Río de la Plata** is the approximately 170-mile (275-kilometer) estuary on the Atlantic Ocean between Argentina and Uruguay, formed by the junction of the Paraná and Uruguay rivers. It is a vital waterway to inland South America. Its chief ports are Buenos Aires in Argentina and Montevideo in Uruguay. The name Río de la Plata is often given to the entire river system that includes the Paraná, Paraguay, and Uruguay rivers.

**The Rio Grande**, about 1,885 miles (3,033 kilometers) in length, rises in the San Juan Mountains of Colorado. It flows through parts of Colorado, New Mexico, and Texas and empties into the Gulf of Mexico near Brownsville. The river forms part of the boundary between the United States and Mexico. See the article RIO GRANDE.

**The Saint John River** is about 418 miles (673 kilometers) long. It rises in northern Maine and empties into the Bay of Fundy at St. John, New Brunswick. The river forms part of the border between the United States and Canada. High tides in the Bay of Fundy cause the river to reverse its flow, resulting in the famous Reversing Falls.

**The Saint Lawrence River** in southeastern Canada flows about 760 miles (1,225 kilometers). An international waterway, it is one of the great rivers of the world. See the article SAINT LAWRENCE RIVER AND SEAWAY.

**The Salween River** of Southeast Asia rises in China (Tibet) and flows through Myanmar to empty into the Andaman Sea. The Salween is about 1,500 miles (2,415 kilometers) long and forms part of the Burma-Thailand border.

**The São Francisco River** rises in Brazil and flows about 1,988 miles (3,199 kilometers) to the Atlantic Ocean. It is the main transportation route into the interior of eastern Brazil. The river supplies hydroelectric power for part of northeastern Brazil.

**The Saskatchewan River** rises in eastern Alberta in Canada, winds eastward across Saskatchewan, and empties into Lake Winnipeg in Manitoba. The upper part of the river is divided into two branches: the North Saskatchewan River, which flows about 760 miles (1,223 kilometers), and the South Saskatchewan River, which flows about 865 miles (1,392 kilometers). After the two branches meet, the river flows about 340 miles (547 kilometers).

The Thames is England's chief water highway. Located in the south of the country, it flows through London and empties into the North Sea.

**The Schelde River** rises in northeastern France. It flows across Belgium and empties into the North Sea through two estuaries in the Netherlands. About 270 miles (434 kilometers) long, it is part of an important network of waterways. Antwerp, Belgium's chief port, is on the Schelde.

**The Seine River**, France's most navigable river, rises in the Langres Plateau and enters the English Channel at Le Havre. The river is about 482 miles (776 kilometers) long. It flows through Paris and divides the city into the Left Bank and Right Bank.

**The Shannon River**, Ireland's chief river, is about 230 miles (370 kilometers) long. It rises near the border of Northern Ireland, flows

south to Limerick, then empties into the Atlantic Ocean. Canals link the Shannon with Dublin on the Liffey River.

**The Songhua (Sungari) River** in Manchuria rises near the Chinese-North Korean border and flows into the Amur River. It is about 1,150 miles (1,850 kilometers) long. Its waters provide power for one of northeastern China's largest hydroelectric plants.

**The Tagus River**, a major river of Spain and Portugal, is about 626 miles (1,007 kilometers) in length. It is the longest river in the Iberian Peninsula. The river rises in eastern Spain, flows west across the country, then forms a section of the Spain-Portugal boundary. It then flows southwest across Portugal and into the Atlantic Ocean near Libson.

**The Thames River** is England's chief water highway. It rises in the Cotswold Hills of Gloucestershire and flows about 210 miles (338 kilometers) before emptying into the North Sea.

**The Tiber River** in Italy rises in the Tuscan Apennines. It flows about 252 miles (405 kilometers) across the Sabine Mountains, through Rome, and into the Tyrrhenian Sea. Dams and reservoirs provide irrigation.

**The Tigris and the Euphrates** are two great rivers of southwestern Asia. They rise in Turkey, flow roughly parallel, and join in Iraq. The Euphrates is about 2,235 miles (3,596 kilometers) long. It is broad and too shallow for navigation except by small boats. The Tigris is about 1,180 miles (1,899 kilometers) long. It is swifter, carries more water, and is more navigable. The rivers are linked by irrigation canals. The historic region between them was once called Mesopotamia ("land between rivers"). It is considered one of the birthplaces of civilization.

**The Ural River** rises in the Ural Mountains of Russia, flows through Kazakhstan where it supplies water to the dry steppes, and empties into the Caspian Sea. It is about 1,575 miles (2,534 kilometers) long. The Ural is partly navigable but freezes over in winter.

**The Uruguay River** rises in the mountains near the southeastern coast of Brazil. It flows

The Zambezi River, the main river in southern Africa, rushes over the spectacular Victoria Falls. The river forms part of the boundary between Zambia and Zimbabwe.

southward along the Brazil-Argentina border and the Argentina-Uruguay border. It is about 1,000 miles (1,609 kilometers) long and forms part of the Río de la Plata estuary.

**The Vistula River**, Poland's longest river, rises near the southern border and flows about 675 miles (1,086 kilometers) to the Baltic Sea. Warsaw is on its banks. Canals link the Vistula with the Oder River.

**The Volga River**, Europe's longest river, is the chief water highway of Russia. It rises in the Valdai Hills west of Moscow and flows for about 2,293 miles (3,689 kilometers), emptying into the Caspian Sea near Astrakhan. It drains much of Eastern Europe.

**The Weser River** in Germany is formed by the joining of the Fulda and Werra rivers, which rise in the Rhön Mountains. The Weser flows 273 miles (439 kilometers) and enters the North Sea near Bremerhaven.

**The Western Dvina River** rises in the Valdai Hills of Russia and flows about 634 miles (1,020 kilometers) through Belarus and Latvia to empty into the Gulf of Riga.

**The Yalu River** rises in northeastern China and flows southwest about 501 miles (806 kilometers) to Korea Bay in the Yellow Sea. The river is a source of hydroelectric power for China and North Korea. The Yalu forms the border between China and North Korea.

**The Yangtze (Chang) River** is the longest river in China and the third longest river in the world. Its name in Chinese, Chang Jiang, means "Long River." It flows about 3,434 miles (5,525 kilometers). See the article YANGTZE (CHANG) RIVER.

**The Yellow (Huang) River** is the largest river in north China. The river was given its name due to its high content of yellow-brown silt. It flows 2,903 miles (4,671 kilometers) before emptying into the Yellow Sea.

**The Yenisey River**, one of the world's longest rivers, rises in Asia's Eastern Sayan Mountains. It flows through Siberia for about 2,566 miles (4,129 kilometers) to empty into the Kara Sea, a branch of the Arctic Ocean.

**The Yukon River**, one of the longest rivers in North America, is about 1,979 miles (3,184 kilometers) long and rises in the Yukon Territory, Canada. The river flows through Alaska, passes the Arctic Circle, and empties into the Bering Sea.

**The Zambezi River** in southern Africa is about 1,700 miles (2,735 kilometers) long and drains a large area. It rises in Angola, flows through Zambia and Mozambique, and empties into the Indian Ocean. The Zambezi forms part of the boundary between Zambia and Zimbabwe; the spectacular Victoria Falls are on this part of the river. Only the lower Zambezi is navigable.

Reviewed by MELINDA D. DANIELS
University of Connecticut

**RIVETS.** See NAILS, SCREWS, AND RIVETS.

Road crossings are often built in several levels to permit traffic to flow safely. Circular entry and exit roads, called cloverleaf crossings, are often used to connect the various levels.

# ROADS AND HIGHWAYS

When we speed along a modern highway, we rarely stop to think what it is we are riding on. To understand what a road is, we must study the ways in which people traveled in the past.

## ▶HISTORY

The very first roads were merely tracks made on the ground by wild animals. People used these animal trails because they provided an easy and quick way to get through forests. In time, people began to improve these trails by filling the ruts with earth and laying logs across wet spots. These attempts were crude, but they were the beginning of road construction.

As people began to carry goods over longer distances, they developed new ways of traveling. First, goods were carried by animals. Then sleds were developed so that things could be pulled. When the wheel was invented wagons were built. Each advancement brought a need for better traveling routes. As time went on, well-traveled routes were made sturdier with rocks and stones and paths were raised above surrounding land to become "high ways."

### Roads in Ancient Civilizations

The great civilizations throughout history were also great road builders. Roads helped these civilizations control and extend their empires because they permitted trade and travel and made it easier to move armies. As early as 3000 B.C., roads were built in Mesopotamia, and later in Egypt, India, and China. Most of these early roads were simply hard-packed dirt, but some were paved with stone blocks or burnt bricks.

The Romans were the most impressive road builders of the ancient world. More than 50,000 miles (80,000 kilometers) of roads—many of them paved—stretched in a vast network throughout the Roman Empire. Some Roman roads are still in existence today, and many modern highways follow ancient Roman routes.

### The Modern Era

For more than 1,000 years after the Roman era, Europe's road system was neglected because of wars, poverty, and little interest in travel. Roman roads were forgotten and left to decay. Then Europe slowly recovered. As trade and travel became important for growth, European nations turned their attention once more to the building of roads.

During the 1700's and early 1800's, France and England took the lead in road building. Pierre-Marie Jérôme Trésaguet (1716–94) was the most prominent French road builder. He built roads in three layers, putting very large rocks at the bottom and smaller stones in each following layer. In 1800, Napoleon began an extensive road-building project to move his armies around Europe. This marked the first organized road-building effort in Europe since the time of the ancient Romans.

The most influential British road builder was John Loudon McAdam (1756–1836). McAdam believed that the most important thing in road building was to make sure a road's foundation was well drained. On top of a dry, firm foundation he put a thick layer of small stones, which were packed down. To finish the surface he added a layer of fine rock.

At about this time in England, private companies began to build roads and charge tolls to pay for the costs of building and maintaining them. These roads were called turnpikes, and the money they produced helped stimulate additional road building.

Despite the efforts of road builders in the 1700's and 1800's, roads in rural areas remained very poor. When it rained, the roads were slippery, and in dry weather they were dusty. During this time, people using horses and wagons accepted these conditions. At the beginning of the 1900's, however, a new invention—the automobile—began to take over the roads. To meet the demands of this new vehicle, roads had to be built better and stronger, and modern roads, highways, and superhighways developed.

▶ BUILDING MODERN ROADS AND HIGHWAYS

The first step in building a modern road is to plan the route. While routes are sometimes determined by the characteristics of the landscape, nature can often be conquered by powerful machinery to make a highway route as direct as possible.

After a general route is chosen, the details are planned by surveyors and engineers. They determine such things as the road's precise route, its width, the number of driving lanes, the number and location of entrances and exits, and the strength of the road surface. Road builders must consider the amount of traffic expected now and in the future. Modern highways are usually planned with twenty years of traffic in mind.

The next step in road building is testing the earth on which the road will be built. Engineers carefully study the soil to learn how solid it is, how much moisture it contains, and how well it drains. Then they decide how the soil should be prepared in order to provide a good sturdy foundation, or **roadbed**. They determine the thickness of the road layers, the size of the rocks in them, and the other materials that should be used.

*Top:* Construction begins on a new road. *Middle:* Paving a highway prepares it for the weight of heavy vehicles. *Bottom:* Roads require regular repair and maintenance.

After all planning and testing is completed, construction crews can begin their work. Giant bulldozers clear the path for the roadbed, knocking over trees and removing large rocks from the ground. Other powerful earth-moving machines, such as loaders and scrapers, move earth and stones into low spots. This **fill**

ROADS AND HIGHWAYS • 249

is then pressed down tightly with large rollers, and the roadbed gradually becomes a long, level band of hard-packed dirt.

Proper drainage is essential in road building. If the foundation were to become soggy, the heavy road might sink into it. If water were to freeze in the ground, it would cause the road to expand and crack. To protect against such damage, drainpipes called **culverts** are laid across the roadbed wherever a strong flow of water is expected. In addition, the roadbed is shaped so that the middle of the finished road will be higher than the sides, allowing water to drain off into the culverts or ditches.

After allowing for drainage, the roadbed is given a final **grading**, or smoothing, and is ready to receive the road itself. Almost all roads are built in two or more **courses**, or layers, of rocks or stones. The bottom course is 4 to 8 inches (10 to 20 centimeters) thick and is usually made up of larger stones. The upper course has smaller stones and is about 3 inches (8 centimeters) thick. The lower course is usually wider so that the edges of the top course do not break off or sink. After each course is laid, it is compacted by large, heavy rollers.

The top, or surface, layer of a road must withstand the weight of heavy vehicles. It must also prevent water from seeping into the roadbed and destroying it. Modern highways are therefore surfaced either with concrete or with **bituminous materials**, such as asphalt, tar, or heavy oils. Asphalt is the most commonly used road-surface material. It is well suited for road surfaces because it needs no water for mixing and water cannot seep through it. Asphalt is generally poured on the road in a layer 2 inches (5 centimeters) thick. Because it has a dark color, roads surfaced with asphalt often are called **blacktop** roads. Sometimes hot asphalt or tar is sprayed on each layer of a road to fill spaces between the rocks. Roads built this way are called macadam roads because they are similar to the roads built originally by John McAdam.

### Concrete Highways

Highways that must carry heavy, high-speed traffic are usually surfaced with concrete —a mixture of cement, sand, gravel or broken rock, and water. Concrete can be poured easily and dries into a hard mass. To strengthen the concrete, steel rods or wire can be placed within the layers of concrete being poured.

When surfacing a highway, concrete is mixed at the construction site in a huge machine called a **paver**. A paver pours loads of wet concrete on the packed layer of stones in the roadbed. A **spreader** follows and spreads the concrete evenly between steel bars that are laid along the sides of the section being poured, to contain it. Finally, **vibrators** shake the concrete to remove air bubbles. The concrete layer may be from 8 to 12 inches (20 to 30 centimeters) thick.

Concrete expands in hot weather and contracts in cold weather. If it were laid in one long, uninterrupted strip, the road would buckle and crack. To prevent such damage, concrete is laid in slabs from 12 to 30 feet (3.5 to 9 meters) long. Tar or asphalt is poured between these slabs to connect them and to keep water from entering the roadbed. These narrow strips, which run across the driving lane, are called **expansion joints**.

### Safety on Highways

Some safety features can be built right into a road. Steep hills can be removed. Curves can be designed to make skids less likely and to allow drivers to see well into the distance. To be safe, roads should be fairly straight, but if a road has many long, straight stretches, a driver may become drowsy. As a result, highways are designed with occasional curves. When a car goes around a curve, however, its speed and weight tend to push it outward and off the road. To counteract this force, the roadbed and surface of a curve is usually tilted, or **banked**, so that the outside of the curve is higher than the inside.

Safety devices can also be added to a finished highway. Warning signs for curves, hills, turn-offs, merging traffic, and other dangers are used on modern highways. Travel lanes are usually divided by lines painted on the road surface. These lines are often painted with light-reflecting paint, as are guide rails at the side of the road. At intersections, dangerous stretches, or heavily traveled areas, traffic lights are often installed. To block out the glare from the lights of oncoming traffic, trees and bushes are often planted in the center strip between opposing lanes of traffic.

GEORGE N. BEAUMARIAGE, JR.
California State University, Sacramento

See also BRIDGES; EARTH-MOVING MACHINERY; TRAFFIC CONTROL.

## ROBERT I (THE BRUCE) (1274–1329)

Robert the Bruce, Scotland's most celebrated national hero, was crowned King Robert I in 1306. His victory in the Battle of Bannockburn in 1314 restored his country's freedom from English rule and led to Scotland's independence in 1328.

He was born on July 11, 1274, the son of Robert de Bruce VII, the Earl of Carrick. Robert followed his father's example in acknowledging Edward I of England as ruler of Scotland, and in 1298 he fought for Edward against the Scottish rebel William Wallace. Robert was still loyal to Edward as late as 1305, the year Wallace was captured by the English and executed.

By 1306, however, Robert believed that Scotland could win its independence from England, and he sought to take the crown for himself. He gathered forces to fight Edward I, and he also murdered John ("Red") Comyn, his chief Scottish rival to the throne. After securing enough support from his countrymen, he was crowned King Robert I at Scone, in eastern Scotland, on March 27. Then, when

Edward I died in 1307, Robert took advantage of the succession of the weak King Edward II and recaptured several castles that the English held in Scotland.

These attacks provoked an English invasion, and on June 23, 1314, Edward II met Robert I at the Battle of Bannockburn. Edward's army failed to break the Scottish defensive line, and Bruce's surprise counterattack the following morning scattered the English forces. This famous battle finally weakened England's hold over Scotland.

Scotland's war for independence continued for 14 years after Bannockburn. On several occasions, Bruce's soldiers penetrated more than 150 miles (240 kilometers) into England. Robert also went to Ireland, where he helped his brother, Edward Bruce, attack the English (1316–18).

England launched a final invasion in 1327, but formally recognized Scotland's independence the following year. Robert I died, possibly from leprosy, 13 months later.

ALAN PALMER
Author, *The Penguin Dictionary of Modern History*

---

**ROBESON, PAUL.** See NEW JERSEY (Famous People).
**ROBESPIERRE, MAXIMILIEN.** See FRENCH REVOLUTION (Profiles).

## ROBIN HOOD

Robin Hood is one of England's most popular legendary figures. No one really knows whether Robin Hood ever lived, but since the Middle Ages many stories have been told about him.

According to legend, Robin was an outlaw who lived in Sherwood Forest, near Nottingham, in central England. He and his carefree band of followers spent their days hunting the king's deer, testing their skill at archery, and robbing the rich to give to the poor. Their chief enemy was the sheriff of Nottingham.

Robin's right-hand man, Little John, was named in jest because he was tremendously tall and strong. Friar Tuck was Robin's chaplain and confessor. Others in Robin's band included Will Scarlet, Arthur-a-Bland, Will Stutely, Much, and the minstrel Allen-a-Dale. Robin's sweetheart was Maid Marian.

One legend says that Robin was the Earl of Huntingdon and lived from 1160 to 1247 dur-

ing the reign of Richard I (the Lion-Hearted). Others place him in the 1400's, during the reign of Edward IV. Robin Hood has been portrayed in plays, motion pictures, and novels, including Sir Walter Scott's *Ivanhoe*.

NANCY LARRICK
Author, *A Parent's Guide to Children's Reading*

**ROBINSON, EDWIN ARLINGTON.** See MAINE (Famous People).

ROBINSON, FRANK. See BASEBALL (Great Players).

## ROBINSON, JACK ROOSEVELT (JACKIE) (1919–1972)

Jackie Robinson was the first African American to play major league baseball. He was also an exceptional and exciting player who faced prejudice with remarkable determination and grace.

Jack Roosevelt Robinson was born on January 31, 1919, in Cairo, Georgia. During his years at the University of California, Los Angeles (UCLA), Robinson starred in many sports, including track and field, basketball, baseball, and football.

During World War II (1939–45), Robinson served in the army. After his discharge, he eventually turned to playing baseball. At that time, however, the sport was segregated (African Americans were not permitted to play with whites), so he joined the Kansas City Monarchs of the Negro American League.

A major change came for Robinson—and all of baseball—in 1945. Branch Rickey, president of the Brooklyn Dodgers, wanted to end segregation in the sport and signed Robinson to play for his organization. Robinson was sent to the Montreal Royals, a Dodger minor league team, in 1946. When he was called up to the Dodgers the following year, Jackie Robinson became the first African American baseball player on a major league team. Although he encountered much prejudice at first, he excelled on the field and was named the major league's first Rookie of the Year in 1947.

In 1949, Robinson was named the National League's Most Valuable Player, as he stole 37 bases, hit for a .342 average, and batted in 124 runs. Robinson played with the Dodgers for ten years, during which time they won six National League pennants and the 1955 World Series. He retired from baseball in 1957 with a career batting average of .311. In 1962 he became the first African American to be elected to the Baseball Hall of Fame. Robinson was active in business and the civil rights movement until his death in Stamford, Connecticut, on October 24, 1972. In 2005, he was posthumously awarded the Congressional Gold Medal.

Reviewed by MONTE IRVIN
Member, Baseball Hall of Fame

---

ROBINSON, SUGAR RAY. See BOXING (Profiles).
ROBINSON CRUSOE. See DEFOE, DANIEL.

## ROBOTS

When we hear the word "robot," we usually imagine a walking, talking, mechanical companion that can do lightning fast calculations and recite many facts. No real robots actually come close to having these abilities. A typical robot looks like a big mechanical arm holding a tool. It performs the same repetitive industrial task hundreds of times each day in a factory.

### ▶ WHAT IS A ROBOT?

A robot is a machine capable of being set up and programmed to perform a wide variety of tasks for which it must physically move itself or other objects. Most tasks that robots do are repetitive, difficult, or hazardous to humans. The technology associated with robots is called **robotics**.

The first use of the word "robot" was by the Czech dramatist Karel Čapek in 1921 for his play *R.U.R.* (for Rossum's Universal Ro-

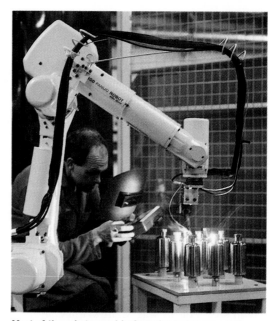

Most of the robots used in factories today are robot arms that have been programmed to perform repetitive tasks such as welding.

bots). The play was about a man who creates human-like machines to work in his factory. Čapek coined the word "robot" from the Czech word *robota*, meaning "work" or "slavery". The first actual robot was developed by American inventors George Devol and Joseph Engelberger in 1958. General Motors purchased the first industrial robot and installed it in a Trenton, New Jersey automobile factory to lift and stack hot pieces of metal.

Today, commercial robots are available in two basic types, manipulator and mobile. A robot manipulator looks like a mechanical arm and may range in length from 12 inches (30 centimeters) to 12 feet (3.7 meters) or more. Robot manipulators, or robot arms, account for the vast majority of robots used for practical purposes today.

Mobile robots roll on wheels from place to place. So far, they have only a few practical applications. However, mobile robots are being extensively developed in research laboratories. Researchers have built a humanoid (human-like robot) that can walk very slowly, turn, and climb stairs, but it does not yet have any practical use.

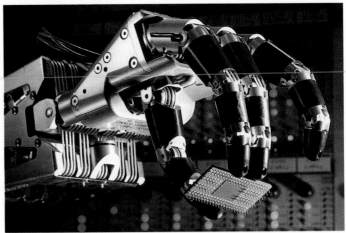

End-effectors on robotic arms may look like hands. Each finger is equipped with a sensor linked to the control computer that allows the robot to manipulate delicate objects, such as this microchip.

### ▶ HOW A ROBOT WORKS

Most robots in factories are stationary (immobile) robot arms. Robot arms are made up of mechanical links connected by joints. The two most common types of robot joints are rotational joints and translational joints. **Rotational** joints move like the elbow of a human arm. **Translational** joints are used for extension and are similar to the ball-bearings that allow a file cabinet drawer or a trombone slide to move in and out.

The specific sequence of joint types from the base of an arm to its end is referred to as its **configuration**. Different configurations are selected depending on the task to be performed by the robot. The three-dimensional area within which a robot arm can move is called its work space.

The joints of a robot arm must be powered in order for the robot to move. The power may be supplied by electricity, air pressure, or fluid pressure. Each joint of a robot arm also has a sensor to measure the joint's position. Each sensor relays information about its position back to the robot's control computer.

The base of a robot arm is usually bolted to the floor or another structure. A tool or other device, called an **end-effector**, is mounted at the end of the robot arm like a hand, to enable it to perform a specific task. The end-effector is chosen based on the task that is to be performed. A gripper is used when the robot must pick up objects. Grippers might be designed to have two fingers, three fingers, or suction cups. Tools such as welders, spray paint guns, gluing guns, and drills are also common end-effectors.

A robot may use sensors and other devices to get information about its environment. Touch sensors give information about objects near the robot. Ultrasonic sensors (sensors that use sound waves) and scanning laser sensors provide information about the distances to objects and their geometric locations and shapes. Force sensors can be built into the end-effector so that the robot has more control when manipulating objects. Video cameras linked to computers can be used to locate, identify, and determine the motion of objects.

Safety is an important concern when programming and operating an industrial robot. Because a robot is nothing more than a big and powerful machine, it cannot know if a human is in its way unless it has an appropriate sensor and is specifically programmed to use the sensor to check for people. Thus, a robot may move anywhere within its work space without regard for humans that might be there. For that reason, physical safety barriers are usually placed around the entire robot work space in order to ensure that humans do not accidentally wander into the area.

Some robots can be programmed to communicate and "learn." Robots equipped with software that recognizes a limited number of spoken words can respond to verbal commands from an operator. And voice synthesizers built into robot systems enable them to talk back to their human users with electronic voices. The robot's control computer may be programmed to exhibit some form of artificial intelligence, such as the automatic avoidance of obstacles in its work space. Some robots can also be programmed with

Scientists learned a great deal about the Martian surface from the mobile robot *Sojourner*, which explored Mars and sent information back to Earth.

the capability to learn a specific skill, such as mastering a sequence of movements that the user teaches it by giving commands from a controlling computer.

▶ ROBOTS IN ACTION

Most people are familiar with fictional robots portrayed in books and films, but few have seen real robots in action. This is due to the types of tasks that robots perform. Industrial robots operating in factories and robots performing tasks in hazardous situations are seldom seen by the public. Medical robots are encountered only by those who need the pro-

cedures they perform, and research robots generally remain within universities or industrial research facilities.

## Industrial Robots

Factories are well suited for robotic automation because many tasks in manufacturing and other industries tend to be repetitive. Robots have been found to be especially useful for welding and spray painting on automotive assembly lines. Robots are also used in a variety of industries to load and unload machines and package products. The assembly of mass-produced products, such as circuit boards and printers, has been automated in some plants using robots. Robots are also used for some machining operations such as drilling and riveting and for tasks such as inspection and testing that make use of a robot's sensors.

Automated Guided Vehicles are mobile robots that travel on wheels and are used in factories to transport parts and materials by following a wire buried in the floor. Special mobile trolley robots have been developed for the semiconductor processing industry to transport loads of integrated circuits from one processing station to another. Other mobile robots perform nontransport tasks such as vacuuming and cleaning floors.

## Robots for Dangerous Situations

Robots are often used in situations that are hazardous for humans. For example, periodic maintenance on nuclear power generators can be performed by a robot arm rather than a person. And robots can also be used to monitor security in office and apartment buildings.

Space travel can be dangerous for humans, so robots are used whenever possible. In 1997, the *Mars Pathfinder* spacecraft landed on Mars and released a small mobile robot called *Sojourner* to conduct experiments. The robot, which was only 11 inches (28 centimeters) high and weighed 25 pounds (11 kilograms), did not need to be returned to Earth. *Sojourner* performed chemical analysis and imaging on several rocks, studied different regions of soil, took more than 16,000 images of the Martian landscape, and logged millions of temperature, pressure, and wind-speed measurements during its three months of operation on the planet. The United States space shuttle also is equipped with a long robot arm that carries out a variety of tasks in the bay area of the shuttle during each mission.

## Medical Robots

Robots are just beginning to aid in the field of medicine. In response to a surgeon's verbal commands, one kind of medical robot will move a tiny video camera inserted inside the body through a small incision. Such a system enables the surgeon to perform the operation through nearby small incisions while viewing the operation site on a video monitor. Such minimally invasive procedures heal much more quickly and with fewer complications than when a large incision is made. Other medical robots perform portions of hip- and knee-replacement surgeries. The robot holds a milling tool that cuts the bone to a predefined three-dimensional shape.

## Research Robots

Many different kinds of robots have been developed for research purposes. In research laboratories, mobile robots outnumber robot arms. In addition to the more common wheeled robots, researchers have developed mobile robots with legs that walk, run, and hop and robots that move by snake-like propulsion. Climbing robots have been devised that scale walls, the outside surface of airplanes, or the insides of pipes and liquid-filled tanks to perform inspection tasks. Researchers are also developing versatile robots that can change shape in order to perform particular tasks.

Other experimental robots have been designed for more specific applications. These include robots for military purposes, farming, and planetary exploration. Robots have also been built to search for meteorites in Antarctica. Scientists in the field of artificial intelligence have designed robots that appear to respond to and express emotions. Other researchers have created tiny micro-robots that can move objects too small to be seen with the unaided eye.

The fictional robots C-3PO and R2-D2 (*above*) were made famous by the 1977 film *Star Wars*. Now, more than two decades later, some humanoid robots (*left*) look similar to C-3PO. Although they can move well, these robots still do not have the intelligence of fictional robots.

## Entertainment and Hobby Robots

Most of the public's awareness of robots has come from the entertainment industries. Perhaps the two best-known fictional robots in American popular culture are R2-D2 and C-3PO from the motion picture *Star Wars*.

Several companies have made small robots for home use that are mainly for educational purposes, and many students have taken up robot building as a hobby. Some hobbyists participate in annual robot competitions in which their creations are scored against each other while finding objects, playing games, and performing other tasks.

## ▶ IMPACT OF ROBOTS ON SOCIETY

The industrial robot was developed to allow the automation of a wide range of practical tasks. Instead of designing a new special-purpose automated machine to handle each new task, we need only select an available robot and an appropriate end-effector, and then set up and program the robot at the work site. This represents a considerable savings in time and resources when constructing new industrial processes and production systems. Businesses can mass-produce high-quality products at lower costs, making them more available to consumers. Robots also enable manufacturers to inexpensively produce small quantities of more specialized items.

Entertainment robots and the fictional portrayals of robots in the media play a role in our society as well. Children and adults are fascinated by the antics of robotic toys and animated electronic figures at amusement parks. Science fiction enthusiasts enjoy movies and books about humanoid robots. These futuristic portrayals of robots can be sources of inspiration for young engineers and scientists. And robot construction as a hobby is a fun way to introduce students to the technologies involved.

In the future, robots may be used for automating even greater numbers of dangerous and undesirable tasks. Because robots are complex engineered systems, the technologies that allow them to operate are difficult to develop. Robots are still not able to perform some seemingly easy tasks, such as consistently selecting a specific part from a bin of assorted parts. Yet robots have successfully performed more complex activities. For example, robot cars have driven through traffic on normal roadways. It is inevitable that robots will play a bigger role in an expanding set of tasks in the future.

PATRICK F. MUIR
Carnegie Mellon University

See also AUTOMATION; COMPUTERS.

---

**ROB ROY.** See OUTLAWS (Profiles).
**ROCHAMBEAU, COMTE DE.** See REVOLUTIONARY WAR (Profiles).
**ROCHESTER (MINNESOTA).** See MINNESOTA (Cities).
**ROCHESTER (NEW YORK).** See NEW YORK (Cities).

## ROCKEFELLER, JOHN D. (1839–1937)

John Davison Rockefeller was an American industrialist and philanthropist. As founder of the Standard Oil Company, he amassed such a fortune that the Rockefeller name came to stand for wealth and power. He was born near Richford, New York, on July 8, 1839, the second of six children. In 1853 the family moved to Cleveland, Ohio.

In 1863, Rockefeller bought an interest in an oil-refining company. The following year he married Laura Celestia Spelman. They had three daughters—Bessie, Edith, and Alta—and one son, John D. Rockefeller, Jr. (1874–1960).

In 1870 he founded the Standard Oil Company with his brother William and three other partners. By the 1880's the business had grown into one of the largest and richest manufacturing concerns in the world. Its large combination of companies, called a trust, almost monopolized the oil business. In 1911 the U.S. Supreme Court ruled that the Standard Oil Company was a monopoly in restraint of trade and ordered it broken up. It was replaced by 38 separate companies.

In spite of his great wealth, Rockefeller lived a simple, thrifty life. He seldom went to the theater or concerts and paid little attention to clothes or food. One of his favorite dishes was bread and milk. He received so many requests for gifts that four organizations were set up to help give his money to worthy causes— the Rockefeller Institute for Medical Research, the General Education Board, the Rockefeller Foundation, and the Laura Spelman Rockefeller Memorial. He also founded the University of Chicago.

Rockefeller died at the age of 97 on May 23, 1937, in Ormond, Florida. He was buried in Lake View Cemetery, Cleveland, Ohio.

Reviewed by GERALD KURLAND
Author, *John D. Rockefeller*

**ROCKEFELLER, NELSON ALDRICH.** See VICE PRESIDENCY OF THE UNITED STATES (Profiles).

# ROCKETS

A rocket is a device used to propel a vehicle, often a spacecraft. Rockets can be used to propel all types of vehicles, including cars, boats, and aircraft. But they are most suitable for use in outer space, where there is no atmosphere. Other forms of propulsion, which need oxygen to work, cannot be used there.

When you think of a rocket, you probably picture a bullet-shaped vehicle several stories tall. However, the only section of this vehicle that can properly be called a rocket is the one that holds the engine and fuel tanks. The section at the pointed end of the vehicle usually carries cargo. It also has equipment to protect the cargo, electronic sensors and computers to monitor and guide the vehicle's flight, and a radio to relay data to flight controllers on the ground. The entire vehicle is called a **launch vehicle**, and the cargo it carries is called the **payload**. Payloads can be anything from bombs to satellites or spacecraft that circle the Earth.

▶ **THE DEVELOPMENT OF ROCKETS**

The first rockets were invented in the 1200's by the Chinese. These early rockets were produced by stuffing gunpowder into sections of bamboo tubing. For centuries, such rockets, which were very small, were used as weapons. They were also used as signaling devices or to create fireworks displays.

In the 1860's, French writer Jules Verne published two science fiction adventures, *From the Earth to the Moon* and *Round the Moon*, that described the use of an enormous cannon for journeys in space. But it was not until the mid-1900's that the principles of rocketry became understood well enough for rockets to be used in that way.

The person who did the most to develop the ideas that eventually made space travel in rockets possible was Russian inventor Konstantin Tsiolkovsky. In 1903, Tsiolkovsky published "The Investigation of World Space with Reaction Machines," in which he predicted the use "of a reaction machine, rather like a rocket" to travel into outer space. He also described ideas for multistage rockets, artificial satellites, and space stations.

An important step in the development of rockets occurred in 1917, when German scientist Hermann Oberth proposed using a liq-

This painting captures the excitement of Robert Goddard's first successful launch of a liquid-fuel rocket.

uid fuel for rockets. The first liquid-fuel rocket to fly successfully was launched by American scientist Robert Goddard in 1926.

During World War II, German scientist Wernher von Braun led a team of scientists in the development of the V-2 rocket, which became the first long-range guided missile. After the war, he and other German scientists and engineers came to the United States and helped develop other missiles and rockets, including the *Saturn V* rocket that launched U.S. astronauts to the moon in 1969. Since then, rockets have become more powerful and efficient and are still an indispensable part of space travel. The most complicated and versatile rocket-propelled vehicle ever built is the U.S. space shuttle.

▶ **HOW ROCKETS WORK**

In its simplest form, a rocket is a tube of fuel closed at one end and open at the other. As the fuel burns, it creates hot gases that expand and emerge rapidly from the open end. The action of the rushing gases causes the rocket to move in the opposite direction. This push is called **thrust**. The faster the gases rush out, the faster the rocket moves.

To understand this principle, imagine a balloon filled with air. If the stem of the balloon is released, the air rushes out and causes the balloon to fly. The balloon continues to fly until most of the air inside it has escaped. That is basically how rocket propulsion works. With rockets, however, the expanding gases are released through a chemical reaction. The chemicals that produce this reaction are called propellants. Rocket propellants may be either liquid or solid.

### Rockets and Newton's Laws

The way a rocket behaves can be explained by the three laws of motion proposed in the late 1600's by English scientist Sir Isaac Newton. Newton's third law of motion describes the force that gives a rocket its power. It states that for every action there is an equal and opposite reaction. In the case of a rocket, the "action" is supplied by gases rushing out of the open end of the rocket. The "reaction" is the motion of the rocket in the opposite direction of the escaping air or gases.

Once a rocket is launched, it accelerates, or gains speed, as long as its fuel continues to burn. This is explained by Newton's second law of motion, which states that acceleration depends on the amount of force applied to an object. The greater the force produced by the gases escaping out of the rocket's exhaust, the faster the rocket will go.

Newton's first law, known as the law of inertia, states that an object at rest will remain at rest unless acted upon by some outside force that puts it in motion, and that a moving object will continue in motion unless acted upon by an outside force that stops or changes its motion. In other words, objects at rest or in motion have a tendency to remain at rest or in motion. This tendency is called **inertia**. In launching a rocket, force must be applied to overcome its inertia. This force comes from the thrust produced by the emerging gases. The thrust required depends on the weight of a rocket. A larger rocket needs more thrust than a smaller one.

### Rockets in Space

Rockets work best in outer space, where there is no air. When a rocket moves through air, the air creates friction, or drag, which causes the rocket to slow down. Since there is no air in outer space, there is almost no drag against the rocket to slow it down. Rockets are ideal in space for another reason. In order to burn, fuels must combine with a type of chemical known as an **oxidizer**. Large quantities of oxygen, the most common oxidizer, are present in the air, but there is almost no oxygen in outer space. Since rockets carry their own oxidizer, in either liquid or solid form, they do not need oxygen from the air in order for their fuel to burn.

### ▶ ROCKET BALLISTICS

You may have seen pictures of a rocket blasting off a launchpad and climbing into the sky. You might think that getting into space is mainly a matter of gaining altitude. In reality, getting into orbit is mostly a matter of **ballistics**, the science and study of the motion of projectiles such as bullets and shells.

If a rocket only gained altitude, the force of gravity would pull it back toward the Earth. That is why shortly after liftoff, a launch vehicle is tipped slightly to follow a flight path in the shape of an arc. To understand why, consider a cannonball fired from a cannon. If fired level to the ground, the cannonball will soon curve downward, pulled by the force of gravity. But if it is aimed slightly upward, it travels in a long arc and much farther before it falls back to the ground. As the cannon is aimed farther upward, the cannonball travels somewhat farther. Moreover, the more powerful the force of the cannon, the farther the cannonball will fly.

Large rockets are, in effect, cannonballs with their own source of power. Like cannonballs, rockets are pulled downward by the force of gravity once they have burned all their fuel. However, their immense power has pushed them into a tremendously long arc, one that reaches beyond the curved surface of the Earth, so they can continue falling without ever touching the Earth's surface. Such an arc is called an orbit.

### ▶ MEASURING ROCKET PERFORMANCE

To place a spacecraft in orbit above the Earth, a rocket must travel 5 miles (8 kilometers) per second. The speed required to escape the Earth's gravity and travel to another planet is even faster. The minimum speed needed to escape the Earth's gravity, known as the **escape velocity**, is 7 miles (11 kilometers) per second. Some rockets can achieve these speeds because of their power.

### Thrust and Impulse

One measure of a rocket's power is the thrust it can produce. This is expressed in pounds. Depending on its size and type, one rocket can produce as little as 1 pound or as much as several million pounds of thrust.

The thrust a rocket produces multiplied by the amount of time its fuel can burn is called **total impulse**. The efficiency of a rocket is expressed in a number called **specific impulse**, which measures pounds of thrust per pound of propellant flow per second. The higher the specific impulse number, the more efficient the rocket.

### Payload

The power of a rocket can also be expressed by its payload, the cargo it carries. Two factors, weight and destination, must be considered in regard to payload. For example, it would take a larger and more powerful rocket to carry a payload of 2,000 pounds (900 kilograms) to the moon than it would to place the same payload in orbit 150 miles (240 kilometers) above the Earth. The space shuttle can deliver a payload of about 52,800 pounds (24,000 kilograms) to an orbit about 185 miles (300 kilometers) above the Earth.

### Launch Site

The location of the launch site is another factor in rocket performance. Because the Earth rotates from east to west, a rocket launched toward the east gets an added push from the force of the Earth's rotation. This push is greatest at the equator, where the Earth is rotating at 1,500 miles (2,400 kilometers) per hour. This is one reason why the United States built a launch site at Cape Canaveral, Florida, one of the southernmost areas of the nation. This site also was chosen because rockets could be launched eastward over the Atlantic Ocean, so that used rocket parts could fall safely into the water instead of onto inhabited regions of the country.

### ▶ ROCKET FUELS AND ENGINES

Rockets are powered by the burning of chemicals. Some rockets use only one chemical, such as hydrazine, a colorless liquid related to ammonia. A single chemical is called a **monopropellant**. But many rockets use two propellants. One is a fuel, such as kerosene, alcohol, or hydrogen. The other is an oxidizer, such as oxygen, fluorine, or nitrogen tetroxide. This combination of fuel and oxidizer is called a **bipropellant**. There are two main types of chemical rockets—solid-propellant rockets and liquid-propellant rockets—and a third type called hybrid rockets.

### Solid-Propellant Rockets

Solid-propellant rockets contain a solid mixture called the **grain**. This propellant, usually a mixture of a fuel and an oxidizer, has a consistency similar to cake batter before it is put into a rocket. After it is poured into the casing, or walls of the rocket, it hardens and has the consistency of a rubber eraser. The hardened grain has a hollow channel at its core. When the rocket is ignited, the surface of this channel begins to burn, producing hot

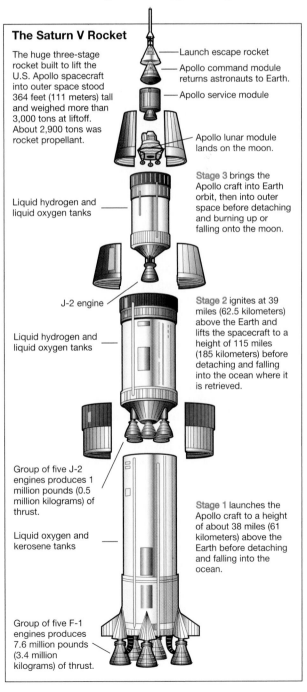

**The Saturn V Rocket**

The huge three-stage rocket built to lift the U.S. Apollo spacecraft into outer space stood 364 feet (111 meters) tall and weighed more than 3,000 tons at liftoff. About 2,900 tons was rocket propellant.

Launch escape rocket

Apollo command module returns astronauts to Earth.

Apollo service module

Apollo lunar module lands on the moon.

Stage 3 brings the Apollo craft into Earth orbit, then into outer space before detaching and burning up or falling onto the moon.

Liquid hydrogen and liquid oxygen tanks

J-2 engine

Stage 2 ignites at 39 miles (62.5 kilometers) above the Earth and lifts the spacecraft to a height of 115 miles (185 kilometers) before detaching and falling into the ocean where it is retrieved.

Liquid hydrogen and liquid oxygen tanks

Group of five J-2 engines produces 1 million pounds (0.5 million kilograms) of thrust.

Liquid oxygen and kerosene tanks

Stage 1 launches the Apollo craft to a height of about 38 miles (61 kilometers) above the Earth before detaching and falling into the ocean.

Group of five F-1 engines produces 7.6 million pounds (3.4 million kilograms) of thrust.

gases that escape through a nozzle at the open end of the rocket. This is what produces the rocket's thrust. Solid-propellant rockets are said to have rocket motors.

### Liquid-Propellant Rockets

Liquid-propellant rockets, which use liquid fuels and oxidizers, are more complicated than solid-propellant rockets. Such rockets are said to have engines because of their elaborate system of tanks, pumps, valves, hoses, and pipes. In a liquid-propellant rocket, the liquid fuel and oxidizer are stored in separate tanks with valves that keep them sealed. Pumps move the fuel and oxidizer through hoses and pipes to a combustion chamber, where they burn. Many liquid propellants have to be ignited in the combustion chamber by a device that produces a spark. Some, however, ignite spontaneously when the fuel and oxidizer are brought together in the combustion chamber. These self-igniting propellants are called **hypergolics**.

Liquid oxygen is an oxidizer often used in liquid-propellant rockets, and liquid hydrogen is sometimes used as a fuel. These are gases that have been compressed and chilled to very low temperatures until they change into liquid form. They are not suitable as rocket propellant in their gaseous form because gas takes up too much space and would require enormous storage tanks. These liquids must be stored in specially designed tanks to keep them cold. Rockets that use liquid oxygen and liquid hydrogen must be fueled shortly before launching in order to prevent the liquid from warming and changing back into a gas. Thus, handling these liquid propellants is difficult and expensive.

Because of their complexity, liquid-propellant rockets can be difficult to design and operate. Yet they have several advantages over solid-propellant rockets. They are usually more efficient than solid-propellant rockets, producing a greater specific impulse. A liquid-fueled engine also can be shut down after ignition, and its thrust can be more readily controlled. Once a solid-propellant rocket is ignited, there is no way to stop the fuel from burning. A liquid-fueled engine can be turned off to abort, or stop, a launch in the event of a problem. It also can be stopped and restarted in space, giving a spacecraft greater maneuverability. For this reason, liquid fuels are used for most satellites and for all spacecraft with astronauts aboard.

### Hybrid Rockets

A third type of rocket, a **hybrid rocket**, uses a solid fuel and a liquid oxidizer. This may be the safest type. Since the solid propellant does not contain an oxidizer, which is often highly flammable, there is less danger of accidental fire or explosion. Moreover, since the oxidizer is liquid, its flow can be varied or stopped as in a liquid-fueled engine. In general, hybrid rockets perform more efficiently than solid-propellant rockets but less efficiently than liquid-propellant rockets.

## ▶ HOW ROCKETS ARE STEERED

There are several methods of steering a rocket, and launch vehicles often use more than one method. One way to steer a rocket is to change the direction of the thrust, known as the **thrust vector**. This can be accomplished by tilting the exhaust nozzle toward the place where the hot gases exit the rocket. The device used to tilt or pivot the nozzle is called a **gimbal**. The thrust vector can also be changed by injecting more gases into the exhaust, which alters its flow, or by diverting the exhaust flow by means of a device called a steering vane. Another way to steer a rocket is with small **thrusters** on the body of the launch vehicle. These thrusters, which act like miniature rockets, emit controlled amounts of exhaust to push the vehicle in a certain direction.

Rockets can also be steered by fins, flaps, and other devices on their outside surfaces. These devices, called **control surfaces**, work by altering the flow of air over the outside of the rocket. Since there is no air in outer space, they are effective only while a rocket is within the Earth's atmosphere.

Computers at control centers on Earth monitor information about a launch vehicle's flight. This is known as **tracking**. Meanwhile, onboard instruments sense and measure data about the flight. Accelerometers measure changes in speed and direction. Gyroscopes measure **attitude**, the direction in which the launch vehicle is pointed. A device called the **inertial measurement unit** (IMU) combines these instruments, providing attitude and acceleration data in all directions. Information from these devices is sent to onboard com-

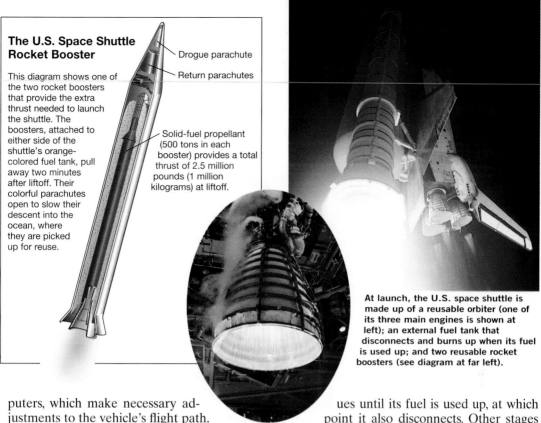

## The U.S. Space Shuttle Rocket Booster

This diagram shows one of the two rocket boosters that provide the extra thrust needed to launch the shuttle. The boosters, attached to either side of the shuttle's orange-colored fuel tank, pull away two minutes after liftoff. Their colorful parachutes open to slow their descent into the ocean, where they are picked up for reuse.

Drogue parachute

Return parachutes

Solid-fuel propellant (500 tons in each booster) provides a total thrust of 2.5 million pounds (1 million kilograms) at liftoff.

At launch, the U.S. space shuttle is made up of a reusable orbiter (one of its three main engines is shown at left); an external fuel tank that disconnects and burns up when its fuel is used up; and two reusable rocket boosters (see diagram at far left).

puters, which make necessary adjustments to the vehicle's flight path.

### ▶ ROCKET STAGES

A launch vehicle must propel its rocket, its fuel, and its payload into space. This requires a tremendous amount of thrust, especially at liftoff, when inertia and gravity must be overcome. Producing this thrust requires large amounts of fuel because much of the weight of a typical launch vehicle is its fuel and the large, heavy tanks that store it. This makes it even harder for the rocket to perform efficiently, since much of the thrust is needed just to lift the fuel and storage tanks.

Rocket designers have developed a clever strategy to help launch vehicles perform more efficiently. Rather than use just one large rocket in a launch vehicle, they use several smaller rockets, each with its own engines, fuel, and fuel tanks. Each of these is called a rocket **stage**. Several rocket stages usually are stacked on top of each other, creating a multistage rocket. The largest stage, the first stage, is at the bottom. It lifts the launch vehicle off the launchpad and propels the other stages for a few minutes. When its fuel is spent and its fuel tanks are empty, the first stage disconnects from the launch vehicle. The second stage then ignites and contin-

ues until its fuel is used up, at which point it also disconnects. Other stages may follow. Each stage is smaller and lighter than the one before it, and it carries less fuel because it needs less thrust. Many launch vehicles have additional smaller rockets attached to the first stage to produce extra thrust. These are known as **strap-on boosters**.

### ▶ REUSABLE ROCKETS

After using their fuel, many rockets fall back to Earth. In some cases, they burn up as they fall through the atmosphere and are thus destroyed. But even if they survive, they are not used again. These throwaway rockets are called **expendable launch vehicles**. However, other rockets, known as **reusable launch vehicles**, are recovered and used again and again. An example of a reusable launch vehicle is the space shuttle. The space shuttle consists of three main parts, not all of which are reusable, however. The airplane-like vehicle that carries the astronauts and payload is called the orbiter. It has three engines in the rear and is reusable. The second part of the shuttle is a large external fuel tank attached to the underside of the orbiter. Liquid propellants stored in this tank are pumped to the engines on the orbiter, which provide thrust to help launch the shuttle. After use, the external tank disconnects from the shuttle, is pulled back toward Earth, and burns up on re-entry into the atmosphere. The third part of the shuttle is a pair of solid-propellant rockets attached to the sides of the external tank. These solid rocket boosters, as they are called, provide most of the initial thrust needed to lift the shuttle off the launchpad and propel it for the first two minutes of flight. After their fuel is used up, they fall back to Earth. Parachutes help slow their descent, to prevent them from being damaged when they hit the surface of the ocean. They are then recovered and reused.

Since the space shuttle was first developed, advances in technology and materials have generated interest in constructing fully reusable launch vehicles. In the 1990's, the United States began short flights of an experimental rocket designed to test the technology for developing a fully reusable, single-stage-to-orbit (SSTO) vehicle.

This computer-generated model shows the experimental design for a new, reusable rocket, the *Venture Star*. It would not need external fuel tanks or boosters and would land on a runway.

▶ **ROCKETS OF THE FUTURE**

In the future, some rockets will probably still use chemical combustion. Meanwhile, scientists are developing ways to propel rockets using nuclear or electrical energy.

**Nuclear Propulsion**

A nuclear thermal rocket would use a small nuclear reactor to heat a monopropellant such as liquid hydrogen, which turns into a gas when it becomes hot. The hot gas rushing through the rocket's exhaust would create the thrust needed to propel the rocket. Such a rocket would be more efficient than a chemical rocket, which must burn both a fuel (such as hydrogen) and an oxidizer.

**Electric Propulsion**

Future rockets might also be powered by a form of electric propulsion that has been tried on some rockets that use the chemical xenon as a propellant. When the xenon enters a special chamber within the rocket engine, it changes into **plasma**, a very hot gas consisting of charged particles of matter called **ions**. As this plasma flows through electrical conductors, it generates the thrust needed to propel the rocket.

A more futuristic form of electric propulsion would use hydrogen or argon heated to tremendous temperatures in a small nuclear reactor, causing them to turn into plasma. When exposed to an electromagnetic force, this plasma would provide thrust.

This type of propulsion would produce only low levels of thrust, making it unsuitable for launch vehicles, which require great thrust and acceleration. But it might be excellent for travel in outer space, where a spacecraft does not need to accelerate quickly. An engine powered by nuclear-electric propulsion would accelerate slowly, but it could run for months at a time. On a long trip, this ability would allow the engine to build more speed than a rocket with greater thrust but less running time.

**Antimatter Propulsion**

Scientists and engineers are always working on new ideas. One idea they have considered is to power rockets with **antimatter**, particles of matter with the opposite electrical charges of ordinary matter. If antimatter and matter could be made to collide, a tremendous amount of energy would be released. This is called antimatter-matter annihilation. Antimatter could provide an efficient and powerful source of energy. But scientists have had only the briefest glimpse of real antimatter, so a rocket engine powered by antimatter is still just a dream.

JAMES R. ASKER
Washington Bureau Chief
*Aviation Week & Space Technology*

See also GODDARD, ROBERT HUTCHINGS; MISSILES; MOTION; SATELLITES, ARTIFICIAL; SPACE EXPLORATION AND TRAVEL; SPACE PROBES; SPACE RESEARCH AND TECHNOLOGY.

**ROCKFORD.** See ILLINOIS (Cities).

A scene from the film Grease (1978), a rock musical about growing up in the 1950's.

## ROCK MUSIC

Rock music is a part of popular music today. It is played and listened to in almost all the countries of the world.

Until the 1950's, American popular music was divided into three separate styles, each with its own performers, musical content, and audience. One style was called pop, and it served most Americans. Pop songs came from movies, Broadway musicals, and pop composers. The songs were mainly simple 32-bar melodies with lyrics about love. They were played by bands in dancehalls, restaurants, and nightclubs and on radio. The bands consisted of anywhere from six to more than twenty musicians playing combinations of trumpet, trombone, saxophone, and clarinet, with a rhythm section of drums, guitar, string bass, or piano. Soloists or small vocal groups generally accompanied the bands.

In the late 1930's and 1940's, there were hundreds of "big bands." The most popular included the white bands of Artie Shaw, Benny Goodman, Glenn Miller, Tommy and Jimmy Dorsey, Harry James, and Woody Herman. There were also the more jazz-style black bands of Jimmie Lunceford, Fletcher Henderson, Count Basie, Duke Ellington, and Lionel Hampton. After World War II, individual singers such as Frank Sinatra, Perry Como, Nat ("King") Cole, Doris Day, Patti Page, and Jo Stafford, most of whom had been band singers, became much more popular than the bands themselves.

The second style, rhythm and blues, came from the blues sung by black performers, along with the fast dance music that had grown out of ragtime and boogie-woogie. It was the popular music of the black people of the United States, played and sung in taverns and clubs or listened to on records in jukeboxes. Later, it was called soul music. A few of the most popular rhythm and blues performers of the 1940's and early 1950's were Chuck Berry, Fats Domino, B. B. King, Dinah Washington, and Willie Mae Thornton. Both the white pop bands and the black rhythm and blues musicians were influenced by jazz and by black spirituals and gospel music.

The third style is now called country and western, or country music. But before World War II it was often called hillbilly music. It includes the commercialized folk music of the rural southern and southwestern parts of the United States. The main center of this music has always been Nashville, Tennessee.

### ▶ HOW ROCK BEGAN

Rock and roll was the name given to the music that developed when these three separate styles came together in the early 1950's. It is widely believed that the term "rock and roll" was first used by a Cleveland disk jockey, Alan Freed. He was one of the first persons to bring rhythm and blues to white audiences. He did this on his radio program and through concerts he produced, beginning in 1952, which presented both black and white performers to audiences of black and white teenagers. But not any one person created rock and roll. Rock was born as a result of changes in the music, broadcasting, advertising, and entertainment industries.

Before World War II the music industry was centered in New York. Music publishers printed the words and music of songs, and people all over the country bought this sheet music to play the songs on their guitars, pianos, or accordions. A hit song might sell 1,000,000 copies, but most songs made little or no money. No one really knew what made a hit, but most people believed in a few rules. One was that success in the immediate past meant success in the immediate future. If last week's hit was about apples, then next week's songs would be about oranges or pears. If last week's hit was sung by Perry Como, next week the music industry would have new songs for him or would be looking for someone who sounded just like him. Another rule was just the opposite—find a new and different song; find a new and different performer.

But finally, only public response could make a hit. Enough of the public had to hear a song often enough to distinguish it from the rest and become familiar with it. So the publishers brought songs to bands playing in and around New York—especially bands that had radio programs. In that way, not only would more people hear the songs, but the newspapers of the entertainment industry could keep count of how often they were played. The publishers also arranged for as many recordings of their songs as possible. Sheet music was still more important than records, but by the early 1950's several things had happened to change this.

First came the disk jockeys. Just before World War II, the Federal Communications Commission, which regulates United States broadcasting, authorized the licensing of new radio stations. These stations needed three things to be successful—inexpensive, interesting material; advertisers who would buy time from them; and a large audience. The answer was found in disk jockeys. They designed programs consisting of pop records with a playing time of about three minutes. They also read "spot" commercials and held the program together with talk.

The disk jockeys soon had local audiences loyal to their stations, products, and musical tastes. This weakened the control of the net-

Elvis Presley combined rhythm and blues with country and western. He became one of the top rock stars of all time.

work stations and of the bandleaders over what songs became hits. The disk jockeys appealed mainly to young people in their teens who were more interested in dancing and listening to music than playing it themselves.

The disk jockeys also held "record hops" (dances) in high schools and invited teenagers into radio studios to listen to new records. The teenagers made it clear which songs they liked and which they did not. Now the music industry could find out more quickly what kind of songs to do next. Now, too, records became more important than sheet music.

Several other things happened in the early 1950's to set the stage for rock and roll. The big dance bands were losing popularity, and dancehalls were closing as record companies followed the charts and recorded individual singers and small groups. Television was replacing radio, and soon disk jockeys had television programs of their own.

Rhythm and blues was expanding, too. During and after World War II many black people moved to northern cities in search of jobs. Because the war improved their economic position, the music industry was responsive to their tastes. This led to an increase in the production of rhythm and blues records. Radio stations played more rhythm and blues and had black disk jockeys. But white teenagers also listened, even in the South, because there was no segregation of the radio audience.

Country and western music was also being more widely heard. At first, rhythm and blues and country and western hits were copied by white pop singers. They used black or hillbilly material, but they often changed the lyrics and smoothed out the "roughness" of the music.

Left: The Beatles—Paul McCartney, Ringo Starr, George Harrison, and John Lennon—revolutionized pop music. Right: Bob Dylan sparked folk rock.

### ▶ HOW ROCK DEVELOPED

In 1955, records by a young singer from Tennessee, Elvis Presley, were heard across the country. After he appeared on nationwide television, Elvis Presley's singing—a combination of rhythm and blues and country and western—and his performing style came to mean "rock and roll" all over the United States. Presley's many hits, including "Heartbreak Hotel" and "Hound Dog," made him an all-time star of pop music. Bill Haley and the Comets—with songs like "Rock Around the Clock"—were a country and western group that also became a rock pacesetter.

At first it was mainly the fast, strong beat of rock songs that appealed to young audiences. Musically, the songs were simple, too, following a one-four-five chord pattern similar to that used in the blues, with chords based on the first, fourth, and fifth notes of the scale. For example, in a song written in the key of C, the first chord would consist of the notes C, E, G, and C; the second of F, A, C, and F; and the third of G, B, D, and G.

Young people identified with the music, and soon songs especially aimed at the lives and problems of teenagers were being written. These included such hits as Chuck Berry's "Sweet Little Sixteen" and "Teen Age Prayer" by Gale Storm. Within a short time, young singers began to replace older entertainers. Ricky Nelson, Paul Anka, Lesley Gore, Bobby Darin, and Dion and the Belmonts were just some of these. New black groups also became successful—the Drifters, the Platters, and the Clovers were typical. But older performers such as Dinah Washington, Bo Diddley, and Fats Domino were also popular.

Rock became mainly the music of the young. They understood its beat and sound, and its lyrics spoke to them. By the early 1960's, rock had spread across the Atlantic to England, and new groups began to emerge there as well. The one that rapidly became most popular was made up of four boys from the industrial port city of Liverpool, on England's west coast. Calling themselves the Beatles, John Lennon, Paul McCartney, George Harrison, and Ringo Starr had been playing together since 1962. At first they did songs by other composers, but John and Paul soon began to write the Beatles' songs. By 1964, when the Beatles were introduced to U.S. audiences, they had revolutionized pop music.

PHILIP H. ENNIS
Wesleyan University
MICHAEL SAHL
Composer

### ▶ ROCK IN THE 1960'S

In the mid-1960's, rock music began to be influenced by certain new and surprising forces. Folk rock brought the gentler sounds of folk ballads into rock. Bob Dylan is generally acknowledged to have sparked folk rock when his song "Mr. Tambourine Man," recorded by the Byrds, became a tremendous hit. This was followed by the release of Dylan's own album, *Bringing It All Back Home*. Other folk rock artists included Donovan and the Mamas and the Papas.

Among black musicians, the 1960's brought about a polishing and speeding up of old rhythm and blues forms. The Supremes, the Temptations, and Stevie Wonder were among the best and most popular of soul music artists.

Janis Joplin

Madonna

**The Beach Boys**, with their songs about surfing, cars, and girls, epitomized the California sound of the early and mid-1960's. The group was formed in 1961 by brothers **Brian Wilson** (1942–  ), **Carl Wilson** (1946–98), and **Dennis Wilson** (1944–83), all born in Hawthorne, California; their cousin **Mike Love** (1941–  ), born in Los Angeles, California; and family friend **Al Jardine** (1932–  ), born in Lima, Ohio. Characterized by rich vocal harmonies, Beach Boy songs such as "Surfin' U.S.A." (1963), "Fun, Fun, Fun" (1964), and "California Girls" (1965) were instant hits. The album *Pet Sounds* and the song "Good Vibrations," both released in 1966, were creative highlights for Brian Wilson, who wrote, arranged, and produced most of the group's music. His participation in the group was limited after 1970, and the Beach Boys continued mainly as a touring "oldies" act.

**The Beatles** were one of the most popular and influential rock groups of all time. An article on the Beatles can be found in Volume B of this encyclopedia.

**Chuck Berry** (1926–  ), a singer, songwriter, and guitarist, was born Charles Edward Anderson Berry in Wentzville, Missouri. Beginning with "Maybellene" (1955), Berry produced a string of hit songs that greatly influenced the development of rock and roll. Combining blues and country-influenced melodies with witty lyrics about teenage frustration, young love, and fast cars, his music was admired and imitated by such later groups as the Beach Boys, Beatles, and Rolling Stones. Many Berry songs, including "Roll Over Beethoven" (1956),

"Rock and Roll Music" (1957), "Sweet Little Sixteen" (1958), and "Johnny B. Goode" (1958), have become classics.

**Eric Clapton** (1945–  ), born Eric Clapp in Ripley, England, is a leading rock guitarist. He first gained fame as a member of the British blues band the Yardbirds. He later played in a number of other notable bands, including Blind Faith and Cream, and also developed a successful career as a solo artist. Clapton's style was much influenced by American blues artists. His later work, which included pop ballads and traditional blues songs, emphasized his singing as much as his guitar playing.

**Bob Dylan** (1941–  ), born Robert Allen Zimmerman in Duluth, Minnesota, became a leading figure of folk rock. Influenced by the folk songs of Woody Guthrie, Dylan began his career as a folksinger in 1960, accompanying himself on acoustic guitar and harmonica. His early folk protest songs, notably "Blowin' in the Wind" (1962) and "The Times They Are a-Changin'" (1963), became anthems of the antiwar and civil rights movements. In 1965, Dylan turned to rock music, angering many of his earlier fans but achieving international celebrity and influencing a younger generation of rock artists.

**The Grateful Dead**, one of the most enduring American rock bands, was formed in 1965. Its original members, all Californians, were guitarists and vocalists **Jerry Garcia** (1942–95) and **Bob Weir** (1947–  ), both born in San Francisco; bassist **Phil Lesh** (1940–  ), born in Berkeley; drummer **Bill**

Chuck Berry

**Kreutzmann** (1946–  ), born in Palo Alto; and keyboardist **Ron McKernan** (1945–73), born in San Bruno. The band's music blended country, blues, and folk sounds with rock and roll. Until the death of Jerry Garcia in 1995, the Dead was the world's most successful touring rock band, known for its long, free-form live performances. The band's concerts attracted large numbers of devoted followers, who were known as Deadheads.

**Jimi Hendrix** (1942–70), born in Seattle, Washington, was an innovative rock guitarist. His experimentation with electronic effects such as distortion changed the way electric guitar was played. A self-taught, left-handed guitarist, Hendrix played with B. B. King and other noted blues artists before moving to New York City and forming his own band. In 1966 he moved to London and started a new band, the Jimi Hendrix Experience. His work with this band, which includes "Purple Haze" (1967) and a famous version of the Bob Dylan song "All Along the Watchtower" (1968), won him international fame. But his career was cut tragically short by his death from a drug overdose in 1970.

**Buddy Holly** (1936–59), born Charles Hardin Holley in Lubbock, Texas, was a pioneer of rock and roll music. His singing and playing style influenced many later musicians. Holly began as a country performer but by 1957 was playing rocking versions of his music with his band, the Crickets. "That'll Be the Day" (1957) was Holly's first hit. It was followed by a number of others, including "Peggy Sue" (1957), "Maybe Baby" (1958), and "Rave On" (1958), before his death at age 22 in an airplane crash.

**Janis Joplin** (1943–70), born in Port Arthur, Texas, was one of the first women rock singers to achieve stardom. She won fame for her raw, heartfelt renditions of blues-rock tunes—notably "Piece of My Heart" (1968)—performed with her band, Big Brother and the Holding Company. But Joplin's drug and alcohol dependence prevented her from reaching her true potential; she died at age 27 of a drug overdose.

**Madonna** (1958–  ), born Madonna Louise Ciccone in Bay City, Michigan, was one of the biggest female pop stars of the 1980's. She first gained fame when her album *Like a Virgin* (1984) became a hit. Her later albums include *True Blue* (1986) and *Like a Prayer* (1989). Madonna also acted in films and on stage. In addition to her recordings, music videos, and concert performances, her ever-changing appearance and often controversial statements kept her at the center of media attention.

**Pearl Jam** was one of the most successful bands to emerge from Seattle, Washington, a center of rock music in the 1990's. Founding members were bassist **Jeff Ament** (1963– ), born in Big Sandy, Montana; rhythm guitarist **Stone Gossard** (1965– ), born in Seattle; guitarist **Mike McCready** (1966– ), born in Pensacola, Florida; drummer **Dave Krusen** (1966– ), born in Tacoma, Washington; and singer **Eddie Vedder** (1964– ), born in Evanston, Illinois. Pearl Jam was originally labeled "alternative," a term used to describe a variety of bands that rejected the commercialism of mainstream rock acts. But the group's powerful guitar-driven sound owed much to classic rock of the 1960's and 1970's.

Pearl Jam's Eddie Vedder

The Rolling Stones

**Elvis Presley** (1935–77), born in Tupelo, Mississippi, was known as the king of rock and roll. He popularized the mingling of blues and country music—the sound that became rock and roll. Presley first gained attention with his recording of "That's All Right (Mama)" (1954) by African American blues singer Arthur Crudup. With a series of hit songs released in 1956, among them "Heartbreak Hotel," "Blue Suede Shoes," and "Hound Dog," he became a teen idol and a national star. He starred in more than 30 films, and his concerts in Las Vegas drew huge audiences. Presley's popularity continued even after his death. Graceland, his home in Memphis, has become a mecca for his fans.

**The Rolling Stones**, one of the most successful and long-lived British rock bands, was formed in 1962. Original members were vocalist **Mick Jagger** (1943– ) and guitarist **Keith Richard** (1943– ), both born in Dartford, England, who together wrote most of the band's music; bassist **Bill Wyman** (1941– ), born in London; drummer **Charlie Watts** (1941– ), born in Islington; and guitarist **Brian Jones** (1942–69), born in Cheltenham. Jones, who left the band shortly before his death, was replaced first by Mick Taylor and later by Ron Wood. The Stones began by playing their interpretations of African American blues music (they took their name from a song by blues singer Muddy Waters). But they soon developed their own distinctive style. Their many hit songs include "(I Can't Get No) Satisfaction" (1965), "Honky Tonk Women" (1969), "Brown Sugar" (1971), and "Start Me Up" (1981). They won their first competitive Grammy Award, for best rock album, for 1994's *Voodoo Lounge* (they had been given a lifetime achievement award in 1986).

**Paul Simon** (1941– ), a singer-songwriter born in Newark, New Jersey, first won fame in the duo Simon and Garfunkel. He began performing with schoolmate Art Garfunkel while still in his teens. Their early songs—most written by Simon—had a folk-music feeling, with intricate vocal harmonies. Simon and Garfunkel had numerous hits, including *The Sounds of Silence* (1966) and *Bridge Over Troubled Water* (1970) before splitting up in 1970. As a solo artist, Simon was known for his explorations of the music of other cultures. For example, his album *Graceland* (1986) showcased South African music and musicians, while *Rhythm of the Saints* (1990) incorporated Brazilian sounds.

**Bruce Springsteen** (1949– ), born in Freehold, New Jersey, achieved great popularity with his songs about the lives of working-class Americans. The long story-songs on his early albums caused him to be compared with Bob Dylan. Later Springsteen songs had similar themes but were shorter and simpler. He began his climb to stardom in 1975 with the release of his third album, *Born to Run*, and his appearance on the covers of both *Time* and *Newsweek* magazines. With *Born in the U.S.A.* (1984) he became a superstar. Springsteen's other work includes the albums *Tunnel of Love* (1987) and *Human Touch* (1992) and the Grammy-winning song "Streets of Philadelphia" (1993). In 2002, he released *The Rising*, a collection of songs inspired by the September 11, 2001, terrorist attacks.

**The Who**, a British rock group, became popular in the mid-1960's. Original members, all born in London, England, were guitarist and composer **Pete Townshend** (1945– ), bassist **John Entwhistle** (1944– ), singer **Roger**

**Daltrey** (1944– ), and drummer **Keith Moon** (1947–78). The Who's early songs, such as "My Generation" (1965), expressed youthful discontent and rebellion. This attitude was underscored by their live performances, during which they frequently destroyed their instruments. Their rock opera *Tommy* (1969) brought them widespread critical recognition. It was made into a film in 1975 and produced on Broadway in 1993.

**Stevie Wonder** (1950– ), born Steveland Morris in Saginaw, Michigan, was one of the most successful artists to record on the famous Motown label. Blind from infancy, he was a musical prodigy and recorded his first hit song at age 12. His early songs, including "Up-Tight" (1966) and "My Cherie Amour" (1969), were outstanding examples of the distinctive pop-soul "Motown sound." As he grew older, Wonder's music incorporated a wide variety of sound—gospel, rhythm and blues, jazz, reggae, and African rhythms—while his lyrics showed his concern with social issues. His albums, on which he often played nearly all the instruments, include *Songs in the Key of Life* (1976), *In Square Circle* (1985), and *Conversation Peace* (1995).

**Neil Young** (1945– ), born in Toronto, Canada, has been a major force in rock music since the 1960's. As a member of Buffalo Springfield (1966–68), he helped shape the sound of country rock. He then joined Crosby, Stills, and Nash (to form Crosby, Stills, Nash, and Young), bringing a harder edge to that group's soft acoustic rock on the hit album *Déjà Vu* (1970). As a solo artist, often backed by his band Crazy Horse, he played both folky ballads and hard-rocking songs. His deliberately simple approach to music influenced alternative-rock musicians.

Rock star Bruce Springsteen is famous for the energy of his live performances. His songs, which often describe the lives of ordinary people, are set to a driving beat.

Major British groups—including the Beatles, the Rolling Stones, and the Who—confirmed their earlier promise by producing mature reflective music. In the United States, bands on the West Coast, such as the Grateful Dead and the Jefferson Airplane (later Jefferson Starship), were influenced by the free-form techniques of jazz.

In the 1960's, too, young people began to think of themselves as a new and different generation because they were the first to grow up with rock and roll. Rock concerts and festivals—such as the one in Woodstock, New York, in 1969—were part of this trend.

Rock went into musical theater with such shows as *Hair* (1968) and *Jesus Christ, Superstar* (1971). Rock musicians also became interested in experimental music, notably electronic music, and in the sound language of modern composers. Rock was moving in new directions. There was no longer any way of telling what was rock except by the community it served.

▶ROCK TODAY

The 1970's were a time of tremendous expansion within the rock industry. Rock became a very big business, earning more money annually than any other form of entertainment, including the film industry. One rea-

son was that the number of rock music fans grew larger all the time. People who were originally excited by it in the 1950's and 1960's continued to buy records and attend concerts. Their children, in turn, were also attracted to this music of youth.

Until the 1970's, a rock performer would have been proud to earn a "gold record," an album that sold 500,000 copies or earned $1,000,000 in sales. Today a performer can also earn a platinum record when a record sells 1,000,000 copies, or a multi-platinum record when 2,000,000 or more copies are sold. Among performers who have multi-platinum records to their credit are Michael Jackson, Bruce Springsteen, and Madonna.

The late 1970's saw the rise of disco, an offshoot of the soul music of the 1960's. It had a steady, almost mechanical beat that was easy to dance to. The most important instrument in the development of disco was the electronic synthesizer.

The increasing sophistication of rock music sparked a cry of protest within the rock world itself. Many struggling rock bands believed that the smoothness and polish of modern recording techniques had drained rock of much of its vigor and daring.

These musicians formed rock bands that rejected extensive musical knowledge and elaborate equipment. Their music, harsh and direct in sound, became known as punk music. Punk, in turn, inspired other musical styles, which together were called new wave. The new music was played by such English bands as the Clash and the Police, and by U.S. groups such as the Ramones, Blondie, and Talking Heads.

The rise of music videos in the 1980's added another dimension to rock music, providing a way for new artists to win almost instant recognition. Other trends of 1980's and 1990's rock included increasing interest in the music of other cultures and the emergence of "alternative" rock—younger bands united mainly by their rejection of the commercialism of mainstream rock.

Rock's energy, its expression of the concerns of young people, and its ability to speak through many musical forms make it a living part of our musical world.

KEN TUCKER
Music Critic, Los Angeles *Herald Examiner*
See also COUNTRY MUSIC.

# ROCKS

Rock is the hard, solid material that makes up the earth. It is everywhere. Mountains are great masses of rock. Stones and pebbles are small pieces of it. In fact, the earth itself is a great ball of rock weighing about 6,600,000,000,000,000,000,000,000 (6.6 sextillion) tons.

All rocks are made up of one or more **minerals**. Minerals are naturally occurring chemical substances. The various kinds of rocks are determined by the kinds of minerals they contain. Along with the kinds of minerals in a rock, the arrangement of the minerals and the amount of each mineral also help give the rock its identity.

**Geologists**, the scientists who study rocks, use information about rocks to understand the history of the earth. They also study rocks and rock formations to find oil deposits, predict earthquakes, and find **ores**. Ore is a rock containing a large enough deposit of a useful metal, such as iron, aluminum, and copper, that the metal can be profitably mined from the rock.

Geologists study rocks, such as the basalt columns of Giant's Causeway in Northern Ireland (*above*) and the grooved rock of the Grand Canyon in Arizona (*right*), to learn about the earth and its history.

## ▶TYPES OF ROCKS

When geologists use the word "rocks," they usually do not mean the stones or pebbles you may find along a road or in a river. They mean the great mass that makes up a mountain or lies beneath a vast area of land. Geologists divide all the different kinds of rock, no matter where they are found, into three types based on how the rock was formed. With this system, rock is classified as either igneous, sedimentary, or metamorphic rock.

No matter how different one kind of rock might look from another, 98 percent of all the rocks in the world are made up of a combination of just eight elements—oxygen, silicon, aluminum, iron, calcium, sodium, potassium, and magnesium.

### Igneous Rock

Try to imagine rocks so hot that they melt and become liquid. For this to happen, the temperatures must reach more than 2192°F (1200°C). The melted, or molten, rock is called **magma**. When the magma cools and becomes solid, igneous rock is formed. Temperatures hot enough to melt rocks are usually found only deep inside the earth. It is there, far below the surface, that most igneous rock is formed.

Magma is often found in huge underground pockets. Because magma is liquid and less dense than surrounding matter, it flows upward, closer to the earth's surface into the cracks, or fissures, of rock. There the magma slowly cools and hardens into rock. Igneous rock formed in this way is described as **intrusive**. Thin bands, veins, or layers of igneous rock show where the magma once flowed. These features often can be seen at the earth's surface, not just deep underground. Natural forces such as erosion, earthquakes, and glacier movements change the earth's surface, exposing intrusive igneous rock.

Sometimes magma flows upward and is forced out onto the earth's surface during a

## Common Igneous Rocks

Igneous rock forms when magma cools and hardens.

Red Granite

Obsidian

Basalt

Pumice

volcanic eruption. Magma that reaches the surface of the earth is called **lava**. When it cools and hardens, it too forms igneous rock. Igneous rock that is formed on the earth's surface is described as **extrusive**.

Granite, obsidian, pumice and scoria, basalt, and felsite are just a few of the many types of igneous rock. The minerals in the magma determine the type of igneous rock formed. Minerals that are made up of the chemical elements silicon, aluminum, iron, calcium, potassium, sodium, oxygen, and magnesium are the ones most commonly found in igneous rock.

Where and how quickly the magma cools also help determine the type of igneous rock formed. As magma cools, the minerals in it form tiny grains, or crystals, almost like ice crystals forming in water that gets colder and colder. It is these mineral grains that give the rock its distinctive appearance.

**Granite.** Granite is the most common igneous rock at the earth's surface. Whole mountains of granite, once the core of much bigger mountains, now lie exposed. Even though it often can be seen at the earth's surface, granite is an example of an intrusive igneous rock. It originally formed far underground. The three main minerals in granite are quartz, feldspar, and mica. The color of granite is either gray or pink, depending on the color of its feldspar.

While most types of granite have mineral grains that are small and about the same size, some types of granite, called **coarse-grained**, have very large mineral grains. It is when granite magma cools very slowly, sometimes taking tens of thousands to millions of years to harden, that the mineral grains grow large.

Other types of granite are a mixture of large and small mineral grains. As magma cools, certain mineral grains may form and grow into large crystals while other minerals are still in the molten phase. For a while, the large crystals float in the magma. When the rest of the magma cools quickly, the large crystals become embedded among the small mineral grains. This type of rock is called **porphyry**. Granite porphyry has large crystals of quartz or feldspar.

Because of its beauty, granite is often used as a decorative stone for statues and monuments. It is also a strong and long-lasting building material.

**Obsidian.** Compared to magma, which cools slowly underground, lava cools quickly. After reaching the earth's surface, most thin lava flows harden within a few weeks, and thick flows, which form pools, take decades. When lava cools exceptionally fast, it forms no mineral grains and becomes a natural glass called obsidian. Obsidian is usually jet black. Because it is glass, its broken edges are very sharp.

**Pumice and Scoria.** Sometimes lava froths and bubbles while it is still molten. The foaming action is caused by gases in the lava as they rise to the surface. The gases may turn the lava into a frothy, spongy mass. When this lava cools, it becomes rock that is full of holes and pockets of gas that did not escape.

Pumice is light gray or cream-colored lava rock. It can float on water because it is full of so many small holes and gas pockets. Pumice is often ground up into a powder to be used for fine polishing. Dentists use it to polish teeth.

Black or dark red lava rock with a glassy appearance is called scoria. It is heavier than pumice, and its holes and pockets are usually bigger. In places where scoria is abundant, it is used as construction material for roads.

**Basalt.** Basalt is the rock that makes up most lava flows. It is a dense, hard rock that is almost always dark gray or black. The mineral grains in basalt are so tiny that they cannot be seen without a magnifying glass or microscope. For this reason, scientists describe basalt as a **fine-grained** rock.

**Volcanic Tuff.** Another fine-grained extrusive rock, called volcanic tuff, can be very colorful. Microscopic particles of glass give volcanic tuff its white, pink, gray, or yellow color. Yellowstone National Park gets its name from the yellow rhyolite, a type of volcanic tuff, that formed its broad plateaus.

## Sedimentary Rock

About three fourths of the earth's land surface is covered with sedimentary rock. Common types include sandstone, limestone, shale, conglomerate, and chert and flint. Most sedimentary rock was once part of some other, older rock. As the older rock was worn down, its particles were carried away by water, wind, or ice. The particles were finally deposited as layers of sediment on sites such as the floor of a lake, a river, or an ocean. Sometimes the loose material was carried to other land sites. But rock particles are not the only materials that formed sedimentary rock. Other kinds of material also accumulated and formed layers of sediment—the shells of tiny sea animals, decaying plants, dissolved minerals that settled out of ocean or lake waters, and ash from volcanoes that erupted long ago.

As many layers of sediment built up, pressure from water and the weight of overlying sediments squeezed the solids at the bottom closer and closer together. Minerals in the water acted as a cement, helping to hold the particles together. Slowly, over hundreds of thousands of years, the sediments were compressed into solid rock.

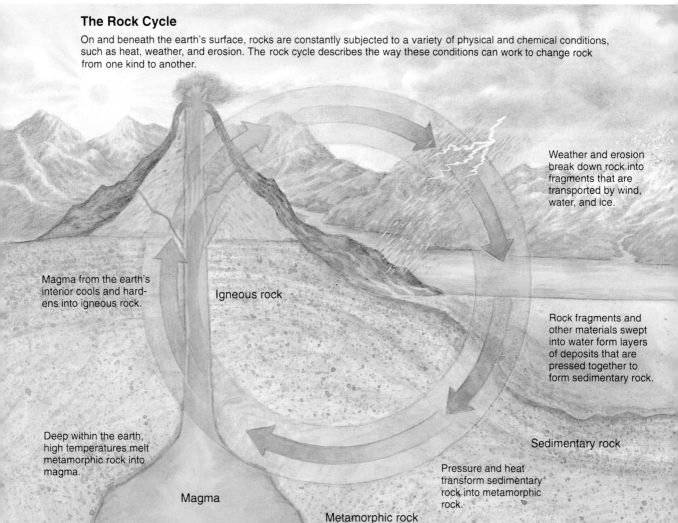

## The Rock Cycle

On and beneath the earth's surface, rocks are constantly subjected to a variety of physical and chemical conditions, such as heat, weather, and erosion. The rock cycle describes the way these conditions can work to change rock from one kind to another.

Weather and erosion break down rock into fragments that are transported by wind, water, and ice.

Magma from the earth's interior cools and hardens into igneous rock.

Igneous rock

Rock fragments and other materials swept into water form layers of deposits that are pressed together to form sedimentary rock.

Deep within the earth, high temperatures melt metamorphic rock into magma.

Sedimentary rock

Pressure and heat transform sedimentary rock into metamorphic rock.

Magma

Metamorphic rock

the oldest known rock ever found is almost 4 billion years old? Scientists have long searched for rock that formed during the earth's earliest history. To find ancient rock, a team led by Dr. Sam Bowring examined a well-exposed belt of the metamorphic rock gneiss (*below*) near Yellowknife, a city in Canada's Northwest Territories. The rock of the area was known to be from the Precambrian era, the geologic time that began with the formation of the earth about 4.5 billion years ago.

Samples of the area's gneisses, together called Acasta gneisses, were taken. When their ages were established, the oldest rock was found to be 3.962 billion years old!

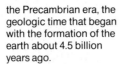

Arctic Circle

Site of find

Yellowknife

CANADA

Many different kinds of sedimentary rock, layered one on top of the other, have been found. This tells scientists that different particles were deposited on the ocean or lake floor at different times in history. Some layers are very thin, and others are hundreds of feet thick. Sedimentary rocks are like a book in which scientists can read the story of the earth's past.

Scientists can also learn about early forms of life on earth from sedimentary rocks. This is because traces of ancient plant and animal life are sometimes found in sedimentary rock. These traces are called **fossils**. Fossils are especially common in a sedimentary rock called shale.

**Sandstone.** As you might guess from its name, sandstone is made of grains of sand cemented together. The sand is made mostly of the mineral quartz. The minerals that cement the grains together are usually limonite, hematite, or calcite. These cementing minerals give sandstone a wide variety of colors—yellow, green, brown, pink, orange, red, gray, or white. Sandstone is a popular building material around the world.

**Limestone.** Limestone is made mostly of the mineral calcite. The shells and bones of millions of tiny sea animals are the source of this material. If you see a piece of common limestone, however, you cannot tell that the tiny mineral grains in it were once part of animal shells. When the animals die, their shells and bones are broken up by waves into tiny powdered shell fragments. The pieces of shell and bone settle on the bottom of the ocean and form a layer there. In time, this layer is covered by other sediments that press down, eventually pressing the calcite and other sediment into solid rock.

Most limestone is gray but it can also be almost white or almost black. Chalk is a form of limestone. So are the rock formations found in many caves. In one type of limestone, called coquina, you can see the small animal shells cemented together by minerals.

Limestone is one of the world's most important rocks. It is widely used as a building stone. When crushed and heated, limestone becomes a white powder called lime that is used in cement and mortar, to make glass, and to extract metals from ores.

**Shale.** More than half of all sedimentary rock is shale. It is formed in quiet water environments, such as lake bottoms, marshes, and deep ocean bottoms, as tiny particles of mud

### Common Sedimentary Rocks

Sedimentary rock forms as layers of plant, animal, and mineral sediment is compressed.

Sandstone

Limestone

Shale

Conglomerate

## Common Metamorphic Rocks

Metamorphic rock forms when rock is subjected to intense heat and great pressure.

Slate

Gneiss

Marble

Quartzite

and clay sink to the bottom and are compressed. It takes hundreds of thousands of years for the mud and clay particles to become shale. As the shale forms, it can capture traces of the surrounding environment. Fossils of plants and animals may be found in shale. It can also contain markings such as dinosaur tracks or ripple marks from the constant motion of waves.

The mineral grains in shale are flat, layered one on top of the other. The alignment of the minerals gives shale its characteristic property of splitting easily into flat layers or flakes. Its color, which ranges from yellow to red, brown, gray, and black, depends on the kind of rock particles and the amount of organic material in the clay and mud. Shale is crushed into a claylike material and is used to make tiles, bricks, and cement.

**Conglomerate.** The word "conglomerate" means "uneven mixture." That is just what this rock is—a mixture of pebbles and gravel cemented together by sand, clay, and silt. The pebbles in conglomerate are smooth and rounded. The way the pebbles are shaped tells geologists that they were worn down by water as they rolled about at the bottom of rivers and oceans.

The color and texture of conglomerates depend on the pebbles, gravel, and cementing material in them. Most are gray, although some conglomerates are dark brown with white quartz pebbles showing clearly.

**Chert and Flint.** Chert is a hard, dense sedimentary rock with very fine mineral grains. It is made mostly of quartz; however, it may also contain clay minerals, iron oxides, and the remains of marine animals. Chert may be white or a variety of other colors— gray, green, pink, red, yellow, brown,

or black. Dark-colored chert is called flint, while brightly colored chert is sometimes called jasper.

The way chert breaks—like glass into smooth, curved flakes with sharp edges—is one of its most recognizable characteristics. For this reason, chert was widely used by prehistoric people to make sharp-edged tools and weapons. They also discovered that flint gives off a spark when struck against hard metal and can be used to start a fire.

### Metamorphic Rock

Although the earth seems to be an unchanging place, great forces are at work within it all the time. These forces produce great pressure on rocks that moves, compresses, and sometimes changes them. Heat from within the earth and chemical reactions can also change rocks. The changes may alter the rocks' appearances in a variety of ways. For example, the mineral grains in a rock may be crushed and broken into smaller grains. Or they may be stretched so that they become long, thin, and flat. Still other minerals may change from one kind to another.

Rock that is changed by heat or pressure is called metamorphic rock. Both igneous rock and sedimentary rock can be changed to metamorphic rock. In fact, metamorphic rock itself can be changed to other types of metamorphic rock.

The minerals most often found in metamorphic rock include calcite, quartz, dolomite, and feldspar. Large mineral crystals may be found embedded in metamorphic rock. Sometimes these large crystals are gemstones, such as garnets. Although metamorphic rock is most often a gray color, small amounts of other minerals, including gemstones, can

## THE USES OF ROCKS

Since prehistoric times, rocks have been valued for their beauty and usefulness. *Clockwise from below:* Some people collect interesting or beautiful rocks as a hobby. Many different cultures designed implements from rock to use in food preparation, such as these stone tools used to grind and crush grain. Water from distant lakes, rivers, and mountain springs coursed through the channels of stone aqueducts to the people of ancient cities. Brownstone row houses, built from sandstone, are found in many cities in the northeastern United States. The beauty of polished marble can be seen in the art and architecture of cities throughout the world. Sharp-edged weapons and tools were made by prehistoric people using the rock called chert.

make the rock more colorful. Slate, schist, gneiss, marble, and quartzite are some of the most common metamorphic rock.

**Slate.** Slate was once the sedimentary rock shale. It is most often found in areas where shale has been subjected to heat and pressure. Like shale, slate is composed of quartz, mica, and chlorite and is often gray; but unlike shale, it has a shiny luster. When broken, this fine-grained rock splits into thin, smooth slabs.

**Schist.** Schist is a dark, sparkling rock. There are various types of schist, depending on the most abundant mineral in it. For example, there are mica schists and hornblende schists, among others.

As schists form, pressure and heat cause the various mineral grains in the rock to lengthen and flatten. The mineral grains grow enough so that they are often visible without a microscope. As the mineral grains re-form, they produce a metamorphic rock that is made up of many thin parallel layers, or bands. Schist breaks readily along these layers.

**Gneiss.** The name "gneiss" (pronounced like the word "nice") is given to metamorphic rock that has light-colored and dark-colored bands next to each other. A gneiss is named for the main mineral in its dark bands or for the rock from which it formed. There is hornblende gneiss, granite gneiss, and so on. The light bands give the gneiss its color, which may be pink, gray, white, or even green. Unlike the banded schists, gneiss does not easily break along its layers.

**Marble.** Marble was once the sedimentary rock limestone. It is formed as heat and pressure cause the minerals in limestone to recrystallize and form large, coarse grains. The minerals calcite or dolomite, which are the main substances found in marble, give it its white or gray color. Small amounts of other minerals found in marble can color it brown, red, or green. Dark streaks in some marbles were caused by layers of shale in the original limestone. As the limestone was heated and compressed into marble, the shale was compressed and twisted into the dark streaks.

Marble, which can be polished to reveal the mineral patterns of the rock, is valued for its strength and its beauty. It is widely used in architecture and to make statues.

**Quartzite.** This common metamorphic rock is made from sandstone, which is made of quartz grains cemented together by other mineral grains. Most kinds of quartzite were made by great pressure and heat. But other kinds were made when quartz grains slowly replaced the cementing minerals holding sandstone together. Thus, quartzite is a rock made of quartz sand cemented together by quartz. It is one of the hardest rocks known.

The color of quartzite depends on what other minerals besides quartz are in the rock. Some quartzite is milky white, but most types are light brown or pink.

▶**FINDING AND PROCESSING ROCKS**

Some rocks have more value than others. Characteristics such as strength, resistance to wear, and beauty give certain rocks a commercial value. These rocks are extracted from the ground and sold for various purposes.

Mining and quarrying are the two ways of obtaining rocks. When rocks are mined, it is usually for the valuable minerals they contain.

Most gemstones are found in rocks. So are valuable metals, such as gold, silver, and platinum. Useful metals such as iron and aluminum are also found in rocks. The rock surrounding the minerals is often considered a by-product or waste product.

Rock that is quarried, such as this granite, is carefully cut and removed rather than broken and scooped out of the earth.

In quarrying, the rocks themselves are sought. Rocks are components in many important products. Ceramics, which are used for dishes, electrical insulators, and engine parts, come from crushed rocks and clays. Many building materials are also made from rock. Clays and crushed shale are used to make bricks and tiles. Limestone is crushed, dried, and mixed with other materials to make cement and concrete for bridges, dams, buildings, and roads. Rocks containing phosphate are crushed and mixed with minerals to make fertilizers. Although most rocks must be broken down before they can be used, some are used whole, such as blocks of granite or marble for buildings and statues.

Some rocks are easy to find at the earth's surface. Others are deep underground or even underwater. The value and usefulness of each kind of rock help determine how much effort is spent to obtain it. Tests and surveys are done before digging to determine the size and quality of a particular rock deposit.

Reviewed by JEFF STEINER
Earth Sciences
City University of New York

See also CRYSTALS; EARTH; EARTH, HISTORY OF; GEOLOGY; ORES; VOLCANOES.

# ROCKWELL, NORMAN (1894–1978)

Norman Rockwell was a leading American illustrator whose professional career spanned more than 60 years. Most famous for the hundreds of covers he painted for the *Saturday Evening Post,* Rockwell specialized in lifelike portrayals of ordinary Americans in everyday situations. His accurate powers of observation and gentle humor gave point to his work.

Rockwell was born in New York City on February 3, 1894. He was the son of a businessman who liked to read the works of Charles Dickens to his children, and his grandfather had been an unsuccessful English artist. Rockwell showed an early talent for drawing and painting. While still attending the Art Students League in New York City, he became a commercial artist and illustrator. In 1916 his work began to appear in the *Saturday Evening Post,* and from that time on he was counted among the first rank of American illustrators.

Rockwell's early cover paintings often featured children, elderly people, and dogs in amusing situations. He continued to draw and paint similar subjects throughout his career. During World War I, he served in the Navy but continued to work for the *Post* and other clients. In the 1920's he made a number of trips to Europe and was briefly influenced by modern art. He quickly returned to his realistic style, but he continued to admire Picasso and other modern artists.

Rockwell reached new heights during World War II when his famous series of paintings *The Four Freedoms* (1943), celebrating democracy, toured the country. From that time until the early 1960's, he was at the peak of his powers. The best paintings of those years, such as *Breaking Home Ties* (1954) and *Marriage License* (1955), are important contributions to the tradition of realist painting in America.

Rockwell's later paintings show well-drawn characters in detailed settings—often in corners of his beloved New England. Many of these paintings recorded an America that was vanishing even as he portrayed it on canvas. It was part of his genius that he gave his vast audience a link with the past at a time when the world was changing rapidly. Yet he did this without losing sight of the everyday events of modern life.

In the last years of his life, Rockwell traveled all over the world, from Mexico to Mongolia, painting wherever he went. But his roots remained in the northeastern United States. He died in Stockbridge, Massachusetts, in 1978.

CHRISTOPHER FINCH
Author, *Norman Rockwell's America*

Left: *Freedom of Speech* is from a Norman Rockwell series of paintings celebrating democracy. Right: In *Breaking Home Ties,* the artist uses details and facial expressions to tell a story about what these people are doing and how they are feeling.

# ROCKY MOUNTAINS

The Rocky Mountains are part of the great mountain system known as the North American Cordillera. The Rockies extend from northern Alaska to New Mexico—a distance of about 3,000 miles (4,800 kilometers). These mountains form the great Continental Divide, which separates river systems flowing to opposite sides of North America.

The Rockies are divided into four major groups. The Arctic Rockies extend from the Brooks Range of Alaska into northwestern Canada. The Northern Rockies extend from British Columbia and Alberta, in Canada, down through northeastern Washington and across Idaho and Montana. The Middle Rockies are found in Utah, Montana, Wyoming, and Idaho. The Southern Rockies, which lie in Wyoming, Colorado, and New Mexico, are separated from the Middle Rockies by the level Wyoming Basin.

The Rockies' highest peaks are in Colorado. Mt. Elbert is the highest, at about 14,433 feet (4,399 meters) above sea level.

During the 1500's, Spanish conquistadores under Coronado explored the Southern Rockies. From 1804 to 1806, Meriwether Lewis and William Clark crossed and recrossed the Northern and Middle Rockies in their exploration of the Louisiana Territory. Trappers and fur traders explored the Middle Rockies between 1800 and 1850.

Some mountain passes used by settlers to cross the Continental Divide are still important. Several highways, as well as a line of the Burlington Northern railroad system, follow the same route into Idaho and Washington used by Lewis and Clark. Other railroads use parts of trails blazed by Coronado and Mormon leader Brigham Young.

The rugged mountains are rich in minerals. Gold, silver, lead, zinc, copper, and tungsten have been found in the Rockies. Also, the mountain landscapes are enjoyed in U.S. and Canadian parks, forests, and wilderness areas.

GEORGE W. CAREY
Rutgers, The State University of New Jersey

See also FUR TRADE IN NORTH AMERICA; MOUNTAINS; OVERLAND TRAILS.

**ROCKY MOUNTAIN SPOTTED FEVER.** See DISEASES (Descriptions of Some Diseases).

**RODDENBERRY, GENE.** See SCIENCE FICTION (Profiles).

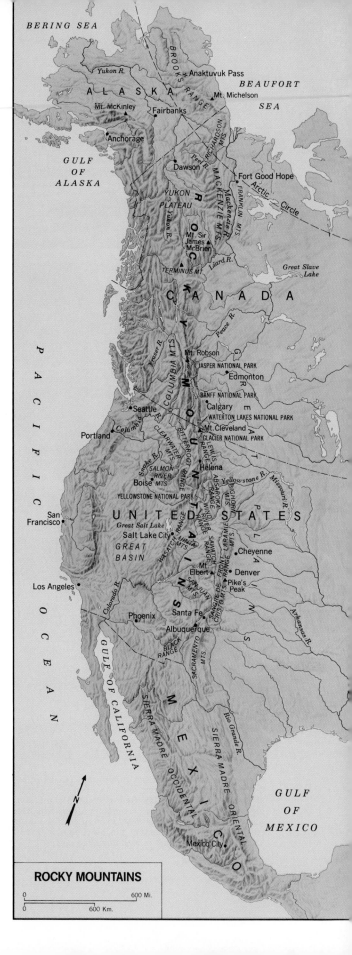

**ROCKY MOUNTAINS**

0        600 Mi.

0        600 Km.

These animals represent the three main groups of rodents. The chipmunk (*top*) enjoys a meal of mountain ash berries. It belongs to the squirrel group. The rat (*middle*) shares its group with mice, lemmings, muskrats, and hamsters. A destructive animal, it often damages food supplies. Long quills identify the porcupine (*bottom*). These prickly rodents are related to guinea pigs.

# RODENTS

Rodents are gnawing mammals. The very word "rodent" comes from a Latin word that means "to gnaw." House mice and rats, squirrels and chipmunks, beavers and porcupines, hamsters and guinea pigs—all are familiar rodents. They are just a very few of the many, many kinds of rodents that live in the world today.

In both variety and total numbers, the order Rodentia is the most successful of all the orders of mammals. There are thousands of different kinds of rodents all over the world—nearly as many as all other kinds of mammals added together.

## ▶CHARACTERISTICS OF RODENTS

Most rodents are less than 20 centimeters (8 inches) long, including the tail. The biggest rodents are the beaver and the South American capybara. The capybara sometimes measures more than 120 centimeters (4 feet) in length and weighs 45 kilograms (100 pounds).

Rodents are most easily identified by their teeth. Every rodent has four chisel-shaped front teeth—two in the upper jaw and two in the lower. These are its gnawing teeth, or incisors. The incisors grow throughout the animal's lifetime, but they wear away against each other and so remain a constant length. The front surface of the incisor is hard enamel, often orange in color. This is backed by softer dentine. As the teeth grind against each other, the dentine is worn away, and the enamel is ground to a sharp cutting edge.

All rodents eat plant food—roots, bulbs, leaves, stalks, fruit, seeds, and nuts. Many rodents have cheek pouches in which they transport food to storage places. Many species—squirrels, rats, and mice, for example—also eat eggs as well as insects and other small animals.

Most rodents do not live very long, but they are hardy and adaptable creatures. They mature quickly and have many big litters of young. Rodents must have big families in order for their species to survive, for they have many enemies. Most of the flesh-eating mammals, birds, and reptiles hunt them.

## ▶HARMFUL RODENTS AND HELPFUL ONES

Some rodents do vast amounts of damage to grain and fruit and other crops. Rats and mice invade buildings, where they ruin stores of food and other products. Porcupines kill many trees by eating the bark. Many rodents are infested with fleas that carry various diseases.

Many rodents, on the other hand, are useful to people. Beavers and muskrats are valued for their fur. Rats, mice, guinea pigs, and hamsters are raised as laboratory animals. Many rodents in the wild eat large quantities of harmful insects and weed seeds. Squirrels aid in the job of tree planting by burying nuts, acorns, and pine seeds. Millions of burrowing rodents help to turn over and condition the soil.

Scientists have separated the many rodents into 32 or more families. These, according to their characteristics, can be grouped into three main divisions:

(1) Squirrels and their relatives
(2) Rats and mice
(3) Porcupines and their relatives

▶ SQUIRRELS AND THEIR RELATIVES

This group includes many of the most appealing and familiar rodents—tree squirrels, chipmunks and ground squirrels, woodchucks, and prairie dogs.

### Tree Squirrels

The familiar tree squirrels are characterized by their thick, plumed tails. The tail acts as a balancer when a squirrel leaps from branch to branch, as a parachute if the squirrel falls, and as a snug blanket when it curls up to sleep.

Tree squirrels live in holes in trees or in bulky leaf nests, which they build high in the branches. They are usually active throughout the year. Their main diet is seeds and nuts and fruit, but many of them eat insects and other small animals as well. Many squirrels gather hoards of nuts for winter use.

A great number of different kinds of squirrels live in Eurasia, Africa, and the Americas. The gray squirrel is the most common species in the eastern United States. The largest of the American tree squirrels is the fox squirrel. Some individuals are mostly rust-brown and tan. Others are gray and black.

The red, or pine, squirrels are smaller than either the gray or the fox squirrels. They are found from coast to coast and usually live in evergreen forests. They are great hoarders and sometimes store several bushels of cones

in one hiding place. The seeds from the cones are their main food.

The little flying squirrels are seldom seen. They live in hollow trees and are active only at night. Flying squirrels have furred membranes of skin joining their front and hind legs. Spreading these like wings, the squirrels glide from tree to tree. Sometimes they travel 45 meters (150 feet) or more in one downward leap.

### Chipmunks and Ground Squirrels

The eastern chipmunk is common throughout southeastern Canada and the eastern United States. It is a small, reddish brown ground squirrel with dark and light stripes on its face and sides. Its tail is not so bushy as the tails of tree squirrels. The chipmunk can climb trees but usually prefers to hunt food on the ground. It stuffs seeds and nuts into its cheek pouches, then unloads its cheeks in an underground storeroom.

Three to five young are born each spring in an underground nursery, about a month after the parents have mated. By autumn the young are nearly full-grown. They dig burrows, which they fill with stores of food, then sleep away most of the winter. Occasionally they wake up, eat some of the food, and then sleep again.

Other species of chipmunks live in western North America. All of them look much like the eastern chipmunk and have similar habits. Many other kinds of ground squirrels are found in this region, too. Some of these are plain-colored, without the chipmunk's stripes. Others have striking patterns. One of the best known is the thirteen-lined ground squirrel. It has a number of alternating light and dark stripes on its back and sides. The thirteen-lined ground squirrel hibernates all winter long, as do many other ground squirrels.

### Marmots and Prairie Dogs

Marmots are large, heavy-bodied relatives of the squirrels. They have short legs and tails. Several species of them live in Europe and Asia, and others in the Rocky Mountains of western North America. The most familiar marmot in eastern North America is the groundhog, or woodchuck.

The woodchuck digs its burrow in fields or clearings. There are usually two or more entrances. A strict vegetarian, the woodchuck

The woodchuck, or groundhog, is common in North America. According to legend the groundhog's shadow on February 2 indicates six more weeks of winter.

Beavers spend most of their lives near the water. They build homes with underwater entrances and construct dams over small streams to form ponds.

stuffs itself with clover and other plant foods all summer long. By early autumn it is very fat. Retiring to its underground sleeping chamber before the first frost, it hibernates there until the following spring.

Prairie dogs look very much like small marmots and have similar habits. They live on the western prairies and plains of North America. They dig fairly deep burrows, often with entrance shafts going almost straight down for 3 meters (10 feet) or more. Sociable animals, prairie dogs live in colonies and often form large towns. Because they damage crops and range grass and because their holes are hazards for horses, prairie dogs have been killed off in many areas.

### Rodents with Fur-Lined Cheek Pouches

The pocket gophers are among the strangest of all rodents. A number of different kinds of these small burrowing animals live in North America. Equipped with short, stout legs and long, powerful claws, pocket gophers are expert diggers. Various individuals have been known to tunnel as much as 90 meters (300 feet) in a single night. Most of their lives are spent underground, where they feed on roots, bulbs, and other vegetable matter.

The most remarkable thing about the pocket gopher is the fact that on the outside of each cheek, it has a slit that leads to a fur-lined pocket. The animal stuffs seeds and other food into its pockets with its front paws. Then it goes off to a storage or eating place and pushes the food out by rubbing its cheeks with its paws.

The kangaroo rats and pocket mice that live in western desert areas also have fur-lined cheek pouches. These attractive little rodents

have tiny front legs, long tails, and long hind legs on which they hop about like miniature kangaroos. They live in burrows, where they retire during the day, often plugging the entrance behind them. Many of them do not drink during their entire lives but obtain moisture from seeds and juicy vegetation.

### The *Aplodontia*, or Mountain Beaver

The *Aplodontia*, or mountain beaver, looks something like a miniature beaver with a stubby tail. This stocky little rodent, usually 30 to 45 centimeters (12 to 18 inches) long, lives along the Pacific coast from southern Canada into California. It has short legs and very small ears. It lives in colonies and builds extensive tunnels. Bark, twigs, and green plant material form the *Aplodontia*'s main food. During the summer it busily stockpiles such food for winter use.

### ▶RATS, MICE, AND THEIR RELATIVES

Thousands of kinds of rats and mice and their relatives populate the earth in untold billions. They are the most abundant of all rodents. Besides the familiar house mouse and brown rat, there are field mice, lemmings, deer mice, pack rats, jumping mice, and many other kinds.

### The House Mouse and Brown Rat

These two rodents are among the most successful of all animal species. Along with the housefly—and human beings—they have populated most of the world. Hardy and resourceful, these two rodents have followed people practically everywhere.

Originally natives only of the Old World, house mice are little gray-brown rodents with long, nearly naked tails. They usually live in houses and buildings, where they build their nests between walls or in holes. They often do great damage to stored foods and other materials. One reason for their success is their high rate of reproduction. Female house mice can mate when they are 40 days old. Their young—four to seven in a litter and sometimes more—are born only 19 or 20 days after their parents have mated. Sheltered from the weather, house mice breed all year round.

The brown rat, also called the house rat or the Norway rat, is much larger than the house mouse. Breeding throughout the year, brown rats bear seven to nine young at a time, about 3 weeks after mating. The young are ready to become parents when they are about 4 months old. The brown rat is the most destructive of all mammals. It not only destroys hundreds of millions of dollars' worth of foodstuffs and other products yearly but also spreads disease. The only kind thing that can be said for the brown rat is that its domesticated strains are used as experimental laboratory animals the world over. As such, they help conquer various diseases.

### Field Mice and Lemmings

Field mice—or voles, as they are sometimes called—are small, stout mice with short tails and short legs. They have small eyes and ears. Mainly seed and plant eaters, they make mazes of tiny runways and shallow tunnels across fields and woodlands. They build globe-shaped nests of grass under logs or rocks. Here several litters of five to eight young are born during the warm months. When the weather is favorable and food is plentiful, field mice tend to have more families and larger ones than usual. Then thousands of mice per acre overrun the area and do great damage to crops.

Lemmings are closely related to field mice. They live in far northern tundra areas of the Northern Hemisphere. They also multiply very fast in favorable years. It is then that their famous travels, or migrations, take place. Moving away from their birthplace in search of less crowded areas, brown lemmings gather into great hordes—sometimes numbering many millions—that sweep across the land. Coming to a river, the tiny rodents swim across. Coming to a cliff, they plunge over. Many swim out to sea and are drowned. Huge numbers of flesh eaters—foxes, wolves, weasels, owls, hawks, and the like—follow the hordes of lemmings and feast on them. Finally the lemming population drops sharply. For several years, lemmings are quite scarce in the area. Eventually, however, the survivors build up to another peak. Then another lemming migration occurs.

### Muskrats, Hamsters, and Other Kinds of Rats and Mice

There are hundreds of other kinds of rats and mice. One of the largest is the muskrat. Equipped with partly webbed feet, it lives in ponds and marshes. There it builds snug, dome-shaped houses of cattails and other marsh plants. The muskrat is an important fur animal.

Many different varieties of attractive little deer mice, or white-footed mice, inhabit North America. These mice have tan-colored bodies with white bellies. They have enormous dark eyes and big ears. Clean and dainty, they build their nests in hollow trees or under logs. Here they store seeds for winter use. Sometimes they invade houses during the winter.

Pack, or wood, rats inhabit woodlands, mountains, and desert areas of North America. Some of them build huge nests of twigs and brush. They are called pack rats because they collect buttons, bits of glass, and other shiny objects in their nests.

Jumping mice are tiny American mice with very long tails and long hind legs used for jumping. They sometimes cover more than 3 meters (10 feet) in one leap. The jerboas form another family of rodents that also hop about on their hind legs. They live mainly in dry or desert areas of the Old World.

The golden hamster, a familiar pet, also belongs to the group of mouselike rodents. It was originally a native of Syria and neighboring areas. It is now kept the world over as a pet and laboratory animal.

### ▶PORCUPINES AND THEIR RELATIVES

The third large group of rodents has only a few species. Many of these are fairly large. Unlike most other rodents, most species in this group bear young that are active, fully furred, and have their eyes open at birth. Beavers, which are also rodents, share these traits. They have a separate article in Volume B.

Domestic guinea pigs come in a variety of patterns and colors. The word "pig" in their name may have come from their high-pitched, piglike squeals.

The capybara, largest of all rodents, may weigh more than 45 kilograms (100 pounds). It eats grasses and other plants found near rivers and lakes.

## Porcupines—Rodents with Quills

The North American porcupine is a large, clumsy-looking rodent with short legs. An adult porcupine may measure 1 meter (about 3 feet) in length and weigh up to 14 kilograms (30 pounds). It is famous for its protective covering of long, sharp quills—as many as 30,000 on a single individual.

Porcupines cannot shoot their quills. The quills are loosely attached and come out on contact with an attacker's skin. Each quill has many tiny barbs at its tip. These dig into the flesh like the barbs on fishhooks.

Many meat-eating mammals that attack porcupines get quills in their faces and mouths. The quills work their way deeper and deeper. Eventually the animal may be unable to eat and may die as a result.

Porcupines live in wooded areas. They make their homes in burrows or in hollow trees. Their main food is the bark of trees. They kill many trees by stripping off rings of bark. A single young porcupine is born in the spring, about 7 months after its parents mate. (You can read more about the North American porcupine in Porcupines in Volume P.)

The prehensile-tailed porcupine lives in tropical North and South America. It has a long tail with a bare spot near the end. It uses the tail to hold onto branches.

Crested porcupines live in Africa and Asia. They are usually a bit larger than North American porcupines and have even longer quills. Those on the neck and back may measure 50 centimeters (20 inches) in length.

## Guinea Pigs and Their New World Relatives

The domestic guinea pig was originally a native of South America. A rat-size rodent, it has short legs, no tail, small ears, and a rabbitlike face. Wild guinea pigs are reddish or gray-brown. Domestic guinea pigs come in many assorted colors and patterns.

Guinea pigs usually bear two to four young at a time. Several litters may be born each year. The babies, born 60 days after the parents mate, are fully furred and active at birth.

Agoutis are another group of tropical New World rodents. They have sleek, reddish or golden fur; small ears; fairly long, slender legs; and practically no tails. They are burrowers, as are their relatives the pacas and the Patagonian cavies.

The South American capybara is the largest of all rodents. About the size of an average pig, it has a blunt face, a stout body covered with brownish fur, rather long legs, and partly webbed feet. The capybara lives near water and is an expert swimmer.

The chinchilla is a native of the high Andes Mountains of South America. Its 38-centimeter (15-inch) body and tail are thickly covered with smoky-blue fur that is silky soft. It is now quite rare in the wild. In the 1920's about a dozen chinchillas were captured in Chile and brought to the United States. They were bred in captivity, and now many thousands are raised on fur farms.

Another famous South American rodent is the coypu, or nutria. It looks very much like a big muskrat and has similar habits. The coypu has been introduced into the southern United States and into Europe, where it is trapped for its fur.

Robert M. McClung
Author, science books for children

See also Beavers; Porcupines; Rabbits and Hares.

# RODEOS

In rodeos cowboys and cowgirls try their luck and riding skill on unbroken horses called bucking broncos. They risk their lives riding raging bulls. And they test the speed and training of their horses in calf roping and team roping.

"Rodeo" is a Spanish word that means "roundup." Rodeos started in the western United States more than 100 years ago as a celebration after the work of roundup had been done. Gradually some cowboys began to choose rodeo as a profession. The competition became more difficult as rules and regulations were made. In 1936, contestants began organizing themselves. In 1945 the Rodeo Cowboys Association—later renamed the Professional Rodeo Cowboys Association (PRCA)—was formed. The association governs procedures and makes the rules for professional rodeos.

The rodeo today is a big business. More than 500 rodeos are held each year in Canada and the United States. They are attended by millions of spectators, and the prize money exceeds several million dollars. Every rodeo has five standard events—bareback bronco riding, saddle bronco riding, bull riding, calf roping, and steer wrestling.

## ▶ BUCKING EVENTS

Usually the first thing you think of when rodeo is mentioned is the bucking bronco. The bronco is a wild, untamed horse. It fights anyone who tries to saddle or ride it.

In bareback bronco riding, the contestant rides with one hand holding onto a thick leather cinch that is strapped around the horse behind its shoulders. The rider must stay on the plunging, bucking horse for eight seconds and must spur the horse continuously during the ride. (Dull spurs are used.)

Saddle bronco riding requires the use of a special saddle. In this event, the rider's balance and timing are more important than physical strength. With one hand, the rider holds onto a soft woven rein that is attached to the horse's halter. As in bareback, the rider must stay on the horse for eight seconds and must keep on spurring. Riders must also keep their feet in the stirrups.

Two judges score the bucking events. Each

A bucking bronco does its best to throw its rider. The rider must stay on the horse for eight seconds.

gives points to both horse and rider. Riders may lose points for not spurring or for simply riding poorly. Horses lose points for not bucking enough. The point scores are added together, and the highest total wins. Riders are disqualified for touching the horse with the free hand or for falling off before eight seconds are up.

Bull riding is considered by many to be the most dangerous rodeo event. The contestant rides bareback with one hand holding onto a rope that is tied around the bull behind its shoulders. Again, the rider must stay on the animal for eight seconds. If a rider falls, rodeo clowns run out and distract the bull so that the rider can get safely out of the arena.

Scoring in the bull-riding event is the same as in bronco riding, except that the contestants do not lose points for not spurring.

## ▶ TIMED EVENTS

The two timed events in a rodeo are calf roping and steer wrestling. In calf roping, the goal is to rope a running calf, throw it on its side, and tie three of its legs together.

To be successful, the contestant must be good with a rope. But teamwork between the horse and rider is just as important. The horse must stand quietly and alertly and must be able to move quickly as soon as the calf is let out of the chute. Once the calf is roped, the horse must stop quickly and try to keep the rope taut while the contestant makes the tie.

Contestants are disqualified for missing the calf with the rope. If they start out of the box too soon, a ten-second penalty is added to their time.

In steer wrestling, the contestants ride up beside running steers, leap off their horses, and grab the animals' horns. They get the steers off balance by twisting the horns and forcing the animals to fall flat.

As in calf roping, good horses are important to success in steer wrestling. The horses must be fast. They are trained to run up next to the steers so that the riders can make their jump.

There is another rider—called a hazer—in the steer-wrestling event. The hazer rides along the other side of the steer and tries to keep the animal running in a straight line. This makes it easier for the contestant to catch the steer.

In both calf roping and steer wrestling, the rider who takes the least amount of time to complete the event is the winner.

Team roping is another timed event that is seen at many rodeos. Two contestants work together. One throws a rope around a steer's horns, and the other ropes the animal's hind legs. Time is called when the steer is roped and the two contestants have pulled their ropes taut and are standing away from the steer facing each other.

## ▶ RODEO SKILLS

Different skills are required in each event. In fact, in competition today you seldom find contestants who ride and rope equally well. They must concentrate on one or the other. Usually the best ropers come from the southwestern part of the United States, where cattle are still roped on the range. In the north, outdoor roping cannot be done during the winter. But a great many indoor or covered arenas have been built so that the northerners can continue their practice sessions unhampered by the cold. Bronco riders are more numerous in Canada and the northwestern United States, where more emphasis is put on their event. There are also more horses broken to ride in those areas. Canadian rodeos always have an amateur bronco-riding event as well as the professional contest. This serves as schooling for the young bronco riders. As a general rule, the horses raised in the northwest and in Canada are heavier than those raised in the southwest. They provide a little more action when they are being "gentled." This factor contributes to the northerners' riding skill.

## ▶ WOMEN IN RODEOS

In most rodeos, women compete only in an event called barrel racing. Each cowgirl races her horse around a course marked by three barrels, weaving in and out among them. The rider with the fastest time is the winner. Penalty time is added for knocking over barrels.

There are all-cowgirl rodeos. In these rodeos, cowgirls compete in calf roping, bareback bronco riding, and bull riding, as well as other riding and tying events.

## ▶ JUNIOR RODEOS

The rodeo is not for adults only. The National Little Britches Rodeo Association sponsors several hundred rodeos a year for youngsters between the ages of 8 and 17. These young people compete in all the rugged events of adult rodeos. The Little Britches Rodeos provide good training for young people who want to go on to become professional rodeo performers.

At the high school level, the National High School Rodeo Association holds about 600 rodeos a year. Each state has championship elimination trials among the various teams. Rodeos are also held at the collegiate level, under the auspices of the National Intercollegiate Rodeo Association.

These college and junior organizations are spread over more than half the United States. They are organized in the same manner as professional rodeos, ending in national finals and annual championship awards. Each year, gold and silver trophy buckles are given to championship winners.

RODEO NEWS BUREAU
Association of Professional Rodeo Cowboys

# RODIN, AUGUSTE (1840–1917)

François Auguste René Rodin—the greatest of French sculptors—was born in Paris on November 12, 1840. At the age of 14 he began taking drawing lessons, and in 1857 he tried to enroll in the École des Beaux-Arts (School of Fine Arts). The admissions director of the school thought that Rodin's work was crude, and he rejected the young artist.

Rodin then took odd jobs making plaster ornaments and casting other sculptors' works. His skill increased, and he was given the opportunity to carve figures on buildings.

By 1875, Rodin had not yet worked on his own. He borrowed money from a friend and went to Italy. The sculpture of the great Italian masters, especially Michelangelo, stirred Rodin. When he returned home, he began to work independently, and the influence of Michelangelo touched all of Rodin's sculpture.

Rodin's first life-size statue was *The Age of Bronze*, a male nude figure. Using a technique new to sculpture, Rodin modeled the surface of the figure with many small, flat areas. Each of these planes acts as a mirror, catching and reflecting light. As the viewer walks around the figure, the light shifts, and the surface appears to be real skin.

*The Age of Bronze* was first shown in an exhibition in Paris in 1877. Visiting critics were so startled by the lifelike effect of the statue that they accused Rodin of having made a mold of a living person. Although this accusation was ridiculous, the sculpture was not widely admired until 1884, when it was shown in London.

Rodin soon began to win recognition because a great many people disagreed with the critics. In 1880 he was commissioned to make a bronze door for the Museum of Decorative Arts in Paris. The door, called *The Gate of Hell*, was never cast during his lifetime. But some of Rodin's later works—*The Thinker*, for example—were based on figures first planned for the door.

Rodin constantly experimented with new techniques and new ideas. He created sculptures of expressive hands alone. Several times Rodin carved part of a body out of a block of stone, leaving much of the original block uncut and unpolished. He was also a portrait sculptor who made busts of some of the most important people of his time. Many young art-

When critics saw *The Age of Bronze* (1877), they thought Rodin had made a mold of a living person.

ists were inspired by Rodin to take up sculpture, a long-neglected art form.

On November 17, 1917, Rodin died. He was buried near his home at Meudon (near Paris), with *The Thinker* as the headstone on his grave. (A photograph of *The Thinker* is included in the article FRANCE, ART AND ARCHITECTURE OF in Volume F.) The Rodin Museum in Paris, which houses much of his work, was built in his honor.

Reviewed by JOSEPH RISHEL, JR.
Philadelphia Museum of Art

**RODNEY, CAESAR.** See DELAWARE (Famous People).

**ROGERS, WILL.** See OKLAHOMA (Famous People).

# ROLLER-SKATING

More than 2,000 years ago in Scandinavia, people started skating over ice as a means of transportation. The first known instance of skating on rollers was in 1760, in England. Unfortunately, the skates could only go straight ahead, and the inventor of the skates, Joseph Merlin, crashed into a mirror at one end of the ballroom where he was giving a demonstration. In 1819 a French inventor named Petitbled devised a skate with two, three, or four wheels in a straight line.

In 1863, James Plimpton, an American, made a four-wheeled skate, and the sport became popular.

The four-wheeled skate kept roller-skating popular for more than 100 years, before in-line skates, with four wheels in a straight line, made "roller blading" popular in the 1990's.

His skates permitted movement sideways as well as forward and backward. When it became apparent that roller skaters could now do all the movements that ice skaters could do, arenas for roller-skating were built. These attracted many people to the sport.

Roller-skate wheels used to be made of steel but are now made of other materials, including plastic, that are quieter and allow skaters to move more quickly and smoothly. Skates are generally riveted, bolted, or screwed to skating boots or bootlike shoes. Skating boots are cut higher and give greater support to the ankle than shoes.

The first contests in roller-skating were races. Speed-skating competitions are similar to ice-skating races, in which competitors follow a track with two corners and two straightaways. In racing, the skill lies in turning corners as swiftly as possible and in passing another skater.

Another form of competition is roller hockey, which is popular in Europe. It is played on a court similar to an ice-hockey rink. Two teams of five people attempt to move a ball into the opposing team's cage. Players control the ball with a stick with one curved end. A good player must have skating skill and stick-handling ability. Roller Derby is a United States sport involving contests of speed, skill, and endurance between two teams of roller skaters. Each team is made up of five men and five women. Women compete only against women, and men against men. Roller Derby contests usually take place in an arena with a specially constructed track. Points are scored when a member of one team overtakes and passes an opposing player. It is a rough game, and players wear protective clothing and helmets. A popular form of competition throughout the world is the artistic form of roller-skating. Contests are held in singles, in pairs, and in dance.

Roller disco developed from the dance styles popular at discotheques. Some disco dance patterns have been choreographed for skaters. But for the most part, roller disco is a freestyle form of dance that is spontaneously developed by the individual skater.

Roller-skating requires a flat, fairly smooth surface. The area must be rather large and uncrowded because the ease of rolling makes a skater travel far. Outdoor rinks usually have a skating surface of smooth concrete. Indoor rinks have floors of flake board, which is a pressed wood that is coated with plastic.

In skating, you control your balance differently from the way you do in walking. Roller-skating differs from walking in that you place your foot flat, rather than your heel followed by your toe. To maintain good balance, you bend your knees whenever you take a step and try to keep your body in line between your head and the foot that is off the floor.

Roller-skating provides good muscular exercise. Since no strenuous movements are required, roller-skating is suited for people of all ages and physical conditions.

GEORGE F. WERNER
Former United States Dance-Skating Champion

# ROMAN CATHOLIC CHURCH

The Roman Catholic Church is one of the three major forms of Christianity. It is also the world's single largest organized religious group, with about 1 billion Catholics worldwide. The Roman Catholic faith is based on the teachings of Jesus Christ, who lived in Palestine about 2,000 years ago. The church is headed by the pope, also known as the bishop of Rome, who governs it in communion with more than 2,000 Roman Catholic bishops around the world (including cardinals, who typically are ordained bishops). It is headquartered in Vatican City, a tiny city-state in Rome.

▶ BELIEFS

Roman Catholics, like other Christians, believe in one God who is a trinity, or a single deity made up of three divine persons: the Father (or Creator), the Son (or Word), and the Holy Spirit. While Catholics accept the trinity as a mystery that cannot be fully understood, they do believe it to be the source of energy and goodness that created the universe, as well as that which inspires love and compassion in humans.

Catholics believe that the Son of God became a human being, Jesus of Nazareth, who became known as Jesus the Christ (messiah or anointed one). Jesus was born of Mary, a Jewish girl who Catholics believe was specially chosen by God. Jesus grew to manhood, preached the gospel, and was crucified (executed by being nailed to a cross) by the Roman authorities occupying Jerusalem at the time. Catholics believe that he was raised from the dead by God the Father and eventually ascended into heaven. They further believe that the life, death, and resurrection of Jesus made it possible for people to be saved from sin.

Sin, according to the Catholic Church, is disobedience toward God and lack of trust in his goodness. The fact that people are born with the capacity for this is considered original sin. Other categories of sin include mortal and venial. Mortal sin, the more serious of the two, includes such actions as premeditated murder. Examples of venial sins are lying, cheating, and stealing.

Catholics also believe in an afterlife and think that those who have committed mortal sins will be in hell when they die if they have not sought and received God's forgiveness. For centuries the church taught that hell was an actual place of eternal—and physical—suffering, but not all Catholics today share this view. Some believe that hell represents complete separation from God.

In 2001, Pope John Paul II created 44 new cardinals at a Mass in Vatican City. The pope is the head of the Roman Catholic Church, the world's largest organized religious group.

Heaven is the opposite. It is defined by the church as "the ultimate end and fulfillment of the deepest human longings, the state of supreme, definitive happiness," as well as "the blessed community of all who are perfectly incorporated into Christ." Before one reaches heaven, however, atonement for sin is often believed to be necessary. Catholics call this process—or place—purgatory.

Catholics regard their church as Christ's continuing presence on Earth. That is, it is not

Baptism, one of seven sacraments in the Catholic church, represents the washing away of original sin.

merely a human institution but a holy entity, led by the Holy Spirit, that is part of God's plan for salvation. Catholics also contend that the church is infallible (free from error) when it teaches matters of faith and morals, and that the pope, as Christ's representative on Earth, can speak for the whole church when proclaiming its central teachings.

This belief in the church's infallibility is based on the doctrine of apostolic succession. Apostolic succession means that the spiritual authority granted by Christ to the Apostles (his original followers) has been passed on to all popes and bishops since then. The Apostles included Saint Peter (?–A.D. 64), who is traditionally considered the first pope.

The pope heads an organization that also includes ordained priests—men who receive their spiritual authority from a bishop. All are viewed as mediators (go-betweens) joining Catholics and God. They are part of a vast global network of parish communities, religious orders, schools, colleges, universities, seminaries, embassies, hospitals, orphanages, and other charitable and religious agencies. The local bishop presides over a **diocese** (a regional religious community) that consists of **parishes** (individual congregations), which are headed by priests. Residing within the boundaries of the diocese are also independent religious groups (orders) such as Jesuits (priests), the Dominicans (monks and nuns), and the Sisters of Mercy (nuns). Nuns are women who, like bishops and priests, have taken vows of poverty, chastity, and obedience, and have devoted their lives to God and the church. They are not allowed to

marry or have families. Nuns often live together in groups in a convent, while priests live in church rectories as well as in private and communal residences.

The doctrines of the Catholic church are based in part on the Bible, Christianity's most sacred book. The Bible consists of the Old Testament—the core writings of Judaism—and the New Testament. The New Testament is made up of the Gospels (four "books" detailing the life and teachings of Jesus), the writings of Saint Paul (?–A.D. 67), the books containing stories of Jesus' immediate followers, and the Revelation of Saint John the Divine.

Catholic beliefs are also a reflection of the ancient creeds that emerged during the early days of Christianity. These creeds include an emphasis on a holy communion of saints, or community of Christians in heaven, which Catholics believe is united in prayer on their behalf. Catholic creeds also stress the importance of Jesus' mother, Mary, who is also called the Blessed Virgin Mary. Catholics believe that she was conceived free of original sin (a doctrine called the Immaculate Conception) and that after her life on Earth she was taken up, body and soul, into heaven (a doctrine known as the Assumption).

### ▶ PRACTICES

The main form of worship in the Catholic church is the Mass. This is a communal service that revolves around specific acts of public worship (liturgies) that include prayers, rituals, hymns, and scriptural readings. Catholics are expected to attend Mass each Saturday night or Sunday (the Christian sabbath), although they may choose to attend more frequently, since Masses are offered every day of the year. Mass is presided over by a priest and includes the Liturgy of the Word, which is the proclamation and preaching of the scriptures, and the Liturgy of the **Eucharist**. The latter, also known as Holy Communion, is viewed as the transformation of bread and wine into the body and blood of Christ (which is consumed by the congregation). It is believed that Jesus instituted the Eucharist the night before his death, instructing his followers to "Do this in remembrance of me." This belief in Christ's real presence in the Eucharist makes the Mass a solemn and wondrous ritual for Catholics.

The Eucharist is one of seven sacraments in the Catholic church. The others are baptism, penance, confirmation, marriage, holy orders, and anointing of the sick.

**Baptism**, which usually takes place in infancy, represents one's entry into the church and the washing away of original sin. During this ceremony, prayers are said and the head is sprinkled with holy water. **Penance**, or the sacrament of reconciliation, takes place when a person confesses his or her sins to a priest and receives absolution (forgiveness in the eyes of God and the church). Like Holy Communion, penance can be repeated many times. **Confirmation** is the completion of the sacrament of baptism. It is a mature expression of faith that usually takes place when a person reaches adolescence. **Marriage** takes place when a man and woman are united as husband and wife, with the blessing of the church and God. The sacrament of **holy orders** is ordination to the priesthood, which is restricted to men. **Anointing of the sick** usually takes place when a person is very sick or close to death. During this sacrament, a priest prays over a person and anoints him or her with oil. It is believed that this sacrament strengthens the soul and grants forgiveness of sins.

What Catholics ultimately seek through the sacraments is God's grace—which they believe is the experience of sharing in God's life. Catholics believe they can become holy and enter into God's presence for all eternity by repeatedly accepting this offer of grace. Catholics also believe that grace is offered through Mass, and through prayer, meditation, and good works.

At the same time, Catholics affirm the concept of free will, which means that the individual can accept or reject the gift of grace. To accept grace, one must choose to follow Christ in his or her day-to-day thoughts and actions. This means showing love, kindness,

**Catholics believe that on Pentecost, the Holy Spirit descended upon Christ's Apostles as tongues of fire and enabled them to speak in many languages.**

and compassion toward others, particularly those in need.

▶ **HISTORY**

The path that Christianity would take first became apparent on the Pentecost following Christ's death. (At the time, Pentecost was solely a Jewish feast). Christians believe that when Christ's Twelve Apostles gathered on that day, the Holy Spirit descended upon them as tongues of fire, enabling them to speak in many languages. As the result, according to the Bible, the early church was able to spread Jesus' teachings far and wide.

The stage was set for what followed: a dramatic expansion of Christianity to the cities and towns on the coasts of the Mediterranean, then to Rome itself and the larger empire. Saint Paul (an early convert) and his fellow evangelists (heralds of the Gospel) embarked on long journeys to proclaim the Gospel to Asia Minor and Greece and perhaps as far as Spain.

Because Christianity was illegal in the Roman Empire, groups of Christians met in secret on the Lord's Day, the first day of the week, often in private homes. Over time, as Christian communities sprang up across the empire, the church developed a three-tiered ministry of bishop (the supervisor and chief teacher of the community), presbyter (or priest, the leader of local worship), and dea-

con (the person responsible for organizing the charitable works of the church, especially the care of widows and orphans).

During the first three centuries of the Christian era, Christians lived under the threat of persecution by the Roman Empire. Some Romans feared and despised them because they would not worship the Roman gods or the emperor. Nor, for a time, would Christians serve in the imperial army. Perhaps most troubling to the Roman authorities was the fact that Christians were able to convert so many slaves and women, including the wives and mistresses of some of the senators. Because of this, Christians were considered dangerous to the state, and some were tortured and killed. They became known as martyrs. The first persecutions occurred under Nero (37–68) in A.D. 64. The last (and worst) occurred under Diocletian (245–313), running from 303 to 305.

Diocletian was eventually succeeded as Roman emperor by Constantine (280?–337), who helped transform Christianity. Although Constantine was hardly a saint, he was a shrewd political leader who realized that Christianity was becoming stronger in the empire. He not only ended the persecutions but in 313 legalized the religion by issuing the Edict of Milan. In addition, he moved the imperial capital east to Byzantine, which he renamed Constantinople (present-day Istanbul), leaving the bishop of Rome, the pope, as the most powerful single individual in the Western part of the empire (today's western Europe).

Those who supported this move took matters a step further when they announced that Constantine had "donated" his political authority in the West to the pope. Although this was not true, many people believed it was, and the Roman papacy (office of the pope) became the final authority for the Christian community worldwide. This gave the Roman Catholic Church far greater strength and power. Its officials, including bishops and priests, as-

sumed important administrative positions in the empire.

By the reign of Emperor Theodosius (347–395) in 380, Roman Catholicism had become the state's official religion. (Now it was unwise not to be a Christian!) Although this represented significant gains for Christians, including the ability to shape culture and political institutions, a certain pure and deeply devotional quality was lost.

### Doctrines and Heresy

After Christianity became a public religion, much more attention was given to doctrinal questions. There were many strong opinions, and disputes were often accompanied by riots and street fighting. To address these matters, Constantine called the first official **ecumenical** (worldwide) council of the church in 325 at Nicaea. At issue were the doctrines of Arius (250–336), a priest of Alexandria, who taught that Jesus was not fully God but merely the "first-born" of all creatures. The bishops who assembled at Nicaea rejected Arius' teachings as **heresy** (unacceptable beliefs) and formulated their own creed that recognized the full divinity of Christ. This, called the Nicene Creed, is still recited by Catholics today.

During the next 500 years, seven more ecumenical councils expanded the basic doctrines of the Nicene Creed. Councils held in Constantinople (381), Ephesus (431), and Chalcedon (451) further explored the beliefs

Many early Christians were persecuted and killed because they would not worship the Roman gods or emperor.

about Christ, the Trinity, and Mary. These councils helped bring about agreement on matters of faith between Christianity in the East (the Middle East and Asia Minor) and in the West (Europe and North Africa), but other factors weakened the sense of unity between these two groups.

These factors included papal claims to supreme religious and political power. In the East, the Christian patriarchs and bishops made no such claims. In the West, however, the papacy not only claimed spiritual and religious authority over all Christian bishops (in both the East and West), but it believed itself to be the ultimate political authority as well. Neither claim was recognized by the patriarchs of the Eastern churches. From the time of Constantine, therefore, the Roman Catholic Church—the form Christianity took in the West—has been somewhat different from Christianity in the East, which came to be known as Eastern Orthodoxy.

### The Christianization of Europe

In the West, the Roman Empire began collapsing in the 400's. Tribal peoples—Goths, Huns, and Vandals—who lived beyond the borders of the empire joined the Roman armies, first as soldiers, then as officers. They eventually launched full-scale assaults on the empire; the Visigoths sacked Rome itself in 410. By the end of the century the empire had crumbled, and the church remained as the one great institution capable of maintaining order and preserving civilization.

Three of the church's great saints—Augustine, Jerome, and Benedict—led the way in preserving and Christianizing the classical art, literature, and philosophy that Europe had inherited from ancient Greece and Rome. Saint Augustine (354?–430), Bishop of Hippo in North Africa, produced many influential theological writings, including a Christian philosophy of history, *The City of God*, and *The Confessions*. Saint Jerome (331?–420) translated the Greek Bible into Latin. This translation became the commonly accepted, or Vulgate, text of Christian Europe for almost 1,000 years. Saint Benedict of Nursia (480?–547) founded a monastic order. This was a community of men called monks who lived in seclusion from the world in a common dwelling called a monastery and who followed the "Rule" Benedict had established.

Saint Augustine, Bishop of Hippo in North Africa, produced many important Christian writings. These included *The City of God* and *The Confessions*.

Benedict's Rule was a set of regulations governing monastic life. The monks took vows of obedience to the head of the community (the abbot) and devoted themselves to constant prayer, manual labor (farming in particular), and the transcribing of ancient Greek, Roman, and Christian texts. The Order of Saint Benedict, or the Benedictines, as these monks were known, established monasteries first in Italy and then throughout Europe. During the early years of the Middle Ages (500–1500), they were among the few places in Europe where both Christian teaching and classical culture were preserved.

Eventually the monasteries produced missionaries (and often a pope), who devoted their lives to spreading the Christian faith. Saint Patrick (389?–461), called the Apostle of Ireland, established a **bishopric** (territory administered by a bishop) in each of the provinces of Ireland. Saint Augustine of Canterbury (?–604) worked hard to convert the Anglo-Saxon invaders of England. Monks from Catholic Ireland preached the gospel throughout Europe. One of the greatest figures of the period was the English Benedic-

Charlemagne, crowned emperor of the Holy Roman Empire by Pope Leo III in 800, ruled over much of Europe. He converted many to Christianity.

tine monk Winfrid (680–754), or Boniface, known as the Apostle of Germany.

As the monks promoted Roman Catholic Christianity in western Europe, a new religion with global ambitions arose in Arabia. This was called Islam and was founded by the prophet Mohammed. In the 600's and early 700's, the Muslims (followers of Islam) conquered vast territories of the eastern world, with the exception of Constantinople. They entered Spain in 711 and invaded southern France. But their attack on France—and the northern regions of Europe—was halted by the victory of the Frankish ruler Charles Martel (689?–741) at Tours in 732.

In 751 the son and successor of Charles Martel, Pepin (714?–768), was consecrated king by Saint Boniface (675?–754) and was reconsecrated and crowned by Pope Stephen III (720–772) in 754. Thus began an alliance between the papacy and France that helped shape medieval Europe. When Rome was threatened by the Lombards (a Germanic people), the pope called upon the Franks for assistance. Pepin responded by invading Italy, driving out the Lombards and handing over the conquered lands—later known as the Papal States—to the pope. The papacy now controlled a sovereign (self-ruled) state as well as the church, and the pope was considered a king in his own right. Not surprisingly, this meant that some of those who wanted to be pope were more interested in power and wealth than in spiritual matters.

### The Medieval Church: 800–1500

Although the pope had become a monarch of sorts, it was Charlemagne (742?–814), Pepin's son and successor, who built up the vast Frankish kingdom and controlled the political destiny of Europe. Yet the popes wanted to establish more political power. To make this point, Pope Leo III (750?–816) dramatically summoned Charlemagne to Rome in 800 and crowned him emperor of the Holy Roman Empire on Christmas Day. The symbolism of this was clear: All political authority must be received from the pope, who was to be considered both the spiritual and political head of Christendom, or the Christian civilization of the West.

Charlemagne rejected the pope's boldest claims to political authority, although he built a truly Christian state and advanced the church's interests. When Charlemagne died, so did his plans for the Christian world. However, the Holy Roman Empire was revived in 962 with the coronation of Otto I (912–73), and it lasted until 1806.

The 800's were chaotic. The Danes overran England, Ireland, and northern Europe, demolishing monasteries and murdering Christians, and they remained a threat to Christendom for about 100 years. Muslim armies invaded France and Italy; in 846, they plundered the basilicas (churches) of Saint Peter and Saint Paul in Rome. Europe was devastated by political disorder and civil war. Education and discipline all but disappeared among the clergy.

Affairs within the church decayed as well. The roots of the evil lay in feudalism. Under this system, bishoprics and monasteries were in the domain of overlords, and laymen (usually nobles, princes, or the king) had the power to appoint bishops (a practice called **lay investiture**). As a result, greedy and immoral noblemen often became bishops, based primarily on political loyalty. Also, several of the popes of the 800's and 900's disgraced the papacy with their immoral lifestyles, particularly Pope John XII (936?– 64).

## Papal Reform

Many Christians were dismayed and scandalized by these developments, and a powerful reform movement originated in the Benedictine monastery of Cluny, founded in 910. The abbots of Cluny had a great influence on popes and kings. With the election of Leo IX (1002–54), who was pope from 1049–1054, a new age dawned for the church. Pope Leo took measures to eliminate **simony** (the sale of sacred things) and lay investiture. The greatest of the reforming popes, however, was Hildebrand, Gregory VII (1020?– 85), who served as pope from 1073–85.

Gregory's accomplishments were many. He continued the development of canon law (the body of law regulating church governance) and also produced documents that specifically defined the obligations of Catholics and the rights of the pope. These rights included the power to eliminate uncooperative rulers. Gregory proved this when Emperor Henry IV (1050–1106) refused to abolish lay investiture and give up control of his bishops. Gregory responded by deposing (taking away the right to rule) and excommunicating (cutting off from the church) Henry.

The result proved a huge political and moral victory for the church. In 1077, Henry journeyed to the castle in Canossa, Italy, where the pope was staying, fell to his knees in the snow, and begged the Pope's forgiveness (which Gregory granted). These and other events that occurred while Gregory was pope sparked a great revival of religion and culture that was the crowning achievement of medieval Christianity.

By the 1200's Roman Catholicism was in the midst of a Golden Age—a time when the Catholic view of the world was reflected in many areas. These included architecture (as in the great cathedrals of Europe) and education (the Catholic universities in Paris, Bologna, Cambridge, and Oxford). The 1200's also saw the rise of two great religious orders (organizations)—the Friars Preachers, or the Dominicans, founded by Saint Dominic (1170?–1221), and the Friars Minor, or the Franciscans, founded by Saint Francis of Assisi (1182–1226). The monks of both orders traveled throughout western Europe and preached in its growing cities, serving the poor and the sick.

The Dominicans, who were scholars, also produced one of Christianity's greatest theologians, Saint Thomas Aquinas (1225?–74). Thomas, influenced by the Greek philosopher Aristotle, created a brilliant system of thought that became known as Thomism, which still influences church teachings.

For all its glories, Christendom was not considered a total success; among its failures was the split between the Christian churches of the West and the East. This split, known as the Great Schism, occurred in 1054, as the old tensions between Rome and Constantinople (the center of Eastern Orthodoxy) reached the breaking point with the excommunication of Michael Caerularius, the Patriarch of Constantinople.

Many Christians also consider the Crusades a black mark on the record of Christendom. In 1071 Jerusalem fell to the Turks, who

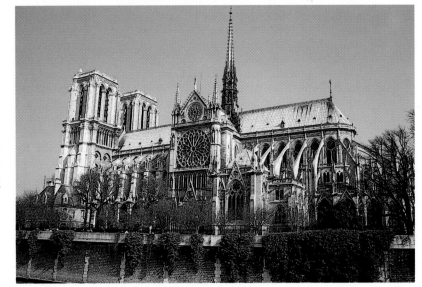

The cathedral of Notre Dame in Paris, begun in 1163, was built at a time when all of Europe was Roman Catholic.

The Crusades were a series of wars fought in the name of Christianity that were launched in 1095. The goal was to recapture the Holy Land from the Turks.

Medieval Christian society revolved around both worldly and spiritual power. By the end of the 1200's, however, the emperors and kings were increasingly unwilling to obey the pope, especially in political affairs. The political importance of the papacy declined further when Clement V (1264–1314), a Frenchman, was elected as pope in 1305 and never moved to Rome. Instead, he took up residence in Avignon, in southern France. Of the 24 cardinals he created, 22 were French. This became known as the Avignon papacy, which lasted for 70 years. All seven Avignon popes were Frenchmen. The papacy had become a puppet of France.

About 1348 a great plague called the Black Death struck Europe, and millions perished. Its damaging effect upon the church cannot be measured. The ranks of the clergy were seriously reduced. In the effort to replace those who died, men who had little preparation were ordained priests. With the decrease in the number of monks, the great monastic estates fell into ruin. The total effect was a lessening of religious feeling and a lowering of moral standards. An uneducated and greedy clergy was not qualified to guide people through such difficult times.

In 1377 the pope, encouraged by Saint Catherine of Siena (1347–80), returned to Rome from Avignon. The exile in Avignon had greatly weakened the papacy, leading to an embarrassing and confusing breakdown within the church. This, known as the Western Schism, was a period in which three separate people claimed the papacy. (Each man called the other two "anti-popes.") The matter was finally resolved when a council of cardinals met in Constance from 1414 to 1418 and demanded the resignation of all three popes. They then elected Martin V (1368–1431), who reigned as pope between 1417 and 1431, bringing the schism to an end.

were Muslims and persecuted the Christians. Pope Urban II (1042?–99) launched the First Crusade in 1095 to recover the Holy Sepulchre, the tomb of Christ in the holy city. The Second Crusade followed in 1147, the Third Crusade in 1189, and a disastrous Fourth Crusade in 1202. Only the First Crusade achieved its goal, but all included the rape and torture of Muslims and the destruction of sacred places.

Another unfortunate consequence of Christendom was the papal Inquisition, which was launched to identify and persecute heretics (those who did not agree with church teachings). Torture was sometimes used to force confessions, and persons found guilty were given to the state for execution.

The church's increasing demands for money were also widely resented—particularly because the money came from taxes that people paid on crops and land and the sale of indulgences (payments believed to release people from punishment for their sins). A growing spirit of **nationalism** (interest in one's own country) led to bitter feelings against the papacy. These feelings were further fueled by the widespread practice of papal **nepotism** (giving special favors to relatives). Popes frequently appointed members of their families to the Sacred College of Cardinals, made them princes, and married them into the royal houses of Europe.

## Renaissance and Reformation

The Renaissance began in Italy about 1300 and gradually developed in other European countries. This period, which would last about 300 years, saw a cultural rebirth in Europe. Scholars rediscovered the classical literature and arts of ancient Greece and Rome. The development of the printing press made books (including the Bible) widely available and fostered the spread of new ideas. People began to question certain practices established by the medieval church, paving the way for the Protestant Reformation.

Martin Luther (1483–1546), an ordained German Augustinian friar, started this revolution. Although he was motivated primarily by religious concerns, the movement he sparked also influenced European political structures and alliances. Religiously, Luther came to believe that human beings are utterly incapable of achieving their own salvation, even with the help of the church. Only the undeserved gift of faith, bestowed directly by God, could redeem the sinner.

Luther also translated the Bible from Latin into German, the language of his people, which made them less dependent upon the clergy for interpretation. This also made them less likely to see themselves as subjects of the pope and Germany a territory of the Holy Roman Empire. Rather, they began to see Germany as a separate nation, important in its own right.

This sense of nationalism would quickly replace religious unity, not only in Germany but in France, Holland, Switzerland, England, and elsewhere in Europe—and, subsequently, in the United States of America. In England, for example, King Henry VIII (1491–1547) decided to reject papal authority and make himself head of the English church after Pope Clement VII (1478–1534) refused to grant him a divorce.

Reformation was not limited to Protestants alone. The Roman Catholic Church underwent a Counter-Reformation during the 1500's to correct abuses, to reaffirm the basic theological principles that had been challenged by the Protestants, and to change the way some of these principles were applied.

Most reforms of the Counter-Reformation were formalized by the Council of Trent and the 19th ecumenical council of the Roman Catholic Church. The Council of Trent, which met three times in 18 years (1545–63), was a turning point for the church. The official decrees of Trent focused on the centrality of the church, the effectiveness of the sacraments, the legitimacy of the ordained priesthood, Purgatory, Mary, and the veneration of saints. It also focused on the role of the church in interpreting the Bible and the doctrine of apostolic succession.

Reform within the church was also brought about by others. These included the Jesuits, a religious order (also known as the Society of Jesus) that was founded by Saint Ignatius Loyola (1491–1556). Marked by intellectual excellence and strict discipline, the order was a fitting response to the issues of the day.

Trent's program of reform failed, however, to bring the Roman Catholic princes of Europe in line with papal policy. They continued to think of their worldly power as absolute,

Saint Ignatius Loyola, a key figure in the Counter-Reformation of the 1500's, founded a religious order of men known as the Jesuits.

# POPES OF THE ROMAN CATHOLIC CHURCH

The pope's titles are bishop of Rome, vicar of Jesus Christ, successor of Saint Peter, prince of the Apostles, supreme pontiff of the Universal Church, patriarch of the West, primate of Italy, archbishop and metropolitan of the Roman Province, and sovereign of the State of Vatican City.

The names of doubtful popes and antipopes, or pretenders, are in italics.

| Year of Conse-cration | Name of Pope | Year of Conse-cration | Name of Pope | Year of Conse-cration | Name of Pope | Year of Conse-cration | Name of Pope |
|---|---|---|---|---|---|---|---|
| 42? | St. Peter | 483 | St. Felix II (III) | 757 | St. Paul I | 984 | *Boniface VII* |
| 67 | St. Linus | 492 | St. Gelasius I | 767 | *Constantine* | | (second time) |
| 76 | St. Cletus | 496 | Anastasius II | 768 | *Philip* | 985 | John XV |
| | (Anacletus) | 498 | St. Symmachus | 768 | Stephen III (IV) | 996 | Gregory V |
| 88 | St. Clement I | 498 | *Lawrence* | 772 | Adrian I | 997 | *John XVI* |
| 97 | St. Evaristus | 514 | St. Hormisdas | 795 | St. Leo III | 999 | Sylvester II |
| 105 | St. Alexander I | 523 | St. John I | 816 | Stephen IV (V) | 1003 | John XVII |
| 115 | St. Sixtus I | 526 | St. Felix III (IV) | 817 | St. Pascal I | 1004 | John XVIII |
| 125 | St. Telesphorus | 530 | Boniface II | 824 | Eugene II | 1009 | Sergius IV |
| 136 | St. Hyginus | 530 | *Dioscorus* | 827 | Valentine | 1012 | Benedict VIII |
| 140 | St. Pius I | 533 | John II | 827 | Gregory IV | 1012 | *Gregory* |
| 155 | St. Anicetus | 535 | St. Agapetus I | 844 | *John* | 1024 | John XIX |
| 166 | St. Soter | 536 | St. Silverius | 844 | Sergius II | 1032 | Benedict IX |
| 175 | St. Eleutherius | 537 | Vigilius | 847 | St. Leo IV | | (deposed) |
| 189 | St. Victor I | 556 | Pelagius I | 855 | Benedict III | 1045 | Sylvester III |
| 199 | St. Zephyrinus | 561 | John III | 855 | *Anastasius* | 1045 | Benedict IX |
| 217 | St. Calixtus I | 575 | Benedict I | 858 | St. Nicholas I | | (second time) |
| 217 | *St. Hippolytus* | 579 | Pelagius II | 867 | Adrian II | 1045 | Gregory VI |
| 222 | St. Urban I | 590 | St. Gregory I | 872 | John VIII | 1046 | Clement II |
| 230 | St. Pontian | 604 | Sabinian | 882 | Marinus I | 1047 | Benedict IX |
| 235 | St. Anterus | 607 | Boniface III | | (Martin II) | | (third time) |
| 236 | St. Fabian | 608 | St. Boniface IV | 884 | St. Adrian III | 1048 | Damasus II |
| 251 | St. Cornelius | 615 | St. Adeodatus I | 885 | Stephen V (VI) | 1049 | St. Leo IX |
| 251 | *Novatian* | | (Deusdedit) | 891 | Formosus | 1055 | Victor II |
| 253 | St. Lucius I | 619 | Boniface V | 896 | Boniface VI | 1057 | Stephen IX (X) |
| 254 | St. Stephen I | 625 | Honorius I | 896 | Stephen VI (VII) | 1058 | *Benedict X* |
| 257 | St. Sixtus II | 640 | Severinus | 897 | Romanus | 1059 | Nicholas II |
| 259 | St. Dionysius | 640 | John IV | 897 | Theodore II | 1061 | Alexander II |
| 269 | St. Felix I | 642 | Theodore I | 898 | John IX | 1061 | *Honorius II* |
| 275 | St. Eutychian | 649 | St. Martin I | 900 | Benedict IV | 1073 | St. Gregory VII |
| 283 | St. Caius | 654 | St. Eugene I | 903 | Leo V | 1080 | *Clement III* |
| 296 | St. Marcellinus | 657 | St. Vitalian | 903 | *Christopher* | 1086 | Victor III |
| 308 | St. Marcellus I | 672 | Adeodatus II | 904 | Sergius III | 1088 | Urban II |
| 309 | St. Eusebius | 676 | Donus | 911 | Anastasius III | 1099 | Pascal II |
| 311 | St. Miltiades | 678 | St. Agatho | 913 | Lando | 1100 | *Theodoric* |
| 314 | St. Sylvester I | 682 | St. Leo II | 914 | John X | 1102 | *Albert* |
| 336 | St. Mark | 684 | St. Benedict II | 928 | Leo VI | 1105 | *Sylvester IV* |
| 337 | St. Julius I | 685 | John V | 928 | Stephen VII | 1118 | Gelasius II |
| 352 | Liberius | 686 | Conon | | (VIII) | 1118 | *Gregory VIII* |
| 355 | *Felix II* | 687 | *Theodore* | 931 | John XI | 1119 | Calixtus II |
| 366 | St. Damasus | 687 | *Paschal* | 936 | Leo VII | 1124 | Honorius II |
| 336 | *Ursinus* | 687 | St. Sergius I | 939 | Stephen VIII (IX) | 1124 | *Celestine II* |
| 384 | St. Siricius | 701 | John VI | 942 | Marinus II | 1130 | Innocent II |
| 399 | St. Anastasius I | 705 | John VII | | (Martin III) | 1130 | *Anacletus II* |
| 401 | St. Innocent I | 708 | Sisinnius | 946 | Agapetus II | 1138 | *Victor IV* |
| 417 | St. Zozimus | 708 | Constantine | 955 | John XII | 1143 | Celestine II |
| 418 | St. Boniface I | 715 | St. Gregory II | 963 | Leo VIII | 1144 | Lucius II |
| 418 | *Eulalius* | 731 | St. Gregory III | 964 | Benedict V | 1145 | Eugene III |
| 422 | St. Celestine I | 741 | St. Zachary | 965 | John XIII | 1153 | Anastasius IV |
| 432 | St. Sixtus III | 752 | Stephen (II) | 973 | Benedict VI | 1154 | Adrian IV |
| 440 | St. Leo I | | (died before | 974 | *Boniface VII* | 1159 | Alexander III |
| 461 | St. Hilarius | | consecration) | 974 | Benedict VII | 1159 | *Victor IV* |
| 468 | St. Simplicius | 752 | Stephen II (III) | 983 | John XIV | 1164 | *Pascal III* |

| Year of Conse-cration | Name of Pope | Year of Conse-cration | Name of Pope |
|---|---|---|---|
| 1168 | *Calixtus III* | 1503 | Julius II |
| 1179 | *Innocent III* | 1513 | Leo X |
| 1181 | Lucius III | 1522 | Adrian VI |
| 1185 | Urban III | 1523 | Clement VII |
| 1187 | Gregory VIII | 1534 | Paul III |
| 1187 | Clement III | 1550 | Julius III |
| 1191 | Celestine III | 1555 | Marcellus II |
| 1198 | Innocent III | 1555 | Paul IV |
| 1216 | Honorius III | 1559 | Pius IV |
| 1227 | Gregory IX | 1566 | St. Pius V |
| 1241 | Celestine IV | 1572 | Gregory XIII |
| 1243 | Innocent IV | 1585 | Sixtus V |
| 1254 | Alexander IV | 1590 | Urban VII |
| 1261 | Urban IV | 1590 | Gregory XIV |
| 1265 | Clement IV | 1591 | Innocent IX |
| 1271 | Gregory X | 1592 | Clement VIII |
| 1276 | Innocent V | 1605 | Leo XI |
| 1276 | Adrian V | 1605 | Paul V |
| 1276 | John XXI | 1621 | Gregory XV |
| 1277 | Nicholas III | 1623 | Urban VIII |
| 1281 | Martin IV | 1644 | Innocent X |
| 1285 | Honorius IV | 1655 | Alexander VII |
| 1288 | Nicholas IV | 1667 | Clement IX |
| 1294 | St. Celestine V | 1670 | Clement X |
| 1294 | Boniface VIII | 1676 | Innocent XI |
| 1303 | Benedict XI | 1689 | Alexander VIII |
| 1305 | Clement V | 1691 | Innocent XII |
| 1316 | John XXII | 1700 | Clement XI |
| 1328 | *Nicholas V* | 1721 | Innocent XIII |
| 1334 | Benedict XII | 1724 | Benedict XIII |
| 1342 | Clement VI | 1730 | Clement XII |
| 1352 | Innocent VI | 1740 | Benedict XIV |
| 1362 | Urban V | 1758 | Clement XIII |
| 1370 | Gregory XI | 1769 | Clement XIV |
| 1378 | Urban VI | 1775 | Pius VI |
| 1378 | *Clement VII* | 1800 | Pius VII |
| 1389 | Boniface IX | 1823 | Leo XII |
| 1394 | *Benedict XIII* | 1829 | Pius VIII |
| 1404 | Innocent VII | 1831 | Gregory XVI |
| 1406 | Gregory XII | 1846 | Pius IX |
| 1409 | *Alexander V* | 1878 | Leo XIII |
| 1410 | *John XXIII* | 1903 | St. Pius X |
| 1417 | Martin V | 1914 | Benedict XV |
| 1431 | Eugene IV | 1922 | Pius XI |
| 1439 | *Felix V* | 1939 | Pius XII |
| 1447 | Nicholas V | 1958 | John XXIII |
| 1455 | Calixtus III | 1963 | Paul VI |
| 1458 | Pius II | 1978 | John Paul I |
| 1464 | Paul II | 1978 | John Paul II |
| 1471 | Sixtus IV | 2005 | Benedict XVI |
| 1484 | Innocent VIII | | |
| 1492 | Alexander VI | | |
| 1503 | Pius III | | |

Source: *Annuario Pontificio (Pontifical Yearbook)*.

and they treated the church as their subject. After the Treaties of Westphalia (1648) following the Thirty Years' War, the pope and the church were no longer forces in the public life of Europe, even in Catholic states.

Still, Catholicism was growing, aided by foreign missionary activity. Spanish missionaries brought the gospel to the New World. Jesuit missionaries reached Africa, India, Japan, and, later, China.

**The Challenge of the Enlightenment**

In the 1600's a system of thought called Deism arose in England. Deists denied that religion was revealed by God and defended "natural" religion based on human reason. Deist ideas quickly spread to France, where they were promoted by Voltaire (1694–1778), Diderot (1713–84), and other intellectuals. By the mid-1700's, the credibility of the church in France had declined even further. Still, the church clung tightly to its alliance with the French monarchy and continued to oppose the new wave of democracy. As a result, it experienced great upheaval during the French Revolution of 1789. The French revolutionaries stole or destroyed church property, imprisoned or executed priests, and demolished monasteries. Their goal was to de-Christianize France, particularly during the Reign of Terror (1793–94).

In 1801, Emperor Napoleon Bonaparte signed an agreement with Rome recognizing the freedom of the church in France. However, this agreement did not last, and the resulting struggle led to the imprisonment of Pope Pius VII (1742–1823). Napoleon's conquering armies carried the ideas of the Revolution with them across Europe. The church, faced with the loss of its religious orders and great universities, embarked upon an enormous task of restoration that continued throughout the 1800's.

▶ **RECENT HISTORY**

As the church struggled to regain its stature, new challenges arose. One of them, modernity, was characterized by the rise of free thinking and the belief that people need not answer to any outside authority (including the church). A number of ideas and trends played a part in this, including Darwinism (the theory of human evolution), materialism (the denial of the importance or

In Indonesia, a bishop and church members gather for Mass. Over the past several decades, the church has increasingly adapted its practices to various cultures.

even the existence of spiritual reality), and atheism (disbelief in God). Socialism, an economic and philosophical system that sought to end the exploitation of workers by capitalists, targeted Christianity as oppressive.

Although some Catholics supported modernity, the church did not. In 1864 Pope Pius IX (1792–1878) issued the famous Syllabus of Errors. This condemned many aspects of modernity. Pius also called the First Vatican Council in 1869, the first ecumenical council since the Council of Trent, which decreed that the pope is infallible.

Pius' successor, Pope Leo XIII (1810–1903), further addressed issues of modernity in his **encyclicals** (letters written to the whole church). One of the most significant encyclicals was *Rerum Novarum* (*Of New Things*), written in 1891. It is a statement of the social teachings of the church. Leo's ability to understand and deal with the issues of the day proved him to be a true spiritual leader.

Meanwhile, other changes were brewing. Following the start of the Franco-Prussian War in 1870, the church lost its papal states to Italian nationalists who sought to unify the country. In protest, Pius IX became a voluntary "prisoner of the Vatican." This was addressed in 1929 by the Lateran Treaty, which established Vatican City—a small separate and independent territory that extends for acres around Saint Peter's Basilica.

In the United States, the church was thriving. As a result of large-scale immigration from Europe, there were many new converts, religious orders, schools, and hospitals. Like the modern state, Roman Catholicism grew more centralized and bureaucratic.

### The Second Vatican Council

Vatican II changed the church's attitude toward the modern world. This gathering of approximately 2,300 Catholic bishops opened in Vatican City in 1962. By the time it adjourned approximately three years later, it had produced 16 official documents which revolutionized Roman Catholicism.

Though the church had been undergoing reforms for decades, Pope John XXIII (1881–1963), who called the council, did more to change the image of the church in the modern world than any previous pope. The council declared the church's respect for different cultures and religions and acknowledged the need for collaboration. It also recognized that in order to spread Christ's message even further, it was necessary to adapt church practices to differing customs, rituals, and cultural values.

In addition, greater importance was placed on "full conscious and active participation" in the Mass among Catholics. That meant, among other things, that Masses could be held in the language of the people, not in Latin as they had been.

An increased emphasis on political activism and human rights was another result of Vatican II. Pope John Paul II (1920–2005) himself hastened the collapse of Soviet communism by his support of Poland's Solidarity movement, and by his vigorous moral and spiritual leadership in general. In many parts of the world today, Catholics are among the leading advocates of democratic values and human rights.

Following John Paul's death, 115 cardinals from 52 countries met on April 19, 2005, and elected Cardinal Joseph Ratzinger as the Supreme Pontiff, or 265th pope of the Roman Catholic Church.

Cardinal Ratzinger chose the title Pope Benedict XVI. The new pope, who worked closely with John Paul II for over two decades, was born in Germany in 1927. He is expected to continue John Paul II's emphasis on the Roman Catholic Church's traditional values.

Reviewed by KEVIN MADIGAN
Harvard Divinity School

Romanesque architecture was well suited for castles and churches. Many such structures from the 1000's and 1100's stand today, complete with sculptural embellishment. *Left:* The church of St. Astor, in Coblenz, Germany. *Right:* Detail from a column in Autun, France.

## ROMANESQUE ART AND ARCHITECTURE

One of the most important styles of European art that developed during the Middle Ages was called Romanesque. This style began during the 1000's and lasted for more than 200 years.

Prior to the Romanesque period, powerful rulers like Charlemagne and Otto the Great helped to lay the foundations for this new style of art. They ordered their builders to design palaces and churches similar to ancient Roman temples. Romanesque architecture is massive, low, and solid-looking. Round Roman arches, thick walls, and small windows are typical of the buildings. Churches were built in the shape of a cross, using the basilica (a type of Roman building) as the basis for the design. Another important feature of Romanesque architecture was the use of a separate bell tower, or campanile, that was built beside the main church.

Although the new architecture used Roman elements in its design, it incorporated other styles as well. Germanic, Asian, Byzantine, Muslim, and Christian forms contributed to its unique appearance.

Both painting and sculpture in the Romanesque age were decorative and highly or-namental, often incorporating strange entwining plant forms and grotesque imaginary animals.

Romanesque painting followed the traditions set by the spiritual art of the Byzantine Empire. Naturalism—painting things as they might really appear—was not emphasized; the artists concentrated mainly on expressive color and rhythmic compositions in order to stir religious emotions within the viewer. Many murals were painted during this period, often in fresco (on fresh, wet plaster), and the production of illuminated manuscripts increased.

In sculpture, for the first time since the days of the ancient Roman world, monumental work was created. Most of the work was religious—statues depicting biblical scenes and statues of saints and martyrs. Sculpture rarely existed apart from architecture. Most Romanesque sculpture decorates the porches, doors, and columns of churches.

Although there were slight variations in each country, the Romanesque style dominated Western Europe until it was replaced by the Gothic style.

Reviewed by LEE HALL
President Emerita
Rhode Island School of Design

See also ARCHITECTURE; CATHEDRALS; SCULPTURE.

# ROMANIA

Romania (sometimes spelled Rumania) is a nation located on the Balkan Peninsula of southeastern Europe. What is now the country of Romania was first settled in ancient times by a people called the Dacians. Later it became a part of the Roman Empire. Over the course of its history, the size of Romania has changed many times as a result of invasions, foreign occupation, and wars. Its present boundaries date from the peace treaties signed following World War I (1914–18). A Communist government came to power in Romania in 1947 and ruled until 1989, when it was overthrown by an anti-Communist revolution. A democratically elected government took office in 1990.

## ▶THE PEOPLE

The Romanians trace their origins to the original Dacian settlers and to the Romans, who colonized the region. Most of the people are ethnic Romanians. Hungarians, who make up nearly 8 percent of the population, and Germans, with about 1.5 percent, are the largest minority groups. They live mainly in the regions of Transylvania and Banat.

**Language and Religion.** Romanian is one of the Romance languages. Like French, Italian, Spanish, and Portuguese, it is derived from Latin, the language of the Romans. Romanian also contains words from the Slavic languages spoken by some of Romania's neighbors.

Most Romanians belong to the Romanian Orthodox Church. The Eastern Catholic (or Uniate) Church, the second largest religious group, was abolished in 1948 and its property was transferred to the Orthodox Church. There are also smaller numbers of Roman Catholics, Protestants, and Jews.

## ▶THE LAND

**Regions.** Romania is divided into six regions: Banat, Transylvania, Moldavia, Bukovina, Walachia, and Dobruja.

Villages dot the lush rolling hills in the northern part of Romania's Moldavia region. The land rises to the Carpathian Mountains, which can be seen in the background.

The Banat region is located in the southwestern corner of the country. Relatively small in area, it consists mainly of a flat, fertile plain.

Transylvania occupies an elevated plateau surrounded by mountains in central Romania. Its mineral and forest resources make it one of the richest parts of the country.

Moldavia, in the northeast, contains high mountains and fertile plains. Bukovina, on the northern edge of Moldavia, has forests and mountains in its northern section but slopes down to a lowland in the south.

The plains region of Walachia, bordering the Danube River, covers a large part of southern Romania. Dobruja, on the Black Sea coast, consists chiefly of marshy plains and hilly lowlands. The Danube River plain, or delta, is in this region. The delta is formed where the Danube turns northward.

**Rivers and Mountains.** The Danube River is Romania's most important waterway. The valley of the Danube also contains some of the most fertile soils in Europe. Except for its northern tributary (branch), the Prut, the Danube is Romania's only navigable river—that is, the only one that can be used by ships. Other tributaries include the Mures, the Jiu, the Olt, the Somes, and the Siret. A 40-mile (640-kilometer)-long canal links the Danube and the Black Sea.

There are a few natural harbors along the Black Sea coast, although most of the shoreline consists of crumbling cliffs and salty marshlands.

The Carpathian Mountains and the Transylvanian Alps (the southwestern extension of the Carpathian chain) stretch across central Romania roughly in the shape of a jagged triangle. Negoi Peak, in the Făgăraş Mountains of the Transylvania Alps, is the country's highest mountain.

**Climate and Natural Resources.** Romania is a land with great extremes of climate, ranging from very hot summers to windy, bitterly cold winters. The average January temperature in Bucharest, the capital, is about 9°F (–13°C). In July it rises to an average of 73°F (23°C). Rainfall is moderate, with most of the rain coming in May. During the months of July and August there are often periods of severe drought.

Romania's natural resources include fertile soils, which make more than 60 percent of its

Romania

land suitable for farming. Another 25 percent of the land, mainly in the Carpathian Mountains and Transylvania, is covered by forests. Romania has traditionally been one of Europe's leading petroleum producers, chiefly from the Ploeşti fields. Although much of this source has been depleted, new offshore deposits of oil and natural gas have been discovered in the Black Sea.

Salt, coal, and iron ore are mined commercially. Deposits of gold, silver, copper, and other minerals are found scattered throughout the mountainous regions.

▶ **THE ECONOMY**

After World War II, emphasis was placed on developing Romania's heavy industry. But agriculture continues to play an important role in the country's economy, and about one half of its people still live in rural (country) areas.

**Agriculture.** Agriculture employs more than 20 percent of the work force. The chief crops are corn, wheat, and other grains, potatoes, and fruits, including grapes for the country's important wine industry. Livestock, particularly sheep and cattle, are also raised.

**ROMANIA** is the official name of the country.

**LOCATION:** Balkan Peninsula in southeastern Europe.

**AREA:** 91,700 sq mi (237,500 km²).

**POPULATION:** 23,000,000 (estimate).

**CAPITAL AND LARGEST CITY:** Bucharest.

**MAJOR LANGUAGE:** Romanian.

**MAJOR RELIGION:** Romanian Orthodox.

**GOVERNMENT:** Republic. **Head of state**—president. **Head of government**—prime minister. **Legislature**—Parliament.

**CHIEF PRODUCTS: Agricultural**—corn, wheat, and other grains, potatoes, fruits (including wine grapes), livestock. **Manufactured**—refined petroleum products, petrochemicals, chemical fertilizers, steel, heavy machinery, locomotives, tractors, electrical products, processed foods, wine, textiles, clothing, shoes, timber and wood products. **Mineral**—petroleum and natural gas, salt, coal, iron ore.

**MONETARY UNIT:** Leu (1 leu = 100 bani).

When the Communist government came to power, the land was taken from the big land-owners. Part of it was divided among poor farm workers. The major part (about 90 percent), however, was taken over by the state. It established state farms, owned by the government; and collective farms (or agricultural co-operatives), in which the farmers pooled their land and equipment. Laws restoring private ownership of land were enacted in 1991.

**Industry.** Industry, including mining, provides some 60 percent of the country's income. Major industries include oil refining and the manufacture of petrochemicals and chemical fertilizers, steel, heavy machinery, locomotives, tractors, and electrical equipment. Food processing and the manufacture of textiles, clothing, and shoes are also of major importance. The country's forests supply timber and wood products.

▶CITIES

Bucharest is the capital and largest city of Romania. With a population of about 2 million, it is the commercial, industrial, and cultural center of the country. Before World War II, Bucharest was known as the Paris of the Balkans—a city of glittering palaces, hotels, cafés, and theaters. It remains a lovely city today, but the luxury for which it was noted is past.

Cluj is the second largest city. It is the capital of Transylvania, which was part of Hungary until the region was acquired by Romania after World War I. About 40 percent of its people are of Hungarian descent. Cluj is a major industrial and cultural center. Because of its location in the foothills of the Apuseni Mountains, it is a popular winter sports resort. The fruits and wines from the countryside around the city are considered among the best in Romania.

Constanta, on the Black Sea, is Romania's chief seaport. It is also the commercial center of the Dobruja region and the country's leading seaside resort. Eforie and Mamaia, small towns near Constanta, are also popular resorts. Jassy, the leading city of Moldavia, is famous for its university, Romania's oldest, and for its academies of art, music, and drama.

The Ploesti fields (*below left*) were long Romania's chief oil-producing area, but new oil deposits have been discovered offshore in the Black Sea. Romanians, like this farmer, claim descent from the ancient Dacians and from the Romans, who colonized the region.

Bucharest (*left*), Romania's capital and largest city, still retains the beauty that once earned it the name Paris of the Balkans, although it has kept little of its former luxury. The frescos, or wall paintings (*below*), in the Voronets monastery in Moldavia date from the 1400's. Considered among the finest examples of early Romanian art, they depict scenes from the Bible and from legend, including the story of St. George and the Dragon, seen at lower left.

## ▶ GOVERNMENT

Under the Communist government that ruled Romania until 1989, the Communist Party was "the leading political force of the whole of society," and it was the only legal political party. It was headed by a general secretary, who was the country's real political leader. This post was held by Nicolae Ceauşescu for some 25 years, until his death in the 1989 revolution.

A new Romanian government came to power following elections in 1990. It is led by a president, who is the head of state and the country's chief executive officer. A prime minister heads the Council of Ministers, or cabinet. The Parliament is the country's legislative body.

## ▶ HISTORY

**Early History.** During the A.D. 100's, Roman legions under the Emperor Trajan conquered and settled in the region called Dacia, northeast of the Danube River. The language and customs of Rome took root, and Dacia became one of the most prosperous provinces of the Roman Empire. Toward the end of the 200's, however, as the Roman Empire began to decline, Dacia was overrun by invading Goths, Huns, and Slavs. Beginning in the 800's, Magyars (Hungarians) swarmed eastward across the Carpathian Mountains. They conquered Transylvania, a territory that was to later be claimed by both Romanians and Hungarians.

**Turkish Rule.** Until the 1800's, what is now Romania consisted of two provinces, or principalities—Walachia and Moldavia (which in-

cluded the region of Bessarabia). By the end of the 1500's, both principalities had fallen under the rule of the expanding Ottoman Turkish Empire. Some grew rich under the Turks, but most of the people of the principalities lived in poverty.

During the 1700's and 1800's, the region became part of the battleground between warring Ottoman and Russian empires. In 1858, Walachia and Moldavia won some degree of independence from Ottoman rule. Alexandru Ion Cuza, a great landowner, was elected prince of Walachia and Moldavia.

Jubilant Romanians in Bucharest (*left*) celebrate the revolution in 1989 that overthrew the Communist regime of Nicolae Ceauşescu, who had ruled Romania since 1965. The hole in the Romanian flag carried by one of the men shows where the Communist emblem has been ripped out. A woman (*below*) rejoices in her country's freedom in a quieter but equally heartfelt manner.

**Romania United.** Cuza united the two provinces under the name of Romania in 1859. During his reign, Cuza made it easier for the peasants to own land, but in 1866, he was forced to abdicate, or give up the throne. In his place the Romanian government chose a German prince, Charles of Hohenzollern-Sigmaringen, who became king as Carol I.

Complete freedom from Turkish control was formally won at the end of the Russo-Turkish war, 1877–78, but it was a weakened Romania that emerged, for Bessarabia had been ceded to Russia in exchange for the much less desirable territory of Dobruja. Carol I played an important role in transforming Romania into a strong nation. Industries were established and railroads were built. Most of the power, however, still remained in the hands of the great landowners. A peasant revolt in 1907 was put down by the government with brutal severity.

**Expansion and Rise of Fascism.** During World War I, Romania sided with the Allies (led by Britain and France), who defeated the Central Powers (headed by Germany and Austria-Hungary). As a result of the peace treaties, Romania acquired Bessarabia from Russia, Bukovina from Austria, and Transylvania from Hungary—doubling both its area and population.

But the new territories were not a complete blessing. The government found it difficult to govern so many non-Romanian minorities. In addition, by 1930 Romania, economically, had

been caught up in the worldwide Great Depression. Carol II was crowned king in 1930, but his reign was marked by continuous intrigues and misunderstandings between himself and the two leading political parties. An organization called the Iron Guard grew up, which had strong sympathies with Nazi Germany and Fascist Italy. The years leading up to World War II were marred by violence and disorder.

**World War II and Communist Rule.** World War II broke out in 1939, and the following year the Soviet Union occupied Bessarabia and northern Bukovina. Romania lost northern Transylvania to Hungary and part of South Dobruja to Bulgaria. King Carol II was forced to abdicate in favor of his young son, Michael, but the country's real ruler was General Ion Antonescu, who established a military dictatorship. In June 1941, Romania entered the war as an ally of Germany. In August 1944, as Soviet armies advanced through Romania, Antonescu was overthrown and King Michael switched Romania to the side of the Allies. But he was unable to prevent the Soviet occupation of the country.

The first government established after World War II included some Communists. But in the 1946 elections, the Communists—backed by Soviet military forces—overwhelmed all opposition. Prominent anti-Communists were sentenced to prison, and Michael was forced to abdicate in 1947. In 1952, Gheorghe Gheorghiu-Dej, Romania's leading Communist, became chief of state. He was succeeded by Nicolae Ceaușescu in 1965. Ceaușescu's policies at first won acceptance, but his rule became increasingly tyrannical as the economy declined in the 1980's.

**Fall of Ceaușescu: Rise of Democracy.** Antigovernment demonstrations erupted in 1989 and soon developed into full-scale revolution. Ceaușescu and his wife, Elena, were tried and executed. Ion Iliescu was elected president in 1990, and a democratic constitution was adopted in 1991. Iliescu, leader of the newly formed Party of Social Democracy in Romania (PSDR), was re-elected in 1992.

Democratization proceeded slowly, mainly because of serious economic problems and ethnic conflicts. In 1996, Emil Constantinescu, leader of the National Peasant Party-Christian Democratic (NPPCD), was elected president. A new policy was instituted to guarantee the rights of ethnic Hungarians, and the nation applied for membership in the European Union (EU) and North American Treaty Organization (NATO). But economic hardships continued. In 2000, former president Iliescu was returned to power. Romania joined NATO in 2004. Later that year, Traian Basescu, representing the Justice and Truth Alliance Party, was elected president.

JAMES CHACE
Managing editor, *Foreign Affairs*
Reviewed by STEPHEN FISCHER-GALATI
Author, *Twentieth Century Rumania*

# ROMAN NUMERALS

If you had lived many centuries ago in ancient Rome, you would have written V to stand for the number five. The symbols V and 5 stand for the same thing—the idea of five. A symbol that stands for a number is called a **numeral**. The number symbols used by the Romans are called **Roman numerals**.

The seven basic Roman numerals are:

| I | 1 |
|---|---|
| V | 5 |
| X | 10 |
| L | 50 |
| C | 100 |
| D | 500 |
| M | 1,000 |

All other numbers are represented by combinations of these numerals. The numbers are written from left to right and are usually formed by adding numerals together. Seventeen, for example, is

$$X + V + I + I = XVII$$
$$10 + 5 + 1 + 1 = 17$$

Roman numerals were formed by subtracting as well as by adding numbers. For example, instead of adding four ones to make four—IIII—the Romans usually subtracted 1 from 5, writing IV. Using this general rule, the Romans were able to simplify many numbers, writing IX instead of VIIII for 9, and CD instead of CCCC for 400.

The origin of the Roman symbols is not known exactly. There are two main theories, for example, about how V developed. Some scholars say that five was first shown by holding up one hand with the thumb held apart from the fingers. The hand was imitated in drawings and was later simplified to V.

Another theory is that the X came from crossing out a row of 10 lines: ▱▭. Five could then be represented by half the X, or V.

Roman numerals are easy to work with when you want to add or subtract numbers, but multiplication and division are very awkward to carry out. This is the main reason Roman numerals are not used very often today.

CARL B. BOYER
Brooklyn College

See also MATHEMATICS; NUMERALS AND NUMERATION SYSTEMS.

*Jacob's Ladder*, by English poet and artist William Blake, has the quality of a dream or vision. Like other romantics, Blake was inspired by his imagination.

## ROMANTICISM

Romanticism was a major international movement that was influential in shaping modern views of art, literature, and music. It was at its height between 1798 and 1830 but came later in some countries, such as Italy, Spain, and the United States. It occurred first in art and literature and later in music. In part, romanticism was a reaction against the artistic styles of classical antiquity, which had been revived in the 1600's and 1700's as **neoclassicism**. Neoclassicists placed great importance on the power of reason as a way of discovering truth; indeed, the neoclassical era is often called the Age of Reason.

The romantics, in contrast, hoped to transform the world into a new Golden Age through the power of the imagination.

### ▶THEMES AND IDEAS

When the English poet and painter William Blake was asked whether he saw a round, shining ball of fire when the sun rose, he replied, "Oh no, no. I see an innumerable company of the heavenly host crying 'Holy, holy, holy is the Lord God Almighty!' " His response shows the importance the romantics placed on the imagination. For them, it was the quality that sets artists apart from other people and allowed them to express their emotions in their art. As exceptional individuals, artists were free to pursue their creativity, unrestrained by the demands of society.

The romantics developed a deep love of nature, which was thought to be mainly good and kind, in contrast to the corruption of society. Many romantic works take nature for their theme or setting. The dark side of nature, such as storms and fire, also fascinated the romantics. Through nature, artists could escape from an unsatisfying present into a better world.

Another escape route was into the past. The romantics were strongly attracted to the distant, the exotic, and the mysterious. They were drawn to the supernatural and to real and imaginary lands of long ago and far away. They rediscovered the heritage of the Middle Ages, collected folk songs and tales, and tried to understand dreams. In this way, romanticism opened up a wide range of new interests and injected into the arts a vitality and urge to experiment that laid the foundation for many later developments.

### ▶ROMANTICISM IN ART

Romanticism was more prominent in painting than in sculpture or architecture. Subjects for paintings were often taken from nature, but biblical, mythological, and supernatural sub-

This portrait of the composer Frédéric Chopin was painted by Eugène Delacroix. Both men were giants of the romantic movement in France. Chopin's pieces for piano greatly expanded the musical possibilities of that instrument. The Delacroix portrait has the expressive brushwork and dramatic lighting characteristic of romantic art.

In *The Cross on the Mountain*, German artist Caspar David Friedrich combines religious symbolism with the beauty of nature to create a solemn, mysterious mood.

jects were also used. Romantic painters generally used radiant colors and unrestrained, expressive brushwork, and showed a preference for curving lines and shapes.

Romantic art differed from place to place, even within the same country. In England, William Blake created dreamlike illustrations for his poetry. But the dominant English romantic style can be found in such landscapes as Thomas Gainsborough's *The Market Cart* (1786), John Constable's *Malvern Hall* (1809), and J.M.W. Turner's *Fire at Sea* (about 1834). These artists captured the beauty and power of nature, often using watercolors to give their paintings a feeling of freshness and immediacy.

The nature paintings of the German artist Caspar David Friedrich create a solemn, mysterious mood. Johann Friedrich Overbeck led a religious brotherhood of German painters, the Nazarenes, in Rome after 1810. Spain's most noted romantic painter is Francisco Goya, whose intense portraits, such as *The Young Girls* (1813), are remarkable for their flowing lines. The Swiss artist Henry Fuseli painted fantastic and nightmarish subjects. In France, Théodore Géricault and Eugène Delacroix painted wild and violent scenes. Another French artist, Théodore Rousseau, led the Barbizon School, a group of landscape painters who depicted rural life.

Beginning in the 1820's American romantic artists, inspired by the optimism of a young, rapidly growing nation, painted landscapes that glorified the country's natural beauty. One group of artists, including Thomas Cole and Asher Durand, painted scenic views of upper New York State and came to be called the Hudson River School.

▶ ROMANTICISM IN LITERATURE

Romanticism in literature was equally varied, developing many new forms. The emphasis on imagination and emotion led to the flourishing of **lyric** poetry—short poems that express personal emotion. The Gothic novel, with its emphasis on mystery and the supernatural, and the historical novel were popular prose forms. Least interest was shown in drama; many plays were written to be read rather than performed. The exception was in France, where the battle for romanticism was fought in the theater, the home of an established neoclassical tradition.

In England all the major romantic poets wrote lyric poetry, each in an individual voice. William Wordsworth and Samuel Taylor Coleridge published a collection of poems called *Lyrical Ballads* (1798). John Keats is famous for his odes, including "To Autumn" and "Ode to a Nightingale" (both written in 1819), as is Percy Bysshe Shelley. George Gordon, Lord Byron, wrote longer narrative poems, such as *Childe Harold's Pilgrimage* (1812). Of the poetry of William Blake, *Songs of Innocence* (1787) and *Songs of Experience* (1797) are the most widely read.

In Germany, romantic literature ranged widely from the difficult theories of Friedrich von Schlegel and his brother August Wilhelm to the fantastic tales of Johann Ludwig Tieck and E.T.A. Hoffmann. The outstanding lyric poets were Novalis (Friedrich von Hardenberg) and, later, Heinrich Heine.

The greatest romantic poet in France was Victor Hugo, whose vast output also included novels, such as *Les Misérables* (1862), and plays. Alfred de Musset wrote both plays and poems, while Alphonse de Lamartine is known for his touching nature poetry. Alexandre Dumas was the author of many lively tales, among them *The Three Musketeers* (1844). Italy's foremost romantic poet was the melancholy Giacomo Leopardi, and Spain's was José de Espronceda.

Romanticism came somewhat later in the United States than in Europe, but it was a vigorous movement with distinctive themes. The love of nature took a philosophical form in the group of New England writers known as **transcendentalists**. Their views are expressed in *Nature* (1836), by Ralph Waldo Emerson, and *Walden* (1854), by Henry David Thoreau. The theme of the American frontier experience was introduced by James Fenimore Cooper in such well-loved tales as *The Last of the Mohicans* (1826) and *The Deerslayer* (1841). This tradition was continued by Henry Wadsworth Longfellow in *The Song of Hiawatha* (1855). The poems of Walt Whitman, published after 1855 under the title *Leaves of Grass*, celebrate the American spirit and remain influential.

American romanticism is particularly rich in prose narratives that have become an important part of the country's literature. These include the novels *Moby-Dick* (1851), by Herman Melville, and *The Scarlet Letter* (1850), by Nathaniel Hawthorne, and the short stories of Edgar Allan Poe.

Romantic opera reached new heights in drama and theatrical effects. This costume design was for a production of *Der Ring des Nibelungen*, an opera cycle by German composer Richard Wagner.

### ▶ROMANTICISM IN MUSIC

The full tide of romanticism in music began in the 1800's with operas that treated old legends or Shakespearean subjects, as in *Otello* (1816) by the Italian composer Gioacchino Rossini. The bold new orchestral sounds invented for opera were then brought into the concert hall. Overtures were written, not as introductions to operas, but as concert pieces with themes suggested by books, plays, or personal experiences. The German composer Felix Mendelssohn wrote an overture to Shakespeare's *A Midsummer Night's Dream* in 1826.

In addition to opera, more intimate kinds of music were also produced by romantic composers. Often, short pieces for the piano expressed the composer's inner thoughts and feelings. Mendelssohn titled some of his collections "songs without words." Another German composer, Robert Schumann, wrote songs both with and without words. Many of Frédéric Chopin's piano pieces were inspired by tunes from his native Poland and the *Hungarian Rhapsodies* (1846) of Franz Liszt by Hungarian gypsy music. Franz Schubert set songs to poems in his song cycles, including *A Winter's Journey* (1827).

Some romantic composers favored **program music**, which tells a story with music and is sometimes explained in a concert program. *Harold in Italy* (1834), by the French composer Hector Berlioz, is a leading example of this type of music. Other program compositions, such as *Don Juan* (1889), by the German composer Richard Strauss, were called **tone poems**.

Later in the 1800's symphony and opera were the dominant forms. The great symphonies of Germany's Johannes Brahms and Gustav Mahler, Russia's Peter Ilyich Tchaikovsky, Czechoslovakia's Antonin Dvořák, and Austria's Anton Bruckner brought full, rich harmonies into the concert hall and are still much loved by audiences today.

Opera, too, tended to become increasingly spectacular. Such operas as *Tannhäuser* (1845), by Germany's Richard Wagner, *Aïda* (1871), by Italy's Giuseppe Verdi, and *Salome* (1905), by Richard Strauss, reached new heights in their theatrical and musical efforts. Mythological and literary subjects were turned into stirring musical dramas that often reflected the national pride of newly emerging countries.

LILIAN R. FURST
University of North Carolina, Chapel Hill
Author, *Romanticism in Perspective*

See also articles on the arts of various countries; biographies of individual artists, writers, and composers.

# ROME

Rome (Roma in Italian) is the capital and largest city of Italy. One of the world's oldest and most beautiful cities, it was founded on the Tiber River in the 700's B.C. and later became the very center of Western civilization. Over the centuries, Rome has served as the capital of the mighty Roman Empire, the seat of the Roman Catholic Church, and the capital of the modern nation of Italy.

Rome is called the Eternal City because it has survived wars, plagues, floods, earthquakes, and the ravages of time. Its often sunny climate and architectural beauty have attracted artists and poets from every era.

## ▶ LAND

The original city of Rome was built on several hills—the Aventine, Caelian, Capitoline, Esquiline, Palatine, Quirinal, and Viminal—the legendary Seven Hills of Rome. But over the course of many centuries, several of them have all but disappeared.

The Tiber River flows through the city and is spanned by many bridges. The sturdiest bridge is also the oldest. Called the Ponte Milvio, it was completed in the 100's B.C.

Rome is generally warm and sunny. Temperatures average 76°F (24°C) in July and 45°F (7°C) in January.

## ▶ PEOPLE

Present-day Rome has a population of about 2.5 million. But even 18 centuries ago Rome is estimated to have been home to more than 1 million people. Its large population reflected its role as the center of the Western world.

**Education and Libraries.** Rome's leading public institution of higher learning is the University of Rome, founded in 1303. The Roman Catholic Church sponsors a variety of theological schools. Universities for foreigners include the American University of Rome.

Rome also has many libraries. By far the most important is the Vatican Library, founded in the 1400's, which today houses more than 1 million books and historical manuscripts.

**Museums and the Arts.** Rome has dozens of museums featuring the history and culture of the city. Among the most visited are the Museum Galleria Borghese on the grounds of the beautiful Villa Borghese, built for the cardinal Scipione Borghese and completed in 1616. The

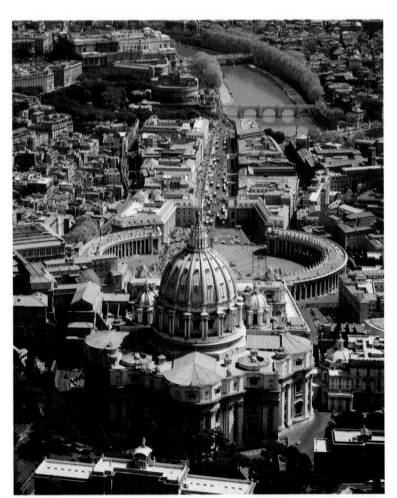

The dome of St. Peter's Basilica rises above the ancient city of Rome, the capital and largest city of Italy.

# Places of Interest

Colosseum

Spanish Steps

**Catacombs** are a network of underground passageways in which the early Christians hid from authorities to worship during the periods they suffered persecution. They also became Christian burial grounds, for which they are best remembered today.

**Colosseum**, properly known as the Flavian Amphitheater, is among the most important monuments remaining from the days of ancient Rome. When the stadium was completed in A.D. 80, it stood 160 feet (49 meters) high with an oval arena measuring 280 by 175 feet (85 by 53 meters). Built as an entertainment complex, it held up to 50,000 spectators, who gathered there to watch gladiator battles and other spectacles.

**Pantheon**, a temple with an enormous dome, is one of the best preserved buildings dating from ancient times. It was built in the A.D. 100's on the site of an earlier temple that celebrated Octavian's (later the emperor Augustus) victory over Marc Antony at the Battle of Actium in 31 B.C. In A.D. 609, the Pantheon became a Christian church. Several Italian kings and the great Renaissance artist Raphael are buried there.

**Piazza di Venezia**, a public square in the heart of Rome, stands at the southern end of Rome's main concourse, the Via del Corso. The piazza is dominated by an enormous white marble monument dedicated to Victor Emmanuel II, the first king of a united Italy. On the west side of the square stands the Piazza Venezia, where the fascist dictator Benito Mussolini once had his office, with a balcony from which he used to address large crowds. It was opened as a museum in 1944.

**Quirinal Palace** is situated atop the Quirinal, the tallest of Rome's Seven Hills. The history of the rust-colored palace reflects the varied history of the city. It was begun in 1574 as a summer residence of the popes. It later became the home of the Italian king, who replaced the pope as the ruler in Rome. It has been the residence of the president of the Italian Republic since 1947.

**Roman Forum**, situated between the Palatine and Capitoline hills along Via dei Fori Imperiali, was once the center of ancient Roman political life. Among the ruins of many triumphal arches, columns, and temples lies the Curia, the seat of the ancient Roman Senate.

**Spanish Steps** (or Scalinata di Spagna) is a popular tourist attraction. Named for the nearby Spanish Embassy, the steps rise to the Trinità dei Monti church overlooking the Piazza di Spagna. On one side sits the Keats-Shelley House, a museum dedicated to the great British poets of the romantic era and the place John Keats spent the last year of his short life.

**Trevi Fountain**, an enormous structure built in the baroque style between 1732 and 1762, is perhaps the most famous of Rome's many fountains. Located near Quirinal Hill, it is the site where water, carried by an ancient aqueduct, flows into the city of Rome. According to legend, any foreigner who tosses a coin into the fountain is destined to return one day to Rome.

**Vatican City**, the world's smallest independent country and the seat of the Roman Catholic Church, is situated on Vatican Hill in northwestern Rome. St. Peter's Square, St. Peter's Basilica, the Vatican Library, and the Sistine Chapel are among its famous landmarks. For more information, see the article VATICAN CITY in Volume UV.

Trevi Fountain

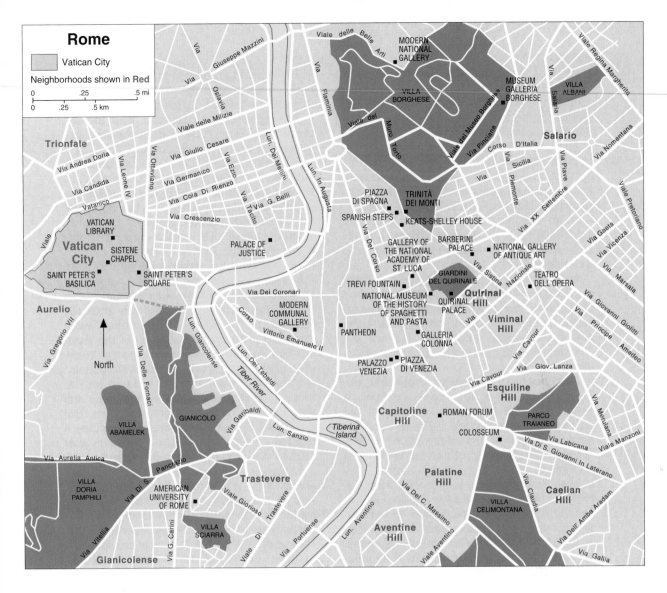

**Rome**

Vatican City

Neighborhoods shown in **Red**

0    .25    .5 mi
0    .25    .5 km

Trionfale

Via Giuseppe Mazzini
Via Oslavia
Viale delle Milizie
Via Andrea Doria
Via Candida
Vatanico
Via Giulio Cesare
Via Germanico
Via Ezio
Via Cola Di Rienzo
Via Taciti
Via Crescenzio
Via G. Belli
Lun. Del Mellini
Lun. In Augusta

VATICAN LIBRARY
Vatican City
SISTENE CHAPEL
SAINT PETER'S BASILICA
SAINT PETER'S SQUARE

PALACE OF JUSTICE

Aurelio

Via Gregorio VII
Via Delle Fornaci

North

Lun. Gianicolense
Lun. Dei Tebaldi

VILLA ABAMELEK
GIANICOLO
Via Garibaldi
Tiber River

Via Aurelia Antica
Lun. Sanzio

VILLA DORIA PAMPHILI
Via Di S. Pancrazio
AMERICAN UNIVERSITY OF ROME
Trastevere
Viale Glorioso
Viale Di Trastevere

VILLA SCIARRA
Via G. Carini

Gianicolense

Viale delle Belle Arti

MODERN NATIONAL GALLERY

VILLA BORGHESE

Viale del Museo Borghese

MUSEUM GALLERIA BORGHESE

VILLA ALBANI

Viale Regina Margherita

Via Flaminia
Muro Torto
Viale del
Via Pinciana
Via Salaria

Salario

Corso D'Italia
Via Sicilia
Via Piave
Via Nomentana

PIAZZA DI SPAGNA
SPANISH STEPS
Via Del Corso
TRINITÀ DEI MONTI
KEATS-SHELLEY HOUSE

Via Piemonte
Via XX. Settembre
Viale Pretoriano

GALLERY OF THE NATIONAL ACADEMY OF ST. LUCA
BARBERINI PALACE
NATIONAL GALLERY OF ANTIQUE ART
Via Sistina
Via Nazionale
Via Gaeta
Via Vicenza
Via Marsala

TREVI FOUNTAIN
GIARDINI DEL QUIRINALE
TEATRO DELL'OPERA

NATIONAL MUSEUM OF THE HISTORY OF SPAGHETTI AND PASTA
Quirinal Hill
QUIRINAL PALACE
Viminal Hill
Via Giovanni Giolitti

PANTHEON
Via Dei Coronari
MODERN COMMUNAL GALLERY
Corso Vittorio Emanuele II
GALLERIA COLONNA
Via Cavour
Via Principe Amedeo

PALAZZO VENEZIA
PIAZZA DI VENEZIA
Via Cavour
Via Giov. Lanza

Capitoline Hill
ROMAN FORUM
Esquiline Hill
PARCO TRAIANEO
Via Labicana
Via Merulana
Viale Manzoni
Via Manzoni

Tiberina Island
COLOSSEUM
Via Di S. Giovanni In Laterano

Palatine Hill
Via Del C. Massimo

VILLA CELIMONTANA
Caelian Hill
Via Claudia
Via Dell' Amba Aradam

Aventine Hill
Viale Aventino
Via Gallia

museum features Borghese's famous collection of Italian Renaissance paintings, including works by such masters as Raphael, Titian, and Caravaggio. The baroque Galleria Colonna, completed about 1700, features works by Bronzino, Ghirlandaio, Veronese, and Tintoretto. Additional museums include the Modern Communal Gallery, the Gallery of the National Academy of St. Luca, the Modern National Gallery, and the Barberini Palace and National Gallery of Antique Art.

The performing arts are well represented in Rome, especially music. Opera and ballet are featured at the Teatro dell'Opera di Roma and the Auditorium Parco della Musica. Additional concert series are offered by the orchestra of the Accademia Nazionale di Santa Cecilia and the Rome Philharmonic Orchestra.

**Parks and Recreation.** Rome is known for its many beautiful parks. Many were once the gardens on the estates of Rome's richest families. Among the best known are the gardens at the villas Borghese, Celimontana, Doria Pamphili, and Sciarra.

Frequent topics of conversation for young Romans include politics, the latest films, and, above all, the current standings of their favorite soccer teams. Soccer is the city's favorite sport, followed closely by bicycle and automobile racing. These and other sports are practiced in Rome's splendid arenas. Many were built for the 1960 Summer Olympic Games.

## ECONOMY

Rome is not one of Italy's main industrial cities, but many sizable factories operate in its suburbs. Food processing and the manufacture of textiles and drugs are among the main industrial activities.

Tourism provides a major source of income. Millions of tourists arrive each year by airplane, railroad, bus, or car. Hundreds of hotels and restaurants operate within the city. Crowds of sightseers provide a livelihood for Roman tour guides, souvenir sellers, and guidebook publishers. Filmmaking, government services, and banking also contribute to the economy.

**Transportation.** Many of Rome's cobbled streets are very narrow, dating from the days of chariots. Because automobile traffic has increased, there are often traffic jams. Laws have been passed to protect Rome's old churches, palaces, and other monuments from damage.

The construction of wider streets and underpasses is often impossible because it would mean destroying or altering an old wall or an ancient temple. Subway construction is limited by the network of underground passageways known as the catacombs.

**Communication.** More than a dozen newspapers and magazines are published in Rome. The daily newspaper *La Repubblica* has the widest circulation. Others include *Internazionale*, *Liberazione*, and *L'Unità*. The Vatican publishes *L'Osservatore Romano*. Rome is also the headquarters of Radiotelevisione Italiana, Italy's principal broadcast network.

## GOVERNMENT

Rome is the seat of the Italian federal government, and many Romans work in government offices. The two chambers of parliament are housed in separate old palaces, a dozen blocks apart. Large buildings in various parts of the city contain government ministries and offices. Many foreign embassies are also located there to maintain diplomatic relations.

The city itself is governed by a group of 80 city council members, from which a mayor is selected to serve as chief executive. The mayor also heads an 18-member City Executive Committee, also chosen from among the city council members. All these public officials are elected to 4-year terms.

## HISTORY

The origins of Rome are lost in the legends of history, but the traditional date for its founding is 753 B.C. Its geographical position in the center of the peninsula, near the sea, contributed to its growth in importance and the adventurous character of its people.

First under the rule of kings and then as a republic, Rome steadily expanded in size. The Roman Empire, founded by the emperor Augustus in 27 B.C., reached its greatest extent by A.D. 117, when it ruled much of the known Western world. Thereafter, ancient Rome began its decline. In A.D. 476 it fell as the capital of the Western empire, although an Eastern empire remained, with its capital at Constantinople (modern Istanbul), until 1453.

The glory of ancient Rome was gradually inherited by the popes. The Catholic Church remained in Rome after the fall of the Western empire, and its popes emerged as rulers of the Papal States, with Rome as its capital.

In the 1800's a movement arose in Italy to unite the peninsula, which at that time still was made up of many separate regions. But the city of Rome and the area surrounding it resisted unification until 1870, ten years after most of Italy had been joined together.

United Italy was governed by a king, and Rome was proclaimed the capital. After World War I (1914–18), Benito Mussolini, leader of the authoritarian, warlike Fascist Party, rose to power. Mussolini ruled from 1922 until 1943. When Italy was proclaimed a republic after World War II (1939–45), Rome, which was little damaged in the war, continued as the capital of the nation.

Since the war, the completion of several major building projects have modernized sections of the city. Among the most important were the Esposizione Universale di Roma (E.U.R.), a complex of businesses, government offices, and residences, and museums constructed in the 1950's; the Palazzo della Sport, built for the 1960 Summer Olympic Games; and the Auditorium Parco della Musica, completed in 2002.

IRVING R. LEVINE
Author, *Main Street, Italy*

Reviewed by JEREMY BLACK
Author, *Italy and the Grand Tour*

See also ITALY, ART AND ARCHITECTURE OF; ROME, ANCIENT; ROME, ART AND ARCHITECTURE OF; VATICAN CITY.

# ROME, ANCIENT

From a small settlement in central Italy, ancient Rome grew into a great city and the heart of one of the largest and most long-lasting empires in history. At its height, the Roman Empire stretched from western Asia to Britain and Spain, and from the Danube River in central Europe to the edge of the Sahara desert in North Africa. The empire in the West lasted for some 500 years. An Eastern empire endured for a thousand years more.

In creating their empire, the Romans were often ruthless in their methods. They destroyed entire cities and enslaved whole populations. At the same time, they brought peace, an advanced culture, and the rule of law to the conquered lands. The many different peoples in the far-flung empire were united by common citizenship. They enjoyed free trade and travel over good roads and safe waterways, a high level of public services (including libraries and museums), and a uniform law code, government, and system of money.

Along with the ancient Greeks, the Romans contributed greatly to the development of Western civilization. Latin, the Roman language, spread to all parts of the Western empire. Even after the fall of the empire in the West, Latin remained a common language of educated people as well as the language of the Roman Catholic Church, the law, medicine, and science. The Latin alphabet was adopted by most European languages. Latin itself is the ancestor of modern French, Italian, Spanish, Portuguese, and Romanian, which are referred to as Romance languages because of their origin in the language of the Romans.

See the article on Latin language and literature in Volume L. An article on Roman art and architecture appears in this volume.

## ▶ BEGINNINGS

**The Rome of Legend.** The traditional date claimed by the Romans for their city's origin was 753 B.C. According to legend, Rome was founded by a descendant of the Trojan prince Aeneas, who escaped to Italy after the city of Troy was destroyed by the Greeks during the Trojan War. The legendary founder was Rom-

The ruins of the Roman Forum (*below*) still stand as a reminder of the grandeur of ancient Rome, which ruled an empire stretching from western Asia to Britain, and from the Danube River in central Europe to North Africa. According to legend, Rome was founded by Romulus, who, with his twin brother, Remus (*right*), had been nursed as an infant by a she-wolf.

The Senate was the chief branch of government under the Roman Republic. Originating as a group of elderly advisors (the name comes from the Latin word for "old man") to the early Roman kings, the Senate held great powers, including control of finances, foreign policy, and religion. It continued to have considerable influence under the early empire, but later lost much of its power to the emperors.

ulus. He and his twin brother, Remus, had been abandoned as infants and rescued by a female wolf, who nursed them. Grown to manhood, they decided to build a city near the spot where the wolf had saved them. Disagreeing over the location, each built at a separate site. Later they quarreled and Remus was killed. Romulus became the first king of the city named after him. According to another legend, the early Romans, who had no wives, kidnapped the unmarried women of the neighboring Sabines to take as their wives.

**Origins.** Legend aside, it is likely that Rome originally consisted of several small villages situated on hills (eventually seven) beside the Tiber River, near the western coast of central Italy. The city lies on a fertile plain called Latium. Rome's location, at a natural crossroads of Italy, favored its growth. The hills guarded the roads and made it easy for the Romans to defend themselves. The plain of Latium provided food for a growing population, which soon expanded across the Tiber.

**The Monarchy (753?–509 B.C.).** Rome was ruled at first by simple kings, who were more like tribal chiefs. The king was advised by a group of elders, who came to be known as the Senate (*Senatus*, from the same root as *senex*, meaning "old man"). On major issues, such as peace and war, the king and Senate had to have the approval of the Roman citizens.

The first four kings were probably native to the region. The last three were a foreign dynasty of Etruscans, a wealthy and powerful people who lived to the north, in what is now Tuscany. The Etruscans had grown rich through trade with the Greeks, who had colonized the coasts of southern Italy as well as Sicily, and the Carthaginians (originally Phoenicians), who had established settlements in Sicily and North Africa. Led by the more advanced Etruscans, Rome grew from a small hill town of farmers and shepherds into an important city.

**The Army.** Under the Etruscans, the Roman army was reorganized into a disciplined force of heavily armed infantry. Soldiers originally fought in deep, tight ranks. They were armed with spears and, later, short swords. For protection, a soldier wore a metal helmet, chest piece, and greaves (shin guards), and carried a shield. Cavalry was used to protect the flanks of the infantry, pursue a fleeing enemy, and act as scouts. The army was composed of landowning citizens at first. It later became a professional army and a flexible, efficient fighting machine. Its basic unit was the legion, made up of from 3,000 to 6,000 men. With it the Romans conquered an empire.

▶**THE ROMAN REPUBLIC**

The Etruscan kings had grown very powerful at the expense of the Senate, whose leaders greatly resented the last Etruscan ruler, Tarquinius Superbus (Tarquin the Proud). In 509 B.C., in a revolt led by Lucius Junius Brutus, Tarquinius was overthrown and a republic was established.

**Government.** The government of the republic had three major parts: magistrates, who were elected each year to lead the army and run the government; the Senate, made up of wealthy aristocrats, the heads of noble families, and hereditary priests, who advised the magistrates; and the popular assemblies, composed of all adult male citizens, who elected the magistrates, passed laws and treaties proposed by the magistrates, and acted as courts in some cases.

Because the wealthier citizens originally made up most of the army, their votes always counted more than those of the poorer classes in the main popular assembly, the Assembly of Centuries. Although the Senate could not pass laws, in early times the hereditary priests claimed the right to approve laws.

The chief magistrates came to be called consuls. There were two elected each year. They had command over the army outside the boundaries of Rome and could punish disobedience with immediate execution. Within Rome, elected officials called tribunes protected citizens from abuse by the magistrates.

**Society.** It has been common to refer to the upper classes of Roman society as patricians and to call the lower classes plebeians. But this concept is too simple. A family's social status depended on how much land it owned and whether any of its ancestors had been senators.

Large landowners (100 acres was considered a large estate) all belonged to the upper class. Within the upper class, those Romans whose ancestors or family members had been senators made up the senatorial aristocracy. Patricians were one part of this class. Under certain conditions, wealthy plebeian families could also belong to the aristocracy. Plebeians who were not part of the aristocracy but were able to afford a horse and thus serve in the cavalry were called *equites*, or knights.

**Slavery.** Slavery was always a part of Roman life and increased as a result of Rome's conquests. Captives taken in war were sold as slaves to work on the farms and in the homes of wealthy Romans, in rock quarries or mines, and in workshops in the cities and towns. Some were well treated, but others labored under brutal conditions. Educated, Greek-speaking slaves were especially valuable as estate managers, overseers, skilled workers, teachers, cooks, or personal servants. Some slaves were freed after years of loyal service. Others were able to earn money with which to purchase their freedom. Freed slaves had the same rights as free-born Roman citizens but could not be elected to public office, although their sons could.

**Patrons and Clients.** Wealthy Romans who helped less fortunate citizens were called patrons. Those they assisted were known as clients. (The word "patron" comes from the Latin *pater*, meaning "father.") The patron-client relationship was a distinctive part of Roman life. Having a large number of clients added to a family's status. Every morning, crowds of clients would wait to greet their patrons at home and ask for favors or offer to perform a service for them.

**The Family: Adults.** The family was the most important part of Roman society. The Latin *familia*, however, does not mean exactly the same thing as the English "family." It refers to the entire household, including slaves and clients. Several generations might live together. The Romans also believed that the spirits of dead ancestors played a role in family affairs, and offerings were made to them each day.

The head of the family was the father (*paterfamilias*), who had absolute power over the household. Only the father could sell family property or make contracts. In practice, however, a father usually consulted other family members, including his wife (*materfamilias*), on important matters.

Upper-class Roman women were treated better than women in many ancient societies. They could appear in public, were not kept in separate quarters at home, owned property, and were relatively well educated. They could not, however, take part in Roman political life. Legally, women were supervised by their fathers or husbands, but such supervision was often light. The lives of poorer women were much more difficult. In the countryside, they labored in the fields and the home. In the cities they worked long hours in laundries, shops, taverns, or markets.

**Children.** Childhood did not last long for young Romans. Poor children began to work almost as soon as they could walk. Those from the upper classes were usually educated at home by slaves; sometimes they were sent to a grammar school run by an educated freed slave or a foreign resident. At the age of 7, girls and boys received separate training. Girls were taught by their mothers how to be wives and run a large household. By 15 they were often married, usually to an older man chosen by their parents for the social and political advantage of the family.

## THE ROMAN EMPERORS

| NAME | REIGNED | NAME | REIGNED |
|------|---------|------|---------|
| Augustus | 27 B.C.—A.D. 14 | Probus | 276–282 |
| Tiberius | A.D. 14–37 | Carus | 282–283 |
| Caligula | 37–41 | Carinus and Numerianus | 283–285 |
| Claudius I | 41–54 | Diocletian | 284–305 |
| Nero | 54–68 | Maximian | 286–305 |
| Galba | 68–69 | Constantius | 305–306 |
| Otho | 69 | Galerius | 305–311 |
| Vitellius | 69 | Constantine I, the Great | 306–337 |
| Vespasian | 69–79 | Constantine II | 337–340 |
| Titus | 79–81 | Constans | 337–350 |
| Domitian | 81–96 | Constantius II | 337–361 |
| Nerva | 96–98 | Julian the Apostate | 361–363 |
| Trajan | 98–117 | Jovian | 363–364 |
| Hadrian | 117–138 | Valentinian I (West) | 364–375 |
| Antoninus Pius | 138–161 | Valens (East) | 364–378 |
| Lucius Aurelius Verus | 161–169 | Gratian (West) | 367–383 |
| Marcus Aurelius | 161–180 | Valentinian II (West) | 375–392 |
| Commodus | 180–192 | Theodosius I, the Great (East) | 379–394 |
| Pertinax | 193 | Maximus (West) | 383–388 |
| Didius Julianus | 193 | Eugenius (West) | 392–394 |
| Septimius Severus | 193–211 | Theodosius I, the Great (sole emperor) | 394–395 |
| Geta | 211–212 | | |
| Caracalla | 211–217 | **ROMAN EMPERORS IN THE WEST** | |
| Macrinus | 217–218 | Honorius | 395–423 |
| Heliogabalus (or Elagabalus) | 218–222 | Valentinian III | 425–455 |
| Alexander Severus | 222–235 | Petronius Maximus | 455 |
| Maximinus | 235–238 | Avitus | 455–456 |
| Gordianus I | 238 | Majorian | 457–461 |
| Gordianus II | 238 | Severus | 461–465 |
| Balbinus and Pupienus | 238 | Anthemius | 467–472 |
| Gordianus III | 238–244 | Olybrius | 472 |
| Philip the Arabian | 244–249 | Glycerius | 473 |
| Decius | 249–251 | Julius Nepos | 473–475 |
| Gallus | 251–253 | Romulus Augustulus | 475–476 |
| Aemilianus | 253 | | |
| Valerian | 253–260 | **ROMAN EMPERORS IN THE EAST** | |
| Gallienus | 253–268 | Arcadius | 395–423 |
| Claudius II | 268–270 | Theodosius II | 408–450 |
| Aurelian | 270–275 | Marcian | 450–467 |
| Tacitus | 275–276 | Leo I | 457–474 |
| Florian | 276 | Leo II | 473–474 |

After age 7, upper-class boys often accompanied their fathers to learn how to manage the family's property or business. They usually also received military and political training. At 15, a boy received his toga of manhood. (The toga was the traditional garment worn by Roman men.) At 17, he usually began two years of military service. After that, he was ready to start a career of his own or to round out his education by the advanced study of oratory (public speaking) or philosophy, frequently by traveling to Greece for such study.

**Religion.** Rome had no special class of professional priests. The father performed priestly duties for the family, while the aristocrats and elected officials acted as priests for the state, along with performing their other duties. There was no distinction between religion and the state. One of the main purposes of the state, in fact, was to interpret the will of the gods for the community. Rituals were performed in public temples to appease the gods and keep them on the side of Rome.

Many Roman religious cults, rituals, and festivals were connected with the fields and home, the centers of early Roman life. Each home had a special niche or place for the household gods. Every aspect of nature had its particular spirit too. Ceres (from whom we get the word "cereal") was the very important goddess of the grain or harvest. The Romans later adopted many of the gods of the Greeks and gave them Latin names. For example, Zeus, the king of the gods to the Greeks, became Jupiter to the Romans.

**Economic Life.** The early Romans were mostly farmers and herders of livestock. Each family raised most of the food it needed and traded any small surpluses for such things as salt, pottery, and metals. The Etruscan kings had promoted trade, but after their fall trade was, for a long time, of less importance. The ideal Roman, for rich and poor alike, was the hardy, self-sufficient farmer who fought to defend his family and community. The only honorable forms of wealth to the Romans were those produced from the land or captured in war.

**Conquest of Italy (509–264 B.C.).** The young republic faced many enemies in 509 B.C. The Etruscans tried to gain supremacy again. Rome warred with neighboring hill tribes, such as the Aequi and Volsci, and with other cities of Latium who resisted Roman attempts to dominate them. A serious defeat for Rome occurred about 390, when Gauls from the north captured most of the city. The Gauls agreed to depart only after a payment of gold. Nevertheless, by 338, Rome had conquered or made favorable alliances with many Etruscan cities, the hill tribes, and the Latin cities. After three wars with the fierce Samnites (343 to 290), the Romans were the masters of central Italy.

The Romans adopted many of the Olympian gods of the Greeks. Jupiter, king of the gods, was the Roman version of the Greek god Zeus.

Meanwhile, the Greek cities of southern Italy, fearing the growing power of Rome, hired Greek generals to defend them. The most famous was King Pyrrhus of Epirus. He won victories over the Romans (280 and 279) but suffered such heavy losses (the origin of the term "Pyrrhic victory") that he returned to Greece. By 264, Rome had captured all of the Greek cities in the south and had gained control of all Italy south of the Po Valley.

**Political Reforms.** Since Rome's safety depended on unity, Roman leaders agreed to a series of reforms that made the government and society more fair for all. The right of tribunes to protect citizens by their veto and the right to appeal sentences of exile or death to a popular assembly were guaranteed. Popular protests forced the patrician senators to draw up Rome's first written code of laws, the Laws of the Twelve Tables (449 B.C.). The ban forbidding plebeians from marrying patricians was ended; the right of patricians to disapprove laws was abolished; and wealthy plebeians were permitted to hold all high government offices, which had previously been denied them.

New laws were also passed to protect the poorer citizens. They prevented large landowners from taking public land for themselves, limited the rate of interest on loans, and stopped the sale of debtors into slavery.

**Reasons for Rome's Success.** There are a number of reasons for Rome's successes. Its central location made it easy for Roman armies to attack anywhere in Italy. The combination of an excellent army and organization, stern discipline learned at home, and a life of hard work made the Romans good in battle. The Romans always improved their army in the face of experience. The importance of the family over the individual also taught the Romans to put the interests of the community above one's own personal interests.

## SOME IMPORTANT DATES IN ROMAN HISTORY

| | |
|---|---|
| 753? B.C. | Traditional date for the founding of Rome. |
| 753?–509 | Period of the monarchy. |
| 509? | The republic established. |
| 509–264 | Conquest of Italy. |
| 449 | Laws of the Twelve Tables published. |
| 264–146 | Defeat of Carthage in the three Punic Wars. |
| 60 | First Triumvirate formed. |
| 44 | Assassination of Julius Caesar; Second Triumvirate formed. |
| 27 | Empire founded; Augustus becomes the first emperor. |
| A.D. 98–117 | Rome reaches its greatest extent under Trajan. |
| 284–305 | Empire reorganized under Diocletian. |
| 313 | Edict of Milan grants religious toleration to Christians. |
| 330 | Capital moved to Byzantium (Constantinople) by Constantine I, the Great. |
| 395 | Division of the empire into Western and Eastern halves. |
| 476 | Last emperor of the West, Romulus Augustulus, gives up the throne; the empire survives in the East. |
| 1453 | Fall of Constantinople to the Ottoman Turks marks the fall of the Eastern (or Byzantine) Empire. |

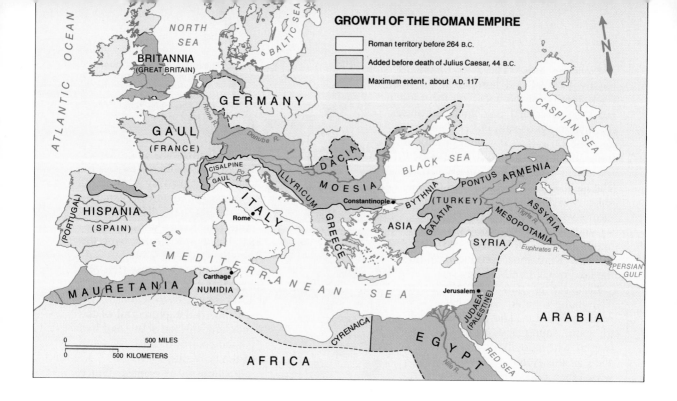

**GROWTH OF THE ROMAN EMPIRE**

- Roman territory before 264 B.C.
- Added before death of Julius Caesar, 44 B.C.
- Maximum extent, about A.D. 117

The Romans also made a point of treating their allies well, even those forced into an alliance through defeat, and protecting them against their enemies. In return, their allies remained loyal and sent men to fight in Roman armies. Faithful allies gradually received more and more of the rights and privileges of Roman citizens. In time many of them became full citizens.

Finally, there was the element of luck. The Romans were fortunate in that some enemies, such as the Gauls, were too far from home to fight against continued Roman resistance, after their earlier capture of Rome. Others, such as the Greek cities of southern Italy, were too disunited to fight more effectively. The Romans always believed that Fortuna, the goddess of good luck, favored them more than other peoples.

**Roman Expansion (264–133 B.C.).** With virtually all of Italy south of the Po Valley united under them, either by alliance or citizenship, the Romans found new worlds to conquer. Between 264 and 133 B.C., most of the independent lands around the Mediterranean Sea, except Egypt, came under the rule of Rome.

In the west, three successful wars—known as the Punic Wars—were fought against Carthage, which turned Sicily, Sardinia, and Corsica, as well as Spain and central North Africa, into Roman provinces. During the second war, the great Carthagenian general Hannibal won several victories over Roman armies, before he was finally defeated (202 B.C.). The Romans completely destroyed Carthage at the end of the third war (146 B.C.).

See the articles on the Punic Wars and Hannibal in the appropriate volumes.

Between 225 and 172 B.C., the Romans conquered Cisalpine Gaul (northern Italy) and extended their domain into what is today France as far as Massilia (Marseilles). The planting of military colonies made these conquests permanent. In the east, the Romans took over Macedon and Greece after four Macedonian wars (between 215 and 148 B.C.), and broke the power of the Seleucid Empire in Asia Minor and Syria (192 to 188 B.C.).

**Influence of Greece.** The Roman conquerors felt culturally inferior to the Greeks, who had created a great civilization. To make Rome look like the famed Greek cities, they imported thousands of statues and other works of art from Greece. Greek artists were hired to copy old works and to make new ones. The Romans began to construct their buildings of marble in the Greek style. They learned the Greek language, read Greek literature, and tried to make their own Latin literature more like the admired Greek models.

**Results of Roman Expansion.** As a result of its overseas conquests, great wealth poured into Rome. The aristocrats used it to build expensive homes, roads, aqueducts (for carrying water), temples, public baths, and monuments to Roman victories. The population of the city swelled with slaves, laborers, artisans, and shopkeepers. The poorer people lived crowded together in large blocks of apartment houses.

In the countryside, aristocrats and *equites* used their new wealth to buy land and create large commercial estates run with cheap slave labor. The small farmers could not compete and many lost their land. They became seasonal farm workers or moved to the city to find work.

The wars had cost the lives of hundreds of thousands of Roman soldiers. To replace them, men with no property were eventually allowed to serve in the army. Most were recruited for long terms of overseas service and developed strong loyalties to individual generals. Rome also demanded increasing numbers of soldiers from its allies, who resented being treated more and more like subjects rather than allies.

**The Roman Revolution (133–27 B.C.).** All of these changes were to play a role in the eventual collapse of the Roman Republic. But other factors were also at work. Roman aristocrats put their personal ambitions above the interests of Rome. Political leaders exploited discontented groups by promising reforms in exchange for votes, and rivals blocked reforms out of political jealousy. Frustration led to violence and assassination.

One political leader, Tiberius Gracchus, was assassinated in 133, when he tried to win re-election as tribune after he had succeeded in gaining passage of a popular land-reform law. His brother Gaius Gracchus won passage of even more popular reforms ten years later, but he committed suicide in 121 to avoid being killed by his rivals.

Corruption of officials in the provinces grew, while successful generals used their loyal client armies to crush rivals in civil war. The first civil wars were fought by Gaius Marius and Lucius Cornelius Sulla. Marius was a popular military hero backed by one group of aristocrats. Sulla was supported by Marius' rivals. After Marius died, Sulla defeated Marius' former followers and briefly ruled Rome as dictator (82–81 B.C.).

**The First Triumvirate.** In 60 B.C., three powerful senators who had been victorious generals joined together to run the government for themselves. They were Pompey the Great, Marcus Licinius Crassus, and Gaius Julius Caesar. They are often referred to as the First Triumvirate (Committee of Three). Crassus was killed while trying to conquer the Parthian empire in Asia. Pompey, a fine general, had previously won much of western Asia for Rome. But Caesar, who conquered Gaul (most of present-day France) between 58 and 49 B.C., is renowned as one of the greatest generals of all time. A devastating civil war between the armies of Pompey and Caesar

At the Battle of Zama (202 B.C.) in the Second Punic War, the Romans defeated one of their greatest foes, the Carthagenian general Hannibal, who used elephants in his campaigns.

(48–45 B.C.) resulted in Pompey's defeat (and later death) and made Caesar dictator of Rome.

**The Second Triumvirate.** In 44 B.C., however, republican opponents, led by Marcus Junius Brutus and Gaius Cassius Longinus, stabbed Caesar to death in the Senate. Further political struggles brought to power the Second Triumvirate, made up of Marcus Antonius (Mark Antony), Marcus Amelius Lepidus, and Gaius Julius Caesar Octavianus (Octavian), Caesar's adopted son. Eventually, a struggle for power developed between Antony and Octavian. It ended in 31 B.C. with the victory of Octavian's forces against those of Antony and his ally, the Egyptian queen Cleopatra. Egypt was made a Roman province, and Octavian became sole ruler of Rome. See the article on Mark Antony in Volume A, and the articles on Caesar and Cleopatra in Volume C.

### ▶THE EMPIRE

**The Age of Augustus.** The Senate honored Octavian with the name Augustus (meaning "revered"). He became the first emperor of Rome, although his many powers and offices were traditional republican ones. During his long reign (27 B.C.– A.D. 14), the army was reorganized, a permanent navy created, the empire expanded, and a 200-year era of peace, the *Pax Romana* (Roman Peace), begun. Most of Rome was rebuilt and a professional civil service was formed to supervise the collection of taxes, public works,

Octavian rose to power in Rome after defeating his chief rival, Mark Antony. As Augustus, a name given him by the Senate, he became the first Roman emperor in 27 B.C.

The Praetorian Guard served as bodyguards of the Roman emperors. They eventually became powerful enough to determine the succession to the imperial throne.

food and water supply, and the minting of coins. It was also a golden age of literature. See the article on Augustus in Volume A.

Augustus founded the Julio-Claudian dynasty of emperors, the first of many dynasties and individual emperors who were to rule the Roman Empire. Some were good. Many were ordinary. Others were incompetent or tyrannical. See the table for a complete list of emperors.

**Augustus' Successors.** Augustus was succeeded by his stepson Tiberius (A.D. 14–37) and his great grandson Caligula (37–41). An unpredictable tyrant, Caligula was noted for his cruelty. He was assassinated by his own bodyguards, the Praetorian Guard, who named his uncle Claudius I (41–54) emperor. Physically disabled but a learned man and an effective administrator, Claudius added Britain to the empire (43). His nephew and adopted son, Nero (54–68), was at first a successful ruler but later became self-indulgent, extravagant, and cruel. See the article on Nero in Volume N.

**Flavian Emperors and Antonines.** After a brief civil war, in which several emperors succeeded one another, a veteran, no-nonsense general, Vespasian (69–79), came to the throne. The first of the Flavian emperors, he quickly restored peace and stability. He was succeeded by two sons, the popular Titus (79–81), and Domitian (81–96), who began well but became tyrannical and was murdered.

They were followed by emperors known as the Five Good Emperors, who ruled during the height of Roman power. Nerva reigned only briefly (96–98). But under Trajan (98–117), a Spaniard and the first non-Italian emperor, who was one of its greatest rulers, Rome reached its farthest extent. Hadrian (117–138), like his predecessor a soldier, founded many provincial cities. The reign of Antoninus Pius (138–161) was a long and prosperous one. Marcus Aurelius (161–180) ruled jointly with Lucius Aurelius Verus (161–169) before he became sole emperor. An able ruler, Marcus Aurelius is also known for his philosophical writings.

**Life During the *Pax Romana*.** The *Pax Romana* was not entirely without conflict. Revolts broke out from time to time as subject peoples sought to regain their independence. A revolt in Britain (60–61) was put down, and two Jewish revolts (66–70 and 132–135) in Palestine were brutally crushed. Titus destroyed the Temple in Jerusalem, and under Hadrian the Jews were forbidden to live in the city.

But for the majority of people, life was peaceful and prosperous in the empire of the first two centuries A.D. The good emperors and wealthy individuals supported benefits and education for the poor, and women gradually gained more legal rights. In general, the provinces enjoyed better government under the supervision of the emperors. Many in the provinces rose through the ranks of the army and civil service to become citizens and even senators. Trade and commerce flourished in the cities, while in the countryside, farming thrived under the peaceful conditions.

**Rise of Christianity.** The old gods of Greece and early Rome were not relevant to Rome's worldwide empire. Gradually, the worship of the emperors themselves grew. Also, as the urban, or city, population grew, the old gods of the countryside lost favor. Many religions from the eastern part of the empire became popular because they promised relief from the cares of a more complex, impersonal world. Christianity was one of these religions.

Christianity began in Roman-ruled Palestine. Jesus was born there during the reign of Augustus and he was crucified there in the time of Tiberius. The early Christians were unpopular with their fellow Romans because they refused to worship the traditional gods or take part in the ceremonies honoring them. This seemed unpatriotic to the emperors, and Christians were often persecuted.

Nevertheless, the new religion gradually spread throughout the empire. Christianity was made legal by the emperor Constantine the Great in the Edict of Milan (313). It became the official religion of the empire under Theodosius the Great (379–395).

**Century of Crisis.** The A.D. 200's were a critical time for the empire, which came under

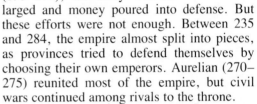

Constantine I, the Great, briefly halted the decline of Rome during the A.D. 300's. He created a new capital at Constantinople (modern Istanbul) and made Christianity legal throughout the empire.

attack from Germanic peoples to the north. Marcus Aurelius had tried to create a stronger border against them, but died before he could do so. His son Commodus (180–192) was an unfit ruler. Under Septimius Severus (193–211), the army was enlarged and money poured into defense. But these efforts were not enough. Between 235 and 284, the empire almost split into pieces, as provinces tried to defend themselves by choosing their own emperors. Aurelian (270–275) reunited most of the empire, but civil wars continued among rivals to the throne.

**Division of the Empire.** Two emperors briefly halted the growing decay of the empire. Diocletian (284–305) reorganized it and shared it with a co-ruler and two junior rulers. Constantine I (306–337), known as the Great, created a new capital for the empire at the old Greek city of Byzantium, which was renamed Constantinople after him. (See the article on Constantine in Volume C.) After the death of Theodosius the Great in 395, the empire was formally divided in two. Constantinople became the capital of the eastern half of the empire and Rome the capital of the western half.

**Fall of the Western Empire.** The eastern half of the empire was richer, had a greater population, and enjoyed more secure borders than the western half. Alone, it could survive. There was not enough strength left to save both halves. The Western emperors bought some time by paying foreigners to fight their enemies. But by A.D. 430, Visigoths and other German invaders had captured most of the Western empire. The last emperor of the West, Romulus Augustulus, gave up the throne in 476. The Eastern empire survived, and at times flourished, as the Byzantine Empire, until the capture of Constantinople by the Ottoman Turks in 1453.

ALLEN M. WARD
University of Connecticut
Co-author, *A History of the Roman People*

See also BYZANTINE EMPIRE.

The Pont du Gard, an aqueduct near Nîmes, France, was built by the Romans in 19 B.C. A notable feature of Roman architecture was the extensive use of the arch.

# ROME, ART AND ARCHITECTURE OF

The Romans wanted their art and architecture to be useful. They planned their cities and built bridges, aqueducts, public baths, and marketplaces, apartment houses, and harbors. When a Roman official ordered sculpture for a public square, he wanted it to tell future generations of the greatness of Rome. Although the practical uses of art were distinctly Roman, the art forms themselves were influenced by the ancient Greeks and Etruscans.

In the late 600's B.C., the most powerful people in Italy were the Etruscans, who had come from Asia Minor and settled in Tuscany, an area north of Rome. Although the Etruscans imported Greek styles of art, they achieved much by themselves. They developed a very realistic type of portrait sculpture. They were also the first to introduce the use of the stone arch into architecture.

## ▶ARCHITECTURE

The Romans put the lessons of the Etruscans to practical use. The baths and arenas are tributes to the skill of Rome's great builders. Because of the use of the arch, the Romans could build on a greater scale than the Greeks, who used the post and lintel (a beam supported by two columns). The arch can support much more weight than the post and lintel. Roman aqueducts were often three levels of arches piled one on top of another. And their buildings, such as the Baths of Caracalla, enclosed huge open areas.

In the 1st century B.C. the Romans developed the use of concrete. It could be poured into any shape for arches, vaults, or domes. Concrete enabled architects to build structures of immense size. One such gigantic construction was the Temple of Fortune at Praeneste, built by the ruler Sulla about 80 B.C. The architect used concrete to support terraces and to build what was in effect a skyscraper. To build their open-air theaters, the Greeks had scooped out the sides of hills, using the hills to support the sloping tiers of seats. But the Roman engineers used concrete to support the three gigantic tiers of the Colosseum, their main stadium for public entertainment. The tiers held seats for more than 45,000 spectators. A picture of the Colosseum is included in the article on Rome.

## SCULPTURE

The Romans used a great deal of sculpted decoration to embellish their architecture. Columns were often placed on the walls of buildings as part of the decoration. (They actually supported no weight themselves.) Many of these decorations were copied from Greek styles. In fact, many Greek forms were simply placed on the facades of Roman buildings without any practical reason for being there.

In portraying their gods, the Greeks had been influenced by their ideas of form and beauty. Roman sculptors were greatly influenced by the Greeks. But the Romans showed their skill and originality in their portraits. They portrayed their emperors, generals, and senators with a degree of realism unknown to the Greeks. Thinning hair, double chins, crooked noses—all the physical traits that make one person look different from another —can be found in Roman portraiture.

## PAINTING

In A.D. 79, an eruption of the volcano Vesuvius destroyed the city of Pompeii, covering it with layers of lava that hardened into rock. The wall paintings preserved in this rock tell us nearly everything we know about Roman painting.

Painting was usually done as a form of decoration. In Pompeii, for example, paintings were executed on the inside walls of the houses in fresco (painting on wet plaster). Often these murals were used to make the room seem larger, by giving the illusion of depth, or to create a pastoral landscape where there was no window or view.

Columns and other forms of architecture were often painted into the compositions or used to frame the murals and add to the feeling of depth. A system of perspective was known and used by the Romans. Red, black, and cream-white were among the most popular colors.

Roman painting achieved a high degree of naturalism through the artists' understanding of perspective and use of light and shade. The Romans painted many charming scenes from nature and portraits of children and beautiful young men and women. Religion, too, inspired their art.

Reviewed by LEE HALL
President Emerita,
Rhode Island School of Design

The detail of a statue of Antinoüs (*above*) shows the combination of realism and simplicity for which Roman sculpture is known. The painting of the youth Narcissus (*below*) is typical of the scenes painted directly onto the walls of the homes of ancient Pompeii.

## ROMMEL, ERWIN (1891–1944)

German General Erwin Rommel was nicknamed the Desert Fox for his brilliant and cunning military campaigns in North Africa during World War II (1939–45). Erwin Johannes Eugen Rommel was born on November 15, 1891, in Heidenheim, Württemberg. After serving as a commissioned officer during World War I (1914–18), he won his country's highest medal for bravery.

In 1933, Adolf Hitler became leader of Nazi Germany. Rommel was quickly promoted to a high rank in the army and helped pioneer the German fighting method known as **blitzkrieg** (lightning war), which used large forces of tanks and dive-bombers to break through enemy lines.

During World War II, Rommel commanded an armored division and participated in the 1940 blitzkrieg that helped win a rapid victory over France. He was then given command of the Africa Corps in North Africa, where he won numerous victories against the British and almost conquered their colony, Egypt. Rommel became a national hero, and in June 1942, Hitler promoted him to field marshal.

But the tide soon turned against him. In October 1942, the Africa Corps was defeated by the British at El Alamein. In December 1943, Rommel was transferred to France. But in spite of his great efforts there, he was unable to prevent the great Allied invasion of Normandy that took place on June 6, 1944.

At that point, Rommel tried to persuade Hitler to end the war. When Hitler refused, Rommel participated in a plot to overthrow him but was found out. Hitler gave Rommel a choice —he could either commit suicide or be tried as a traitor and face certain execution. Rommel poisoned himself on October 14, 1944. To preserve public morale, the German people were told that their popular general had died from battle wounds, and Rommel was buried with full military honors. Today he is remembered, even by his enemies, as a brave and honorable man.

MICHAEL HUGHES
Author, *Nationalism and Society: Germany 1800–1945*

## ROOSEVELT, ELEANOR (1884–1962)

Social activist, humanitarian, and crusader for human rights, Anna Eleanor Roosevelt was known as the First Lady of the World. The wife of one United States president, Franklin D. Roosevelt, and the niece of another, Theodore Roosevelt, she was born in New York City on October 11, 1884.

In 1905, Eleanor married her distant cousin, Franklin Delano Roosevelt. They had six children—one girl and five boys. Eleanor devoted herself to her family while her husband developed his political career. But after Franklin was stricken with polio in 1921, Eleanor herself became politically active. She worked for the New York League of Women Voters and the women's division of the state Democratic committee. She also established the Val-Kill Furniture Shop in Hyde Park, New York, to provide jobs for the unemployed.

Franklin Roosevelt became president in 1933, and Eleanor began her twelve-year career as the most active first lady the country had ever known. Because of her husband's paralysis she traveled for him and reported on

what she had observed. A tireless advocate for social causes, including civil rights for blacks and women, she held press conferences, had her own radio program, and wrote a daily newspaper column called "My Day."

Franklin Roosevelt died in 1945. That year, Eleanor Roosevelt was appointed a United States delegate to the United Nations (1945–52; 1961–62). She also served as chairman of the United Nations Commission on Human Rights (1946–51) and helped draft the U.N. Declaration of Human Rights. She died in New York on November 7, 1962, and was buried at the Roosevelt home at Hyde Park.

Reviewed by WILLIAM JAY JACOBS
Author, *Eleanor Roosevelt: A Life of Happiness and Tears*

See also FIRST LADIES.

# FRANKLIN D. ROOSEVELT (1882–1945)
## 32nd President of the United States

FACTS ABOUT
FRANKLIN
ROOSEVELT
Birthplace: Hyde
   Park, New York
Religion:
   Episcopalian
College Attended:
   Harvard
   College
Occupation: Lawyer, public official
Married: Anna Eleanor Roosevelt
Children: Anna, James, Franklin (died
   1909), Elliott, Franklin, Jr., John
Political Party: Democratic
Office Held Before Becoming President:
   Governor of New York
President Who Preceded Him:
   Herbert Hoover
Age on Becoming President: 51
Years in the Presidency: 1933-1945
Vice President: John Nance Garner
   (1st and 2nd terms); Henry A. Wallace
   (3rd term); Harry S. Truman (4th term)
President Who Succeeded Him:
   Harry S. Truman
Age at Death: 63
Burial Place: Hyde Park, New York

DURING FRANKLIN ROOSEVELT'S
PRESIDENCY
*Left:* The National Recovery Administration (NRA), symbolized by a blue
eagle, was created (1933) as one of the
early New Deal programs to combat
the Great Depression. The 20th Amendment to the Constitution (the "lame
duck" amendment), establishing new
beginning dates for terms of office for
the president and Congress, went into
effect (1933). The 21st Amendment,
which repealed the 18th (or Prohibition)
Amendment, was ratified (1933). Germany's invasion of Poland (1939) set off
World War II. *Below:* The Japanese
attack on Pearl Harbor, Hawaii, (1941)
brought the United States into the war.

**ROOSEVELT, FRANKLIN DELANO.** Franklin D. Roosevelt served longer than any other president of the United States. He held office from 1933 until his death in 1945, at the beginning of his fourth term. During his presidency he led the United States through two great crises —the Great Depression of the 1930's and World War II.

Roosevelt was a man of unusual charm and great optimism, which he was able to communicate to others. He had a broad smile and an easygoing way of nodding agreement to whatever proposals were made to him. But beneath his outward friendliness was an inner reserve and an iron will. He became one of the most beloved as well as one of the most hated of U.S. presidents. His admirers emphasized the way in which he met the nation's problems. They praised him for insisting that the federal government must help the underprivileged and that the United States must share in the responsibility for preserving world peace. Roosevelt's opponents denounced him for increasing the role of the government in the eco-

nomic life of the country and claimed that he unnecessarily involved the United States in World War II. Yet friend and foe alike agreed that Roosevelt made a vital impact upon his times and that his policies exerted great influence on the future.

▶**EARLY YEARS AND MARRIAGE**

Roosevelt was born on a comfortable estate overlooking the Hudson River at Hyde Park, New York, on January 30, 1882. He had a pleasant, sheltered childhood. His father, James Roosevelt, was a well-to-do investor and vice president of a small railroad. His mother, Sara Delano Roosevelt, came from a wealthy family of New England origin. During his childhood Franklin was taught by a governess and was taken on frequent trips to Europe. Once his father took him to the White House to see President Grover Cleveland. Cleveland, saddened and worn by the burdens of office, said he hoped that young Franklin would never have the misfortune of becoming president.

The Roosevelt family in 1919: Franklin and Eleanor are at center, with their children (from left to right) Anna, Franklin, Jr., James, John, and Elliott.

At 14, Roosevelt entered Groton School in Massachusetts. From Groton he went to Harvard College, where he became chief editor of the Harvard *Crimson*, the student newspaper. He graduated in 1904 and went on to Columbia University Law School. Meanwhile, he had become engaged to his distant cousin, Eleanor Roosevelt. At the wedding in 1905, Eleanor's uncle, President Theodore Roosevelt (who was Franklin's fifth cousin), gave her in marriage. See the biography of Eleanor Roosevelt preceding this article.

Roosevelt was an indifferent law student and did not bother to complete work for his degree after passing his bar examination. Nor was he much interested in his work with a prominent Wall Street law firm.

▶ HE ENTERS POLITICS

In 1910 the Democratic leaders in Dutchess County, New York, persuaded Roosevelt to run for the state senate. The senate contest seemed hopeless for a Democrat. Nevertheless, Roosevelt conducted an energetic campaign, touring the Hudson River farming communities in a red Maxwell automobile. The Republicans were split that year,

and the 28-year-old Roosevelt won his first election.

Roosevelt supported Woodrow Wilson for the presidential nomination in 1912, and when Wilson became president in 1913, Roosevelt was appointed assistant secretary of the navy. He was especially successful as an administrator during World War I. He was also achieving a reputation as a rising young progressive. In 1920, at the age of 38, he won the Democratic nomination for vice president, running with the presidential candidate, James M. Cox (1870–1957). But the Democrats were buried in the landslide victory of the Republican Warren Harding.

▶ ILLNESS STRIKES

Biding his time, Roosevelt entered private business. Then, in the summer of 1921, while vacationing at Campobello Island in Canada, he was suddenly stricken with what was believed to be polio, which paralyzed him from the waist down. (More recent medical analyses suggest his symptoms may have been more consistent with Guillain-Barré syndrome, an illness that was scarcely known in Roosevelt's day.) Not yet 40, he seemed finished in politics. But his wife, Eleanor, and his private secretary, Louis Howe, felt that his recovery would be aided if he kept his political interests. Eleanor, now the mother of five children (a sixth child had died in 1909), cast aside her acute shyness and learned to make appearances for her husband at political meetings. In spite of his illness,

His legs paralyzed by illness, Roosevelt found relief in swimming and refused to let his disability end his political career. The smile was a Roosevelt trademark.

which left him unable to walk without leg braces, a cane, and a strong arm upon which to lean, Roosevelt remained one of the dominant figures in the Democratic Party.

### FROM GOVERNOR TO PRESIDENT

In 1928, Roosevelt ran for governor of New York at the urging of the then-governor, Alfred E. Smith (1873–1944), who was the Democratic candidate for president. Although Smith was defeated by Republican Herbert Hoover, Roosevelt was elected governor by a narrow margin. His re-election in 1930 by a record majority made him the leading candidate for the Democratic presidential nomination in 1932.

During the 1932 election campaign, the Depression overshadowed all other issues. In accepting the nomination, Roosevelt had promised the American people a "new deal," and they voted for him in overwhelming numbers. Roosevelt defeated Hoover, running for re-election, by more than 7 million popular votes and received 472 electoral votes to Hoover's 59.

Conditions became worse between Roosevelt's election on November 8, 1932, and his inauguration on March 4, 1933. (The 20th Amendment to the Constitution, changing the presidential inauguration date to January 20, did not go into effect until October 1933.) Thousands of banks failed as depositors, fearful of losing their savings, withdrew their money. A quarter of the nation's wage earners were unemployed. Families on relief sometimes received no more than 75 cents a week for food. Farmers were in an equally desperate plight because of low prices on basic crops.

### HIS PRESIDENCY

**First New Deal Measures.** Amid these grim conditions Roosevelt took his oath of office as president. "The only thing we have to fear is fear itself," he said in his inaugural speech. The words were not new, but the way Roosevelt said them gave people new hope. As a first step he closed all U.S. banks to prevent further collapse. Then he called Congress into special session to pass emergency banking legislation. Within a few days most banks were reopened, and people who had withdrawn their money redeposited it. The Federal Deposit Insurance Corporation was established soon after. It insured bank deposits and protected people from losing their savings.

During the first one hundred days of his administration, Roosevelt presented to Congress a wide variety of legislation. This became the first New Deal program. These early measures contained one notable reform —the creation of the Tennessee Valley Authority (TVA). The TVA provided flood control, cheap electricity, and better use of the land for the entire poverty-stricken Tennessee River area.

A political cartoon of the 1930's depicts Roosevelt as a doctor treating the country's economic ills. The bottles reflect the president's many New Deal measures.

For the most part the early New Deal measures were meant to bring immediate relief to the needy and recovery to the economy. A federal agency was set up to provide the states with funds to feed the hungry. Legislation was passed to aid farmers and homeowners in danger of losing their property because they could not keep up mortgage payments. The Civilian Conservation Corps (CCC) was organized, providing jobs for unemployed young men in forest conservation and road construction work.

At the president's urging, Congress took the United States off the gold standard and devaluated the dollar. This lowered its exchange value, allowing American products to be sold to better advantage abroad.

**The AAA and NRA.** At the heart of the recovery program of the early New Deal were the Agricultural Adjustment Administration (AAA) and the National Recovery Administration (NRA). Under the AAA, production of basic crops and livestock was limited in order to raise prices and thus increase farmers' incomes. Farmers were rewarded by benefit payments for reducing production.

The NRA, created by the president under the National Industrial Recovery Act of 1933, it was meant to aid both business and labor. The NRA established codes of fair competition in major industries. In turn, businessmen were expected to pay at least minimum wages and to work their employees for no more than established maximum hours. Furthermore, under the terms of the Recovery Act, workers were given the right to bargain collectively—that is, to join unions of their choice, which would negotiate wages and working hours with employers. These collective bargaining provisions were replaced in 1935 by the National Labor Relations Act (the Wagner Act), which gave strong protection to unions and encouraged the growth of the labor movement.

None of Roosevelt's recovery measures worked quite satisfactorily, and the road to recovery was one of ups and downs. In 1935 the Supreme Court declared the NRA code system unconstitutional, and in 1936 they ruled against part of the AAA. Still, the economy was showing a marked improvement.

**Other Measures.** But although recovery seemed on the way, unemployment remained high. In 1935, Roosevelt undertook a large-scale work program—the Works Progress Administration (WPA). Then, in the summer of 1935, he pushed through Congress three important reform measures. The Public Utility Holding Company Act placed restrictions on gas and electric utilities. The Revenue Act of 1935 placed heavier tax burdens on those in the upper income brackets. Roosevelt's opponents, who criticized the government's heavy spending, called it the "soak the rich" tax. Most important of the three was the Social Security Act. This provided for unemployment insurance, pensions for the aged, and aid to widows and orphans.

**Second Term.** In the 1936 election, Roosevelt won re-election over the Republican can-

In the economic collapse that began the Great Depression of the 1930's, one quarter of American workers lost their jobs. With little government aid then available, these unemployed men probably thought themselves fortunate to receive a skimpy meal at one of the many soup kitchens that sprang up across the United States. Roosevelt's early New Deal measures were intended to bring immediate help to the needy and recovery to the economy.

As president, Roosevelt frequently addressed the American people, in what he called his "fireside chats," to reassure a troubled nation and to win support for his political program. A combination of charm, optimism, and effective leadership enabled Roosevelt to win election to four terms of office, more than any other U.S. president.

didate, Alfred M. Landon (1887–1987), sweeping every state except Maine and Vermont. The electoral vote was 523 for Roosevelt to 8 for Landon, with Roosevelt receiving nearly 11 million more popular votes than Landon. Re-election by such an overwhelming margin seemed a call for further reform. "I see one third of a nation ill-housed, ill-clad, ill-nourished," Roosevelt declared in his second inaugural address.

**The Supreme Court Crisis.** As a first step, Roosevelt wanted to end the Supreme Court's invalidation of New Deal measures. Roosevelt felt that these laws were constitutional but that the Supreme Court's interpretation of them was sadly out of date. In February 1937, he asked Congress to authorize him to appoint as many as six new justices to the Court.

A great controversy swept Congress and the country. Many people denounced the proposal to "pack" the Court. Roosevelt's plan failed, but the gradual retirement of the older justices brought more liberal ones to the Supreme Court. Even while the debate was going on, the Court had modified its decisions. Thereafter it approved of most government regulation of the nation's economy.

**Toward Recovery.** By 1937 the economy had reached almost the prosperity levels of the 1920's, although unemployment continued to be high. When Roosevelt cut New Deal spending in an effort to balance the federal budget, a sharp recession followed. He re-turned to heavy spending, and the trend toward recovery resumed. Large sums were provided for a vast public works project—the Public Works Administration. Roosevelt also obtained from Congress the Fair Labor Standards Act of 1938. This set a national standard of minimum wages and maximum hours for workers and prohibited the shipping in interstate commerce (commerce between states) of goods made by child labor. It was the last important piece of New Deal reform legislation. Thereafter, Roosevelt and the American people were concerned with events in Europe and Asia, where the aggressive policies of Nazi Germany, Italy, and Japan, known as the Axis powers, threatened to lead to war.

**The Approach of World War II.** In taking office in 1933, Roosevelt had pledged the United States to a "good neighbor" policy. Roosevelt had carried out this pledge in Latin America. Indeed, he tried to follow a policy of goodwill throughout the world. As the threat of war became more ominous during the mid-1930's, both the president and the American public wished to remain neutral. But at the same time, Roosevelt did not want to see the aggressors triumph. When Japan invaded northern China in 1937, he declared in a speech that war, like a dangerous disease, must be quarantined.

War finally broke out in Europe when Germany invaded Poland in 1939. Roosevelt wished to help the democratic nations—Brit-

Roosevelt met with chief U.S. World War II allies, Britain's prime minister Winston Churchill (left) and Soviet leader Joseph Stalin (right), at Yalta in 1945. He died that same year, near the war's end.

ain and France—without involving the United States in war. But gradually, as the crisis deepened, he took greater risks of involvement. After the fall of France in 1940, Roosevelt, with the approval of Congress, rushed all possible weapons to Britain in order to help the British in the fight against Germany.

**Third Term.** In the 1940 election, Roosevelt's Republican opponent was Wendell Willkie (1892–1944), who held similar views on aid to Britain. Isolationists, who wished the United States to keep out of European affairs, campaigned vigorously against Roosevelt. In spite of their opposition, he was elected to a third term, winning 449 electoral votes to Willkie's 82. He also received over 5 million more popular votes than Willkie.

Early in 1941, at the president's urging, Congress passed the Lend-Lease Act. This provided further aid to Britain and other nations fighting the Axis.

**U.S. Entry in the War.** At the same time, Roosevelt was trying to block Japan's ad-

vances into China and Southeast Asia. The Japanese felt they faced a choice of giving up their policy of expansion or fighting the United States. On December 7, 1941, Japanese planes attacked U.S. air and naval bases at Pearl Harbor, Hawaii. The next day Congress declared war on Japan. On December 11, Germany and Italy declared war on the United States. With the United States now involved in a world conflict, Roosevelt sought to increase U.S. war production and to lead the country in a great alliance against the Axis powers. As commander in chief of the armed forces, he helped plan major offensives in Europe, leading to the Normandy invasion in 1944. At the same time, the Japanese were gradually pushed back in the Pacific.

Even before the United States entered the conflict, Roosevelt had been concerned with planning a better postwar world. As the war progressed, he hoped that an international organization could be created to prevent future wars. This organization was to be the United Nations. Roosevelt felt that the keeping of peace would depend to a considerable extent upon goodwill between the United States and the Soviet Union. He thus tried to establish friendly relations with the Soviet leader Joseph Stalin at the Tehran Conference (in Iran) in 1943 and at the Yalta Conference (then part of the Soviet Union; now in Ukraine) in 1945.

**Fourth Term and Death.** In 1944, Roosevelt was nominated for a fourth term, running against Thomas E. Dewey (1902–71), the governor of New York. Roosevelt appeared thin, worn, and tired, but late in the campaign he seemed to gain renewed energy. Again he was re-elected by a substantial margin, with 432 electoral votes to 99 for Dewey and close to 4 million popular votes. But his health, which had been declining since early in 1944, did not improve. After returning from the Yalta Conference, he went to Warm Springs, Georgia, to rest. There, on April 12, 1945—less than a month before the war in Europe ended—he died of a cerebral hemorrhage. As the world mourned Roosevelt's death, Vice President Harry S. Truman took over the duties of office as the new president.

FRANK FREIDEL
Harvard University
Author, *Franklin D. Roosevelt*

See also NEW DEAL; TRUMAN, HARRY S.; WORLD WAR II.

# THEODORE ROOSEVELT (1858–1919)

## 26th President of the United States

### FACTS ABOUT THEODORE ROOSEVELT

**Birthplace:** New York City
**Religion:** Dutch Reformed
**College Attended:** Harvard College, Cambridge, Massachusetts
**Occupation:** Cattle rancher, writer, public official
**Married:** Alice Hathaway Lee (died 1884); Edith Kermit Carow
**Children:** Alice Lee (by Alice Hathaway Roosevelt), Theodore, Jr., Kermit, Ethel, Archibald, Quentin
**Political Party:** Republican
**Office Held Before Becoming President:** Vice President
**President Who Preceded Him:** William McKinley
**Age on Becoming President:** 42
**Years in the Presidency:** 1901-1909
**Vice President:** Charles Warren Fairbanks
**President Who Succeeded Him:** William Howard Taft
**Age at Death:** 60
**Burial Place:** Oyster Bay, New York

*Theodore Roosevelt* (signature)

### DURING THEODORE ROOSEVELT'S PRESIDENCY

The Department of Labor and Commerce (later separate departments) was created as a cabinet post (1903). The United States recognized the independence of Panama from Colombia (1903). *Above:* Orville and Wilbur Wright made the first successful airplane flights in a powered, controllable, heavier-than-air craft (1903) at Kitty Hawk, North Carolina. Construction of the Panama Canal was begun (1904). The president's role as a mediator in the Russo-Japanese War won him the Nobel peace prize (1906). *Left:* Much of San Francisco was destroyed by an earthquake and fire (1906). Oklahoma became the 46th state (1907).

**ROOSEVELT, THEODORE.** Theodore Roosevelt was one of the most popular American presidents as well as one of the most important. With his zest for life and his love of controversy, he captured the public's imagination as no president since Andrew Jackson had done. His willingness to shoulder the burdens of world power and to struggle with the problems caused by the growth of industry made his administration one of the most significant in U.S. history.

Roosevelt was a strong nationalist and a dynamic leader, who greatly expanded the power of the presidency at the expense of Congress, the states, and big business. He made the United States the guardian of the Western Hemisphere, especially in the Caribbean. Roosevelt was also the first president-reformer of the modern era. He increased regulation of business, while encouraging the labor movement. He led a long, hard fight for the conservation of natural resources, and he broadly advanced the welfare of the people as a whole. At the same time he was a compelling preacher of good government and responsible citizenship.

Roosevelt was sworn in as president on September 14, 1901, following the assassination of President William McKinley. At 42 years of age he was the youngest person ever to become president of the United States. Fortunately, 15 years of public service, particularly as governor of New York, had also made him one of the best prepared presidents.

### ▶ EARLY YEARS

No president led a more varied, interesting, or adventurous life than Theodore Roosevelt. He was a hunter, rancher, and explorer as well as a soldier, naturalist, and author. As a youth, however, he had to struggle against poor health. From his birth in New York City on October 27, 1858, until his late teens, he suffered from asthma and was generally weak and frail. Otherwise he had many advantages. His father, after whom he was named, came from an old New York Dutch family of moderate wealth and high social position. His mother, Martha Bulloch, belonged to a prominent family from Georgia. Both parents were kind and affectionate. His father, in particular, concerned himself actively with Theodore's development. He encouraged Theodore to build up his body by doing hard exercises and engaging in sports. He arranged for his son to be educated by excellent private tutors until it was time to enter college. And most important of all, he taught Theodore the difference between right and wrong and gave him an unusually strong sense of responsibility. When Theodore entered Harvard College in 1876, he was healthy in body and mind, except for a trace of snobbishness, which he later lost.

At Harvard, Roosevelt wrote a senior honors thesis and was elected to Phi Beta Kappa, the student honor society. He graduated 21st in a class of 158. He probably would have done even better, for his intelligence was high and his memory keen, but he spent much of his time in outside activities. He played tennis and boxed, read hundreds of books not related to his courses, and wrote the first two chapters of a quite good book, *The Naval War of 1812*, published after he graduated. He also became interested in politics and government.

▶**FIRST MARRIAGE, ASSEMBLYMAN, RANCHER**

In 1880, a few months after graduation, Roosevelt married a charming young lady, Alice Hathaway Lee of Chestnut Hill, Massachusetts. After a short honeymoon he started to study law at Columbia University. He had little interest in legal details, however. In 1881, he gave up the study of law upon his election to the first of three terms in the New York State Assembly.

Roosevelt was only 23 years old when he took his seat in January 1882. But his courageous support of good government soon earned him a statewide reputation, and he rose rapidly in influence. He became the leader of a group of reform-minded Republicans and pushed through several bills strengthening the government of New York City. At the same time, he overcame a belief that government should not interfere in the economy and fought successfully for the regulation of tenement workshops.

Early in his third term, in 1884, Roosevelt's mother died. A few hours later his wife, who had given birth to a baby girl a short while

<table>
<tr><th colspan="2">IMPORTANT DATES IN THE LIFE OF THEODORE ROOSEVELT</th></tr>
<tr><td>1858</td><td>Born in New York City, October 27.</td></tr>
<tr><td>1880</td><td>Graduated from Harvard College; married Alice Hathaway Lee.</td></tr>
<tr><td>1882–1884</td><td>Served in the New York State Assembly.</td></tr>
<tr><td>1886</td><td>Married Edith Carow, his first wife having died in 1884.</td></tr>
<tr><td>1889–1895</td><td>Member of U.S. Civil Service Commission.</td></tr>
<tr><td>1895–1897</td><td>President of New York City board of police commissioners.</td></tr>
<tr><td>1897–1898</td><td>Assistant secretary of the Navy.</td></tr>
<tr><td>1898</td><td>Organized and then commanded the 1st U.S. Volunteer Cavalry Regiment ("Rough Riders") during Spanish-American War.</td></tr>
<tr><td>1899–1901</td><td>Governor of New York.</td></tr>
<tr><td>1901</td><td>Inaugurated vice president of the United States, March 4; sworn in as president upon the death of President William McKinley, September 14.</td></tr>
<tr><td>1901–1909</td><td>26th president of the United States.</td></tr>
<tr><td>1909–1910</td><td>Hunted in Africa.</td></tr>
<tr><td>1912</td><td>Organized the Progressive ("Bull Moose") Party; was defeated as its presidential candidate by Woodrow Wilson.</td></tr>
<tr><td>1913</td><td>Explored in South America.</td></tr>
<tr><td>1919</td><td>Died at Oyster Bay, Long Island, January 6.</td></tr>
</table>

before, also died. Though grief-stricken, Roosevelt carried on his duties until the end of the session. As he wrote to a close friend, "It was a grim and evil fate, but I have never believed it did any good to flinch or yield for any blow, nor does it lighten the blow to cease from working." That summer he retired temporarily from politics and went out to the Dakota Territory to raise cattle on his ranch on the Little Missouri River.

When Roosevelt first appeared in the West, veteran cowboys and hunters were amused by his thick glasses, eastern accent, and gentlemanly manners. But after he had knocked out a drunken stranger who threatened him with two pistols and had proved himself in a half dozen other incidents, he was accepted. Within a year he was regarded as one of the region's ablest young leaders. Besides running cattle, Roosevelt spent his time in the West writing a biography of Thomas Hart Benton (1782–1858), a Missouri senator of the pre-Civil War period. He also planned a four-volume history of the westward movement, later published under the title *The Winning of the West*.

### ▶ PUBLIC SERVICE

Roosevelt returned from the West in the fall of 1886 to suffer defeat in a race for mayor of New York. That same year he married a childhood sweetheart, Edith Carow, and settled in a great rambling house on Sagamore Hill, overlooking Oyster Bay, Long Island. Four sons and a daughter were born to them.

But Roosevelt's energy was too great and his ambition too driving for him to be satisfied with life as a sportsman and writer. Besides, he felt that men of independent means were obligated to serve the public. So in 1889 he accepted an appointment to the United States Civil Service Commission. Roosevelt at once gave the commission new life, and for 6 years he enforced the laws honestly and fearlessly. When he resigned in 1895 to accept the presidency of the New York City Police Board, the civil service system had become an important part of American government.

As New York police commissioner, Roosevelt prowled the streets after midnight, overhauled the promotion system, and modernized the force. In 1897 he resigned from the Police Board to become assistant secretary of the Navy.

### ▶ ROUGH RIDER AND GOVERNOR

Roosevelt's service in the Navy Department and in the war against Spain brought out his aggressive qualities. He believed at the time that power was necessary for a country to achieve greatness, and that war was a test of manliness. He also believed that civilized nations had a right to interfere in the affairs of less advanced nations in order to forward the march of civilization. He demanded that the United States build up its fleet, drive Spain from the Western Hemisphere, and acquire colonies of its own.

Soon after the Spanish-American War broke out in 1898, Roosevelt helped organize the First United States Volunteer Cavalry Regiment (the "Rough Riders"). He took command of the regiment in Cuba, and on July 1 he led an assault on a hill outside Santiago. For hours he braved withering gunfire from the heights as he rode up and down the line urging his men, who were on foot, to press the attack. His elbow was nicked, a soldier was killed at his feet, and he had several other narrow escapes. But he rallied his own and other troops, and the hill was captured.

As soon as Roosevelt returned to New York in the fall of 1898, Republican bosses nominated him for governor. They hoped that his war record and reputation as a reformer would cause the voters to overlook a series of recent scandals within the party. After being elected by a narrow margin, Roosevelt compelled the bosses to accept a

The Roosevelts in 1903. From left are Quentin, Theodore Roosevelt, Theodore, Jr., Archibald, Alice, Kermit, Edith Roosevelt, and Ethel.

Roosevelt (*center*) and his Rough Riders in Cuba in 1898.

number of reform measures. These included a tax on corporation franchises, regulation of sweatshops, a raise in schoolteachers' salaries, and a conservation program. This angered the businessmen who supported the bosses. So Republican leaders practically forced Roosevelt to accept the vice-presidential nomination in 1900, although he wanted a second term as governor. In the election McKinley and Roosevelt defeated the Democratic candidates, William Jennings Bryan and Adlai E. Stevenson (1835–1914).

Roosevelt was a vigorous public speaker. This picture was taken in 1902, during a speech in Concord, N.H.

Six months after their inauguration McKinley was dead and Roosevelt was the new president of the United States.

## ▶ PRESIDENT

The main drive of Roosevelt's administration was toward a balance of economic interests. He believed that he should represent all the people—farmers, laborers, and white-collar workers as well as businessmen. Roosevelt called his program the Square Deal. He began to put it into effect 5 months after he took office by starting antitrust proceedings against the Northern Securities Company, a giant holding company. Holding companies controlled other companies and were thus able to reduce competition. Then in the fall of 1902, Roosevelt helped settle a long coal strike on terms favorable to the workers. This marked the first time that a president who took action in a strike had failed to side with management.

Despite his popular fame as a "trustbuster," Roosevelt continued to believe that bigness was good economically. He felt that large corporations should be regulated rather than destroyed. In 1903 he pushed through Congress a bill to form a Bureau of Corporations. That same year he gave his support to the Elkins Bill to prohibit railroad rebates. This was a practice in which railroads returned part of their payment to favored customers.

## Foreign Policy

Roosevelt's foreign policy was guided by the belief that the United States must police the Western Hemisphere and should accept the responsibilities of world power. He felt that the United States was morally bound to uplift the people of the Philippines, which the United States had acquired from Spain. He worked conscientiously to improve the economy of the Filipinos and prepare them for self-government. In 1902 he persuaded Germany to arbitrate a dispute with Venezuela. In 1903 he acquired the Canal Zone after Panama broke away from Colombia. The circumstances left a feeling of ill will in Colombia.

In 1905, at the request of the government of Santo Domingo (now the Dominican Republic), Roosevelt took over control of customs collections in that misgoverned country. He did not want to do so. But he feared that European powers might take control for nonpayment of debts if the United States did not act. He then announced in a public letter that the United States had a right to intervene in the internal affairs of Latin-American countries unable to keep order. This policy became known as the Roosevelt Corollary to the Monroe Doctrine.

## Second Presidential Term

Roosevelt's flair for the dramatic combined with his solid achievements to assure him a term in his own right. In the election of 1904 he won a landslide victory over his conservative Democratic opponent, Judge Alton B. Parker (1852–1926) of New York. The most productive years of his presidency followed. In a masterful display of leadership, Roosevelt forced the conservative Republicans into line by threatening to lower the tariff, or tax, on imports. (The Republicans generally favored a high tariff to protect American industry.) As a result, he won conservative support for a number of reforms in 1906—among them the Hepburn Act to regulate railroads, the Pure Food and Drug Act, and employers' liability legislation.

Meanwhile, Roosevelt and his chief forester, Gifford Pinchot (1865–1946), pushed conservation forward. Their program was based on the theory that natural resources belong to all the people, that scientific forestry would provide a constant supply of timber, and that river valleys should be developed as

This cartoon, entitled "Hands Off," illustrates Roosevelts's determination to enforce the Monroe Doctrine.

entire units. Roosevelt and Pinchot were bitterly opposed by small lumber companies, electric power corporations, and states' righters. But progress was made. The Reclamation Act of 1902 provided for a large irrigation project in the southwestern United States. Many big lumber companies were won over to scientific forestry. More than 125 million acres (over 50.5 million hectares) were added to the national forests, and the number of national parks doubled. Sixteen national monuments were created, and 51 wildlife refuges were established.

In foreign affairs Roosevelt's second term saw a retreat from his earlier imperialism. He tried mainly to protect the Philippines, support a balance of power in the Far East, and build up friendship with the Japanese. In 1905 he offered his good offices to end the Russo-Japanese War. His mediation proved successful and earned him the Nobel peace prize. On the other hand he served notice that he still carried a "big stick" by sending the American fleet on a world cruise in 1907.

As Roosevelt's term of office neared its end, Congress grew more and more resentful of his strong leadership and progressive policies. Again and again during his last 2 years Congress refused to do what he asked. Roosevelt's insight into the nation's problems continued to deepen, however. On January 31, 1908, he sent Congress the most radical message written by a president to that time. It called, among other things, for better conditions for workers and for the arrest of businessmen who broke the law.

In spite of his troubles with Congress, Roosevelt's great energy and straightforward speeches appealed more than ever to the man in the street. He could have been renominated easily had he chosen. But he decided instead to support the candidacy of one of his dearest friends, Secretary of War William Howard Taft. Soon after Taft was inaugurated in 1909, Roosevelt left for Africa to hunt big game and collect wildlife specimens for the Smithsonian Institution.

### ▶THE BULL MOOSE PARTY

While Roosevelt was in Africa, progressivism was gaining new force in the United States. But instead of encouraging its growth as Roosevelt had done, President Taft tried to hold it back. This put him on the side of the Republican conservatives who had opposed Roosevelt's policies.

In 1910 Roosevelt returned to the United States. Although irritated at Taft's policies, he at first tried to avoid hurting his old friend. But it was not in Roosevelt's nature to keep silent. In a series of speeches in the Midwest he set forth his own views, which he called the New Nationalism.

The New Nationalism was an extension of the progressive program he had urged in the last years of his presidency. It called for steeply graduated income and inheritance taxes and a long list of other social and political reforms. Finally, in 1912, Roosevelt yielded to the pleas of progressive midwestern Republicans and challenged Taft for the presidential nomination. But the Republican Convention failed to nominate Roosevelt in spite of his two-to-one victory over Taft in the primary elections. Roosevelt then organized the Progressive Party, better known as the Bull Moose Party. ("I am as strong as a bull moose," he had once commented.) The new party was supported by most of the country's social workers, intellectuals, and progressive-minded citizens.

Roosevelt's leadership of the progressive movement stirred the social conscience of middle-class America. Though Woodrow Wilson, the Democratic candidate, won the three-cornered contest with about 42 percent of the popular vote, Roosevelt ran far ahead of Taft. In a sense, too, Roosevelt was vindicated in defeat. For by 1916 Wilson had written a great deal of Roosevelt's New Nationalism into law.

### ▶RETURN TO WRITING AND EXPLORATION

After his defeat in 1912 Roosevelt wrote his autobiography. It is a colorful and vigorously written book and still the most informative memoir ever written by a former president.

Then, in 1913, Roosevelt decided to indulge his love of adventure once more by exploring an unknown South American river, the River of Doubt. It was a harrowing experience. He almost died of an injury suffered in a heroic effort to save two capsized boats. He was then stricken with malaria. Realizing that he was a burden, Roosevelt begged his companions, who included his son Kermit, to go on without him. But they insisted on bringing him out of the jungle.

### ▶FINAL YEARS

Upon the outbreak of World War I in 1914, Roosevelt at first refused to take sides. But after a few months, he decided that the interests of the United States and the world would best be served by U.S. support of the Allies, led by Britain and France, against Germany, which he feared would dominate the European continent. Early in 1915 he became a leader of the movement to prepare the United States for possible entry into the war. When the United States declared war against Germany in 1917, Roosevelt asked Wilson for permission to raise a volunteer division. But Wilson refused, and Roosevelt devoted himself to spurring the war effort at home.

Bouts of malaria sapped Roosevelt's health in his last years. He was also greatly saddened by the death of his youngest son, Quentin. An aviator, he was killed in an air battle over France in 1918, the last year of the war. Roosevelt himself died a year and a half later, at Sagamore Hill on January 6, 1919.

WILLIAM H. HARBAUGH
University of Virginia
Author, *Power and Responsibility: The Life and Times of Theodore Roosevelt*

See also PANAMA; PANAMA CANAL.

The way rope will be used determines the kind of rope that is needed. Nylon rope is used to moor a ship because it is strong, durable, and elastic.

# ROPE

A rope is made up of fibers that are twisted together into many small yarns. The yarns are gathered together into strands (hanks) that usually are twisted into three- or four-strand ropes. Sometimes they are braided, or plaited. Rope fibers usually come from plants, but the fibers may be of almost any material that can be cut or combed into strips and twisted, such as nylon, wire, or leather.

"Rope" is a general term used to describe any kind of cordage or line. But to a rope-maker, a rope is at least 3/16 inch (5 millimeters) thick. Large ropes generally are called cables. A rope large enough to moor a ship is called a hawser. When yarns are single or when two or three are twisted together, they are called twine.

Rope is usually classified by its circumference (the distance around it), but sometimes it is classified by its diameter. For example, a rope 5/16 inch (8 millimeters) in diameter measures 1 inch (25 millimeters) around and is called a 1-inch rope. The circumference is about three times the diameter.

## ▶HOW ARE FIBER ROPES MADE?

Ropemaking is almost entirely a process of twisting. When a bundle of fibers is twisted, the fibers pack together, and friction helps to hold them in place. But the twisting must be done just right. Too tight a twist makes the fibers cut each other. Too loose a twist gives a weak rope. Ropemaking is an art as well as a science.

Single fibers are twisted together to make a yarn; yarns are twisted together to form strands; strands are twisted together to make rope. Every time a unit of rope is put through one of these twisting operations, it is twisted in the direction opposite to the direction in which it was twisted before. This makes the rope hold together because each twist binds the other.

The basic steps in making rope are the same whether they are done slowly by hand or rapidly by huge, powerful machines:

(1) Fibers are separated and put in parallel formation on a combing machine. This machine puts them into the form of a continuous ribbon.

(2) The ribbon of fibers is spun out into a thin, round, twisted yarn.

(3) Groups of yarn are twisted into strands.

(4) The strands, tightly stretched, are passed through a tight, cone-shaped die in groups of three and twisted to make rope. This is the final step in the process of making most ropes.

(5) To make cables, groups of three-strand ropes are again twisted through a die.

(6) Cables are passed through dies and twisted under severe tension to form hawsers.

## ▶KINDS OF ROPE

Ropes are grouped together according to the materials that are used to make them. Some ropes are made from natural fibers, such as abaca, sisal, or cotton. Others are made from wire. Still other ropes are made from synthetic fibers, such as nylon or dacron.

### Natural-Fiber Rope

**Abaca**, often called Manila hemp, is the fiber most often used in ropes, but synthetics are slowly replacing it. Actually abaca is not hemp at all. (Hemp used to be an important rope fiber, but it was replaced by abaca.) Abaca fiber comes from the abaca plant, which was discovered in the Philippines. The plant is related to the banana plant. Abaca ropes are durable, strong, flexible, and reasonable in price. They resist weather and rot.

Swordlike sisal leaves are harvested for the 20 to 50-inch (51 to 127-centimeter)-long fibers they yield. The fibers will be used to make twine.

The other important rope fibers are **sisal** and **henequen**. Sisal comes from Haiti, South America, and Africa. Henequen comes from Mexico. Both are fairly strong and hard plant fibers that come from the spiny leaves of similar semitropical plants. Sisal and henequen baler twines tie well. They are used in the automatic knotters of the harvesting machines that form bales. Sisal ropes are also good utility ropes for general-purpose use. They are widely used by farmers.

High-grade **flax** fiber (linen) makes a beautiful, smooth rope that does not stretch, wears well, resists weather, and takes up very little room. It is used for signal ropes and pennant ropes on yachts.

**Cotton** rope is fairly strong, wears exceptionally well, and wedges snugly into grooved pulleys. It is well suited for use as window sash cord and for small pulleys. It is also used in crafts, such as macramé.

For a rope that is moderately strong, very supple, long-wearing, and weatherproof, **leather** is used. In addition, leather can take a severe jerk. Leather, or rawhide, rope is made by hand from strips of untanned cowhide. The strips are braided carefully together so that they are perfectly even and free of kinks. Oil, lanolin, or wax is rubbed into them to make them supple and to preserve them. Rawhide was once used to make the lariat, the cowboy's rope.

### Wire Rope

When tremendous strength and little bulk are needed in a rope, **wire** is used. Wire ropes are used for elevator cables, towlines used by tugboats, and guy lines that brace telephone poles and masts. They are also used for suspension lines on bridges. Wire rope can be used even when there are rapid changes of load due to quick starts and stops or sudden, violent motions. Huge fiber hawsers could carry great loads and absorb the jerk, but they are too large to be handled practically.

Wire ropes come in all sizes—they may be very fine and supple or big enough for a load of 100 tons. Wire ropes are made by the same general methods used in making fiber ropes. They have the advantage of being smaller than fiber ropes of the same strength, and of wearing longer. But larger wire ropes are very heavy. Some are too stiff and heavy for people to use easily and are used only on machines.

### Synthetic-Fiber Rope

**Nylon** is a synthetic fiber that makes a very strong, lightweight, stretchable rope. Nylon ropes are very elastic—that is, they can stretch a long way under strain and then recover their size and shape. Their ability to absorb a violent jerk is important in the climbing ropes used by mountaineers, the lines used by waterskiers, fishing lines, and mooring lines.

A fiber forms as the stream of liquid pulled from the nylon solution hits the air and hardens.

**Dacron** and **polypropylene** are strong synthetic fibers that are also weatherproof. When hemp rope was used on sailing ships in the early 1800's, it had to be repeatedly coated with pine tar to prevent rotting. Abaca rope must be oiled during manufacture. But Dacron and polypropylene rope

do not rot because the fibers are synthetic—they are manufactured from chemicals and do not break down like natural fibers.

Reviewed by HAROLD M. WALL
Chairman of the Board
Wall Industries, Inc.

See also KNOTS.

# ROPING

To the working cowboy, roping means throwing a rope so that a loop at the end of it encircles and catches cattle or horses. This form of roping is called catch-roping or lassoing. The word "lasso" comes from a Spanish word, *lazo,* meaning "slipknot" or "snare."

Since the early days of cattle ranching in the American West, catch-roping has been one of the cowboy's most useful skills on the ranch and on the range.

A newer form of roping is rope spinning. This is enjoyed as a sport or hobby both on and off the ranch. In rope spinning, the roper tosses a loop of rope into the air and quickly turns the loop so that it widens into a circle. The roper keeps this circle spinning while doing tricks and stunts.

The art of rope spinning developed in Mexico and was introduced in the United States in the late 1800's. Cowboys, who were already skilled in rope handling, began to practice rope spinning in their spare time. Today people in many areas enjoy rope spinning as a hobby.

If you have ever been to a rodeo, you have seen a demonstration of the third and most difficult kind of roping: trick and fancy roping and horse catching. Rodeo performers do a number of stunts with a spinning rope and then throw the rope to catch a horse or steer. The humorist Will Rogers (1879–1935) was one of the greatest trick and fancy ropers of all time.

## ▶ ROPING AS A HOBBY

To enjoy roping as a hobby, you need only a rope and a small outdoor area in which to practice. You must start, though, with the right kind of rope. An old clothesline or string will not do.

**(1)**

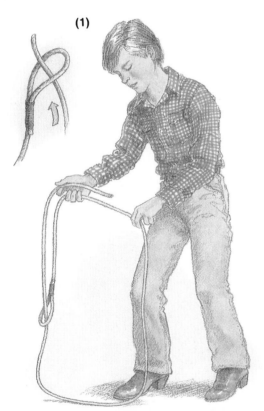

**(2)**

**The Flat Loop: (1)** Stand bent forward. With both hands a little below waist level, hold the loop about a foot from your body. Let the bottom of the loop rest on the ground. The spoke should go straight up into the right hand from the honda. The spoke is held with the thumb and forefinger, and the loop rests on the other fingers of the right hand. **(2)** With your right hand holding both the loop and spoke, toss the loop out to the left and away from you. Let go of the loop with your left hand as you toss.

In the early days of the West, ropes were made of horsehair. Later they were made of buffalo, buck, or elk hide. Today cowboys and cowgirls use an extra-quality hemp rope about ⅖ inch (1 centimeter) thick and about 40 feet (12 meters) long as a catch-rope or lariat. (The term "lariat" comes from *la reata,* meaning "the rope" in Spanish.)

For spinning, the best rope is a braided cotton rope known as spot cord. The spinning rope is about 20 feet (6 meters) long. In trick and fancy roping, a four-strand maguey rope 35 to 50 feet (10½ to 15 meters) long is used. The ropes can be bought in a well-stocked hardware or Western-goods store.

The three ropes are similar in construction. All three have a honda, or small loop or eye, at one end. ("Honda" means "sling" in Spanish.) The length of rope from the honda to the end held in the hand is called the spoke or stem.

The first step in roping is learning to coil the rope neatly, so that it runs out smoothly when it is thrown. Before starting, loosen up a hemp or maguey rope by softening the fibers. Pull it back and forth over a fence or post a few times.

A rope may be spun in circles that are parallel to the ground (flat spins) or in circles that are at right angles to the ground (vertical spins).

For beginners, the first spins to master are the flat spins. The basic flat spin is the flat loop. To learn to do this spin, pass the end of the rope through the honda and form a loop, using about 10 feet (3 meters) of rope. Follow the sequence of steps shown in the drawings, beginning on the previous page.

GENE AUTRY

See also RODEOS.

**ROSENBERG, JULIUS and ETHEL.** See SPIES (Profiles).

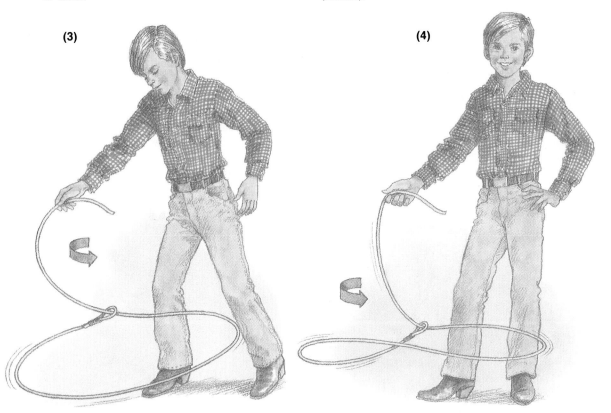

**(3)** Immediately move your right hand in a counterclockwise circle parallel to the ground and about the size of the loop you want to spin. As you complete the circle, let go of the loop with your right hand. Holding only the spoke, raise your hand a little and continue to make circles in the air. **(4)** As the loop spins, you can make smaller and smaller circles (the size of the loop remains the same), until you are spinning the loop with just a circular motion of the wrist. Hold the spoke end loosely, so that it can turn in your hand as you spin. This prevents the rope from kinking.

According to legend, Philadelphia seamstress Betsy Ross sewed the first American flag in June 1776, at the request of General George Washington.

## ROSS, BETSY (1752–1836)

Schoolchildren all over the United States are familiar with the legend that the first Stars and Stripes flag was designed by a Philadelphia woman named Betsy Ross. The account of the part she played in creating the flag was first told by her grandson, William Canby, in 1870. But no one has been able to prove that the story is true.

Elizabeth (Betsy) Griscom was born in Philadelphia, Pennsylvania, on New Year's Day, 1752, the eighth child of a devout Quaker couple. When she was a young woman, Betsy married a furniture upholsterer named John Ross. Ross was not a Quaker, and Betsy's parents objected to the marriage.

John Ross opened an upholstery shop on Arch Street in Philadelphia. He also served in the militia. While on guard duty, Ross was wounded by an explosion of gunpowder. He died of his wounds, and Betsy was left to carry on her husband's business, to which she added flag making. Next, Betsy married Captain Joseph Ashburn, who was captured by the British and died a military prisoner. They had two daughters. Then, in 1783, Betsy married John Claypool. They lived happily and Betsy had five more daughters. She died in Philadelphia on January 30, 1836.

Betsy Ross has become a folk heroine because of the story her grandson, William Canby, told about her. According to Canby, General George Washington and two aides came into the Arch Street shop one day in June 1776. They asked Betsy Ross to make a new flag for the 13 states. They brought with them a rough design. According to the legend, Betsy Ross made the flag but changed the design by making five-pointed stars instead of the proposed six-pointed stars.

The Arch Street shop still stands in Philadelphia, and thousands of people visit it each year.

Reviewed by JOHN J. WATERS
University of Rochester

**ROSS, SIR JAMES CLARK.** See NORTHWEST PASSAGE.

**ROSS, JOHN (Cherokee chief).** See INDIANS, AMERICAN (Profiles).

**ROSS, SIR JOHN (Scottish explorer).** See NORTHWEST PASSAGE.

**ROSS, NELLIE TAYLOE.** See WYOMING (Famous People).

Drawing of Christina by her brother Dante Gabriel.

## ROSSETTI FAMILY

Dante Gabriel, Christina Georgina, Maria Francesca, and William Michael were the children of the Italian poet Gabriele Rossetti. He fled from Italy after the revolution of 1820 and became a professor of Italian at King's College, London.

Dante Gabriel, who was called Gabriel, was born in London on May 12, 1828. He began to write and draw when he was very young. His imagination was stirred by tales of adventure and terror. When he was 13, he left school and studied drawing.

By the age of 20, Gabriel was the leader of a group of young artists who admired the realistic style of Italian painting of the time before Raphael (1483–1520). They called themselves the Pre-Raphaelite Brotherhood. In 1850 they published *The Germ,* a magazine of art and poetry. In it appeared original poems by three Rossettis—Gabriel, Christina, and William.

In the 1850's and 1860's, Gabriel spent most of his time painting, but he also continued to write. The publication of a collection of his poems in 1870 established his reputation as a major Victorian poet. In his last years, he was mentally unstable and dependent on drugs. But he stood at the center of a new Pre-Raphaelite circle of writers who followed his poetic example. In 1881 he published *Ballads and Sonnets,* a fine volume of new and revised work. He died on April 9, 1882.

Gabriel's sister Christina was born on December 5, 1830. She was educated at home and began writing verses in early childhood. Her grandfather, Gaetano Polidori, owned a private press, and he printed her first book of poems in 1847. Christina's contributions to *The Germ* three years later showed a fine sense of form and a musical ear. In 1862 she published *Goblin Market and Other Poems,* with two illustrations by Gabriel. The title piece tells an exciting story in rollicking rhymes and colorful detail.

As a young woman, the beautiful Christina often modeled for the Pre-Raphaelite painters. In later life she suffered a long, painful illness. But she kept active as a poet and storyteller until her death on December 29, 1894. She is remembered as the author of charming nursery rhymes, love lyrics and sonnets, and hymns of great religious intensity.

"Who Has Seen the Wind?" is one of Christina Rossetti's best-known poems for young readers.

Who has seen the wind?
  Neither I nor you:
But when the leaves hang trembling
  The wind is passing thro'.

Who has seen the wind?
  Neither you nor I:
But when the trees bow down their heads
  The wind is passing by.

Maria, born on February 17, 1827, was the most practical of the children. She helped in the home and had a gift for educational work. Her best book, *A Shadow of Dante* (1871), carries on the work of her scholarly father. Her lifelong interest in religious teaching appears in *Letters to My Bible-Class* (1872). Maria entered an Anglican convent in 1873 and died there on November 24, 1876.

William was born on September 25, 1829. From 1845 to 1894 he worked in a government office, and his salary was the chief support of the family. He was editor of *The Germ* in 1850, and for the rest of a long life he edited family diaries and journals, as well as collections of the works of Gabriel and Christina. His own poems are less important than his literary essays. He remained, until his death on February 5, 1919, the faithful recorder of Pre-Raphaelite life and art.

JEROME H. BUCKLEY
Harvard University

# ROTHSCHILD FAMILY

Mayer Amschel Rothschild, the founder of the great banking house of Rothschild, was born in the ghetto, or Jewish section, of Frankfurt am Main, Germany, in 1743. The family took its name from the red shield (*rotes Schild* in German) that was painted above the door of an ancestral home. Mayer was given a Jewish education. Instead of becoming a rabbi, as his father had hoped, he became a dealer in old coins.

Mayer's business grew. He started a small banking establishment and was soon making business loans. When he was successful enough to support a wife, he married Gutele Schnapper. The couple had ten children, five girls and five boys.

One of Mayer's clients, Prince William of Hesse-Kassel, was so impressed by Mayer's keen business sense that he made Mayer his personal adviser. Mayer's business grew so large that he sent four of his sons to open offices abroad. Salomon went to Vienna, Nathan to London, Karl to Naples, and James to Paris. The fifth son, Amschel, stayed in Frankfurt. The offices flourished, and the Rothschild name was soon known in banking circles around the world.

Mayer's sons carried out their father's deathbed instructions to work harmoniously and keep the business together. Their banks made huge loans to businesses and governments. In 1822, Emperor Francis I of Austria made all five of them barons.

From these beginnings the house of Rothschild continued to grow. The family produced doctors, writers, scientists, and philanthropists. Mayer's grandson Lionel took his seat as the first Jewish member of the British House of Commons in 1858. Lionel's son Nathan became a member of the House of Lords in 1885. Another grandson, Alphonse, served in the French Senate. The house of Rothschild, headquartered in London and Paris, is still a powerful force in international finance.

Reviewed by GERARD BRAUNTHAL
University of Massachusetts, Amherst

---

# ROUSSEAU, JEAN JACQUES (1712–1778)

The philosopher, novelist, and essayist Jean Jacques Rousseau was born in Geneva, Switzerland, on June 28, 1712. His mother died about a week after his birth. His father, a watchmaker, was his first teacher.

When Jean Jacques was 10, his father was forced to leave Geneva after a duel. He moved to Nyon, leaving Jean Jacques in Geneva in the care of relatives. Young Rousseau attended a boarding school and was later apprenticed to an engraver. But he became restless, and in 1728 he ran away. In France he met Madame de Warens of Annecy, who befriended him. He spent long periods in her house, reading, writing verse, and composing music.

In 1741, Rousseau went to Paris. Through friends he obtained the position of secretary to the French ambassador in Venice. After a year and a half he returned to Paris.

His first fame came in 1750, when he won an essay contest with his *Discourse on the Arts and Sciences*. This was followed in 1754 by his *Discourse on the Origin and Foundations of Inequality* and in 1762 by *The Social Contract*. In these works, Rousseau stated that unjust laws and customs were harmful to society because they deprived people of their natural equality and freedom.

Rousseau also wrote a successful operetta, which was presented before the king and at the Paris Opéra. Further success came with a novel, *The New Héloïse* (1761), and a book on education, *Émile* (1762), which describes the growing up of a child. Rousseau believed that a child should remain in a "state of nature," learning from experience and example rather than from books. Rousseau's ideas were so revolutionary that the government ordered his arrest. He fled to Môtiers in the principality of Neuchâtel (now in Switzerland).

In 1765 a booklet attacking him so aroused the people of Môtiers that they stoned his house. Rousseau moved to England in 1766. He returned to France finally and spent his last years writing his autobiography, the *Confessions*. He died on July 2, 1778.

Reviewed by RAMON M. LEMOS
Author, *Rousseau's Political Philosophy: An Exposition and Interpretation*

**ROWAN, CARL.** See JOURNALISM (Profiles).

Rowing is an exciting sport and an excellent form of exercise.

# ROWING

Rowing—moving a boat through water with oars—was an important means of transportation to early people. The ancient Greeks and Romans used galleys (huge boats) for transportation and warfare. These boats had oars arranged in tiers, one above the other. Some had as many as three tiers. They were rowed by slaves. The largest galleys had as many as 80 oarsmen.

Today rowing is popular as a pleasant exercise and as a means of transportation around small lakes and coves. With a little patience and practice almost anyone can learn to handle a small rowboat.

The oars fit into oarlocks on the sides of the boat. The rower sits between them facing the stern, or back. To row a straight course, you must pull equally on the two oars. To turn slightly, you must use more power and stroke on the side opposite the direction in which you wish to turn. For a sharper turn, you must row with one oar only. To row backward, you must reverse the stroke, pushing the oar handles away from yourself. A good rower rows smoothly and rhythmically and is careful not to splash water on passengers in the boat.

## ▶RACING BOATS

Modern racing boats are called shells. They are long, narrow boats made of a thin wooden or fiberglass skin over a frame. The rowers sit on sliding seats facing the stern. They tie their feet into shoes fixed into the boat.

Racing shells are of two types—sweeps and sculls.

In **sweep rowing,** each rower uses one oar, or sweep, 3.7 meters (12 feet) long. There are three basic sweep boats—pairs (with two rowers), fours (four rowers), and eights (eight rowers). Pairs and fours may be with or without coxswain. A coxswain is always used in eights. In crews without coxswain, one of the rowers steers the boat with a toeplate attached to the rudder lines.

In **sculling,** each rower uses two oars, or sculls, which are each 2.7 meters (9 feet) long. There are three basic sculling boats—single sculls (one rower), double sculls (two rowers), and quadruple sculls (four rowers). Scullers steer by varying the pressure on their oars.

## ▶THE COXSWAIN

In some races, a coxswain sits in the stern, facing forward, and steers with the tiller ropes. The coxswain also directs the timing of the oar strokes, which usually range from 28 to 45 strokes a minute. Since the coxswain does not row, he or she should be light in weight. The coxswain should also be keen, decisive, and able to inspire the crew.

## ▶ROWING RACES

Men's races are 2,000 meters (1.24 miles), and women's are 1,000 meters (0.62 miles). The course must be straight, wide enough for six crews, and of even depth. Crews begin rowing on the signal from the starter. The boats must stay in their lanes. But crews that

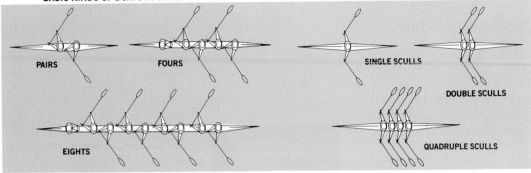

stray out of their lanes are not penalized if they do not hinder other boats.

The race is followed by a referee in a motorboat. Judges at the finish line determine the order of finish and take times. The winning boat is the one whose bow (front) first crosses the finish line.

### ▶ ROWING ACTION

A single stroke of the oar takes two seconds or less. Rowers use their legs, backs, and arms to generate the power needed to propel the shell to speeds as great as 24 kilometers (15 miles) an hour. In addition to strength and endurance, the rowers must possess grace and coordination in order for the boat to move smoothly through the water.

There are three parts to the rowing stroke—catch, pull-through, and finish. At the beginning of the stroke, you move your seat to the front of the slide as you take the oar back. This brings your knees up in front of you. Then you dip the oar to the full depth of the blade and push with your legs. This sends the seat sliding back. You complete the stroke with a backward body-and-arm swing. At the finish, you bring the blade cleanly out of the water, moving your hands first quickly, then slowly, away from your body.

### ▶ RACING HISTORY

During the 1500's, the Thames River in England was one of the world's busiest inland waterways. Accidents became so common that King Henry VIII ruled that only licensed oarsmen could row on the river. More than 3,200 licenses were issued. These professionals took great pride in their skill. Soon races were held to decide who were the best oarsmen.

In 1715, Thomas Doggett, an Irish comedian, offered a silver badge and orange livery to the winner of a race from London Bridge to Chelsea. This 7.2-kilometer (4½-mile) race was first held in the early 1700's. The prize is known as Doggett's Coat and Badge, and the race is still one of the most popular in the world.

English university students became interested in rowing early in the 1800's. Cambridge and Oxford met in the first intercollegiate rowing race on June 10, 1829. This race continues to be held every year. The most famous of all rowing races is the annual Henley Royal Regatta at Henley-on-Thames. Rowers from all over the world now compete in this colorful regatta, which was first held in 1839.

In the United States, Harvard and Yale met in the first intercollegiate regatta on Lake Winnipesaukee, New Hampshire, in 1852. The Intercollegiate Rowing Association, founded in 1895, gave the sport its great popularity in the United States. Colleges and universities from all over the country enter the association's annual regatta on the Cooper River in Camden County, New Jersey.

In 1858 several boat clubs around Philadelphia formed the "Schuylkill Navy." They made the first rules for amateur rowing in the United States. In 1872 the National Association of Amateur Oarsmen was organized. In 1982 this organization was combined with the National Women's Rowing Association to become USRowing, which is the governing body for rowing in the United States.

Rowing has been included in the Olympics since 1900. In that year, nine countries entered the rowing events. In recent Olympic Games, many more countries have competed in the rowing contests. Women's rowing made its first Olympic appearance in 1976.

ERIC E. STOLL
USRowing

See also BOATS AND BOATING; OLYMPIC GAMES.

## ROWLING, J. K. (1965– )

J. K. Rowling is known worldwide as the author of the phenomenally popular Harry Potter books. Her stories about the adventures of the boy wizard have captured the imagination of children and adults alike.

Joanne Kathleen Rowling was born on July 31, 1965, in Chipping Sodbury, England. She started writing stories at the age of 6 and wrote her first novel when she was 11. She later graduated from the University of Exeter and worked for the human rights organization Amnesty International.

Rowling was struck with the idea of Harry Potter while riding on a train in 1990. She worked on the first book for the next four years, during which time she married, had a daughter, divorced, and moved to Edinburgh, Scotland. She often wrote in local cafés with her young daughter sleeping at her side. Published in 1997, *Harry Potter and the Philosopher's Stone* (published in the United States in 1998 under the title *Harry Potter and the Sorcerer's Stone*) introduced readers to the magical world of the Hogwarts School of Witchcraft and Wizardry, where Harry and his friends Hermione and Ron learn spells and try to defeat the evil Lord Voldemort.

Rowling envisioned seven Harry Potter books. Each of the next four books—*Harry Potter and the Chamber of Secrets* (1999), *Harry Potter and the Prisoner of Azkaban* (1999), *Harry Potter and the Goblet of Fire* (2000), and *Harry Potter and the Order of the Phoenix* (2003)—was eagerly awaited by readers and proved to be even more popular than the one before it. The first two installments in the series were named the British Book Award's Children's Book of the Year, and *Goblet of Fire* became the fastest-selling book of all time after 3 million copies were sold in the first two days of its release.

The books have been translated into more than 60 languages and inspired a series of successful motion pictures, the first one released in 2001.

Reviewed by WILLIAM E. SHAPIRO
Consultant, children's encyclopedias

---

# ROYAL CANADIAN MOUNTED POLICE

The Royal Canadian Mounted Police (RCMP) is Canada's national police force. Its purpose is to enforce laws, prevent crime, and maintain peace, order, and security. It handles all federal policing in Canada, as well as provincial and municipal policing in three territories, eight provinces (except Ontario and Quebec), parts of Newfoundland and Labrador, and more than 200 municipalities. The RCMP also provides police services to nearly 200 First Nations communities, which are made up of native peoples.

The RCMP was originally called the North-West Mounted Police. Officers, nicknamed "Mounties," typically traveled on horseback and wore distinctive scarlet jackets. Today, officers are more likely to travel by car, plane, or even snowmobile, although horses are ridden during special ceremonies. The traditional uniform is also reserved for special occasions, such as the RCMP Musical Ride. (For more information, see the Wonder Question accompanying this article.) The working uniform of the RCMP now consists of blue trousers and a gray shirt.

▸ SCOPE OF OPERATIONS

More than 22,000 people are employed by the RCMP, including some 3,000 civilians. The organization is headed by a commissioner in Ottawa. It is divided into four regions, each headed by a deputy commissioner, then further divided into 14 divisions, plus its national headquarters. At the local level, there are more than 750 detachments.

As a federal police force, the RCMP has a scope of operations that includes fighting organized crime, terrorism, crimes related to the illicit drug trade, and economic crimes. It protects Canada's borders, as well as public figures, and provides the government with security services.

The RCMP also operates the National Police Services, which provides resources to other Canadian law enforcement agencies and international police organizations such as Interpol. These resources include computer databases of fingerprints, criminal records, missing children, and firearms, as well as Forensic Laboratory Services, which analyzes evidence from crime scenes, and the Canadian Bomb Data Centre. National Police Services also operates the Criminal Intelligence Service Canada, which coordinates the gathering and sharing of information on organized crime and similar activities. In addition, it provides specialized training to Canadian and foreign police agencies.

Each year, approximately 10,000 people apply to become RCMP officers. To qualify, an applicant must be a Canadian citizen of good character and at least 19 years old, have a high school diploma, and be able to speak and write in English or French (both official languages). He or she must also be able to meet the physical requirements and be willing to relocate anywhere within Canada. Once selected, applicants undergo an intensive six-month training session at the RCMP Training Academy in Regina, Saskatchewan. This is followed by another six months of on-the-job training.

▶ HISTORY

The RCMP was conceived by Sir John A. Macdonald, Canada's first prime minister and

Royal Canadian Mounted Police perform a riding drill in traditional dress. The RCMP, originally called the North-West Mounted Police, was formed in the 1870's.

minister of justice. Macdonald wanted to establish law and order on the vast western Canadian plains, then known as the North-West Territories (the present-day provinces of Alberta and Saskatchewan). On May 23, 1873, Parliament passed a bill authorizing the creation of a police force, the North-West Mounted Police (NWMP). It called for the enlistment of able-bodied men of good character between the ages of 18 and 40 who could ride a horse.

NWMP detachments were established throughout the West. Their mission included establishing friendly relations with the Indians, enforcing prohibition and eliminating the illegal whiskey trade, and ensuring the health and welfare of the rapidly growing immigrant population.

In 1904, the NWMP became the Royal North-West Mounted Police. In 1905, it began provincial police work for Alberta and Saskatchewan and by 1950 was policing all provinces except Ontario and Quebec. In 1920 it became authorized to enforce federal laws in the entire country and changed its name to the RCMP. At this time, it also merged with the Dominion Police, which had been responsible for Canada's eastern regions, and established its headquarters in Ottawa, Ontario.

Royal Canadian Mounted Police

**RUANDA-URUNDI.** See BURUNDI; RWANDA.

## WONDER QUESTION

### What is the Musical Ride?

The Musical Ride is a complex set of traditional riding drills performed to music by the Royal Canadian Mounted Police. It is performed by 32 riders dressed in the traditional scarlet coats and broad-brimmed hats. The Musical Ride was originally developed so that the Mounties could display their riding ability and entertain the local community. The first known display was held in 1876, and the first Musical Ride performance was held at the Regina barracks in 1887. Regular public performances of the Ride started in 1904. Today the Musical Ride is based at the RCMP Rockcliffe, Ontario, facility. It is performed throughout Canada and around the world.

Rubber—both natural and synthetic—is used to make thousands of products, from diving gear and raincoats to toys and balloons. It is particularly valued for its elasticity, as well as its ability to hold air, keep out noise, resist moisture, and grip surfaces without slipping. Rubber is also important because it does not conduct electricity.

# RUBBER

Rubber is one of the world's most widely used and important raw materials. It is used to manufacture thousands of products that make our lives safer, more comfortable, and more convenient. About 1.4 million tons of rubber products are produced each year. Of this, about 75 percent consists of tires.

Natural rubber is obtained from trees. In addition, people have learned to manufacture various types of synthetic rubber.

Rubber is particularly valued for its elasticity; that is, it stretches easily and quickly returns to its original form. It is also important because it is waterproof, does not conduct electricity, holds air (as in tires), grips surfaces without slipping, and keeps out noise. Both natural rubber and synthetic materials with these properties are called **elastomers**.

### ▶ NATURAL RUBBER

Natural rubber comes from **latex**, a white fluid found in rubber trees. Latex is made up of tiny rubber particles in a watery liquid plus small amounts of other materials.

Most of the world's supply of natural rubber comes from plantations in Thailand, Indonesia, Malaysia, and other countries of Southeast Asia. There are also important plantations in India, China, the Philippines, the Ivory Coast, Sri Lanka, Nigeria, and Brazil. Although there are many kinds of rubber trees, most plantations grow a type that is native to Brazil, the *Hevea brasiliensis*.

Large plantations grow millions of trees. Most reach a height of about 65 feet (20 meters). They have smooth, light-colored bark and dark, shiny leaves. Latex is first taken from a tree when it is 6 to 7 years old. The average rubber tree reaches its period of highest yield in about its 14th year. After 20 to 30 years, the amount of rubber a tree yields becomes less and less. The old tree must then be replaced with a new one.

The job of obtaining and processing latex for shipment involves many steps. The first is to tap the tree. The tappers, as the workers are called, start at dawn because latex flows most freely in the coolness of the morning. Using a sharp knife, the tapper cuts a narrow groove in the tree bark, sticks a V-shaped metal spout in the lower end of the cut, and then hangs a small cup under the spout. Once the groove has been cut in the tree, the latex begins to ooze out. A worker can tap about 500 trees per day, with each tree yielding about a cupful of latex.

When returning to a tree to tap it again, the tapper slices off another thin shaving of bark, slightly below the first groove. This re-opens the latex veins. The latex from the tappers' pails is carried by truck to a factory, where the latex can be processed either in liquid form (concentrated latex) or in solid form (crepe, smoked sheet, or block rubber).

If the latex is to remain in liquid form, it is run through centrifuges similar to the separators used on a dairy farm. These machines spin the latex at high speed, removing most of the water. To protect the latex from bacteria and to keep it from coagulating (thickening or clotting), a preservative such as ammonia is added at various stages, from the collection cup through final processing. Products such as rubber gloves, tubing, balloons, and toys are made by dipping a mold into liquid latex. Some latex is forced through tiny tubes and coagulated to make rubber thread.

If processed into a solid form, the latex is first coagulated into a solid mass called coagulum, which has the appearance and consistency of gelatin. If crepe or smoked sheets are to be made, the coagulum is passed between rollers that squeeze out most of the water. The remaining water is removed by drying.

In making crepe, the rollers roughen and crinkle the sheets of coagulum. This gives them ridges, like thick crepe paper. The sheets are then hung to dry in the sun or a heated room. This type of rubber is used to make crepe-rubber soles for shoes and many other products.

To make smoked sheets, the coagulum is passed through rollers that give the sheets a ribbed appearance. The sheets are hung in a hot smokehouse to dry. The smoke colors the rubber and helps preserve it. To make block rubber, the coagulum is formed into small crumblike particles and dried. These particles, called crumb rubber, are then pressed into small bales. Smoked sheets and block rubber are used primarily for tires.

## ▶ SYNTHETIC RUBBER

Synthetic rubber accounts for about two-thirds of all rubber currently used in the United States, Canada, and Mexico. North America now produces nearly one-third of the world's supply. The development of synthetic rubber in the mid-1900's can be traced to earlier discoveries by English scientists Michael Faraday and Charles Grenville Williams.

In 1826, Faraday found that rubber is a hydrocarbon—that is, a combination of the elements hydrogen and carbon. This was the

Rubber trees are grown on large plantations, where tappers (*below*) collect latex from the trees. Most of the world's rubber supply comes from plantations in Southeast Asia.

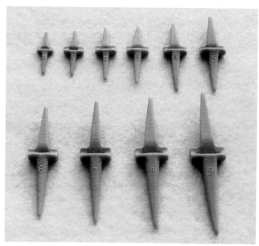

Many types of synthetic rubber have been developed for different purposes. One kind is silicone, which is used for implants such as these replacement finger joints.

Most of the synthetic rubber produced is a general-purpose type of rubber called **styrene-butadiene rubber**, or SBR. It is made by pumping butadiene and styrene gases into a large reactor or tank filled with a soapy mixture that makes it easier for the rubber particles to form. A **catalyst** (a chemical that speeds up the reaction) is added. As the mixture in the reactor is stirred, it gradually changes to a milky white liquid. This is synthetic latex, which looks similar to natural latex from rubber trees. When the synthetic latex has developed to a proper state, a chemical is added to stop the reaction. The latex is then coagulated, and the resulting synthetic rubber is dried and pressed into bales.

Other kinds of synthetic rubber can be produced by using other ingredients or by combining or processing the ingredients in different ways. To produce a product that wears better, for example, lower temperatures are used in the reactor.

Some synthetic rubbers have been developed that can better withstand solvents, chemicals, and other harsh conditions. **Neoprene**, for instance, is used for gasoline hose and to cover electrical wires that come in contact with oil or are exposed to sunlight. It is made from acetylene gas and hydrogen chloride. **Butyl** rubber, made from the gas isobutylene and the liquid isoprene, is much better than any other rubber for holding air and is therefore used for automobile inner tubes and linings for tubeless tires. **Nitrile** rubber, made of butadiene and acrylonitrile, is exceptionally resistant to oil and is used for seals, gaskets, fuel hose, and other products that must resist oil.

Specialty rubbers that can withstand very high or low temperatures have also been developed. These include **silicone**, **fluorocarbon**, and **phosphazene**. These rubbers are often expensive and difficult to produce. But they are vital for parts used in such products as jet engines and pollution-control devices.

The production of **polyurethane** rubber involves a different way of making the giant polymer needed to get rubberlike properties. An intermediate-molecular-weight liquid, called a prepolymer, is formed first. Then a chemical is added that rapidly joins the prepolymer molecules together to form the high-molecular-weight rubber. This technique is especially useful for making soft foam rubber

beginning of the formal study of rubber's chemistry. In 1860, Williams found that rubber was composed of a basic material that he called **isoprene**. Each isoprene molecule was found to contain five atoms of carbon and eight atoms of hydrogen. Chemists write this in a formula as $C_5H_8$.

Later, chemists learned that rubber is a giant molecule formed by joining together many isoprene molecules. They join together like the links of a chain. When the isoprene molecules link together, they no longer behave as separate molecules. They form a material with entirely different properties. This new material is called a **polymer**, from the Greek *poly* ("many") and *meros* ("part").

Early attempts to produce rubbery materials by synthetically linking together isoprene molecules were not very successful. The resulting rubber was of poor quality and costly to produce. But when supplies of natural rubber from the Far East were cut off from the United States during World War II (1939–45), chemists tried even harder to make synthetic rubber. As a result, a commercially successful process was quickly developed.

Some products, such as gaskets, washers, and wire coating, can be made entirely of synthetic rubber. Other products, such as tires used for trucks, airplanes, and earth-moving equipment, are best made almost entirely from natural rubber. Many other products, such as automobile tires, are made from a combination of both.

for cushions and mattresses and very large molded rubber items such as automobile body parts.

## MAKING RUBBER PRODUCTS

In manufacturing rubber products, natural rubber and synthetic rubber are treated in much the same way. The bales are cut into small pieces for easier handling. Various ingredients are added to the rubber to give it qualities such as strength and elasticity. Pigments may be added to color the rubber.

Most rubber must be treated with sulfur and heat to make it tougher and more durable. This process is called **vulcanization**. Without vulcanization, rubber products would be sticky in the heat and stiff and brittle in the cold. (Some synthetic rubbers called **thermoplastic elastomers** have recently been developed that do not require vulcanization. But the materials needed to produce them are relatively expensive, so scientists are looking for ways to make them with less expensive materials.)

Carbon black (a soft, powdery form of carbon) is another important ingredient added to rubber. It makes the rubber tougher and more resistant to abrasion (wearing away by friction). Newer products also contain silica, which can keep items such as contact lenses colorless and transparent.

When all the necessary chemicals have been added to the rubber, it is emptied into a large mixer. After it is thoroughly mixed, the batch goes to a mill, where it is rolled into a sheet about ¼ inch (6 millimeters) thick.

Rubber is made into a finished product by **calendering**, **extrusion**, or **molding**.

A calender is a machine with a series of huge rollers. Its main use is to press rubber into fabric and sheets for tires.

Extrusion is the most widely used method of forming rubber products. The soft rubber is pushed out through holes in a metal shaping device called a die. The shaped rubber is squeezed from the die

much as toothpaste is squeezed from a tube. Examples of extruded products are inner tubes and tire treads.

In molding, the rubber is placed in a metal form and heated until it has taken on the shape of the mold. Many small products, such as handlebar grips, foot pedals, and mats, are made this way. Any molded rubber product must be vulcanized so that it will keep its molded shape.

The possibilities for new products and new uses of rubber are limitless. Scientists in the rubber industry are continually developing new kinds of rubber and new uses for it.

## HISTORY OF NATURAL RUBBER

When Europeans first went to the New World more than 400 years ago, they saw people in Central and South America playing a game with a bouncing ball. They learned that the ball had been made out of a white liquid that oozed from certain trees. But Europeans did not pay much attention to this material until nearly 200 years later.

In 1735 the French scientist Charles de La Condamine traveled up the Amazon river in South America. He asked about the tree that could produce balls that bounced. The Indians told him they called the tree *cau-uchu*, meaning "weeping wood." The drops of sticky fluid oozing out of the tree reminded them of tears. La Condamine named the fluid *caoutchouc* (kow-chook) after its native name. The English word "rubber" came from the discovery that the gummy material could erase, or rub out, pencil marks on paper.

La Condamine showed his samples of dried rubber to another French scientist, François Fresneau, and the two men began to experiment with the strange material. Fresneau decided to tap a rubber tree himself and study the liquid before it dried. To show how rubber could be used, he coated a pair of old

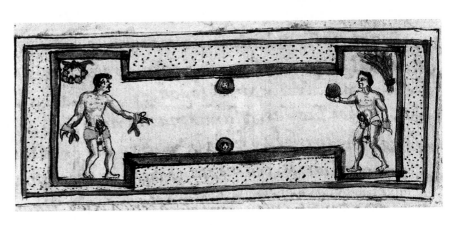

An early manuscript shows Aztec men playing a game with a rubber ball. Early people of Latin America collected and used the latex that oozed from certain trees.

boots with the liquid, creating one of the first pairs of waterproof boots.

When La Condamine and Fresneau returned to France, they published reports on rubber. Although Europeans were very interested in its commercial possibilities, it was clear that a method had to be found to make the dried rubber soft and workable. Fresneau tried soaking it in turpentine. The turpentine turned the rubber into a liquid solution that could then be brushed over shoes and clothes to make them waterproof. Other scientists and some manufacturers experimented further on rubber with different solvents.

Solid rubber had a limited commercial value. Thomas Hancock, an Englishman, cut strips of rubber from large balls shipped from South America. He covered the strips with cloth and sold them as elastic bands. However, there seemed to be no way to use the scraps of rubber left from the cuttings.

In 1820, Hancock designed a machine, called a masticator, to chew the scraps into tiny bits. Instead it pressed them into a large ball. This gave Hancock a large amount of solid rubber, which he could cut into different shapes. The masticator also made the rubber softer by kneading it. This invention marked the beginning of rubber manufacturing as we know it today.

Three years later Charles Macintosh introduced a new process to waterproof cloth with rubber. Macintosh first dissolved the rubber in a solution of coal-tar naphtha, which was a better solvent than turpentine. The liquid was brushed over two pieces of fabric, and the rubber-coated pieces were laid back to back and squeezed together. Rain and sleet could not penetrate this inner layer of rubber.

Many U.S. companies started producing rubber goods. But, although rubberized coats were practical and could be marketed successfully, many rubber products were useless because they stiffened in the winter and became soft and sticky in the summer. The rubber companies were soon in financial trouble.

A young inventor, Charles Goodyear, became interested in the changeable nature of rubber and started looking for a way to improve it. In 1838 he heard that Nathaniel M. Hayward had discovered a way to make rubber less sticky by mixing it with sulfur. Goodyear hired Hayward to continue experimenting with rubber. He also bought the rights to Hayward's patent.

One day Goodyear accidentally dropped some of the rubber-and-sulfur mixture on a hot stove. Instead of melting, the rubber turned into a leatherlike strip that did not become sticky or brittle as the temperature changed. From this accident Goodyear was able to work out the processing method he called vulcanization, named after Vulcan, the Roman god of fire. This discovery was the turning point in the rubber industry. With vulcanized rubber, manufacturers were able to make reliable products, and the rubber industry began to grow rapidly.

Rubber solved many problems in the developing industrial age. Leaks in a steam engine could be quickly and effectively sealed with elastic, airtight rubber. Wires carrying

Natural rubber did not have many practical uses until the 1830's, when Charles Goodyear (*left*) invented a way to improve its strength and stability. His process, called vulcanization, paved the way for the rise of the rubber industry.

A worker (*above*) prepares crushed tires for recycling. Researchers continue to seek ways to dispose of the millions of worn tires discarded each year.

electricity were made safer by insulating them with rubber. Air brakes for trains were connected by hoses of fabric and rubber, strong enough to stand heavy pressure and yet flexible enough to carry the braking system from car to car.

The demand for rubber increased during the last half of the 1800's. Many new uses were found and many factories opened. As automobile manufacturing got under way, rubber became even more important.

But rubber was difficult and expensive to obtain; practically the only sources were the jungles of South and Central American countries, mainly Brazil. As a result, growers began to look elsewhere for a supply. In 1861 the Dutch started a rubber plantation in Java, using native trees. Rubber could be gathered more easily and economically from trees planted in orderly rows on a plantation than from those scattered around the jungles.

The next major attempt to domesticate rubber trees was made by the British. In 1876, Sir Henry Wickman planted seeds from Brazilian Hevea trees in greenhouses near London. The seedlings were replanted in what is now Sri Lanka and Malaysia, where the growing conditions were similar to Brazil's. After that, rubber became an important plantation crop in southeastern Asia.

### ▶ CURRENT AND FUTURE TRENDS

As the demand for rubber increases, people are looking for new sources of this material. One possibility is a bush called guayule (wy-OO-lee), which grows in Mexico and the southwestern United States. Through careful plant breeding and techniques such as genetic engineering, researchers have developed new varieties of faster-growing guayule that yield more latex than the wild varieties. One advantage of guayule rubber is that it produces no allergic reactions in people who are allergic to products (such as surgical gloves) made from Brazilian rubber trees. However, it is still relatively expensive to extract the rubber from the plant.

At the same time, researchers are seeking practical ways to dispose of used rubber—mainly the millions of worn tires discarded each year. Some of these tires are ground up, and the rubber is reclaimed for use in new products. Some are used as artificial reefs on ocean bottoms, to provide havens for fish. Still others are ground up and used in asphalt for paving.

There is also another way to dispose of used tires. By burning them in specially designed, pollution-free incinerators, old tires could become a source of energy. But this method is extremely costly.

One new approach is to use high-energy sound waves to break up the linkages between the molecular chains, which is basically the reverse of the vulcanization process. These regenerated polymers can be used like new materials, or used in blends with other elastomers.

JAMES E. MARK
University of Cincinnati

# RUBBINGS

Have you ever put a piece of paper on top of a coin and then rubbed a pencil over it until the pattern of the coin appeared? That is a very simple form of rubbing. Rubbing is an easy way to reproduce many designs and textures—even very complicated ones.

You can rub all kinds of things, from small coins to large wall carvings, manhole and sewer covers, and even stained-glass windows. In the United States old gravestones are often good subjects. The stones in New England graveyards are especially popular because of their interesting designs. In Britain the floors of churches are often set with brass plaques, some of which date back to medieval times. Many plaques mark the graves of important people. People enjoy doing rubbings of these plaques, with their designs of knights and ladies or religious subjects.

Rubbing is an exciting way to learn about history and architecture. It may help you to notice things in your town that you never noticed before. It is also a way to preserve, on paper, images of things that may one day be destroyed or worn away. Frame your rubbings and hang them on your walls, or use them as patterns for needlepoint, block printing, and other crafts.

There are two basic rubbing techniques.

The wax method is used for rubbing flat surfaces or surfaces with designs carved into them. The graphite method is used on surfaces with raised designs.

## ▶ THE WAX METHOD

To do a rubbing with this method, first decide what you want to rub and get all your materials together. You will need a sheet of paper large enough to cover your subject. The paper should be fairly strong but not too thick. Brown wrapping paper, newsprint, and rice paper are all good. You will also need masking tape, scissors, a natural-bristle brush, and a crayon. Special rubbing wax is available in some art-supply stores. It is less likely to smear than crayons.

Go over your subject with the brush so that it is cleaned of dirt. (Never use a metal-bristle brush, as the bristles may damage the object.) Cut your paper to a size that will completely cover the design you want to rub. Then tape it down securely at the edges. Next, rub the colored wax or crayon lightly over the entire surface of the paper to block in the design. Feel around on the paper with your fingers to make sure you have covered all parts of the design. When you can see the whole design, decide where you want to darken the rubbing. If you press harder with the wax, the rubbing will become darker, and more details will show up.

**To do a rubbing by the wax method, first get all your materials together. Use a natural-bristle brush to clean dust and dirt from the object you plan to rub.**

**The paper you use should be strong but not too thick. Cut the paper to a size that will completely cover the design, and then tape it down securely at the edges.**

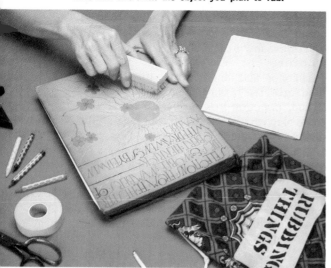

Continue rubbing until you think you have all the details you want. To see if you have missed any, you can peek beneath the paper by lifting one section of tape. But make sure that the rest of the tape is tightly attached. Never lift the paper all the way off—it will be impossible to put it back exactly the way it was. When your rubbing is finished, gently remove the tape by peeling it toward the edges of the paper.

For a different effect, try metallic or white wax on black paper. Fabric may be used instead of paper, but you will need special fabric-dying crayons.

### ▶ THE GRAPHITE METHOD

In this method, rubbing is done with a paste of mineral oil and graphite. (Graphite is the soft, black carbon that is used in pencils.) Working with graphite is messy. You should wear old clothes and use utensils that can be thrown away. Cover your work area with newspapers or a plastic drop cloth.

You can buy mineral oil at a drugstore and powdered graphite at an art-supply or a hardware store. Find an old but clean can and a mixing stick. Put some graphite in the can and slowly stir in mineral oil until the mixture is thick and pasty, like canned shoe polish. If the mixture gets too thin, add more graphite. Store the mixture in a covered plastic bowl to keep it from drying out.

Rub crayon or colored wax over the entire surface to block in the design. Then darken the rubbing and bring up details by going over it with the crayon again.

The finished rubbing. Different colors of wax and crayon have been used to highlight the design.

You will also need scissors, masking tape, a natural-bristle brush, two small pieces of cloth, a spray bottle filled with water, and paper. The paper must be strong when it is wet, like the paper used in tea bags. Paper made with hemp or some other fiber is good.

To begin, brush the object clean, and tape the paper loosely but securely over it. Use the spray bottle to dampen the paper, but do not soak it. The idea is to soften the paper so that it will mold to the design underneath. Now wrap one of the small cloths around your finger, and dip it into the graphite mixture. Wipe most of the mixture off onto the second cloth. This will remove large clumps of graphite that might smear and spoil your rubbing. With the first cloth, apply the graphite to the dampened paper, blocking in the design lightly. Darken areas of the rubbing by going over them again in the same way. When the rubbing is completed, gently remove the tape by pulling it toward the edge of the paper.

CECILY BARTH FIRESTEIN
Author, *Rubbing Craft*

## RUBENS, PETER PAUL (1577–1640)

The Flemish painter Peter Paul Rubens was one of the greatest artists of northern Europe. He was also an honored scholar and a respected diplomat.

Rubens was born on June 28, 1577, in Siegen, Germany. After his father died, his mother returned with her family to her native Antwerp in Flanders (now part of Belgium). Rubens was apprenticed at the age of 14 to an artist in the city. From 1600 until 1608, he lived in Italy as court painter to the Duke of Mantua. There he fell under the influence of such Italian masters as Titian, Michelangelo, and Caravaggio.

On his return to Antwerp in 1608, Rubens was appointed court painter to the Spanish governor of Flanders. In 1609, he married Isabella Brant.

Rubens was in great demand by the leading rulers of Europe. He decorated churches and palaces and painted countless portraits, landscapes, and events in classical mythology. He had to employ many assistants to complete his numerous commissions. Rubens was known above all for the brilliant color of his works. Even today we admire the robust, pink-cheeked beauty of the women he painted.

After his wife died in 1626, Rubens entered the diplomatic service. He went on several missions to Holland and England. On his return to Antwerp in 1630, Rubens mar-

*Hélène Fourment and Her Children,* by Peter Paul Rubens.

ried the young and beautiful Hélène Fourment—the subject of many of his later and gentler paintings. He died in Antwerp on May 30, 1640, at the height of his popularity.

Reviewed by ARIANE RUSKIN BATTERBERRY
Author, *The Pantheon Story of Art for Young People*

## RUGBY

Rugby is an outgrowth of a kicking game that was originally called football. Rugby rules allow players to advance the ball by either kicking or carrying it. Lateral—but no forward—passing is permitted. A player carrying the ball may be tackled, as in American and Canadian football.

In 1823, William Webb Ellis, a student at the Rugby School, England, picked up the ball during a soccer game and ran with it. Students at other schools heard of Ellis' mistake and developed a new game that allowed players to carry the ball. This new game was called "the Rugby game."

Some athletes preferred the old rules. In 1863, they formed the London Football Association and called their game Association Football. Later it was called soccer.

Rugby players discovered that their rules varied. In 1871, representatives from 20 teams met in London and formed the Rugby Union. They made game rules that have changed little since.

There are 15 players on a team. Eight are forwards and seven are backs. The forwards usually are the biggest and strongest players. Their main job is to control the ball with their feet and dribble it forward. Or, in a formal scrummage, they attempt to pass the ball back to their own halfback.

A player fights his way out of a dangerous position in front of his own goalposts.

## The Scrummage

A formal scrum, or scrummage, is called by the referee after a minor rule infraction. It is a little like a scrimmage in American football. The forward players of both teams line up opposite each other, parallel to the goal lines. They are usually in a 3-2-3 or 3-4-1 formation. All are bent down from the waist. The front rows of each team are in shoulder-to-shoulder contact. Their teammates are braced together behind them. When the ball is tossed into the scrum, between the front rows of each team, the players surge forward. Their object is to gain possession of the ball, either by pushing the other team away from it or by feeding it back with their feet through the scrum to a halfback. No one may touch the ball with his hands until it is clear of the scrum.

## Scoring

There are two basic ways to score. One,

called a **try**, is like a touchdown in American football and counts 5 points. To score a try, a player must carry the ball into the other team's in-goal area and touch it to the ground before being tackled. If the player does not touch the ball to the ground, no try is scored. After a try, the scoring team attempts a **conversion**. This is a placekick or a dropkick from a spot directly opposite the point where the ball was grounded. The ball, when kicked, must pass between the uprights and over the crossbar of the goalposts, as in American football. A successful conversion adds 2 points to the try, for a total of 7.

All other kicked goals count 3 points. A player on the attack may drop-kick a goal. Goals also may be made on penalty kicks and awarded after rules violations.

A fair catch is made when a player catches the ball directly from an opponent's kick while in a stationary position. The player may then call for a scrummage or take a free kick. The

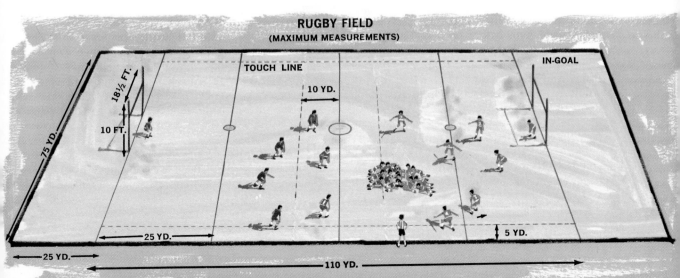

### RUGBY FIELD
#### (MAXIMUM MEASUREMENTS)

TOUCH LINE

IN-GOAL

18½ FT.

10 YD.

10 FT.

75 YD.

25 YD.

25 YD.

5 YD.

110 YD.

free kick may be simply a downfield punt, or it may be a dropkick or placekick. It may not be kicked for points.

### Equipment

The rugby ball is oval. It is leather and is inflated with a rubber bladder. The ball is rounder at the ends and thicker in the middle than the American football.

The players wear light uniforms—shorts and jerseys—and cleated leather shoes. Hard protective equipment, which could injure another player, is illegal.

### The Game

A rugby match consists of two 40-minute halves. Time out is permitted in case of serious injury. But the injured player must resume play or leave the field within 1 minute. Substitutions are allowed for injured players.

The game is started by a kickoff from midfield, somewhat as in American football. A kickoff is also used to continue play after scores and at the start of the second half.

Play is interrupted only for violations and out-of-bounds. When the ball crosses a touch line, it is said to be "in touch," which means out-of-bounds. It is returned to play by a **line-out** where it crossed the touch line. In a line-out the forwards of both teams form two rows at right angles to the touch line. The ball is thrown in by a member of the team that did not send the ball into touch. It must go at least 5½ yards (5 meters) before it is considered in play.

Players must stay behind the ball when a teammate of theirs is controlling it. If they are ahead of the ball, they are offside and may not participate in the play until they return to onside position.

Rugby is a game of continuous action. A player who is tackled must release the ball immediately.

Speed, stamina, and quick thinking are the assets of a good rugby, or "rugger," player. There is little individual stardom. The best players are those who work best for the team.

ROBERT L. ("DINK") TEMPLETON
Member, 1920 United States
Olympic Rugby Team

Reviewed by NEIL SORBIE
Executive Director
Ontario Rugby Union

# RUGS AND CARPETS

Rugs and carpets are heavy fabrics used to cover floors. The words "rug" and "carpet" can be used for one another. Today, however, "carpet" is often used for a fabric that covers the entire floor and "rug" for a fabric that covers part of the floor. The first rugs were made long before recorded history. People probably began weaving rugs by hand from animal hair and wool to protect themselves from the damp floors of their primitive homes. By the time of the early Babylonians and Egyptians, rug weaving was an established craft.

For many centuries only a very rich person could afford a rug because it was woven by hand, and hours of skilled labor went into each

A scene of early settlers in the United States is woven into this rug, which dates from the 1700's or 1800's.

rug. Today rugs and carpets are made on machines that rapidly turn out a wide variety of floor coverings. As a result, rugs and carpets are sold at prices that most people can afford.

Many rugs are considered valuable works of art because of their beautiful colors, textures, and patterns. In some countries they are hung on walls. Nomadic tribes of the Middle East use rugs as beds, tent flaps, and saddle blankets and bags.

### ▶HISTORY OF RUGS AND CARPETS

The basic steps of hand weaving have not changed much since people first wove carpets.

Vertical strands of yarn, called the **warp**, are first strung on a rectangular frame called a **loom**. Other strands of yarn, called the **weft**, are passed under one warp thread and over the next across the loom. This creates a rug or carpet fabric known as **flat fabric**.

Threading the weft yarn over and under warp yarn by hand is very time consuming. Early weavers wound the weft yarn on a piece of wood, called a **shuttle**, which was passed over and under the warp threads. The **weave shed**, another early invention, is created by raising alternate sets of warp yarns so that the shuttle can be quickly passed across the loom.

As early as 2000 B.C., rug makers had learned how to work in another layer of yarns, called the **pile**. Pile adds thickness, diversity of pattern, and durability to a carpet. In rugs woven on a hand loom, the pile is made by taking several strands of yarn and knotting them around one or two warp threads. The strands of yarn are cut, and the weft yarn is inserted and forced tightly against the pile knots to hold them in place. The protruding ends of the knots are called **tufts**. The size of the yarns, the number of knots, and the length of the tufts determine the quality of the rug.

Rugs were made by these painstaking methods for thousands of years. Throughout the Middle East and in India, whole villages made their living by the slow, laborious creation of luxurious rugs. The yarn for the rugs was dyed in beautiful colors and woven into elaborate patterns. Each pile knot was tied by hand, and the value of the rug was judged by the number of knots. Some rugs contained more than 400 knots per square inch (60 knots per square centimeter).

Crusaders returning from the religious wars brought rugs and other rich possessions of the East into medieval Europe. The rugs added welcome color and warmth to the cold stone floors and walls of European castles. Because these rugs came from the East, they were called Oriental rugs.

European artisans developed a rug-weaving style, too. They wove patterned rugs for the few nobles who could afford them. By the 1500's, Europe's center of weaving was Brussels, Belgium.

Many of the weavers were Protestants. As the 1500's progressed, these weavers were forced to flee from Brussels because of their religious beliefs. Many weavers settled in France until the French government also tried to stamp out Protestantism. Some of the weavers finally found a safe refuge in England, where they helped establish a highly skilled carpet-weaving trade.

France, however, remained a very important center of weaving. Jean Baptiste Colbert (1619–83), Louis XIV's finance minister, gathered expert weavers together in state-operated workshops. For the next three hundred years beautiful rugs and tapestries were woven at the Gobelins workshop in Paris and workshops in the towns of Aubusson and Beauvais.

These rugs were woven on **draw looms**. For each part of the pattern, different sets of warp threads had to be raised. An assistant known as a drawboy studied a chart of the pattern and then pulled the master cords that raised the proper warp yarns. This was a difficult and lengthy process, and the drawboy could easily ruin the pattern by pulling the wrong cord. The mistake in the design would not be seen until the pattern began to take shape.

During the 1700's various artisans worked on a mechanism that would set the pattern threads automatically. Eventually a system was developed that worked somewhat like a player piano. The master cords were attached to needles that moved across a card. The card had the pattern outlined in tiny holes. When a needle reached a pattern hole, it dropped in and held the right warp yarn ready for the drawboy.

In 1801, the French weaver J. M. Jacquard (1752–1834) invented an automatic mechanism for pulling the pattern cords. Jacquard's device combined many of the features of the card-and-needle system, but his cord-selecting system could be worked directly from the loom. The Jacquard loom used for weaving patterns today is based on the French weaver's invention.

### The Development of Power Looms

England was the center of mass-produced carpets from the mid-1700's through the mid-1800's. Towns such as Wilton, Kidderminster, and Axminster turned out rugs in such quantities that the names of the towns were given to the different weaving techniques developed there. But even though carpet making was a growing industry, the looms were still powered by hand.

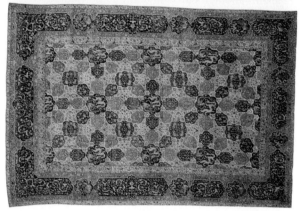

These Oriental rugs all date from about the 1500's. *Above:* Mamluk rugs from Egypt are known for their lustrous wool and translucent colors. *Top right:* In Persia (now Iran), rug making was a fine art. Skilled painters created intricate designs that were turned into rugs by master weavers. *Bottom right:* This fine Persian rug, made of silk and wool, has 625 knots per square inch.

The great revolution in carpet making occurred in the United States when Erastus Brigham Bigelow (1814–79) invented the first power loom for carpets in 1839. Power looms did away with hours of painstaking work by hand. The industry rapidly became mechanized, and the United States took the lead in carpet production.

### ▶ MANUFACTURE OF CARPETS AND RUGS TODAY

There are two basic methods used to manufacture carpets and rugs: weaving and tufting.

### Weaving

The structural foundation of a woven carpet is made on a loom by interlocking warp and weft yarns. These backing yarns are usually spun from jute or cotton fibers and are hidden from sight when the carpet is laid on the floor. (Jute is a fiber used in making burlap.) In most woven carpets, pile yarns are added during the weaving process.

**Velvet Loom.** The velvet loom is the least complex of the specialized weaving equipment used for making carpets. The loom is very similar to Bigelow's original power loom. The pile yarns are lifted. Then a strip of flat steel, called a wire, is mechanically inserted by the loom. The pile yarns are then pushed down over the wire to form them into loops. Some of the wires may have sharp knives at their ends. As these sharp knives are pulled out, they cut the pile and produce a **cut-pile**. Velvet carpets are usually solid colored, but the texture of the yarn may vary.

**Looms for Pattern Carpets.** Carpets that are patterned may be made on either Wilton or Axminster looms, which are named after the towns where the carpets were first made. Wilton carpets are woven on velvet power looms adapted with the Jacquard system. A series of cards punched with holes automatically regulates the feeding of two to five different-colored yarns to form the pattern in the carpet. In Wilton carpets the pile is normally thick and may be made in different heights, which gives the appearance of a carved design in the rug. The Axminster loom is used for carpets that have complex designs with many colors. It does mechanically what a weaver making an Oriental carpet does by hand. Each tuft of yarn for the pile is inserted separately into the carpet by the loom. These carpets have floral, geometric, scroll, leaf, and other intricate patterns and may contain as many as a hundred different-colored yarns.

## Tufting

Tufting is a high-speed method of carpet manufacturing that originated in the United States in the 1920's. Today's machines use hundreds of fast-moving needles to punch the pile yarns through the preformed backing fabric. The pile yarns are anchored to the backing by coating the carpet back with liquid latex.

The tufting process was at first used mainly for manufacturing solid-color or **tweed** carpets. Tweed carpets are made by using two or more different-colored yarns or by using yarns containing plies (a ply is a unit of yarn) of different colors. Now carpets of many different colors and textures can be made with the tufting process. Detailed patterns can be created in tufted carpets by inserting colored yarns into the carpet with a hand-tufting machine. This process is known as **overtufting**.

Tufted carpets can be produced at lower costs than woven carpets because they can be made more quickly and with fewer workers. The tufting industry has grown so rapidly that it now accounts for more than 95 percent of the total amount of carpets made in the United States. Tufting also has increased in Canada, the United Kingdom, and Germany.

## Handmade Rugs

Although the power loom has replaced the hand loom for mass-produced rugs and carpets, the ancient craft of hand weaving still continues. Among the most beautiful are the Oriental rugs made in Iran, India, Egypt and other Arab countries, the southern part of the former Soviet Union, and China.

An important characteristic of handwoven rugs is the wealth of pattern and color they contain. Since each tuft of yarn is added by

Handmade rugs from around the world show a variety of designs and weaving styles. Each is unique to the region where it was made. *Clockwise from top:* A Kurdish rug from Turkey, made about 1900; a French rug dating from the 1600's; a Navajo rug from North America in a pattern known as "Eye Dazzler"; and a Chinese rug woven during the late 1600's or early 1700's.

355

hand, weavers can use as many colors as they wish to make a design.

Two other methods are also used in handmade rugs—hooking and braiding. For a hooked rug, a piece of sheet or heavier material is used as a backing fabric. Then a hook is used to pull pieces of colored fabric or yarn through the backing. For a braided rug, long pieces of fabric are braided into long cords. The cords are then coiled into spirals or ovals and sewn together to make the rug.

▶ **MATERIALS USED IN RUGS AND CARPETS**

Wool has long been the most important natural fiber used in carpets and rugs. In some countries, linen and silk have also been used as rug materials, and cotton has been used for inexpensive rugs.

The wool used in carpets is very different from the soft, fine wool used for clothes. Carpet wool must be strong, springy, and coarse. Wool for rugs and carpets comes from sheep raised in countries where the climate is severe and the countryside is rugged. Major producers of carpet wools include New Zealand, Argentina, India, Pakistan, Iraq, Syria, Scotland, and Ireland.

The wools are first scoured and washed to remove grease, dirt, and other impurities. Different kinds of wool are often blended together. It is not uncommon for the pile yarns in a carpet to be made from wools grown in as many as five different countries.

In the United States, most carpets and rugs have face yarns made from human-made fibers. These fibers made their appearance in the late 1940's. Their use has grown until today they represent 99 percent of the fibers used for face yarns. Nylon, polyester, and polypropylene are the main fibers used. Each has definite characteristics. Special properties —such as resistance to soil, static electricity, and flammability—can also be built into them.

RICHARD NED HOPPER
The Carpet and Rug Institute

See also TAPESTRY.

---

**RULES OF ORDER.** See PARLIAMENTARY PROCEDURE.
**RUMANIA.** See ROMANIA.

## RUSSELL, BERTRAND (1872–1970)

In 1918, Bertrand Russell wrote, "I want to stand at the rim of the world and peer into the darkness beyond, and see a little more than others have seen. . . . I want to bring back into the world of men some little bit of new wisdom."

Bertrand Arthur William Russell was born on May 18, 1872, in Trelleck, Wales. Before he was 4, both his parents died, and he and his elder brother went to live with their grandparents. When his brother died in 1931, Bertrand inherited the title 3rd Earl Russell.

Bertrand was tutored at home until he entered Trinity College, Cambridge, in 1890. He had been a shy, silent boy, but at Cambridge he became a great talker and a student who questioned everything. He studied mathematics and philosophy.

In 1894, he married Alys Pearsall Smith, the first of his four wives. His first book, *German Social Democracy* (1896), was written after a trip to Germany. In *The Principles of Mathematics* (1903) he outlined a theory presenting logic as a foundation for mathematics. He demonstrated this theory in *Principia Mathematica* (1910–13), a three-volume work written with Alfred North Whitehead.

Russell also made time for politics and social problems. In 1918, Russell was jailed for criticizing the United States Army in a newspaper article. He spent his time in prison writing *Introduction to Mathematical Philosophy* (1919). After visiting the Soviet Union and China, he wrote *The Practice and Theory of Bolshevism* (1920) and *The Problem of China* (1922). *A History of Western Philosophy* (1945) was based on lectures he gave in the United States.

Russell's beliefs are stated in *Human Knowledge: Its Scope and Limits* (1948). In 1950, he received the Nobel Prize for literature. In later years he led demonstrations against the nuclear bomb. *The Autobiography of Bertrand Russell* was published in three volumes in 1967–69. Russell died on February 2, 1970, in his native Wales.

Reviewed by HOWARD OZMON
Author, *Twelve Great Philosophers*

**RUSSELL, CHARLES M.** See MONTANA (Famous People).

# RUSSIA

Russia (officially, the Russian Federation) is the world's largest country. Extending over two continents, Europe and Asia, it stretches from the Gulf of Finland (part of the Baltic Sea) in the west to the Bering Strait (separating the Arctic and Pacific oceans) in the east—a distance of more than 5,000 miles (8,000 kilometers). In all, it contains more than one-tenth of the world's land surface.

The history of Russia dates back more than one thousand years. In the A.D. 800's and 900's, Vikings from Scandinavia ruled over a Slavic people then known as the Rus. Tatars, a Mongol people from the east, conquered the Rus in the 1200's and ruled until Ivan III, the grand duke of Moscow, defeated them in 1462. Ivan became the sole ruler over central Russia and began the first dynasty of Russian imperial rulers. In 1613, the Russian aristocracy elected Michael Romanov czar (or emperor), beginning a second dynasty that lasted for three hundred years.

Under the Romanovs, the Russian Empire more than tripled in size, expanding to the south, east, and west. The czars, impressed by the wealthy and sophisticated nations of western Europe, tried to copy western ways. But Russia's entry into the modern industrial age was hindered by its medieval labor system. Russian peasants, called serfs, remained bound in a state of servitude to the landowners.

The Romanov Dynasty remained in power until 1917, when the empire was swept away by a people's revolution that established the Communist Union of Soviet Socialist Republics, more commonly known as

*Clockwise from top:* A Russian patriarch, or bishop, of the Eastern Orthodox Church. St. Basil's Cathedral in Red Square, a notable landmark in Moscow, the capital of Russia. Chukchi children in the far reaches of eastern Siberia.

the Soviet Union, or U.S.S.R. Russia, the largest of the republics, formed the core of the Soviet Union and contained about half its population. Communists ruled the country until the union collapsed in 1991. Since that time, Russia has struggled to overturn the effects of the failed Communist system and build a strong democratic government and capitalist economy.

## ▶ PEOPLE

About 80 percent of Russia's population is made up of ethnic Russians, who are descended from East Slavs. Slavs probably first appeared in Europe about 2,000 years ago and later divided into western and southern as well as eastern branches.

Although East Slavs form a majority, Russia also has a number of non-Slavic minorities. The second largest ethnic group includes peoples of Turkic origins, such as the Tatars, the Chuvash, and several smaller groups in Siberia. People in the third largest group, the Finno-Ugric, are concentrated along the border with Finland, in the eastern plains and Ural Mountains, and in northern Siberia.

Most ethnic Russians are descended from an East Slavic people known as the Rus.

### Language

All Russians speak Russian as their primary language. Russian belongs to the East Slavic group of languages, a branch of the larger Indo-European family of languages. Tatar, Chuvash, and other languages are spoken within distinct ethnic groups.

The Russian language is written in the Cyrillic alphabet, also used by other East Slavs and some South Slavs. The Cyrillic alphabet is based on Greek letters with a few additions to convey Slavic sounds. It was probably developed in the 800's by a student of St. Cyril, a Byzantine missionary after whom it is named. For more information, see the article RUSSIA, LANGUAGE AND LITERATURE OF in this volume.

### Religion

Although religion was officially banned during the years of Soviet rule, Russians historically have belonged to the Eastern Orthodox Church. Today about 40 percent of ethnic Russians consider themselves orthodox Christians.

Most Tatars and other minority peoples in the Russian Federation are Muslims. Russia also has a significant number of Jews, although large numbers have immigrated to Israel and the United States. Russia also has a relatively small number of Buddhists among the Mongols of the lower Volga River (the Kalmyks) and in the vicinity of Lake Baikal (the Buriats). A small Baptist denomination is the only sizable Protestant group. There are, in addition, even smaller groups of evangelicals such as Pentecostals, Seventh-Day Adventists, and Jehovah's Witnesses.

Most Russian city dwellers live in apartment buildings built during the Soviet era.

## Education

In Russia, education is mandatory between the ages of 6 and 17, and almost everybody over the age of 15 can read and write. Schooling from the first grade through college is free. However, only a small percentage of the best students are able to pass the entrance examinations required to gain admission to a university. Of the approximately 40 universities in Russia, Moscow State University in Moscow is the largest.

Under the Soviet system, schools were noted for their difficult curriculum, and students excelled in the sciences, mathematics, foreign languages, physical education, and the arts. But the downfall of Communism and the collapse of the Russian economy dramatically affected education. Today schools are underfunded and suffer from a lack of basic

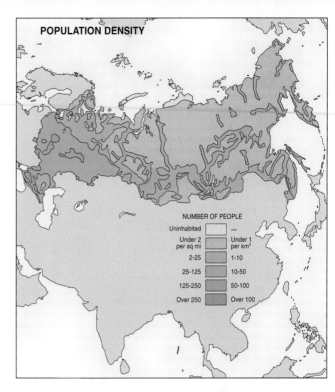

POPULATION DENSITY

| NUMBER OF PEOPLE | |
|---|---|
| Uninhabited | — |
| Under 2 per sq mi | Under 1 per km² |
| 2-25 | 1-10 |
| 25-125 | 10-50 |
| 125-250 | 50-100 |
| Over 250 | Over 100 |

Russian elementary schoolchildren learn English in a language laboratory. Education in Russia is mandatory through the age of 17.

materials. Often the government has difficulty paying the teachers' salaries.

## Libraries and Museums

Nearly every town or village in Russia has a public library. The country has two national libraries, the National Library of Russia in St. Petersburg and the Russian State Library in Moscow. The largest library in Siberia is the Tomsk State University Library.

Russia contains several of the world's finest museums. Moscow alone has approximately 100 of them, notably the State Museums of the Moscow Kremlin and the Pushkin State Museum of Fine Arts at Moscow University. Notable institutions in other cities include the Nizhniy Novgorod Art Museum and the Novosibirsk Art Gallery, which is renowned for its collection of Russian icons. The State Hermitage Museum, located in St. Petersburg, is one of the largest and most famous art museums in the world. For more information, see the article HERMITAGE MUSEUM in Volume H.

## Way of Life

The great majority of Russians are city dwellers. City people, for the most part, live in apartments. The typical Russian family has two wage earners—the husband and wife—and one or two children. Often, one or more grandparents may also live with the family. Although luxuries are few, most homes have television sets and electric appliances.

About one-quarter of the population lives in villages scattered across the vast area of the countryside. Most of the villages were established as collective, or state, farms during the Communist era. Almost all villagers have electricity but many lack running water. Water must be drawn from wells, often at some distance away.

# FACTS and figures

**RUSSIAN FEDERATION** is the official name of the country.

**LOCATION:** Eastern Europe and northern Asia.

**AREA:** 6,592,850 sq mi (17,075,481 km²).

**POPULATION:** 146,000,000 (estimate).

**CAPITAL AND LARGEST CITY:** Moscow.

**MAJOR LANGUAGE:** Russian.

**MAJOR RELIGIOUS GROUP:** Eastern Orthodox.

**GOVERNMENT:** Republic. **Head of state**—president. **Head of government**—premier (prime minister). **Legislature**—Federal Assembly, made up of the Federation Council and the State Duma.

**CHIEF PRODUCTS: Agricultural**—grain, sugar beets, sunflower seeds, vegetables, fruits, beef, milk. **Manufactured**—Mining equipment and machinery, aircraft, space vehicles, ships, road and rail transportation equipment, communications equipment, agricultural machinery, tractors, and construction equipment, medical and scientific instruments, textiles, foodstuffs, handicrafts. **Mineral**—coal, iron ore, petroleum, natural gas, gold, bauxite, and other metals.

**MONETARY UNIT:** Ruble (1 ruble = 100 kopeks).

the cities, bread, kasha (made from buckwheat), and sausage are commonly eaten. Other favorite dishes include borscht (a soup made from beets or other vegetables), beef Stroganoff (made with sour cream), bliny (stuffed pancakes), and *golubtsy* (meat wrapped in cabbage leaves).

Caviar, probably the country's most famous and expensive gourmet delicacy, is enjoyed when available and affordable. The best is obtained from the roe (eggs) of sturgeon from the Caspian Sea.

Russians everywhere drink much tea and vodka. Mineral water is preferred to tap water. Soft drinks have become increasingly popular.

### Sports and Recreation

Soccer (Europeans call it football) is the most popular team sport in Russia, as in many other countries, followed by basketball, volleyball, and hockey. *Lapta*, a popular bat-and-ball game similar to baseball, has been played for a long time and is mentioned in old Russian literature.

Russians also enjoy spectator sports, such as boxing, wrestling, skiing, ice-skating, swimming, and gymnastics. In past years, the government provided financial support for a wide variety of sports teams in international competitions.

### Food and Drink

For Russians in the countryside, black bread and cabbage soup are staple foods. In

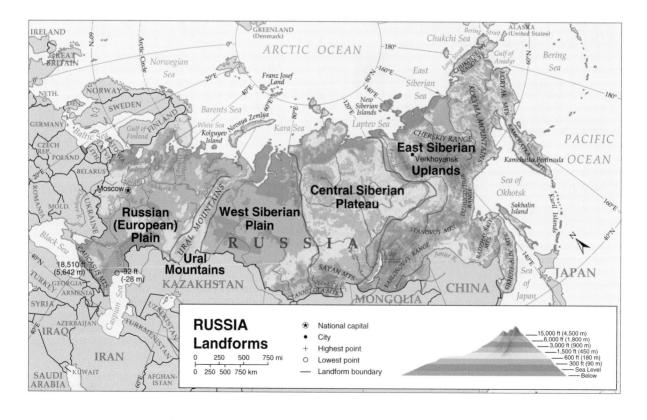

**RUSSIA Landforms**

0    250    500    750 mi
0  250 500 750 km

⊛ National capital
• City
+ Highest point
○ Lowest point
— Landform boundary

15,000 ft (4,500 m)
6,000 ft (1,800 m)
3,000 ft (900 m)
1,500 ft (450 m)
600 ft (180 m)
300 ft (90 m)
Sea Level
Below

*Above:* Reindeer graze on the summer tundra in the Siberian Arctic. *Right:* Lake Baikal in Siberia is the world's deepest freshwater lake.

## ▶ LAND

Russia's enormous landmass is bounded on two sides by oceans—the Arctic on the north and the Pacific on the east. Its neighboring countries are North Korea, China, Mongolia, and Kazakhstan on the south; Azerbaijan and Georgia on the southwest; Moldova, Ukraine, Belarus, Poland, Lithuania, Latvia, and Estonia on the west; and Finland and Norway on the northwest.

The Arctic north, which extends from Norway to the Bering Strait, consists of tundra, much of which is permafrost, or permanently frozen land. Just below the tundra and stretching across the country, barely interrupted by the modest-sized Ural Mountains, is the wide belt of forest known as the taiga. South of the taiga is an extensive region of steppe, or plains, containing some of the country's most fertile soil. The steppe reaches as far south as the Black Sea and Caucasus Mountains and extends, more narrowly, east of the Urals, where it merges into the semi-desert regions of Central Asia.

### Land Regions

Russia's landscape is marked by broad plains (or steppes), rugged plateaus, and towering mountain ranges. The western half of the country includes two vast plains: the Russian (or European) Plain and the West Siberian Plain. The Russian Plain is separated from the West Siberian Plain by the Ural Mountains, which form part of the traditional boundary between Europe and Asia. In the east, the land rises to the Central Siberian Plateau and the uplands and mountains of East Siberia.

The Asian part of Russia, although many times larger in area than European Russia, is much more sparsely populated, because of its harsher climate and less fertile soil.

**The Russian Plain.** The great Russian (or European) Plain is Russia's westernmost region. Watered by the Volga and Northern

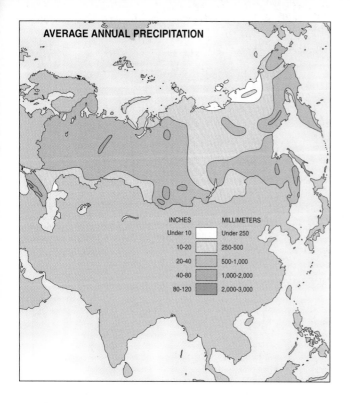

**AVERAGE ANNUAL PRECIPITATION**

| INCHES | MILLIMETERS |
|---|---|
| Under 10 | Under 250 |
| 10-20 | 250-500 |
| 20-40 | 500-1,000 |
| 40-80 | 1,000-2,000 |
| 80-120 | 2,000-3,000 |

**The Central Siberian Plateau.** Rising 2,000 feet (610 meters) or more above sea level, the Central Siberian Plateau covers the vast region between the Yenisey and Lena rivers.

**The East Siberian Uplands.** Farther east are the mountains of the East Siberian Uplands and the varied terrain of the Pacific coastal region. The largest ranges in this region are the Kamchatka, Kolyma, and Chukotskoye Nagor'ye. For more information, see the article SIBERIA in Volume S.

### Rivers and Lakes

Russia has an extensive network of rivers. The Volga, the longest river in Europe, flows 2,293 miles (3,689 kilometers) across the Russian Plain, south to the Caspian Sea. The Dnieper, Europe's third longest river, rises in Russia and flows south into Ukraine. Other major rivers in western Russia include the Don, Oka, and Sukhona. Several others flow north into the Arctic Ocean—the Northern Dvina and Pechora in Europe and the Ob', Yenisey, and Lena in Asia. The Amur River, which forms part of the border with China, flows into the Pacific.

The two largest lakes in Europe, Ladoga and Onega, lie within Russia, not far from St. Petersburg. The magnificent Lake Baikal in Russian Asia is the world's deepest lake. It is estimated to contain one-fifth of all the fresh water on the planet but is threatened with pollution. Russia borders on the Caspian Sea (actually a salt lake), the world's largest inland body of water, situated just east of the Caucasus, on the boundary between Europe and Asia.

### Climate

Russia's climate ranges from the frozen north to a small subtropical area in the south. The average monthly temperature in the tundra is 50°F (10°C) or less, and for at least eight months of the year it is below freezing. Precipitation (rain and snow) is usually less than 16 inches (410 millimeters) per year. The taiga may even be colder, falling to –90°F (–68°C) at Verkhoyansk in Siberia, the coldest spot on Earth outside of Antarctica. Precipitation there varies from 8 to 20 inches (200 to 500 millimeters) a year.

In the steppe region around Moscow, agriculture is possible, although the temperature remains below freezing for much of the year.

Dvina rivers and their tributaries, the plain extends as far east as the Ural Mountains. The Russian Plain is Russia's heartland. It contains its most fertile lands and supports the largest population.

The country's highest peaks lie within this region, mainly in the Caucasus Mountains along Russia's southern border between the Black and the Caspian seas. With an elevation of 18,510 feet (5,642 meters), Mount Elbrus, in the Caucasus Range, is the highest mountain peak in Europe.

**The Ural Mountains.** The Ural Mountains, along with the Caucasus Range in the southwest, are the traditional boundaries between Europe and Asia. The mountains are densely forested and rich in mineral resources. The highest peak among them, Mount Narodnaya, rises 6,214 feet (1,894 meters).

Historically, the relatively low Urals were not a useful natural barrier against invasion from the east. Nomadic peoples from Asia, including the war-like Mongols, crossed into Russia in its early centuries.

**The West Siberian Plain.** East of the Urals, the West Siberian Plain continues as far as the Yenisey River. This region, formed by glacial deposits from the last Ice Age, is forested and swampy.

### Natural Resources

The precise extent of Russia's vast underground mineral deposits is still unknown. But in petroleum reserves alone, Russia ranks at least second to the Persian Gulf region. Most of its petroleum and natural gas are found in western Siberia and carried by pipeline westward to Europe and eastward to the Pacific coast. It has huge deposits of coal and iron ore. Gold, bauxite (aluminum ore), and many other metals have long been mined or are known to be present in the lands east of the Urals. Russia has the largest forest reserves of any country. The swift-flowing Siberian rivers are a primary source of hydroelectric power.

Russia has a great variety of animal life. In the north are found polar bears, seals, musk oxen, and reindeer. The taiga supports elk and small fur-bearing animals, such as sable and ermine. Farther south are wolves, foxes, beavers, otters, and deer as well as small brown bears. Siberian tigers, found along the Pacific coast, are protected.

### ▶ ECONOMY

Throughout most of the 1900's, during the years of Soviet rule, Russia's economy was controlled by the state, meaning the leaders of the ruling Communist Party. Their policies were based on socialist philosophy, which rejected the capitalist system, claiming it "en-

Nesting dolls are lined up for sale at a Moscow flea market. These painted wooden figures are a traditional Russian folk art.

slaved" workers to the owners of private industry. The socialists believed that every citizen should equally contribute to and benefit from the nation's productivity.

The Communists decided what goods and services would be produced, how much they should cost, and even who could obtain them. Extreme emphasis was placed on heavy industry, particularly the manufacture of military weapons and equipment.

Radical economic reforms were begun immediately following the breakup of the Soviet Union in 1991. However, the transition from collective (state-owned) to private (individually owned) enterprise has been difficult, and many Russians have suffered the hardships of inflation, falling wages, food shortages, and unemployment.

### Services

About 55 percent of Russia's workforce is employed in the service industries. These include financial services, wholesale and retail sales, government and social services, transportation, communication, and other public utilities. Tourism, which feeds a variety of service industries, has been on the rise since the early 1990's.

### Manufacturing

About 30 percent of Russia's workforce is employed in manufacturing industries. Chief products include the equipment and machines needed to mine and process coal, oil, and natural gas. Steel is also produced for the manufacture of aircraft, space vehicles, ships,

Manufacturing industries, such as the production of bread and other foodstuffs, employ about one-third of all Russian workers.

road and rail transportation equipment, communications equipment, agricultural machinery, tractors, and construction equipment. Medical and scientific instruments, textiles, foodstuffs, and handicrafts are also produced.

### Agriculture

More than half of Russia's cropland is devoted to growing grains—rye, barley, and oats, in addition to wheat. One-third is sown with fodder crops—grasses and corn—used to feed livestock. The remainder is used to produce commercial crops, notably sugar beets, sunflower seeds, and vegetables. Cattle are raised for beef and dairy products.

### Foreign Trade

Russia is a major exporter of petroleum and petroleum products, natural gas, wood and wood products, metals, chemicals, and a wide variety of military goods.

At one time, Russia exported wheat and other grains to Western Europe. But today it must import grain from the United States and elsewhere in order to feed its people with the most common staple, bread. Other imports include machinery and equipment, consumer goods, medicines, meat, and sugar. Most fruits must also be imported.

### Transportation

Workers in Russia usually commute by public transportation, since there are few private automobiles and only a sparse network of good roads. The subways in Moscow and St. Petersburg are clean, attractive, reliable, and cheap.

Russia has an extensive railway network, although it is increasingly in need of repair. It includes the Trans-Siberian Railroad, the world's longest continuous railroad, which runs between Moscow and the Pacific coast port of Vladivostok. Nearly half of all freight is carried by truck, in spite of the generally poor condition of highways. About one-third is transported by railroad and the rest by water and pipeline. About 70 percent of Russia's international air transport is handled by Aeroflot-Russian International Airlines.

Ships provide transportation on inland and international waters. Although Russia has an enormous coastline, much of it remains ice-bound for many months of the year and is of limited use for shipping. The only seaport with year-round ice-free access to the open ocean is Murmansk, near the border with Norway. Other northern ports are kept open only with icebreakers.

### Communication

Russia has more than 7,300 television broadcast stations and 850 radio stations. Newspapers with large circulations include *Izvestia*, *Moskovsky Komsomolets*, *Pravda*, and the English-language *St. Petersburg Times*. Technically advanced communications, such as the use of computers, has grown as access to digital lines has improved and the number of Internet service providers (ISP's) has increased.

## ▶ MAJOR CITIES

**Moscow,** which dates from the 1100's, was the capital of the Grand Principality of Muscovy for centuries before the Russian Empire was founded in 1721. It became the capital of the Soviet Union in 1918 and of the Russian Federation in 1991. Although the city was burned during a French invasion of Russia in 1812, much of it was preserved, and Moscow still contains many monuments and treasures from the time of the czars. For more information, see the article MOSCOW in Volume M.

Farmers plant oats in the Krasnodar region near the Black Sea. More than half of Russia's cropland is devoted to growing grains.

Russia's Trans-Siberian Railroad, which runs between Moscow and Vladivostok, is the world's longest continuous railway.

The Nevsky Prospekt is a busy commercial center in St. Petersburg, Russia's second largest city.

**St. Petersburg** was built on a marsh by Czar Peter the Great, beginning in 1703, and served as the Russian capital from 1712 to 1918. In 1924 it was renamed Leningrad, after the Communist leader V. I. Lenin. But its original name was restored in 1991. It remains to a considerable extent the beautiful city it was in the 1700's, complete with the canals that inspired its nickname, Venice of the North. See the article SAINT PETERSBURG in Volume S.

**Nizhniy Novgorod**, formerly known as Gorki, is one of Russia's most important industrial cities. It was founded in 1221 on the south bank of the Volga River about 250 miles (400 kilometers) east of Moscow.

**Novosibirsk**, a major industrial center in Russian Asia, prospered as a terminus of the Trans-Siberian Railroad. Situated on the Ob' River, it is a major producer of steel and mining equipment.

**Yekaterinburg**, or Ekaterinburg, is another major mining center along the route of the Trans-Siberian Railroad. It was founded as a fortress in 1721 and named for Empress Catherine I, wife of Peter the Great. Czar Nicholas II and his family were held there as prisoners and executed in 1918.

**Volgograd**, once known as Stalingrad, is an industrial center and the eastern terminus

along the Volga-Don Canal. Founded as a Russian fort in 1589, it was the site in 1942 of one of the most crucial battles against the Germans during World War II.

▶ **CULTURAL HERITAGE**

For most of Russia's early history, its culture was largely religious in nature. Russian art, in particular, was characterized by religious themes, especially during the Middle Ages, when the creation of icons, or religious paintings on wood, flourished. Unaccompanied vocal music was part of Eastern Orthodox worship. Russian architecture was influenced in large measure by that of the Byzantine Empire, centered at Constantinople (modern Istanbul).

Western artistic and literary forms were introduced in the 1700's, and by the 1800's and early 1900's, Russian poets, novelists, playwrights and directors, painters, composers, musicians, and ballet dancers and choreographers had gained world renown. For more information on Russia's cultural heritage, see the articles RUSSIA, ART AND ARCHITECTURE OF; RUSSIA, LANGUAGE AND LITERATURE OF; and RUSSIA, MUSIC OF following this article.

▶ **GOVERNMENT**

The government of the Russian Federation is based on a constitution that was approved by popular vote in 1993. It replaced the 1978 constitution, which had been amended many times. The country is divided into 49 oblasts, or administrative divisions.

Russia's chief of state is its president, who is elected by the people to serve a 4-year term. The prime minister serves as head of government. The Security Council reports directly to the president. The 1993 constitution strengthened the power of the president. He may appoint and dismiss the prime minister (with parliamentary approval), veto legislation, and dissolve parliament.

The legislative branch consists of a parliament called the Federal Assembly. It is made up of two houses, the Federation Council and the State Duma. The Federation Council has 178 deputies, two from each of the 89 republics, regions, and other administrative divisions of the Russian Federation. The State Duma has 450 members, half elected from single-member constituencies and half according to proportional representation by the various political parties.

Russia's judicial system is made up of the Constitutional Court, the Supreme Court and the Superior Court. All the judges are appointed for life by the Federation Council on the recommendation of the president.

▶ **HISTORY**

Among the earliest peoples to inhabit what is now Russia were the Cimmerians, about 1000 B.C. They were displaced about 700 B.C. by the nomadic Scythians, who left traces of their art in gold treasures that now reside in the Hermitage Museum in St. Petersburg. The Scythians were in turn overwhelmed by the Sarmatians about 200 B.C. The Goths, a Germanic people, erupted into the region from the Baltic area about A.D. 200 but were pushed westward by the Huns in A.D. 370. The Huns were followed by other invaders from Asia. The Slavs probably appeared at

---

## INDEX TO RUSSIA POLITICAL MAP

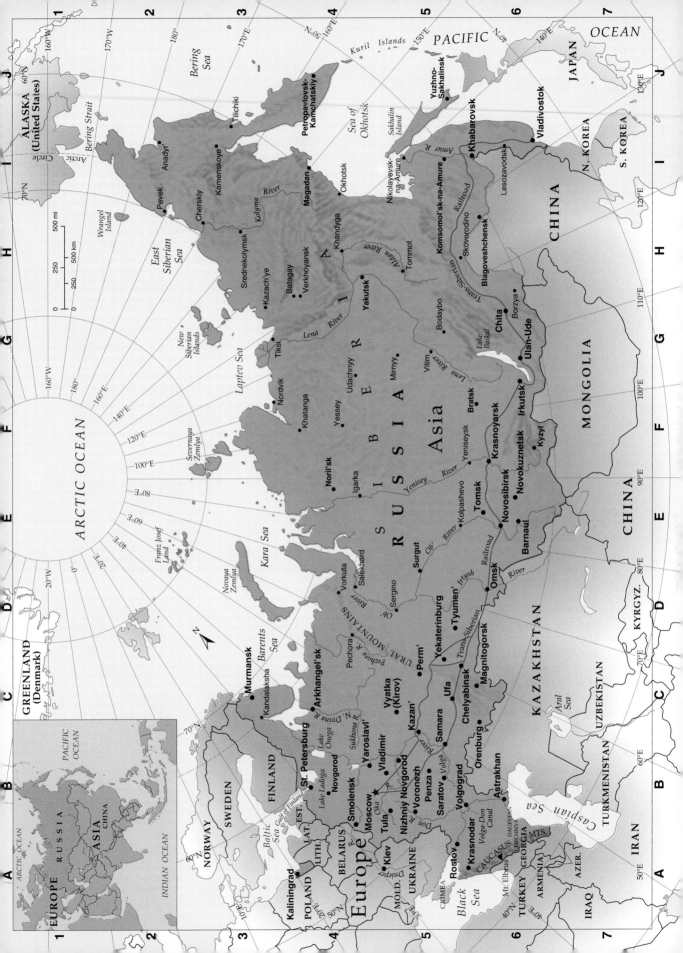

**RUSSIAN EXPANSION WESTWARD (IN EUROPE)**

Moscow in 1462

Acquisitions by 1505

Acquisitions by 1689

Acquisitions by 1801

Acquisitions by 1914

Dividing line between European and Asian Russia

lated the scriptures into the Slavic tongue, gave the Kievan Christians their alphabet, known as Cyrillic, which was based on the Greek alphabet. The other East Slavs soon followed, and a Christian civilization of high achievement developed.

**Alexander Nevsky.** In its early history, Kievan Rus was invaded often. In 1240, Alexander, prince of Novgorod, defeated the Swedes in a famous battle on the Neva River, near St. Petersburg. Thereafter he became known as Alexander Nevsky. Then in 1242, on the winter ice of Lake Peipus, he defeated an invading Germanic army of Teutonic Knights. Three hundred years later, Nevsky was made a saint of the Russian Orthodox Church. Today he is still considered a national hero.

**Mongol Rule.** Persistent wars with successive waves of nomadic peoples weakened the Kievan state. In 1240, conquerors from the Mongol Empire to the east overran its lands. For more than two centuries, the Mongols (or Tatars, as they were often called) remained the overlords of the region. Kiev itself was devastated and did not recover until years

the beginning of the 1st century A.D., or perhaps even earlier.

**Kievan Rus.** There is a historical legend that the East Slavs invited Scandinavians, known as Varangians, to rule over them in the 700's or 800's. In 882 a Viking chieftain from the north named Oleg captured the city of Kiev (in present-day Ukraine), situated on the Dnieper River, which became the capital of the state of Kievan Rus. Under Oleg's descendants, Kievan Rus became an important power that for a time extended as far west as present-day Bulgaria. It had a flourishing trade with the Byzantine Empire as well as with western European and Asian states. About 988 or 989, Prince Vladimir of Kievan Rus accepted Eastern Orthodox Christianity from the Byzantines. Two monks, Cyril and Methodius, who a century earlier had trans-

**RULERS OF THE RUSSIAN EMPIRE**

**Rurik Dynasty**

| | |
|---|---|
| 1462–1505 | Ivan III (the Great) |
| 1505–33 | Vasily III |
| 1533–84 | Ivan IV (the Terrible) |
| 1584–98 | Fyodor I |

**Time of Troubles**

| | |
|---|---|
| 1598–1605 | Boris Godunov |
| 1605 | Fyodor II |
| 1605–06 | False Dmitri |
| 1606–10 | Vasily Shuisky |
| 1610–13 | Interregnum (vacant) |

**Romanov Dynasty**

| | |
|---|---|
| 1613–45 | Michael Romanov |
| 1645–76 | Alexis I |
| 1676–82 | Fyodor III |
| 1682–89 | Sophia (regent) |
| 1682–96 | Ivan V (co-czar) |
| 1682–1725 | Peter I (the Great) |
| 1725–27 | Catherine I |
| 1727–30 | Peter II |
| 1730–40 | Anna |
| 1740–41 | Ivan VI |
| 1741–62 | Elizabeth |
| 1762 | Peter III |
| 1762–96 | Catherine II (the Great) |
| 1796–1801 | Paul I |
| 1801–25 | Alexander I |
| 1825–55 | Nicholas I |
| 1855–81 | Alexander II |
| 1881–94 | Alexander III |
| 1894–1917 | Nicholas II |

later. After the initial destruction and death produced by the conquest, however, the Mongols generally left the Slavs alone, so long as they continued to recognize the Mongols' authority.

During the period of Mongol rule, such cities as Novgorod in the northwest and Vladimir in the northeast developed in different ways. But it was Moscow, or Muscovy, first mentioned in chronicles in 1147, that emerged as the chief principality of the Russians. This was partly because the Mongols came to trust the princes of Moscow more than

Ivan IV (the Terrible) conquered lands to the east, enabling Russian settlement as far as the Pacific Ocean.

others, and partly because the head of the church settled there.

**The Rise of Moscow.** Moscow effectively became independent in 1450 and finally ceased to pay tribute to the Mongols in 1480, after a confrontation with Mongol troops. Grand Prince Ivan Rurik, who reigned as Ivan III (the Great) from 1462 to 1505, took the title "czar" (from *caesar,* a title used by Roman emperors) and greatly added to Moscow's domains. Ivan IV (the Terrible), ruler from 1533 and crowned czar in 1547, conquered the Tatar states of Kazan', Astrakhan, and Sibir', opening the way for Russia to cross the continent to the Pacific Ocean. He also did much to suppress the boyars, or hereditary nobles. But by killing his eldest son in a fit of rage, he ended the dynasty, or ruling family, that had begun in the 800's. See the biography of Ivan in Volume I.

A period of turmoil followed the death of Ivan IV's successor, Fyodor I, in 1598. Known as the Time of Troubles, it was an era of domestic strife and invasions by the Poles and Swedes. Calm returned with the election in 1613 of Michael Romanov as czar. He was the first of the Romanov dynasty, which was to rule Russia until 1917.

During the 1600's the institution of serfdom was formalized, especially by the Code of 1649, under which the peasants were bound by law to the land owned by absentee landlords.

**The Russian Empire.** Peter the Great, who became czar in 1682, had been influenced by western European traditions as a young man. To symbolize the direction he wished his

country to take, he established St. Petersburg as its new, western capital. His successes, which included military victories over Sweden, led to the proclamation of the Russian Empire in 1721. That same year, he brought the last remaining independent body in his country, the Orthodox Church, under his control.

Peter also created Russia's first institutions of higher education. He opened a network of orthodox seminaries (for training priests) and founded the Academy of Sciences. The first Russian university was founded in Moscow in 1755.

Peter, like Ivan IV, was responsible for the death of his only surviving son. As a result, the period that followed Peter's death in 1725 was one of a quick succession of weak rulers. But after the death of Czar Peter III (a grandson of Peter the Great) in 1762, his German wife, Catherine II, emerged as a powerful monarch and the last ruler to be called the Great. Among her achievements was the conquest of a wide band of territory stretching from the Baltic to the Black Sea, including half of Poland, and the annexation of the Crimea, the last remaining Tatar state.

Peter the Great brought Western ideas and culture to Russia. His military successes formed the foundation of the Russian Empire, proclaimed in 1721.

She sought to bring the aims of the Enlightenment, the era of intellectual change in Western Europe, to Russia, but she was only partly successful.

**Invasion, Reform, and Reaction.** During the 1800's, a number of attempts at political and social reform were made, but these were followed by reaction, or the return to the old, ultraconservative ways.

Alexander I, who came to the throne in 1801, put aside consideration of constitutional reform in 1812 to deal with a French invasion of Russia, led by Napoleon I. Although Napoleon was able to occupy Moscow, the destruction of much of the city by fire forced him to retreat, during which most of his army was lost.

With Napoleon's eventual defeat in 1814–15, Alexander played an important role in settling the political affairs of Europe. He was succeeded in 1825 by his brother, Nicholas I.

In December 1825—alarmed by a revolt of army officers (known as the Decembrists)—Nicholas attempted to suppress discontent by imposing censorship and forming a society of secret police. At the same time, he improved the condition of peasants on state lands and codified (put down in writing) Russian laws for the first time.

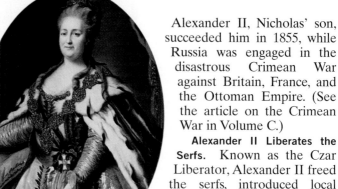
Catherine II (the Great)

Alexander II, Nicholas' son, succeeded him in 1855, while Russia was engaged in the disastrous Crimean War against Britain, France, and the Ottoman Empire. (See the article on the Crimean War in Volume C.)

**Alexander II Liberates the Serfs.** Known as the Czar Liberator, Alexander II freed the serfs, introduced local self-government, reformed the court system, and greatly improved the conditions of military service. However, he held back from creating a national representative government until 1881. A few hours after signing such a measure, he was assassinated by terrorists. Alexander III succeeded his murdered father. He had little sympathy for reform and sought to suppress the growing revolutionary movement that had been responsible for Alexander II's death. For more information, see the biography of Alexander in Volume A.

**The Last Czar.** Nicholas II, the eldest son of Alexander III, came to the throne in 1894. Like his father, he was bent on maintaining absolute rule. However, the civil disturbances known as the Revolution of 1905, which occurred in the wake of Russian defeats in a war with Japan, forced Nicholas to grant an

In 1812, the defeated French soldiers of Napoleon I's Grand Army retreated from Moscow through the snows of the harsh Russian winter.

Czar Nicholas II and Czarina Alexandra (seated center) posed with their children (clockwise from left) Maria, Tatiana, Olga, Anastasia, and Alexis. The family was executed by the Bolshevik Communists in July 1918.

elective national assembly, called the Duma, and other civil rights. Four Dumas met from 1906 to 1917 and passed several progressive measures, including a land reform program. But Nicholas II was unable to halt the disorder that overcame the government before and during World War I (1914–18).

Russia had entered the war at its outbreak as an ally of Britain and France, opposing the Central Powers, headed by Germany and Austria-Hungary. The war went badly for Russia, and by February 1917, the government and army were near collapse, and Nicholas II was forced to abdicate (give up) the throne. For more information, see the biography of Nicholas in Volume N.

**Revolution.** In February 1917 (under the old calendar then in use; March under the present calendar), bread riots broke out in Petrograd (present-day St. Petersburg). Two governing bodies were established in place of the monarchy. One was the Provisional Government, which was to last only until a constituent assembly could be called and a new form of government decided upon. The other was the Soviet of Workers' (and later Soldiers') Deputies. Soviets (which means "councils") soon spread to other cities. The Provisional Government was too weak to govern effectively, although its last head, Prime Minister Alexander Kerensky, did his best. The leaders of the moderate socialist parties, the Mensheviks and Social Revolutionaries, who controlled the Petrograd Soviet, refused to take responsibility for governing. They believed a transitional period of government was necessary before socialism could be established in Russia.

**The Bolshevik Coup.** The Bolshevik Party, led by Vladimir Ilich Lenin, had no such qualms. In October 1917 (November in the new calendar), the Bolsheviks overthrew the Provisional Government and seized power throughout the country. All other political parties were banned. A constituent assembly, elected by popular vote and strongly anti-Bolshevik, met for only one day in January 1918, but it was quickly dispersed by troops loyal to the Bolsheviks. The Bolshevik Party then renamed itself the Communist Party.

*The history of Russia that follows, up until 1991, is also largely the history of the Soviet Union. For supplementary information, see the article on the Union of Soviet Socialist Republics in Volume UV.*

**Lenin's Policies.** In 1918, the Communists under Lenin were forced to conclude a disastrous peace treaty with Germany, the Treaty of Brest-Litovsk, under which Russia lost much of its western territories. (The treaty was later nullified.) They also had to fight a civil war, which lasted until 1921, against anti-Communist forces, who wished to undo the October Revolution. Nicholas II and the royal family became victims of the civil war; taken prisoner after the revolution, they were murdered by the Communists in July 1918.

Lenin at first sought to achieve socialism by taking complete control of the economy.

Vladimir Ilich Lenin, the leader of the Bolshevik Communists, overthrew Russia's Provisional Government in the October Revolution of 1917.

But he soon recognized that he had acted too hastily. With the economy in ruins and the regime facing revolt, he introduced the New Economic Policy (NEP) in 1921. Under the NEP, peasants were allowed to farm as they pleased, small private businesses flourished, and trade revived. In 1922 the Union of Soviet Socialist Republics was officially founded. See the biography of Lenin in Volume L.

**The Stalin Era.** When Lenin died in 1924, he was succeeded as Soviet leader by Joseph Stalin. Under Stalin, farms were forcibly collectivized, industry nationalized, and many new factories built.

Collectivization of agriculture, in which individual farms were joined together, was achieved at a dreadful human cost, and poor production led to the deaths of millions of people from starvation. While heavy industry grew under state control and the strength of the armed forces increased greatly, the standard of living of the peasants and working class fell sharply.

During the 1930's, Stalin began a series of purges that led to the deaths of many old Bolsheviks, most of the former leadership of the Communist Party, labor leaders, and nearly all of the senior officer corps.

It is estimated that Stalin was responsible for the deaths of more than 20 million of his own people. Millions more were sent to labor camps, where many died under the harsh conditions.

**World War II.** The chaos that resulted from Stalin's policies was one of the reasons for the quick successes won by the Germans, when Nazi Germany invaded the Soviet Union in 1941, beginning a 2½-year siege on Leningrad (present-day St. Petersburg). The attack came in spite of a nonaggression pact between the two countries, signed in August 1939. The wartime Soviet losses were enormous: At least 18 million—and possibly as many as 27 million—Russian soldiers and civilians are believed to have died.

Stalin emerged as one of the victors in the war, along with the United States and Britain. With Soviet troops controlling much of Eastern Europe at the war's end in 1945, Communist governments quickly came to power in most of the countries of the region. Because of this and other disputes, a long period of hostility, known as the Cold War, developed between the Soviet Union and its former Allies. See the article on the Cold War and the biography of Stalin in the appropriate volumes.

**Stalin's Successors.** Stalin was eventually succeeded by Nikita Khrushchev, who began the process of "de-Stalinization" in 1956 by revealing some of Stalin's crimes. In 1964 he was toppled from power by a group of old Stalinists, headed by Leonid Brezhnev.

Under Brezhnev, Soviet nuclear power grew to match that of the United States, and the expansion of Communism in Asia and Africa was startling.

Yuri Andropov, who succeeded Brezhnev in 1982, died in 1984. His successor, the elderly Konstantin Chernenko, survived only 13 months into his term. See the biographies of Khrushchev, Brezhnev, and Chernenko in the appropriate volumes.

**The Breakup of the Soviet Union.** An era of great change began when Mikhail Gorbachev became Soviet leader in 1985. Between 1987 and 1988 he began a limited venture into private enterprise as part of his attempt to revive the economy. He loosened the bonds of government censorship by encouraging *glas-*

Boris Yeltsin, president of the former Russian Soviet Republic, was elected president of the Russian Federation in 1991. Throughout the 1990's he tried to guide his country in its transition from Communism to a free-enterprise system.

*nost*, or openness, in the media. He allowed the people of Eastern Europe to go their own way, politically, which they proceeded to do by ending Communist regimes in their countries by democratic means.

In August 1991 a group of hardline Communist leaders, displeased with Gorbachev's political reforms, attempted to overthrow the government. The attempted coup failed after three days, but its results were dramatic. Boris Yeltsin, president of what was then the Russian Soviet Republic, became a popular hero for leading the resistance to the coup. By December, Gorbachev had resigned as president of the Soviet Union, and the Soviet Union ceased to exist. For more information, see the biographies of Gorbachev and Yeltsin in the appropriate volumes.

**Formation of the Russian Federation.** Boris Yeltsin was elected president of Russia in June 1991. When the Soviet Union fell apart that December, Yeltsin faced a Russian Supreme Soviet that was led by opponents of his reform program. The struggle between them culminated in a political crisis in 1993. Yeltsin dissolved the Supreme Soviet and set new elections; the Supreme Soviet responded by voting to oust him as president and finally called for an armed revolt. Yeltsin sent in military units, who cleared the parliament building and arrested his chief opponents.

Yeltsin then became president of a new Russian Federation. Immediately he faced the tasks of converting the formerly Communist country to a free-market economy and developing a new foreign policy. To this was added political opposition at home, a civil war against separatists in the republic of Chechnya, and his own poor health. Still, he won re-election by a wide margin in 1996.

**Recent History.** In 1998, the nation's currency lost its value. Parliament's desperate attempts to stabilize the economy failed, resulting in a rapid succession of prime ministers. Furthermore, in 1999 dozens of terrorist bombings in Russia, believed to be authorized by radical Islamic warlords in Chechnya, reopened the civil war. Yeltsin resigned on December 31, 1999, and named Prime

Vladimir Putin replaced Boris Yeltsin as president of Russia on December 31, 1999. He was elected in his own right by popular vote in 2000 and 2004.

Minister Vladimir Putin acting president. Putin was elected president in his own right by popular vote in 2000. See the biography of Putin in Volume P.

In 2001, Putin signed a treaty of friendship with China and negotiated with the United States to reduce the number of nuclear weapons. Soon after, Russia signed a historic agreement, pledging cooperation with NATO as a limited partner in the Western alliance. Putin also supported action against terrorists. Russia's war against Chechnya escalated after Chechen rebels seized a theater in Moscow in 2002. Approximately 120 civilian hostages died in the rescue attempt.

Putin was re-elected by a landslide in 2004. But the beginning of his second term was marked by mounting attacks by Chechen terrorists. On August 24, they claimed responsibility for bringing down two passenger jet airplanes, killing 90 people. On September 1, they seized an elementary school in Beslan, in the region of North Ossetia, which shares a border with Chechnya. For 62 hours they held hostage hundreds of students, parents, and teachers, demanding the withdrawal of Russian troops from Chechnya. The standoff came to a brutal end, and more than 300 people, many of them children, were killed.

Putin cited an increased need for control and security as he announced plans to take greater control of the country's central government by eliminating democratic elections for governors and other regional leaders and substituting them with government appointees. The State Duma approved the plan in October. That same month, the Federation Council approved the Kyoto Protocol, an international agreement to reduce global greenhouse gas emissions

DONALD W. TREADGOLD
Author, *Twentieth Century Russia*
Reviewed by ILYA PRIZEL
University of Pittsburgh

See also COMMONWEALTH OF INDEPENDENT STATES.

The *Vladimir Mother of God* was painted in Constantinople in the early 1100's and later brought to Russia. It became the most treasured of all Russian icons.

# RUSSIA, ART AND ARCHITECTURE OF

The arts of Russia reflect the country's long history and vast size. They have been shaped by Russia's contacts with cultures to the east and west as well as by its periods of isolation.

## ▶ ANCIENT SOURCES

Early Slavic tribes in the lands around the Black Sea created some of the first Russian art. Beautifully designed jewelry, leather sword sheaths and harnesses, embroidered wall hangings, and other objects have been found in the burial mounds of chieftains and nobles. The artists often used animal forms, and they decorated their work with intricate patterns. Some designs stood for natural forces: zig-zag lines for lightning, circles and diamonds for the sun.

From the 100's to the 600's, the Slavs moved north and east into areas we now call Russia. Settling in forested areas along rivers and lakes, they worshipped nature spirits and made wooden figures to represent their gods. Although the old beliefs were suppressed when Christianity became the state religion, these spirits remained important. Their images continued to appear in folk art.

## ▶ KIEV AND CHRISTIAN RUSSIA

Scandinavian traders entered Russia in the 700's, seeking river routes from the north to the Black Sea. One of their outposts, Kiev, became a major city and the capital of an important state. The Kievan rulers gained wealth and strength through a treaty with the powerful Byzantine Empire. Constantinople (now Istanbul), the Empire's capital, was the center of the Eastern (Greek Orthodox) Church. It was partly to strengthen ties with the Empire that Prince Vladimir of Kiev decided to adopt the Eastern Christian faith in 989.

But ancient records suggest other reasons, too. Before deciding which form of worship to make the official religion of his kingdom, Vladimir studied those of other countries. He sent envoys to the Muslims in the south and to the German Christians in the west, but they returned to say that they found "no beauty" there. At last, in Constantinople, they attended a service in the Cathedral of Holy Wisdom (St. Sophia). "We did not know whether we were in heaven or on earth," they reported. "For on earth there is no sight or beauty to equal this. . . . We know only that God abides there with his people. . . . We cannot forget that beauty."

This feeling that the beauty of a church expresses the glory of God is a key to Russian religious art. Vladimir wanted his city to glorify God, and he brought teams of masons and painters to build palaces and churches modeled on those of Constantinople. The most important cathedral, begun in 1037, was dedicated to St. Sophia. Its roof was formed by 13 domes. The largest symbolized Christ, and the twelve smaller domes around it stood for the Apostles. Inside, the walls were covered with **mosaics**, pictures made up of small pieces of polished stone or glass. Most of the cathedral artists were Greeks from Constantinople. As they worked, they trained helpers, and within a few years Kiev had several workshops of local artists. The city grew in magnificence. At its height, with nearly four hundred churches, Kiev rivaled the Byzantine capital.

## THE NORTHERN CENTERS

Two northern centers, Novgorod and Vladimir, developed distinctive styles of architecture. Novgorod was famous for its woodcarvers and for its wooden architecture. Wood was used to build churches, houses, and even the fortress (*kremlin*) that stood at the highest point of each town. No early wood churches have survived, but the Church of the Transfiguration (1714) on Kizhi island, with its pointed tent roof and clustered domes, gives an idea of how they looked.

In the 1100's the capital was moved from Kiev to the city of Vladimir. Churches and palaces were built there of local white limestone, their outside walls decorated with carvings of figures, animals, and plants. Vladimir became the home of a famous **icon** of the Mother of God. (An icon is a religious image, usually painted on a wood panel.) This icon, which became known as the *Vladimir Mother of God*, had been painted in Constantinople and was cherished as a symbol of the Kievan state. It was the most treasured of all Russian icons.

## THE MONGOL INVASION AND ISOLATION

During the 1200's, nomadic tribes called the Mongols (or Tatars) conquered the Byzantine Empire and swept over south and central Russia. By 1240 both Kiev and Vladimir had been destroyed, and hundreds of churches and early icons were burned.

The Mongol occupation, which lasted for nearly 250 years, cut Russia off from Constantinople and from Western Europe. This meant that Russian artists could no longer imitate Byzantine models. Gradually, Russian builders and painters began to develop their own styles. Regional schools of icon painting were established in Novgorod and other cities, bringing new types of figures and color combinations to religious images. Northern artists invented the **iconostasis**, a carved wooden choir screen on which rows of icons were hung. The iconostasis came to be the outstanding feature of Russian churches.

In the early 1400's several masterful painters emerged, including Theofanes the Greek, his assistant Prokhor of Gorodets, and Andrei Rublev. One of the most deeply moving icons is Rublev's *Old Testament Trinity* (about 1410–20), in which three angels represent the three figures of the Holy Trinity—the Father,

The Church of the Transfiguration (1714) in Kizhi, with its clustered onion domes, is an outstanding example of Russia's traditional wooden architecture.

the Son, and the Holy Spirit. The feeling of serenity and joy in this icon echoes the rising hopes of Russians as the Mongols were finally being driven from the land.

## THE RISE OF MOSCOW

The princes of Moscow took the lead in driving back the Mongols. Under Ivan I (ruled 1325–41), the city rose in power. As it did, new building projects were begun. In 1462, Ivan III took the title of Czar (meaning Caesar, or emperor), and called Moscow the "third Rome." He hired architects from Italy to build new churches and palaces in the Kremlin. Aristotele Fioravanti, the Italian architect who built the Cathedral of the Dormition (1475–79), based his design on the churches of Vladimir but used new building techniques from Italy. Italians also designed the Cathedral of the Archangel Michael, the Annunciation Cathedral, the banquet hall known as the Faceted Palace, and the towers of the Kremlin walls.

The Cathedral of the Dormition (1475–79) was built in Moscow during the city's rise as a powerful center. Its architect based his design on the stone churches of Vladimir but used building techniques from Italy.

The Cathedral of the Intercession (1555–60, known as St. Basil the Blessed), on Red Square, was built in honor of Ivan IV's capture of the Mongol capital of Kazan. The Russian architects Postnik and Barma combined forms of the Kievan domed churches with the tent-shaped roof of northern wooden churches. Their striking use of brightly glazed tiles on the domes may have been inspired by styles of Kazan and the East.

The czars were also patrons of icon painting, metalwork, and manuscript illumination (illustration). After a fire destroyed much of Moscow in 1547, the Czar called in architects, painters, and craftsmen to replace the lost works and to establish a permanent school and workshops in the Kremlin.

During the 1500's and 1600's, the czars promoted trade and artistic contact with other lands. The styles of Germany, Holland, England, Italy, Turkey, and Persia began to influence the ways Russian artists decorated buildings and ceremonial objects. In icons painted by Simon Ushakov and other Kremlin masters, figures appeared rounded and naturally shaded in the manner of Western European art.

While the arts of the church and the czars' courts were absorbing Western influences, the art made by peasants to decorate their houses, clothing, and tools kept older forms alive. Some designs on carved and painted wood articles and on embroidered textiles can be traced back to the early Slavic tribes.

## ▶ ST. PETERSBURG AND WESTERNIZATION

Peter the Great (ruled 1682–1725) continued the Westernization begun under Ivan III. In 1703, Peter founded a new capital, St. Petersburg, near the Gulf of Finland. To build the new city, his "window" on the West, Peter summoned architects and artisans from all over Europe and Russia.

Peter worked with his chief architect, Domenico Trezzini, to create buildings modeled after those of Holland and other countries of Western Europe. One of the first projects was the Cathedral of Saints Peter and Paul (1712–13). Its tall gilt spire, still a landmark today, contrasts sharply with the domed churches of Moscow.

Peter's daughter Elizabeth (ruled 1741–62) also loved architecture. Her chief architect, Bartolomeo Rastrelli, built palaces and churches in an ornate but lively style known as Elizabeth's rococo. The buildings were painted in bright colors and trimmed in white. The most famous example is the Winter Palace, on the south bank of the Neva River.

Catherine the Great (ruled 1762–96) preferred a more restrained, classical style of architecture. Like Peter, Catherine was international in outlook. She sent young artists to study abroad, and through her ministers, she purchased works of art in every major European city. Other Russian rulers followed Catherine's example in collecting art. Their collections later formed Russia's art museums, which are among the finest in the world.

The Academy of Arts was founded in 1757 under Elizabeth and given its permanent form in 1764 by Catherine. It was established to provide Russian artists with training equal to European standards. The Academy had its most dramatic effect on painters. Because of the long-standing icon tradition, painting was slower than architecture to adopt foreign styles. Russian painters had to learn new forms and techniques if they were to gain a place in the new, international art world.

▶ THE 1800'S

Contrasting trends can be seen in Russian art of the early 1800's. The most successful artists, like Karl Briullov, mastered all aspects of European painting and spent many years abroad. Briullov was most famous for his dramatic painting *The Last Day of Pompeii* (1830–33). The best portrait painters, Orest Kiprenski and Vasili Tropinin, were both peasants' sons who were given the chance to study at the Academy. Alexander Ivanov was an important painter of religious subjects.

Alexei Venetsianov was the first trained artist to abandon historical and religious subjects. Instead, his main subjects were the peasants who worked on his estate. Venetsianov's careful observation of everyday scenes paved the way for the realist movement.

*Above: The Rider* (1832), by Karl Briullov, shows the influence of Western European painting traditions. *Below:* The palace at Tsarskoye Selo (now Pushkin) is typical of the ornate buildings designed by Bartolomeo Rastrelli for the Russian Empress Elizabeth I.

*Above:* In the later 1800's, many Russian painters began to express social concerns through their art. *Barge Haulers on the Volga,* by Ilia Repin, dramatically depicts the exhausting work of the boatmen.

*Left:* Elaborately decorated Easter eggs, crafted from gold and other precious materials, were made for the Russian royal family at the turn of the century by goldsmith Karl Fabergé.

By the 1860's, many artists were concerned about the hard lives of the peasants and other social issues. Ivan Kramskoi and Vasili Perov worked in a style known as critical realism. They wanted to paint works that showed what life in Russia was really like, and they wanted to exhibit them throughout the country.

In 1871, Kramskoi and others founded the Association of Traveling Art Exhibitions. Ilia Repin was the most gifted and best known of this group. His *Barge Haulers on the Volga* (1871–73) showed the hard toil of the bargemen and the vastness of the river in a way that was both familiar and striking. The Association remained active into the 1900's. However, by the late 1800's many Russian artists had begun to look beyond realism toward new artistic values.

Outstanding younger painters, including Valentin Serov, Isaak Levitan, and Mikhail Vrubel, had studied with Repin and other realists. But these artists cared more about style than about the content or message of a work. Their paintings, whether portraits, landscapes, or subjects from literature, often emphasized a mood or impression.

One group went even further in promoting "art for art's sake." Led by Alexander Benois and the art and dance patron Sergei Diaghilev, they formed a society known as the World of Art in 1898. Through art exhibitions and a magazine, this group introduced modern European art into Russia. It also brought Russian art to a European audience.

In architecture and the decorative arts, European styles were combined with those of early Russia. Churches, stores, public buildings, and homes were built in this style, which became known as the Russian Revival. Early painting and decorative styles used by the Kremlin masters and by folk artists were also revived. The love of precious materials and fine craftsmanship is best seen in the jeweled enamel Easter eggs made for the royal family by the goldsmith Karl Fabergé.

▶ **THE 1900'S**

Russian artists were involved in many of the art movements of the early 1900's. Thanks to the World of Art exhibits and to adventurous collectors, young artists could see the works of modern European painters in Russia. Many artists also traveled abroad. Mikhail Larionov and Natalia Goncharova invented neoprimitiv-

*Above:* In *Couple on Horseback* (1907), by Vasili Kandinsky, dots of glowing color create a mosaic-like effect. *Right:* Soviet laborers and farm workers are celebrated in *Worker and Collective Farm Woman* (1937), a socialist realist sculpture by Vera Mukhina.

ism and rayonnism, styles that were inspired by both Russian folk art and French cubism.

Two artists whose influence extended outside Russia were Vasili Kandinsky and Marc Chagall. Both used color to express feelings and visions comparable to those of early icons and mosaics. Kandinsky at first painted recognizable scenes and images. Later he became one of the first artists to paint completely abstract works: compositions of lines, shapes, and colors that do not represent any real object. Chagall's dreamlike images recall his Jewish upbringing in a small Russian village.

Kazimir Malevich created suprematism, a form of abstract art, about 1913. Slightly later, a group of artists developed constructivism, a combination of sculpture and architecture based on modern building materials, which they believed would help in constructing a new society.

The artistic "revolution," with its new visual ideas, occurred before the political revolution of October 1917. But the artists' goals were similar to those of the Bolshevik leaders. They believed that art could work with new social theories to build a new society. The constructivists designed monuments to express the hopes of the Soviet regime.

In the 1930's the government began to limit personal and artistic freedom. Artists were allowed to work only in a style called socialist realism, which celebrated the values of socialism and patriotism. Abstract art and other experimental styles were forbidden. No foreign art was shown in Russia for more than thirty years. A few artists tried to work according to their own ideals, but they were denounced, and their work was suppressed. Many artists left the country.

Nevertheless, an "unofficial" art movement began in the 1960's, led by the sculptor Ernst Neizvestny; the painters Mikhail Chemiakin, Oskar Rabin, and Evgeny Ruhkin, and others. Exhibits were held in parks and social clubs in the mid-1970's and early 1980's. But it was still difficult and dangerous to work outside the official system. After 1985, the cultural policy of *glasnost*, or "openness," encouraged artists to experiment with new styles and themes and to show their work abroad. The breakup of the Soviet Union in 1991 seemed certain to further the process of bringing Russia once again into the larger world of art.

ALISON HILTON
Georgetown University
Author, *Russian Folk Art and the Patterns of Life*

# RUSSIA, LANGUAGE AND LITERATURE OF

Russian is the native tongue of more than 140 million people. This language has been the medium for such literary masterpieces as Tolstoi's *War and Peace* and Dostoevski's *Crime and Punishment*. The histories of Russian language and Russian literature are as distinguished as they are long.

## ▶RUSSIAN LANGUAGE

In prehistoric times a people known as Slavs probably spoke a common tongue. This language was one of the Indo-European family of languages. The Slavs settled in the East European plain, and then they moved westward over the Carpathian Mountains and southward into the Balkan Peninsula. Their one language was replaced by a number of languages, each of which was based on the dialect of a region.

Today the Slavic languages can be divided into three main groups. The Western group includes the language of Poles, Czechs, and Slovaks, among others. The Southern group takes in the Bulgarians, Serbs, Croats, and Slovenes. The Eastern group, the largest, includes the language of the three branches of Russians. These are Russians, Ukrainians, and Belarusians (also known as White Russians). Latins, Greeks, Turks, Mongolians, Finno-Ugrians, and Scandinavians influenced the different Slavic languages. Although many changes crept in, all the Slavic tongues had many word roots in common.

The Eastern group of the Slavic tongues came to be known as Russian. In various parts of Russia the differences in dialect are slight. For almost 2,000 years Russian was the principal language of the Kievan and Moscow states. It is the principal language of present-day Russia and was widely used throughout the former Union of Soviet Socialist Republics. Schools in many Eastern European countries teach Russian as a foreign language.

The Russian language is written with an alphabet of 33 letters, many of which resemble Greek and Latin ones. It is a Cyrillic alphabet, based on the one devised by Saints Cyril (827–69) and Methodius (826–85).

## ▶RUSSIAN LITERATURE

The Slavic tribes had an oral tradition of myths, songs, fairy tales, and sayings, passed on from generation to generation. Their epic stories about "men of might" came to us in a more modern form in the 1500's and 1600's. Commonly called *byliny*, they stem from the ancient poetry of the Slavs.

### From the Beginnings to the 1600's

Written literature started only after Prince Vladimir of Kiev officially accepted Christianity, in 988, and forced it on his subjects. Kiev, in Ukraine, was the center of Slavic culture. Its literature was written in a language called Old Church Slavonic. Surviving manuscripts include lives of saints, legends, and apocrypha (religious tales, which are not part of the Bible). Among them was the moving *Virgin's Journey Through Suffering*.

Russian medieval literature has two remarkable monuments. One, Nestor's *Chronicle*, completed in the 1100's, relates important events in a lively style. Numerous chronicles followed it. The second outstanding piece of medieval literature is *The Tale of Igor's Campaign*, an epic poem of the late 1100's. Filled with beautiful word pictures, the poem depicts the struggle of the people against Asian invaders.

In the 1200's, Kiev fell to the Tatars. Their rule, from 1240 until 1480, slowed the development of literature. The writings of the period are of great historical interest but have little literary value.

### The Rise of Moscow

A new cultural upsurge began with the defeat of the Tatars and the rise and growth of Moscow. Ties with the West were resumed, and political writing took on great importance. The best example is the *Correspondence* (1563–79) between Ivan the Terrible and Prince Andrei Kurbsky.

The most realistic, lively, and daring work of the 1600's was the *Autobiography* of Archpriest Avvakum (1621–82). A defender of his church's ancient traditions, he was burned at the stake. Simeon of Polozk (1629–80) represents Western trends in literature that came from Poland and Bohemia. A whole poetic

| THE RUSSIAN (CYRILLIC) ALPHABET | RUSSIAN | А | Б | В | Г | Д | Е | Ё | Ж | З | И | Й | К | Л | М | Н |
|---|---|---|---|---|---|---|---|---|---|---|---|---|---|---|---|---|---|
| | ROMAN EQUIVALENT | a | b | v | g | d | e or ye | e or yo | zh | z | i | y | k | l | m | n |

school copied his style of verse, and his plays were performed in the first national theater, established in 1672 in Moscow.

Poetry and dramatic literature blossomed in the 1700's after the reforms of Peter the Great. He freed literature from the rules of the Church Slavonic language and modernized the Cyrillic alphabet. He brought Western customs and ideas into Russia and encouraged Russian writers to follow European models.

Russia enjoyed a literary renaissance. This rebirth of literature began with satires by Prince Antiokh Kantemir (1709–44), the odes of Mikhail Lomonosov (1711–65), and the dramas of Aleksandr Sumarokov (1718–77). Of greatest importance was the shift in verse-making from the arrangement of lines by syllable count to the writing of accented verse. Although the great Russian poets of the 1700's followed the strict rules of French classicism, they gave their works a national spirit and an original form. This is especially evident in the impressive poems of Gavrila Derzhavin (1743–1816) and in *The Minor* (1782), a realistic comedy by Denis Fonvizin (1745–92) that became a highlight of the Russian stage.

The end of the 1700's produced a leading literary figure, Nikolai Karamzin (1766–1826). A historian and traveler, Karamzin also wrote the popular sentimental tale *Poor Liza* (1792).

### The 1800's

The first half of the 1800's is known as the golden age of Russian poetry. The foremost writer of the period was Aleksandr Pushkin (1799–1837), Russia's greatest poet.

Pushkin absorbed fully the fruits of European culture. The settings of his poetic dramas range from Germany (*The Covetous Knight*, 1830) to Scotland (*The Feast During the Plague*, 1830). The historical chronicle *Boris Godunov* (1824–25) recaptures the "times of trouble" of the 1600's. This work was made into an opera, as was Pushkin's masterpiece, *Eugene Onegin* (1823–31), a novel in verse. It goes to the very soul of Russian cultural tradition, literature, and way of life. Passion and clarity, realism and romanticism, are in all Pushkin's works, especially his lyrical poems. His magical verse, as well as the perfection of

his tales in prose, helped to shape Russia's literary language.

The second great poet of the period is Mikhail Lermontov (1814–41), whose work differs greatly in tone from that of Pushkin. Lermontov's narratives in verse, *The Novice* (1840) and *The Demon* (1841), and his lyrical pieces and plays are filled with bitterness and anger. His novel *A Hero of Our Times* (1841) portrayed the "superfluous man," of no use to his society.

**Gogol, Turgenev, and the Realists.** There was a great deal of intellectual and artistic activity in Russia between 1830 and the 1860's. Russian literary criticism got its start through Vissarion Belinsky (1811–48). In his writings Aleksandr Herzen (1812–70) gave a new prominence to philosophical and political thought.

Among numerous prose writers emerged the central figure of Nikolai Gogol (1809–52). Gogol was a government clerk and teacher in St. Petersburg before he began his writing career. Upset by criticism of his work, Gogol left Russia and traveled widely in Europe. He returned to Russia four years before he died.

Gogol's novel *Dead Souls* (1842–52) takes a humorous look at Russian provincial life and is filled with portraits of freaks and knaves. *The Inspector General* (1836), a satirical play, exposes the dishonesty of small-town officials. Both these works show the rare qualities of Gogol's imagination, as do his tales *The Nose* (1835) and *The Overcoat* (1842), among oth-

Aleksandr Pushkin was Russia's greatest poet. His masterpiece is *Eugene Onegin* (1823–31), a novel written in verse. Pushkin's brilliant use of the language set the standard for later poets and novelists.

| О | П | Р | С | Т | У | Ф | Х | Ц | Ч | Ш | Щ | Ъ | Ы | Ь | Э | Ю | Я |
|---|---|---|---|---|---|---|---|---|---|---|---|---|---|---|---|---|---|
| o | p | r | s | t | u | f | kh | ts | ch | sh | shch | (∗) | y | (∗) | e | yu | ya |

★ No Roman Equivalent

ers. They also reveal Gogol's sense of fantasy, his religious longings, and his mixture of laughter and tears. The flow of his witty, rich language created a new style of writing.

Ivan Turgenev (1818–83) came of well-to-do parents, who sent him to universities in Moscow, St. Petersburg, and Berlin. From 1845 on he devoted his time to writing, and he spent a great deal of time in France.

The label "realist" aptly fits Turgenev, whose works, translated into many languages, were among the first to introduce Russian literature to the Western world. His *Notes of a Hunter* (1847–52), depicting peasants in their true environment, promoted the freeing of the serfs. His tales and novels—*Rudin* (1856), *Gentlefolk's Nest* (1859), *Fathers and Sons* (1862), *Smoke* (1867), and *Virgin Soil* (1877) —reflecting shifting ideas and moods in mid-century Russia, formed a history of its educated class.

realistic school reigned in prose, but even its best representatives, such as Alexei Pisemsky (1821–81) and Nikolai Leskov (1831–95), were overshadowed by two literary giants.

### Dostoevski and Tolstoi

These two writers are Fëdor Dostoevski (1821–81) and Leo Tolstoi (1828–1910). Dostoevski's four greatest novels are *Crime and Punishment* (1866), *The Idiot* (1868), *The Possessed* (1872), and *The Brothers Karamazov* (1880). *Notes from the Underground*, a combination of philosophy and fiction, was written in 1864. These works, some of which are disguised as mystery stories and crowded with turbulent events and frantic characters, raised problems of freedom and evil in people. Dostoevski probed deep into the human mind and spirit. The suspense of his plots and his sweeping style make him one of the most fascinating masters of world literature.

*Far left:* In novels such as *Crime and Punishment* (1866), Fëdor Dostoevski explored the complexities of the human mind and spirit. His portrayal of the inner lives of his characters greatly influenced later novelists.

*Near left:* Leo Tolstoi's great novel *War and Peace* (1869) describes historic military campaigns and intimate scenes of family life with equal skill and liveliness. Toward the end of his life, when this photograph was taken, Tolstoi renounced his wealth and adopted the life-style and simple dress of a peasant.

Next to Turgenev stands Ivan Goncharov (1812–91), author of *Oblomov* (1859). In this and other novels, such as *Common Story* (1847), Goncharov excels in detailed representation of people and their environment.

What Turgenev and Goncharov accomplished in fiction, Aleksandr Ostrovsky (1823–86) did in the theater. He wrote 47 plays, national in style and spirit, showing mainly the old-fashioned merchant class (*Poverty No Disgrace*, 1854) and the decline of the nobility (*Wild Money*, 1870).

After the serfs were freed in 1861 and after a series of reforms, many authors showed radical and socialist tendencies in their work. The

Leo Tolstoi, in the size and range of his epic works, can be compared with Homer and Shakespeare. His great novel *War and Peace* (1869) has more than 500 characters. Each plays a part in an enormous historical picture —Napoleon's 1812 invasion of Russia and his defeat. The novel is also an intimate chronicle of family life. Among Tolstoi's many other novels and tales are *Anna Karenina* (1877), a novel of a tragic love affair, *The Death of Ivan Ilyich* (1886), *The Kreutzer Sonata* (1890), and *Resurrection* (1899). In all his writings Tolstoi emphasized individual search for truth, which is a fundamental theme of all Russian literature.

### From Chekhov and Gorky to the Symbolists

The start of the 20th century brought a new renaissance of arts and letters. Traditional realism continued in lively short stories and novels by Aleksandr Kuprin (1870–1938). The work of Ivan Bunin (1870–1953) offered something more. A brilliant storyteller, Bunin was the first Russian to win the Nobel prize for literature (1933). A marvelous stylist, he moved from realism (*The Village*, 1909) to thoughtful prose (*The Life of Arseniev*, 1930) and moving tales of love. In drama Leonid Andreyev (1871–1919) went toward the fantastic and tragic with *The Life of Man* (1906) and *He Who Gets Slapped* (1914).

The plays and short stories of Anton Chekhov (1860–1904) had a great influence on writers everywhere. Chekhov received a medical degree from the University of Moscow. While a student, he began writing short pieces (some of which he signed "The Doctor Without Patients"). Chekhov's reputation as a writer grew, and he soon gave all his time to literature. He blended humor and melancholy in his subtle plays of understatement. He created lyrical dramas of moods and telling details in *The Sea Gull* (1896), *Uncle Vanya* (1897), *The Three Sisters* (1901), and *The Cherry Orchard* (1904).

In his numerous works, Maxim Gorky (1868–1936) depicted the lower classes' sufferings and dreams of a better life. The power of his writing and its revolutionary spirit made him the leader of a whole literary movement, before and after the Revolution of 1917. Gorky's major novel is *Mother* (1906). *The Lower Depths* (1902) is his most famous play.

Symbolists changed the literary climate. They searched for the hidden meaning of images and saw in them and in words the reflection of a higher reality. Between 1890 and 1917 the symbolists dominated Russian poetry and established a vast and brilliant school. Its leader was Aleksandr Blok (1880–1921). His musical poems of love and despair charmed a whole generation. Another important symbolist was Andrei Bely (1880–1934). One of his best-known novels is *Petersburg* (1914).

### After the 1917 Revolution

Between 1917 and 1932 prerevolutionary trends continued under the Soviets, who replaced rule by czars with a Communist government. Vladimir Mayakovski (1893–1930) devoted his great talent to the service of the Revolution and reflected in his poems the events of his times. He was a futurist—that is, one against all tradition in art. Sergei Esenin

*Right:* Boris Pasternak won the Nobel prize for literature for his novel *Dr. Zhivago* (1955). But, under pressure from the Soviet government, he refused the award. The novel was not published in the Soviet Union until 1988.

*Below:* A scene from *The Cherry Orchard* (1904), a play by Anton Chekhov. One of modern literature's leading playwrights, Chekhov was also a master of the short story.

(1895–1925), the "peasant poet," wrote of nature, grief, and rebellion.

In his dynamic and highly imaginative poems Boris Pasternak (1890–1960) remained an individualist, always trying new forms and techniques. Pasternak's writings displeased the Soviets. Government officials would not allow the publication of his novel *Dr. Zhivago*, which describes the turmoil of the 1917 Revolution and later events. The novel received worldwide acclaim after it appeared in an Italian translation in 1957. Pasternak won the Nobel prize for literature but was forced to refuse it. *Dr. Zhivago* remained banned in the Soviet Union until 1988. That same year, plans were announced to turn Pasternak's home into a memorial museum.

Important works of early Soviet prose included civil war stories by Isaac Babel (1894–1941), humorous sketches by Mikhail Zoshchenko (1895–1958), and tales by Aleksei Tolstoi (1882–1945). The Communist approach to events was fully expressed in *The Quiet Don* (1928–40), a monumental chroni-

Aleksandr Solzhenitsyn won the 1970 Nobel prize for literature. His dramatic accounts of life in Soviet prisons were secretly circulated in the Soviet Union and openly published abroad. The Soviet government expelled him in 1974 but began to publish his works about prison in 1989. He returned to Russia after the Soviet Union collapsed in 1991.

cle of civil war by Mikhail Sholokhov (1905–84), winner of the 1965 Nobel prize for literature. A Communist outlook is also present in *The Rout* (1927), by Aleksandr Fadeev (1901–56).

After 1932, Soviet literature was channeled into "socialist realism," an official school of writing controlled by the Communist Party. Literature focused on problems of labor, industrialization, and social change. Its aim was the education of the masses according to the Communist doctrines of Marx and Lenin.

Despite the restrictions on writers during this period, Mikhail Bulgakov (1891–1940) did not give up his artistic convictions. His play *The Days of the Turbins* (1926) and his novels *The White Guard* (1924) and *The Master and Margarita* (1940; published 1967) are masterpieces. Two poets, Anna Akhmatova (1899–1966) and Marina Tsvetaeva (1892–1941), created lasting and highly personal poems.

The ordeals of the Russians during World War II and their struggle against Hitler were the subject of many works, among them the novels *Days and Nights* (1944), by Konstantin Simonov (1915–79), and *In the Trenches of Stalingrad* (1946), by Viktor Nekrasov (1911–87), and the poem *Vassily Tyorkin* (1946), by Alexander Tvardovsky (1910–71).

After the death of Stalin in 1953, writers became freer, and a new generation of poets and prose writers came to the fore. Yevgeny Yevtushenko (1933– ) attacked aspects of Soviet society in poems such as "Stalin's Heirs" (1962). One of Yevtushenko's best-known poems is "Babi Yar" (1962), written in memory of Jews killed by Germans in the Ukraine during World War II. Andrei Voznesensky (1933– ) and Bella Akhmadulina (1937– ) also attained national and international prominence for their poetry.

Notable prose writers of recent times include Yuri Kazakov (1927–83), Valentin Rasputin (1937– ), Yury Trifonov (1925–81), Chingiz Aitmatov (1928– ), and Aleksandr I. Solzhenitsyn (1918– ). A number of Solzhenitsyn's books, including *One Day in the Life of Ivan Denisovich* (1962) and *The Gulag Archipelago* (1973–75), describe Soviet prison life. Solzhenitsyn won the Nobel prize for literature in 1970. In 1974, he was expelled by the Soviets. He took up residence in the United States in 1976, where he continued to write. He finally returned to Russia in 1994, three years after the collapse of the Soviet Union. An important but separate section of Russian literature was formed by writers, such as Vladimir Nabokov (1899–1977), who left Russia after the Revolution and continued their writing abroad.

Since the early 1990's, less restrictive government policies have provided greater freedom of expression for Russian writers.

Reviewed by NICHOLAS RZHEVSKY
Author, *Russian Literature and Ideology*

# RUSSIA, MUSIC OF

For hundreds of years music in Russia consisted mainly of church music and the songs and dances of the peasants. Then, in the 1700's, foreign musicians brought Italian opera to Russia. It was widely performed and was supported by the aristocracy.

In the 1800's Mikhail Glinka (1804–57), a Russian musician, decided to compose a national opera. He wanted to write music that was genuinely Russian and that every Russian could understand. Basing his style on Russian folk music, he composed *A Life for the Tsar* (1836) and *Russlan and Ludmilla* (1842). These two operas were taken as models by many later Russian composers.

Glinka had a young friend named Mily Balakirev (1837–1910), who believed strongly in the future of Russian music. A born leader, Balakirev gathered a little group of friends about him and taught them, firing them with his own ideals. The oldest member of the Mighty Handful, as the group was called, was an eminent scientist, Alexander Borodin (1833–87). Two younger members were Modest Mussorgsky (1839–81), an army officer, and Nikolay Rimsky-Korsakov (1844–1908), a naval officer. Borodin had little time for composing. He never finished his opera *Prince Igor* or his third symphony. However, his second symphony is considered one of the finest of all Russian symphonies.

Mussorgsky wrote no symphonies. His best work consisted of operas and songs with piano accompaniment. Mussorgsky was much more interested in writing music to go with words than in composing beautiful melodies. He often wrote his own words for songs on subjects that had never been used by song composers before. His operas, such as *Boris Godunov* (1869), contained scenes from real life that were very unlike the more conventional love scenes and pageantry. One of Mussorgsky's best-known works is his set of pieces for piano, *Pictures at an Exhibition* (1874).

Rimsky-Korsakov was a great teacher and above all a superb orchestrator. His *Scheherazade* (1888) and *Capriccio espagnol* (1887), although not great music, are among the most brilliant pieces of orchestration composed in the 1800's. Songs and dances from his best-known operas—*The Snow Maiden* (1881),

A dancer's costume for an early production of *The Firebird*, a ballet by the Russian composer Igor Stravinsky. The costume was designed by the artist Léon Bakst.

*Sadko* (1894), *Tsar Saltan* (1900), and *The Golden Cockerel* (1906)—are familiar to many people.

The most famous of all Russian composers, Peter Ilyich Tchaikovsky (1840–93), studied at Russia's first official school of music. It was in St. Petersburg. Most of the staff, headed by pianist-composer Anton Rubinstein (1829–94), did not care at all about Glinka's ideal of writing music that was Russian. Tchaikovsky's training took him nearer to the styles of German, French, and Italian music and made him less purely Russian. He wrote music of every kind. Two of his operas, *Eugene Onegin* (1878) and *The Queen of Spades* (1890), are among the best Russian operas. Tchaikovsky's three ballets—*Swan Lake* (1876), *The Sleeping Beauty* (1889), and *The Nutcracker* (1892)—and three of his six symphonies are world-famous. His First Piano Concerto is probably the most popular piano concerto ever written.

Many composers followed Tchaikovsky and the Mighty Handful, but only a few became world famous. These included three composers who emerged during the years before World War I—Sergei Rachmaninoff (1873–1943), Alexander Scriabin (1872–1915), and Igor Stravinsky (1882–1971). Rachmaninoff, who was thought to be old-fashioned by many, continued to write music in a style similar to Tchaikovsky's. Two of his piano concertos became especially popular, along with several shorter pieces for piano. He was also a fine pianist and conductor.

Scriabin began by writing beautifully polished short piano pieces. Then his music became more complicated and very much influenced by his religious ideas. Examples are *Poem of Ecstasy* (1908) and *Prometheus* (1911), two works for orchestra.

Stravinsky's first notable composition, the ballet *The Firebird* (1910), is a little in the style of Scriabin but much more in the style of Stravinsky's teacher, Rimsky-Korsakov. Stravinsky's next two ballets, *Petrouchka* (1911) and *The Rite of Spring* (1913), were revolutionary in their highly original use of folk music. In fact, *The Rite of Spring* was so daring that the audience in Paris at the first performance got angry and caused a riot in the theater. Within a year, however, the work was hailed as a masterpiece. When World War I broke out, Stravinsky was in Western Europe and could not return to Russia. After the Russian Revolution of 1917 he stayed in the West, and his music became less and less Russian in character. After 1939 Stravinsky lived in the United States.

### After the Revolution

The 1917 Revolution made a break in Russian musical life. Some composers, such as Rachmaninoff, disliked the new government and left Russia for good. Others stayed on for a number of years and then left. Some of the composers, such as Reinhold Glière (1875–1956) and Nikolai Miaskovsky (1881–1950), remained in Russia and passed on the great Russian tradition to their pupils.

The most gifted of all the younger composers who had grown up just before the revolution, Sergei Prokofiev (1891–1953) left Russia at once but changed his mind and returned home in the 1930's. Like Tchaikovsky, Prokofiev was successful at writing many different kinds of music, including operas, symphonies, concertos, and ballets. His most popular work is *Peter and the Wolf* (1936), a musical version of a Russian fairy tale.

Before long, a new generation began to grow up that had never known the Russia of the czars. One of these composers was Dmitri Shostakovich (1906–75). Another was the Armenian Aram Khachaturian (1903–78), best known for his exciting *Saber Dance* (1942).

At first, many Communists wanted to ban the works of such great Russian composers as Tchaikovsky. They felt that music should be understandable to ordinary concertgoers and that it should fill people with courage, patriotism, and hope. In the early 1930's, however, the government realized that the classics were too precious to ban.

But composers living in the Soviet Union soon found themselves in difficulties unknown to composers in non-Communist countries. Though the Communists saw to it that composers were well-paid and spent great sums of money to put on fine opera, ballet, and concerts, the government kept a firm watch on all new music. Shostakovich's opera *Lady Macbeth of the District of Mtsensk* was taken off the stage after Stalin heard it in 1936. But his Seventh Symphony, inspired by the defense of Leningrad against the Germans, was warmly received. So were his Eleventh, about the attempted revolution of 1905, and his Twelfth, about the Revolution of 1917.

Gradually, restrictions on the arts were relaxed, especially with the introduction of the cultural policy of *glasnost* ("openness") after 1985. However, the adventuresome spirit that has characterized much modern music was discouraged in the Soviet Union prior to its breakup in 1991. Rodion Shchedrin (1932–   ) emerged as a leader of a movement to allow composers more artistic freedom.

As in earlier generations, some contemporary Russian composers, such as Alexei Volkonsky (1933–   ), have lived and worked outside the country. Others, such as Alfred Schnitke (1934–   ), achieved worldwide recognition without leaving Russia.

GERALD ABRAHAM
Author, *Studies in Russian Music*
Reviewed by RAYMOND KNAPP
Conservatory of Music, Oberlin College

**RUSSWURM, JOHN BROWN.** See ABOLITION MOVEMENT (Profiles).
**RUSTIN, BAYARD.** See CIVIL RIGHTS MOVEMENT (Profiles).

# RUTH, GEORGE HERMAN (BABE) (1895–1948)

In the long history of baseball, no one stands near him. He is big and alone, like a giant. He is known wherever baseball is played as the Babe.

Just a glance at the things he did tells why he looms so large. Ruth held more than 50 records. Known as the Sultan of Swat, he hit 714 home runs. From 1919 to 1931, except for two years, he led the American League in home runs. In 1927 he hit 60. His career batting average of .342 is one of the highest.

George Herman Ruth was born in Baltimore, Maryland, on February 6, 1895. When he was 7, his father placed him in St. Mary's Industrial School in Baltimore. There Ruth learned to play baseball. And there he developed his lifelong love for children.

The Babe started his professional career with the Baltimore Orioles of the International League in 1914. He was soon sold to the Boston Red Sox. Ruth was a pitcher then, and one of the best. The record book shows 94 wins and 46 losses. In 1920 he was sold to the New York Yankees. There he became an outfielder and started slugging his way into the hearts of millions of fans. Ruth stayed with the Yankees until the end of the 1934 season. He finished his playing career with the Boston Braves. He had become a legend. In 1936 he was one of the five original players named to the Baseball Hall of Fame.

The Babe—big, colorful, ever ready with a handshake for any child—died of cancer in New York City on August 16, 1948.

Reviewed by MONTE IRVIN
Member, Baseball Hall of Fame

See also BASEBALL.

---

# RUTHERFORD, ERNEST, LORD (1871–1937)

Ernest Rutherford was a British scientist whose work led to our knowledge of the atom's structure and of nuclear energy. He was born in New Zealand—near Nelson, on August 30, 1871—and received his education through college in New Zealand.

By 1893, Rutherford had begun research in physics—the study of matter and energy. In 1895, he won a scholarship to Cambridge University, England. At its Cavendish Laboratory, under the great physicist J. J. Thomson, he began to study X rays, which had just been discovered. He also studied radiation from the element uranium.

In 1898, Rutherford became a professor at McGill University in Montreal, Canada. He continued research in radioactivity. This is a process in which certain atoms give off "bullets" of energy called beta rays and gamma rays. As a result of this process, one element may change to another—for example, uranium changes to a form of lead. Rutherford discovered that a radioactive element also gives off another "bullet," which he called alpha particles.

In 1900, Rutherford was married in New Zealand and then returned with his wife to McGill. That same year he was joined in his research by the English scientist Frederick Soddy. In 1902, Rutherford and Soddy published a new theory. It stated that radioactivity results from the breakdown of atoms of an element.

Rutherford returned to England in 1907 as a professor at the University of Manchester. In 1908, he received the Nobel prize in chemistry for his work in radioactivity. This work led to the theory on which we base our present idea of the structure of the atom. It stated that an atom is composed of a small but heavy nucleus surrounded by one or more electrons.

In 1919, Rutherford announced that he had bombarded nitrogen atoms with alpha particles to produce oxygen and hydrogen atoms. This was the first time a scientist had succeeded in changing one element into another.

Rutherford became head of the Cavendish Laboratory in 1919. There, many who later became great scientists studied under him. He was made a peer (1st Baron Rutherford of Nelson) in 1931. He died in Cambridge on October 19, 1937.

JOHN S. BOWMAN
Author and Science Editor

See also ATOMS; NUCLEAR ENERGY; RADIOACTIVE ELEMENTS.

# RWANDA

Rwanda is a nation in east central Africa, located just south of the equator. It is bordered by Uganda on the north, Tanzania on the east, Burundi on the south, and the Democratic Republic of Congo on the west. Although small and largely mountainous, Rwanda is one of the most densely populated countries in Africa. It was at one time a colony of Germany and then governed by Belgium, before winning independence in 1962.

Millions of Rwandans became refugees in 1994 following the outbreak of ethnic violence between the country's two major peoples, the Hutu and the Tutsi.

### ▶ PEOPLE

Rwanda's population is made up of three main ethnic groups—the Hutu (or Bahutu), the Tutsi (also called Batutsi or Watutsi), and the Twa (or Batwa).

The great majority of the people are Hutu. Most are farmers, who live mainly in the western part of the country. Hutu homes have a distinctive beehive shape and thatched roofs. They are usually built individually on hills rather than grouped in villages.

The Tutsi are generally slender in appearance and often quite tall. They are traditionally herders of cattle. Although much smaller in numbers, the Tutsi long dominated the majority Hutu, who were forced to work the land for them. Political and ethnic tensions between them have erupted into violence several times, the most serious outbreak occurring in 1994.

Only a few thousand Twa still exist. Most live in the northern mountains as hunters and as gatherers of fruits and nuts.

The Hutu and Tutsi speak Kinyarwanda, a Bantu language, which is one of the country's two official languages. The other is French, which dates from the time of Belgian rule. About half the people are Christians, mostly Roman Catholics. The remainder practice traditional African religions.

### ▶ LAND

Most of Rwanda consists of mountains and plateaus, with an average elevation of more than 6,000 feet (1,830 meters). The highest peak, Mount Karisimbi, rises to 14,780 feet (4,505 meters) in the Virunga mountain range in the northwest. Lake Kivu, the largest of the country's many lakes, is situated on the western border.

Although close to the equator, Rwanda has a generally moderate climate because of its elevation. The average annual temperature is about 68°F (18°C) throughout much of the country. The Lake Kivu region is much warmer, however, and the mountainous areas cooler. Average annual rainfall ranges from 40 to 60 inches (1,000 to 1,500 millimeters).

Rwanda has only one major city, Kigali, the capital. Much of its population, estimated at about 250,000, fled during the recent civil strife and are only slowly returning.

### ▶ ECONOMY

Most of Rwanda's people are subsistence farmers, growing food for their own use. The main food crops are cassava, sorghum, millet, and bananas. In addition to cattle, goats and sheep also are raised as livestock. The leading commercial crop is coffee, Rwanda's chief export. Other cash crops are cotton, tea, and pyrethrum, used in making insecticides.

Tin ore (cassiterite) is the country's chief mineral resource. Rwanda also has deposits of tungsten ore and gold and is thought to have large reserves of natural gas beneath Lake Kivu. Industry is limited mainly to processed agricultural products.

## ▶ HISTORY AND GOVERNMENT

What is now Rwanda became part of the colony of German East Africa in the late 1800's. After Germany's defeat in World War I (1914–18), Rwanda and what is now Burundi were administered by Belgium. The combined territory was then called Ruanda-Urundi. Belgium continued to govern the region as a trust territory of the United Nations following the end of World War II (1939–45). The first ethnic clashes broke out in 1959, when the Hutu revolted against the Tutsi. After much bloodshed, the Tutsi king was deposed, and many Tutsi fled the country. In 1961 a majority of the people voted to establish a republic. Separated from Urundi (now Burundi), it formally gained independence as the Republic of Rwanda in 1962.

Rwanda's first president, Gregoire Kayibanda, governed until 1973, when he was overthrown by the military. General Juvénal Habyarimana became president under a new one-party constitution, approved in 1978. He was re-elected in 1983 and in 1988.

**Recent History.** In 1990, Rwandan exiles, mainly Tutsi, invaded the country from

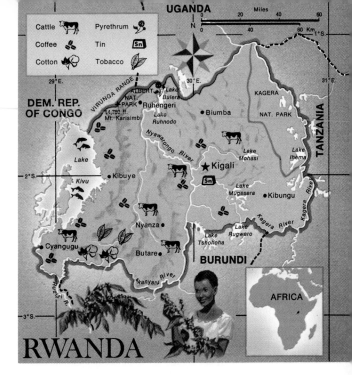

RWANDA

## FACTS and figures

**RWANDESE REPUBLIC** is the official name of the country.

**LOCATION:** East central Africa.

**AREA:** 10,169 sq mi (26,338 km²).

**POPULATION:** 7,800,000 (estimate).

**CAPITAL AND LARGEST CITY:** Kigali.

**MAJOR LANGUAGE:** Kinyarwanda, French, English (all official).

**MAJOR RELIGIOUS GROUPS:** Christian (mostly Roman Catholic), traditional African religions.

**GOVERNMENT:** Republic. **Head of state**—president. **Head of government**—premier. **Legislature**—National Assembly.

**CHIEF PRODUCTS: Agricultural**—coffee, cotton, tea, pyrethrum, cassava, sorghum, millet, bananas, livestock. **Manufactured**—chiefly processed agricultural products. **Mineral**—tin ore, gold, tungsten ore.

**MONETARY UNIT:** Rwandan franc (1 franc = 100 centimes).

Uganda, setting off a civil war. A 1991 constitutional revision provided for multiparty elections, and in 1993 the government signed a peace accord with the rebel Rwandan Patriotic Front (RPF). In 1994 Habyarimana, a Hutu, died in a plane crash under suspicious circumstances. The Hutu militia then began massacring Tutsi and moderate Hutu. But the RPF resumed the civil war and quickly occupied most of the country. In July 1994 a primarily Tutsi government, dominated by the RPF, was installed, and many Hutu fled to the Democratic Republic of Congo. Since 1990, the number of dead has been estimated in the hundreds of thousands and the number of refugees in the millions. Many refugees have since returned, but tensions remain high.

In 1998, a United Nations war crimes tribunal sentenced a former premier, Jean Kambanda, a Hutu, to life imprisonment for his part in the 1994 massacres. He was the first person in history to be sentenced by a nonmilitary international court for genocide. In May 2000, RPF chairman Paul Kagame became Rwanda's first Tutsi president. He was re-elected, to a 7-year term, in 2003. The first multiparty parliamentary elections since 1994 were also held, bringing an end to the transitional period of government.

ROBERT O. COLLINS
Williams College

# RYE

Rye is a hardy cereal grass closely related to wheat. It is hardier than wheat and is often grown where wheat would fail because of low soil fertility. Rye is widely cultivated as a food grain, especially in central and northern Europe. It is the chief ingredient of the "black bread" common there.

Rye seems to have first appeared after 1000 B.C. It grew as a weed in the wheat fields of the kingdoms around the Black Sea. Rye seeds were often accidentally mixed in with the wheat seeds saved for the next year's planting. Where the soil or the climate was not good, the rye grew better than the wheat. Each year there was more rye and less wheat in the grain that was harvested. After a time the rye crowded out the wheat entirely. For hundreds of years the people who worked in the rye fields believed that wheat turned into rye after several seasons of planting.

The culture of rye spread from the lands around the Black Sea through the northern areas of Europe and Asia. During the Middle Ages the sour, gummy black bread made from whole rye kernels was one of the main foods of the peasants. It was not until the 1700's that wheat production increased, as a result of better agricultural practices. In England and western Europe black bread was eaten only by the very poor. But in central and eastern Europe rye ranked with wheat as a bread cereal.

▶ **CULTIVATION**

Most rye is sown in the fall, although a little is planted in the spring. Rye usually grows about 5 feet (1.5 meters) tall. The grain is harvested by combines. In poor soil, rye yields about 12 bushels per acre (750 kilograms per hectare). But if rye is properly cared for, the yield may be twice as high. It is difficult to grow a pure variety of rye because the pollen from the flowers of one rye plant can fertilize only the flowers on another rye plant.

Ergot, leaf and stem rust, stalk and head smut, and some root rots are common enemies of rye. But except for ergot these diseases do little serious damage. Ergot is a fungus that makes the young rye kernels become very hard and turn a purplish-black color. Infected kernels are poisonous to both humans and livestock. One of the best ways of controlling ergot is to rotate rye with crops that are immune to the fungus.

Among the largest producers of rye are Poland, Russia, Germany, and Belarus. In the United States, North Dakota, Georgia, Oklahoma, and South Dakota are among the leading rye-producing states.

▶ **USES OF RYE**

In making rye flour, rye is milled very much like wheat. But it is not so carefully graded or purified. Rye is first cleaned and then ground between rollers into pieces called middlings. These are sifted to remove the bran, which is the outside covering of the kernel. The rye bran sticks very closely to the seed and is almost impossible to remove completely. The highest grades of rye flour are produced by special rolls that crush the middlings into powder. Dark rye flour with a strong rye flavor is made from middlings that still carry bits of bran. Pumpernickel bread is baked from a coarse, unsifted rye flour.

Rye flour is inferior to wheat flour in baking quality because rye cannot form the elastic gluten that helps bread rise. Since rye does not have all of the proteins that make up gluten, the dough is sticky and claylike. In the United States and Canada, rye bread is made from mixtures of rye flour and an equal or even greater amount of wheat flour. The gluten in the wheat dough makes the rye bread lighter. Usually a sourdough (dough left over from an earlier mixing) is used instead of yeast as leavening for rye bread.

A large percentage of the yearly crop is made into mash for whiskey. The rye is crushed into a meal and soaked in a specially prepared liquid until it ferments.

Generally, animals do not like rye as much as they do wheat and other cereals. Lambs sometimes fatten on rye. But it is fed to most animals in limited amounts because they tend to have some difficulty digesting it. Since rye can be grown under difficult conditions, it makes good emergency pasture. Tough, fibrous rye straw makes excellent bedding for animals.

C. HAMILTON KENNEY
Canada Department of Agriculture

See also GRAIN AND GRAIN PRODUCTS; WHEAT.

**RYLANT, CYNTHIA.** See CHILDREN'S LITERATURE (Profiles).

# Index

HOW TO USE THE DICTIONARY INDEX

See the beginning of the blue pages in Volume 1.

**Quasi-stellar radio sources** *see* Quasars
**Quaternary period** (in geology)  **E**:25; **P**:434
  *picture(s)*
    drifting continents  **G**:113
  *table(s)*  **F**:384
**Quayle, James Danforth (Dan)** (vice president of the United
    States)  **V**:331 *profile*
**Quebec** (Canada)  **Q**:10–17
  Anticosti Island  **I**:362
  Champlain, Samuel de  **C**:80, 185
  civil law  **C**:78
  education  **C**:52
  federal senators  **C**:75
  founding of and early history as part of New France  **C**:80
  labor movement  **L**:18
  Magdalen Islands  **I**:366
  Montreal  **M**:444–45
  provincial government  **C**:77–78
  Quebec Act of 1774 and British Canada  **C**:82
  Quebec City  **Q**:17–19
  Revolutionary War, American  **C**:82; **R**:201
  separatist movement  **C**:69, 85
  Supreme Court of Canada  **S**:506
  *map(s)*  **Q**:12
  *picture(s)*
    Château Richer  **C**:71
    dairy cows on Gaspé Peninsula  **C**:54
    Daniel-Johnson Dam  **D**:17
    Montreal  **F**:13; **M**:444, 445; **Q**:13, 14
    Quebec City  **N**:299; **Q**:14, 18, 19
**Quebec, Battle of** (1759)  **F**:465
  *picture(s)*  **C**:81; **F**:465
**Québec, Université de** (Quebec)  **Q**:11
**Quebec Act of 1774**  **C**:82
**Quebec City** (capital of Quebec)  **C**:67–68; **Q**:16, 17–19
  first North American library  **L**:174
  places of interest  **Q**:13
  Saint Lawrence River, history of  **S**:14
  *picture(s)*  **N**:299; **Q**:14
    Château Frontenac  **H**:258
    Citadel  **Q**:18
    Winter Carnival  **Q**:19
**Quebec Railway Bridge** (Canada)  **B**:401
**Quebracho** (tree)  **A**:386; **L**:111
**Quechan** (Indians of North America)  **I**:183
**Quechee Gorge** (Vermont)
  *picture(s)*  **V**:309
**Quechua** (Indian language of South America)  **I**:108, 110;
    **L**:49; **P**:160; **S**:285, 288
**Quechua** (Indians of South America)  **B**:306–7; **I**:173, 196;
    **P**:161
**Queen, Ellery** (American author)  **M**:565 *profile*
*Queen Anne's Revenge* (Blackbeard's ship)  **P**:262
**Queen Anne style** (in art and architecture)  **A**:315; **E**:260;
    **F**:511–12
  *picture(s)*  **F**:511
**Queen Anne's War** (1702–1713)  **C**:81; **F**:463; **I**:203; **U**:175
**Queen ants**  **A**:319, 320, 321, 323
**Queen bees**  **B**:116, 117, 119; **H**:211
  *picture(s)*  **B**:118
**Queen Charlotte Islands** (British Columbia)  **B**:402, 403,
    406b; **C**:56
  *picture(s)*  **C**:58
*Queen Elizabeth* (ocean liner)  **O**:31
*Queen Elizabeth 2* (ocean liner)  **O**:31
  *picture(s)*
    cutaway view  **O**:30–31
*Queen Mary* (ocean liner)  **O**:31
  *picture(s)*  **T**:284
*Queen Mary 2* (ocean liner)  **O**:33
**Queens** (borough of New York City)  **N**:226, 227–28
**Queensberry rules** (of boxing)  **B**:351–52
**Queen's Birthday** (holiday)  **H**:165, 168
**Queen's Dolls' House, The** (of Queen Mary of England)  **D**:263

**Queensland** (Australia)  **A**:506, 511–12, 514
  *picture(s)*  **A**:505, 512
**Queens-Midtown Tunnel** (New York City)  **N**:233
**Queenston Heights, Battle of** (1812)  **W**:9
**Queequeg** (character in *Moby Dick*)  **M**:215–16
**Quemoy** (island off China's mainland)  **T**:8
**Quenching** (of metals)  **M**:236
**Quercia, Jacopo della** (Italian sculptor)  **F**:393; **S**:100
**Querendí** (Indians of South America)  **I**:198
**Querns** (revolving mills)  **F**:277
**Question mark butterfly**
  *picture(s)*  **B**:476
**Question marks** (punctuation)  **P**:542
**Questionnaires** (used in opinion polls)  **O**:170
**Quetelet, Adolphe** (Belgian astronomer and statistician)
    **S**:443
**Quetico Provincial Park** (Ontario)  **C**:54
**Quetta** (Pakistan)  **P**:40
**Quetzal** (bird)  **B**:245
**Quetzalcóatl** (Aztec god)  **A**:244, 578; **I**:172; **M**:248, 443
  *picture(s)*  **M**:568
**Quetzaltenango** (Guatemala)  **G**:397
**Quevedo, Francisco de** (Spanish poet)  **S**:389
**Quezon, Manuel** (Philippine statesman)  **P**:188; **Q**:20
**Quezon City** (Philippines)  **P**:187
**Quick breads**  **B**:386
**Quick-freezing** (of food)  **F**:341–42
**Quicksand**  **Q**:20–21
**Quicksilver** *see* Mercury
**Quiet Revolution** (in Quebec)  **Q**:17
**Quiet viruses** *see* Latent viruses
**Quileute** (Indians of North America)  **I**:188
**Quill pens**  **C**:463; **P**:142
**Quills** (of animals)  **M**:74; **P**:389; **R**:278
**Quilting** (form of needlecraft)  **F**:297; **N**:101
  *picture(s)*  **F**:297, 305; **N**:380
**Quimbaya** (Indians of South America)  **I**:195
**Quince** (tree)
  *picture(s)*  **G**:36
*Quinceañera* (Hispanic American girl's 15th birthday
    celebration)  **H**:146
  *picture(s)*  **H**:145
**Quincy Grammar School** (Boston, Massachusetts)  **S**:60–61
**Quincy Market** (Boston, Massachusetts)  **A**:376; **B**:342
  *picture(s)*  **B**:340
**Quinine** (drug)  **D**:196; **P**:297
**Quinoa** (plant)  **G**:286
**Quinolones** (antibiotics)  **A**:309
**Quintilian, Marcus Fabius** (Roman rhetorician)  **L**:76; **O**:191
**Quintuplets** (multiple birth)  **T**:364
**Quipus** (knotted strings, record keeping of Inca Indians)
    **I**:108
**Quirinal Palace** (Rome, Italy)  **R**:306
**Quirino, Elpidio** (Philippine statesman)  **P**:188
**Quiroga, Jorge** (president of Bolivia)  **B**:310
**Quirt** (riding whip)  **C**:577
**Quisling, Vidkun** (Norwegian Nazi)  **U**:14; **W**:296
**Quito** (capital of Ecuador)  **E**:64, 67, 69; **L**:61
  *picture(s)*  **E**:65; **L**:56
**Quixote, Don** *see* Don Quixote
**Quiz shows** (on television)  **T**:70
**Qumran** (community on northwest shore of Dead Sea)  **D**:47
**Qumran texts** *see* Dead Sea Scrolls
**Quoits** (lawn game)  **H**:246
**Quokas** (small kangaroos)  **K**:174
**Quorum** (number of members needed to conduct business
    legally)  **L**:89; **P**:81
**Quota Act** (United States, 1921)  **I**:91; **U**:193
**Quotas** (trade barriers)  **I**:271; **O**:228
**Quotation marks** (punctuation)  **P**:543
**Quotations**  **Q**:21–22 *see also* Epigrams; Proverbs (traditional
    sayings); individual sayings by the first word of the
    quotation
  famous quotes from Shakespeare's plays  **S**:135–39

**Radio telescopes**   R:51, 66–69, 71–72, 73; **T:**59
  electric waves   **L:**220
  search for life on other planets   **A:**476b; **L:**211
  sun, observation of   **S:**489
  *picture(s)*
    Very Large Array (near Socorro, New Mexico)   **N:**187
**Radiotherapy** (cancer treatment)   **C:**93–94
  *picture(s)*   **C:**94
**Radio waves**   **R:**44, 50, 51, 52–53, 54, 58 *see also* Radio
    astronomy
  electromagnetic spectrum   **L:**220
  ice thickness measured by radio waves   **I:**7
  Jupiter   **J:**161
  microwaves   **L:**46d; **M:**287–88
  pulsars   **A:**474; **S:**433
  radar   **R:**38, 39, 40
  reflected back to Earth by the ionosphere   **E:**21
  telegraph messages   **T:**52
  television   **T:**63
  travel through a vacuum   **V:**263
  universe, study of   **U:**217
  *diagram(s)*
    electromagnetic spectrum, place on   **R:**44
**Radishes**   **V:**287, 290
**Radisson, Pierre** (French explorer)   **F:**520; **O:**137; **S:**14
**Radium** (element)   **C:**614; **E:**176; **U:**230
**Radius** (bone of the forearm)   **S:**183
**Radius** (of a circle)   **G:**122
**Radon** (radioactive gas)   **G:**61
  diseases caused by   **D:**186
  radioactive elements   **E:**176; **N:**105, 106
**Radula** (tongue of snail)   **M:**406
**Radura** (symbol indicating irradiated food)   **R:**47
**Radwastes** *see* Radioactive wastes
***Ra* expeditions** (of Thor Heyerdahl)   **H:**125
**Raffarin, Jean-Pierre** (premier of France)   **F:**420
  *picture(s)*   **F:**420
**Raffia** (fiber)   **A:**74
**Raffles, Sir Thomas Stamford** (English colonial administrator)
    **M:**58; **S:**181
**Rafflesia plants**
  *picture(s)*   **F:**283
**Rafsanjani, Ali Akbar Hashemi** (Iranian president)   **I:**309
**Raft foundation** (in construction) *see* Mat foundation
**Rafts** (watercraft)   **T:**281
  ancient ships   **S:**155
  Heyerdahl, Thor, explorations of   **H:**125
  *picture(s)*
    Colorado River   **R:**240
    white-water rafting   **C:**435; **W:**336
***Raftsmen Playing Cards*** (painting by Bingham)
  *picture(s)*   **M:**380
**Raga** (in Indian music)   **I:**143; **M:**544
**RAGBRAI** (*Register*'s Annual Great Bike Ride Across Iowa)   **I:**290
  *picture(s)*   **I:**291
**Rag dolls**   **D:**268
**Raggedy Ann doll**
  *picture(s)*   **D:**272
**Ragnarok** (battle in Norse mythology)   **N:**278, 279, 280, 281
  *picture(s)*   **N:**281
**Ragtime** (music rhythm)   **A:**419; **J:**57–58; **U:**208
**Ragweed** (plant)
  *picture(s)*   **W:**105
**Ragworms** *see* Bloodworms
**Ragwort** (plant)
  *picture(s)*   **P:**292–93
**Rahman, Hasim** (American boxer)   **B:**351
**Rahman, Tunku (Prince) Abdul** (Malaysian statesman)   **M:**59
**Rahn, Johann Heinrich** (English mathematician)   **M:**165
**Rail fence cipher**   **C:**394
**Rail fences**   **P:**255
**Railroads**   **R:**77–90 *see also* the transportation section of
    country, province, and state articles
  airports   **A:**128

Andes mountain region   **A:**251
armies' use of   **B:**103f
Asia   **A:**452
canal traffic affected by   **C:**90
Casey Jones memorial   **T:**82
Cass Scenic Railroad (West Virginia)   **W:**134
Colorado's historic railroads   **C:**438
cowboys' job changed by   **C:**579
Debs, Eugene V., and labor issues   **D:**53
Federal Railroad Administration   **T:**293
Finland and Russia share wider gauge than standard
    European tracks   **F:**137
flanged wheels   **W:**160
high-speed trains   **F:**410; **O:**235; **R:**77
lanterns   **L:**233
locomotives   **L:**285–88
lumbering industry   **L:**341
maglevs   **M:**33; **S:**141; **T:**291–92
model railroads   **R:**91–92
Montana, immigration to   **M:**432–33
Mount Washington's cog railway   **N:**158
postal service   **P:**397
rail expansion and contraction   **H:**92–93
Russia   **R:**364
Siberia   **S:**170
transcontinental, United States *see* Transcontinental
    railroad
transportation, history of   **T:**285–86
tunnels   **T:**339
United States   **U:**95
Vanderbilt family   **V:**276–77
Westinghouse's air brake   **W:**125
Why does the standard gauge measure 4 feet 8 1/2 inches
    (1.4 meters)?   **R:**78
*picture(s)*   **R:**79, 81, 82
  Australian maglev train   **M:**33
  Cass Scenic Railroad (West Virginia)   **W:**134
  Chinese railroad tracks buckled by earthquake   **E:**38
  Civil War, United States   **R:**86
  dispatch center   **R:**85
  early mining railroad   **R:**87
  Eurostar trains   **E:**361; **L:**288
  freight yard   **R:**85
  incline railway   **T:**82
  Japanese bullet train   **A:**452
  Mount Washington Cog Railway   **L:**288
  Nevada State Railroad Museum   **N:**126
  Panama Railroad   **P:**45
  rails, expansion and contraction of   **H:**92
  Trans-Siberian Railroad   **R:**365
**Railroads, model**   **R:**91–92
**Railroad ties**   **W:**226
**Rails, steel**   **I:**336
**Railways** *see* Railroads
**Rain** (kind of precipitation)   **R:**93–94; **W:**84 *see also* Clouds;
    the climate section of country, province, and state
    articles
acid rain   **A:**9–10, 124
affects the food supply   **F:**351
Africa   **A:**49
Asia   **A:**443
cave formation by erosion   **C:**155
climate   **C:**361, 362
cloud seeding to create rain   **W:**95
deserts   **D:**124
floods   **F:**254, 255, 257
hurricanes   **H:**302–6
Ice Age distribution   **I:**11
measurement   **R:**96
mountains influence rainfall   **M:**507
nimbostratus clouds bring rain   **C:**385
prairies   **P:**426
rain forest amounts   **R:**99
rainmaking   **W:**54

**Rain** (cont.)
    record greatest rainfall   **W:**95
    trade winds' influence   **T:**268
    Vancouver Island's average is heaviest in North America
        **B:**402
    Waialeale, Mount, has average rainfall of 460 inches
        **H:**53
    water shapes the land   **W:**51
    water supply   **W:**73, 75
    weather, creation of   **W:**87, 88
    What is the shape of a falling raindrop?   **R:**97
    *map(s)*
        North America, average precipitation in   **N:**288
    *picture(s)*   **R:**93
        frozen rain   **R:**95
        nimbostratus clouds bring rain   **C:**384
**Rainbow**   **R:**45, **98**
    *picture(s)*   **P:**229; **R:**98
**Rainbow Bridge National Monument** (Utah)   **U:**250
**Rainbow Coalition** (political organization formed by Jesse
        Jackson)   **A:**79p; **J:**8
**Rainbow snakes**   **S:**216
**Rainbow trout** (fish)
    *picture(s)*   **F:**213
**Raindrops, shape of**   **R:**97
**Rainey, Joseph Hayne** (American politician)   **A:**79c; **U:**142–43
        *profile*
**Rainfall** *see* Rain
**Rainforest Action Network**   **E:**210
**Rain forests**   **R:**99–100 *see also* Jungles
    Africa   **A:**52
    animals adapted to   **A:**273
    biomes   **B:**210, 212; **P:**319
    Brazil's Amazon Basin   **B:**378
    climate, types of   **C:**362, 363
    Colombia   **C:**405
    Costa Rica's national parks   **N:**56
    destruction of   **E:**304–5
    endangered species   **E:**209
    equator   **E:**308
    Honduras   **H:**207
    Indians, American   **I:**198
    Ivory Coast   **I:**419–20
    jungles compared to   **J:**157
    Olympic National Park (Washington)   **W:**18, 22
    South America   **S:**282–83, 291
    Southeast Asia   **A:**442
    *picture(s)*   **A:**49
        Amazon Basin   **S:**290
        Australia   **A:**505
        Belize   **B:**137
        Borneo   **S:**331
        Brazil's Amazon Basin   **L:**202
        Canada   **C:**58
        Central America   **N:**284
        Costa Rica   **R:**99
        destruction of   **P:**317
        Hawaii   **H:**50
        Mexico   **M:**244
        Olympic National Park (Washington)   **W:**22
        researcher studying canopy   **R:**99
        Southeast Asia   **A:**438f
        Thailand   **T:**150
        worker clearing land   **R:**100
**Rain gauges**   **R:**96, 97; **W:**88
    how to make a rain gauge   **W:**92
    *picture(s)*   **R:**97; **W:**88
**Rainier, Mount** (Washington)   **W:**16, 18, 22
    *picture(s)*   **S:**112; **W:**15, 23
**Rainier III** (prince of Monaco)   **M:**410
**Rain shadow effect** (on climate)   **C:**363–64
    *picture(s)*   **W:**87
**Rainy River** (Minnesota)   **M:**328
**Raisins** (dried grapes)   **F:**340; **G:**297
**Rajang River** (Malaysia)   **M:**56

**Rajasthan** (state, India)   **I:**121
**Raj Path** (avenue in New Delhi)   **D:**104
    *picture(s)*   **D:**104
**Rajputs** (a people of India)   **I:**137
**Rakapakse, Mahinda** (prime minister of Sri Lanka)   **S:**416
*Rake's Progress, The* (series of paintings by William Hogarth)
        **E:**260; **H:**159a
**Rakhine** (a people of Myanmar)   **M:**557
**Raleigh** (capital of North Carolina)   **N:**311, 315
    *picture(s)*   **N:**315, 317, 319
**Raleigh, Sir Walter** (English soldier, courtier, and poet)
        **E:**272; **R:**101; **T:**165
    *picture(s)*
        miniature portrait by Hilliard   **E:**258
**Ralik** (chain of islands in the Marshall Islands)   **M:**112
**Rall, Johann** (German soldier)   **R:**202
**Ram** (constellation) *see* Aries
**RAM (Random-access memory)** (of computers)   **C:**481, 491
    *picture(s)*
        RAM chips   **C:**482
**Rama** (hero-god of Hinduism)   **H:**139, 141; **I:**140
**Rama I** (king of Thailand)   **B:**47
**Ramadan** (month of religious fasting for Muslims)   **I:**122,
        349; **P:**37; **R:**155
**Ramámuri** (Indians of North America) *see* Tarahumara
*Ramayana* (Hindu epic poem)   **H:**139, 140, 141; **I:**140;
        **T:**162
    Tamil version   **I:**141
**Ramazzini, Bernardino** (Italian doctor)   **O:**13
**Rambert, Marie** (English ballet director)   **B:**30–31
**Rambi** (volcanic island in South Pacific)   **K:**265
*Rambler, The* (essays by Samuel Johnson)   **J:**124
**Rameau, Jean-Philippe** (French composer)   **F:**446; **O:**142,
        196
**Rameses** *see* Ramses
**Ramie** (natural fiber)   **F:**109
**Ramillies, Battle of** (1706)   **S:**377
**Ramjet engines**   **J:**91
**Ramm, Mount** (highest point in Jordan)   **J:**130
**Ramon, Ilan** (Israeli astronaut)   **S:**352
**Ramones** (American rock group)   **R:**264
**Ramos, Fidel V.** (Philippine president)   **P:**188
**Ramos-Horta, José** (East Timorese independence leader)
        **T:**208
**Ramprasad** (Indian poet)   **I:**142
**Rams** (in metalworking)   **M:**234
**Rams** (male sheep)   **S:**147
**Rams** (projections on ships for smashing into enemy vessels)
        **S:**156
**Ramsay, Sir William** (British chemist)   **N:**106
**Ramses II** (king of ancient Egypt)   **E:**104, 109
    Abu-Simbel temple   **E:**114, 115
    *picture(s)*
        mummy   **M:**512
        statue   **A:**234
**Ramses III** (king of ancient Egypt)   **E:**114
    *picture(s)*   **E:**107
**Rana family** (of Nepal)   **N:**110
**Ranariddh** (prince of Cambodia)   **C:**38
**Ranch life**   **R:**102–6 *see also* Cattle; Livestock
    Australia   **A:**500
    cowboys   **C:**577–79
    desert ranchers   **D:**128
    prairies, land use of   **P:**427
    roping   **R:**335–36
    Uruguay   **U:**238
    *picture(s)*
        Arizona   **A:**396
        New Mexico   **N:**186
        prairies, land use of   **P:**429
        Wyoming   **U:**93
**Rand** (South Africa) *see* Witwatersrand
**Randolph, A. Philip** (American labor leader and civil rights
        activist)   **A:**79k; **L:**17 *profile;* **S:**115

Randolph, Martha Jefferson (acting first lady in Jefferson's administration)  F:165–66; J:68
  *picture(s)*  F:165; J:69
Randolph, Peyton (American political figure)  C:536; V:359
Randolph family (prominent Virginia family)
  *picture(s)*
    Edmund Randolph at Washington's first Cabinet meeting  C:2
Random access memory *see* RAM
*Random House Book of Poetry for Children, The*
  *picture(s)*
    Lobel illustration  C:240
Random sampling (in statistics)  S:439
Random triangles (in geometry)  G:121
Rangeland (open land for grazing)  R:102–6
Rangeley Lakes (Maine–New Hampshire)  M:38
*Ranger* (moon probes)  S:357, 359
Rangers (United States Army)
  *picture(s)*  U:100
Ranges (of mountains)  M:501
Ranging (measuring the distance from a radar system to its target)  R:38
Rangoon (Myanmar) *see* Yangon
Rankin, Jeannette (American legislator and suffragist)  M:441
  *profile;* U:143 *profile*
Rankine scale (of temperature)  T:163
Rankin Inlet (Nunavut)  N:412
Ransom (payment for freedom from captivity)  K:273–74; P:263
Ransom, John Crowe (American poet and critic)  A:216
Rao, P. V. Narasimha (prime minister of India)  I:134
*Rape of the Lock, The* (poem by Pope)  E:277
Raphael (Italian painter)  R:106
  Italian art in Florence and Rome  I:397–98
  Renaissance art  R:167, 169
  style of his paintings of the Madonna and Child  P:21
  tapestry designs  T:21
  Vatican City frescoes  V:281
  *picture(s)*
    *Baldassare Castiglione* (painting)  W:264
    *Madonna della Sedia* (painting)  R:106
    *The Miraculous Draught of Fishes* (tapestry)  J:87
    *The School of Athens* (painting)  I:398; R:168
    *The School of Athens* (painting), detail from  P:330
Rapid City (South Dakota)  S:312, 319, 321, 324
  *picture(s)*  S:322
Rapid eye movement (REM) (during sleep)  B:367; D:319–20
Rapp, Gertrude (American textile manufacturer)  T:146
  *picture(s)*
    ribbons  T:145
Rappel (descent of a mountain by means of a rope)
  *picture(s)*  M:500
Raptors (birds) *see* Birds of prey
"Rapunzel" (fairy tale by Grimm brothers)  G:382–84
Rare-earth elements  E:170
Rare gases *see* Noble gases
Raritan River (New Jersey)  N:167
Rarotonga (island in the Cook Islands)  P:8
Rashes (skin irritations)  A:190
Rashid, Harun al- (Muslim caliph)  B:15
Rashtrapati Bhavan (president's residence in Delhi, India)  D:104
Rask, Rasmus (Danish language scholar)  L:39
Raspberries  G:298, 301
  *picture(s)*  G:299
Rasps (tools)  T:229
Rasputin, Grigori Efimovich (Russian faith healer)  N:249
RAST *see* Radioallergosorbent test
Rastafarians (Jamaican religious sect)  J:16
Rastatt, Treaty of (1714)  S:378
Rastelli, Enrico (Russian-born juggler)  J:151
Rastrelli, Bartolomeo (Italian architect)  R:376
  *picture(s)*
    palace at Pushkin  R:377
Ratak (chain of islands in the Marshall Islands)  M:112

Ratels (honey badgers)  O:257
  *picture(s)*  O:257
Rate-of-climb indicator (in airplanes)  A:118
Ratification (of treaties)  T:297
Ratings (of television programs)  T:68, 69
Rating systems
  motion pictures  M:495
  video games  V:332c
Ratio (in mathematics)  R:107
  map scales  M:95
  time, definition of  T:199–200
  trigonometry  T:312–13
Rational numbers (quotients of two integers)  N:401–2
Ratites (group of flightless birds)  O:243–45
Rat kangaroos  K:174
Ratline hitch *see* Clove hitch
Ratoon crop (of pineapples)  P:249
Rats (rodents)  R:276–77
  aging experiment  A:84–85
  disease prevention and rat control  D:212
  household pests  H:264
  pack rats  R:277
  *picture(s)*  R:274
Ratsiraka, Didier (president of Madagascar)  M:9
Rat snakes  S:210, 212
  *picture(s)*  S:210
Rattan palm trees  J:157
Rattigan, Terence (English dramatist)  E:290
Rattle (for a baby)
  *picture(s)*  C:410
Rattlesnakes  S:212, 213, 215, 216
  hunt small mammals  A:280
  *picture(s)*  S:216
Rauschenberg, Robert (American artist)  D:318; M:396b; P:31
Rauwolfia (plant)  P:297
Ravalomanana, Marc (president of Madagascar)  M:9
Ravana (demon in Hindu literature)  I:140
Ravel, Maurice Joseph (French composer)  C:184; F:447; O:148, 155
Ravenna (Italy)
  Byzantine art of  B:488; I:392
Ravens (birds)  H:116
  *picture(s)*  Y:370
Rawalpindi (Pakistan)  P:39
Rawalt, Marguerite (American attorney)  W:213
Rawhide rope  R:334
Rawlings, Jerry J. (president of Ghana)  G:198
Rawlings, Marjorie Kinnan (American novelist)  F:266, 275
  *profile*
  *picture(s)*  F:275
Raw materials  M:87 *see also* the names of agricultural products, as Corn
  forests  F:374–77
  industry's needs  I:225
  mines and mining  M:318–24
  primary products in international trade  I:270–71
  recycling reduces the need for  R:125
  wood  W:222–27
Raw score (of a test)  T:119
Ray, Charles B. (American publisher)  A:79c
Ray, Dixy Lee (American governor)  W:27 *profile*
Ray, Man (American artist)  M:393; P:205 *profile*
  *picture(s)*  P:205
    *Cadeau, Le (The Gift)* (dada sculpture)  M:394
Ray, Satyajit (Indian motion picture director)  M:494, 495
  *profile*
Ray, Ted (British golfer)  G:257
Rayburn, Samuel Taliaferro (American statesman)  J:120; T:140; U:144 *profile*
Ray craters (on Mercury)  M:228
Ray-finned fish  F:184, 185–86, 188
Ray florets (of composite flowers)  F:283
Rayleigh, Lord (British chemist)  N:106
Rayon (synthetic fiber)  F:110, 112; N:436, 440
  first synthetic fiber  C:381; T:141

Rayonnism (in art)   R:379
Rays (fish)   S:142, 143, 145
Rays (of light)   L:213
Rays (on the moon)   M:452
Rays, cosmic see Cosmic rays
Raystown Lake (Pennsylvania)
    picture(s)   P:128
Raza, El Día de la see Dia de la Raza, El
Razor clams (mollusks)   O:291
    picture(s)   S:150
RBI see Runs batted in
RCA see Radio Corporation of America
RDA's see Recommended Daily Allowances
RDX (explosive)   E:423
Re (Ra) (Egyptian sun god)   A:235; E:107, 108
    picture(s)   M:569
Reaching (in sailing)   S:11
    diagram(s)   S:10
Reaction (force in direction opposite to action)   M:476
    jet propulsion   J:90–91
    reaction engines   E:229, 231
Reaction, chemical   C:199, 202, 204
    catalysis   C:200
Reaction engines   E:229, 231
Reaction time (time it takes to respond to a change in the
        environment)   E:389
Reaction turbines   T:341
Reactive armor (on tanks)   T:14
Read, George (American political leader)   F:392
Read, Mary (British pirate)   P:262–63 profile
    picture(s)   P:262
Reader's Digest, The (magazine)   M:20
Readers' Guide to Periodical Literature   R:129
    indexes to magazines   I:115
Reading   R:108–11 see also Children's literature
    book reports and book reviews   B:314–17
    kindergarten activities   K:246
    language arts reading program   L:36
    learning disorders   L:107
    learning to write   W:330
    nonsense rhymes need to be seen   N:273
    phonics in teaching reading   P:194
    testing comprehension   T:121
    vocabulary, how to increase   V:374
Reading readiness   R:108–9
Read-only memory see ROM
Read through (first rehearsal of a play)   P:337
Ready-to-wear clothing   C:378, 380, 381
Reagan, Nancy Davis (wife of Ronald Reagan)   F:180a;
        R:112b
    picture(s)   C:125; F:180a; R:112c
Reagan, Ronald Wilson (40th president of the United States)
        R:112–12c; U:202, 204
    Bush's vice presidency   B:464–65
    Cold War   C:401
    Iran-Contra Affair   I:310
    picture(s)   C:32; P:453; R:112, 112c
        with George Bush   B:464
        governor of California   R:112b
        with Jimmy Carter   C:125
        with Mikhail Gorbachev   U:204
        with Nixon, Ford, and Carter   F:368
        political cartoon   H:291
        signing INF treaty   I:267; U:43
Real estate   H:189–90; R:112d–113; S:519
Real images (light pictures)   L:144, 214, 215
Realism (in art and literature)   R:114–15
    American art   U:130
    American literature   A:212
    baroque art   B:63, 64, 65
    children's literature   C:236, 238, 240
    China, literature of   C:279
    composition   C:478
    drama   D:303–4

drawing, history of   D:317, 318
Dutch and Flemish art   D:358–59, 360
Eakins, Thomas C.   E:3
fiction   F:114
French painting   F:429
German literature   G:179–81
Greek art   G:349, 351
Italian literature   I:408
modern art   M:386–87
Russian literature   R:382
socialist realism   N:363; R:379
Spanish literature   S:390
Real numbers (include rational and irrational numbers)
        N:402
Real property see Real estate
Realtors   R:113
Reamers (tools)   T:234, 235
Reaper (harvesting machine)   F:17; M:190
    picture(s)   U:183
Rear-fanged snakes   S:211, 214
    picture(s)
        skull and teeth   S:212
Reason, Age of see Enlightenment, Age of
"Reason for the Pelican, The" (poem by John Ciardi)   N:275
Reasoning see Thinking
Réaumur, René Antoine de (French naturalist)   P:58
Rebec (Arabic musical instrument)   M:297; V:345
Rebekah (Rebecca) (Biblical character)   B:161; I:345
Reber, Grote (American engineer)   R:73
Rebounding (in basketball)   B:95d
Rebuses   W:236–37
Rebuttal (in a debate)   D:52
Recall see Impeachment; Initiative, referendum, and recall
Recapitulation (in music)   M:541
Receivers (in electronics)
    high-fidelity systems   H:133
    radar systems   R:38
    radio   R:53–54
    radio telescopes   R:67
    stereo systems   S:267b
    telephone   T:53, 55
    television   T:61, 63–64, 65
    diagram(s)
        television receiver   T:62
    picture(s)
        early television receiver   T:65
Receptive language disorders   L:107, 108
Receptors (on cell membranes)   D:334; H:227; V:364, 366
    diagram(s)   H:228
Receptors (specialized nerve cells)   B:366
    body, human   B:289, 292
    brain cells   B:362
    parts of insects that receive sensation   I:234–35
    tongue   B:290
Recessions see Depressions and recessions
Recessive traits (in genetics)   G:79
    picture(s)   G:79
Recharge wells (wells that pump water into the ground)
        W:122
Recharging of batteries see Charging
Recife (Brazil)   B:381
Recipes   C:540, 541, 544
    bread, how to bake a loaf of   B:386–87
    peanut butter, how to make your own   P:112
    pumpkin seed snacks   H:13
Recipient countries (receiving foreign aid)   F:370
Reciprocals (fractions)   F:400
Reciprocating engines   A:115; E:229; I:262; T:342
Reciprocity Treaty (1854)   C:83
Recitals (of art songs)   V:378
Recitatives (sung dialogues or speech-songs)   B:70; M:539;
        O:141
Reclaimed water   W:75
Reclamation, land   B:131, 339; N:119, 120a
Reclamation, United States Bureau of   D:21

Redgrave, Lynn (English actress) **T:**161 *profile*
Redgrave, Michael (English actor) **T:**161 *profile*
Redgrave, Vanessa (English actress) **T:**161 *profile*
Redgrave family (English actors)
  *picture(s)* **T:**161
Red Guards (militant Communist Chinese youth organization)
  **C:**272; **J:**108
Redhead ducks **B:**231
"Red-Headed League, The" (story by Arthur Conan Doyle)
  excerpt from **D:**292
Redi, Francesco (Italian physician and scientist) **L:**209–10
Red Jungle Fowl (ancestor of chickens) **P:**414
Red kangaroos **K:**174; **M:**113
Red Lion (first public theater in England) **D:**300–301
Redman, Don (American jazz composer) **J:**60
Red maple trees
  *picture(s)* **R:**213
*Red Mill, The* (operetta by Herbert) **0:**168
Red oak trees
  *picture(s)* **N:**165
Redonda (island, Antigua and Barbuda) **A:**314
Redox reactions (in chemistry) **0:**287
Red Paint people (early inhabitants of Maine) **M:**48
Red pandas (Lesser pandas) (animals) **C:**263; **P:**52; **R:**27
*Red Petals* (mobile by Alexander Calder)
  *picture(s)* **D:**136
Red (Norway) pine trees
  *picture(s)* **M:**327
Red Planet *see* Mars
Redpoll (bird)
  *picture(s)* **B:**221
Red Poll (breed of dual-purpose cattle) **C:**154
Red raspberries
  *picture(s)* **G:**299
"Red, Red Rose, A" (poem by Robert Burns) **B:**455
*Red River* (motion picture, 1948) **M:**492
Red River (Southeast Asia) **R:**245; **V:**334a–334b
Red River (United States) **L:**316, 323; **0:**85; **T:**127
  *picture(s)* **L:**323
Red River colony (Canada) **C:**84; **R:**232
Red River of the North **M:**328; **N:**324
Red River Resistance (1869, Canada) **R:**232
Red River Valley (North Dakota) **N:**322, 325, 326
  *picture(s)* **N:**323
*Red Room, The* (novel by Strindberg) **S:**467
Red Sea **0:**46
Red shift (change in galaxy spectrum) **L:**226; **U:**215–16
Redshirts (guerrilla band led by Italy's Garibaldi) **G:**56; **I:**389
Red-spotted newt
  *picture(s)* **A:**224
Red Square (Moscow, Russia) **M:**466–67
  *picture(s)* **M:**468; **R:**357
Red squirrels (rodents) **R:**275
  *picture(s)* **B:**209
Redstone Arsenal (Huntsville, Alabama) **A:**137, 143
*Red Studio, The* (painting by Matisse)
  *picture(s)* **M:**389
Red supergiant stars **S:**430
Red-tailed hawks (birds) **A:**276; **H:**64
  *picture(s)* **B:**241; **H:**64; **I:**49
Red tides (marine organisms) **A:**181; **E:**209; **F:**221
Reductants (Reducing agents) (in chemistry) **I:**330, 331;
  **0:**287
Reduction (of metals) **M:**233
  smelting **M:**233–34
Redware (pottery) **A:**316a
*Red Wheelbarrow, The* (poem by William Carlos Williams)
  **W:**176
Red wines **W:**190, 190a
Red wolves **W:**210
Redwood (tree) **T:**300
  California forests **C:**21
  plant fossils **P:**300
  why called sequoias **S:**122

  *picture(s)* **C:**19
  uses of the wood and its grain **W:**224
Redwood Library (Newport, Rhode Island) **R:**217
Redworms **W:**320
Reed, John Silas (American political radical) **0:**215 *profile*
  *picture(s)* **0:**215
Reed, Thomas Brackett (American politician) **U:**144 *profile*
Reed, Walter (American doctor) **R:**128
Reed boats (water craft) **S:**155
  *picture(s)* **B:**306
Reed College (Portland, Oregon)
  *picture(s)* **U:**222
Reedfish **F:**185
Reed instruments **M:**549–50; **W:**184, 185
Reed organs **K:**239
Reed pipe (African musical instrument) **A:**79
*Reed v. Reed* (1971) **W:**213
Reef knots *see* Square knots
Reefs (coral) **C:**556; **J:**77
  Pacific islands **P:**3
  What is a reef community? **J:**75
Reelfoot Lake (Tennessee) **T:**76
Reels (for fishing) **F:**209–10, 214
Reel-to-reel tape recording **R:**123
Re-enactments, historic *see* Living history museums
Re-entry (of spacecraft) **S:**340d, 340i–340j
Reese, Harold Henry (Pee Wee) (American baseball player)
      **K:**225 *profile*
Reeve, Tapping (American lawyer and educator) **C:**514
Reeves, Steve (American bodybuilder and actor) **B:**294
Referee (in sports)
  boxing **B:**350b
  football **F:**357
  soccer **S:**221–22
Reference librarians **L:**176
Reference materials **R:**129 *see also* Textbooks
  dictionaries **D:**156–57
  encyclopedias **E:**206–7
  indexes and indexing **I:**114–15
  libraries **L:**176–77, 185, 186
  magazine lists **M:**19
  quotations **Q:**21
  reports, how to write **C:**476, 477
  word origins, source books for **W:**241
Referendum *see* Initiative, referendum, and recall
Referent (in semantics) **S:**116
Refining (of metals) **M:**234
  aluminum **A:**194f
  coal used in refining **C:**391
  gold **G:**249
Refining (of petroleum) *see* Petroleum and petroleum refining
Reflecting telescopes **A:**475; **0:**180; **T:**57, 58–59
  lenses **L:**147
  *diagram(s)* **T:**58
Reflection (in physics)
  color is determined by light wavelengths **C:**424; **L:**216
  light **L:**212, 213
Reflection nebulas (in astronomy) **N:**96
Reflectors (of radio telescopes) **R:**67
Reflex action (Reflexes) (in psychology)
  experiments and other science activities **E:**396
  nervous system **N:**116, 118
  sleep **S:**198
  spinal cord functions **B:**366–67
  yawning **L:**345
Reforestation **F:**376–77
  Asia **A:**452
  logging companies required to replant trees **L:**342
Reform, social *see* Social reform
Reformation **R:**130–32; **W:**264
  baroque art, influence on **B:**63–64
  Calvin, John **C:**34
  Christianity, history of **C:**291–93, 294
  Christmas carols outlawed in England by Puritans **C:**299

clothing, history of   C:376
Geneva   G:92
Germany's early religious divisions   G:160
Huguenots   H:279
Hus, Jan   H:306
Knox, John   K:289
Luther, Martin, led Protestant movement   L:346
Protestantism   P:492
Puritans   P:550
reforms for Roman Catholic Church   R:291
Renaissance and humanism   R:160
Switzerland   S:546; Z:395
What was the Counter-Reformation?   R:132
**Reformation Sunday** (Protestant holiday)   C:288
**Reformatories** (prisons that attempted to reform inmates)
      P:482
**Reform Bill** (1832, England)   E:250
**Reformed faith** see Calvinism
**Reform Judaism**   J:143, 145–46, 146a, 146b, 147, 148,
      149
**Reform Party** (in the United States)   P:372
**Reform schools** (for juvenile offenders)   P:482
**Refracting telescopes**   A:475; L:147; O:180; T:57–58
      diagram(s)   T:58
**Refraction** (of light)   L:213, 215
      hummingbirds' feathers   H:288
      lenses   L:142–43
      optical instruments   O:178
      prisms reveal spectra of light   C:424
      rainbow   R:98
**Refractive index** (of light)   F:106; G:69; O:184–85
**Refractometer** (optical instrument)   O:184–85
**Refractories** (ceramics that can hold up under high
      temperatures)   C:178
**Refractors** (optical instruments)   O:182
**Refractory brick**   B:390, 392
**Refrain** (in music)   M:537
**Refreshments** (for parties)   P:89, 91
**Refrigerants** (substances that do the cooling in refrigerators)
      R:133, 135
      air conditioning   A:102
      fluorocarbons   G:61
      liquid nitrogen   N:262
      used in heat pumps   H:96
**Refrigeration**   R:133–35
      air conditioning   A:102
      dairying, history of   D:11
      food preservation   F:340–41
      ice-skating and artificial rinks   I:44–45
      leather, preparation of   L:110
      liquid gases   L:253
      diagram(s)   R:133
**Refrigerator magnets**   M:33
**Refrigerators**   R:133, 134–35
      refrigerator cars of railroads   R:84
      trucks   T:320
      diagram(s)   R:134
**Refugees** (people who flee their countries for their own safety)
      R:136–37
      Afghanistan   A:44, 45
      Africa   A:69
      aliens in the United States   A:189
      anthropologists' study of   A:305
      Cambodia   C:38
      Cuba   C:610
      exodus from East to West Germany   G:166
      famine   F:45
      Florida   F:275
      foreign aid   F:370
      homelessness   H:183
      immigration   I:87–94
      India   I:133
      Jews after World War II   J:106
      Jews expelled from Spain   J:104

Kosovo   Y:369
Palestinian Arab refugees   H:307; I:375; J:129; L:122,
      123; P:42
poverty, victims of   P:419
Rwanda   R:389
picture(s)   R:136
      Albanian woman   P:418
      Ethiopia   E:334
      Kosovo   S:127
      Kurds from Iraq   A:305; I:315
      Rwandan refugees   A:60–61; R:388
      United Nations High Commissioner for Refugees
            U:71
**Refuse and refuse disposal** see Solid-waste disposal
***Regarding the Meaning of "Persons"*** (Canadian Supreme Court
      case, 1928)   S:506
**Regattas** (races)
      rowing   R:340–41
      sailing   S:12
**Regency style** (of furniture)   F:513
**Regenerated fibers**   N:436, 439–40
**Regeneration** (in biology)
      crustaceans replace lost appendages   C:602
      deer's antlers   H:220
      hydra   J:74–75
      liver   L:270
      lizards replace broken-off tails   L:276
      nervous system   N:118
      starfishes   S:427
**Regent's Park** (London, England)   L:296; P:76
**Regina** (capital of Saskatchewan)   S:47, 49
      picture(s)   S:50
**Regionalism** (in American art)   B:144a; U:132
**Regional libraries**   L:178
**Regional literature** (American)
      Canada, literature of   C:86–87
      folklore   F:314–15
      local-color short stories   S:162
**Regional theater** (in the United States)   D:307; T:159
**Regions** (in geography)   G:98
**Registan, I.** (Russian poet)   N:18
**Registered mail**   P:399
**Registered nurses (RN's)**   N:417
**Registration** (of trademarks)   T:266
**Registration of voters**   V:392
**Regis University** (Denver, Colorado)   C:435
**Regs** (gravel plains)   S:6
**Regular polygons** (in geometry)   G:121
**Regular polyhedra** (in geometry)   G:123
      diagram(s)   G:123
**Regulatory taxes**   T:25
**Regulus** (star)   C:531
**Regurgitation** (of food)
      owls   O:285
      wild dogs   D:254
**Rehabilitation** (after illness)   H:248
**Rehabilitation** (of people with disabilities) see Disabilities,
      people with
**Rehabilitation Act** (United States, 1973)   D:180
**Rehabilitation programs** (in prisons)   C:586; P:481
**Rehearsals** (of plays)   P:336, 337–38
**Rehnquist, William Hubbs** (American jurist)   S:508 profile
      picture(s)   U:171
**Rehoboam** (Biblical character)   B:161
**Rehoboth Beach** (Delaware)   D:88, 90
      picture(s)   D:89, 92
**Reich** (German word for empire)
      First Reich founded by Charlemagne   G:158
      Second Reich (of Germany)   G:161
      Third Reich (of Germany)   G:162–63
**Reich, Steve** (American composer)   M:544; U:210
**Reichenbach Falls** (Switzerland)   W:58, 59
**Reichstadt, Duke of** see Napoleon II
**Reichstag** (lower house of German parliament)   B:146
**Reichstag fire** (1933)   H:173; N:79

**Reign of Terror** (in the French Revolution)    **F:**416, 472; **P:**74; **R:**293; **T:**114

**Reiki** (type of alternative therapy)    **A:**194e

**Reims Cathedral** (France) *see* Rheims Cathedral

**Reincarnation** (rebirth of the soul in a new body)    **D:**51; **R:**149
Hinduism    **H:**140; **I:**118
Jainism    **R:**150
Sikhism    **R:**151

**Reindeer and caribou**    **D:**80, 81; **H:**216, 218–19; **R:138**
Alaska    **A:**149
Inuit's traditional way of life    **I:**273
Lapland    **L:**44, 45
livestock    **L:**273
migration    **H:**200; **M:**75
milk    **M:**307
tundra    **T:**331
*picture(s)*    **B:**209; **C:**60; **K:**255; **T:**331
    Lapland    **E:**351; **F:**134; **L:**44; **R:**138
    migration route    **H:**201
    reindeer sleds in North Asia    **A:**440
    on Siberian tundra    **R:**361

**Reindeer moss** (lichen)    **M:**473

**Reinforced concrete**    **B:**437, 438; **C:**165–66
architectural possibilities    **A:**373
building material    **B:**433
homes of    **H:**187
modern architecture    **A:**375

**Reinforcement** (in learning)    **L:**98–99
homework tips    **L:**99

**Reinhardt, Jean Baptiste "Django"** (Belgian jazz musician)    **J:**61 *profile*, 64
*picture(s)*    **J:**61

**Reisen, Abraham** (Yiddish author)    **Y:**361

**Rejection of organ transplants** *see* Organ transplants

**Relative** (relationship between musical keys)    **M:**537

**Relative humidity** (in meteorology)    **W:**83–84

**Relative pronouns**    **P:**93

**Relatives** (in grammar)    **G:**289

**Relativity** (theory in physics)    **R:139–44**
Einstein, Albert    **E:**119–20; **G:**325; **P:**236–37; **S:**67
Einstein's theory and quasars    **Q:**9
modern physics    **P:**230–31
science, milestones in    **S:**73
time and relativity theory    **T:**203–4

**Relay races** (in cross-country skiing)    **S:**184f

**Relay races** (track events)    **T:**255
team racing    **R:**34a
world records    **T:**261

**Release agents, silicone**    **S:**173

**Relics** (of saints)    **K:**273; **S:**18c

**Relief** (for famine victims)    **F:**45

**Relief** (in sculpture)    **G:**349–50; **S:**90
Assyria    **A:**462
Byzantine carving    **B:**490
Egypt, ancient    **E:**112, 116
France, architecture of    **F:**422
Ghiberti's doors    **I:**395
*picture(s)*
    Assyrian stone carving    **A:**462
    Ghiberti's doors    **R:**165

**Relief, public** *see* Welfare, public

**Relief maps** *see* Physical maps

**Relief printing**    **G:**302
letterpress printing    **P:**472–74
linoleum-block printing    **L:**251
woodcut printing    **W:**229

**Reliever airports**    **A:**126

**Religion, freedom of** *see* Freedom of religion

**Religion, primitive**    **D:**297; **P:**437; **R:**147

**Religion, Wars of** (in French history)    **F:**425; **H:**111, 279

**Religions**    **R:145–52** *see also* the facts and figures and people sections of continent and country articles
Africa    **A:**57, 60
African Americans    **A:**79c

ancient civilizations, characteristics of    **A:**229
Andean civilizations    **A:**244–45
angels    **A:**258
art, the meanings of    **A:**428
art as a record    **A:**431
Asia    **A:**448–49, 453
Asian Americans    **A:**457–58
Aztecs    **A:**244, 577
birds in religion    **B:**216
Buddhism    **B:**423–27
Christianity    **C:**287–95
colonial America    **C:**417–18, 419
Communist Yugoslavia allowed practice of religion    **Y:**365
Confucius' teachings    **C:**498
death, beliefs about    **D:**51
Eastern Orthodox churches    **E:**45–47
Egypt, ancient    **A:**235; **E:**107, 108, 109
ethics    **E:**328
Europe    **E:**356
evolution and religious beliefs    **E:**379
fire worship in primitive religions    **F:**142
freedom of *see* Freedom of religion
French schools ban wearing of religious symbols    **F:**405
fundamentalism    **F:**492
funeral customs    **F:**493–95
Greece, ancient    **G:**342
Harappan beliefs    **A:**240
hats worn for religious reasons    **H:**46–47
Hinduism    **H:**139–42
Incas    **I:**109
Indians, American    **I:**182
Inuit religion    **I:**275
Islam    **I:**346–53
Judaism    **J:**143–49
Maya    **A:**243; **M:**185–86
Middle East    **M:**299
Minoans and Mycenaeans    **A:**237
Mormons    **M:**457
mythology    **M:**568–77
peace movements    **P:**105
*philosophes'* view of    **E:**295
pioneer life    **P:**258
prayer    **P:**430–31
Protestantism    **P:**490–94
Renaissance and humanism    **R:**160
Roman Catholic Church    **R:**283–94
Rome, ancient    **R:**312
Soviet Union, life in the    **U:**34–35
wedding customs    **W:**100–103
witchcraft and nature spirituality    **W:**209
Zoroastrianism    **Z:**394

**Religious art** *see also* Christian art; Islamic art and architecture
Africa, art of    **A:**70, 71–72, 73
Chagall, Marc    **C:**182
Egyptian tomb paintings    **E:**108
India, art and architecture of    **I:**135–39
Japanese art and architecture    **J:**48–49
Russian cultural heritage    **R:**365
sculpture    **S:**90, 96–98

**Religious drama**
autos sacramentales    **D:**301
Middle English literature    **E:**270–71
miracle, morality, and mystery plays    **D:**299–300

**Religious education**
church-controlled colleges    **U:**223
colonial America    **E:**82
Middle Ages    **E:**79
parochial schools    **E:**76, 87
Renaissance    **E:**81

**Religious freedom** *see* Freedom of religion

**Religious Freedom Restoration Act** (United States, 1993)    **F:**163

**Religious holidays**    **H:**164; **R:153–55**
Buddhism    **B:**426; **L:**42

Christianity **C:**288
Christmas **C:**296–301
Easter **E:**43–44
Hanukkah **H:**28–29
Hinduism **H:**141
Japanese **J:**32
Judaism **J:**146a–146b
New Year celebrations around the world **N:**208–9
origin of the trade fair **F:**17, 18
Passover **P:**95–96
Purim **P:**549
Shinto **R:**152
Taoist festivals **R:**151
**Religious liberty** *see* Freedom of religion
**Religious literature** *see also* Sacred books
colonial American Puritans **A:**202, 203
**Religious music** *see also* Church music
Christmas carols **C:**118, 299
folk music **F:**324
Germany **G:**183–84
hymns **H:**320–26
Renaissance music **R:**172, 173–74
Spain **S:**392a
spirituals and other folk hymns **H:**324–26
**Religious orders** *see* Monks and monasticism; Nuns
**Relocation camps** (in World War II) *see* Detention camps
**REM** *see* Rapid eye movement
**Remagen** (Germany)
battle for the Rhine bridge (1945) **W:**315
**Remarque, Erich Maria** (German-born American novelist)
**G:**182
**Rembrandt** (Dutch painter) **R:**156
art of the artist **A:**432
*The Blindness of Tobit* (etching) **G:**304
drawing, history of **D:**318
Dutch and Flemish art **D:**365–66
etching technique **G:**305–6
importance to baroque period **B:**67–68
importance to history of painting **P:**24
signature reproduced **A:**528
*picture(s)*
*Abraham's Sacrifice* (etching) **D:**366
*The Anatomy Lesson of Dr. Tulp* (painting) **M:**208a;
**W:**266
Dutch countryside, drawing of the **D:**316
*Faust in His Study, Watching a Magic Disc* (painting)
**F:**73
*The Jewish Bride* (painting) **A:**432
*The Polish Rider* (painting) **P:**25
*Self-Portrait* (1661–1662) **R:**156
*The Syndics of the Cloth Merchants' Guild* (painting)
**B:**68; **D:**367
**Remedial reading** **R:**111
**Remembering** (in psychology) **L:**100–105; **T:**204
**"Remember the Alamo"** (battle cry) **H:**272; **T:**139
**"Remember the *Maine*"** (Spanish-American War slogan)
**S:**392c
**Remembrance Day** (in Canada) **H:**169
*Remembrance of Things Past* (novel by Marcel Proust) **F:**442;
**N:**361
**Remi, Georges** (Belgian cartoonist) *see* Hergé
**Remineralization** (effect of fluoride on teeth) **T:**44
**Remington, Frederic Sackrider** (American artist) **U:**130;
**W:**347 *profile*
*picture(s)* **W:**347
*Coming and Going of the Pony Express* (painting)
**P:**383
painting of Hudson's Bay Company store **F:**521
*Trooper of the Plains* (sculpture) **U:**130
**Remond, Lenox** (American anti-slavery lecturer) **A:**79c
**Remoras** (fish)
*picture(s)* **F:**188
**Remote broadcasting** (taking place outside the studio) **R:**53

**Remote control systems**
hydraulic systems **H:**312
model airplanes **A:**105–6
model racing cars **A:**535
radio, uses of **R:**51
televisions **G:**60; **T:**67
*picture(s)*
toy race cars **R:**51
**Remotely operated vehicles (ROV's)** (submersibles) **U:**24, 27
*picture(s)* **U:**23
**Remote Manipulator System** (on space shuttles) **S:**349
**Remote observing** (using computers to control distant
telescopes) **T:**60
**Remote-sensing instruments** **G:**106
**Remote viewing** (kind of extrasensory perception) **E:**428
**Removable disks** (computer peripherals) **C:**482, 491
*picture(s)* **C:**483
**Removal Act** (United States, 1830) **A:**140; **I:**179; **M:**362
**Remus** *see* Romulus and Remus
**Renaissance** **R:**157–62; **W:**264–65
archaeology, history of **A:**358
biology, history of **B:**201
châteaus **F:**379
Christianity, history of **C:**291
cities, history of **C:**317; **U:**236
clothing, history of **C:**376
dance and pantomime **D:**24–25
education **E:**81
exploration during **E:**403
Florence was the cradle of **F:**259
historical writings **H:**151
humanism **H:**284
inventions **I:**280
Italy **I:**388
Jews, history of the **J:**105
Leonardo da Vinci **L:**152–54
libraries **L:**173–74
Medici **M:**201–2
medicine **M:**208–8a
Roman Catholic Church **R:**291
science, milestones in **S:**70–71
upholstery began to be used **U:**228
Venice was chief power in the Mediterranean **V:**301
**Renaissance architecture** **R:**163–71
architecture, history of **A:**371–72
building during the Renaissance **R:**160
cathedrals **C:**135
Giotto's bell tower (Florence) **G:**211
homes **H:**193
humanism **H:**284
Michelangelo **M:**257
Spain **S:**383
Venice **V:**301
**Renaissance art** **R:**163–71
art, the meanings of **A:**428
art collections **M:**525, 527–28
Bellini family **B:**140
Botticelli, Sandro **B:**345
decorative arts **D:**75–77
Donatello **D:**285
drawing, history of **D:**316–17
Dürer, Albrecht **D:**354
Florence (Italy) **F:**259
flower arranging **F:**278
France **F:**424–25
furniture **F:**509
German painting and sculpture **G:**168–70
Giorgione **G:**210
Giotto di Bondone **G:**211
golden age of **R:**160–61
humanism **H:**284
humanism in **A:**430
interior design **I:**257
Italian art and architecture **I:**395–99

**Renaissance art** (cont.)
    Italian painting  **P:**20–21, 23
    jewelry making developed  **J:**98–99
    Michelangelo  **M:**255–57
    Raphael  **R:**106
    sculpture  **S:**98, 100
    Spain  **S:**383
    tapestries  **T:**20–22
    Titian  **T:**212–13
    Uffizi Gallery  **U:**2–3
    Venice  **V:**301
**Renaissance Center** (Detroit, Michigan)
    *picture(s)*  **D:**142; **M:**259
**Renaissance literature**
    drama  **D:**300–301
    France  **F:**437
    Italy  **I:**406–7
    Spain  **S:**387–88
**Renaissance man**  **R:**159
**Renaissance music**  **R:**161, **172–74**
    choral music  **C:**283
    Dutch and Flemish music  **D:**371–73
    France, music of  **F:**444–45
    history of Western musical forms  **M:**538–39
    Italian music  **I:**410
**Renaissance revival** (art style)  **F:**514
**Renal dialysis treatment** (medicine) *see* Hemodialysis
**RENAMO** (Mozambican political party)  **M:**509
**Rendering** (extracting oils and fats from animal tissues)  **O:**80
**Rendezvous** (of spacecraft)  **S:**340d
**Rendezvous** (system of fur trading)  **F:**523; **U:**254
    *picture(s)*  **F:**524; **W:**142, 335
**René, France Albert** (president of Seychelles)  **S:**131
**Renewable resources** (replaceable by natural processes)
    automobiles' power sources  **A:**556
    biotechnology and the environment  **B:**214
    conservation  **C:**523–24
    energy sources  **E:**221–23; **F:**490; **N:**63
    solar energy  **S:**239–40
    waterpower  **W:**69–70
**Renin** (enzyme)  **K:**244
**Renner, Paul** (German type designer)  **T:**369, 370
**Rennet (Rennin)** (enzyme used for curdling milk)  **D:**10
**Rennin** (digestive enzyme)  **S:**461
**Reno** (Nevada)  **N:**122, 125, 129, 131, 132
**Reno, Jesse** (American inventor)  **E:**188
**Reno, Jesse Lee** (American general)  **N:**132
**Renoir, Jean** (French film director)  **M:**493
**Renoir, Pierre Auguste** (French painter)  **F:**430–31; **I:**103, 104; **P:**29; **R:174**
    *picture(s)*
        *A Girl with a Watering Can* (painting)  **N:**37
        *The Luncheon of the Boating Party* (painting)  **I:**103
        *Two Sisters* (painting)  **R:**174
**Rental housing**  **H:**190
**Reparations** (payment for damages caused by war)
    Versailles Treaty (1919)  **W:**291
**Repartee** (humorous speedy dialogue)  **H:**290
**Repeaters** (on telephone lines)  **T:**54
**Repeating decimal fractions**  **F:**401
**Repeating rifles** (guns)  **G:**422
**Repeat signs** (in musical notation)  **M:**537
**Repentance** (in religion)  **J:**144
**Repertoire** (collection of songs)  **F:**320
**Repertory theaters**  **T:**159, 160
**Repetitive stress injuries (RSI's)**  **O:**13
**Repin, Ilia** (Russian painter)  **R:**378
    *picture(s)*
        *Barge Haulers on the Volga* (painting)  **R:**378
**Replacement** (fossilizing process)  **F:**381
**ReplayTV** (video recording service)  **V:**332i
**Repletes** (liquid-storing ants)  **A:**323
**Replication** (process by which cells copy their DNA)  **B:**299
    *diagram(s)*  **B:**299

**Reporters and reporting**  **N:**199–200
    Bly, Nellie  **B:**264
    investigative reporters  **J:**136
    Pulitzer Prizes in journalism  **P:**533
    radio news broadcasting  **R:**57
**Reports** *see also* Compositions
    book reports  **B:**314–17
    how to write a report on an experiment  **E:**382, 383
    how to write reports  **C:**476
    opinion polls  **O:**170
    outlines  **O:**265–67
    proofreading  **P:**487
    research methods  **R:**182–83
    science-fair experiments  **S:**78
**Repotting of plants** *see* Potting
**Repoussé** (decorative art)  **D:**70
**Representative fraction (RF)** (of maps)  **M:**95
**Representative government**
    beginnings in America  **T:**169, 173
    democracy  **D:**105–7
    differences between the House and the Senate  **U:**137–39
    parliaments  **P:**83–84
    problems of local governments  **M:**517
    proportional representation  **E:**130
    state governments  **S:**438
    United States, government of the  **U:**161
**Representatives, United States House of** *see* United States House of Representatives
**Repression** (in psychology)  **P:**511
**Reprieve** (suspension of the execution of a legal sentence)  **L:**89
**Reproduction**  **L:**198; **R:175–79**
    algae  **A:**181
    animals  **A:**284–85
    baby  **B:**2–3
    bacteria  **B:**11
    bees  **B:**119–20
    biology  **B:**196–97
    birds  **B:**224
    birth control  **B:**250a–251
    body, human  **B:**286–87
    breeding and migration  **H:**197–202
    cats, wild  **C:**145–46
    cell division  **C:**161–62
    cloning  **L:**210
    coelenterates  **J:**74, 75, 76, 77
    corals  **C:**555–56
    dogs  **D:**254
    earthworms  **E:**42
    eggs and embryos  **E:**95–98
    endangered species  **E:**211
    ferns  **F:**94–95
    fish  **F:**191, 195–98, 205
    flowers  **F:**280–87
    frogs and toads  **F:**478
    fungi  **F:**497
    genetics and heredity  **G:**77–91
    grasses  **G:**316–17
    human  **R:**178–79
    lizards  **L:**276
    mammals  **M:**67–70
    marsupials  **M:**114
    menstruation  **M:**219–20
    mollusks  **M:**406–7
    mosses  **M:**473
    plants  **P:**308, 310
    primates  **P:**456–57
    protozoans  **P:**496
    spiders  **S:**406
    starfish  **S:**427
    turtles  **T:**357–58
    twins  **T:**363–64
    viruses  **V:**364–67
**Reproductive mycelium** (of fungi)  **F:**497

**Repros** (in printing)  **B:**330
**Reptiles**  **A:**266; **R:**179–80
  Antarctica, fossil remains in  **A:**293
  crocodiles and alligators  **C:**592–94
  desert animals  **D:**124
  dinosaurs  **D:**166–77
  dormancy  **H:**128
  Earth's history  **E:**27, 28
  estivation  **H:**128
  evolution  **E:**374; **F:**386
  life spans  **A:**83
  lizards  **L:**275–77
  locomotion  **A:**278
  ocean life  **O:**25
  prehistoric animals, development of  **P:**433, 434
  reproduction  **R:**178
  snakes  **S:**209–18
  turtles  **T:**355–58
**Republican Party** (of the United States)  **P:**371
  Depression, Great  **D:**120
  elections  **E:**128
  formation in Wisconsin  **W:**205
  fundamentalist Protestantism  **C:**295; **P:**494
  Lincoln, Abraham, was first elected president  **L:**244
  Nast popularized elephant as symbol  **N:**17
  Roosevelt, Theodore, and the Bull Moose Party  **R:**332
  United States, history of the  **U:**185, 205
  *picture(s)*
    political cartoon on party symbol  **P:**371
**Republic Day** (holiday in India)  **H:**168
**Republics** (governments of elected representatives)  **D:**105; **G:**273; **U:**161
*Repulse* (British warship)  **W:**304
**"Requiem"** (poem by Robert Louis Stevenson)  **S:**449
**Requiem mass** (musical form)  **C:**284
*Rerum Novarum (Of New Things)* (papal encyclical)  **R:**294
**Resaca de la Palma, Battle of** (1846)  **T:**32
**Resaws** (tools)  **L:**342
**Rescue breathing** *see* Artificial respiration
**Rescue dogs**  **D:**256
  *picture(s)*  **D:**257
**Rescue organizations** (to help dogs)  **D:**251
**Research**  **R:**181–83
  advertising, research in  **A:**34
  debates and discussions  **D:**52
  encyclopedias  **E:**206–7
  indexes, how to use  **I:**114–15
  market research  **S:**20
  planning a science fair project  **S:**76
  reference materials  **R:**129
  research libraries  **L:**178–79
  tracing a family tree  **G:**76b–76d
**Research, scientific**  **S:**64–75
  agricultural research  **A:**96, 100
  airplane engines and propulsion  **A:**116–17
  balloons and ballooning  **B:**37
  basic and applied  **R:**181
  botanical gardens  **B:**342–43
  cancer research  **C:**94–95
  chemical industry  **C:**197
  computers, uses of  **C:**485
  cosmic rays: how observed  **C:**563
  disease prevention  **D:**213
  Edison's "invention factory"  **E:**71–72
  Forest Service  **N:**30, 32
  foundations  **F:**391
  four-step process  **R:**139–40
  ghosts and science  **G:**200
  identical twins raised apart  **T:**364
  livestock  **L:**273
  medicine  **M:**208d–208h
  methods of the sociologist  **S:**232
  museums' research programs  **M:**522
  National Institutes of Health  **N:**43

  New Jersey, concentration in  **N:**164, 170, 179
  observatories  **O:**7–12
  oceanography  **O:**34–42
  opinion polls  **O:**169–70
  psychological research, methods in  **P:**501–3
  public health  **P:**513
  robots  **R:**255
  satellites, artificial  **S:**54
  Smithsonian Institution  **S:**206
  solar energy  **S:**239–40
  space research and technology  **S:**361–63
  underwater exploration  **U:**21–27
  Veterans Health Administration  **V:**322
  veterinarians and medical research  **V:**323
  zoology  **Z:**388
  zoo research  **Z:**393
**Research and Special Programs Administration**  **T:**294
**Research libraries**  **L:**178–79
**Research Triangle** (of North Carolina)  **N:**306, 321
**Reserpine** (drug)  **P:**297
**Reservations, Indian** *see* Indian reservations
**Reserves** (of the United States armed forces)  **U:**101 *see also* National Guard
  Air Force Reserve  **U:**107, 108, 109
  Army reserve components  **U:**105
  Marine Corps Reserve  **U:**119, 122
  Naval Reserves  **U:**112, 113–14
**Reservoir** (of a hydraulic jack)  **H:**312–13
**Reservoir rocks** (containing oil)  **P:**167
**Reservoirs** (for storing water)  **P:**521
  artificial lakes  **L:**27
  dams  **D:**16, 18; **D:**19; **D:**20
  flood control  **F:**255, 257
  water supply  **W:**73, 74
**Resettlement Administration (RA)**  **D:**356
**Resident aliens**  **A:**189
**Resident doctors** (in hospitals)  **D:**238; **H:**249
**Residential hotels**  **H:**257
**Residential property**  **R:**113
**Residual oil** (petroleum product)  **F:**487
**Residual powers** (of state governments)  **U:**162
**Residual volume** (air remaining in lungs)  **L:**344
**Resins**  **R:**184–85
  aquatint, used in  **E:**327
  paints and pigments  **P:**32
  synthetic adhesives  **G:**243
**Resistance** (in biology)  **A:**311–12; **P:**291
  antibiotic-resistant bacteria  **D:**199, 332
  disease-resistant organisms  **G:**85
  insect-resistant crops  **B:**213, 214
  tuberculosis, drug treatment of  **T:**329
  vectors and pathogens  **V:**285
**Resistance** (in electricity) *see* Electric resistance
**Resistance, air** *see* Drag
**Resistance arms** (of levers)  **W:**249
**Resistance heating systems**  **H:**96
**Resistance movements** (against the Nazis in World War II)  **F:**419
**Resistance welding**  **W:**118
**Resist method** (of printing textiles)  **D:**378; **T:**143
**Resnik, Judith A.** (American astronaut)  **S:**352
*Resolution* (Captain Cook's ship)  **C:**539
**Resolution** (in music)  **M:**537
**Resolution** (of photographs)  **P:**205
**Resolving power** (of a microscope)  **M:**282, 284; **O:**180
**Resonance** (in physics)  **S:**261; **T:**196
**Resort hotels**  **H:**256–57
**Resources, natural** *see* Natural resources
**Respighi, Ottorino** (Italian composer)  **I:**412
**Respiration** (act of breathing)  **B:**283 *see also* Breathing
  amphibians  **A:**222
  artificial respiration  **F:**158
  circulatory system's role in  **C:**304, 305
  Lavoisier's studies  **L:**83

Ride, Sally Kirsten (American astronaut)   A:467; C:33 *profile*;
   S:347 *profile*
   *picture(s)*   A:466; S:347
Rideau Canal (Ontario)   O:247–48, 250
   *picture(s)*   O:249
*Rider, The* (painting by Karl Briullov)
   *picture(s)*   R:377
*Riders to the Sea* (play by Synge)   I:327
Rides (at carnivals)   C:117
Ridge lift (type of updraft)   G:237
Ridges, oceanic (underwater mountain chains)   G:113; O:21
Ridgway, Matthew Bunker (American army officer)   K:306;
   V:359 *profile*
   *picture(s)*   V:359
Riding *see* Horseback riding
Riefenstahl, Leni (German film director)   M:495 *profile*
Riel, Louis (Canadian métis leader)   C:84; M:3, 86; R:232;
   S:51
Riemann, Bernhard (German mathematician)   G:128;
   M:168–69
Riemenschneider, Tilman (German sculptor)
   *picture(s)*
      altarpiece   W:228
Rif (mountains, Morocco)   M:460
Rifampin (drug)   D:204
Rifles (guns)   G:418–19, 422, 423, 424; H:300
   *picture(s)*   D:68; G:415, 419, 421, 425
Rifling (of guns)   G:418
Rift Valley (Africa) *see* Great Rift Valley
Riga (capital of Latvia)   L:79
   *picture(s)*   L:80
Riga, Gulf of (arm of the Baltic Sea)   O:43
Riga, Treaty of (1921)   B:129
Rigging (lines and ropes used to work sails)   S:11, 157–58
Right angles (in geometry)   G:121
   *diagram(s)*   G:121
Right Bank (of the Seine, Paris)   P:68
Righteous Gentiles (non-Jews who helped Jews survive the
      Holocaust)   H:174
Right lymphatic duct (in the human body)   L:349
Right of deposit (in Spanish territories)   T:105
Right of way (in boating)   B:267
Rights, animal *see* Animal rights
Rights, civil *see* Civil rights
Rights, consumer   C:533–34
Rights, human *see* Human rights
Rights of Man and of the Citizen, Declaration of the *see*
      Declaration of the Rights of Man and of the Citizen
Right to bear arms (in the Second Amendment to the United
      States Constitution)   B:183; G:426
Right to die (of patients)   E:329
Right-to-life movement (believing abortion should be restricted
      or prohibited)   A:8
Right to vote *see* Suffrage
Right to work *see* Open and closed shop
Right triangles   G:121; T:312
   *diagram(s)*   G:121
   *picture(s)*
      Egyptians used for measurements   G:120
Right whales   W:151–52, 154, 155
   *picture(s)*   W:152
Right wing   P:372
Rigid airships *see* Zeppelins
*Rigoletto* (opera by Giuseppe Verdi)   O:161
*Rig Veda* (Hindu religious text)   H:139; I:140
Riis, Jacob (Danish-American journalist)   C:318; N:233
   *profile*
Rijeka (Croatia)   C:589
Rijksmuseum (Amsterdam)   B:142; M:525
Rila Monastery (Bulgaria)
   *picture(s)*   B:445
Riley, Bennett (American army captain)   O:275
Riley, James Whitcomb (American poet)   I:157 *profile*
Rilke, Rainer Maria (Austrian poet)   G:182

Rilles (twisting, valleylike clefts on the moon)   M:452
   *picture(s)*   M:450, 451
Rillieux, Norbert (American engineer)   A:80
Rimfire cartridges (for guns)   G:419
Rimpa school (of Japanese painters)   J:49
Rimsky-Korsakov, Nikolay (Russian composer)   O:146; R:385;
   S:467
Rimstone (cave formations)   C:156
Rindjani, Mount (Indonesia)
   *picture(s)*   I:208
Rinehart, Mary Roberts (American novelist)   M:564
"Ring around the rosy" (children's song)   F:325–26
*Ring des Nibelungen, Der* (music dramas by Richard Wagner)
   O:161–63
   *picture(s)*
      costume design   R:304
Ringer (game of marbles)   M:99
Ringling, John (American circus owner)   F:275 *profile*
Ringling Brothers (American circus family)   W:206–7 *profile*
   *picture(s)*
      Ringling, Mr. and Mrs. Charles   W:207
Ringling Brothers and Barnum & Bailey Circus   B:61; C:307,
   310; W:206–7
Ring Nebula (in the constellation Lyra)   N:96
   *picture(s)*   S:432
Ring-necked pheasant   S:312, 316
   *picture(s)*   S:313
Ring of Fire (Circle of Fire) (volcanoes of the Pacific Ocean rim)
   E:15; V:386
Rings (around planets)
   Jupiter   J:162; P:280; S:360
   Neptune   N:114; P:282
   Saturn   A:470; P:280, 281; S:55, 56–57, 58, 360
   Saturn: where did Saturn's rings come from?   S:57
   Uranus   P:281; U:232–33
   *picture(s)*
      Saturn   P:280; S:55, 57
      Uranus   U:232
Rings (jewelry)   J:94, 98
Rings (use in gymnastics)   G:432
   *picture(s)*   G:431
Ringstrasse (circular boulevard in Vienna)   V:332j
Ringtails (animals related to raccoons)   R:28
   *picture(s)*   R:28
Ringworm (skin infection)   D:123, 200
   *picture(s)*   D:200
Rio de Janeiro (Brazil)   B:375, 379, 381, 383; R:232–33;
   S:289
   Carnival   B:375; H:163
   influence of geography on the city's character   C:319
   *picture(s)*   B:381
      Carnival   B:374
      Carnival costumes   S:284
      *Christ the Redeemer* (statue)   C:320; R:233; S:285
      slums   S:289
      soccer fans   B:375; S:284
Río de la Plata (South America) *see* Plata, Río de la
Rio Grande (river, United States–Mexico)   C:433; N:182;
   R:234; T:126
   *map(s)*   R:234
   *picture(s)*   R:245; T:126
Río Muni (province of Equatorial Guinea)   E:309
Rioni River (republic of Georgia)   G:147
Riopelle, Jean-Paul (Canadian artist)   C:73
Riots (in African American history)   A:79i, 79j, 79o–79p
   New York City   A:79g, 79k
   Wilmington (North Carolina)   A:79i
Ripken, Cal, Jr. (American baseball player)   B:94
Riposte (counterattack in fencing)   F:86
Ripsaws (tools)   T:228
Ripton (Vermont)
   memorial to Robert Frost   F:480
"Rip Van Winkle" (story by Washington Irving)   A:208; S:161
   excerpt from   I:343–44

**"Rip Van Winkle"** (cont.)
    fairies  **F:**12
    *picture(s)*  **A:**204
**Risorgimento** (Italian national unity movement)  **I:**389, 408
**Risotto** (rice dish of Italy)  **I:**382
**Ritalin (Methylphenidate)** (drug)  **A:**23; **D:**332
**Ritardando** (musical term)  **M:**537
**Ritchie, Albert C.** (American public official)  **M:**133 *profile*
*Rite of Spring, The* (ballet by Stravinsky)  **M:**398; **R:**386;
    **S:**467
**Rites and ceremonies** *see also* Religious holidays; individual
      religions by name; the people section of country articles
    Corn Maidens in Native American mythology  **M:**576–77
    folklore  **F:**311
    funeral customs  **F:**493–95
    Hindu samskaras  **H:**141
    knights and knighthood  **K:**272–77
    marriage rites  **W:**100–103
    myth and society  **M:**570
    prayer  **P:**430
    rituals honoring Dionysus  **D:**298
    tea ceremony of Japan  **J:**29
**Rittenhouse, William** (American clergyman who built the first
      paper mill in America)  **P:**58
**Ritter, Karl** (German geographer)  **G:**105
**Ritter, Tex** (American actor and singer)  **C:**572
**Rituals** *see* Rites and ceremonies
*Rivals* (play by Richard Brinsley Sheridan)  **E:**277
**Rivas, Duke of** (Spanish writer)  **S:**389
**Rivera, Diego** (Mexican painter)  **M:**247; **R:**235
    *picture(s)*  **R:**235
        *Detroit Industry* (frescoes)  **M:**264
        mural painting  **L:**64
**Rivera, Juan María Antonio de** (Spanish trader)  **U:**254
**Riverbanks Zoo and Botanical Gardens** (Columbia, South
      Carolina)  **S:**304
**River blindness** *see* Onchocerciasis
**River City** (nickname for Jacksonville)  **J:**10
**River dolphins**  **D:**275
**River hogs** *see* Bushpigs
**Riverine rabbits**  **R:**26
**River Road** (Louisiana)  **L:**322
**Rivers**  **R:**235–47 *see also* the land section of country,
      province, and state articles; the names of rivers
    Amazon River  **A:**197–98
    Atlantic Ocean drainage area  **A:**478
    Canada's drainage basins  **C:**56–57
    changing flow to create new water supplies  **W:**55
    channels deepened to control floods  **F:**257
    dams  **D:**16–21
    erosion caused by  **E:**318
    experiments and other science activities  **E:**392
    Ganges River (India)  **G:**25
    lake basins, formation of  **L:**26–27
    Mississippi River  **M:**364–65
    Missouri River  **M:**382
    national rivers of the United States  **N:**55
    national wild and scenic rivers  **N:**32, 34, 55
    Nile River  **N:**260–61
    Rio Grande  **R:**234
    systems in Africa  **A:**48
    systems in Asia  **A:**438f, 438g
    systems in Europe  **E:**345–46
    systems in North America  **N:**287
    systems in South America  **S:**280
    tidal bores  **T:**196–97
    waterfalls  **W:**58–59
    water shapes the land  **W:**51
    *table(s)*
        longest rivers in the world  **R:**238
**Riverside Church** (New York City)  **B:**142
**River system** (a large river and its tributaries)  **R:**235
**Rivets** (fasteners)  **N:**3
    *picture(s)*  **N:**3

**Riviera** (Mediterranean resort area)
    *picture(s)*  **E:**358
**Riyadh** (Saudi Arabia)  **S:**58b, 58d
    *picture(s)*
        airport  **B:**439
**Rizzio, David** (Italian secretary of Mary, Queen of Scots)
    **M:**118
**Rjukanfoss** (falls, Norway)  **W:**59
**RNA (Ribonucleic acid)**  **G:**79, 90
    cell nucleus  **C:**160
    chemical composition of viruses  **V:**362, 367
    found throughout cells  **L:**200
    function in body chemistry  **B:**297–98, 299
    *diagram(s)*  **B:**298
**RN's** *see* Registered nurses
**Roaches** (insects)  **H:**263
**Roadbeds** (under tracks of railroads)  **R:**79
**"Road map" peace plan** (in Middle East)  **I:**376; **P:**43
**"Road Not Taken, The"** (poem by Robert Frost)  **F:**480
**Road racing** (running event)  **T:**256
**Roadrunners** (chaparral birds)
    *picture(s)*  **B:**241; **N:**181
**Roads and highways**  **R:**248–50 *see also* the transportation
      section of country, province, and state articles
    Alaska Highway  **A:**152, 158
    bridges  **B:**395–401
    Buenos Aires' Avenida 9 de Julio is one of the widest
      streets in the world  **B:**428
    buses  **B:**460–61
    computer-controlled highways of the future  **A:**556
    driver education  **D:**326–27
    early travel and trade  **T:**282–83
    earth-moving machinery for construction  **E:**32
    explosives used in construction  **E:**423
    Federal Highway Administration  **T:**293
    Going-to-the-Sun Road (Glacier National Park)  **M:**435
    interstate highway system is a large engineering project
      **E:**224
    Los Angeles has more miles of roads than any other city in
      the world  **L:**306
    Mount Evans (Colorado) reached by America's highest
      paved highway  **C:**438
    Natchez Trace  **M:**358
    national parkways  **N:**55
    overland trails  **O:**268–82
    paints for highways  **P:**34
    Pennsylvania Turnpike was first American superhighway
      **P:**133
    Roman *see* Roman roads
    Rome's traffic problems  **R:**308
    Route 66  **O:**90
    salt, uses of  **S:**23
    Sous le Cap (Quebec City) may be narrowest street in North
      America  **Q:**19
    traffic control  **T:**269–70
    traffic problems in modern cities  **T:**288–89
    Trans-Canada Highway  **C:**66
    trucks and trucking  **T:**318–22
    tunnels  **T:**337–40
    *picture(s)*
        Buenos Aires' Avenida 9 de Julio  **B:**429
        California expressway  **N:**283
        construction  **E:**422
        highway overpass  **B:**396
        log roads in Siberia  **S:**170
        road map  **M:**93
**Roan coats** (of dogs)  **D:**242
**Roanoke** (Virginia)  **V:**355
**Roanoke Island** (North Carolina)  **N:**318; **T:**165–66
    *picture(s)*
        American colonial settlement  **C:**409
**Roaring Twenties** *see* Jazz Age
**Roark, Helen Wills** (American tennis player) *see* Moody, Helen
    Wills
**Roasting** (method of cooking)  **C:**541

Roasting (of ores)  M:233
Robbery (crime)  C:584
  juvenile crime  J:167
  outlaws  O:263
  pirates  P:262–64
Robbia, della, family (Italian sculptors and ceramists) see Della
    Robbia, Luca; Della Robbia family
Robbins, Jerome (American choreographer and director)  B:33;
    D:34
Robbins, Marty (American singer)  C:572
Rober, Lewis (American inventor of softball)  S:233
Robert, Nicholas Louis (French paper manufacturer)  P:58
Robert II (duke of Normandy)  H:107–8
Robert I (The Bruce) (king of Scotland)  K:275; R:251; S:88
Robert Mills Historic House and Park (Columbia, South Carolina)
    S:304
  picture(s)  S:304
Roberts, Bartholomew (British pirate) see Black Bart
Roberts, Charles G. D. (Canadian writer)  C:86
  picture(s)
    illustration from Red Fox  C:87
Roberts, Joseph Jenkins (Liberian statesman)  L:168
Robertson, James (American pioneer)  N:16; T:84, 87 profile
Robertson, Oscar (American basketball player)  B:95j profile
  picture(s)  B:95j
Robert's Rules of Order (for parliamentary procedure)  P:81
Robert the Bruce see Robert I (The Bruce) (king of Scotland)
Robert W. Woodruff Arts Center (Atlanta, Georgia)  G:137
Roberval, Jean François de la Rocque, Sieur de (French
    colonizer)  C:126
Robeson, Paul (American singer and actor)  N:179 profile
  picture(s)  N:179
Robespierre, Maximilien (French revolutionary leader)  F:471
    profile, 472
Robie House (Chicago, Illinois) see Frederick C. Robie House
Robin Hood (legendary English hero and outlaw)  A:362;
    F:309; L:134–36; O:263; R:251
Robin Hood (operetta by DeKoven and Smith)  M:553
Robins (birds)  E:385
  picture(s)  B:246; C:509; M:259; W:193
Robinson, Edward G. (American actor)  M:491
Robinson, Edwin Arlington (American poet)  A:214b; M:49
    profile
Robinson, Frank (American baseball player and manager)
    B:90 profile
  picture(s)  B:90
Robinson, Jack Roosevelt (Jackie) (American baseball player)
    A:79c; B:92; R:252
  picture(s)  A:79L
Robinson, Sugar Ray (American boxer)  B:353 profile
Robinson Crusoe (novel by Daniel Defoe)  D:84; E:279; F:115;
    N:359
  books for children  C:232
  excerpt from  D:85
  setting is an island off Chile  C:254
Robinson Crusoe Islands see Juan Fernández Islands
Robot-assisted surgery  M:208f
Robots (automatic machines)  A:530–31; C:484–85;
    R:252–56
  hoisting and loading machinery  H:159c
  manufacturing  M:89
  milking machines  D:11
  plastics manufacturing  P:325
  pneumatic systems  H:314
  robot submersibles in oceanographic research  O:40
  spacecraft  S:362; T:50
  underwater exploration  U:21, 23
  word and concept invented by Karel Čapek  D:304
  picture(s)
    automobile industry  A:531, 554; M:266; N:301
    garment factory  E:61
    Kismet  I:286
    robotic arm  R:253
    volcano exploration  C:485
    welding  R:252

Rob Roy (Scottish outlaw)  O:264 profile
  picture(s)  O:264
Robson, Mount (British Columbia)  J:54
Robusti, Jacopo see Tintoretto
Roca, Cape (Portugal)  L:256
Rochambeau, Jean Baptiste Donatien de Vimeur, comte de
    (French military commander)  R:208, 209 profile;
    W:41
Rochester (Minnesota)  M:326, 335
Rochester (New Hampshire)  N:159
Rochester (New York)  N:214, 220
  picture(s)  N:220
Rock, John S. (American lawyer)  A:79c
"Rock-a-bye Baby" (lullaby)  L:336, 337
Rock and roll music see Rock music
Rock art (Cave paintings; Petroglyphs)
  Africa, art of  A:70, 73, 75
  art as a record  A:428–29; C:463
  Australian Aboriginal rock carvings  A:498
  earliest known drawings  D:315
  painting's earliest artists  P:14–15
  prehistoric art  P:435–37
  prehistoric people  P:441
  Spain, art of  S:380
  watercolor paintings in caves  W:55
  picture(s)  I:186
    Arizona's rock inscriptions  A:393
    France  E:365
    painting of hunting with bows and arrows  A:360
    San people  A:70
    Valley of Fire State Park (Nevada)  N:134
Rock bass (fish)  F:213
Rock climbing see Mountain climbing
Rock Creek Park (Washington, D.C.)  W:33–34
Rock crystal (crystalline quartz)  G:74; Q:8
Rock dredge (in oceanography)  O:39
Rock dusting (in coal mining)  C:391
Rockefeller, John D. (American industrialist)  C:356; P:140;
    R:256
  picture(s)  R:256
Rockefeller, Nelson Aldrich (vice president of the United States)
    L:106; R:224; V:331 profile
Rockefeller Center (New York City)
  Christmas tree  C:298
Rockefeller Empire State Plaza (Albany, New York) see Nelson
    A. Rockefeller Empire State Plaza
Rockefeller Foundation  P:391
Rocker (tool used in print making)  G:307
Rocket (early locomotive)  R:87, 88
Rocket engines  A:116; E:231; J:92; S:502
Rockets  R:257–62
  airplane design  A:567
  artificial satellites, launching of  S:54
  engines  E:231
  fuel stored under refrigeration  R:135
  Goddard, Robert Hutchings  G:244–46; I:286
  Huntsville (Alabama) called the Rocket City  A:137
  hydrogen fuel  H:316
  jet propulsion  J:92
  liquid gases  L:253; O:289
  missiles  M:343–49
  model kits of rockets  A:106
  spacecraft, launching of  S:340e
  space research and technology  S:361–62
  space shuttles  S:364
  Von Braun, Wernher  V:391
  diagram(s)
    Saturn V rocket  R:259
  picture(s)  O:289
    Cape Canaveral  F:270
    Goddard's first successful launch  R:257
    reusable rocket model  R:262
    Saturn  S:340c, 340h
Rockfalls  A:558
Rockford (Illinois)  I:71

Rock gardens  J:28
   *picture(s)*  G:35
Rock Hill (South Carolina)  S:306
Rockhopper penguins  P:120b
*Rocking Chair II* (sculpture by Henry Moore)
   *picture(s)*  D:137
Rock music  R:262a–264
   Beatles, The  B:108
   Cooke, Sam  C:221
   country rock  C:573
   dancing  D:28
   Freed, Alan, coined term "rock and roll"  R:60
   fusion  J:64
   guitar  G:412
   Hall of Fame  O:70
   United States, music of the  U:210
   *picture(s)*
      hall of fame (Cleveland, Ohio)  O:70
Rockne, Knute (American football coach)  F:359, 364; I:157
   *profile*
   *picture(s)*  I:157
"Rock of Ages" (hymn)  H:323
Rock of Gibraltar *see* Gibraltar
Rock pigeons (birds)  D:289
   *picture(s)*  D:289
Rockport (Massachusetts)
   *picture(s)*  M:144
Rock rabbits *see* Pikas
Rock River (Wisconsin–Illinois)  W:194
Rocks  R:265–71 *see also* Sedimentary rocks; Stone
   Can changes in temperature break up rocks?  S:234
   coal  C:388–91
   contain fossils  F:380–89
   crustal rocks  E:10
   Do growing plants break up rocks?  S:235
   Earth, history of  E:22, 23, 24
   erosion  E:16
   geodes  G:97
   geology  G:109, 111, 112–13, 117–18
   How do geologists learn about the history of planet Earth?
      E:28
   ice ages  I:8, 14
   Idaho's City of Rocks  I:54
   mines and mining  M:318–24
   moon (lunar) rocks  M:453, 455; S:340h, 342
   mountain building  E:13
   oldest rock ever found  R:268
   ores  O:217
   quarrying  Q:6
   radiometric dating  R:74–75
   tunnel building through rock  T:337
   volcanic rocks  V:383
   water shapes the land  W:51
   *picture(s)*
      rock cycle  R:267
      rock inscriptions  A:393
Rock salt  S:22
Rock Springs (Wyoming)  W:341
Rockwell, George Lincoln (American Nazi)  N:81
Rockwell, Norman (American artist)  I:82; R:272
   *picture(s)*
      *Breaking Home Ties* (painting)  R:272
      *Freedom from Want* (painting)  T:154
      *Freedom of Speech* (painting)  R:272
      *Saturday Evening Post* cover  I:82
*Rocky Landscape* (painting by Cézanne)
   *picture(s)*  M:389
Rocky Mountain bighorns *see* Bighorns
Rocky Mountain Fur Company  F:523
Rocky Mountain National Park (Colorado)  C:433, 438
   *picture(s)*  C:432; I:13
Rocky Mountains (North America)  R:273
   British Columbia  B:402
   Canada  C:55, 58, 60

climate  U:88
Colorado  C:430, 432, 433
Denver is the business center of  D:116
Glacier National Park  G:220
gold discoveries  G:251–52
Idaho  I:48
Jasper National Park  J:54
Lewis and Clark Expedition  L:164
Montana  M:430
mountains of the world  M:503–4
New Mexico  N:182
North American Cordillera  N:284
United States  U:79, 81
upslope fog  F:290–91
Utah  U:242
Washington  W:17
westward movement  W:144
Wyoming  W:336, 337
*map(s)*  R:273
*picture(s)*  N:282
   Banff National Park  C:56
   Colorado  C:431
   Pikes Peak  C:439
   United States  U:72
Rocky Mountain sheep (Bighorns)  H:219; S:147
Rocky Mountain spotted fever  A:348; D:200; T:192
Rococo (art style)
   clothing, history of  C:377
   decorative arts  D:77
   drawing, history of  D:318
   Fragonard, Jean Honoré  F:402
   France  F:427
   furniture design  F:511
   Germany  G:170
   Italy, art and architecture of  I:402
   painting  P:24
   sculpture  S:101
   *picture(s)*
      furniture design  F:510
Rococo revival (art style)  F:514
Rocroi, Battle of (1643)  S:377
Roddenberry, Gene (American writer)  S:81 *profile*
Rodentia (order of mammals)  R:274
   *picture(s)*
      beaver as example  M:67
Rodents  R:274–78 *see also* Hares; Rabbits
   beavers  B:110–12
   estivation  H:128
   gerbils  G:410
   guinea pigs  G:409
   hamsters  G:409–10
   hibernation  H:126, 127
   pets  P:178
   porcupines  P:389
   rabbits a separate order  R:24
   terriers once used to hunt  D:248
Rodeos  R:279–80
   cowboys  C:578
   Pro Rodeo Hall of Champions  C:438
   roping demonstrations  R:335
   *picture(s)*  M:429; N:128; O:206; W:340
      Calgary Exhibition and Stampede  A:170
*Roderick Hudson* (book by Henry James)  J:20
Rodgers, Jimmie (American singer)  C:571
Rodgers, Mary (American writer)  C:238
Rodgers, Richard (American composer)  M:554
Rodin, Auguste (French sculptor)  R:281
   Brancusi, influence on  B:370
   French art of the 20th century  F:429
   modern art  M:387–88
   museums devoted to his work  M:523; P:70
   place in the history of sculpture  S:102–3
   *picture(s)*
      *The Age of Bronze*  R:281

Burghers of Calais (sculpture)   **S:**102
Monument to Balzac   **M:**387
The Thinker (statue)   **F:**429
**Rodman, Dennis** (American basketball player)
picture(s)   **B:**95d
**Rodney, Caesar** (American statesman)   **D:**101 profile
picture(s)   **D:**100
Delaware's commemorative quarter   **C:**400
**Rodó, José Enrique** (Uruguayan essayist)   **L:**69; **U:**240
**Rod (Stick) puppets**   **P:**545
**Rodrigo, Joaquín** (Spanish composer)   **S:**392b
**Rodríguez, Abelardo** (Mexican president)   **M:**251
**Rodríguez, Andrés** (Paraguayan president)   **P:**66
**Rodríguez, Eduardo** (Bolivian president)   **B:**310
**Rodriguez, Miguel Angel** (Costa Rican president)   **C:**567
**Rodríguez de Francia, José Gaspar** see Francia, José Gaspar
Rodríguez de
**Rodríguez Freyle, Juan** (Colombian writer)   **L:**67
**Rodríguez Zapatero, José Luis** (prime minister of Spain)   **S:**379
**Rods** (for fishing)   **F:**209, 210, 214
**Rods** (of nuclear reactors) see Control rods
**Rods** (of retina of the eye)   **E:**430
**Rods, steel**   **I:**337
**Roe** (fish eggs)   **F:**191
**Roebling, John Augustus** (American engineer)   **B:**398, 400
**Roe deer**   **D:**82
**Roehm, Ernst** (German Nazi leader)   **N:**80
**Roentgen, Wilhelm Conrad** (German scientist)   **I:**85;
**L:**221–22; **M:**208e; **P:**236; **X:**351
picture(s)   **M:**208e; **X:**351
**Roentgenology** see Radiology
**Roentgen rays** see X-rays
**Roe** v. **Wade** (1973)   **A:**8; **I:**74; **S:**509; **W:**213
**Rogers, Carl** (American psychologist)   **P:**511
**Rogers, Fred (Mister Rogers)** (American entertainer and
educator)   **P:**140–41 profile
**Rogers, Kenny** (American singer)   **C:**573
**Rogers, Mount** (Virginia)   **V:**348
**Rogers, Roy** (American singer and actor)   **C:**572, 579
**Rogers, Will** (American actor and humorist)   **O:**88, 95 profile;
**R:**335
picture(s)   **O:**95
**Rogerus** (French architect)   **G:**267
**Roget's Thesaurus** (book of synonyms and antonyms)   **S:**548
**Roggeveen, Jakob** (Dutch explorer)   **I:**364
**Rogue elephants**   **E:**182
**Rogue novels** see Picaresque novels
**Rogue River** (Oregon)   **O:**205
**Rohe, Ludwig Mies van der** see Mies van der Rohe, Ludwig
**Roh Moo-hyun** (president of South Korea)   **K:**303
**Rohrer, Heinrich** (German scientist)   **E:**164; **M:**285
**Rojas, Carlos** (Spanish novelist)   **S:**392
**Rojas, Fernando de** (Spanish writer)   **S:**387
**Rokeby Museum** (Ferrisburgh, Vermont)   **V:**314
**Roland** (French missile)   **M:**349
**Roland** (hero of epic poem)   **F:**436; **P:**354
**Roland and Oliver** (legend)   **L:**131–34
**Roldán, Amadeo** (Cuban composer)   **L:**73
**Role-playing video games**   **V:**332c
**Rolfe, John** (English colonist)   **J:**23; **T:**170, 214; **V:**358
**Rolland, Romain** (French novelist)   **F:**442
**Rolled gold plate**   **G:**248
**Rolled oats**   **G:**284
**Roller blading**
picture(s)   **B:**366; **R:**282
**Roller coasters** (amusement-park rides)
picture(s)   **P:**78
**Roller Derby** (sport)   **R:**282
**Roller disco** (dance)   **R:**282
**Roller hockey** (sport)   **R:**282
**Roller printing** (on textiles)   **T:**143
**Roller-skating**   **R:282; S:**5
picture(s)   **R:**282; **S:**4
**Rolling** (of metals)   **M:**235
**Rolling-ball pens**   **P:**143

**Rolling hitches** (knots)
picture(s)   **K:**288
**Rolling mills** (for steel shaping)   **I:**335–37
**Rolling stock** (cars pulled by a locomotive)   **R:**77
**Rolling Stones** (English rock band)   **R:**263 profile, 264
picture(s)   **R:**263
**Rollo** (duke of Normandy)   **V:**342
**Roll on-roll off ships**   **S:**154–55
**Rolls Royce Silver Ghost** (automobile)
picture(s)   **A:**541
**ROM (Read-only memory)** (of computers)   **C:**481, 491
**Roma** (people) see Gypsies
**Romains, Jules** (French novelist)   **F:**442
**Romaji** (method of writing Japanese)   **J:**30
**Roman** (typeface design)   **T:**369
**Roman architecture** see Rome, architecture of
**Roman art** see Rome, art of
**Roman Britain** see Britain
**Roman calendar**   **C:**14–15
**Roman Catholic Church**   **R:**283–94 see also the names of
saints, popes, and Christian leaders
Apocrypha   **B:**163
Argentine president must be Catholic   **A:**383
art as a record   **A:**430
baroque art, influence on   **B:**64, 66
Bible, versions of the   **B:**158
birth control, acceptable methods of   **B:**251
Brazil has the largest Catholic population   **B:**373
canon law   **L:**85
choral music   **C:**283
Christianity, history of   **C:**287–95
Counter-Reformation   **C:**293; **R:**132
duelists refused burial by   **D:**349
ecumenical movement   **P:**494
education, history of   **E:**81
England, history of   **E:**240, 243, 252
forms of address for the clergy   **A:**22
fundamentalism   **F:**492
Germany's early religious divisions   **G:**160
hats indicate rank of leaders   **H:**46–47
Henry VIII's break with the Church   **E:**242; **H:**114
Hispanic Americans   **H:**144, 145
Holy Roman Empire   **H:**175–79
Hus, Jan   **H:**306
Hussites   **C:**622
hymns   **H:**321–22, 324
Ireland   **I:**317
Italy   **I:**380, 388
Kennedy was first Catholic U.S. president   **K:**204
Latin America   **L:**50, 58; **S:**293
Latin is its official language   **L:**74
Luther excommunicated from   **L:**346
marriage rites   **W:**102
Middle Ages   **M:**290, 294–95
North America   **C:**294
Northern Ireland   **N:**336, 337
Philippines has a Christian majority   **P:**184
and Protestantism, differences between   **P:**490, 491
Protestant Reformation   **C:**291–93; **R:**130–32
Quebec (Canada)   **C:**80; **Q:**16, 17
religious holidays   **R:**155
Rhode Island   **R:**216
saints   **S:**18c–18d
Thirty Years' War   **T:**179
Vatican City   **V:**280–82
witches, persecution of   **W:**208–9
picture(s)
medieval church service   **M:**293
Spanish colonial mission   **H:**144
Ugandan priest   **A:**57
Vietnamese outdoor Mass   **C:**294
**Romance languages** (derived from Latin)   **L:**40, 74–75; **R:**309
Europe   **E:**353
French   **F:**433–35

**Romance languages** (cont.)
   Italian  **I:**404–5
   Romanian  **R:**296
   Spanish  **S:**386
***Romance of the Rose*** (poem) *see* Roman de la rose
**Romancero** (Spanish ballad tradition)  **F:**309
**Romances** (story poems, songs, and novels)
   Arthur, King, legends of  **A:**438–38c
   ballad cycles  **B:**24
   early novels  **N:**358–59
   fiction, origins of  **F:**114
   medieval tales of chivalry in German literature  **G:**176
   "Song of Roland"  **F:**436
   Spanish ballads  **S:**387, 392a
***Roman de la rose*** (poem)  **F:**436
   *picture(s)*  **F:**433
**Roman Empire** (27 B.C.–A.D. 476)  **I:**388; **R:**316–17 *see also*
      Byzantine Empire; Rome, ancient
   Attila  **A:**490
   Augustus  **A:**494–95
   Austria, history of  **A:**523
   battles  **B:**103d
   Britain, conquest of  **E:**235–37
   Caesar laid the foundation for  **C:**6
   Christianity became its official religion  **C:**289
   cities, history of  **C:**315
   citizenship  **C:**324
   clothing, history of  **C:**375
   Constantine the Great  **C:**528
   Eastern *see* Byzantine Empire
   emperors, list of  **R:**312
   exploration by ancient civilizations  **E:**400
   feudalism follows decline of Roman Empire  **F:**99–103
   France  **F:**412
   Greece  **G:**337, 344, 358
   Herodian dynasty and  **H:**123
   Holy Roman Empire, naming of the  **H:**175, 179
   imperialism  **I:**100
   Jerusalem destroyed by the Romans  **J:**103
   loss of power in western Europe  **M:**289
   Nero  **N:**114
   Palestine  **P:**40c
   persecution of Christians  **R:**285–86
   postal service, history of  **P:**397
   road builders  **R:**248
   Spain  **S:**370, 375
   Tunisia  **T:**336
   *map(s)*
      growth of the empire  **R:**314
**Romanesque art and architecture**  **R:**295
   architecture, history of  **A:**370–71
   cathedrals  **C:**134
   England  **E:**257
   France  **F:**422
   furniture  **F:**508–9
   Germany  **G:**167–68
   Gothic architecture based on  **G:**264
   Italian churches  **I:**392–93
   sculpture  **S:**97–98
   Spain  **S:**381–82
**Romanesque Revival** (in American architecture)  **U:**131
**Roman Forum** (ruins)  **R:**306
   *picture(s)*  **R:**309
**Romania**  **R:**296–301
   Balkans  **B:**22
   Bucharest  **B:**421
   Moldova  **M:**402, 403
   World War I  **W:**285
   World War II  **W:**299, 312–13, 318
   *map(s)*  **R:**297
   *picture(s)*
      Bucharest  **B:**421
      flag  **F:**238
**Romanian language**  **B:**22
**Romanian Orthodox Church**  **R:**296

**Roman law**  **A:**239; **L:**84
**Roman numerals**  **A:**2; **N:**397, 404; **R:**301
**Romano, Giulio** (Italian painter and architect)  **I:**399
**Romano cheese**  **C:**195
**Romanovs** (Russian ruling family)  **I:**413–14; **R:**357, 369–71;
   **U:**41
   Nicholas (emperors)  **N:**248–49
   *picture(s)*
      Nicholas II and his family  **R:**371
**Roman Peace** (in Roman history) *see* Pax Romana
**Roman Republic**  **A:**317; **R:**310–16
**Roman roads**  **A:**239; **E:**227–28, 235–36; **T:**282
**Romans** (book of the New Testament)  **B:**166
**Romansch language**  **S:**540
**Romantic fiction**  **F:**114
**Romanticism** (in art, literature, and music)  **R:**302–4 *see also*
      Classical age in music
   American literature  **A:**208–9
   Delacroix, Eugène  **D:**87
   drama  **D:**302
   English literature  **E:**280–84
   France, literature of  **F:**440–41
   France, music of  **F:**446–47
   French art  **F:**428–29; **P:**29
   German art  **G:**171
   German composers  **G:**186–88
   German literature  **G:**178–79
   historical writing  **H:**152
   history of Western musical forms  **M:**542–43
   Keats, John  **K:**202
   Latin America, literature of  **L:**67–68
   modern art  **M:**386–87
   opera  **O:**144
   operetta  **O:**166–68
   romantic poetry  **L:**259
   sculpture  **S:**102
   Spanish literature  **S:**389
**Romanus** (pope)  **R:**292
**Romany (Gypsy) language**  **G:**434
**Romberg, Sigmund** (Hungarian-born American composer)
   **O:**167, 168
**Rome** (capital of Italy)  **I:**385, 390; **R:**305–8
   art and architecture  **I:**396, 399–400
   Egyptian obelisks  **O:**5
   fountains  **F:**393–94
   painting  **P:**21
   Renaissance art and architecture  **R:**167
   Vatican City  **V:**280–82
   World War II  **W:**309
   *map(s)*  **R:**307
   *picture(s)*
      Colosseum  **I:**387; **R:**306
      Forum  **R:**309
      Saint Peter's Basilica  **C:**135; **E:**356; **R:**305
      Spanish Steps  **I:**385; **R:**306, 309
      Trevi Fountain  **F:**394; **R:**306
      World War II  **W:**309
**Rome, ancient**  **A:**239; **R:**309–17 *see also* Roman Empire
   alphabet  **A:**194b–194c; **C:**463
   Antony, Mark  **A:**317
   archaeological specialties  **A:**350
   architecture *see* Rome, architecture of
   armor  **A:**423
   art *see* Rome, art of
   banks and banking  **B:**52
   beekeeping  **H:**212
   bookmaking  **B:**319
   bottles, history of  **B:**346
   breadmaking industry  **B:**388a
   bridge building  **B:**396
   burning of (A.D. 64)  **C:**288
   Caesar, Gaius Julius  **C:**6
   calendar  **C:**14–15
   canal builders  **C:**89

**Roosevelt, Franklin Delano** (cont.)
    Hull, Cordell  **H:**280
    Japanese Americans, internment of  **W:**304
    memorial (Washington, D.C.)  **W:**32
    modifies capitalism  **C:**103
    New Deal  **D:**122; **N:**138h
    New York, governor of  **N:**225
    presidential leadership  **P:**448–49
    quotation from First Inaugural Address  **Q:**22
    Roosevelt Campobello International Park  **N:**138f
    Supreme Court  **H:**275; **S:**510
    vice presidency upgraded by  **V:**330
    World War II  **W:**301–2
    *picture(s)*  **N:**225; **P:**194, 452
        with family  **R:**322
        fireside chats  **R:**325
        with Johnson, Lyndon B.  **J:**120
        in swimming pool  **R:**322
        Tehran conference (1943)  **W:**293
        Yalta conference (1945)  **R:**326
**Roosevelt, Theodore** (26th president of the United States)
    **R:**327–32
    Bull Moose Party  **P:**372
    conservation movement, history of the  **C:**526
    football rules to make game safer  **F:**361
    Kipling's correspondence with  **K:**261
    Monroe Doctrine  **M:**427
    national parks  **N:**45
    New York, governor of  **N:**225
    Panama Canal  **P:**51
    ranching in North Dakota  **N:**334
    Sagamore Hill National Historic Site (Oyster Bay, New
      York)  **N:**214
    Spanish-American War  **S:**392c, 392d
    Taft, feud with  **T:**5–6
    "the Trust Buster"  **C:**103
    vice presidency  **V:**328 *profile*
    White House  **W:**166
    *picture(s)*  **P:**451
        cartoon on "Big Stick Policy"  **U:**190
        cartoon on Panama Canal  **P:**51
        cartoon on party symbols  **U:**190
        with Muir, John  **N:**50
**Roosevelt Corollary** (to Monroe Doctrine)  **M:**427
**Roosevelt families**
    *picture(s)*
        Franklin D. Roosevelt family  **R:**322
        Theodore Roosevelt family  **R:**329
**Roosevelt River** (formerly **River of Doubt**) (Brazil)  **R:**332
**Roosters** (male chickens)  **P:**414
**Root** (in music)  **M:**533
**Root, George F.** (American composer)  **N:**23
**Root caps** (of plants)  **P:**304
**Root crops**
    potatoes  **P:**403–4
    vegetables  **V:**286–87
**Root hairs** (of plants)  **P:**303–4; **T:**306
**Root-knot nematode** (plant pest)  **P:**289
*Roots* (book by Alex Haley)  **G:**76
**Roots** (of plants)  **P:**303–4
    food from plants  **F:**329; **P:**296
    houseplants  **H:**265–66
    plant pests  **P:**288, 289
    rain-forest plants  **R:**99
    trees  **T:**305–6
    weeds  **W:**104
**Roots** (of teeth)  **T:**43, 44
**Roots** (of words)  **W:**239
*Roots* (television miniseries)  **T:**70
**Rootstocks** (seedlings)  **O:**188
**Rope**  **R:**333–34
    knots  **K:**286–88
**Rope jumping** (game)  **G:**19
    *picture(s)*  **F:**315; **G:**18
**Rope spinning**  **R:**335, 336

**Rope tows** (kind of ski lift)  **S:**185
**Roping**  **R:**279–80, **335–36**
**Roquefort** (cheese)  **C:**195; **D:**10; **F:**499
**Roraima, Mount** (Venezuela–Guyana)  **S:**277
**Rorquals** (whales)  **W:**152–53
**Rorschach Test** (personality test)  **T:**119
    *picture(s)*  **P:**502
**Rosario** (Argentina)  **A:**386, 386a
**Rosas, Juan Manuel de** (Argentine dictator)  **A:**386b
**Rose, Pete** (American baseball player)  **B:**93
    *picture(s)*  **B:**94
**Roseau** (capital of Dominica)  **D:**279
**Rose Bowl** (football game, Pasadena, California)  **F:**360–61;
    **R:**60
**Rosecrans, William Starke** (American army officer)  **C:**342
**Rose garden**
    *picture(s)*  **G:**31
*Rose Marie* (operetta by Friml)  **O:**168
**Rosenberg, Julius and Ethel** (American husband and wife
    convicted of espionage)  **S:**409 *profile*
    *picture(s)*  **S:**409
**Rosenfeld, Morris** (Yiddish poet)  **Y:**361
*Rosenkavalier, Der* (opera by Richard Strauss)  **O:**163
**Rosenwald, Lessing J.** (American merchant and art collector)
    **N:**38
**Rose of Lima, Saint**  **S:**18d *profile*
**Rose quartz** (gemstone)  **G:**74; **Q:**8
**Roses** (flowers)  **G:**46, 49
    Bulgaria is center of rose-growing industry  **B:**443
    Portland (Oregon) called City of Roses  **P:**390
    Texas agriculture  **T:**133
    *picture(s)*  **G:**27, 31; **K:**256; **N:**211
        Bulgaria  **B:**444
        wild rose  **A:**165; **I:**291; **N:**323
**Roses, Wars of the** (1455–1485)  **E:**241; **H:**110
**Rose-shaped ears** (of dogs)  **D:**241
**Rosetta** (branch of the Nile River)  **N:**261
*Rosetta* (space probe)  **C:**452
**Rosetta Stone** (first clue to understanding Egyptian
    hieroglyphics)  **A:**351; **H:**131; **M:**525
    *picture(s)*  **A:**351
**Rosette sampler** (in oceanography)  **O:**39
**Rosé wines**  **W:**190, 190a
**Rosewood trees**
    *picture(s)*
        uses of the wood and its grain  **W:**224
**Rosh Hashanah** (Jewish religious holiday)  **J:**146a, 148;
    **N:**208; **R:**154
**Rosin** (resin of certain pine trees)  **R:**184
**Ross, Betsy** (American maker of the first Stars and Stripes flag)
    **F:**243; **R:**337
**Ross, Sir James Clark** (English polar explorer)  **E:**415; **N:**339
**Ross, Jerry L.** (American astronaut)  **S:**348 *profile*
    *picture(s)*  **S:**340b
**Ross, John** (Cherokee chief)  **I:**178 *profile;* **T:**87 *profile*
**Ross, Sir John** (Scottish Arctic explorer)  **N:**339
**Ross, Malcolm** (American military balloonist)  **B:**36
**Ross, Nellie Tayloe** (American political figure)  **W:**347 *profile*
    *picture(s)*  **W:**347
**Rossellini, Roberto** (Italian film director)  **M:**493
**Rosselló, Pedro** (Puerto Rican political leader)  **P:**532
**Rossetti, Christina** (English poet)  **E:**285; **R:**338
    "Who Has Seen the Wind?" (poem)  **R:**338
    *picture(s)*
        "Goblin Market" (poem)  **F:**12
**Rossetti, Dante Gabriel** (English painter and poet)  **E:**263,
    285; **R:**338
    *picture(s)*
        drawing of Christina Rossetti  **R:**338
**Rossetti, Gabriele** (Italian poet)  **R:**338
**Rossetti, Maria** (English writer)  **R:**338
**Rossetti, William** (English art critic and essayist)  **R:**338
**Ross Ice Shelf** (Antarctica)  **G:**224; **I:**5–6

**Royal Gorge** (Colorado)
*picture(s)* **C:**438
**Royal Greenwich Observatory** *see* Greenwich Observatory
**Royal Highland Games** (Scottish festivities) **U:**50
*picture(s)* **U:**51
**Royal Institution of Great Britain** **T:**180
**Royal jelly** (food of bees) **B:**118, 119; **H:**212
**Royal Montreal Golf Club** (Canada) **G:**257
**Royal Mosque** (Isfahan, Iran)
*picture(s)* **A:**438d
**Royal Ontario Museum** (Toronto) **T:**244
**Royal Opera House** (London, England) **L:**296
**Royal Road** (network of roads in ancient Persia) **P:**155
**Royal Shakespeare Company** (Stratford-on-Avon, England)
**T:**160; **U:**49
**Royal Society of London** **B:**354
**Royalty** (payment to the creator of a work) **C:**555; **P:**524
book contracts **B:**324
check on royalties if you charge admission to your play
**P:**335
**Royal walnut moth** (insect)
*picture(s)*
caterpillar **I:**242
**Royal Winnipeg Ballet** (Canada) **B:**32; **C:**69
*picture(s)* **C:**68
**Rozier, Jean François Pilâtre de** (French balloonist) *see* Pilâtre
de Rozier, Jean François
**R.S.V.P.** (on an invitation requiring a reply) **L:**160a; **P:**88
**RU-486** (abortion-inducing drug) **A:**8
**Rua Cana Falls** (Angola) **W:**59
**Ruanda-Urundi** *see* Burundi; Rwanda
*Rubáiyát of Omar Khayyám, The* **E:**285
**Rub' al Khali** (desert region of Saudi Arabia) **S:**58c
*picture(s)* **A:**438f
**Rubato** (musical term) **O:**198–99
**Rubber** **R:**344–48a
dolls made of **D:**268
first rubber balls **B:**23
Goodyear's vulcanization process **G:**262; **S:**486
Liberia **L:**168
rubber-powered airplane models **A:**105
silicones **S:**173
Thailand is leading producer **A:**450
tires **T:**210–12
**Rubber boas** (snakes) **S:**217
**Rubber trees** **R:**344–45, 347; **T:**306
*picture(s)* **R:**345; **S:**332
**Rubbing alcohol** **A:**172; **H:**92
**Rubbings** (reproductions of designs and textures) **R:**348b–349
**Rubbish** (solid waste) **S:**33
**Rubble masonry** **B:**393
**Rubella** (disease) *see* German measles
**Rubens, Peter Paul** (Flemish painter) **D:**360; **R:**350
baroque art **B:**66; **P:**24
drawing, history of **D:**317–18
English art and architecture **E:**259
etchings of his paintings **G:**305
gallery in the Louvre **L:**331–32
Luxembourg Palace (Paris) **F:**425
*picture(s)*
*Adoration of the Magi, The* (painting) **B:**67; **D:**364
*Hélène Fourment and Her Children* (painting) **R:**350
*Marie de Medicis, Queen of France, Landing in*
*Marseilles* (painting) **P:**25
**Rubeola** *see* Measles
**Rubicon** (river in northern Italy) **C:**6
**Rubidium** (element) **E:**176
**Rubidium-87** (radioactive element) **R:**75
**Rubies** (gems) **G:**69, 70, 71, 73
amulets **G:**72, 74
lasers **L:**46b
*picture(s)* **G:**72, 74; **M:**316
**Rubik's Cube** (puzzle) **P:**554
**Rubinstein, Anton Grigorievich** (Russian composer and pianist)
**R:**385

**Rublev, Andrei** (Russian artist) **R:**375
**Ruby, Jack** (American murderer) **K:**210; **O:**246
**Ruby Mountains** (Nevada) **N:**124
**Ruby Ridge** (Idaho) **F:**77
**Ruby-throated hummingbird** **H:**289
*picture(s)* **B:**234
**Rudbeckias** (flowers)
*picture(s)* **G:**28
**Rudders** (steering devices)
airplanes **A:**113
sailboats and sailing ships **S:**11, 156, 157
**Ruddle, Frank** (American geneticist) **G:**91
**Ruddy duck** (bird) **D:**346
**Rude, François** (French sculptor) **S:**102
**Rudolf, Lake** (east Africa) *see* Turkana, Lake
**Rudolf I** (Holy Roman Emperor) **A:**523; **H:**2, 179
**Rudolph, Wilma** (American track star) **T:**87 *profile*, 260
*profile*
*picture(s)* **T:**260
**Ruffed grouse** (bird) **A:**284, 286; **B:**242
*picture(s)* **P:**127
**Rufous hummingbird**
*picture(s)* **B:**208
**Rugae** (folds in the stomach wall) **S:**460
**Rugby** **R:**350–52; **U:**51 *see also* Football
*picture(s)* **A:**500; **N:**237
**Rugs and carpets** **R:**352–56
carpet tacks **N:**2
interior design **I:**259, 260
Islamic art **I:**359
Kurds **K:**307
*picture(s)*
Chinese carpet **D:**68
Chinese carpet factory **E:**59
cotton rug from Sierra Leone **A:**75
Persian rugs of Iran **I:**307
rug maker in Turkmenistan **T:**351
**Ruhr district** (of Germany) **G:**154, 155, 157
**Ruins** *see* Archaeology
**Ruisdael (Ruysdael), Jacob van** (Dutch painter) **D:**365
**Ruiz, José** (Spanish planter in Cuba) **A:**221
**Ruiz, José Martínez** (Spanish writer) *see* Martínez Ruiz, José
**Ruiz, Juan** (Spanish poet) **S:**387
**Ruiz Cortines, Adolfo** (Mexican president) **M:**251
**"Rule, Britannia"** (patriotic song) **E:**278
**Rule of Saint Benedict** **C:**290
**Rulers** (measuring tools) **T:**230, 234
**Rules Committee** (United States Congress) **U:**167
**Rules of order** *see* Parliamentary procedure
*Rules of the Game* (motion picture, 1939) **M:**493
**Rules of the road**
boats and boating **B:**267
sailing **S:**11
**Rum** (distilled beverage) **C:**419; **W:**161
*picture(s)*
Puerto Rican bottling plant **C:**114
**Rum, Romanism and Rebellion** (election campaign catch-words)
**C:**359
**Rumania** *see* Romania
**Rumba** (dance) **D:**27–28; **L:**72
**Rumelhart, David** (American psychologist) **P:**507
**Rumelia oil field** (Iraq-Kuwait) **I:**313
**Rumen** (first chamber of the stomach of a ruminant) **H:**218
**Rumford, Count** (British scientist) *see* Thompson, Benjamin
**Rumford medals** (awards in physics) **T:**180
**Ruminants** (order of cud-chewing mammals) **H:**218–19
antelopes **A:**297–98
cattle **C:**151
deer **D:**81
llamas **L:**278
*diagram(s)*
stomach **H:**219
**Rummy** (card game) **C:**111

Russian music *see* Russia, music of
**Russian Orthodox Church** **R:**358, 368, 369; **U:**34
New Year **N:**208
Saint Michael's Cathedral (Sitka, Alaska) **A:**148
*picture(s)*
Alaska **A:**145
patriarch **R:**357
wedding **W:**100
**Russian Orthodox Church in America** **E:**47
**Russian Republic** *see* Russia
**Russian Revolution and Civil War** (1917–1921) **R:**371;
**U:**40–41
Communism **C:**473
famine a cause of **F:**45
underground movements **U:**14
World War I **W:**288–89
*picture(s)* **W:**289
**Russian Security Service** **S:**407
**Russian thistle** (weed)
*picture(s)* **W:**105
**Russification** (in Russian history) **A:**177
**Russo-Finnish War** (1939) **W:**296
**Russo-German Pact** (1939) **W:**296
**Russo-Japanese War** (1904–1905) **N:**249; **U:**39–40
*picture(s)*
Tsushima Strait, Battle of **J:**45
**Russo-Turkish War** (1877–1878) **B:**445
**Russwurm, John Brown** (American journalist and educator)
**A:**6a *profile,* 79c
**Rust** *see also* Corrosion
combustion **F:**141
oxidation and reduction **O:**287, 288
phlogiston, theory of **C:**208
*picture(s)* **C:**199; **F:**140; **O:**287
**Rustin, Bayard** (American civil rights leader) **C:**329 *profile;*
**S:**115
**Rustlers** (cattle thieves) **C:**577
**Rusts** (fungi) **F:**499; **O:**4; **P:**288
**Rutan, Dick** (American pilot) **A:**567
**Rutgers–The State University** (New Brunswick, New Jersey)
**N:**169
**Ruth** (Biblical character) **B:**161, 163
**Ruth, Babe (George Herman Ruth)** (American baseball player)
**B:**91; **R:**387
signature reproduced **A:**528
*picture(s)* **B:**91; **M:**133; **U:**193
with Harding **H:**31

**Ruthenia** (region in Europe) **S:**201, 202
**Ruthenium** (element) **E:**176
**Rutherford, Daniel** (Scottish chemist) **N:**262
**Rutherford, Ernest (1st Baron Rutherford of Nelson)** (New
Zealand-born British physicist) **A:**486; **C:**211; **R:**47,
**387**
*picture(s)* **A:**486
**Rutherfordium** (element) **E:**176
**Rutland** (Vermont) **V:**315
**Rutledge, Ann** (American historical figure) **L:**242
**Rutledge, Edward** (American political leader) **S:**311 *profile*
**Rutledge, John** (American jurist) **S:**311 *profile*
**Ruutel, Arnold** (president of Estonia) **E:**325
**Ruwenzori Mountains** (central Africa) **A:**48; **C:**500; **M:**502,
505–6; **U:**5
What and where are the Mountains of the Moon? **A:**61
**Ruysdael, Jacob van** (Dutch painter) *see* Ruisdael (Ruysdael),
Jacob van
**RV's** *see* Recreational vehicles
**Rwanda** **R:**388–89
genocide of Tutsi **G:**96, 97; **U:**71
independence from Belgium **B:**135
*picture(s)*
flag **F:**238
poverty and illness **P:**418
refugees **A:**60–61
**Ryan, Nolan** (American baseball player) **B:**90 *profile,* 94
*picture(s)* **B:**90
**Rydberg, Abraham Viktor** (Swedish poet) **S:**58i
**Ryder, Albert Pinkham** (American painter) **U:**130
**Ryder Cup** (golf) **G:**260
**Rye** (grain) **R:**390
cereal grasses **G:**318
grain and grain products **G:**281, 284, 285, 286
*picture(s)*
grain and grain products **G:**283
**Rye** (New Hampshire) **N:**160
**Rye-an' injun** (colonial American bread) **C:**411
**Ryerson, Adolphus Egerton** (Canadian educator) **O:**137
**Rylant, Cynthia** (American author) **C:**235 *profile*
**Rynearson, Edward** (American educator) **N:**42
**Ryukyu Islands** (Pacific Ocean) **J:**35
Okinawa **P:**10
Okinawa in World War II **W:**314–15, 316
**Ryun, Jim** (American track athlete) **T:**260 *profile*
*picture(s)* **T:**260

## PHOTO CREDITS

The following list credits the sources of photos used in THE NEW BOOK OF KNOWLEDGE. Credits are listed, by page, photo by photo—left to right, top to bottom. Wherever appropriate, the name of the photographer has been listed with the source, the two being separated by a dash. When two or more photos by different photographers appear on one page, their credits are separated by semicolons.

### Q-R

Cover © Wei Yan—Masterfile
2 © Fethi Belaid—AFP/Getty Images
3 © Kazuyoshi Nomachi—HAGA/The Image Works
4a © Tom Vezo—Peter Arnold, Inc.
4b The Granger Collection; © Johnny Van Haeften Ltd., London/The Bridgeman Art Library.
5 © Touhig Sion—Corbis Sygma
7 © Russ Kinne—Photo Researchers
8 © Smithsonian Institution—"Visions of Einstein;" © Jodrell Bank—Science Photo Library—Photo Researchers.
9 © Anthony Tyson—AT&T Bell Labs and W. A. Baum and T. Kreidel, Lowell Observatory
10a © Reflexion
10b © Wolfgang Kaehler; © Michel Gagné—Reflexion.
11 © Victoria Hurst—First Light, Toronto
13 © Derek Caron—Reflexion

14 © Perry Mastrovito—Reflexion; © Janet Dwyer—First Light, Toronto.
18 © Yves Tessier—Reflexion
19 © Ken Straiton—First Light, Toronto
24 © Leonard Lee Rue III—Bruce Coleman Inc.; © Steve Maslowski—Visuals Unlimited.
25 © Lynn M. Stone—Bruce Coleman Inc.
26 © Larry Ditto—Bruce Coleman Inc.; © Michael Quinton—Minden Pictures.
27 © Erwin & Peggy Bauer—Bruce Coleman Inc.
28 © Phil A. Dotson—Photo Researchers; © Doug Mason—Earthtrek/Woodfin Camp & Associates.
29 © N. Smythe—Photo Researchers; © Stephen Dalton—Photo Researchers.
30 © Ed Honowitz—Stone
33 © David R. Frazier
34 The Bettmann Archive
34a © Focus on Sports
34b © AllanTannenbaum—Corbis-Sygma
34c © Owen Franken—Corbis-Sygma
34d © Jerry Wachter—Photo Researchers

37 © Kathy McLaughlin—The Image Works
38 © Andrej Reiser—Bilderberg/Peter Arnold, Inc.
40 © Jim Reed—Science Photo Library/Photo Researchers
41 © Colin McPherson—Corbis Sygma
42 © Garry Black—Masterfile; © Jose Luis Pelaes, Inc./Corbis; © David Young-Wolff—PhotoEdit; © David R. Frazier—Photo Researchers.
46 © Manfred Vollmer—Peter Arnold, Inc.
47 Courtesy, Food Safety and Inspection Service/USDA
50 © David Young-Wolff—PhotoEdit; © Philip Rostron—Masterfile; © Gloria Wright—Syracuse Newspapers/The Image Works.
51 © David Frazier—The Image Works; © Bob Daemmrich—The Image Works.
56 © Tom Pantages; © Jessica Griffin—AP/Wide World Photos.
58 Taxi/Getty Images
59 © John Chillingworth—Hulton/Archive by Getty Images